Contents

A lightning tour of the

What we now know as Bristol Civic Society began back in 1905 as the Bristol Kyrle Society. It was named after John Kyrle, an 18th century merchant who devoted his life to beautifying Ross-on-Wye, his native town.

The Bristol Kyrle Society set out to beautify Bristol by preserving fine historic buildings, discouraging bad new building, improving waste spaces by planting trees and shrubs and providing seats, encouraging the cultivation of window boxes and persuading schools and clubs to help preserve trees, flowers and wildlife.

Some things never change: the Kyrle Society was much exercised by the mindless vandalism of young people who deliberately destroyed young plants, trees and shrubs. Litter, too, was a continuing irritant.

In addition to improving the environment, the Kyrle Society also promoted public interest in the arts, arranging for schoolchildren to attend a concert and to be given talks at the Bristol School of Architecture about the city's interesting buildings.

Following the First World War, the Society began to play a larger role in the city, joining with the Design and Industries Association to prepare and present to the Council proposals for the improvement of the Centre.

It also worked for years – with sadly little success – to secure improvements to neglected squares and public green spaces.

A much fuller history of the Kyrle Society, written by Vincent Waite in 1965, is to be found on the Civic Society's website.

When the Second World War began, Bristol was heavily bombarded by the Luftwaffe, destroying much of the city, including its historic shopping area (which lay between Wine Street and Castle Street).

Mr Lionel Fox, Chairman of the Prison Commission, on a visit to Bristol prison, wrote in his diary for April 1945:

> *'…I had my first sight of the ruins of Bristol. This exceeds anything of the sort I have yet seen except perhaps the worst part of the City of London.*
>
> *'From Temple Meads towards the centre is just a normal badly blitzed area, though it was memorable to see the graceful grey lines of St Mary Redcliffe soaring unbroken from the rubbled ruins all around.*
>
> *'But the view from the centre up to the right, where the worst of the devastation fell, was astonishing – it surpassed even what I remember of Ypres at its most desolate. One looks up this broad slope and sees acre upon acre of mere rubble or broken breast-high brick, and out of this emerge the grey shells and battered towers of several ancient churches, upstanding against the sky and accentuating the scene as perhaps they have done since*

irst hundred years

houses were built in brick and stone. For the rest, I was glad to find the Cathedral and College Green unhurt, though the beautiful Park Street leading up to the university was sadly gapped and battered. I wonder what sort of city will take the place of what is now irrevocably gone. It is a splendid opportunity.'

A new society

Mr Fox was not alone in seeing this opportunity. Following the blitz, it was clear that there was a tremendous amount of work to be done to revive the city and bring it back from the terrible devastation it had suffered. The enormity of the task ahead was clear, and thus it was that in June 1943 the Kyrle Society merged into the new Bristol Civic Society, which was founded specifically to help with re-planning the ruined city and to carry out an extended field of activity.

As the Western Daily Press commented:

> *'A new Society was formed in Bristol yesterday to cope with the vital need for re-planning and civic development.'*

Remains of Union Street after bombing, November 1940. Picture by Bristol Evening Post.

The sleeping giant awakes

Generally speaking, until after the end of the Second World War the public was expected to put up and shut up, and be grateful for whatever those in authority felt it appropriate to do with the city. Perhaps as a result of the desperate days that Bristolians had been through, however, there arose a groundswell of critical opinion, expressed by people who were not entirely happy with what was being planned for their city, and wanted their opinions to be taken into account.

A customers' revolt

As Sir Hugh Casson, the architect brought in by the Council as consultant on the future of the bombed-out area of Wine Street/Castle Street, and, later, on the future of City Docks, observed:

> *'What has happened...is the beginning of a customers' revolt – a refusal any longer to be totally the victims of experts, a growing insistence on having more say in the shape of our surroundings.'*

This new, questioning spirit of the public found official expression in a 1967 government report called *People and Planning*. It established that the public should be involved in local planning, and be consulted about proposed developments and road plans.

From the 1970s onwards, Bristol Civic Society and like-minded allies successfully led the resistance to the break-up of cities in general and Bristol in particular. They challenged the pseudo-scientific principles of 'separate zones' and 'predict and provide' as justification for destructive new road schemes. In place of these, the Society presented credible and attractive alternatives.

A new era dawns

This was the dawn of a new era, one which has seen an ever-increasing growth in the importance and influence of public participation – although even now it is still not always as well-organised or as influential as it ought to be.

Nearly 40 years on, a Civic Society Broadsheet* dealt with the 'river of new legislation, policy statements, guidance, regulations and codes of practice [which] flow towards Local Authorities and the public'.

Amongst this welter of government pronouncements one particular point occurs again and again: the key importance of involving local people in decision-making. This means actually involving the public in planning rather than just producing a plan and then 'consulting' them. Government has shown its commitment by providing a £350m grant over three years (2003–2006) to help local planning authorities promote public involvement.

We can only hope that this will result in a truly positive relationship between the local planning authority and the public, in place of the repeated pattern of the past forty years, when proposals for inappropriate development have often been followed by public protest – which has by no means always been successful.

* Souls on Fire, written by Civic Society committee member David Farnsworth, January 2004

d Newspaper of the Year

ENING POST

ST

THE PAPER AT THE HEART OF BRISTOL

No. 20,628

Thursday, January 27, 2000

eld

rong?

SOMERFIELD

Harry Potter

Is the little wizard too lowbrow?

– See Pages 26 & 27

RAISSA HEADS FOR POP STARDOM — SEE FULL ON

ople as docks' plan is thrown out

plan, applauded, right, by Bristol Civic Society chairman Alan Elkan

PERED

by IAN ONIONS

Kershaw, one of the driving forces behind the giant Harbourside scheme. She asked for an early retirement package last year because of a civic departmental shake up.

She represents the council on the Harbourside Sponsors' Group, the consortium of landowners for the rundown site.

The decision to ditch the Crest Nicholson scheme prompted thunderous applause from about 200 campaigners who crammed the council chamber to hear the debate.

But planning refusal now means a public inquiry is likely to be held over what was described as the city's biggest planning issue since the Second World War.

The council will have to defend its decision to turn down the scheme at the inquiry, which has already been set for April 18.

A Government planning inspector will have to decide the

▶ Turn to Page 2

OF THE ROAD: TURN TO PAGE 8

INSIDE TONIGHT

Man knifed to death

ST PAUL'S: A murder hunt is under way today after a man was stabbed to death after a row in City Road.

● Full story: Page 7.

Stores stay

BRISTOL: Campaigners were celebrating today after Somerfield said it would keep open stores in Knowle and Downend.

● Full story: Page 3.

Trucker clear

EASTON: A man has been cleared of assaulting police after he was wrongly accused of stealing his own lorry.

● Full story: Page 5.

Taken off

FILTON: A disabled grandfather who has struggled to see his RAF memoirs published has finally found success.

● Full story: Page 13.

Front page, Bristol Evening Post.

Some disasters that Bristol Civic Society, working with local amenity groups, helped to avert

Post Office Tower

This 1972 proposal for a 300 foot tower block would have dwarfed the Old Vic Theatre, historic King Street and the old city. It was abandoned because of fierce public opposition to the scheme.

Canon's Marsh

A huge, rigidly-zoned scheme for Canon's Marsh would have obscured views of the Cathedral and turned the best site in Bristol into a most unattractive quarter of the city. This scheme was thrown out by the City Council after a protracted and highly effective campaign.

Avon Gorge Hotel

A proposed massive extension to the existing building would have destroyed the view of the Clifton Gorge and the Suspension Bridge. A lively national campaign eventually saw this proposal withdrawn.

The Inner Circuit Road

This proposal would have entailed closing the City Docks and filling-in the Floating Harbour. The scheme was withdrawn following to powerful and sustained public objection.

Campaigns past and

Historic buildings an obstruction to progress

The first campaign waged by the Civic Society was against a proposal by Bristol Corporation to buy up and demolish some 771 acres (312 hectares) of buildings in the middle of the city. In order to redevelop the city comprehensively as a 'business zone', the Council proposed to demolish an area including Orchard Street, Berkeley Square, Great George Street, Redcliffe Parade, Queen Square and far more besides.

Queen Square

Vandalism or idealism?

Although this probably strikes the modern reader as shocking vandalism, it was an approach that was being adopted all over the country in this era of post-war reconstruction. Idealistic local authorities wanted to create a better world, with fine civic buildings in the middle of town and 'homes fit for heroes' in 'housing zones' on the outskirts.

Alas, their plans, however well intentioned, were often unsuccessful, and many beautiful old buildings were demolished to make way for ham-fisted and failed attempts to forge a brave new world.

Death of a dream

A statement by the Civic Society pointed out that the threatened streets were full of fine historic buildings which 'it would be calamitous to destroy.'

Thanks to the subsequent campaign by local groups led by the Civic Society, the Council's compulsory purchase order was finally reduced to 245 acres (99 hectares).

Much to the City's chagrin, a 1948 government circular stipulated that land should be compulsorily purchased 'only for essential and immediate needs'. This lack of government support for comprehensive redevelopment meant that the Council had to drop its ambitious plans.

In the end, the total amount of land compulsorily purchased by the City Council was a mere 19 acres (7.69 hectares) in Broadmead for a new shopping development to replace the devastated former shopping area between Wine Street and Castle Street.

Thus died the Council's dream of a whole brand-new centre for Bristol.

Orchard Street

Pictures by John Trelawny-Ross.

present

erkeley Square

The Civic Centre that never was:

proposed redevelopment of the Castle Street/Wine Street area

Castle Street, Wine Street and the network of smaller streets between them were wiped out by Hitler's bombs. This once thriving and colourful historic shopping centre, where Bristolians loved to spend their Saturdays parading up and down and doing some leisurely window-shopping, was reduced to rubble. Some of it was eventually flattened and surfaced to provide a large open-air car park.

A new Civic Centre for Bristol

The Corporation's plan for the area was to turn it into a civic and cultural centre, including a museum and art gallery, a guildhall, a conference hall, a library of commerce and a college of technology.

The Council promised not to depart from this grand civic plan without public consultation.

A fragile promise

Alas, this promise proved all too fragile: in 1958 the Council gave permission to both the Norwich Union and the Bank of England for new commercial buildings on the site.

This met with a furious reaction from the Civic Society, as well as from professional, political and commercial associations and the general public. The secretary of the Society wrote:

> *'The Civic Society committee were unanimously of the opinion that the planning permission in principle granted to*

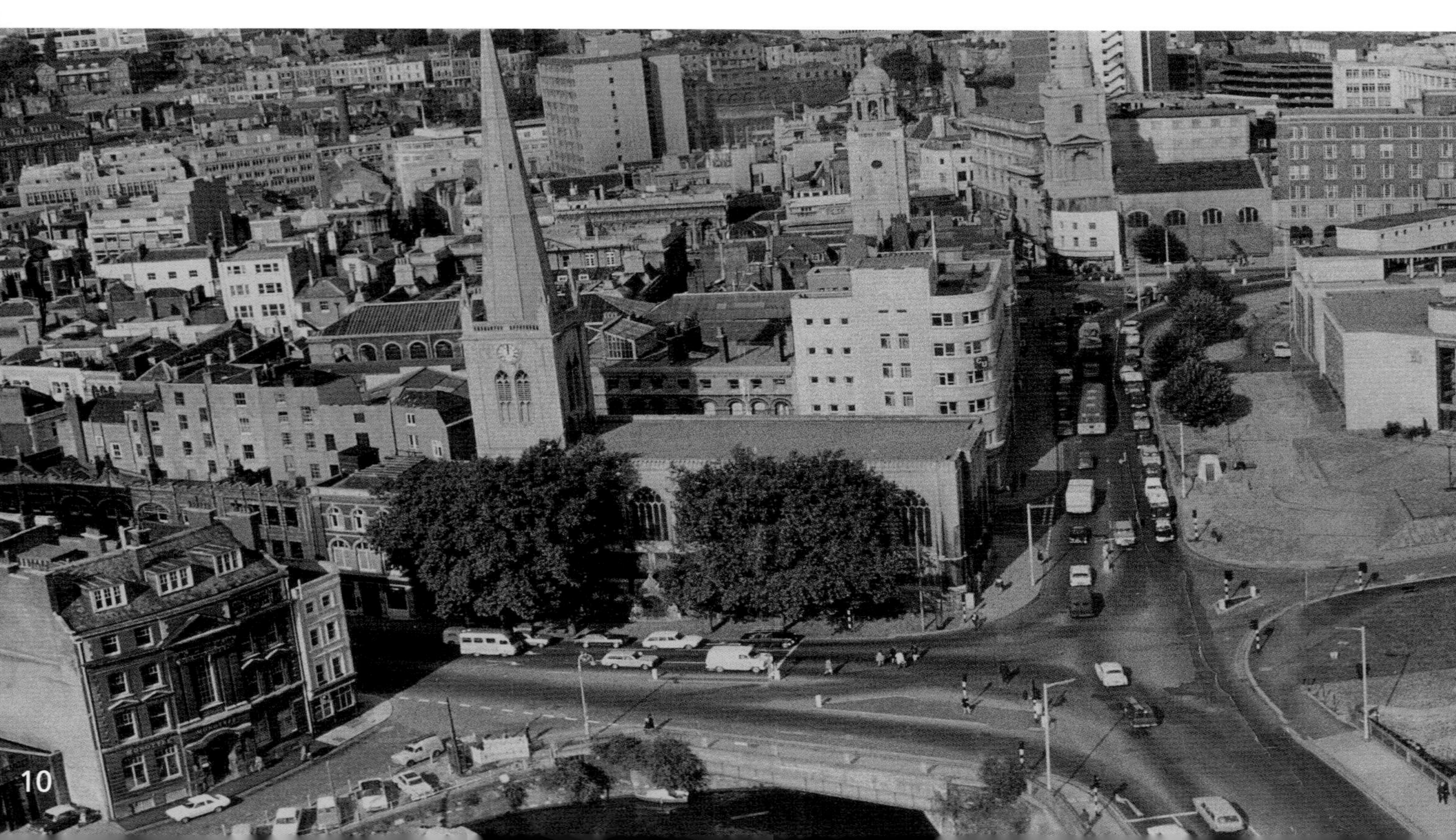

commercial developers should be held in abeyance and rescinded.'

An eminent expert

Arguments about what to do with this important part of the city rumbled on and on, and – at the insistence of all the organisations and associations consulted – an outside expert, the eminent architect Sir Hugh Casson (who had been Director of Architecture for the 1951 Festival of Britain), was drafted in by the City Council to create a coherent plan for the area. This was accepted by the planning committee, but came to naught, stymied by lack of funds.

Arrogance

An interesting sidelight is provided by a small news item in the September 1961 edition of the Bristol and Somerset Society of Architects' Journal. It reports on a meeting to discuss the Council's proposals for the Wine Street area:

> *'The Council spokesman would not discuss the Bank of England or Norwich Union buildings.'*

Would such arrogance and high-handedness be accepted without a murmur today?

It's not over yet

At the time of going to press, the future of the Wine Street area is still unresolved. The Norwich Union and Bank of England buildings remain marooned and alone (although the other side of Bristol Bridge looks more compact and permeable to pedestrians).

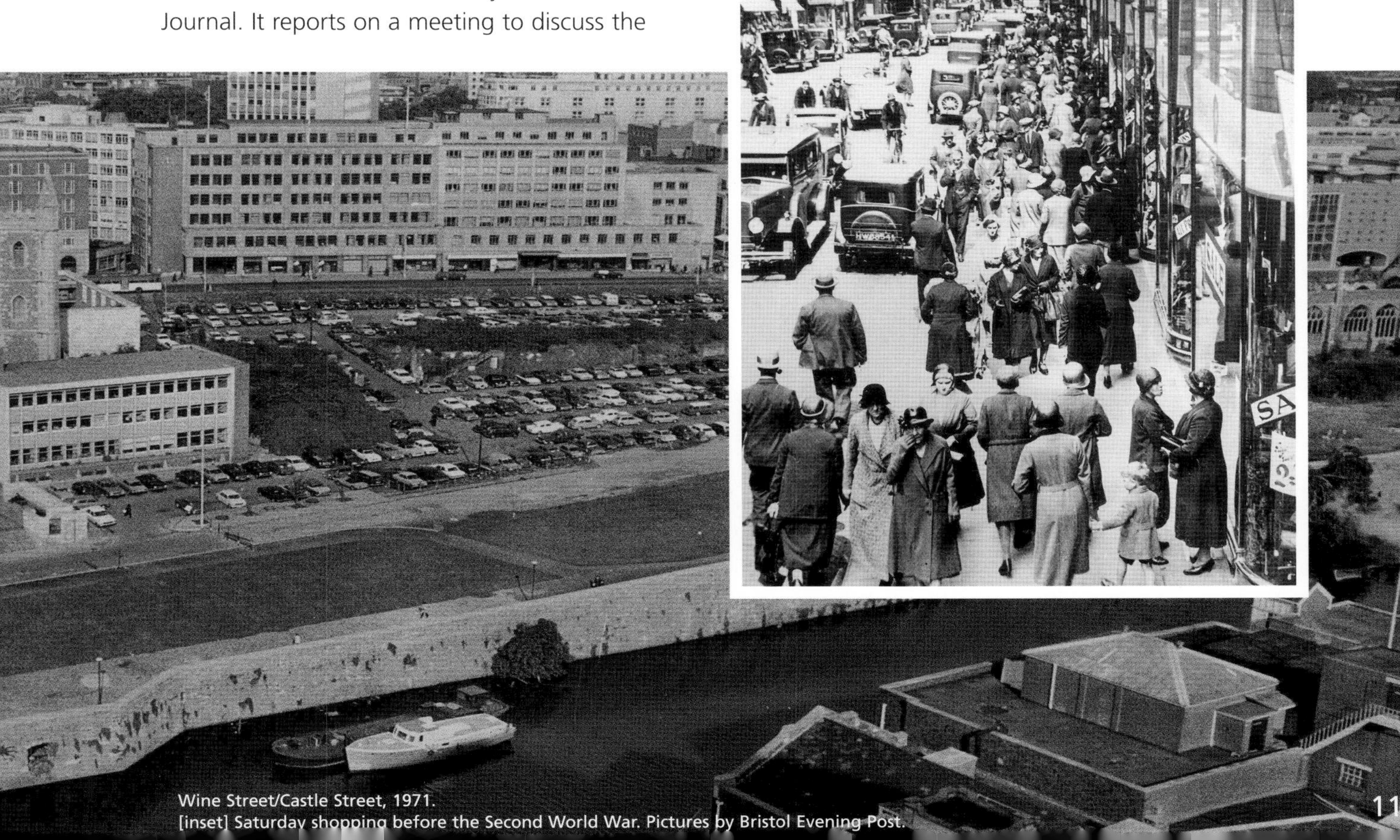

Wine Street/Castle Street, 1971.
[inset] Saturday shopping before the Second World War. Pictures by Bristol Evening Post.

Splendid new car park for the Avon Gorge

From this distance, it is hard to imagine that anybody could have thought it would be a good idea to build a 260-foot long, eight-storey building, comprising a multi-storey car park with a hotel extension on top of it, in the dramatically beautiful Avon Gorge right next to the Clifton Suspension Bridge – but they did.

Picture reproduced by kind permission of Redcliffe Press.

What's more, in January 1971, outline permission for this monstrous development was rushed through by the planning committee so that the hotel-owners could benefit from an English Tourist Board grant of £1,000 per bedroom. The offer of this grant was about to expire, so the heat was really on.

Alarm bells

The Clifton and Hotwells Improvement Society (CHIS) was the first amenity society to get wind of this planning application, and they lost no time in sounding alarm bells. A meeting of interested people was called and an action group, STAG (Save the Avon Gorge), was formed.

In no time at all, 174 individual letters were sent to the Council objecting to the proposal, but this did not stop the planning committee from granting outline planning approval for the hotel extension.

Strike!

Nothing daunted, STAG went national, invoking the power of the national press. In spite of a postal strike, letters from objectors to the Secretary of State calling for a public inquiry were delivered every other day to the Department for the Environment by STAG's very own courier service. No fewer than 1,200 letters were delivered.

The minister announced that he would be calling a public inquiry. Last-ditch attempts by the planning committee and the hotel-owner to get full planning permission for the hotel extension were thwarted at the eleventh hour by a direct intervention from the Minister of the new Department of the Environment.

The Inspector's decision

The Inquiry was an impressive affair. The brilliant local QC Paul Chadd presented a strong case against the development, summoning as witnesses a host of Bristolians, as well as such distinguished national figures as the poet John Betjeman and architects J M Richards and Berthold Lubetkin.

In the end, the Inspector's report recommended that permission for the proposed hotel extension should be revoked.

At the time of going to press, a new plan for the hotel is being mooted by the current owner. It involves creating a car park in the Gorge and building four new town houses on top of the ballroom.

City Docks? **Fill them in!**

In 1969 the Council announced it would promote a Parliamentary Bill enabling the City to withdraw navigation rights in the City Docks. The idea was to fill in large parts of the Floating Harbour to create more space for roads and commercial development.

No more ships in the Docks

Although the proposed scheme was officially described as 'a lagoon system', it soon became all too clear that yachts and tall ships would be banished from the Docks. Bristolians, who have always had a great tenderness for the city's maritime heritage, didn't like this idea one little bit.

The Civic Society, Cabot Cruising Club, Inland Waterways Association, the Kennet and Avon Canal Trust and the Clifton and Hotwells Improvement Society came together at a public meeting which ended with objectors carrying a motion to abandon the Bill that would stop boats from using the docks.

Barrister Paul Chadd concluded a hard-hitting article in the Evening Post (22 August 1969) with the words:

'It is wrong to embark on a vast outlay to destroy what any sane person wants to save.'

DODO in Bristol

DODO drawing by Jerry Hicks

Seasoned campaigner Jerry Hicks promoted the theory that an organisation called DODO (run by covert members of Dada*) was subversively working (in the words of Tony Aldous, writing in *The Times*, 29 June 1971) to subject the city 'to every atrocity of bad planning and non-planning imaginable, in the hope that this ghastly example would bring public and planners elsewhere to their senses'.

The next step of the City Council was to hold a public poll after a campaign to persuade Bristolians that if the docks were ever to be enjoyed as a public space, the Bill had to go through. The council won: the majority of those polled supported the Bill.

*Dada was a group of early twentieth-century artists and writers who used the absurd as a means of protesting against The First World War and the bourgeois society of the day. Among them were François Picabia, Marcel Duchamp and Tristan Tzara.

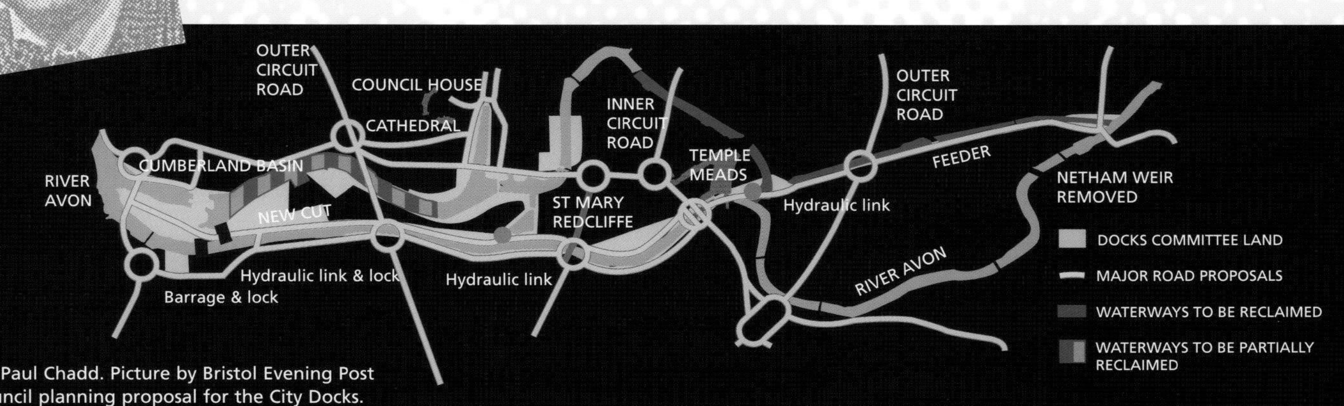

above] Paul Chadd. Picture by Bristol Evening Post
City Council planning proposal for the City Docks.

The fight continues

In spite of this, the fight went on, moving from Bristol to the Houses of Parliament, where vigorous campaigning and distinguished advocacy ensured preservation of the entire water surface and navigation rights for recreational craft. Thus, the Bill was totally emasculated.

Having saved the docks from being filled in, the protestors demanded that a master planner be invited to prepare a study of the area.

Outright criticism

Once again, Sir Hugh Casson was brought in. His report, published in 1972, included outright criticism of the proposed road scheme including an urban motorway, the Outer Circuit Road*, which was to have cut straight across the filled-in Floating Harbour.

Casson also recommended the introduction of a public transport system geared to users' requirements.

It is depressing to observe that we are still not within spitting distance of achieving that; indeed, there is a strong case for saying that public transport is in an even worse state now than it was 30 years ago.

From protest to positive action

The tide turned after the Bristol City Docks Group was founded from the people and groups who had worked so hard to prevent the concreting over of the Docks. Drawing upon the inspiring writing of Jane Jacobs[†], they proposed a return to mixed-use, pedestrian-friendly cities for people. This group transformed the protest movement into a positive forward planning exercise.

* The Outer Circuit Road, which was to have bridged the Floating Harbour, was killed off because the Ministry of Transport refused to finance it, influenced by yet another campaign in which the Civic Society played an important role. Nevertheless, the Outer Circuit Road remained an aspiration for many years.

The Bristol City Docks Group produced a series of seven reports and ideas from the general public – exhibited at the City Art Gallery – for the future of Bristol and its City Docks. 'Twenty ideas for Bristol' was the first of many subsequent invitations to public visionaries.

At the same time, new life was brought to the Docks by the return of the SS Great Britain to the city of its birth. Bristolians were thrilled, though the Council was less certain, since the ship's original dock was on the line of the proposed Outer Circuit Road.

Then, the popular Arnolfini gallery moved into W Shed (before its final move to the Bush warehouse), and when E Shed (now The Watershed) was saved from demolition, the future of the Floating Harbour was assured.

These events, together with enthusiastic public support for keeping the docks open, helped decide the City Council to abandon the 'Docks Bill'. Since then, many of Anne Hicks' illustrations for the Bristol City Docks Group have become reality.

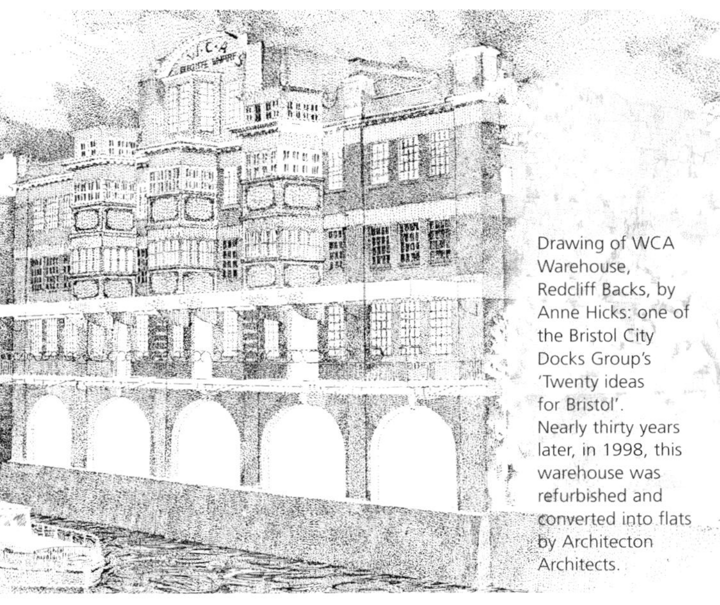

Drawing of WCA Warehouse, Redcliff Backs, by Anne Hicks: one of the Bristol City Docks Group's 'Twenty ideas for Bristol'. Nearly thirty years later, in 1998, this warehouse was refurbished and converted into flats by Architecton Architects.

† Jane Jacobs (born 1916) has written extensively on the subject of cities and how they function. She maintains that local initiatives work better than diktats from central bureaucracies, and that cities should consist of human-scale, sustainable communities.

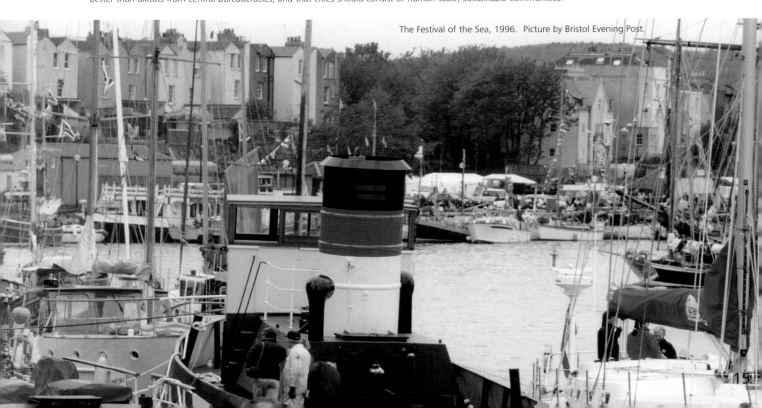

The Festival of the Sea, 1996. Picture by Bristol Evening Post.

A monster looms over King Street

Jerry Hicks from Bristol Evening Post.

A proposal in 1972 to construct a 93 metre high slab block for the Post Office on the site of the Central Telephone Exchange, where it would dwarf the surrounding area including King Street, Queen Square, Corn Street and St Stephen's Street, was rapidly countered by a colourful publicity campaign. This included a scheme to fly barrage balloons at 93 metres to show the general public just how tall the proposed tower would be.

The planning committee rejected the application, so the Post Office changed its plans – and found that its needs were adequately met by a six-storey telephone exchange in place of the proposed behemoth.

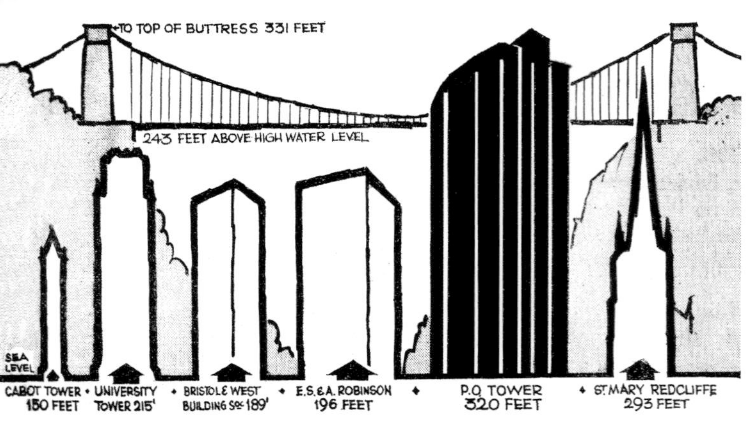

A brief sunlit episode

In April 1974, the County of Avon came into being, sweeping away the old boundaries and taking over the ancient City and County of Bristol.

This was more than a symbolic change: it signalled the end of the post-war era, with its 'Brave New World' politicians and officers. A new breed of planners and politicians soon made itself felt, setting up formal links with the Civic Society and other amenity groups. Bristol won a Europa Nostra award for development in the harbour, and the city's first Local Plan incorporated much of the 'mixed-use' thinking which is current today.

Sadly, this sunlit episode lasted only until March 1996, when the County of Avon officially ceased to exist. A new regime arrived, determined to secure development at all costs, leaving considerations of quality, appropriateness and the wishes of the public trailing behind in the dust.

Canon's Marsh: Bristolians say **NO**

When in 1998 property developers Crest Nicholson launched a scheme, designed by architects Arup Associates*, for the comprehensive redevelopment of Canon's Marsh, the City Council, as one of the joint owners of the Canon's Marsh site, advised councillors to vote in favour of the scheme. Little could the developers or the Council officers foresee the impassioned and furious reaction that these plans would stir up in the people of Bristol.

The proposed development would have been rigidly 'zoned', in the manner which was fashionable in the 1970s, keeping different uses away from each other. There was to be a zone for private housing, an office quarter, a massive commercial leisure centre including a casino, bowling alley, night club and multiplex cinema (of which Bristol already has a plethora) as well as a multi-storey car park.

Outdated and unsuccessful

This was by now generally recognised as an outdated and unsuccessful approach to urban design; the current view is that all new developments should be mixed-use, with lively and attractive uses at ground level (shops, cafés, bars and restaurants), and offices and flats above. This approach keeps a development alive all the time, making it more vibrant and also more secure because of the 'natural surveillance' provided by residents living on the upper floors.

Not Bristol fashion

The planners had so much going for them — but they've lost the urban plot

Tonight the burghers of Bristol must decide the fate of almost a quarter of their city centre. At issue is Canons Marsh, a triangle of mostly derelict land between Bristol Cathedral and the old Floating Harbour. The location should rank in sensitivity with London's South Bank or the Oosterdok in Amsterdam. But tonight's decision faces a greater challenge. Have Britain's cities at the start of the 21st century learnt anything from their recent past?

London normally gazes at provincial Britain with contempt. Unless the country cottage is at stake, or the v... of a recently adopted football team, the provinces can go hang. To Britain's new rulers, the nation beyond the M25 is a no man's land of dreariness and prejudice, to be traversed quickly in search of Tuscany, Provence or the Dordogne. It is pockmarked with cities which, for half a century, have been the most abused and uglified in Europe. How unlike the admired Barcelona, Florence or Nice are Leeds or Nottingham.

Yet the tide is turning. Cities are now good news and British ones are frantically struggling to recover some of their Victorian panache. The ridicule that greeted Manchester's Olympic bid deeply shocked its leaders; they discovered that they had made their city ugly and that it hurt. People do not li... hideous ...

dreadful shopping centre, Broadmead. Amsterdam preserved its wharfs and re-used them for houses and offices. Bristol's wharfs were neglected and demolished. A dual carriageway was driven across Georgian Queen Square. A large roundabout was dumped in front of the finest parish church in England, St Mary Redcliffe. Bristol seemed set on suicide.

Not a vista in this superbly scenic city was left unblighted. A hideous hospital, a students' union, offices and flats went up without care for townscape or horizon. The walk from Temple Meads station to the centre must sink the stoutest heart. The last straw was added by Nicholas Ridley in the 1980s, allowing the giant Cribbs Causeway ...

Simon Jenkins

... medieval alderman. Compare the old and new quarters of any city: the old is alive with congregation, the new is dead. Our age builds magnificent suburbs, but city cen...

... each other". This double-t... help to explain the cyni... afflicts the present image government. Such thin walls" would be unthinkab... other field of regulation. protests that development o...

... mostly it ... medieval neighbourh... across Europe were being rel... after bombing, Bristol build... half its blitzed core and bui...

simon.jenkins@the-times.co.uk

Plan didn't do justice to city heritage

CREST Nicholson's £200 million plan to revive Bristol's docklands lies in tatters today. As the inquest begins into its failure to push through the controversial Harbourside scheme, one fundamental question must be answered.

What is it that the people of this city want to see on what is arguably the most prestigious and important site in Bristol?

Clearly, the current plan has failed to win over the public.

And one overriding factor for that must be its failure to reflect our great maritime heritage.

Nothing contained in the Crest Nicholson proposal did justice to the site's historic links. It was, quite simply, a plan which would have looked equally at home in Milton Keynes.

Today, we applaud the city's planning committee for having the courage to turn it down in the face of a powerful alliance of business and political interests.

Moreover, we support the way in which last night's decision was reached.

Rightly, the city's planning committee is free of political persuasion. It is a legal requirement that its members consider applications on merit, rather than being told how to vote by the Whip.

It also reaffirmed our long-held belief that there is no place in local government for party politics.

Democratically elected councillors should be free to vote with their conscience at all times rather than having to doggedly toe the party line.

If councillors are allowed to vote freely on this issue, then why not on equally important decisions such as school closures and transport policy?

Now that really would be a victory for democracy.

Evening Post Editor MIKE LOWE
Deputy Editor KEVIN BOOTH
Assistant Editor ROB STOKES

SAVE CANONS MARSH!

This is the eleventh hour - together we CAN defeat the Crest Nicholson scheme.

TOWN PLANNING

The dockside site in Bristol is an architect's dream, but there are fears that its development could be a nightmare. Mark Espiner reports

Harbouring doubts

It is the harbour from which Long John Silver set sail for Treasure Island and where Daniel Defoe met the castaway who inspired him to write Robinson Crusoe. But the dockside in Bristol is now at the centre of a different kind of story. It highlights the conflict between business and building development — government utopian directives and funding, the city council's need to realise its land assets, and the wishes of the people of Bristol to see their city shaped in a way that they can enjoy as a community.

Cannon's Marsh, a 16-acre patch of land running along the dockside, complete with listed industrial buildings and in the shadow of the city's cathedral, is up for development. It is the kind of site architects dream about — the ultimate brownfield site ready for urban regeneration to inject life into the city, in line with Lord Rogers' Urban Taskforce document, Towards an Urban Renaissance.

The city council, one of the land owners of the site, was anxious to see it developed. It had to raise matching funding for the million of Millennium Commission mo... the city received to build its edu...

PROFITS RIDING CREST OF WAVE

by CHLOE RIGBY

CREST Nicholson, the building company behind development plans for Bristol's Harbourside, has announced its pre-tax profits soared by more than 40 per cent.

For the second year in a row it announced record house sales, up to 2,422 from 2,210.

The company reported a 42 per cent rise in pre-tax profits from £28.1 million the previous year to £40 million for the year to October 31, 1999.

Operating profits were up from £35.9 million to £49 million, a 36 per cent increase.

Its turnover was £512.5 million compared to £465.4 million.

The firm, which also owns Stoke Gifford company Pearce Construction and sister company MW Pearce, last night had its bid for a £250 million scheme at Harbourside turned down by Bristol City Council.

The development is one of the company's biggest urban regeneration projects. It is also involved in business park developments as well as a major regeneration project at Portbury Dock, Portishead.

In the last year Crest Nicholson says its most significant achievement has been to improve the size and quality of its land holdings.

During the year the company spent £122 million to acquire 48 sites for 2,659 plots compared to 3,155 plots acquired the previous year.

* The architectural practice responsible for designing the Lloyds TSB building.

The proposed new buildings were up to seven storeys in height, very bulky, and would have obscured all views of the Cathedral from the south.

In an attempt to save the beautiful dockside from inappropriate and ugly development, a national publicity campaign was mounted by the Friends of Canon's Marsh. FOCM, in which the Civic Society played a key role, comprised hundreds of individual citizens as well as seven different local amenity societies.

Massive publicity campaign

The FOCM campaign extended to radio, television and the local and national press. On the very day in January 2000 when the planning committee met to make a final decision on whether or no to give planning permission for the Canon's Marsh scheme, Simon Jenkins of The Times wrote a powerful article roundly condemning the proposed development.

FOCM observers in the Council Chamber watched with mounting excitement as, one after the other, members of the planning committee declared against the proposed scheme for Canon's Marsh. The voting was decisively against it, and at last the unpopular proposal was laid to rest.

Once this was out of the way, a master-planner, Ted Cullinan, an architect with a fine national reputation, was appointed as the result of a very limited public consultation exercise, to produce a new plan for Canon's Marsh.

At the time of going to press, the site is being prepared for the start of construction. The Cullinan masterplan plan will transform Canon's Marsh into a place that people will enjoy and want to visit. It will be far more humane and attractive than it could ever have been had the original, rigidly-zoned Arup Associates scheme been implemented.

More trouble and strife down at the Docks

The Docks have been the scene of much planning conflict around the turn of the twenty-first century – perhaps because, at long last, the huge potential value of waterside sites has been recognised by landowners and developers out to make a killing.

If the city were to take a firm line with developers and refuse to countenance any divergence from their own planning guidance, perhaps such conflicts would be fewer and further between.

As it is, developers put forward schemes which do not conform to the planning recommendations, and it is left to the Civic Society and others to try to defend our beloved city against inappropriate development.

At the time of going to press, two proposed developments in particular are hanging in the balance, the subject of lively public discussion and dissent: Wapping Wharf and the McArthur's Warehouse site (the latter lies behind the mooring of the SS Great Britain).

The SS Great Britain in her dock. Picture by Bristol Evening Post.

Both these sites were bought during boom times, so high land prices were paid by the developers. This means that, if the developers are to make a profit, they must squeeze into these sites the maximum possible number of saleable units. Inevitably this brings them into conflict with local residents and the Civic Society, who do not want very tall buildings in an area still dominated by ships' masts; furthermore, they do not think that the exceptionally high densities proposed for Wapping Wharf would create a pleasant environment or comfortable living conditions for the residents.

Massive new development behind SS Great Britain

McArthur's warehouse is a large, handsome brick building, constructed in the early twentieth century, but badly neglected. It may have been the warehouse's state of dilapidation that accounts for its not having been listed.

An application by the developer Quada to demolish the warehouse and replace it with a massive new mixed-use development was given permission in January 2001.

Council's own planning guidelines ignored

It was surprising that the Council accepted this scheme, since the proposed new buildings, designed by Barlow Henley Architects, did not respect the guidelines set out in the Council's own Harbourside Planning Brief: they were taller than recommended; they created more than twice the suggested floorspace and they interfered with a variety of very important views of Brunel's ship SS Great Britain, its masts silhouetted dramatically against the sky. This interference was made glaringly evident by the use of computer-generated images, commissioned by the Civic Society.

The public was very unhappy when the planning committee resolved to grant outline permission for this scheme. A campaign involving the Civic Society and others resulted in the Secretary of State 'calling in' Quada's proposals. A public inquiry was held in January 2002, and in July of that year the Secretary of State rejected the Quada scheme on the grounds that it was out of keeping with the low-lying maritime nature of the surroundings, and that such bulky buildings behind the Great Britain would distract the eye from the funnel and masts of the ship.

The developer went away and got his architects to amend the proposal, making the buildings less obtrusive. The Civic Society still objected strongly to the proposal as being far too big for the site and having a damaging effect upon the setting of the SS Great Britain. When, however, English Heritage withdrew its objection, the Council narrowly agreed that the scheme should go ahead.

Picture by James Barke.

Whopping development on Wapping Wharf

Right behind the Industrial Museum, the 4.15 hectare former NCP car park site has been bought by Umberslade, a developer who proposes to put up housing which would be more than 50% denser than any other new housing on the Docks.

The proposal is for between 500 and 700 residential units on a site which the local plan suggests might accommodate 200 units.

The four blocks of flats are crammed together so closely that there will be little privacy for residents – and all in the interests of maximising profits.

Local residents and members of the Civic Society have together formed the Spike Island Futures Group, which is arguing forcefully for the improvement of Umberslade's scheme. They want more green space, an element of social housing (not pushed out of the way at the back of the site), more space between blocks and a significant reduction in the ridiculously high density proposed.

Negative? not us!

The Civic Society is sometimes accused of being negative and opposed to progress. This could not be further from the truth, but we can see how the opinion may have come about.

After all, when we are involved in a high-profile campaign, it is usually against what we consider to be an ill-judged development proposal, and it is as objectors that we come to public attention. Yet there is much positive work going on, too, aimed at encouraging development which enhances the quality of our environment.

Environmental Awards

One example of positive action by the Civic Society is our annual environmental award scheme, sponsored in recent years by SWRDA, The Institute of Physics Publishing, and Bristol Water, who are our centenary year sponsors. Every year, we ask members of the public to send us their nominations for the city's best new buildings, new public spaces and refurbishments of old buildings. A panel of judges decides which of these nominated projects deserve one of our awards, then there is a presentation ceremony attended by building owners together with members of the construction team. This event is always much enjoyed by those who take part, and is given extensive coverage in the Evening Post. The winners take away an elegant plaque to be displayed at the site for all to admire.

Pictures by Bristol Evening Post.

The greening of Bristol

For close on 30 years, the Civic Society has contributed to the greening of the city by planting thousands of trees. It began in 1973 with the hugely successful 'Plant a tree in '73' campaign, and has encompassed planting throughout the city, including Easton Way and Greville Smyth Park.

The Society also played a leading role in mounting a national campaign (Save Our Sports Grounds) to protect playing fields from being sold off to developers. We briefed MPs and helped draft national Planning Policy Guidance No. 17. This, however, is a continuing battle.

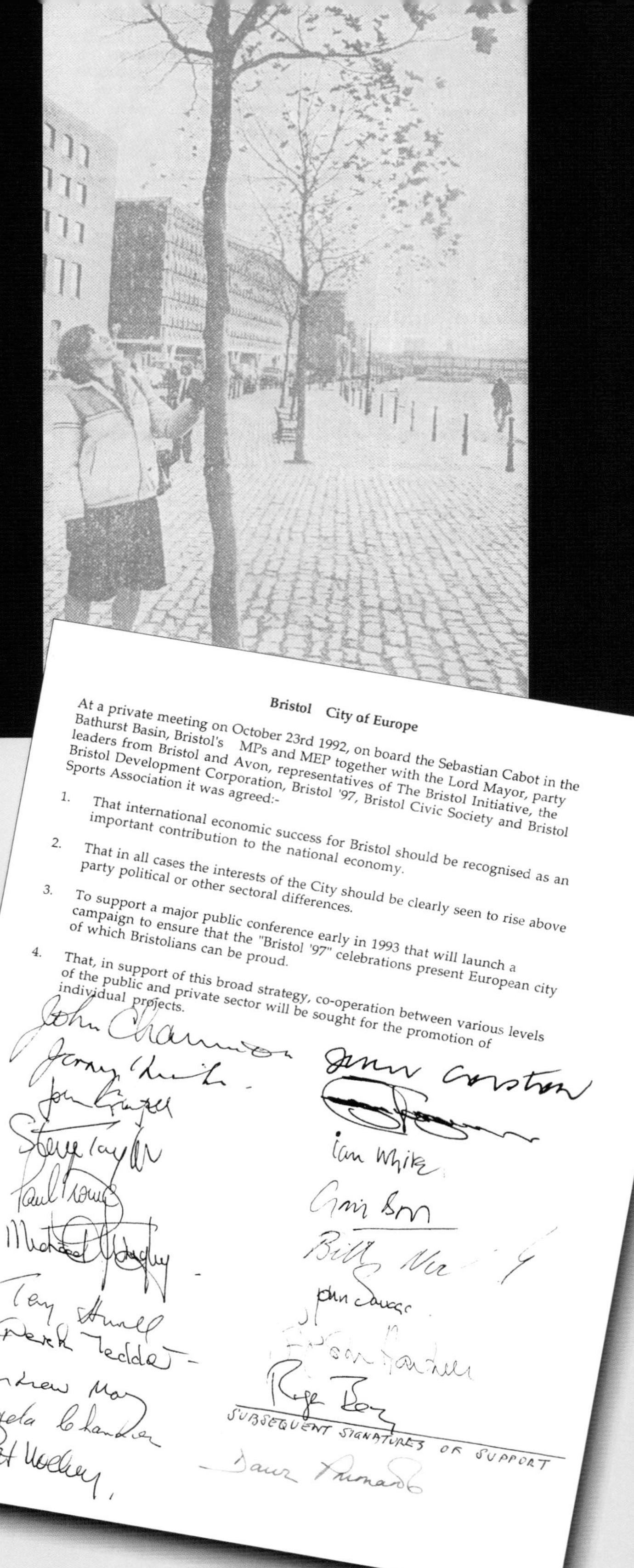

Bristol City of Europe

At a private meeting on October 23rd 1992, on board the Sebastian Cabot in the Bathurst Basin, Bristol's MPs and MEP together with the Lord Mayor, party leaders from Bristol and Avon, representatives of The Bristol Initiative, the Bristol Development Corporation, Bristol '97, Bristol Civic Society and Bristol Sports Association it was agreed:-

1. That international economic success for Bristol should be recognised as an important contribution to the national economy.
2. That in all cases the interests of the City should be clearly seen to rise above party political or other sectoral differences.
3. To support a major public conference early in 1993 that will launch a campaign to ensure that the "Bristol '97" celebrations present European city of which Bristolians can be proud.
4. That, in support of this broad strategy, co-operation between various levels of the public and private sector will be sought for the promotion of individual projects.

SUBSEQUENT SIGNATURES OF SUPPORT

The Bathurst Declaration

In October 1992, the Civic Society joined with the Bristol Sports Association to cajole the city's movers and shakers into sinking their differences and working together for the benefit of the city.

All these important people gathered together on board the Sebastian Cabot, moored in the Bathurst Basin, and signed the declaration shown on the right.

Amongst the signatories were the Lord Mayor, MPs and MEP, representatives of Bristol Civic Society, Bristol Sports Association, Bristol Society of Architects and Bristol Initiative as well as councillors, council officers and other important figures.

Never before (or since) has such an assemblage of important people agreed to set aside their disagreements and work together for the greater good of the city.

The future

Redcliffe – real public involvement at last

It was in 2001 that the Redcliffe Futures Group was formed, comprising 16 local organisations, including several residents' groups, representatives of Bristol City Council and of the Civic Society.

Together they worked out a radical plan for the regeneration of the traffic-blighted no-man's-land that is the Redcliffe area. Their new scheme will remove the traffic from in front of St Mary Redcliffe and create a fine new public square surrounded by a network of buildings, pedestrian routes and facilities for the community and for tourists.

These changes will serve to reunite Redcliffe, currently chopped up by roads, and re-create the tight street pattern of old Bristol, bringing Redcliffe back to life and turning it into a beautiful place where people will want to be.

'But will it ever happen?'

In July 2002, a public exhibition showing what the group had come up with was given an enthusiastic reception – but as the Redcliffe Community Forum commented, 'Exactly what we have wanted for years, but will it ever happen?'

At the time this book goes to press, two and half years on, there is still a major obstruction to the Redcliffe community's plan for the regeneration of their locality.

This stumbling block is the refusal of the Transport Department to allow the removal of through traffic.

The delay is frustrating, but it seems that the tide of opinion in national government and amongst many in the City Council is beginning to turn. The Redcliffe Futures Group is a model of effective public involvement.

Civic society unveils blueprint for 21st Century European city

Bright new future

Queen Square: Calls for a continental look with pavement cafes, restaurants and illuminated fountains

High Cross: The society wants to install a new High Cross at the junction of Corn Street and High Street – the focal point of the Medieval city

St Mary Redcliffe: Society supports city council's desire to take traffic away from one of the finest parish churches in England.

By Rachel Carlyle

GUARDIANS of Bristol's heritage yesterday produced an ambitious vision to take the city into the 21st Century.

Members of the Civic Society have listed 30 ideas they want to see take shape up to the year 2000 to promote Bristol as a key European city.

The document called Our City's Future has received an enthusiastic response from MPs and councillors, and society members hope funding will come from Millennium or Lottery sources.

The society has appealed to people to forget political differences and past mistakes, and work together to create a better Bristol.

Its main ideas include a transformation of Queen Square to give it new life with pavement cafes, restaurants and illuminated fountains, connecting with another smaller square at Welsh Back.

It also backs the city council's plan to take traffic away from the historic St Mary Redcliffe church, including removal of the controversial flyover near Temple Meads railway station.

But in addition it wants to see a whole range of schemes to improve the city's appearance and give it a new vitality.

It feels the city's Festival of the Sea in May and celebrations in 1997 to mark the 500th anniversary of explorer John Cabot's voyage to America gives Bristol a unique opportunity to attract tourists from all over the world.

Jerry Hicks, chairman of the society's urban design group, thinks both events will give Bristol a chance to market itself as a great European city and boost tourism for years to come.

He said: "An awful lot of people are going to be visiting Bristol and first impressions last.

"There is the will to make things happen, but people work in isolation and some feel beleaguered. But if everyone put their backs into it and put aside any political differences, then Bristol could be transformed."

Other ideas include:

- Installing a new High Cross at the top of Corn Street 200 years after the original was removed to Stourhead in Wiltshire.
- Display Welcome-to-Bristol signs, and provide maps and information at key points.
- Restore St Nicholas Street and use St Peter's Church for amenities.
- Erect a statue in King Street, opposite the Llandoger Trow, of Long John Silver reputedly the owner of the pub.
- Rejuvenate run down approaches to the city such as Stokes Croft and Victoria Street.

Some of the ideas are the society's own, but others are from Bristol city council and architects and are already advanced in the planning process.

"We are drawing together the various schemes around to create a real vision of what the future could be like," said Mr Hicks.

"Some of them do not require large funding at all, but just a little thought."

The society is hoping to work with the city council and other groups to apply for funding from the Millennium and Lottery funds.

A city council spokesman said: "Support from the society is very useful."

The council has set up a city centre committee to draw up a strategy for area, which is expected to be published in the next few months.

Ian White, MEP for the city, said he was impressed and believed there was a chance of European funds.

How we work – the nuts and bolts

Bristol Civic Society works on many different fronts at once, and we've found the best way to cope with everything that needs to be done is to split up into various different working groups, all of which report regularly to the Executive Committee. The groups are:

- the **Planning Applications Group**, which keeps a keen eye on the register of planning applications, commenting upon on schemes which would be likely to have a significant impact on their surroundings. The group examines close on 400 applications a year, an enormously demanding task.
- the **Urban Design Group** (combined with the independent **LA21 Land Use Group**, affiliated to the Civic Society), which works to encourage attractive and sustainable new developments in Bristol.

  The LA21 Land Use Group has recently produced a widely-admired guide to best practice in sustainable development. This guide (which has been adopted by national government) is aimed at members of the general public who want to become involved in planning the future of their own neighbourhoods. The guide helps by showing examples of what is possible in the real world.

  Membership is represented on a Scrutiny Commission, the Select Committee on Planning Reform and an advisory group to the Bristol Partnership.
- the **Amenity and Trees Group**, which concentrates on such fundamental matters as the condition of pavements, and the quality and condition of street furniture, while also monitoring Bristol's magnificent parks and open spaces. This group has organised tree-planting in streets, public areas and school grounds, going right back to the long-ago but not forgotten 'Plant a tree in '73' campaign.

  The trees lining St Augustine's Reach are a fine example of the group's contribution to Bristol.
- the **Transport Group**, which considers all aspects of transport in Bristol, whether by foot, water, bicycle, road or rail. A successful transport strategy is one of the keys to making Bristol a more pleasant place, and a vital aim is to ensure that motor vehicles do not continue to dominate the city.

  This group's publication, 'Go Public', inspired new thinking about transport throughout the country.
- the **Futures Group**, which runs our annual environmental awards scheme; this celebrates quality in new developments in the city.

The Futures Group produces and distributes our newsletter, organises visits and meetings for members and looks after publicity and exhibitions. The creative thinking generated by this group has an effect beyond the confines of the Society.

Whenever the Civic Society is 'seen' by the public (rather than working quietly and anonymously), it's probably because of the work of the Futures Group.

- In addition, we have a representative on the **Conservation Advisory Panel**. The advice of this panel is valued by the City Council.
- Finally, we have had a representative on the city's **Public Rights of Way Liaison Group** since it was founded in the late 1990s. The work involves attending meetings and making site visits to assess the current state of some of Bristol's hundreds of rights of way, and to comment upon any proposed changes.

These working groups are always delighted to welcome new members, so if you would like to join any of them, do please let us know.

Picture by James Barke.

All hands on deck

Although this is a history of the Bristol Civic Society, it would be a serious mistake to imagine that the Society works all on its own. On the contrary, as well as working with private developers in the early stages of proposed developments, the Society also has a long history of collaborating with other organisations, from the City Council to a wide variety of lively local amenity and special interest groups. The famous campaigns described in this booklet were the work of many hands.

When something in the city cries out for public action, sometimes amenity, special interest groups, concerned individuals and the Civic Society come together as a new group with its own name, formed for that specific campaign.

For example, when Bristolians were campaigning against a very unpopular plan for the redevelopment of Canon's Marsh (see pages 17–18), a group called Friends of Canon's Marsh was formed to co-ordinate the campaign. It comprised a number of different local amenity societies:

- Brandon Hill Play and Development Group
- Brandon Hill Residents' Association
- Bristol Visual and Environmental Group
- Clifton and Hotwells Improvement Society
- Redland and Cotham Amenity Society
- Sustrans

– and Bristol Civic Society.

Picture by the Brandon Hill Play and Development Group.

Managing Information in Financial Services

Phil Fawcett MBA, FCIB

& **Graham Flower** FCIB

Financial World Publishing
c/o The Chartered Institute of Bankers
Emmanuel House
4-9 Burgate Lane
Canterbury
Kent
CT1 2XJ
United Kingdom

Telephone: 01227 762600
e-mail: editorial@cib.org.uk

Financial World Publishing publications are published by The Chartered Institute of Bankers, a non-profit making registered educational charity.

Typeset by Kevin O'Connor

Printed by Communications in Print, Basildon, Essex

ISBN 0-85297-569-4

Contents

INTRODUCTION

The Concept of the Book

This study text has been written for students of The Chartered Institute of Bankers' ACIB/BSc subject Managing Information in Financial Services and also for practitioners in financial services who are looking for a practical refresher.

Each chapter is divided into sections and contains learning objectives and clear, concise topic-by-topic coverage.

Syllabus

The key sections of the Managing Information in Financial Services syllabus are:

- Strategy and Information Technology Management;
- System and Process Development;
- Customer Knowledge Management;
- Delivery Channels.

Your contribution

Although this study text is designed to stand alone, as with most topics certain aspects of this subject are constantly changing. Therefore it is very important that you keep up-to-date with these key areas. For example, you should read the quality press and financial journals and look out for relevant websites.

We anticipate that you will study this course for one session (six months), reading through and studying approximately one unit every week. However, note that as topics vary in size and as knowledge tends not to fall into uniform chunks, some units are unavoidably longer than others.

Study plan

If you are a distance-learning student and have not received your study plan by the beginning of the session, please contact the CIB Tuition Department.

Tel: 01227 818637

Fax: 01227 453547

e-mail: tuition@cib.org.uk

Part 1

Strategy and the Business Environment

This part of the book considers how financial services organizations develop and formulate both their business strategy and their information strategy.

Strategy formulation is a complex process that needs to take account of the external and competitive environment and the organization's own capabilities, as well as the organization's objectives. We can illustrate this as a diagram:

Figure 1: Strategy Formulation Context

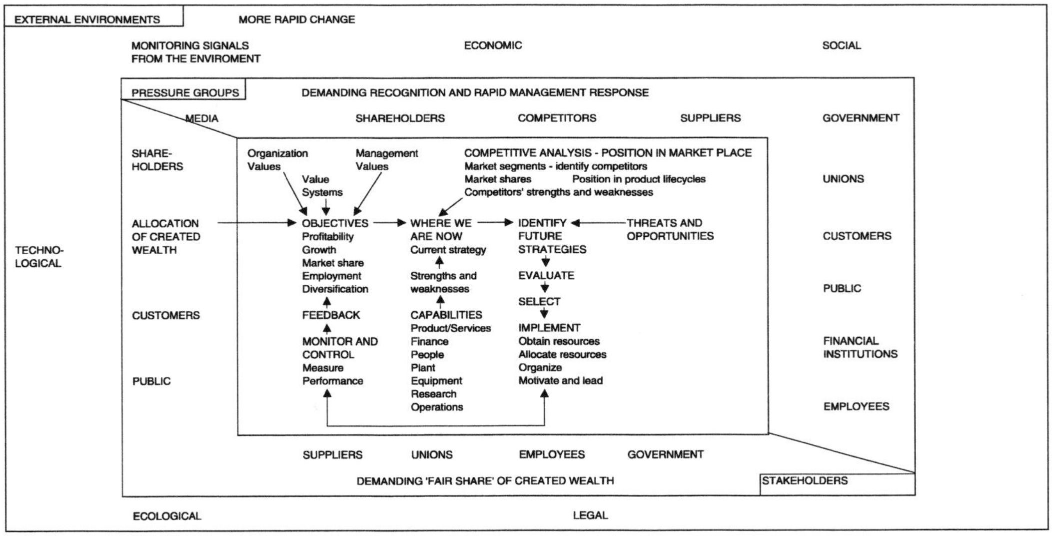

EXTERNAL ENVIRONMENTS
MORE RAPID CHANGE
MONITORING SIGNALS FROM THE ENVIROMENT
ECONOMIC
SOCIAL
PRESSURE GROUPS
DEMANDING RECOGNITION AND RAPID MANAGEMENT RESPONSE
MEDIA
SHAREHOLDERS
COMPETITORS
SUPPLIERS
GOVERNMENT
SHARE-HOLDERS
Organization Values
Management Values
Value Systems
COMPETITIVE ANALYSIS - POSITION IN MARKET PLACE
Market segments - identify competitors
Market shares
Position in product lifecycles
Competitors' strengths and weaknesses
UNIONS
ALLOCATION OF CREATED WEALTH
OBJECTIVES
Profitability
Growth
Market share
Employment
Diversification
WHERE WE ARE NOW
Current strategy
IDENTIFY FUTURE STRATEGIES
THREATS AND OPPORTUNITIES
CUSTOMERS
TECHNO-LOGICAL
Strengths and weaknesses
EVALUATE
SELECT
PUBLIC
CUSTOMERS
FEEDBACK
CAPABILITIES
Product/Services
Finance
People
Plant
Equipment
Research
Operations
MONITOR AND CONTROL
Measure
Performance
IMPLEMENT
Obtain resources
Allocate resources
Organize
Motivate and lead
FINANCIAL INSTITUTIONS
PUBLIC
EMPLOYEES
SUPPLIERS
UNIONS
EMPLOYEES
GOVERNMENT
DEMANDING 'FAIR SHARE' OF CREATED WEALTH
STAKEHOLDERS
ECOLOGICAL
LEGAL

Therefore we spend this part of the book discussing the business environment. The traditional way of remembering this is LePEST & Co., but we shall slightly change the order and consider:

- The competitive environment in Chapter 1;
- The legal environment in Chapter 2;

- The political environment in Chapter 3;
- The economic environment in Chapter 3;
- The social environment in Chapter 3;
- The technological environment in Chapter 4.

This is background to the discussion of the development of the business and information strategy that occurs in Chapter 5.

1

THE COMPETITIVE ENVIRONMENT

Objectives

After studying this chapter, you should be able to:

- understand the 'five forces' model and be able to apply it to analyse the competitive conditions in the financial services industry;
- understand convergence in the financial services industry and the problems this causes in defining markets and identifying competitors;
- understand the characteristics of financial services and be able to take them into account when evaluating competitive advantage;
- understand the potential sources of competitive advantage and be able to analyse competitive position in terms of these sources;
- understand the impact of information technology on mergers and acquisitions;
- understand how to assess market power.

1 Introduction

The competitive environment defines the competitive conditions financial services organizations face. A useful starting point is to define competition. A senior banker has given the following definition:

> *Competition is rivalry in selling among sellers acting completely independently within the same time period: that is two or more suppliers striving simultaneously to achieve the same objective. Their effort is to win business from rivals and in many cases to attempt to extend the total market by influencing the environment in which they operate by marketing activity.*
>
> *Marketing can be described as all forms of competitive activity including both price and non-price competition. Such activities as advertising, public relations, sales promotion, product/service development and sponsorship are all forms of marketing activity.*

Competition has the effect of limiting process and profits: generally, the greater the degree of competition in the market the less the likelihood of abnormal profits being earned in the market.[1]

Figure 1.1: The Five Forces Model

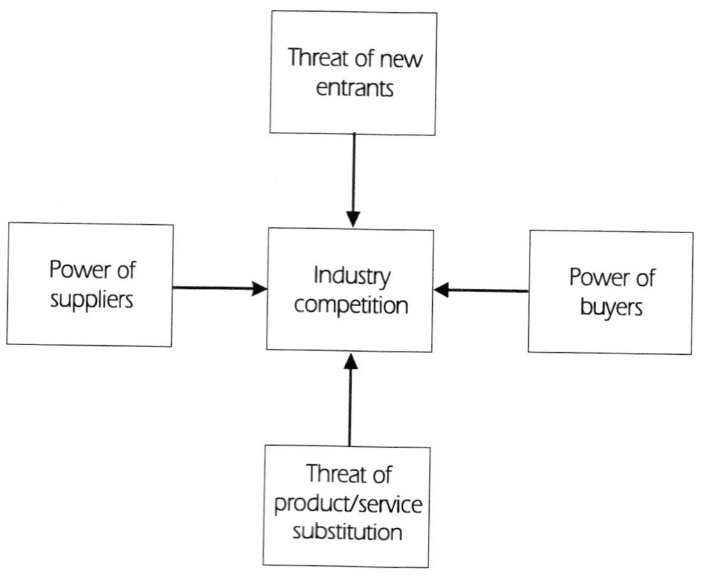

2 The 'Five Forces' Model

One of the most important tools for analysing the competitive environment is Michael Porter's 'five forces' model:

Under this model, the competitive conditions in an industry are determined by five forces:

Table 1.1: The 'Five Forces' Model

Force	Competition is high if ...	Competition is low if ...
Power of suppliers	There are few suppliers with high market power	There are many suppliers with fragmented market power
Power of buyers	There are many customers with fragmented buying power	There are few customers with monopoly buying power
Threat of new entrants	There are low entry barriers for new competitors	There are high entry barriers for new competitors

1 *Source:* Ian Lindsay

Table 1.1: The 'Five Forces' Model (continued)

Threat of product/ service substitution	There are few alternatives to the product or service	Customers can easily switch to alternatives for the product of service
Industry competition	There are many competitors	There are few competitors

3 Defining the Market

The definition we used to introduce this chapter assumes that we know in what market we are operating. But this is not easy in the financial services industry.

Let us consider Coutts and Co. as an example. Is it a very small player in a saturated banking market? Is it a large player in a relatively fast-growing private banking market? Should it be assessed as an independent organization at all or simply regarded as part of its parent bank? Is its marketplace local or global, and are its competitors global or local?

Why is it so difficult to define the market? If we consider this in terms of Porter's model, the problems arise through the threat of new entrants and the threat of product/service substitution.

New Entrants

Sir John Quinton, in his 1989 Presidential Address, pointed out that technology has lowered the entry barriers to the financial services industry and raised the exit barriers. The main entry barrier used to be the cost of building up a large branch network, but ATM reciprocity and direct banking have reduced this. The main exit barrier is the existence of large amounts of 'single-purpose' assets – for example branches that cannot easily be converted to other uses and equipment for clearing cheques and bank giro credits. Technology has raised the exit barriers by increasing the amount of such equipment needed by financial services organizations.

Deregulation in financial services has focused on lowering entry barriers by removing restrictions on competition between providers of different types of financial service. Until Competition and Credit Control (1971) there was a clear distinction between banks, building societies and other types of financial services organization. These have been progressively relaxed through measures such as the 'Big Bang' (1986) and the Financial Services and Markets Act 2000, and a wide range of organizations are now able to offer financial services.

One effect of this has been to encourage globalization. Size is generally seen as a source of competitive advantage because larger organizations can spread their fixed costs across more customers and transactions. Size is of particular benefit in wholesale commercial services, because large financial resources enables financial services organizations to offer customers a single point for all their financing needs and global coverage allows financial services organizations to meet the needs of their multinational customers. This has encouraged financial services organizations to operate on a continental or global scale, with the most obvious examples being Citigroup, HSBC and the American 'bulge bracket' investment banks.

There is a point where the diseconomies of scale outweigh these benefits, and this limits the size of the largest financial services organizations. These diseconomies include the problems of managing a wide range of activities across many locations as well as regulatory and anti-trust pressures.

Industry convergence is a result of deregulation and globalization. The diagram on page 6 illustrates the increasing overlap in financial services.

One effect of these changes has been an oversupply of financial services. This has resulted in industry consolidation, as financial services organizations merge to acquire customer share and reduce industry capacity.

Figure 1.2: Overlap in financial services

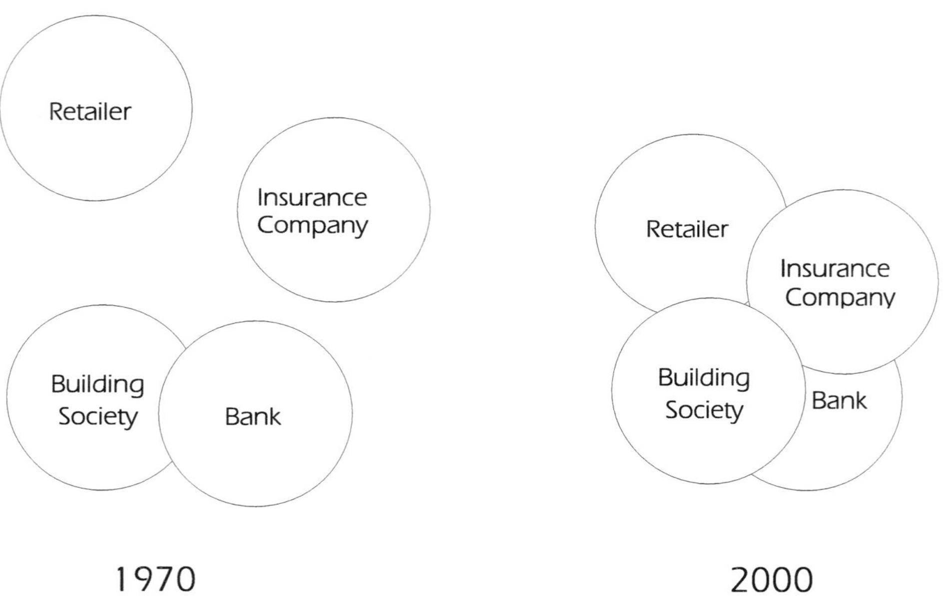

Substitution

The raw material for financial services products is money. An obvious statement, but one that explains why the threat of substitution is so great for the financial services market. Manufacturing organizations can gain control over the sources of supply of their raw materials, but this is not an option available to financial services organizations.

A characteristic of money is fungibility. Money obtained for one purpose can be used for another. Therefore it is very difficult to restrict financial products to one purpose. An example is the mortgage – originally restricted to house purchase, this is increasingly used for a wide range of financing and products are being introduced that link mortgages with other credit and savings products. The removal of product-specific tax breaks (such as those for life assurance and mortgages) has helped to encourage substitution.

4 Characteristics of Financial Services

Despite deregulation, globalization and convergence, there are a number of characteristics unique to the financial services industry:

- The customer relationship is fiduciary – a relationship of trust;
- The characteristics of service industries in general. De Bretani defined these as intangibility, simultaneity, heterogeneity and perishability.

Fiduciary Nature

Financial services are of a 'fiduciary nature'. This means that there is an element of trust between buyer and seller. Therefore the usual rule of *caveat emptor* (let the buyer beware) is less prominent in financial services. Both case law and legislation support this.

For example, insurance contracts are *uberrimae fidei* (of the utmost good faith). This places an obligation on both parties to disclose all information that may affect the decision of the other party to enter into the contract. Most obviously, individuals taking out life assurance must fully disclose any existing health problems, and the contract may be voided if they do not.

The decision in *Lloyds Bank Ltd. v. Bundy* provides another example. The judgement was that 'confidential trust is placed in them [banks] because of a combination of status, goodwill and knowledge' and implied a requirement to give careful, independent advice. Other cases such as *Woods v. Martins Bank Ltd. and Another* support this.

In practice this has limited financial services organizations' ability to move to a purely transaction-based approach.

Intangibility

Services are intangible. This means that they do not involve the creation of a physical product that can be used as evidence of quality of service.

This is not to say that physical objects are not used in financial services. Examples include credit cards and chequebooks. However, the physical object is not the product – customers will assess credit cards on their acceptance and on the accuracy or otherwise of processing, not on the physical card. These objects can perhaps best be thought of as the packaging – the attractiveness of the design and quality of the object may have a small effect on the initial customer buying decision but the customer's needs are satisfied by the product itself.

Simultaneity

Services are simultaneous. This means that they are created and consumed at the same time – the 'process' of creating the service and the 'product' of its consumption occur simultaneously.

An important implication of this is that changes to the process will affect the product.

Heterogeneity

Services are heterogeneous. This means that each service is unique and there is a natural variation in quality. One issue with all services is how much variation is acceptable.

Financial services organizations have invested heavily in reducing this quality variation, most recently by centralizing back-office functions into service centres that operate on a factory basis.

Perishability

Services are perishable. This means that services cannot be 'built for stock'. The simplest example is from outside the financial services industry. A hairdresser with no customers cannot 'create' a stock of haircuts to be fitted to customers when they eventually do arrive.

The consequences of this are quite important. At any time there is no demand for services, the assets that would be used to create those services are unproductive. Therefore the organization is not earning a return on them.

This is one driver behind the development of direct financial services and 'any time, any place, anywhere' banking (sometimes called Martini banking). Financial services organizations tend to have high fixed costs (premises, equipment and staff) and low marginal costs (for example, fees paid to payment schemes). To improve profitability, financial services organizations must 'sweat the assets' by making as much use of their fixed assets as possible.

5 Competitive Advantage

Financial services organizations view information technology as a potential source of competitive advantage. What do we mean by competitive advantage and how can we use information technology to achieve it?

Competitive advantage is any means by which gain an advantage over our competitors. We can seek to win business from our competitors and/or to extend the market in a number of ways.

The simplest classification is that of Xavier Gabriel and Paul Strebel:

- Lowest delivered cost;
- Highest perceived quality.

Another well-known classification is that of Michael Porter:

- Cost leadership;
- Differentiation;
- Focus.

Other potential sources of competitive advantage are:

- Creating a new market. The first entrant in a new market becomes the standard against which all later entrants are judged. This is called 'first mover advantage';
- Logistics. The ability to use distribution channels as a source of competitive advantage;
- Information;
- Mergers and acquisitions;
- Possession of complementary assets. These are also called network effects;
- Market power.

Lowest Delivered Cost/Highest Perceived Quality

Lowest delivered cost is the ability to deliver a product or service at a lower cost than competitors. Organizations that are able to achieve this can either gain market share by reducing prices below those of competitors or can charge the market rate and earn additional profits.

Highest perceived quality occurs when customers believe that the organization's products or services are better than those of its competitors. Such organizations are able to charge a price premium and earn additional profits or, more rarely, to price their products and services competitively to build market share.

The price elasticity of the product or service being sold affects how the relative benefits of lowest delivered cost and highest perceived quality can be used as sources of competitive advantage. If its price elasticity is low, an increase in price will not have much effect on the demand for the product or service. Basics such as foodstuffs have low price elasticity. If its price elasticity is high an increase in price will lead to a large fall in demand, reducing total income from the product or service.

We can classify products and services as commodity or branded goods:

- Commodities are seen by customers as virtually the same irrespective of supplier. Nails are an example – they are bought by weight and the customer does not differentiate between manufacturers. The price elasticity of commodities is often high and the ability to produce the lowest delivered cost creates competitive advantage;
- Branded goods are seen by customers as very different. Confectionery bars are an example – the customer will specify a Mars Bar or a Kit Kat rather than simply asking for a piece of confectionery. The price elasticity of branded goods is usually low and manufacturers are able to charge a premium which represents the value of the brand.

  Some retailers have succeeded in creating universal brands by building an image as a supplier of high-quality goods. Examples of such brands include Marks and Spencer, John Lewis and Tesco. These firms are able to charge a premium across a wide range of own-label products.

Retail financial services in general are now seen as a commodity product, although some areas (most obviously credit cards) are strongly branded. Financial services organizations have generally been more successful in building universal brands than in branding individual products.

Cost Leadership/Differentiation/Focus

Although there are some similarities with Gabriel and Strebel's classification, they are not equivalent.

Cost leadership corresponds to lowest delivered cost.

Differentiation can be on perceived quality but can also be on other factors such as price. Another 'differentiation' strategy is undifferentiation – producing products and services identical to those of competitors. Undifferentiation allows the organization to save marketing and development costs and focus on low-cost production.

Because differentiation can cover so many factors, there are no simple rules as to how best to exploit differentiation once achieved. Differentiation on factors such as perceived quality, quality of support, quality of design or brand image are usually exploited by charging a premium price.

Price differentiation can include charging a *higher* price to build an image. A well-known example of this concerns a perfume manufacturer who increased sales by raising prices, attracting buyers who were interested in buying the most expensive perfume available as a special present. This is unusual and the usual reason for price differentiation is to build market share by undercutting competitors.

Undifferentiation usually involves using the demand for the original product created by competitors' marketing activity. Competitors may have created a niche market or may have developed a unique product position. The organization can exploit this by charging a lower price to build market share – the supermarkets have been accused of this by marketing own-label products similar in appearance to leading brands. An example from financial services might be the development of gold and platinum cards. These created niche markets which were entered by competitors and have now become standard products.

The idea of focus allows us to choose to compete only in parts – or 'segments' – of the market. A financial services organization expects to compete more effectively by concentrating on a small part of the market.

The benefits of focus are:

- Specialization. By specializing in a single market segment the organization expects to have a better understanding of the segment's needs and to be able to tailor the way it works to this segment;
- Possession of complementary assets. Complementary assets include anything that may add value to transactions involving customers in the market segment. We discuss

complementary assets later in this chapter.

Creating a New Market

These models assume that the market size is limited and we can gain competitive advantage only by taking market share away from our competitors or by charging a premium price. An alternative way of securing competitive advantage is to create a completely new market.

Say's Law states that supply creates its own demand. Developing a new product can create a market for it. This is a high-risk strategy – most new products fail – but can be a powerful source of competitive advantage.

One reason for this is 'first mover' advantage. Organizations who are the first to enter a market can create an enduring market lead. Obvious examples – where the brand became synonymous with the product - are Hoover and Biro.

Another reason is that the creator of the market can impose standards on the market. This is harder in financial services than in some other industries, because standards are usually agreed by industry-wide bodies or by regulators, but it is possible. Perhaps the clearest example is the introduction of electronic funds transfer at point of sale (EFTPOS), where the industry-wide initiative EFTPOS UK failed to achieve a viable standard and was overtaken by Switch, introduced by Midland Bank. Switch became the standard for EFTPOS in the UK until the introduction by Visa of the Electron and Delta cards.

The characteristics of services we discussed above allow scope for creating new markets. For example:

- Because services are intangible it is relatively simple to create a new service or to modify an existing service to better meet the needs of the customer. Manufacturing industries need to set up expensive factories to make new goods before they gain any commercial return. Service industries can roll out new services relatively quickly;
- Because services are simultaneous any change to the process of creating the service directly affects the customer's experience of having the service delivered. Service industries can use this to differentiate themselves on the basis of the quality of the experience offered. Some industries – notably leisure – are selling the experience as a product in its own right;
- Because services are heterogeneous, service industries can customize the service to meet the exact needs of the customer. The ability to offer a bespoke service is itself a new product;
- Because services are perishable the ability to deliver the service to where the customer needs it when the customer needs it is a source of competitive advantage. The rise of telephone banking and the emergence of PC banking and Internet banking are examples of new markets created as a result of this time- and location-based competition.

The role of information in the creation of new markets is ambiguous. Traditional market research and market forecasting techniques are notoriously unreliable when applied to new markets. In the early days of the computer industry, the head of IBM forecast that the *worldwide* demand for mainframe computers would be no more than 25 units. There were similar errors in forecasting the demand for personal computers and home computers.

On the other hand, organizations rely on information to reach potential customers. A profile can be developed based on the marketing concept and customers for 'similar' products. This is difficult for any really innovative products and test markets and focus groups are important to understand the buyers' behaviour.

Many recent innovations in the financial services industry have relied on information technology. A good example is the 'electronic wallet' smartcard such as Mondex or VisaCash. It is worth noting that although these smartcards are physical objects, the services they offer are getting (electronic) cash and payment for goods and services. Therefore they do not break our rule about services being intangible.

It has proved very difficult for financial services organizations to protect their competitive advantage by protecting the underlying technology. There are two reasons for this:

- Financial services organizations usually need to develop these services in partnership with organizations that can provide the technology. For example, Mondex was developed by the National Westminster and Midland banks in partnership with BT. It is in the technology partners' interests to promote and license the use of the technology, even though the financial services organization may prefer the technology to remain proprietary;
- New financial services need to achieve a general level of acceptance before they can be used. For example, Mondex becomes useful only once a significant number of retailers are prepared to accept it. However, retailers are willing to accept Mondex only if a significant number of customers are likely to use it. Therefore National Westminster Bank, which originally developed Mondex, allowed a competitor, Midland Bank, to join the consortium to ensure a sufficiently large number of potential customers to make it attractive to retailers.

Distribution Channels

The supply chain is the link between the original supplier and the ultimate customer. For example we can show a simple supply chain for advances:

Figure 1.3: Distribution Channels

Depositors → Financial services organizations → Borrowers

Another way of gaining competitive advantage is to gain control of the supply chain. Organizations that achieve this benefit in a number of ways:

- They may be able to transfer costs or risks from themselves to suppliers or customers. Manufacturing techniques such as just-in-time delivery (JIT) or zero defect achieve this by transferring inventory and inspection costs to suppliers. These transfers are sometimes called upstream and downstream effects;
- They may achieve process efficiencies by automating part of the process. Links between the WalMart and Proctor and Gamble computer systems mean that products are automatically re-ordered when stocks reach re-order point. This saves on administration costs. Straight-through processing, by which the customer enters an order that is processed and fulfilled automatically, produces the greatest efficiency benefits;
- They may benefit from greater information about the customer. We discuss this in Chapter 12;
- They may be able to lock customers or suppliers into their systems. If customers use personal financial management products such as Money or Intuit they are unlikely to switch to a supplier of PC financial services that does not offer this option;
- They may be able to increase product penetration. By making it easier for customers to buy additional products, it is more likely that they will continue with their existing supplier.

Direct banking is the main method financial services organizations are currently using to control the supply chain, although they are also looking at the potential for involvement in e-commerce.

Information

Information as a source of competitive advantage includes information about customers and the organization's own know-how.

We discuss the importance of customer knowledge in Chapter 12 and of know-how in Chapter 19.

Mergers and Acquisitions

We have discussed industry consolidation above. Mergers and acquisitions deliver competitive advantage by increasing market share and by improving product penetration. As the merged organization combines the customer bases of its components, it has more customers. This automatically increases its market share, allowing fixed costs to be spread across more customers, and provides a basis for cross-selling of products to the newly acquired customers, increasing product penetration. It also allows the merged organization to reduce costs by eliminating duplication.

IT is often a factor in inhibiting mergers and acquisitions, and at least one UK financial sector merger is believed to have failed because of the difficulty in combining the organizations' IT systems. There are four main approaches:

- To continue to use the organizations' existing, separate systems, but to build 'bridges' between them to allow the consolidation of management information. This does not produce any cost savings, and differences in the way the systems work may affect the quality of the management information – we end up comparing apples and pears, to use a common analogy;
- To choose one organization and use its systems exclusively. This usually happens where the merger is a clear take-over of a weaker organization by a stronger. There may be significant difficulties in moving the second organization's data onto the systems of the first and this approach badly affects morale in the second organization;
- To choose the best individual systems from each of the organizations and combine these. For example, the first organization's customer information system may be used with the second organization's accounting system. This approach is called 'best of breed'. Although this is the most popular approach for mergers of equals, there are often major technical difficulties in combining the systems;
- To ignore both existing systems and build a new system for both organizations. The existing systems can be retained with bridges – the first option we considered – but will be put on a 'care and maintenance' basis. The major disadvantage of this approach is the delay before the merged organization can respond to new demand for IT systems.

Complementary Assets

It is possible to gain competitive advantage through the possession of complementary assets. This occurs when two separate products or services complement each other in some way – an example of 2+2=5.

An important recent example is the anti-trust trial of Microsoft, where the judge used the term 'network effects'. The argument is that Microsoft's ownership of both the Windows operating system and the Office suite of office products is complementary – that Microsoft can exploit its understanding of how Windows operates both to improve the performance of its own office software and to prevent its rivals from developing superior products.

An example relevant to the financial services industry in the UK is the Cruickshank report into competition in the UK banking industry. This suggested that the major banks' ownership of the major credit card networks was a complementary asset to their main operations and had the effect of restricting competition in the credit and debit card markets.

Market Power

Given the problems of defining the market for any particular financial services organization, how can we define its market power? John Kay has suggested that one measure is the organization's ability to influence pricing decisions.

Basic economic theory tells us that monopolies can charge whatever price the market is prepared to accept and will earn excess returns – the 'monopoly rent' – as a result. It is also known that the established market leader can charge a premium price, and that its pricing decisions set the general level of prices for the market.

Therefore organizations seek to increase market share to allow them more control over pricing decisions. The ability of organizations to achieve this depends not only on market share but also on Porter's five forces.

2

THE LEGAL ENVIRONMENT

Objectives

After studying this chapter, you should be able to:

- understand financial services organizations' duty of confidentiality to the customer;
- understand the main data protection legislation and be able to use it to analyse scenarios and case studies;
- understand the main intellectual property legislation and be able to use it to analyse scenarios and case studies;
- understand the main provisions of financial regulation as they apply to information technology;
- understand the main provisions of competition law and corporate governance as they apply to information technology;
- understand the legal issues associated with electronic commerce and the relevant legislation;
- understand the conditions that must be fulfilled for computer records to be admissible in a court of law;
- understand your organization's own rules as they apply to information technology.

1 Introduction

The legal environment defines the rules within which financial services organizations operate. It includes a mix of case law, statute law, regulation, codes of practice and internal rules. We can consider the legal environment under the following headings:

- Data Protection Legislation
- Intellectual Property Legislation
- Financial Regulation
- Competition Law and Corporate Governance

- Electronic Commerce
- Criminal Justice Act 1984 and Police and Criminal Evidence Act 1984
- Bank Rules.

2 Data Protection Legislation

Until recently, financial services organizations' legal responsibilities have been concerned mainly with data privacy. This was based on case law (*Tournier v. National Provincial and Union Bank of England* 1924) and the Consumer Credit Act 1974.

UK government legislation implementing European directives led to the strengthening of data privacy provisions and imposed on financial services organizations a legal responsibility for data security. These obligations were specified in the Data Protection Acts of 1984 and 1998 and the Computer Misuse Act 1990.

Case Law

Tournier v. National Provincial and Union Bank of England 1924 defined the banker's obligation not to disclose information about customers without their consent. This applies to all information the bank may obtain provided that this arose out of the banking relationship, for example it includes records of interviews and telephone calls as well as financial records. It continues after the closure of the account or accounts, although any new information obtained after closure would not be covered.

This covers all bank records irrespective of whether they are electronic or manual – computer systems were not an issue in 1924! It has now been largely superseded by later legislation, in particular the Data Protection Acts of 1984 and 1998, although it continues to form the basis of the confidentiality provisions of the code of banking practice.

Code of Banking Practice

The code of banking practice and the mortgage code are voluntary codes of practice followed by banks, building societies and mortgage lenders, and monitored by an independent review body. The codes incorporate the conditions under which disclosure was permitted in *Tournier v. National Provincial and Union Bank of England* and restrict the circumstances under which financial services organizations will provide information to credit reference agencies.

Other obligations under the code of banking practice include explaining customers' right of access under the Data Protection Act and advising customers when bankers' references are given. Although the code is voluntary, it is authoritative and financial services organizations take compliance very seriously.

Consumer Credit Act 1974

The Consumer Credit Act 1974 (CCA) was designed to control organizations involved in the granting of credit, with the particular objective of protecting borrowers from unfair lending practices.

The main relevance of the CCA to financial services is with regard to the use of credit reference agencies. The Act defines a credit reference agency as a business whose function is to provide information relevant to the financial standing of individuals. This includes both profit making and non-profit making organizations such as trade associations. All credit reference agencies must be licensed by the Office of Fair Trading. Although financial organizations also provide financial information, this is not their main business and they are not regarded as credit reference agencies under the CCA.

The CCA covers printed information as well as information held in machine-readable form. The CCA gives individuals four rights:

- It places a duty of disclosure on businesses (including financial services organizations) using the services of a credit reference agency. An individual may apply in writing within 28 days of completion of negotiation of a credit agreement and has the right to be informed of the name and address of any credit reference agency consulted;
- It gives the individual a right of access to the information held. The individual must request this in writing and pay a small fee. The credit reference agency must supply all information held about the individual (which may include information about other individuals – for example the husband or wife – if this is considered relevant to the individual's credit-worthiness);
- It gives the individual the right to have information deleted or corrected where it is factually incorrect and likely to damage the individual (for example by making it less likely that credit will be granted). The individual may give the credit reference agency written notice requesting removal or amendment, to which the credit reference agency must respond within 28 days;
- If the credit reference agency does not accept the removal or amendment of the information, it may serve a counter-notice of non-action. The individual has the right to add a 'notice of correction' to the information held. This is a short statement to show why the information held is incorrect. The credit reference agency may apply to the Office of Fair Trading to have the notice of correction quashed if it believes it to be incorrect or if it has other reasons for not publishing it (for example it is libellous or frivolous).

Data Protection Act 1984 and Data Protection Act 1998

The 1984 Data Protection Act was passed to comply with European Union restrictions on cross-border data processing and to meet public concern about the use of data held on computer systems. It protects personal data recorded in a form which can be processed automatically – usually a computer system, although any data that can be identified using computer-readable media (for example a bar code) would be covered.

This has now been superseded by the 1998 Data Protection Act, although there are transitional periods lasting until 2001 for some data held electronically and until 2007 for some data held in manual systems. All references to the DPA in this book refer to the 1998 Data Protection Act.

The main changes under the Data Protection Act 1998 are:

- It has been extended to cover 'relevant filing systems' including paper filing systems and microfiche;
- The principles now include a requirement that personal data shall not be transferred outside the European Economic Area except to countries that ensure an adequate level of data protection;
- Individuals can give notice in writing that the data user must not use their data for marketing purposes;
- There are restrictions on the use of automated decision systems. They can still be used as a condition for entering or performing a contract (therefore credit scoring a new loan application is still permitted) but in other circumstances individuals must be informed when a decision is made on this basis and have the right to have it reassessed manually.

Personal data is defined as statements of fact or opinion and statements of intention about identifiable, living individuals. This excludes information about limited companies although information about sole traders – treated as individuals in law – is covered.

The DPA defines a data subject as being the person about whom data is held. It defines a data controller as a person or organization holding data. Where people access data as part of their jobs, the organization (rather than the individual) would be the data controller. A data processor is defined as someone who processes data on behalf of a data controller, excluding employees of the data controller.

Its definition of processing includes obtaining, holding and disclosing data, as well as amending, deleting or adding to data.

All data users must register with the Data Protection Registrar, who ensures compliance with the DPA. Information to be registered includes, who the data user is, what personal data is held, the purpose for which it is held, where the data subject may apply to look at this data, to whom the data may be disclosed and any foreign countries to which the data may be transferred.

Data subjects' rights include a right of access to data about them; a right to take action for compensation for damage suffered as a result of the Act being contravened; a right to rectify, block, erase or destroy inaccurate data and a right to have an assessment by the Data Protection Registrar as to whether any provisions have been contravened.

In addition, data subjects have the right to prevent processing likely to cause damage or distress; the right to prevent processing for the purposes of direct marketing and the right to have any decision taken by automated means reviewed. There are some exemptions from the review requirement.

There are a wide range of exemptions from various provisions of the DPA, covering areas such as national security, crime, taxation, health, education, social work and regulation. There are also some exemptions covering purposes such as journalism, art, literature, research, history and statistics.

There is an exemption from the non-disclosure provisions where disclosure is required by law.

Financial services organizations must register with the Data Protection Registrar and have appointed compliance officers responsible for ensuring that their obligations under the DPA are met.

Principles of the Data Protection Act

The principles of the DPA are:

- Personal data shall be processed fairly and lawfully and, in particular, shall not be processed unless:
  - at least one of the conditions in Schedule 2 is met, and
  - in the case of sensitive personal data, at least one of the conditions in Schedule 3 is also met.

  (Schedules 2 and 3 establish that either the data subject has given consent for processing or that the processing is necessary, for example to fulfil a contract or for legal reasons. Schedule 3 is concerned with sensitive data such as racial origin, religious belief or sexual preference for which a stricter definition of necessary is applied);
- Personal data shall be obtained only for one or more specified and lawful purposes, and shall not be further processed in any manner incompatible with that purpose or those purposes;
- Personal data shall be adequate, relevant and not excessive in relation to the purpose or purposes for which they are processed;
- Personal data shall be accurate and, where necessary, kept up to date;
- Personal data processed for any purpose or purposes shall not be kept for longer than is necessary for that purpose or those purposes;
- Personal data shall be processed in accordance with the rights of data subjects under this Act;
- Appropriate technical and organizational measures shall be taken against unauthorized or unlawful processing of personal data and against accidental loss or destruction of, or damage to, personal data;
- Personal data shall not be transferred to a country or territory outside the European Economic Area, unless that country or territory ensures an adequate level of protection for the rights and freedoms of data subjects in relation to the processing of personal data.

Data Safe Harbours

The United States has adopted a different approach, using data 'safe harbours'. These rely on a mix of legislation, regulation and self-regulation. The safe harbour principles are:

- Notice. Individuals must be informed about the purposes for which organizations collect information about them;
- Choice. Individuals have the opportunity to prevent information about them being used or disclosed for purposes other than that for which it was collected;
- Onward transfer. Organizations may only disclose information in a manner consistent with the principles of notice and choice;
- Security. Organizations must take reasonable measures to protect data from loss, misuse, unauthorized access, disclosure, alteration and destruction;
- Data integrity. Organizations should take reasonable steps to ensure that data is accurate, complete and current;
- Access. Individuals must have reasonable access to data held about them and must be able to correct or amend it where it is inaccurate;
- Enforcement. There must be adequate mechanisms for ensuring compliance with the safe harbour principles.

The safe harbour principles are voluntary, but are binding on organizations accepting them. At the time of writing it is thought that this will provide an acceptable level of protection to allow data transfers from the EU to the US.

Computer Misuse Act 1990

The Computer Misuse Act was passed in 1990 after some highly-publicized cases of 'hacking' – unauthorized access to data held on computers. The Act introduced three new criminal offences:

- Unauthorized access to computer programs and data;
- Unauthorized access with intent to commit or facilitate the commission of a further crime;
- Unauthorized modification of computer material, that is programs and data held in a computer.

The first offence is relatively minor and allows the prosecution of people who simply want to look at data to which they have no right of access. If convicted, such people can be fined up to £2,000 and/or imprisoned for up to six months. The other two offences are far more serious and cover actions such as industrial espionage, attempted fraud and the introduction of computer viruses. People convicted of these two offences may be imprisoned for up to five years and/or may be given an unlimited fine. Prosecution for these offences does not prevent someone also being prosecuted for the first offence, where the requirement for proof is lower.

For a conviction under the Act, the person must be aware that he or she was not authorized to access or modify the data. This is why financial services organization systems now display warning messages when people log on to use them. It must also be shown that the person's actions caused the computer to carry out some function – even if only to reject the access attempt.

EU Directives 95/46/EC and 97/66/EC

European Union directive 97/66/EC has extended to scope of the earlier directive 95/44/EC in respect of data privacy in telecommunications.

The most important part of the directive is Article 12, which states 'the use of automated calling systems without human intervention or facsimile machines for the purposes of direct marketing may only be allowed in respect of subscribers who have given their prior consent'. In other words, unsolicited marketing faxes are not allowed unless the subscriber has expressly agreed to accept them.

Another important part of the directive is that it defines the subscribers' right to block caller line identification, although this can be overridden by the emergency services and for purposes such as tracing malicious calls. Caller line identification is discussed later in this book and allows someone receiving a call to identify the caller's telephone number.

This directive has been implemented in the UK through the Telephone Preference Service (TPS) and the Fax Preference Service (FPS). Telecommunications regulator Oftel has licensed the Direct Marketing Association to operate the TPS and the FPS, which complement the existing Mailing Preference Service (MPS – formerly the Mail Order Preference Service or MOPS).

The TPS gives individuals the right to opt out of unsolicited direct marketing calls. This is less strict than the EU directive. The FPS complies with the directive by requiring that individuals must opt in before they can be sent unsolicited direct marketing faxes.

The European Commission is currently looking at the use of e-mail for direct marketing and there is discussion as to whether an 'opt out' system or an 'opt in' system should be adopted. This is likely to be covered in a future directive.

3 Intellectual Property Legislation

Intellectual property rights are protected through the Copyright Act 1956, the Copyright (Computer Software) Act 1985 and the Copyright Designs and Patents Act 1988.

Contract law provides additional protection for software purchased from external vendors.

Copyright and Patent Law

Computer programs are the 'intellectual property' of the author and copyright law exists to protect the author's rights. Under the Copyright Act 1956 and the Copyright (Computer

Software) Act 1985, original works such as computer programs cannot be copied, without the permission of the author, for 50 years after publication.

As far as computer software is concerned, the author is usually the organization that produced or commissioned it. The individual or software house who wrote the computer programs usually waives any rights in favour of the organization.

Copyright law also prevents the production of programs which do the same thing as the originals. These design rights are protected under the Copyright Designs and Patents Act 1988. This is important in IT where the identification of requirements and design of the system accounts for much of the cost of systems development.

Patent law protects inventions. Software is not normally covered by patent law in the UK, but it is covered in the USA and there has been discussion in the European Union about adopting a similar approach in the EU. Halifax has applied for patent protection for some of the techniques used in its IF electronic banking system.

Law of Contract

Software purchased from external vendors is also covered by contract law. This takes the form of a licence agreement, which the purchaser accepts as part of the purchase of the software, limiting the purchaser's rights to copy or to sell the software.

As an example, consider purchase of 'shrink wrapped' package software for a personal computer. The CD-ROMs (or, occasionally, floppy disks) which contain the software are usually in a sealed envelope. By breaking the seal the purchaser agrees to the terms of the licence. This restricts the number of copies that can be made and if the purchaser makes more than the licence allows he or she can be sued for breach of contract.

In the UK, an organization called the Federation Against Software Theft (FAST) represents the interests of the software producers and has prosecuted some very large companies for breaches of copyright and contract law. The Business Software Alliance (BSA) is the US equivalent.

4 Financial Regulation

Financial regulation is largely outside the scope of this book, but there are aspects that are relevant to IT. Relevant legislation includes the Financial Services Act 1986 and the Money Laundering Regulations 1993.

Financial Services Act 1986

The Financial Services Act 1986 regulates the provision of financial services in the UK. Although this is largely outside the scope of this subject, two requirements of the Act should be noted:

- Financial services organizations are required to give best advice unless they are dealing with experienced investors or providing services on an execution-only basis. In the context of information management, this restricts our ability to provide direct banking services except on an execution-only basis;

- Financial services must be provided on a best execution basis – financial services organizations must provide the service using the best value method. This may have implications as cheaper methods of service execution become available over the Internet.

Money Laundering Regulations 1993

The 1993 Money Laundering Regulations were introduced to combat money laundering and there are equivalent European Union regulations and global conventions. Again, these are largely outside the scope of the subject but three requirements should be noted:

- Financial services organizations are required to obtain customer identification. This has an impact on providing direct financial services, where physical forms of identification may be difficult to obtain or validate;
- Large movements must be reported;
- Unusual transactions must be reported.

The Joint Money Laundering Steering Group in the UK and the Financial Action Task Force worldwide monitor compliance with the regulations.

5 Competition Law and Corporate Governance

Competition Law in the UK is governed by the Competition Act 1998. This implements the provisions of articles 81 and 82 of the European Community treaty, by prohibiting agreements between firms which distort competition and by limiting the behaviour of dominant firms. The Competition Commission oversees the structure with the Office of Fair Trading (OFT) responsible on a day-to-day basis.

The Financial Services and Markets Act 2000 disapplies some aspects of the Competition Act 1998 from the financial services industry, but includes additional provisions relating to market abuse.

OFT regulation does sometimes affect the financial services sector. For example, it is an OFT ruling that has inhibited financial services organizations from using information from standing orders for marketing purposes. Although this covered only one specific circumstance, the financial services sector has been reluctant to test this ruling.

Corporate governance was the subject of a series of enquiries, of which the first was the Cadbury Committee in 1992. The Turnbull Committee reported in 1999 on the implementation of the 'supercode'. This placed two relevant obligations on directors:

- It extended the responsibility of directors for risk. This now includes non-financial risk in areas such as the environment, markets and technology;

- It placed a focus on ongoing internal control. Companies are now required to satisfy their auditors that these controls are embedded in their operations and that they can respond rapidly to change.

6 Electronic Commerce

The main legal issues associated with e-commerce are:

- How to establish identity and legal capacity;
- Legal jurisdiction;
- Content ownership and legal responsibility for content;
- Taxation;
- Contractual status.

The issues with *identity and legal capacity* arise because of the difficulty of unambiguously establishing the identity of the parties to an e-commerce transaction. Physical proofs of identity such as a passport or driving licence cannot be presented over the Internet and the parties are not physically present, which makes it difficult to establish age.

This can lead to problems such as fraud and to individuals entering into contracts that are illegal or which cannot be enforced against them – for example, minors entering into loan contracts.

The issue with *legal jurisdiction* is which set of laws should apply if the parties to an e-commerce transaction are in different countries. At the time of writing there are three possibilities:

- For business-to-business e-commerce, the contract will specify which legal code applies. Unlike business-to-consumer e-commerce, consumer protection legislation is not applicable;
- The provision of information to consumers. The general view appears to be that the laws of the country of the information provider apply – if a business is allowed to provide information in its country of domicile it is allowed to provide the same information over the Internet;
- The provision of a service to consumers. The general view appears to be that the laws of the country of the consumer apply. Therefore a business may be breaking the law because its service offering does not comply with local consumer protection legislation.

The situation on business-to-consumer e-commerce is clearly inconsistent.

The issues with *content ownership and legal responsibility for content* include:

- Responsibility for illegal material. This category can include material governments regard as seditious and material that is banned under national laws or international conventions;

- Responsibility for libel. This includes the publication of libellous statements on the Internet;
- Responsibility for copyright violations. This is further complicated by differences in copyright law between different countries, and because copyright may be held by different people or organizations in different countries;
- Intellectual property rights in domain names or 'assigned names'. 'Cybersquatting' is the practice of registering as a domain name the name of a famous individual or a well known organization, with the intention of selling the name to the individual or organization at a high price;
- Deep linking. The Internet allows links to be built to any web page. Deep linking occurs when a link is built to a page that would normally be accessible only through an entry screen, as in Figure 2.1.

Figure 2.1: Deep Linking

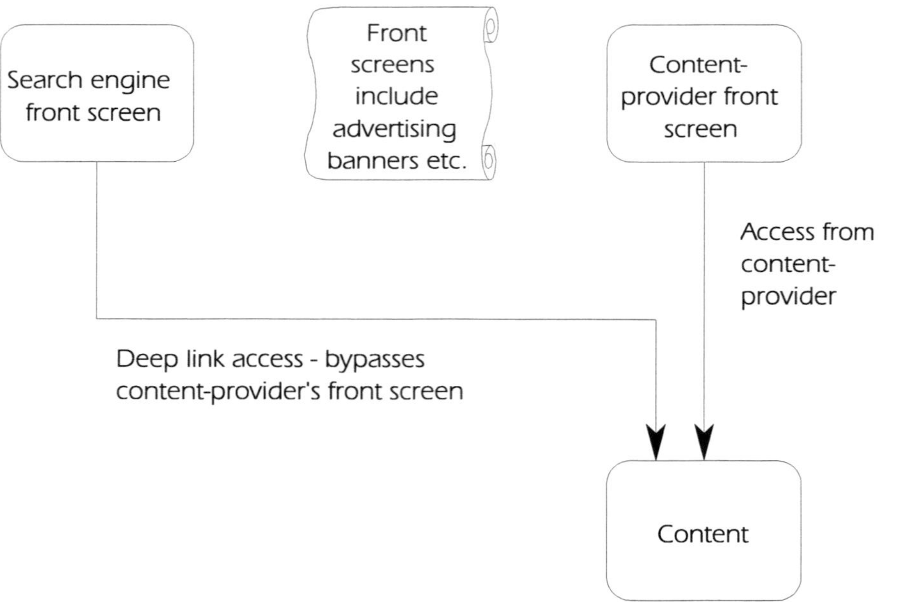

The problem with the first three issues is, who has legal responsibility for ensuring that the content of the Internet complies with local legislation? In particular if an Internet service provider (ISP) 'hosts' material which violates local legislation, is this the ISP's responsibility?

The current view appears to be that the ISP is not a 'publisher' in the legal sense but does have a duty of care and is required to remove illegal or libellous material if this is brought to the ISP's attention. In the USA, ISPs are regarded as 'carriers' similar to the Post Office or courier companies rather than as a publisher. However, there has been a case in Germany in which the ISP was held liable for publishing illegal material.

The World Intellectual Property Organization (WIPO) has set up an arbitration service to address the issue of cybersquatting. Arbitration is binding, which prevents the more flagrant abuses of the domain names registration system. The WIPO is also looking at extending this to prevent registration of domain names unless there is a legitimate interest.

The issue with deep linking is that this allows Internet users access to material without going through warnings screens or seeing advertising banners. Therefore the site providing the content may be in breach of local legislation by failing to provide warnings about unsuitable material and may lose advertising income as there is a lower 'click through' rate.

The position on deep linking is currently unclear, although there has been at least one successful lawsuit to prevent this.

The issues on *taxation* include whether electronic commerce transactions should be liable to tax and where and how tax should be collected.

There is currently an international agreement that these transactions should not be taxed. However there are exceptions – the US State of Michigan requires that purchases made over the Internet should be listed on individuals' income tax returns and the state sales tax should be paid. Courts in France have ruled that on-line auctions should be subject to French law for French residents – which includes tax liability and a requirement that they should be conducted by an auctioneer licensed to conduct auctions in France. The European Union favours taxation of electronic commerce transactions.

The issue on *contractual status* is whether advertising goods and services on the Internet is legally an offer or an invitation to treat. This became an issue in a case in which televisions were advertised for sale at a very low price, due to an error in setting up the web page.

The position on this is not entirely clear. The current view seems to be that this is an invitation to treat (and therefore legally similar to displaying goods in a supermarket). Therefore the customer will make an offer for the goods, which the seller must accept to make the contract legally binding.

There is some uncertainty whether an acknowledgement of the order is legally an acceptance. Many Internet retailers (or e-tailers) have systems that automatically produce an acknowledgement of the order. Because this is a purely automatic process, its legal validity as an acceptance is uncertain.

Electronic Communications Act 2000

The Electronic Communications Act 2000 was introduced to provide a legal framework for e-commerce in the UK. The original bill contained provisions on encryption which proved controversial and have now been put forward as separate legislation, the Regulation of Investigatory Powers Bill.

The act contains two main provisions:

- A register of suppliers. All suppliers of cryptography must be registered and licenced;
- Recognition of digital signatures and digital certificates as legally admissible evidence of identity. The act also gives the Secretary of State the power to amend existing legislation to allow the use of digital signatures and digital certificates where these are not currently allowed.

Regulation of Investigatory Powers Act 2000

Governments around the world are concerned about the potential use of the Internet by criminals, terrorists or those opposed to the government. This resulted in the US government restricting the export of encryption technology by classing it as a munition.

The UK government attempted to restrict the use of encryption in the Electronic Communications Bill. Some of these provisions proved controversial and were taken out of the Electronic Communications Bill and proposed separately as the Regulation of Investigatory Powers Bill. This allowed the passage of the Electronic Communications Act 2000.

The main requirements of the Act are:

- A requirement to provide the key or the information. Internet Service Providers (ISPs) carrying e-mail or electronic data are required to supply 'black box' technology to intercept and copy it, and to provide either a decryption key or the information in decrypted form. This does not require a court order.

  This replaced an earlier proposal that all decryption keys should be held centrally ('key escrow').
- A provision against 'tipping off'. This prevents ISPs receiving a request for the key or the information from making this known. Such a request will form part of an investigation and this provision is intended to prevent the person under investigation becoming aware of the fact.

Civil Evidence Act 1995

The Civil Evidence Act 1995 extended the acceptability of computer records as evidence into civil law. The Act was particularly concerned with the acceptability of images of documents stored on microfiche or optical disk to a court of law.

The Act requires that the recording system is proven and the computer was operating correctly. It also requires that a complete audit trail is kept and that the recording medium is of a form that cannot be altered undetectably. For example write once read many optical disk (WORM) and compact disk-recordable (CD-R) are acceptable whereas compact disk-rewritable (CD-RW) is not. Provided that the requirements laid down in the British Standards Institute's code of practice are met, images are acceptable although they are considered less good than the original documents.

7 Criminal Justice Act 1984 and Police and Criminal Evidence Act 1984

The computer's own records (for example a list of attempts to log on to a system) can be used as evidence provided it can be shown that the recording system is proven and the computer was operating correctly. This must be certified to the court by an expert witness in order to meet the requirements of the Criminal Justice Act 1984 and the Police and Criminal Evidence Act 1984.

8 Bank Rules

Bank rules were originally written to ensure that banks complied with the *Tournier v. National Provincial and Union Bank of England* case. These were then modified to meet the requirements of subsequent legislation. They typically cover areas such as:

- Who is responsible for data and what controls need to be put in place in order to ensure that data remains confidential and available and retains its integrity;
- Measures to protect computer equipment from damage or theft, and to ensure that any equipment failure does not result in a loss of data;
- Measures to protect telecommunications links from unauthorized access, including rules relating to accessing and receiving data from the Internet;
- Rules governing relationships with suppliers to ensure competitive tendering, to protect the organization against unfair contracts and to ensure that the organization's intellectual property rights and rules of non-disclosure are respected.

3

Political, Economic and Social Environment

Objectives

After studying this chapter, you should be able to:

- understand the concept of 'exclusion' and be able to discuss the various types of exclusion;
- understand and be able to discuss the concept of the 'new economy';
- understand the impact of information technology on customers, employees and managers;
- be able to distinguish between relationship and transaction banking;
- understand and be able to discuss technophobia;
- be able to describe the technical options to support teleworking, telecottaging and hot desking, and be able to assess their suitability in scenarios and case studies.

1 Introduction

The political and social environment defines the norms and values of the society in which financial services organizations operate. The main impact of the political environment is felt through legislation and we shall discuss the political environment itself only briefly. The social environment has a profound effect, through customers, employees and other stakeholders, and forms the subject of the majority of this chapter.

The economic environment defines the economic conditions in which financial services organizations operate. This also has relatively little impact and we shall discuss this only briefly.

2 The Political Environment

Introduction

The political environment is perhaps the most changeable part of the business environment and we shall not discuss this in any detail. However, one area of particular interest is exclusion.

Exclusion

Exclusion occurs when individuals or communities are unable fully to participate in the activities of the society in which they live. Historically, exclusion has often been the result of racial or religious prejudice, or of sex discrimination. As these issues have been addressed, there is an increasing emphasis on exclusion arising as a result of poverty or differences in educational standards.

The current UK government is attempting to address the issues of social and financial exclusion. Social exclusion is outside the scope of this book and we shall not consider it any further. Financial exclusion occurs when an individual or community's access to financial services is limited. There are two common types of financial exclusion:

- Exclusion from access to financial services, typically as a result of branch closures. Although direct channels can meet many financial needs, many customers prefer to use branches and these are essential for business customers;
- The withdrawal of financial resources from a community. This may happen in impoverished areas where financial services organizations take deposits from communities but do not re-invest these as lending because individuals and businesses in the area are seen as a poor credit risk. This is often the unintended result of centralized credit assessment systems.

This has been addressed in the USA through the Community Reinvestment Act, which requires financial services organizations to reinvest in communities in which they operate, for example by supporting community-based organizations. A voluntary approach has generally been taken in the UK to date.

Exclusion from access to the 'knowledge economy' is increasingly recognized as a global problem and has been recognized by bodies such as the G8 group of the leading international economies. The Internet increases price transparency and price competition, reducing prices. However, those who do not have access to the Internet are unable to take advantage of this and incur higher costs. This is also called the 'digital divide'.

3 The Economic Environment

The economic environment is also subject to change. The economy also seems to be broadly neutral in its impact on technology in the financial services industry – in bad times organizations invest in technology to reduce costs, in good times organizations invest to increase market share. We shall not discuss the economic environment in any detail.

One aspect of the economic environment is of interest, however. This is the 'new economy'.

The New Economy

The term new economy has been coined to describe the current state of the US economy, which has enjoyed a long period of above-trend growth without high inflation. The issues round the new economy are whether it really represents an increase in the trend growth rate and, if so, what has caused this.

The usual explanation for the cause is that it is due to improved productivity resulting from the effect of new technology on the economy. The rise in productivity is clearly established – US productivity, which rose by 1.42% per annum between 1972 and 1995, has risen by 2.75% per annum since 1995.

It is known that major changes in technology can lead to a permanent improvement in the trend growth rate of an economy. The best-studied such changes relate to the introduction of steam power during the industrial revolution in the UK and the introduction of electric motors in the US. Neither of these is very recent but both show a time lapse of about thirty years between the technology being introduced and a dramatic improvement in the economy.

Therefore one possible explanation for the new economy is that it reflects the introduction of PCs in the early 1970s. This is attractive, not least because it overcomes one of the great paradoxes of information technology – that studies through the 1980s failed to show any significant productivity improvements in service industries in spite of very high levels of investment in technology.

An alternative explanation would be that the new economy is due to the 'e-conomy' – the development of e-commerce in the US. The strongest argument in favour of this is that the potential benefits of e-commerce are so large that we should expect this to have a large impact on the economy. Against this, e-commerce is still a very small part of the overall US economy and it would be surprising for any new technology to have such a large effect so soon after its introduction.

The argument against the new economy, at least as it applies to the service sector, is expressed by Robert Gordon[1]. The recorded productivity improvement is 1.33% per annum. The effects of the economic cycle and various measurement effects account for over half of this. Of the remaining 0.64% per annum, all but 0.07% per annum can be accounted for by the consumer durable sector. The service sector has increased capital investment over this period, and this 'capital deepening' should have increased productivity growth by 0.33% – which suggests that productivity in this sector has improved by much *less* than expected. This is consistent with earlier studies such as those of Gregory Hackett[2] and Paul Strassmann[3].

Professor Gordon suggests a number of reasons for this, with a particular focus on why the high level of investment in the Internet has apparently produced so few benefits:

- Market share protection. The argument is that organizations have been forced into becoming 'clicks and mortar' organizations to protect their market share against pure Internet rivals. High levels of investment have had little effect on the underlying economics of these organizations;
- Re-creation of old activities. The argument is that much information provided over the

1 R Gordon: *Not much of a new economy* Financial Times 26 July 2000
2 G Hackett: 'Investment in Technology – the Service Sector Sinkhole?' *Sloan Management Review* Winter 1990
3 P Strassmann: *The Squandered Computer: Evaluating the Business Alignment of Information Technologies* The Information Economics Press

Internet is simply an alternative form of publication of 'public domain' information. Although this may be a cheaper and more convenient method of distribution, it does not create wealth in its own right;

- Duplication of activities. The argument is that the Internet is simply a new channel, duplicating the functions of existing channels (notably mail order). This increases costs without necessarily increasing the size of the market;
- Personal Internet use at work. The argument is that the level of personal Internet use at work is damaging productivity. One research service found that time spent using the Internet at the office is twice as much as time spent using the Internet at home.

At the time of writing, the issues raised above are still unresolved. There has been a very marked improvement in US productivity and this has produced a high-growth, low-inflation economy. This phenomenon is confined to the USA and has not been tested over a full economic cycle.

4 The Social Environment

Most of this chapter will consider the social environment. We need to consider the impact of technology on the financial services organizations' main stakeholders:

- Customers
- Employees
- Managers.

Customers

Relationship Banking and Transaction Banking

Financial services organizations traditionally operated according to the 'relationship banking' model. This was based on the assumption that 'the banker knew his customer' and this is the legal basis of the banker-customer relationship. The term relationship banking implies this level of knowledge as well as a relationship of trust – a fiduciary relationship – between banker and customer.

Financial services organizations found it difficult to sustain the relationship banking model for mass-market customers. Competitors with lower cost bases prevented them from charging high enough margins to support relationship banking. The financial services organizations found staff costs growing faster than their income and were forced to introduce automation to allow them to service larger numbers of customers in order to remain competitive.

The automation resulting from the first two generations of information technology allowed financial services organizations to handle increased number of customers without increasing staff numbers. However, this increase in numbers and other changes in banking practice such as the more frequent rotation of managers between branches made it impossible for banks to have the personal knowledge of their customers implied by relationship banking.

This resulted in a switch to 'transaction banking'. The fiduciary relationship was replaced by a simple buyer-seller relationship and the application of the principle of *caveat emptor* ('let the buyer beware').

Transaction banking had its disadvantages:

- Courts were not always willing to accept that financial services organizations had no fiduciary duty towards their customers;
- Transaction banking undermined traditional customer loyalty. This allowed new entrants to the financial services market to cherry pick the most profitable customers and products, reducing financial services organizations' ability to subsidize less profitable operations;
- There is an increasing recognition that financial services organizations need to reinvest in the communities in which they operate and the model of transferring deposits out of poor areas to finance lending in wealthier areas (exclusion) is under challenge. Legislation similar to the US Community Reinvestment Act is a possibility should the financial services industry fail to address these issues.

Re-Personalizing the Relationship

Has the traditional banker-customer relationship gone forever? Although we may not know our customer in the traditional sense we can use information to behave as if we do. We can describe this as 're-personalizing' the relationship. Instead of relying on staff knowledge, financial services organizations are increasingly relying on capturing this knowledge in computer systems.

One of the earliest examples of this is the 'customer view'. Early computer systems often viewed the banker-customer relationship as based on the account. There was no attempt to connect different accounts held by the same customer. This led to absurd situations such as customers with thousands of pounds in their deposit accounts having cheques referred if they exceeded agreed limits by a few pounds. The customer view gives us the ability to take an overall view of the relationship with the customer.

A more sophisticated approach is to take account of customer preferences. Customers do not want to be offered insurance products every time they enter a branch, nor do they want to receive large numbers of unsolicited mailings and telephone calls. Financial services organizations can maintain contact histories for their customers, allowing them to avoid repeated offers to the same customer. In addition, customers can specify that they do not want to receive unsolicited mailings or telephone calls.

We have gone from a simple view of the customer's affairs to the ability to react to past events. The next stage is to anticipate future developments.

One example is the extension of credit scoring techniques into propensity and attrition scoring:

- Propensity scoring predicts the probability of a customer buying a particular product. It uses historic information to develop a profile of those customers who are most likely buy this product in the next 1-2 years. This profile can be used to target marketing activity on these customers;

- Attrition scoring predicts the probability of customers closing their accounts or allowing their accounts to go dormant. The high cost of recruiting new customers often makes it beneficial for financial services organizations to take action to retain existing customers.

It is important to understand that propensity and attrition scoring does not attempt to *predict* the future actions of individual customers. What it does is to indicate customers with a *higher probability* of buying a product or ending their account relationship.

Another example is the use of technology for customer identification. This includes:

- The use of smart cards. Private banking customers can be issued with smart cards. These give access to branch premises but also identify the customer to staff, who can greet him or her by name and call up all the necessary details as the customer enters the premises. This has been used in the Middle East;
- Caller line identification. Call centre technology can identify the number from which a call has been made, unless it is withheld for privacy reasons. This can be used with computer telephony integration (discussed in Chapter 17) to call up the customer's details on the agent's screen when the call is put through. This must be used with caution – there are privacy issues and the caller must be positively identified before any information is given – but it can reduce the delay in call handling;
- The use of biometrics. Biometrics are discussed in Chapter 9 and are physical characteristics used to identify an individual. Where biometrics give positive identification they can eliminate the need to ask customers for forms of identification such as a driver's licence and they can also be used to identify customers to staff.

All of these can produce benefits in terms of customer service. They give us a better understanding of our customers' financial affairs and needs. They produce a more personal feel, both by showing customer knowledge and in avoiding sales approaches which the customer may regard as aggressive. They also benefit customers by improving security – providing customers with more effective means of identification without a requirement for papers, identification numbers and verification information that may get lost, forgotten or stolen.

Technophobia

There is a general perception that customers suffer from 'technophobia' – a fear and dislike of technology. It is not clear that there is any real evidence for this (some surveys have suggested that many customers prefer using ATMs for balance enquiries and withdrawals), but financial organizations need to take care when they introduce new methods of service delivery.

Customers are cautious about innovations. There is a relatively small number of 'early adopters' and a significant minority of 'laggards'. This applies to any form of innovation and does not necessarily imply any fear of technology as such.

It is also clear that some customers prefer traditional branch delivery. Some 20% of customers have never used an ATM and 70% of customers in the USA express a preference for using branches as their main delivery channel.

Consultants Forrester Research have developed an approach to market segmentation that specifically considers attitudes to technology. They classify customers according to:

- Whether they are 'technology optimists' or 'technology pessimists';
- Their income;
- Whether their primary motivation is career, family or entertainment.

From these categories they develop ten market segments.

In this model high-income technology optimists represent the primary market for technology innovation, corresponding to the early adopters. Low-income technology optimists generally wait for prices to fall but follow as quickly as their economic circumstances allow. High-income technology pessimists will buy new technology but spend less time using it. They also place high importance on ease of use and reliability. Low-income technology pessimists are disconnected from technology.

Low-income technology pessimists correspond to technophobic customers. Forrester data is based on a survey of US consumers and shows this group representing about 30% of consumers – a significant minority but less than a third of the potential customer base. High-income technology pessimists are willing to use technology – Forrester shows PC ownership in excess of 50% – provided they have confidence both in it and in their ability to use it.

Technophobia may be a result of bad experiences with technology. We need to be aware of the problems that can arise and to treat customer concerns sympathetically.

The main sources of concern include:

- ATMs that are not available;
- 'Phantom withdrawals';
- Fraudulent EFTPOS transactions;
- Fraudulent Internet transactions;
- Errors in standing orders.

ATM Failure

Customers rely on ATMs for cash and can find ATM non-availability very irritating. There are three possible reasons for ATM failure:

- The failure of the ATM itself. This is quite rare. ATMs are very robust devices and it is unusual for them to fail;
- The failure of the telecommunications links to the main computer or of the main computer itself. This is rather more common;

- Running out of money. This is the most common reason for ATM unavailability.

Financial services organizations manage these risks by providing customers with information about alternative ATMs. Stickers can be used to remind customers of those other organizations whose ATMs they can use through reciprocity arrangements, or to direct customers to the location of alternative ATMs.

The amount of money loaded into an ATM depends on the anticipated demand, but financial services organizations also need to consider the cost of using money in this way. Money held as notes in an ATM cannot earn interest. Financial services organizations can reduce the risk of ATMs running out of money by:

- Developing models to predict the expected pattern of demand for ATM withdrawals. The systems which control the ATM maintain statistics about the actual pattern of demand, which can be used to refine the models. This allows ATMs to be loaded with the minimum amount needed to ensure that the ATM will not run out of money provided there is no major departure from normal patterns of demand;
- Using the controlling software to check that the ATM still has money and is still functioning. If the ATM runs out of money a local branch can be notified and instructed to fill it. This can also be carried out by a central group. Other sources of failure can also be notified and an engineer sent.

Phantom Withdrawals

Phantom withdrawals are ATM withdrawals which the card holder denies making. There is concern that either the system is making an error and debiting the wrong account or a fake card has been produced.

The majority of phantom withdrawals have been traced to unauthorized use of the card by a family member or friend. There are no instances where the system is known to have made an error.

Fake cards are reasonably easy to make and, if the PIN is known, can be used to withdraw cash. There have been some elaborate fraud attempts including:

- Using fake ATMs to steal the card and to get the customer to type in the PIN;
- Attaching a device to an ATM which will read the magnetic strip (to be copied later) and ask the customer to type in the PIN.

Financial services organizations have been slow to answer customer concerns on phantom withdrawals. The use of video cameras hidden in ATMs and improved methods to prevent cards being forged or copied make it easier to prove that phantom withdrawals do not happen, but it is the responsibility of the staff to deal with complaints in a helpful and informed way.

Fraudulent EFTPOS Transactions

Fraudulent EFTPOS transactions may be due to fake, lost or stolen cards. There is also the possibility of collusion between the retailer and the fraudster.

Precautions against fraud fall into three main categories:

- Card-based precautions
- System precautions
- Procedures.

Card-based precautions are designed to make cards more difficult to counterfeit and to make stolen cards more difficult to use. The main card-based precautions are:

- Tamper-proof signature strips, which prevent a signature being erased;
- Holograms on the card, which make it more difficult to counterfeit;
- Photographs on the card, which make stolen cards more difficult to use;
- Card Verification Value (CVV - Visa) or Card Validation Code (CVC - Mastercard), additional information making the card difficult to counterfeit.

The first two of these are already widely used. Photocards and CVV/CVC are relatively recent developments which have been shown to be effective in cutting fraud.

The use of signature verification as the primary means of confirming the customer's identity means that personal identification numbers (PINs) are rarely used to protect EFTPOS transactions in the UK.

Smart cards, discussed in Chapter 17, are more difficult to counterfeit and contain more identification information. They are currently used in countries such as France and Japan and they are planned to replace magnetic strip cards in the UK in the near future.

System precautions are designed to prevent counterfeiting of cards or to detect when a card is stolen. The main system precautions are:

- Hot card files, held either locally or centrally, which record lost or stolen cards and prevent their being used;
- On-line authorization, preventing cards being used beyond the funds and credit available;
- Expert systems, which detect patterns of use that may indicate fraudulent behaviour.

All of these are widely used. Expert systems used in the UK include Fraudwatch (Barclaycard) and Falcon (MasterCard).

Procedures are designed to ensure that stolen cards are not misused. The main procedures include:

- Floor limits, which can be used to force authorization of all transactions in retailers particularly likely to be targeted by fraudsters;
- Advising customers that they will shortly be receiving a new card and to contact the issuer if it does not arrive by the validity date;
- Requiring customers to validate cards before use;

- Card collection from branches, which prevents cards being intercepted in the post.

The first three of these are widely used. Card validation is common for new issue of a card but not for renewals. Requiring customers to collect cards from branches has service implications and financial services organizations generally prefer to use secure alternatives such as courier delivery.

Fraudulent Internet Transactions

The Internet is a new medium and stories about fraud and breaches of security seem to be a daily occurrence. Although there are many similarities between Internet fraud and EFTPOS fraud, there are three significant differences:

- The Internet is an open network. Therefore it is exposed to the additional dangers of hacking and virus infection. There have been cases of credit card or debit card numbers being stolen, with their secondary verification details, and posted on the Internet;
- The Internet is global. Internet fraud may be perpetrated by people in different countries, which may make it difficult and time-consuming to recover any losses and which limits the legal protection available under the connected lender liability provisions of the Consumer Credit Act 1974;
- Internet fraud can affect banking transactions as well as e-commerce. Internet banks have, in some cases, refused to limit customers' responsibility for losses due to fraud, on the grounds that these services are offered over a secure link and any fraud is presumed to be a result of the customer's carelessness.

Internet security is discussed at greater length in Chapter 9.

Standing Orders

Errors in standing orders are a common cause of customer complaint. The main problems are standing orders being paid twice, standing orders not being paid at all, or cancelled or expired standing orders being paid.

This is an example of a problem that was less common when standing orders were processed manually because the standing orders clerk would notice if the payment was incorrect. With IT used to automate the process, an error made when the standing order is set up will not be detected until after the payment has been made. This means that it is particularly important to ensure that care is taken when standing orders are set up and that the application software carries out all reasonable checks.

Overcoming Technophobia

How do we overcome technophobia?

Advertising can help. One US bank advertised its new ATMs as 'Tillie the Teller' to make them seem friendlier to its customers. More recently the emphasis has been on the convenience technology offers – in particular, the availability of 24-hour access.

We need to ensure that our systems are easy to use. This applies to all computer systems, of course, but is particularly important for systems which customers are expected to use without assistance.

Systems designed to be used by customers must be very easy to use. This includes the following:

- Screen designs must be clear. Too many colours should be avoided and colours should contrast well. The screen should be legible even if sited in sunlight or where there are reflections from internal lights;
- The screen should give clear instructions to the customer. Courtesy words such as 'please' and 'thank you' may be used at the start and end of a transaction where appropriate;
- It should be clear when the customer is expected to enter something. If there is likely to be a delay while the system carries out some processing a message such as 'busy – please wait' should be displayed;
- Navigation – the way the customer moves from one screen to another – should always be clear. The customer should always be able to cancel a transaction if he or she wishes;
- Transactions should not take too long. Not only is there a risk of the customer forgetting what he or she wants to do, the effect on other customers who may be queuing to use the system also needs to be considered.

New technology such as touch-sensitive screens and multimedia has made it easier to design systems that are customer-friendly.

Staff should be willing and able to help customers – if staff do not understand how to use the equipment, how can customers be expected to? If equipment is located in branches, staff should be trained to deal with enquiries and problems. If possible, staff should be available to assist customers who are not happy to use the equipment unaided.

We must never lose sight of the fact that financial services organizations exist to provide services to their customers. Even where technology is introduced for reasons such as cost control, it should not undermine this fundamental customer service ethic.

Employees

Many of the changes that have affected employees have been IT-enabled rather than IT-led. For example, the move from 'teller to seller' was a result of business changes – the move away from relationship banking and the bancassurance model – rather than IT changes, but IT systems such as sales prompts enabled and supported this change.

The effects of IT and IT-enabled change on employees includes:

- Increased workload

- Career development
- Industrialization
- Teleworking.

Increased Workload

IT has allowed work to be done much faster, hence increasing the amount of work individuals are expected to do. The introduction of IT has also had an impact on the nature of jobs staff are being asked to undertake. This is often called 'teller-to-seller' and describes how the job of branch staff increasingly involves selling products to the customer, rather than simply waiting for the customer to ask what is available. The emphasis now is on selling skills rather than the traditional skills of the teller.

Staff have also been required to take on many more IT-related responsibilities, varying from an awareness of the main data protection and intellectual property legislation, through taking system back-ups to quite technical responsibilities such as system upgrades.

It is possible for staff to take on too much work and *karoshi* or death from overwork is a well documented phenomenon in Japan and elsewhere. As a reaction to this, there is an increasing emphasis on a better balance between work and family responsibilities, and initiatives such as work-life balance in the UK and quality of working life in the US have received a high level of support from governments and major companies.

One good effect of IT is to make information much more freely available to first-line managers and supervisors. They now have the information to take decisions that would have had to be referred to middle management. This is often called 'empowerment'.

Another benefit is that IT may prompt employee development, by requiring a wider range of skills and more use of intellectual skills such as abstraction. This in turn leads to a requirement for continuous learning and for skill sharing. This effect has been called 'informating'[4].

Career Development

Banks and building societies used to offer a 'job for life' – a career with a steady progression through the organization until the employee reached the limit of his or her abilities or ambitions. There were many reasons for this including the organizational culture of banks and building societies – large bureaucracies which placed a high value on staff loyalty.

Another reason was the type of skills required to work in a bank or building society. These did not change – lending assessment now is practically the same as it was one hundred years ago. An employee would become more valuable over time because he or she would still be using the same skills but would also be improving them through experience.

The large-scale introduction of IT has completely changed this. Tasks such as lending

4 S Zuboff: *In the Age of the Smart Machine* Heinemann London 1988

assessment are now largely carried out through credit scoring. Employees are finding the skills for which they were recruited and trained are increasingly unimportant to their employers.

The most obvious effect of this is on job security. Bank and building society staff no longer feel that their jobs are secure. Managers need to consider the effect on staff motivation and to find ways to motivate staff who are worried about the future.

One response to this has been a stress on lifetime employability rather than lifetime employment. As financial services organizations are no longer able to offer the latter, they try to offer the former by keeping employees' skills up to date and by offering transferable qualifications such as national vocational qualifications (NVQs). The emphasis on continuing professional development (CPD) by The Chartered Institute of Bankers is part of the same overall trend.

Industrialization

Call centres and processing centres are a recent feature of the financial services industry. These have introduced a factory or industrial way of working into the industry.

Some important features of the industrial model are:

- Narrower skill requirements. Staff working in traditional branches may well use a large number of different skills during the day, as they carry out a variety of tasks. Staff working in centres are typically trained in a maximum of six different work types;
- Machine measurement and pacing. The amount of work carried out is measured, either manually or through the use of IT. IT may also be used to control the pace of work, by setting up personal work queues of outstanding items.

Some of the issues connected with these environments are discussed in Chapters 16 and 17.

Teleworking

Teleworking involve employees working away from the office. Telecommuting is an alternative term for teleworking. We can identify three main forms:

- Homeworking
- Knowledge working
- Mobile working.

We need to look at these together with the related topics of telecottaging and hot desking.

By homeworking we mean relatively simple processing tasks carried out by employees at home. Data entry tasks such as entering details from application forms provide a common example. Another example is a 'virtual call centre' by which calls into a call centre can be routed to agents working at home. BT ran a virtual call centre pilot for their directory enquiries service in Scotland.

The technology required is relatively simple. A workstation with a built in modem is connected to a server in the financial services organization's data centre, usually through a dial-up line. Where fast response is required a digital line may be used. Security is very important and the workstation has passwords to get into the workstation, to use the application software and to access the data centre. Messages are usually encrypted to prevent their being intercepted, and there may be a firewall between the workstation and the server to prevent attempts at 'hacking'. These security measures are discussed in Chapter 9.

We can show the technology as follows:

Figure 3.1: Homeworking Technology

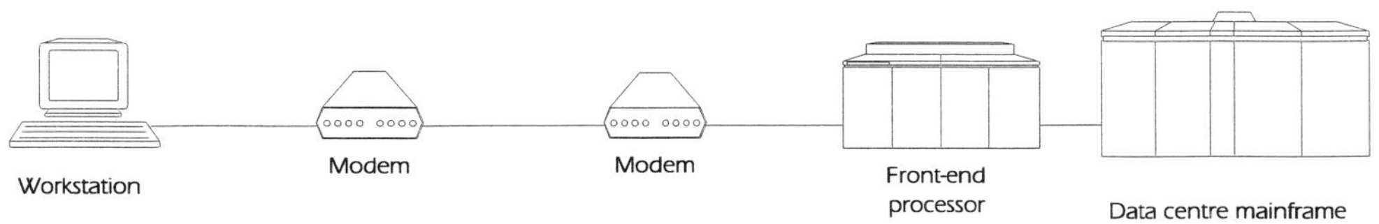

By knowledge working we mean more complex roles such as consultancy and research. Management – especially project management – is possible on a teleworking basis. The requirement is usually to use a range of software tools such as word processors, spreadsheets, databases, presentation tools and Internet browsers.

The technology required is very similar. The workstation is a powerful PC with a wide range of software. Knowledge workers may require access to customer or commercially sensitive data, in which event there may be additional security devices attached to the PC.

We can show the technology as follows:

Figure 3.2: Knowledge Working

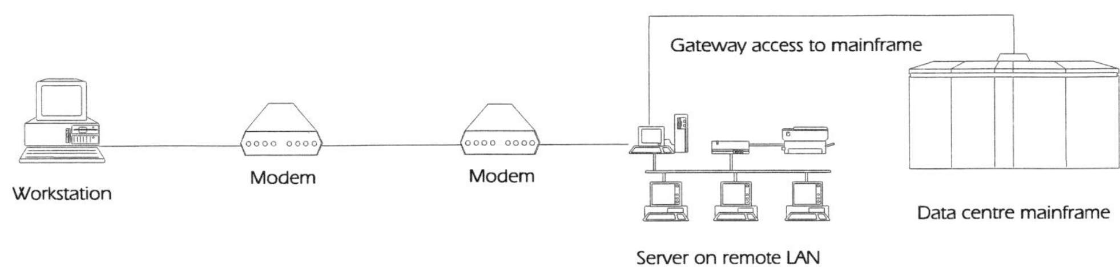

Mobile working refers to employees who travel for a large part of their working day and need to process information while on the move. This is becoming increasingly important as financial services organizations deliver services to their customers rather than expecting customers to visit them.

A number of technologies can be used including:

- The simplest option is to use a stand-alone laptop or notebook computer. The employee returns to a central office from time to time to transfer the data into the organization's systems. The main disadvantage of this approach is that the data may be lost or damaged before it is transferred;
- An alternative is to transfer information from the portable computer to the organization's systems using a dial-up connection over the public telephone network. Messages need to be encrypted because of the risk of interception. A variation on this is to use a mobile phone link to transfer the information. These are probably the most common forms of mobile working;
- Another alternative is to transfer information over the Internet. The security issues associated with the Internet are discussed in Chapter 9 but messages need to be encrypted and a virtual private network can be used to provide a higher level of security.

Teleworking has both advantages and disadvantages. If we consider the advantages and disadvantages for the organization first:

Table 3.1: Advantages and Disadvantages of Teleworking

Advantages	Disadvantages
Savings on premises costs	More difficult to control
Employees do not have to travel	Higher equipment costs
Access for employees who cannot travel	Higher telecommunications costs
	Security issues
	Health and safety issues
	Perceived as 'skiving'

There are *savings on premises costs* because employees are providing their own place of work.

Employees do not have to travel to work. This reduces the risks of lateness or disruption due to travel problems. Some organizations expect employees who are teleworking to work longer hours to reflect the saving in travelling time.

Access for employees who would not find it easy to travel to work. These included carers and disabled people.

It may be more difficult to *control the work* being done. Control must be in terms of what is produced rather than the way the employee works and this is not suitable for all jobs. Employees may suffer from distractions, affecting the quality or quantity of their work.

There are *higher equipment costs*. If employees are sick or on holiday, the equipment is idle and cannot be used by others. The equipment may be more likely to suffer damage either accidentally (for example from children or pets) or through environmental factors (dust and humidity levels may be higher in domestic premises). The cost of supporting and repairing equipment will be higher because the equipment will need to be brought in to a centre or an engineer will need to be sent to the employee's home.

There are *higher telecommunications costs* because employees must connect to the office over public telephone lines.

There are *security issues*. Data confidentiality may be difficult to guarantee because family members, visitors and others may have access to the equipment. There is a risk of viruses being introduced. It is difficult to ensure that backups are taken. There may also be data security issues associated with documents and forms sent to or produced by the employee.

The are *health and safety issues*. It is difficult to ensure that employees use appropriate office furniture providing adequate support. Problems may be more difficult to detect because employees may change their pattern of work to hide problems.

Other employees and managers may *perceive working at home as 'skiving'*, which can damage morale.

The advantages and disadvantages for employees are:

Table 3.2

Advantages	**Disadvantages**
Control over working hours	Isolation
Reduced travel time	Overwork
Control over working environment	Access to support services

Better *control over their working hours*. Employees are not restricted to 9-5 working and can choose to work predominantly early in the morning or late at night. They can also split their work – this can be useful for parents with school-age children, who may choose to work (for example) 10-3 together with a two-hour period either early morning or late evening. This is also useful for staff who work predominantly 9-5 but have the option to stretch their day by doing additional work in the evening or at weekends.

Reduced travel time. As we have discussed, this benefit may need to be shared with the organization. Teleworking is also useful for employees who spend a lot of time travelling as part of their job, because it provides them with a base for administrative tasks without additional travelling.

Better control over their working environment. Employees can organize their working environment in the way that best suits them, without the constraints provided by the office. This freedom must be used with care to minimize distractions and avoid health and safety risks.

Isolation. Employees can feel very isolated. This is partly physical – they are no longer part of a team – but it is also partly an isolation from information. Employees do not know what is going on in the office, they have no access to the grapevine or to their network of colleagues and mentors. Employees who telework can find it difficult to secure promotion simply because they are never in the office – their achievements are less noticeable than those of their peers. It may also be more difficult to secure access to training because training needs may be less apparent.

Overwork. Because employees can work extended hours they may be under pressure so to do. This pressure may come from the organization although it is more usually self-imposed. An anecdote appeared in the *Financial Times*. A senior manager in an organization sent out an e-mail at midnight. He started to receive replies *immediately*. Although the ability to work at unusual hours is one of the main benefits of teleworking, it is unhealthy should this start to be regarded as normal practice.

Access to support services. Employees do not have access to support services such as photocopying.

Telecottaging is a variant on teleworking. Instead of employees working at home they work in office premises close to their homes. Financial services organizations can use spare space in branches for this purpose, or local business centres can be used.

Telecottaging overcomes many of the disadvantages of teleworking. Although the organization still incurs premises costs these are often cheaper than the premises released (for example out-of-town sites rather than city centre) and may be in buildings that are underutilized. They have disadvantages of their own, of which the most important is probably the need for the telecottager to conform to the culture of the premises in which he or she is located.

Hot desking allows employees to work away from the office much of the time but to book a desk (and sometimes an office) for when they need to come in. Again this overcomes many of the disadvantages of teleworking.

In practice, hot desking is often done badly. Successful hot desking requires:

- An effective system for booking desks, offices, meeting rooms and equipment;
- Storage space for employee's possessions which can be moved into position quickly and easily;
- Equipment must be set up in a standard way so that it does not need to be individually reconfigured for each employee.

Managers

Another effect is to take away layers of middle management. One of the main functions of middle management used to be processing information – deciding what information was sufficiently important to be passed on to higher management. IT can now do this. This has produced a flatter organization, with less opportunities for promotion. Employees looking for promotion now need to be willing to move 'sideways' – broadening their experience in other areas of the organization – because they can no longer rely on a regular series of promotions within the same branch or department.

4

The Technology Environment

Objectives

After studying this chapter, you should be able to:

- understand Moore's Law and Meredith's Law and be able to use them to explain the importance of information technology in financial services;
- be able to trace the development and evolution of information technology in general, and in particular the evolution of:
  - approaches to processing – you must be able to describe and distinguish between batch, remote batch, on-line and real time processing
  - data storage – you must be able to describe and distinguish between file-based systems, hierarchical databases, network databases and relational databases
  - data structure
  - topologies
  - the Internet;
- understand the concept of client server and be able to compare client server and Internet/intranet technology;
- understand and explain how the Internet is accessed;
- distinguish between open and proprietary systems.

1 Introduction

The technology environment defines the technology potentially available to financial services organizations. The main focus of this book is on Information Technology.

Information Technology (IT) is a term that encompasses all forms of technology used to create, exchange and use information in its various forms (business data, voice conversations, still images, motion pictures, multimedia presentations and other forms).

It is perhaps worth noting that IT is not the only relevant technology. Devices such as cheque reader/sorters and ATMs also use mechanical technology for physical paper handling. Communications technologies are also very important for financial services organizations and the convergence between IT and communications technology (among others) is discussed later in this chapter.

Moore's Law

A unique feature of information technology is the speed of technological innovation. This is reflected in Moore's Law.

Gordon Moore was one of the founders of computer chip maker Intel. Moore's Law predicts that the processing power of computer chips will double every 18 months. This rule has held true since the mid-1960s and is predicted to continue until at least 2010.

As well as this increase in processing power, there has also been an increase in the amount of storage available and the amount of information that can be transmitted over data communications networks. This itself has increased the use of information within organizations. Fourth-generation systems and the Internet now provide individuals with access to a quantity of information which is, for all practical purposes, unlimited.

Businesses have exploited this opportunity and collect an increasing amount of information which is now critical to their operations. Computer Associates' Chief Executive Officer Charles Wang says:

> *Your core business is information. I don't care if your operation makes doorknobs or services fire alarms, your core business is information.*

In this view, information is not only the business's most important asset but is also a tradable asset. This has been described as the 'information economy'.

Meredith's Law

The Internet is undoubtedly the most significant recent development in IT. Why is there so much interest in the Internet?

Bob Meredith was one of the founders of the Internet. Meredith's Law states that the value of a network is proportional to the square of the number of nodes or users. Therefore, as the size of a network increases its value increase exponentially.

This is the point about the Internet. It is already very large and it is still growing very fast, with the number of users predicted to reach 268 million computers by 2001. The value of the Internet as a method of contacting customers and suppliers is only exceeded by the value of the telephone network. Comparing this to the (very low) cost of connecting to the Internet shows why the Internet has become the most important current technology.

Evolution of IT

Many authors classify the evolution of IT into a number of eras or generations. We shall use a classification based on that of Robin Bloor, a leading UK authority on IT:

- Early developments;
- First generation – batch;
- Second generation – on-line;
- Third generation – client/server;
- Fourth generation – web/Internet.

2 Early Developments

We shall say very little about early developments. World War II stimulated developments in electronics and work on codebreaking at Bletchley Park led to the development of Colossus, the first stored-program computer. Early commercial computers were developed after the war, for example Leo (Lyons Electronic Office) developed by J Lyons and Manchester University.

The development by John Von Neumann of the Von Neumann architecture also followed the war. The Von Neumann architecture represented a different approach to that used in Colossus and other early computers such as ENIAC and is still used today:

Figure 4.1: Von Neumann Architecture

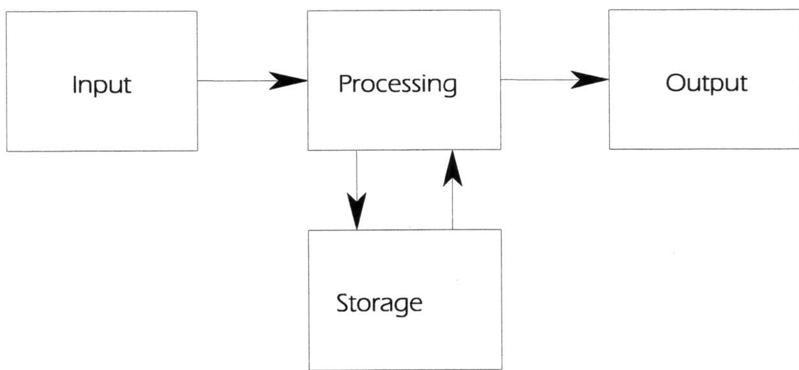

3 Subsequent Generations

Each of the subsequent generations has been characterized by the development of new enabling technologies to meet changing business needs. We can summarize these as a table:

Table 4.1: Computer Generations

	First generation	Second generation	Third generation	Fourth generation
Generation	Batch	On-line	Client/server	Web/Internet
Duration	1965-1975	1975-1985	1985-1995	1995-????
Business driver	Automation	On-line/real time	Re-engineering	e-business
User interface	Paper	Terminal	Workstation	Browser/Java
Enabling technology	Mainframe	Communications Database	Workstation Local area network	Internet
Topology	Stand-alone	Centralized	Distributed	Network
Transaction processing	Batch	Remote batch On-line Real time	Client/server	Internet
Data storage	Files	Hierarchical and network database	Relational database	Relational and object database
Data structure	Rigid	Fixed	Structured	Unstructured

Duration

The durations are approximate and show the period when the technology was at its most dominant. These technologies continue to coexist with their successors and there are still first-generation systems in existence.

Enabling Technology

The enabling technologies shown are the technologies that most clearly distinguish the generation from its predecessors. However, each of these generations has been made possible by a large number of technological developments.

Transaction Processing

A transaction is a logical piece of work such as an account opening or a cheque encashment. Transactions are applied against a master file, for example in a cheque encashment the amount is applied against an accounts file. Systems that process transactions are often called applications.

Data Storage and Structure

Data storage considers how data is organized and accessed.

Data structure is concerned with how 'structured' the data is. Early in the evolutionary process data was highly structured – only characters (such as letters and numbers) could be stored and data had to be presented to the computer according to very rigid rules. As IT has evolved, it has become possible to process other types of data including multi-media data such as pictures, voice recordings, video and music.

We shall not in this chapter discuss the physical storage media used to hold data. These have remained relatively constant over the generations and most data is still held using magnetic storage media such as magnetic tape and magnetic disk.

4 First Generation

The first generation was concerned with data processing and was the dominant model from the mid-1960s until the mid-1970s.

Business Driver

The main business driver was the need for automation to support existing manual processes. These were almost entirely back-office processes and many financial services organizations developed their clearing and core accounting systems during this period.

Users interacted with the systems through paper. Data was entered into the computer using punched paper tape, punched cards or magnetic ink character recognition (MICR). Computers read punched cards and punched paper tape by shining lights through the holes, which were detected using sensors. MICR was magnetized and the computer was able to read the numbers or letters – special shapes were used to make the magnetic ink easier for the machine to read.

Printed reports were produced which contained the same information as the manually produced reports they replaced.

Enabling Technology

The advance in technology that made this possible was the availability of reliable, affordable mainframe computers. The mainframe computers were stand-alone – there were no connections between them and the rest of the business. They were located in special-purpose buildings called data centres.

We can show how these operated as follows:

Figure 4.2: Data Centres

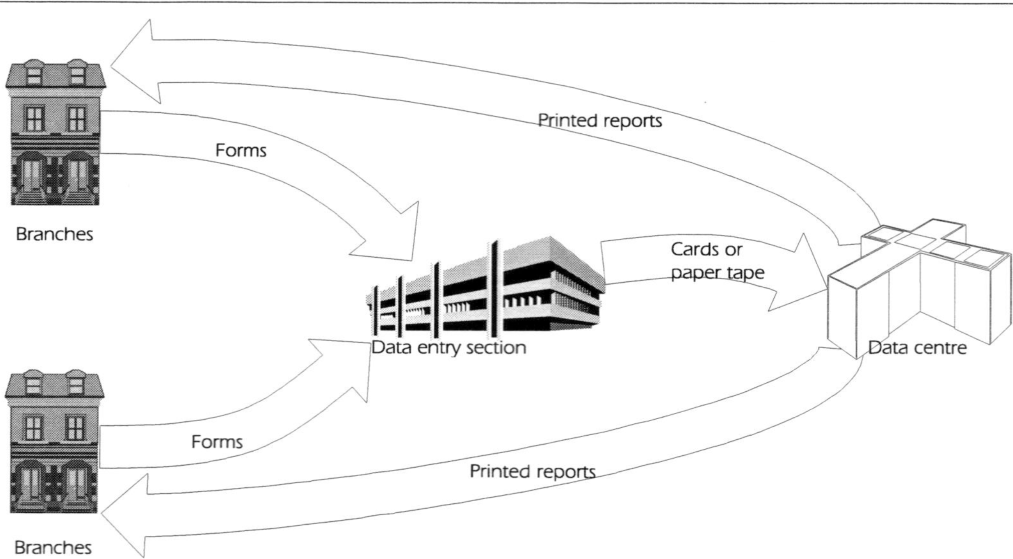

Transaction Processing – Batch Processing

Transactions were processed in batches. Information was sorted into batches of the same type of form and sent to a data entry section, which would type the information onto punched cards for input into the computer.

In batch processing, transactions are collected into batches of similar items. For example, a batch might contain all cheques presented over the counter. These are entered into the computer and recorded on a transaction file, which is used to update the master files at a later time – often overnight.

The simplest form of batch processing works as follows:

- Forms and documents that need processing are collected during the day;
- At the end of the working day, the forms and documents are sorted by type. Each separate type of form or document forms one or more separate batches. If there are a large number of forms or documents of a specific type, this may be split into a number of batches each containing (typically) between twenty and one hundred forms or documents;
- A batch header slip is completed. This may contain a batch number (which allows the batch to be identified), a batch type (indicating the type of form or document), a count of the number of items in the batch and a batch total (the total of the amounts on the forms or documents in the batch);
- The batch is entered into the computer. The batch entry system also checks the batch header information (item count and batch total). The items in the batch are written to

a transaction file, which may also include a batch header record (containing the batch header information) and a batch trailer record to tell the system when it has finished processing a batch;

- The transaction file is used to update a 'master file'. This may be a sequential file, for example a file of accounts sorted in account number order, in which event the update process involves the following steps:
  - The transaction file is sorted into the same order as the master file;
  - The transaction file is then matched against the master file, with the changes recorded on the transaction file being applied to the master file record which has the same key;
  - A new copy of the master file is created, based on the original master file and the changes from the transaction file;
  - Input and error reports are produced, allowing the results of the update to be checked.

We can show the batch update process as a diagram (Figure 4.3 opposite):

Financial organizations used batch systems for three reasons:

- Batch processing uses IT resources very efficiently, especially where very large numbers of transactions are involved and where there is a high 'hit rate' – a high proportion of records on the master file will be changed by the transaction file;
- Many financial processes naturally take place outside the normal working day (e.g. interest calculation, charges calculation, statements, standing orders) and would not benefit from the higher costs associated with on-line or real-time processing;
- Other financial processes were designed round the use of batch processing. A good example of this is clearing, where the traditional 3-day clearing cycle was based on the physical delivery of cheques outside working hours. As a result, financial services organizations have a considerable investment in batch systems to be maintain.

Figure 4.3: Batch Update Process

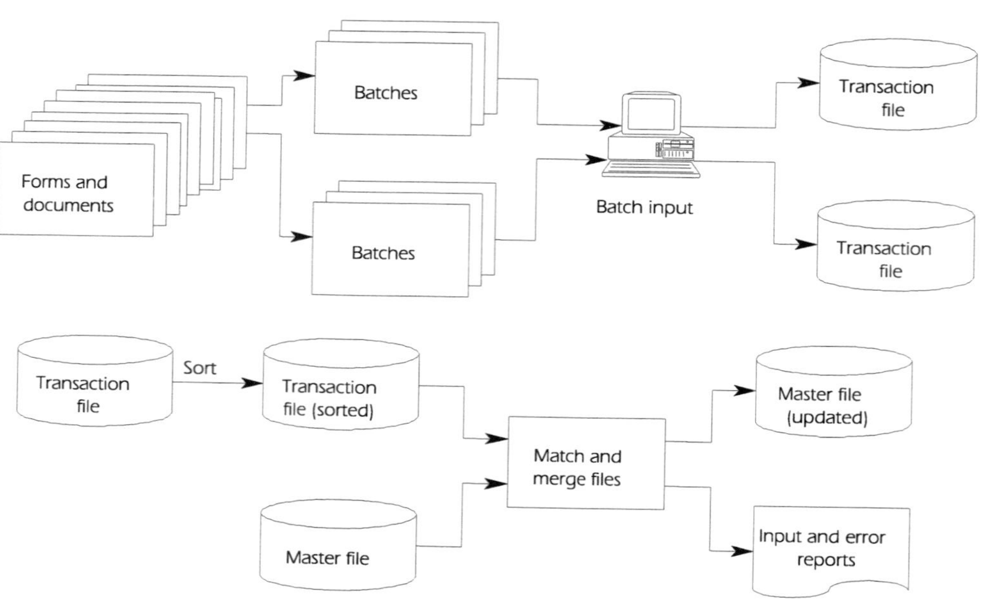

Where the hit rate is low, this may be inefficient. In this event, we could store the master file either as a random access file or as a database, allowing us to go directly to the record we want to change. Instead of creating a new master file, we will make the changes directly to the master file we are using. We could enter batches in exactly the same way as described above, or we could use remote batch. Both databases and remote batch processing are discussed under the second generation.

Data Storage and Structure

First-generation systems usually stored data as files.

The word 'file' sometimes causes a bit of confusion. Manual filing systems have files that hold all the information we have about a customer and 'Mr. Smith's file' will hold a record of all our dealings with Mr. Smith over the years.

IT does *not* use the word in this way. A file in IT is more like a card index file, possibly holding customer addresses for a mailing campaign. Within this file there will be a record card for Mr. Smith.

This is how IT uses the words file and record. A file holds similar data – such as all customer addresses or all customer accounts. A record within the file refers to a particular customer or a particular account. So 'Mr. Smith's file' in our manual filing system could be a record (or a series of records – one for each letter sent or received) in our customer correspondence file on the computer.

Records are made up of pieces of data called 'fields'. A customer record will usually contain fields called Customer Name, Date of Birth, Sex etc. which are pieces of information about the individual customer.

Each record may have a 'key' field, which allows it to be identified. We usually use numbers such as a customer number or account number. We could use names instead, but these might change (by deed poll or marriage) and it could be difficult to find the record afterwards. There are three types of key:

- The primary key uniquely identifies a record. For example, the primary key for an account file will generally be the account number;
- There may be one or more secondary keys. These can be used to identify a record but are not necessarily unique. For example, a secondary key for an account file might well be the account holder's surname;
- There may be one or more foreign keys. A foreign key is a piece of data on one record which is the same as the primary key of another record. For example, a foreign key on an account record may well be a currency code. This will be the primary key for the currency file.

We use foreign keys to define relationships between files. The ability to define such relationships is an important feature of file-based systems and is of critical importance to databases.

There are four types of computer file:

- Serial
- Sequential
- Indexed sequential
- Random.

Serial files are the simplest type of file. Records are stored in the order in which the data comes in. Serial files are very limited because the only way we can access data is to read through the file until we find it – this is called 'sequential access'. They are important for applications where it is important to store the data in the order it comes into the system, for example 'log files' which keep a record of all transactions. Another use of serial files is for applications where every record has to be processed – payroll systems sometimes use serial files.

Sequential files are slightly more complicated. Records are stored in order of the key. A sequential file can be thought of as a serial file which has been sorted and, as we have seen, batch processing systems rely on sorting the (serial) transaction file and then matching it against the (sequential) master file.

We can access sequential files serially, by reading through every record. However, if we are looking for a record with a particular key we can use a 'binary chop' or a 'spaced sequential search' to find the record. We shall not discuss these in detail but they are rather like looking something up in a dictionary – rather than looking at every entry we might open the dictionary at random and decide whether the word we are looking for is earlier or later than the page we have found. We can repeat this process until we are very close to the word, and only then do we start to look at every word.

Indexed sequential files are sequential files that also have an index. This stores the value of the primary key and the 'address' of the record – where the record is in the file.

We can read through the file sequentially, and this is useful for batch processing. However, to find one particular record in the file we can use the index to find out where it is and then go straight to it – this is called random access and is usually much quicker than reading through the entire file.

Random files store records at a location decided by the key. Random files have a 'hashing algorithm' which allows us to work out the address of the record from the key.

It is *not* possible simply to read right through a random file so they are less useful for batch processing than sequential or indexed sequential files. On the other hand, if we know the key of the record we want, we can apply the hashing algorithm and go straight to it.

Very early first generation systems could process only a small amount of data. Such systems generally held data as serial files and many systems from this generation limited records to 80 characters – the amount of information which could be held on a punched card.

This period was relatively short and sequential files rapidly became the most important file type. There was no relationship between files and data was usually compared by sorting the files into the same order and then matching them, as described above. Batch processing could be speeded up using a technique called 'blocking', in which a large number of records were read at the same time.

Random access only really became important in the second generation, as the need for a direct relationship between files developed. Indexed sequential files and random files were introduced towards the end of the first generation and the first type of database – the hierarchical database – marked the transition to the second generation.

5 Second Generation

The second generation provided the bridge from data processing to information technology and was the dominant model from the mid-1970s until the mid-1980s.

Business Driver

The main business driver was the need to access information on-line or in real-time. At the start of the period on-line enquiry systems were developed to allow financial services organizations' staff to access the information held in their mainframe systems.

Another business driver was the desire to allow data to be entered into the system locally, rather than being sent to a separate data entry section. This reduced the time before the computer records were updated and made it easier to resolve any errors. The first-generation approach to batch processing was increasingly replaced by remote batch, on-line transaction processing and real-time processing.

This generation saw the use of IT being extended into the front office. This occurred mainly in wholesale applications such as foreign exchange dealing rooms where the benefit of up-to-date information was sufficient to justify the costs of the system.

Users interacted with the system using a computer terminal. This is a screen and keyboard with no processing or data storage capability of its own. Unlike the paper interface of the first generation, the terminal is both an input and an output device, allowing users to interact directly with the computer for the first time. However, reports continued (and continue to this day) to be one of the most important forms of output.

Enabling Technology

The main advance in technology that made this possible was the availability of affordable data communications networks. The network was arranged on a centralized basis with terminals connected to the central mainframe computer, still located in a data centre. Later in the second generation, smaller computers were introduced between the terminals and the mainframe computer either as front-end processors to reduce the workload on the mainframe or as data concentrators to allow the telecommunications links to be used more efficiently. Front-end processors carried out tasks such as validation, preventing transactions with errors from reaching the mainframe. Data concentrators collected the information from a number of terminals, allowing it to be sent over a single telephone line. A telecommunications device called a multiplexor could be used instead of a data concentrator.

We can show how this type of network operated as follows:

Figure 4.4: Data Communications Network

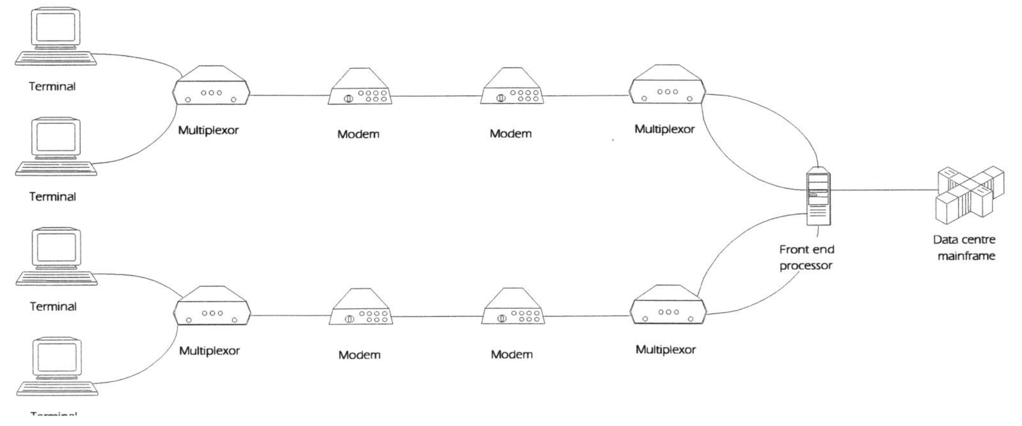

Another important technology was the development of the database, which had a critical role in transforming data into information.

Transaction Processing

With batch processing, the master files are not updated until the overnight processing run. This leads to two possible problems:

- There is a limited 'processing window' between the point at which the on-line systems are closed to allow batch processing and the point at which they re-open. As financial services organizations have moved closer to '24x7' (24 hours a day 7 days a week) processing, this window has grown shorter;
- The information on the master file is out-of-date during the day, because the transactions are not processed until the evening. This creates a significant risk for financial services organizations because of the possibility of fraud or of customers going over-limit.

Remote batch processing was an approach to overcoming the processing window limitations. Remote batch allowed data entry to take place during the day and, as the technology evolved, it also allowed the master file updates to take place during the day. However, remote batch does not generally support 24x7 processing.

A number of technologies were used to address the problem of out-of-date information. 'Shadow files' were used in conjunction with remote batch processing, and on-line and real-time processing were introduced.

A shadow file is a random access file holding information that needs to be kept up-to-date – for example account balances. The transactions were stored and used as remote batch files to update the mainframe systems overnight.

On-line and real time processing both update the master file when the transaction is entered (this is also called demand processing).

The processing of transactions using on-line transaction processing (OLTP) increased during this period, although batch processing was still important. Hybrid approaches were also common, for example using OLTP only for a small amount of processing.

One example – an approach that is still used – is to process house cheque encashments on-line while other cheques are processed in batch or remote batch. The additional cost of on-line processing could be justified for house cheque encashments as these carry more risk, because they involve paying out money immediately and the bank does not have the normal paying banker protection.

Remote Batch Processing

Remote batch processing differs from the older form of batch processing in that transactions can be entered into the computer immediately they are received. However, when they have been entered they are still placed on a transaction file and the master files are updated at the end of the day.

Remote batch systems do not include the batch checking (record counts, batch totals) described above and may work as follows:

- Forms and documents that need processing are entered when they are received or at any convenient point during the day. There is no batch checking so the data entry system carries out some validation;
- If a shadow file is used, the transaction code is used to decide what action to take and the key is used to look up the corresponding record. The balance on the shadow file is updated;
- The items are stored on a transaction file during the day;
- The processing is carried out at the end of the day. The master file can be sequential or allow direct access;
- If a shadow file is used, the balances are either ignored or reconciled against the master file after the transactions have been applied. The shadow file is then rebuilt from current balances for the following day's processing.

Many early ATM networks operated in this way, with transactions being recorded at the ATM and sent to the mainframe at night. This minimized telecommunications costs and fitted with the batch processing approach used in the other mainframe systems. This approach has been reintroduced as part of the VisaCash system, with transactions being stored at the merchant's till and sent to the bank's mainframe system at the end of the day.

Another form of remote batch processing, which is becoming increasingly common, processes transactions as a 'background' task during the day when sufficient computer resources are available:

- As transactions are entered into the computer, they are placed on a 'queue'. In effect, this is a temporary transaction file. Records on the queue are processed in the order in which they are received.
- When the transaction reaches the front of the queue and the computer has sufficient spare resources to process it, the record(s) to be changed will be read and updated. Note that remote batch processing as a background task is effective only where the master file records can be accessed directly – usually through a database.

Again a shadow file can be used to ensure balances are completely up-to-date, as described above.

On-Line Transaction Processing

On-line transaction processing also involves transactions being entered into the computer when they are received. However, the transaction immediately updates the master file.

On-line processing works as follows:

- As forms and documents are completed, they are entered into the system;

- Each item entered has a transaction code. The system uses this to decide which program will be needed to process it;
- The program validates and processes the item and updates the master file, which must be stored as a database.

Real-Time Processing

Real-time processing applications are a special type of on-line processing application. The important difference is that an application involves real-time processing only if *the event which causes* the transaction is almost simultaneous with its being entered into the computer and the database being updated.

Consider a dealing system as an example. If the dealer enters the details into the system while carrying out the deal, and the payment instructions and account updates are produced immediately, this is a real-time system. If the dealer completes a dealing slip and the details are entered by the back office, this is either an on-line transaction processing system (if payment instructions and account updates are produced immediately) or a remote batch system (if account updates are processed later – for example overnight).

Real-time systems work in much the same way as on-line systems. Because the originating event is taking place at the same time as the real-time transaction, it is important that the system performance is acceptable and that the user is not kept waiting for a response. This requires a database.

If forms are used they are completed on the computer screen. Some real-time transactions, such as ATM withdrawals, do not require forms.

In practice there is often little difference between on-line transaction processing systems and real-time systems. Even though the data is not updated simultaneously with the event causing the transaction, the update usually happens seconds or minutes later. This is sometimes called 'pseudo-real-time' or 'near time'.

Data Storage and Structure

Second-generation systems needed on-line access, perhaps to more than one file at a time. Therefore they needed to be able to link a record in one file to the corresponding record in another file, without the need to sort the files. Second-generation systems used databases to achieve this.

Hierarchical Databases

The hierarchical database was the earliest type of database. We can think of a hierarchical database as storing data as a 'tree' structure:

Figure 4.5: Hierarchical Database

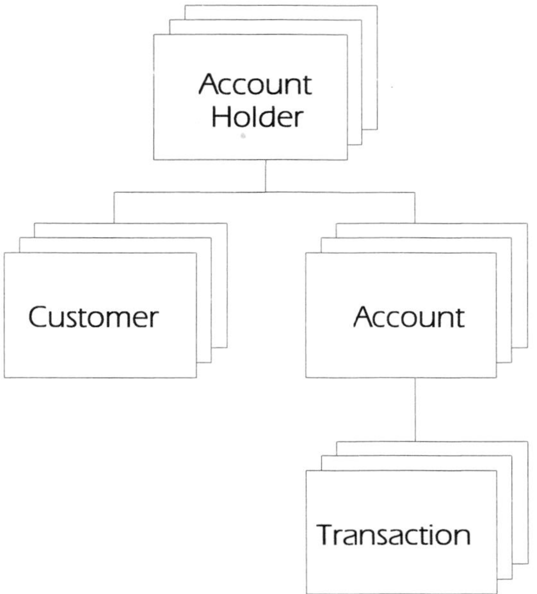

Data stored in hierarchical databases can only be accessed by going up and down the tree. In the example given, we can only find out which accounts the customer holds by going through the account holder. It is very inefficient to access data that is not held on the same 'branch' of the tree. The implications of this are:

- The database needs to be designed specifically for the application. The data must be organized to store the data in the order it will be required when transactions are processed;
- Data may need to be duplicated – the same data may need to be held on different branches to allow it to be accessed efficiently.

Hierarchical databases are very efficient provided that the way the data is needed conforms to the tree structure, and they are still used for applications that need rapidly to process large amounts of data. Their great disadvantage is that are inflexible – they have to be designed specifically for the application for which they will be used.

6 Third Generation

The third generation completed the transition to information technology and was the dominant model from the mid-1980s until the mid-1990s.

Business Driver

The main business driver was the requirement to allow staff to work on more than one task at a time. The processes automated in the first and second generations were labour intensive, with different people required for each different task. Third generation technology allowed these processes to be 're-engineered' so they could be carried out by a single individual.

Users interacted with the system using a workstation capable of displaying multiple windows.

Enabling Technology

The advance in technology that made this possible was the availability of workstations capable of storing data and carrying out processing without reference to the central mainframe computer. The network was distributed – data and processing was shared between the workstations, the server and the central mainframe computer. Workstations could also be used independently of the mainframe computer, as a local area network or as stand-alone personal computers.

This resulted in networks as follows:

Figure 4.6: Wide Area Network with Local Area Network

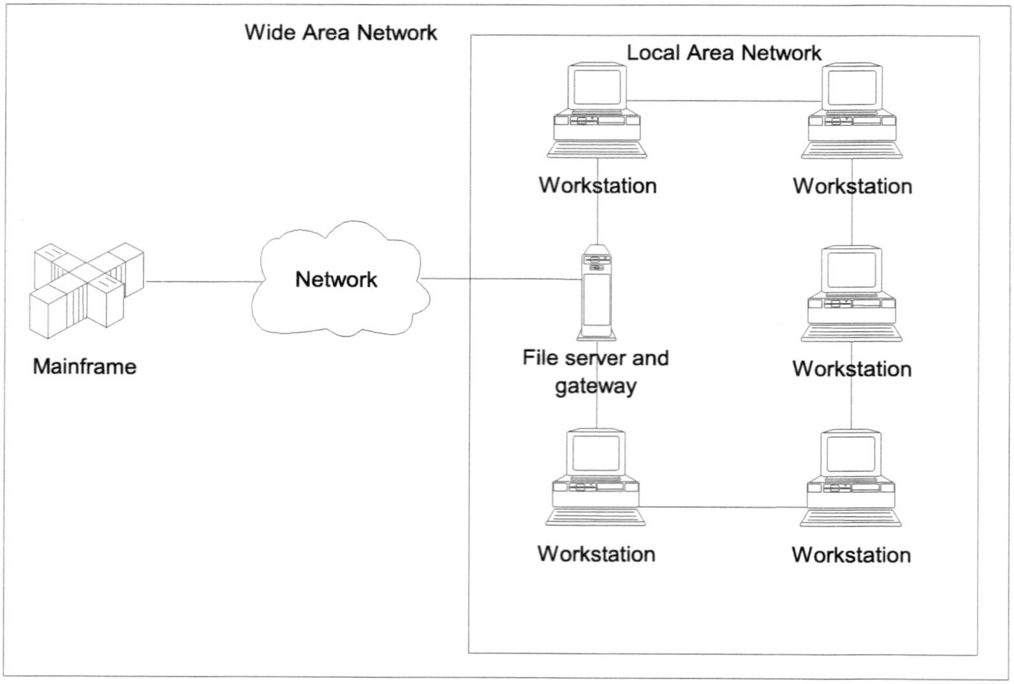

Wide Area Network
Local Area Network
Workstation
Workstation
Network
Mainframe
File server and gateway
Workstation
Workstation
Workstation

Windows and Multitasking

A computer with a single processor, for example a PC, can carry out only one task at a time. PCs are able to use 'multitasking' to carry out several tasks apparently simultaneously.

The operating system schedules work such that only one task is using the processor at any one time. Other tasks in the computer may be suspended or they may be using an input, output or storage device. As the processor can carry out only one process at a time it needs to switch between these tasks to achieve this. There are three main approaches:

- Context switching. Processing takes place only on the 'foreground' task. Any other tasks are in 'background' and will not be processed unless the operator switches them into foreground. The foreground task would be the active window on a PC running a windowing operating system such as Windows or Apple OS;
- Cooperative multitasking. Processing takes place on the foreground task. If the foreground task is not using the central processor unit (CPU) the background tasks will be processed until the foreground task needs the CPU again. Again, the operator can switch any of the background tasks into foreground.

  Tasks do not use the CPU when they are waiting for a peripheral device to complete its processing. Peripheral devices include input devices such as the keyboard, storage devices such as disk drives and output devices such as printers;
- Timeslice multitasking. Each task is allocated a certain amount of time. Processing takes place until either the task runs out of time or it no longer needs the CPU (e.g. because it is waiting for a peripheral). The next task – usually chosen on the basis of a priority level – is then processed.

Context switching and cooperative multitasking are mainly used by older microcomputer operating systems and some would not regard them as 'real' multitasking at all. Timeslice multitasking is used by some microcomputer operating systems and all minicomputer and mainframe computer operating systems.

Both cooperative multitasking and timeslice multitasking rely on the operating system's ability to handle 'interrupts'. When a peripheral device wants to attract the CPU's attention (perhaps because it has completed an input or output operation) it sends a special signal called an interrupt. The operating system identifies that an interrupt has taken place and takes action accordingly. One of the actions that the operating system may take is to stop processing the current task and start processing either the foreground task (cooperative multitasking) or a higher priority task (timeslice multitasking).

Timeslice multitasking also relies on the idea of priorities. Tasks that access peripherals more often will, all other things being equal, get less CPU time. This is because they will be stopped because they are waiting for input or output more often. We can overcome this by giving these tasks a higher priority. This ensures that they will get immediate access to the CPU when the interrupt is received advising the operating system that the input or output operation is complete. The amount of peripheral access is not the only criterion for setting priorities but it is one of the most important.

The terms multiprogramming and multiprocessing are also often used. Multiprogramming means that the computer can run more than one program apparently at the same time. It is very similar to multitasking. Multiprocessing means that the computer has more than one processor and can run more than one task at the same time – it can run one task for each processor. Minicomputers and mainframes usually have a number of processors, each of which is capable of multitasking. Most microcomputers now have a second processor for mathematical calculations known as a maths co-processor.

Windows were developed by Xerox at their Palo Alto Research Centre (PARC) and were first commercially used by Apple in their Lisa and Macintosh computers. Windows are one of the four main components of a Graphical User Interface (GUI):

- Windows. A window is an area of the computer screen. A GUI can have several windows on the screen at the same time, each of which may contain information about a different computer program. We can copy information between windows – for example, copying a table from a spreadsheet into a word processor.

  Windows were particularly important to the third generation because they allowed one person to use a workstation to carry out a number of tasks simultaneously. This was not practical with terminals, where the operator would have needed to log off from one system and log on to a different one, which would greatly increase the time needed to carry out the transaction;

- Icons. An icon is a picture that represents a computer program or some data. We can use the mouse to start the computer program from the icon (by moving the cursor to point at the program icon and clicking twice), or to move or copy the data (by moving the cursor to point at the icon, holding the mouse button down and 'dragging' the icon to where we want it);

- Mouse. We can move the mouse until the cursor is pointing to the right place on the screen. We can then press (or 'click') one of the buttons on the mouse to tell the computer to carry out an action. We have discussed the use of the mouse to start programs and to move or copy data, but it can be used for a number of other reasons including:

  - To press a button on the screen instructing the computer to carry out an action
  - To choose items from a list offered by the computer
  - To position the cursor on an input form so the user can enter data;

- Pull-down menus. GUIs have a 'menu bar' – a list of options – which is usually across the top of the computer screen. If we use the mouse to point at one of the options and click the left mouse button, a more detailed list of options appear below the option chosen. This is a pull-down menu. We can use the mouse to select the option required.

GUIs are also sometimes called WIMPs after the initial letters of these four components.

Client Server Technology

Client server allows a distribution of work where a 'client' can request a 'server' to carry out a task on its behalf. The client and server are usually computers – for example a terminal or workstation as a client requesting information from a mainframe computer as the server. The client and server can also be software – for example an application program requesting data from a database management system.

If we go back to the idea of the client and server as computers, we can identify four forms of work sharing:

Figure 4.7: Worksharing

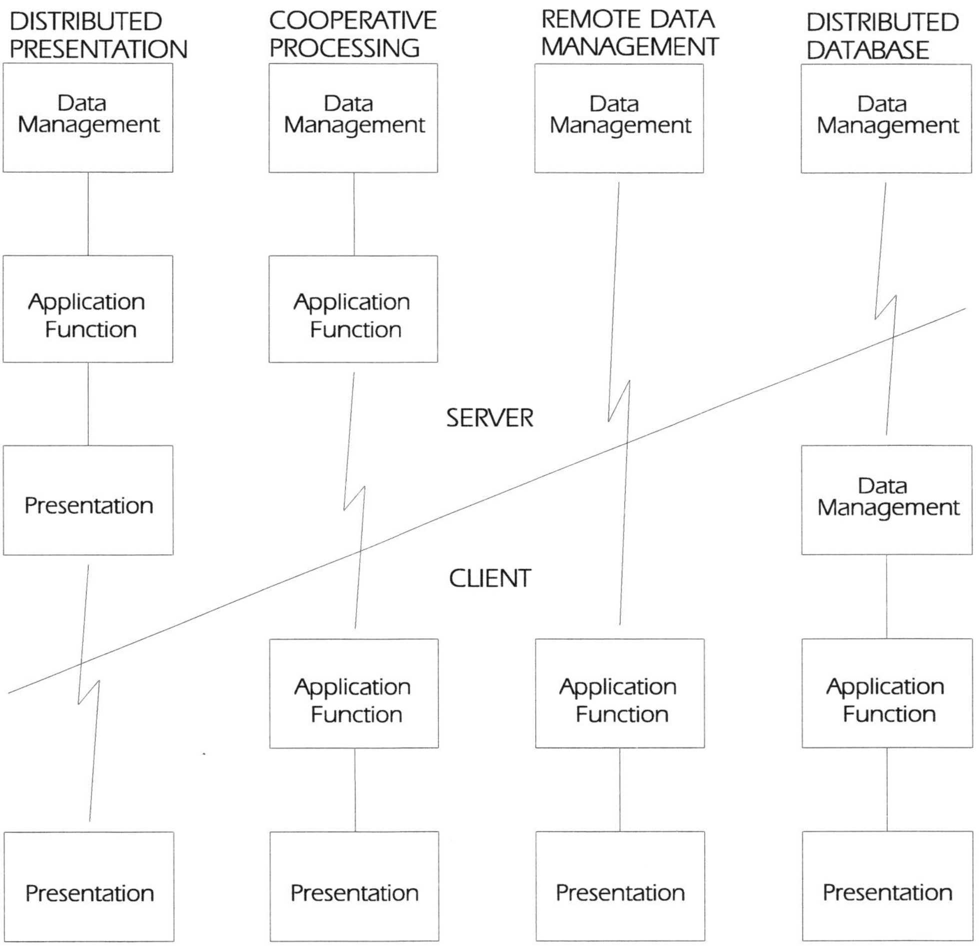

We would not usually regard distributed presentation as client server in any real sense. Almost all of the work is carried out by the server with the client taking only a minor role. The other three forms of work sharing are forms of client server:

- Cooperative processing splits the application processing between the client and server. This makes use of the client's processing power without risking the integrity of data due to the weaker data protection offered by a workstation. This approach was very common in the early stages of the third generation;

- Remote data management uses the server purely as a source of data with all processing carried out on the client. This approach is similar to the use of data warehouses, datamarts or the Internet as sources of reference information;
- Distributed database shares management of the data between the client and the server. To achieve a distributed data environment, we must be able to manage a database spread across different computers. The main concerns with this approach are data protection and data integrity.

  If the data held about customers is not carefully controlled this may give rise to problems with the Data Protection Act. Data integrity problems can occur if the data held on the clients is inconsistent with that held on the server, and a technology called 'replication' should be used to ensure consistency.

Financial services organizations invested heavily in client server technology during the third generation. Telecommunications costs were high, but server and workstation processing power was cheap so it made sense to move from the centralized approach of the second generation to the use of client server – generally cooperative processing.

Using this approach, application processing was split between the mainframe and the workstations. The applications themselves were stored on the file server and loaded onto the workstations when needed. Some data was stored on the server to save telecommunications costs, but this was a copy of data from the mainframe and so was not a true distributed database. The data stored locally was usually either data specific to the local environment – for example, security information about the users on the local network – or 'high usage low volatility' data such as currency codes and country names.

We show how this type of network operated in Figure 4.8.

The problem was that any changes made to data or programs on the branch servers had to be rolled out to every branch. Depending on the amount of information to be sent this could take days or even weeks – which presented a significant problem if the changes were being made to correct a fault.

Although financial services organizations developed various strategies to get round these problems, they increased these organizations' costs. For example:

- One strategy is to keep processing on the mainframe computer as programs held on the mainframe do not need to be rolled out. This increases costs because it uses expensive mainframe processing power rather than relatively cheap workstation processing;
- Another strategy is to allow new versions of software on the server to be switched on and off. This avoided problems with errors on the software – if there was a problem the new version could be switched off and the branch could go back to using the old version. However it also meant that the branch servers had to hold several versions of the software, increasing storage costs.

Figure 4.8: Cooperative Processing

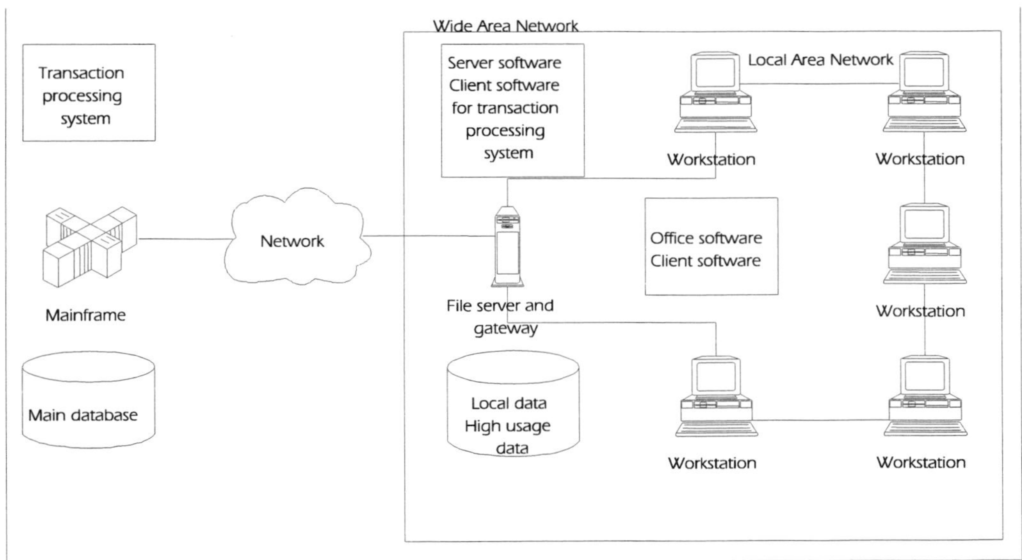

Large roll outs also directly increased telecommunications costs and there were further costs associated with managing the roll out.

Transaction Processing

The technology introduced during the third generation did not greatly change the approach to transaction processing. The ability to share work between the central computer and an intelligent workstation allowed an updated form of remote batch processing, with transactions entered and validated at the workstation before being sent to the mainframe for final validation and updating. However, on-line and real time transaction processing using the power of client/server to split the work was the dominant approach.

Data Storage and Structure

Second-generation databases were very limited. The introduction of network and relational databases during the third generation was an attempt to overcome the problems associated with hierarchical databases.

Network Databases

Network databases stored data as files. Relationships could be created between any two files, without the need for a hierarchy. In a network database, the relationship is defined by adding to the records on one file a pointer to the related records on the other file. The pointer is, in effect, the address of the related records. Pointers could be one-way or two-way.

We can show a network database as follows:

Figure 4.9: Network Database

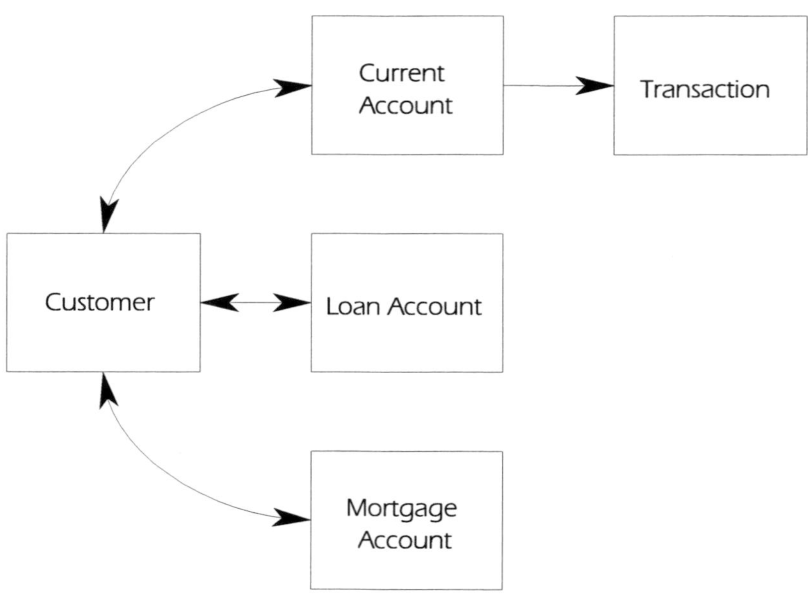

Relational Databases

A relational database holds data in tables, rather like a spreadsheet. To set up a relationship between two tables, we put a common item of data in both tables. Let us consider an example:

Table 4.2: The Relational Database

Customer Table

Customer No.	Customer Name	Date of Birth	Sex	Occupation
111111	Ann Barrow	12-Mar-45	Female	Manager
222222	Colin Davies	03-Apr-56	Male	Accountant

Account Table

Account No.	Customer No.	Account Type	Currency	Balance
12345678	222222	Current	Sterling	376-00
23456789	111111	Deposit	US Dollar	5,000-00
34567890	222222	Deposit	Sterling	528-00

Here we have two tables. There is a common item of data (Customer No.) in both tables and this defines the relationship between them. Ann Barrow has Customer No. 222222 and this can be used to find her record on the Customer Table and the record of all her accounts on the Account Table.

In a relational database, holding this common item of data creates the relationship. This makes it much easier to create relationships between rows in different tables (in relational databases, records are called 'rows' and files are called 'tables').

Customer No. is the *primary* key for the Customer Table and will be unique – only one record in the table can have a particular value of Customer No.

Customer No. is the *foreign* key for the Account Table. It is not unique but provides a way of getting from the account details to the customer details. Account No. will be the primary key for the Account Table .

Relational databases are much more flexible than network databases. In a network database, a relationship needs to be specifically defined through the creation of a pointer. The pointer is an address which must be changed as the database changes. In a relational database, the relationship exists because there is common data. There is no need to define it explicitly or to keep the address up-to-date.

The data in a relational database must be normalized. This is a process which ensures that all data (except for keys) is held in only one place. Problems that may be encountered if data is not normalized include:

- Poor data integrity. For example, if the customer address is held more than once, there is a risk that an update may not be applied to all of them. The data will be inconsistent and confidential information may be sent to an old address;
- Loss of data. For example, if information about currencies is held with the accounts, rather than as a separate currency table, this information may be lost when the last account denominated in that currency is deleted;
- Items must be stored and updated in more than one place, which requires more storage and leads to higher processing costs.

Relational databases allowed much more information to be held and, for the first time, it became feasible to store data other than text and numbers. An early example was the Model 204 database, which was used by the US Navy to store naval charts. Relational databases increasingly became capable of holding multimedia data such as pictures and drawings.

7 Fourth Generation

The fourth generation is the bridge from information technology to knowledge management and is emerging as the dominant model from the mid-1990s.

Business Driver

The main business driver is the growth in electronic commerce, or e-commerce. This is the use of electronic channels (such as the Internet) for ordering and delivering goods or services. Another factor is the continuing fall in telecommunications costs which has undermined the cost justification for the client server approach.

Enabling Technology

The most important enabling technology was the development of the Internet. This is of sufficient importance to be discussed below as a separate section. Another enabling technology was object orientations.

Object Orientation

Most approaches to IT kept data and processes separate. For example, the data was held in files or as a database and the processes were incorporated in computer programs that used the data.

Object orientation is a different approach, in which data is associated with the processes that can use it. These are called methods and a method must be defined for every process that is allowed for the data. Programs cannot access the data directly but must call the appropriate methods using a 'message'. This has the advantage of protecting the integrity of the data – programs can only use the methods for which they are authorized.

Associating data with processes in this way is called encapsulation or wrapping.

The biggest impact of object orientation has been on PCs, through Object Linking and Embedding (OLE). OLE provides a way of linking a document created in one PC application with a document created in a completely different application, in such a way that the first document can be read and changed through the second document.

For example, if we regard a word processor document as the 'data', then the word processing capabilities are the 'methods'. The encapsulated document can be linked to or embedded in another type of document – for example a spreadsheet. This allows us to read and change the word processor document through the spreadsheet.

OLE embeds a *copy* of the document, so changes would be applied to the copy and not to the original. Another approach called Dynamic Data Exchange (DDE) allows a link to be established to the original document so any changes would affect that as well.

Object orientation has also been seen as a way of improving the development of computer systems by 'reusing' proved components. Because objects link data and processes, they are seen as easier to reuse than either data or processes on their own.

This allows financial services organizations to build up 'libraries' of objects that they can combine when they want to develop a new computer system. A technical architecture called the Common Object Request Broker Architecture or CORBA allows the objects to be linked together. Objects can be developed by other organizations and, provided they comply with the CORBA architecture, linked to objects in the organization's own library or objects developed by other organizations. This is called 'componentware'.

Although CORBA, object libraries and componentware offer very large potential savings to financial services organizations, their use has been somewhat limited. The financial services organizations have a very large investments in their existing systems, which do not comply with CORBA, and this limits their ability to use componentware.

Transaction Processing

Fourth-generation technology has not fundamentally changed the approach to transaction processing, where on-line transaction processing continues to dominate.

The major change has been the growth in 'outsourcing to the customer', with customers entering information into the computer themselves over the Internet. Customers are not trained to use the system and this has placed an emphasis on designing simple and easily understood transactions.

This has, in turn, encouraged financial services organizations to develop straight-through processing. This allows the processing of information with no requirement for manual intervention by staff, unless a problem is detected.

Data Storage and Structure

The relational database continued to be the dominant form of data storage.

Object databases were also found. These were hierarchical in structure. Important characteristics of object databases were:

- Classification. Objects were categorized into classes and super-classes to create the hierarchy;
- Inheritance. Objects inherited the methods of the objects above them in the hierarchy – objects inherit the methods of their class and classes inherit the methods of their super-classes;
- Polymorphism. Although objects inherited the same methods, they were able to interpret incoming messages in different ways.

Fourth-generation data storage systems were able to hold a wide range of different types of unstructured data. The fourth generation drew on the technology of the Internet and the web, which was designed to hold multimedia data. In addition to pictures and drawings, other forms of multimedia such as video, animation and sound could be held.

Another difference between the third and fourth generations was the ability of the latter to understand multimedia data. Relational databases typically held this data as objects – binary large objects or 'blobs'. The relational database management system could store multimedia data but it would have to be interpreted by a different computer program. Fourth generation technology such as Internet browsers can both access and interpret multimedia data.

8 The Internet

The Internet is characteristic of the fourth generation as well as being the most important development in information technology of the last decade. What is the Internet and why is it so important?

The Internet is the name given to a world-wide network of computer networks. The term Internet refers to the physical computers – the hardware – and the telecommunications links. In order to use the Internet we need to access the software of which the best known is the 'World Wide Web' (WWW or the web) which allows the Internet to carry text, pictures, audio and video.

The term 'Information Super Highway' is often used and refers to the process of integrating computer networks into a world-wide network which makes best use of technology such as fibre optic data-communications links. The German term 'Infobahn' is sometimes also used. The Internet is the position that has currently been reached in this process.

History and Evolution

The Internet's history is closely tied up with the USA's military requirements. In 1969, the US Department of Defense's Advanced Research Projects Agency (ARPA) constructed a research network called ARPAnet, which linked together military and university staff to facilitate the quick and easy exchange of government information via electronic means. One important feature of ARPAnet was that it was designed to withstand possible destruction, e.g., from a fire, bomb or nuclear attack, and could easily send information from A to B, bypassing the damaged or destroyed section of the network. That is, it was a distributed, non-centralized and robust communication medium. ARPAnet was also designed to be as flexible as possible to cater for the wide variety of computers and equipment that would be plugged into the network.

The main features of both ARPAnet and the Internet were:

- It did not need a central controlling computer. The Internet is an example of a peer-to-peer network in which computers send messages addressed directly to each other without going through a central computer. One reason for this was to allow the network to function even in the event of a nuclear attack – the network did not contain a 'single point of failure' the destruction of which would close down the entire network;
- It sent information over the telecommunications network using packet switching, developed in the UK. Packet switching allows much more information to be sent over a telecommunications network than other methods;
- It allowed computers to instruct other computers in the network to carry out actions. This is called interoperability and was developed at Bell Laboratories in the USA. This was the ancestor of client/server, and computers attached to the Internet are able to request services that they would be unable to carry out themselves.

ARPAnet grew in size over the years to accommodate the ever-increasing number of institutions that had adopted the technology. One key player here was the US Government's National Science Foundation (NSF), which had built several supercomputers for use within selected US universities.

The military decided to pull out of the project because the network had become too popular, and created its own network (Milnet) for its own exclusive use. NSF then maintained and developed this non-military, or citizen's, side of ARPAnet, now referred to as 'NSFnet'. Other partners and companies were soon involved in developing NSFnet. It was eventually decided that the NSFnet should be available to any university, company or organization wishing to use it, and it should not just be available to the elite.

This decentralized the NSFnet forever, and by the late 1980s the NSFnet had become the Internet (an abbreviation for 'Internetworking'). It took the introduction and development of the World Wide Web (WWW) in the early 1990s for more companies, individuals, countries, institutions and organizations to get themselves connected onto the Internet. The web provided a distributed network of information and resources, accessible via mouse clickable 'hyperlinks' contained in web documents. This easy way of linking together associated information resources proved to be a major breakthrough in raising the profile, facilities and benefits of the Internet.

The involvement of research organizations such as NASA greatly expanded the amount of information available through the Internet. The US Government, in particular, played an important role in encouraging the use of the Internet by subsidizing telecommunications costs.

The WWW was developed in 1990 by Tim Berners-Lee at the European nuclear research agency CERN in Switzerland. Scientists had the problem of cross-referencing large amounts of information, which could include diagrams and photographs as well as text. He created a browser that would enable his colleagues to access up-to-date academic information on his research held on his own computer – eliminating the need to constantly distribute printed material. From these early beginnings, the WWW has probably been the sole service that has generated today's huge interest in the Internet.

The WWW allows individuals, organizations, and companies – indeed, anyone – to publish all manner of information on the Internet in the form of a web site. The contents of this web site are linked together by a serious of so-called hyperlinks, which can be text or graphics. Clicking on such a hyperlink displays new information, which again can be text, graphics, sound, video, etc. The effect of these links is to create a 'web' of information and resources on a site – hence the name. These links do not have to point to information within the same web site – the WWW is a distributed information resource, so these links can point to other web sites located anywhere in the world, thus forming the web structure of this Internet service.

More and more companies and organizations are getting a web presence. Indeed, early web sites merely included the company's product brochure, background information, a contact address and generally little else. However, with the accelerated adoption of this Internet service, web sites are becoming increasingly more sophisticated, and offer access to complex information sources such as online databases, multimedia information, Internet telephony facilities, etc.

In recent years, commercial information providers have become increasingly involved in offering services on the Internet. This may result in a greater proportion of Internet services being charged for – a move away from the principle of free access.

But perhaps the most important aspect of web site adoption and development is that companies are realizing the potential of their web site as a central means of conducting business (e-commerce). The Internet can provide a powerful method for presenting products, services and company profiles to a global audience.

Accessing the Internet

Internet Service Providers

Although it is possible to access the World-Wide Web directly, most subscribers register with an Internet service provider (ISP). The ISP will offer one or more telephone numbers (also known as points of presence) through which we can connect to the Internet. ISPs usually offer at least one local number and are increasingly offering connection through a single 0345 (local rate) number.

Many of the older ISPs are relatively small organizations but multinational corporations such as Microsoft and British Telecom are now acting as ISPs. The introduction of free Internet access, initially by Dixons' Freeserve, has changed the economics of Internet service provision and it is likely that the trend towards larger organizations acting as ISPs will continue.

An alternative business model is to offer connection through a free (0800) number outside peak hours, in return for a subscription. This also favours larger ISPs.

Most subscribers still use modems to connect with the Internet over analogue telephone lines. However, other possible forms of connection include digital lines (such as ISDN or ADSL), fibre-optic cable (which can be analogue or digital), power lines or wireless connection. Digital subscriber line technologies such as asynchronous digital subscriber line (ADSL) offer very high connection speeds and are of increasing importance. Many of these technologies have the advantage that the subscriber is permanently connected to the Internet.

Internet Devices

Most people access the Internet through a PC with a modem. The PC's hard disk stores the web browser and the other software (word processor, spreadsheet, database etc.) that we might want to use. We also copy information from the Internet onto the PC's hard disk.

This has a number of disadvantages. There are a lot of things that can go wrong with a PC. The PC is a complicated and expensive piece of equipment. The software loaded on the

PC soon gets out-of-date and it is expensive and time consuming to upgrade to the latest version. Research by consultants Forrester Research shows the annual support cost of a typical PC is $2,680 on top of the original purchase price in the range $2,000-$3,000.

The alternative is to access the Internet using simpler – and cheaper – devices. These are called 'thin clients' because most of the work is carried out on the Internet servers. So instead of having a word processor installed on a PC we might access a word processor located on a server through the Internet. We would not have to buy the word processor and we would always be using the latest version. The PC is called a 'thick client' by comparison.

PC banking provides another example of thick client and thin client. We can deliver PC banking in two main ways:

- We can provide customers with the software to load on their PCs;
- We can provide customers with access through the Internet.

The first is a thick client approach. Before the PC banking system can be used, the customer must load the software onto his or her PC where it takes up hard disk space. If we want to change the software we have to send this out to the customer who then has to reinstall it.

The second is the thin client approach. The client gets access to the software when it is needed. Little or no information is stored on the customer's hard disk and the customer always accesses the most up-to-date version of the banking system.

The thin client approach is not used only for banking systems. The only software that would be stored on the thin client would be the operating system and browser with all other software – including such standard software as electronic office products – accessed through the Internet. Even the operating system and browser might exist only as 'bootstraps' offering the most basic of facilities with the remainder of the software loaded from the Internet.

The first serious attempt at a commercial thin client device was the network computer (or NC). This had a powerful processor but no hard disk storage. Annual support costs for the NC would be about $800 on top of the initial purchase price in the range $700-$1,000. A commercial response to this was the Net PC, a low-power, low-cost PC designed to access the Internet but with a lower total cost of ownership than a fully functional PC. Annual support costs would be $1,480 on top of an initial purchase price in the range $1,200-$2,000.

Neither the NC nor the Net PC were particularly successful, although the NC was used by organizations such as insurer General Accident (now part of CGU) and the Association of British Insurers (ABI) to replace terminal computers.

A new generation of thin client devices is emerging as a result of the convergence of computing with telephony and consumer electronics. Important thin client devices are:

- TV set-top boxes. These allow a television set to be used as an Internet access device;
- Some mobile telephones have a built in keyboard and can be used to access the Internet. 'Third-generation' mobile telephones using wireless access protocol (WAP) technology

have this capability as do some older mobile telephones (the technology was pioneered by Nokia with the Nokia 9000 series, and another approach called I-mode is very popular in Japan);

- Smart phones. These can work in a number of ways, including using a touch-sensitive screen as a keyboard or having a fold-out keyboard;
- Windows-based terminals. These are successors to the Net PC. They include the Java virtual machine but run under Microsoft's Windows operating system.

The relative advantages and disadvantages of the approaches depend on cost and convenience. For example the advantages of thick clients include:

- Telecommunications costs are lower because the device can be used on a stand-alone basis, being connected to the Internet as required;
- Similarly the device can be used if the telephone network is not available or Internet performance is unacceptably slow;
- The user has more control over data which can be stored locally.

The advantages of thin clients include:

- The total cost of ownership is lower because a less complicated device with less software is needed;
- The latest versions of programs and data are always available.

To date, thin clients have made little progress in the marketplace. There are a number of reasons for this including the large number of PCs already in use, customer concerns about the performance of the Internet and the additional facilities available to PC users such as CD-ROMs.

It might be expected that thin clients would be successful in the corporate market. The lower cost of ownership is obviously attractive and the inability to store data or programs long term has security benefits – there is no possibility of out-of-date information being stored and there is less likelihood of virus infection. So far this has not happened, with organizations continuing to use a mix of fully functional PCs and terminal computers. The growth in the use of Internet technology for internal networks – the intranet – may change this.

Internet Connection

There are several ways of connecting to the Internet, each with its own associated costs and tariffs.

At the simplest level there is a dial-up account. This requires a computer, a modem, a telephone line and an account with an Internet Service Provider (or ISP). To access the Internet the PC dials into the ISP network using the telephone line and, after successfully connecting, will be able to access and use most – or all – of the Internet's services. The dial-up number is usually charged at local rate or some suppliers offer free access at off-peak or as part of a telephone service package. The number of ISPs offering free (or local call charge) Internet access is gathering pace; as is the number of 'non-Internet' companies who become ISPs. These companies have realized the increasing importance of e-commerce, and are positioning themselves in the Internet field to gain a large user base and become 'Portal' owners controlling the access to the web. Freeserve (created by Dixons) is the largest of this new breed, with two million users.

At the other end of the spectrum it is also possible to connect to the Internet via a leased line. These are permanent connections to the Internet, and usually allow much faster Internet access rates – anything from 128k to several Megabits. Costs for a leased-line service vary among ISPs, but we may expect to pay several thousand pounds a year for a 128k leased line. Every line upgrade thereafter (to 512k, 1024k, etc.) will cost a few thousand pounds increment each time. Leased lines are usually charged at an annual flat rate, so there are no running charges for actually using the leased line on a daily basis.

Somewhere between these two extremes are several other methods of accessing the Internet, most notably ISDN (Integrated Services Digital Network), offered by most telecommunications providers. ISDN has been around for years, and at the basic level offers speeds of 64k and 128k, and can even let us surf the Internet while simultaneously making conventional telephone calls. ISDN also needs an ISDN modem – although it is actually referred to as a terminal adapter – which allows us to send and receive digital signals through the ISDN lines. There is a one-off installation cost and a monthly line rental of approximately £30-50. There will also be the usual connection charges every time the ISDN service is used.

It is also worth mentioning ADSL, an abbreviation for Asymmetric Digital Subscriber Line, which is currently being rolled out to a number of cities in the UK. ADSL will turn an ordinary telephone line into a high-speed digital connection, offering communications speeds between 10 and 40 times the speed of a conventional modem. British Telecom plan to upgrade 600 exchanges in 2000.

Wholesale prices will range from £40 to £100 per month to service providers for every customer they wish to connect. Actual retail prices, and services offered, will be determined by the service providers. One important benefit of ADSL is that service is 'always switched on' to provide customers fast, convenient and constant access to their service provider[1].

Other technologies for connecting to the Internet are available but of lesser importance. Cable modems can be used to allow high-speed connection through cable television lines. Power line technology – using mains electricity lines – allows high-speed connection and is 'always switched on'. The technology has been trialled but not commercially deployed. Wireless connection – for example satellite broadcast – can be used to allow the high-speed transfer of information from the Internet to PCs.

Web Browsers

1 More information can be found at: http://w.w.w.bt.com/adsl.

Most software is designed to use data of one specific type. For example, a word processor will read and change files either created using that word processor or exported into that word processor format. Browsers can understand a range of different types of data and can be used to look at files of different types. Browsers are becoming increasingly important and much recent software is able to view files in a number of different formats.

Browsers are a very effective way to access data stored on the web. Web browsers use the links provided by HTML both to move between different places on the web (navigation) and to access files of different types (for example, pictures, video and audio) which are then interpreted using the browser technology.

Most people access the Internet through a web browser. The two most important web browsers are Netscape Navigator and Microsoft's Internet Explorer. Web browsers also have standard buttons allowing access to common functions such as e-mail and locations such as the Internet Service Provider's home page and the main search engines.

Push Technology

We use browsers to request information, but we can also ask for information to be sent to us. This is called push technology and was originally developed by Pointcast although it is now a standard feature in browsers.

Push technology allows us to say what information we want and when we want it – usually when telephone charges are low and the Internet relatively quiet. This will be sent to our computer at the specified time.

The effectiveness of push technology depends on its ability to customize the information it delivers to meet the needs of the user. This requires it to categorize and filter.

- Categorization is the ability to look for types of information that may be of interest.
- Filtering is the ability to exclude items from the category if they are not of interest.

These feature are also found in search engines. They are discussed at the end of this chapter under knowledge management.

One problem with push technology is that that it can use telecommunications resources – bandwidth – very heavily. Because it requires no effort to get the information users are less selective about what they ask for. There are technical solutions to this problem ('caching' – moving the data through additional servers to distribute the workload) but these incur additional costs. This may be a factor which explains the limited take up of push technology within organizations despite its obvious potential for distributing information.

Do not confuse push technology with mail enabling, although there are some similarities. Mail enabling allows an e-mail message to be sent in response to an event. Push technologies send data rather than messages and this is sent at a specified time rather than being in response to an event. E-mail messages are delivered to a server whereas push technology delivers the data directly to the PC.

Search Engines

One of the main problems with the Internet is that it contains so much information. Links between sites provide one way of getting around the Internet but are of little use for finding anything new.

One approach is to build an index. This was taken by Yahoo! and yahoo.com is the most popular site on the Internet. Information is classified into about twenty main categories and each category is further broken down into a number of sub-categories. These may be further broken down. Therefore we should be able to find any piece of information by following it through its categories and sub-categories.

This works well for most routine enquiries. But sometimes there is not a category that matches what we are looking for. Alternatively, it may fall into two or three categories. Although we could use the index to find what we are looking for we may have to try several different categories, which is time-consuming and can be frustrating. Search engines allow a search for a word or words within an item of information. Yahoo! combines a search engine with an index, allowing us to search the entire web or to search only within a category or sub-category.

Even using a search engine, there may still be a very large number of items found. Some search engines can group similar items together – they will show one of the items with the option to look at the similar items. This is a knowledge management technique and is discussed in Chapter 19.

The most popular index and search engine sites now offer additional services such as e-mail. These are called portals to show that they offer a wider range of services. For example, Yahoo! offers services such as a currency calculator and a global weather service.

Intelligent Agents

Intelligent agents are a development of search engines. A search engine is passive – we have to ask it a question before it will provide the information we need. It does not tell us when the information changes and we may need to access the search engine again in order to identify any new sites relating to our topic of interest.

Intelligent agents are dynamic. They know the topics in which we are interested and they can carry out periodic searches to identify more up-to-date information and even new sites. Intelligent agent technology is still quite new but it has immense potential to ensure that users of the Internet have access to the latest information.

They can also understand the information. For example, an intelligent agent can be used to identify the lowest price from suppliers of a product. It is this ability that distinguishes intelligent agents from push technology.

9 Open and Proprietary Systems

We can distinguish between:

- Open systems. These are systems about which sufficient information is published to allow others to use them and to develop complementary products. A licence fee may be payable. Note that a system can be open without everything about it being published. Mondex and VisaCash do not publish information about how their security systems work because this would increase the risk of fraud.

  Because open systems allow others to enter the market with complementary products this increases the acceptance of the system;
- Proprietary systems. These are systems about which no information is published and which only the vendor is allowed to develop. Most early IT systems were proprietary.

  Proprietary systems lock customers in to the vendor. This protects the vendor's competitive advantage provided that customers are prepared to accept being restricted to a single supplier;
- Public domain systems. Public domain systems are a form of open system in which the specification is freely published and can be used with no restrictions and no licence fee. The Internet is an example of a public domain system.

Most first- and second-generation systems were proprietary. IT suppliers provided a 'bundle' including the hardware and the system software. Organizations would develop applications software themselves or buy packages from their IT supplier or one of the supplier's business partners.

This had the effect of restricting customers' choice of supplier. This became increasingly unacceptable to both customers and the authorities, and the US Department of Justice brought anti-trust proceedings against IBM – then the world's largest computer company – to prevent them from bundling computer hardware and software.

Most systems are now open and public domain systems such as the Internet and the Unix operating system are becoming increasingly important.

Part 2

System and Process Development

This part of the book considers how systems and processes are developed and implemented within financial services organizations.

Systems theory considers systems in terms of inputs, outputs and the processes required to convert the inputs into the outputs. These can include both manual systems and automated systems such as information systems.

When the word 'system' is used in this book it generally refers to an information system, but it is important to remember that this is only part of a wider processing system. This wider system also includes the manual processes required.

Information systems development is one activity in a broader business and information context. We can show this as:

Figure 1: Information Systems Development

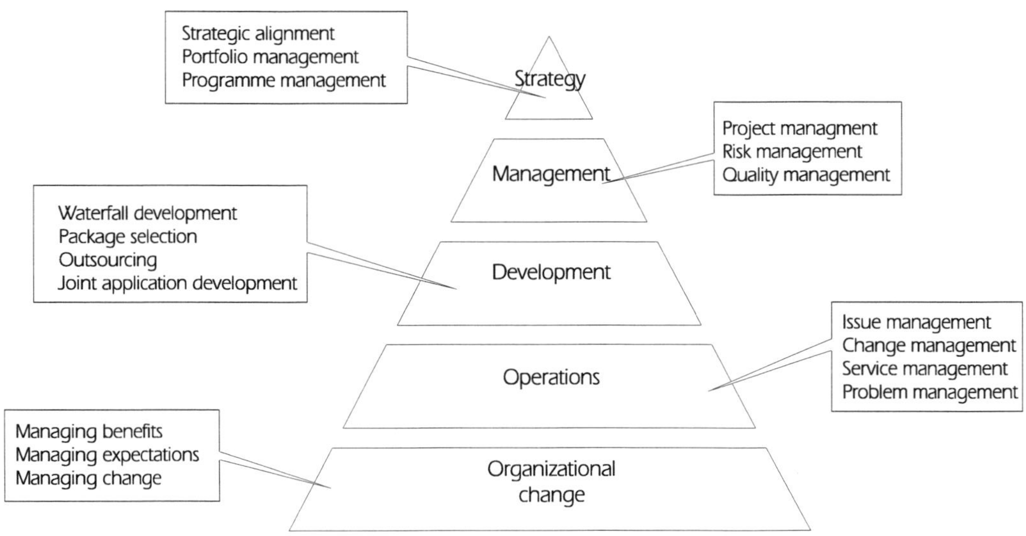

Strategy includes:

- Strategic alignment. This is the process of ensuring that the systems developed are consistent with the overall objectives of the organization. This is discussed in Chapter 5;
- Programme management. This is the overall management of a number of interdependent projects to achieve a single overall purpose. This is discussed in Chapter 6.

Management includes:

- Project management and control. This is discussed in Chapter 6;
- Risk management. This is discussed in Chapter 9;
- Quality management. This is discussed in Chapter 10.

Development is discussed in Chapters 7 and 8.

Operations and *organizational change* are discussed in Chapter 10.

This model describes a general business context, which encompasses process development as well as information systems development. The application of this to processes is largely outside the scope of this book, but we discuss process design in Chapter 8.

5

STRATEGY

Objectives

After studying this chapter, you should be able to:

- be able to distinguish between strategic, tactical and operational information;
- understand and be able to describe and compare the main schools of thought about corporate strategy;
- be able to trace the evolution of corporate strategy;
- understand the overall approach to the development of corporate strategy, and important tools and techniques including:
    - SWOT analysis
    - the Boston matrix
    - product lifecycles;
- understand and be able to describe the relationship between the business strategy and the information strategy (the information systems strategy and the information technology strategy);
- understand and be able to discuss whether information is a strategic resource;
- understand the main approaches to developing an information strategy;
- understand and be able to describe the components of the information strategy and the relationship between these components;
- understand and be able to describe the components of the information technology strategy;
- be able to distinguish between emerging, pacing, key, base and obsolete technologies;
- understand and be able to describe the components of the information systems strategy;
- understand the concept of portfolio management as applied to the information systems strategy;
- understand and be able to discuss strategic alignment and the strategic disconnect;

- understand and be able to distinguish the strategic positioning that organizations may adopt;
- understand and be able to describe how new technologies develop, diffuse and are acquired by organizations;
- understand the particular issues service industries face when innovating.

1 Introduction

What is strategy? The word strategy comes from the Greek *strategea* (generalship), which in turn comes from *strategos* (a General). Webster's Dictionary gives the following definition of strategy:

1) The science of military command, or the science of projecting campaigns and directing great military movements; generalship.
2) The use of stratagem or artifice.
3) A plan of action encompassing the methods to be adopted from beginning to end of a task or endeavour, focusing on the general methods; — contrasted with tactics, which is a plan for accomplishing subgoals of lesser extent than the primary goal. Thus, a strategy is a plan for winning a war, and a tactic is a plan for winning a battle.
4) Biol. A behavior evolved and exhibited by a living organism to accomplish some important goal, as a foraging strategy.

It is the third of these definitions that is most important to us. Strategy is 'a plan of action ... adopted from beginning to end ... focusing on the general methods'. It is contrasted with tactics which accomplish 'subgoals of a lesser extent'.

Military terms are often found in management – for example marketing campaigns or takeover battles – and the analogy of directing a business and directing an army is self-evident. It is perhaps worth noting that the term *strategea* started to be used for administration at a very early stage.

The fourth definition, which looks at strategy in behavioural terms, is also of interest and we shall return to this later in this chapter.

We shall take the following diagram[1] as the starting point for our consideration of strategy:

1 Based on R N Anthony: *Planning and Control: A Framework for Analysis* Harvard University Press 1965

Figure 5.1

Management information can be strategic, tactical or operational. We can summarize some of the differences between these:

Table 5.1

	STRATEGIC INFORMATION	TACTICAL INFORMATION	OPERATIONAL INFORMATION
Used by	Senior Managers	Middle Managers	First-line Managers
Time horizon	1-10 years	3-18 months	Up to 1 month
Sources of data	External and strategic management information systems	Operational and tactical management information systems	Operational systems
Internal or external	Internal and external	Mainly internal	Entirely internal
Frequency of decision	Infrequent and at irregular intervals	Weekly, monthly, quarterly or yearly	Very frequent during the day
Basis for decisions	Facts, projections and judgements	Facts and projections	Facts
Type of decision	Unprogrammed – each decision is unique	Programmed – follows overall policies and precedents	Prescriptive – follows defined rules and procedures
Presentation	Summaries and trends	Summaries and supporting detail	Usually detailed
Examples	Market share and product profitability	Actual costs and revenues *v.* budgets	Customer financial histories

2 Corporate Strategy

There are four schools of thought about corporate strategy:

- The 'content' approach, which regards corporate strategy as a coherent, top-down process;
- The 'political' approach, which regards strategy as a political process between executives;
- The 'logical incrementalism' of Quinn and others;
- The 'organizational learning' approach.

The content approach views strategy as a coherent plan. There is typically an overall corporate strategy, representing a defined route from the organization's current situation to a desired future state, and each business unit has a strategy that explicitly contributes to the corporate strategy. This is consistent with the military analogy for strategy and with the strategic triangle, and it is probably the most common view.

The political approach assumes that executives have different goals and that an overall strategy is reached through processes including bargaining, negotiating and coalition building[2]. The objective of the decision-making process is to reach a solution that is acceptable to the executives rather than necessarily to reach the optimal solution.

Logical incrementalism[3] regards corporate strategy as 'the pattern of decisions in a company that determines and reveals its objectives, purposes, or goals, and defines the range of business the company is to pursue, the kind of economic and human organization it intends to be, and the nature of the economic and noneconomic contribution it intends to make to its shareholders, employees, customers, and communities'[4].

In other words, the organization's strategy is based on the perceptions of the senior management group (what Mintzberg calls perspective[5]). The success of the organization will depend on the quality of these perceptions. The formal planning process exists alongside the tacit strategy but its main function is to provide a structure for the process.

It is perhaps worth noting that this is consistent with Webster's fourth definition, which sees strategy in terms of behaviour.

The organizational learning approach is most often associated with Peter Senge. The organization – which includes staff at *all* levels – adapts and responds to changing

2 J B Quinn: 'Strategic Change: 'Logical Incrementalism' *Sloan Management Review* I Number 20 Fall 1978 quoted in *The Strategy Process* Second Edition (Prentice-Hall International 1991 page 97

3 JB Quinn, Strategic Change: 'Logical Incrementalism' *Sloan Management Review* I Number 20 Fall 1978 quoted in *The Strategy Process* Second Edition (Prentice-Hall International 1991) page 96.

4 KR Andrews, *The Concept of Corporate Strategy* revised edition Richard D Irwin 1980 quoted in *The Strategy Process* Second Edition (Prentice-Hall International 1991) page 44.

5 H Mintzberg, Five Ps for Strategy *California Management Review* Fall 1987 quoted in *The Strategy Process* Second Edition (Prentice-Hall International 1991) page 16.

circumstances. The pattern of these adaptions is the strategy. This is clearly similar in concept to logical incrementalism, but places a stronger emphasis on the organization's response to the business environment.

Perhaps the most accurate view is that strategy has elements from *each* of these approaches – and that opportunism also forms part of most strategy. This is reflected in the following diagram[6]:

Figure 5.2: Strategy – A Consolidated View

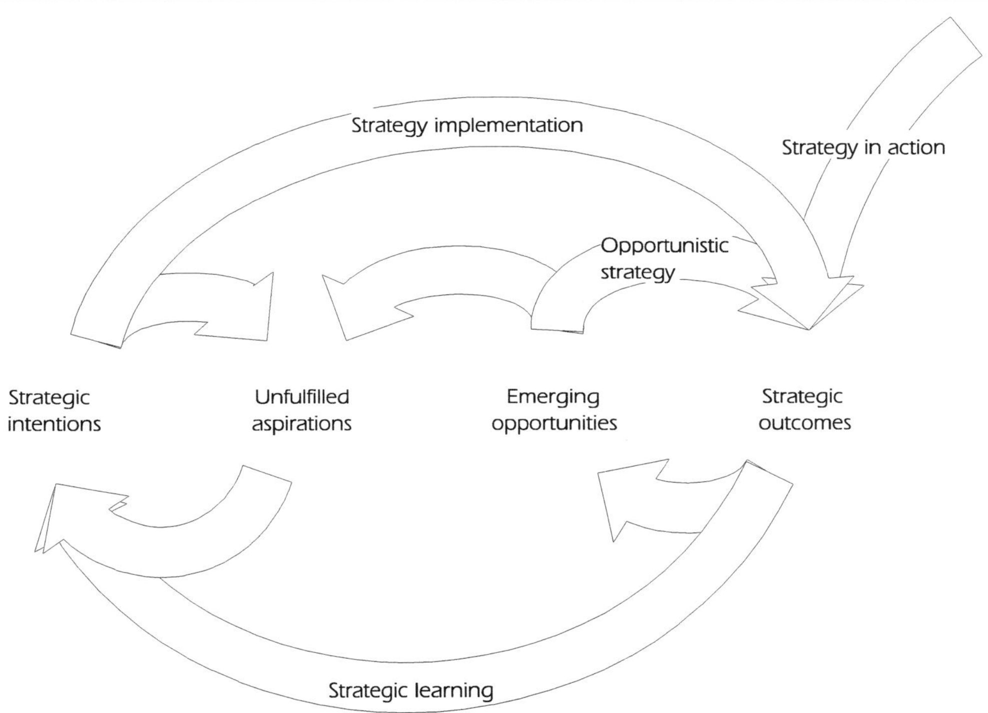

Strategic outcomes may arise as a result of the implementation of the planned strategy, but may also arise from an opportunistic strategy resulting from the exploitation of emerging opportunities, or from 'strategy in action' – the development of strategic responses to day-to-day problems.

Similarly there may be unfulfilled aspirations, resulting from the failure of the planned strategy or because emerging opportunities cannot be exploited as we would wish.

The strategic learning process involves learning from both success and failure. Finally, the strategic outcomes themselves affect our ability to respond to emerging opportunities – this is considered later when we discuss innovation.

The focus of corporate strategy has changed over time. Until quite recently, the main focus

6 J Moncrieff 'Making a Difference' *The Ashridge Journal* November 1998

of business strategy was logistics – organizational efficiency and 'moving stuff out the door'[7]. This changed in the 1980s – partly as a result of Japanese business practice[8] – and it is the current view that competitive advantage is the key subject of business strategy[9].

In parallel with this change of focus, the strategic management processes have changed. The strategic management maturity model[10] reflects this evolution:

Figure 5.3: Strategic Management Maturity Model

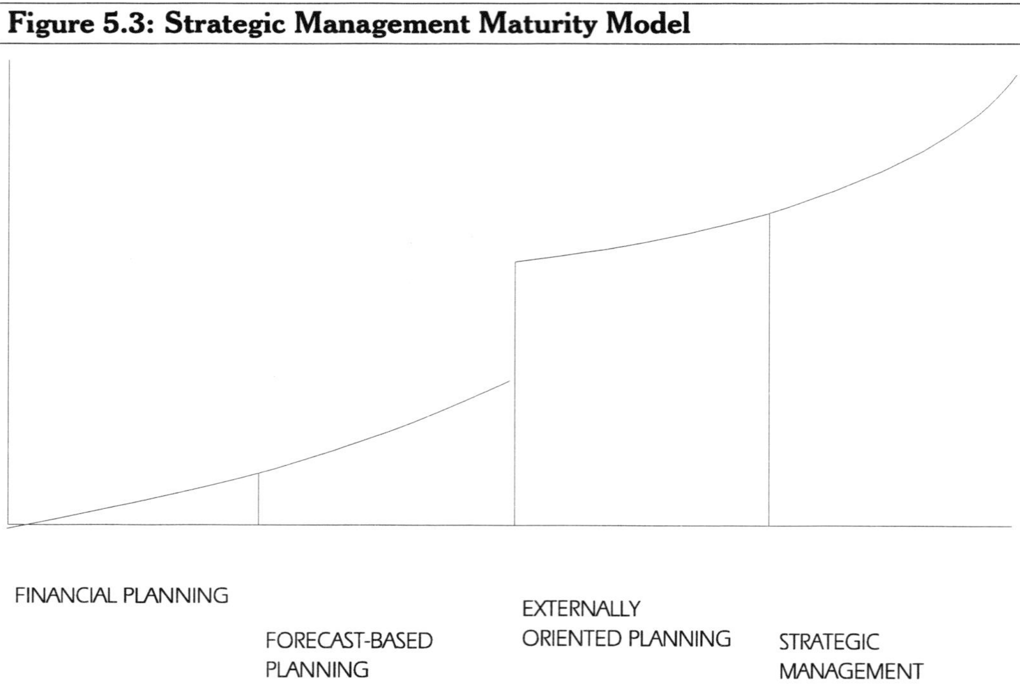

The first phase of this is financial planning, allowing organizations to meet their budgets. There is a functional focus and an annual budget cycle.

As organizations mature they enter the phase of forecast-based planning, allowing them to predict the future. This phase is characterized by budgets spanning several years and techniques such as gap analysis.

The third phase represents a move towards the view of strategy as the search for competitive advantage. This is the externally-oriented planning phase in which organizations think strategically. This phase involves the evaluation of strategic options and a change from

7 CW Stern and G Stalk Jr. *Perspectives on Strategy* (John Wiley & Sons) reviewed in the *Financial Times* 25 June 1998.

8 JC Abegglen and G Stalk *Kaisha: The Japanese Corporation* (Harper & Row 1985).

9 K Ohmae *The Mind of the Strategist - The Art of Japanese Business* (McGraw-Hill Book Company 1982) page 36.

10 FW Gluck, SP Kaufmann and AS Walleck 'Strategic planning for competitive advantage' *Harvard Business Review* July / August 1980

allocating resources statically to dynamic resource allocation. Techniques such as situation analysis and competitive assessment are features of this phase. Moving from the second to the third phase is accompanied by a step jump in efficiency.

The fourth phase is the strategic management phase in which organizations seek to create the future. There exists a well-defined strategic framework and a strategic thinking capability is spread throughout the organization. This is reinforced by the management process and supported by the organizational climate and value system.

3 Developing the Strategic Plan

Overall Approach

Johnson and Scholes described strategic planning as a three-stage process:

- Strategic analysis
- Strategic choice
- Strategy implementation.

The strategic analysis stage involves analysing and understanding the organization's business environment and internal capabilities. The strategic choice stage involves formulating and evaluating strategic options, and selecting a preferred option. The strategy must then be implemented.

One framework for strategic analysis is the three-layer model[11]:

- External environment
- Pressure groups and stakeholders
- Internal business planning.

We discussed the **external environment** in Chapters 2 to 4 of this book.

We have also discussed some important **pressure groups and stakeholders**. We discussed the role of the Government as part of the political environment. Our discussion of the social environment included consideration of customers, staff and managers. All of these are important stakeholders. 'Corporatism' – the view that society as a whole is a stakeholder and that organizations have a duty to the community – is less fashionable than it was in the 1970s but still has a role to play. Competitors are also stakeholders and we discussed these in the chapter on the competitive environment.

We shall go on to consider the **internal business planning** process and some of the most important tools and techniques.

11 J Ward and P Griffiths *Strategic Planning for Information Systems* (John Wiley 1996) based on a structure suggested by John Constable, Visiting Professor of Business Policy Cranfield School of Management

Tools and Techniques

There are a number of tools and techniques for strategic analysis, including:

- SWOT analysis
- The Boston matrix
- Product lifecycles.

SWOT Analysis

SWOT stands for strengths, weaknesses, opportunities and threats, and SWOT analysis analyses these factors for the organization. Strengths and weaknesses are analysed relative to the organization's competitors, which means that its markets – the competitive environment – must be defined. We discussed some of the issues this causes in Chapter 1.

It is possible to consider threats and opportunities in isolation, in which event SWOT analysis produces a simple list of the four components. A more sophisticated approach is to map threats and opportunities against strengths and weaknesses. Clearly it is difficult to exploit an opportunity if it occurs in an area of relative weakness, and a threat may be less dangerous if it occurs in an area of relative strength.

SWOT analysis provides a basis for organizations to understand their capabilities and the possible impact of external factors on them.

Boston Matrix

One of the most common and important strategic planning tools is the Boston matrix[12], named after its inventors the Boston Consulting Group. The Boston Matrix maps an organization's products according to market growth and market share, to produce a matrix as follows:

Table 5.2: Boston matrix

	High market share	Low market share
High market growth	Stars	Wild cats
Low market growth	Cash cows	Dogs

Stars are products with high profit and growth potential. Although they generate high revenues, the competitive nature of the market means that they also incur heavy costs and may not be particularly profitable.

Cash cows are found in more mature markets. They generate high revenues but the market

12 J Ward and P Griffiths *Strategic Planning for Information Systems* (John Wiley 1996)

is less competitive and hence costs are much lower. Cash cows are very profitable but have little long-term growth potential.

Wild cats (also called problem children) have a lot of growth potential but have low current market share. In a high-growth market this also means that they are very unprofitable.

Dogs have very little growth or profit potential, but are not necessarily unprofitable because costs may be very low.

Product Lifecycle

The Boston matrix has ideas in common with the product lifecycle[13]. This describes the typical 'lifecycle' followed by a new product. One version has four stages:

Figure 5.4: Product Lifecycle

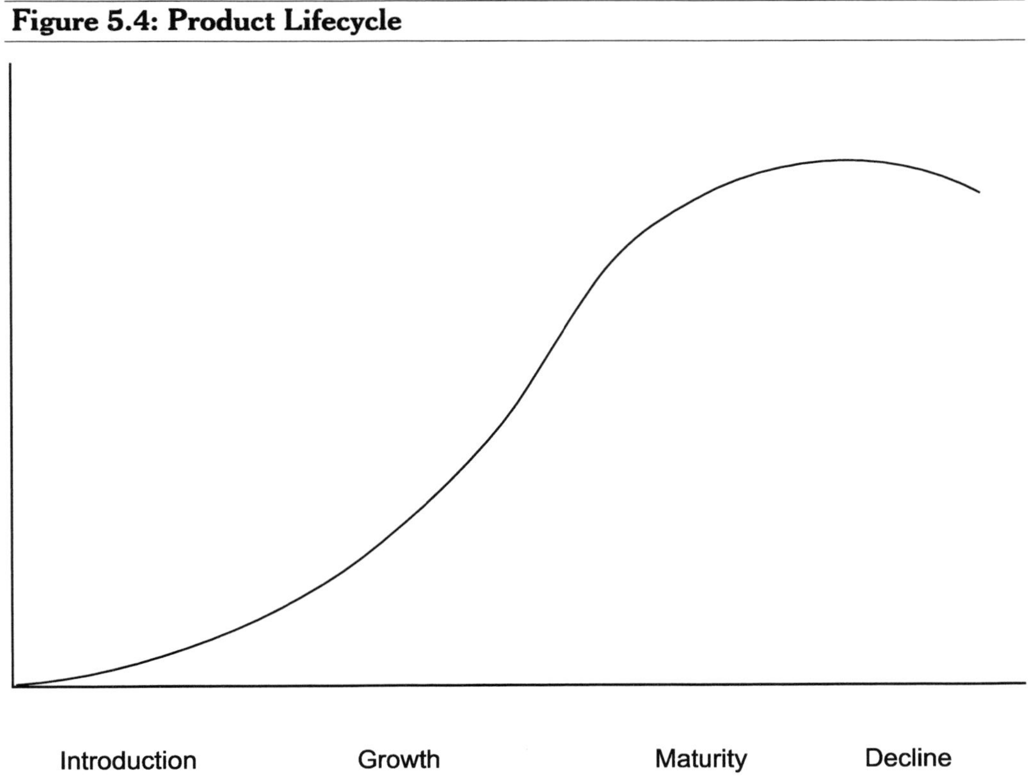

During the introduction stage, market share is low. If the product is launched into a growing market this will correspond to the 'wild cat' placing. The product will be unprofitable because revenues are low, marketing costs are high and development costs will not have been recovered.

The market continues to develop rapidly during the growth stage. If the product establishes

13 JM Higgins *Strategy – Formulation, Implementation and Control* (Dryden Press New York 1985)

itself, it will become a 'star'. Marketing costs will still be high and the product may still not be profitable.

Market growth slows as products enter the maturity part of the lifecycle. If the product has established itself, it will become a 'cash cow' and generate profits that can be reinvested into the next generation of products. If it failed to establish itself, it will become a 'dog' at maturity.

The product enters the decline stage as the market becomes saturated. It may remain a 'cash cow' or it may gradually lose market share and become a 'dog'.

4 Information Strategy

So far we have been discussing strategy at the corporate level. We now turn our discussion to the information strategy. We are adopting this term to cover both the 'equipment' side (the Information Technology or IT strategy) and the 'applications' side (the Information Systems or IS strategy).

One model that describes the relationship between business strategy, IS strategy and IT strategy is as follows[14]:

Figure 5.5: Business Strategy and Information Strategy – Relationship

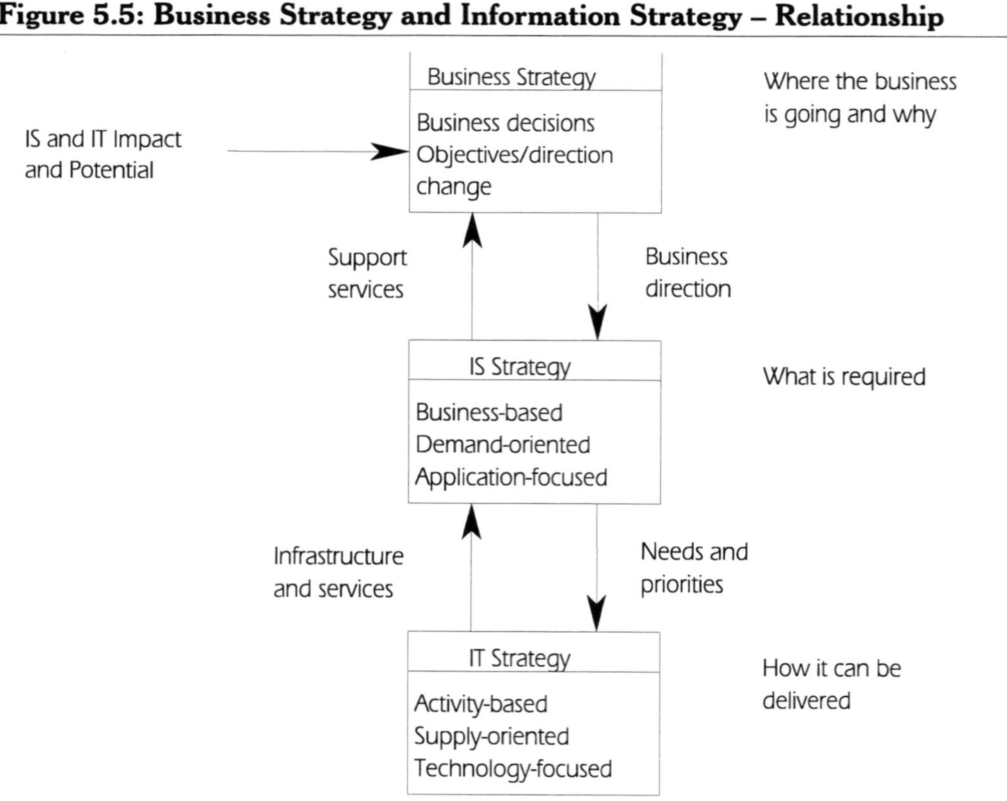

14 J Ward and P Griffiths *Strategic Planning for Information Systems* (John Wiley 1996) page 31

The IS strategy is driven from the business strategy, and in turn drives the IT strategy. Note, however, that the flows are not simply top-down. The IS strategy is affected by the IT strategy and affects the business strategy.

We can show this at a more detailed level, as a process[15]:

Figure 5.6: Business Strategy and Information Strategy – Process

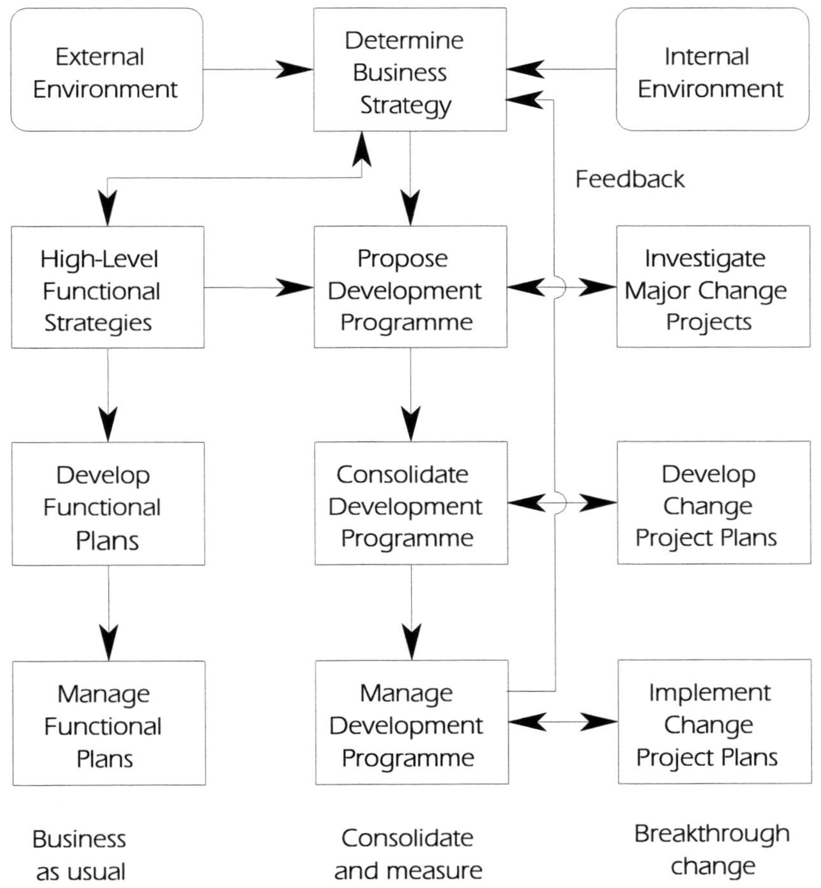

The overall *business strategy* is determined from the external and internal business environment.

This is broken down into a number of *functional strategies* corresponding to the organization's functional or departmental structure. These also affect the overall business strategy. These functional strategies are then broken down into action plans.

Both the overall business strategy and the individual functional strategies give rise to a series

15 J Ward and P Griffiths *Strategic Planning for Information Systems* (John Wiley 1996) page 103

of development *programmes*. These may be consolidated into an overall programme for the organization. The progress of these plans also affects the overall business strategy.

These development programmes in turn give rise to individual *change project plans*.

Do We Need an Information Strategy?

We have shown that the information strategy affects the business strategy, but should it? Is there a distinct information strategy, or is it simply 'to do what the business wants'?

It is now generally agreed that there should be an information strategy for reasons including:

- IS and IT are major cost factors, accounting for about 14½% of costs in the financial services industry. Therefore IS and IT must be managed strategically to ensure that this investment is used in the most effective way;
- IS and IT are 'strategic enablers', which means that other business strategies can only be implemented if the appropriate IS and IT capabilities are available. IS and IT must be managed strategically to ensure that they provide the capabilities to support other strategies;
- Similarly, IS and IT are 'strategic inhibitors', which means that the lack of IS and IT capabilities can prevent business strategies from being implemented. One extreme example of this is that at least one planned merger in the financial services industry has been called off because of the technical incompatibility of the organizations' systems;
- IS and IT decisions have a long-term impact. A decision to invest in a particular technology will be accompanied by a wide range of related decisions on training and information systems that are designed to support and exploit the technology. It is very difficult simply to abandon the investment and go back to the old technology;
- It is now generally accepted that the financial services industry is dependent on information. Organizations must manage their business-critical resources within a strategic framework;
- IS and IT are scarce resources. Organizations' ability to introduce new systems is usually constrained more by a shortage of development resource than by cost and the available resource must be deployed in the most effective manner. This requires a strategic approach.

In support of this, a 1992 survey that included both IS and non-IS managers ranked improving IS strategic planning as a top issue[16].

In spite of this, there are barriers that inhibit top managers from taking a strategic view of IS and IT. These include[17]:

16 RD Galliers, Y Merali, L Spearing 'Coping with information technology' *Journal of Information Technology* 9 (3) 1994

17 AL Lederer and AL Mendelow 'Convincing top management of the strategic potential of information systems' *MIS Quarterly* September 1988

- A lack of top management awareness of the impact of IS and IT on the business;
- A credibility gap between the promises of IT and past performance;
- Information is not always viewed as a business resource;
- The difficulty of expressing benefits in financial terms – financial cases are often seen as weak;
- Top management may take a short-term focus. This militates against an understanding of the long-term implications of IS and IT.

There may also be a 'culture gap' between the IT function and the business. One survey[18] showed that 47% of IT managers saw the culture gap as their main problem and 56% believed that it was inhibiting their companies from achieving competitive advantage from IS and IT. The gap was seen as arising from:

- Different objectives, with IT professionals seeking 'technical excellence' and driven by their own career development options whereas the business is driven to achieve 'functional excellence' and business results;
- Lack of shared values, lack of agreed strategy and a history of failed projects and systems.

However, the failure to treat IS and IT strategically leads to a number of problems[19]:

- A loss of control of IS and IT investments, leading to individuals or departments striving to reach incompatible objectives;
- Problems caused by IS and IT investments can become a cause of friction within the organization;
- Localized justification of investments can produce benefits that are counterproductive for the organization as a whole. The investment may solve the sponsoring department's problems but create more problems elsewhere in the organization;
- Systems on average have a shorter than expected business life and need to be redeveloped more frequently than should be necessary.

A survey of UK companies suggested that failure of the Information strategy planning process leads to[20]:

- Resource constraints;
- Strategy not fully implemented;
- Lack of top management acceptance;

18 K Grindley *IT in the Boardroom* (Pitman Publishing London 1991)

19 Kobler Unit *Regaining Control of IT Investments – A Handbook for Senior UK Management* (Imperial College 1990)

20 MJ Earl 'Approaches to strategic information systems planning: experience in 21 UK companies' *MIS Quarterly* 17 (1) 1993

- Increased length of time involved;
- Poor user-IS relationships.

Approaches

There are a number of theories and approaches towards information strategy. We can broadly classify these into business-driven approaches and partnership approaches.

Business Driven

Business-driven approaches are essentially reactive, regarding the business strategy as a defined starting point rather than trying to influence it. However, this fails to take account of how technology changes the bases of competition and incurs the risk that the vision underpinning the business objectives may already be obsolete.

An example of a business-driven model is[21]:

Figure 5.7: Business-driven Information Strategy Model

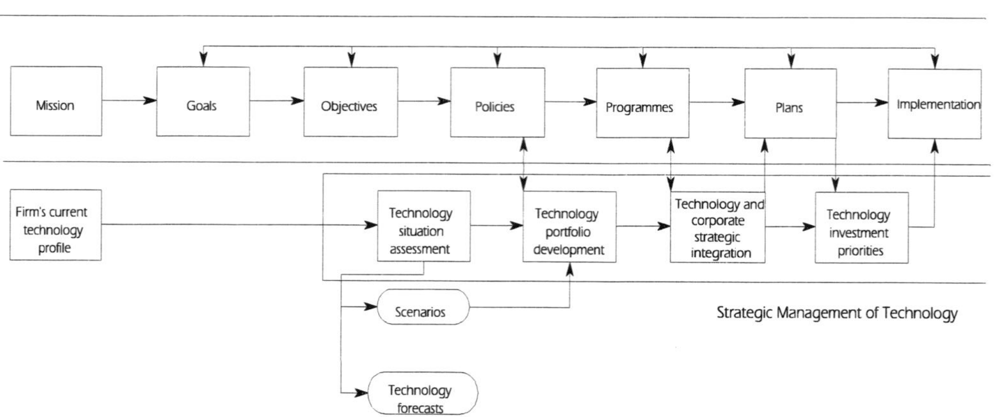

The business strategy follows the typical 'content' approach, giving a hierarchy of mission, goals etc.

The technical portfolio development stage takes account of the organization's current technology profile and uses scenario modelling and technology forecasting to project the future. A dialogue takes place between the business policies and the technology portfolio development process.

Finally the technology portfolio is integrated with business programmes and plans to determine priorities for technology investment.

Note, however, that the technology strategy has no impact on the organization's mission, goals and objectives.

21 NK Sethi, B Movsesian and KD Hickey 'Can Technology be Managed Strategically?' *Long Range Planning* volume 18 number 4 1985 pages 89-99.

Partnership

A key feature of partnership approaches is the dialogue between the overall strategy and the Information strategy.

Enterprise-wide Information Management[22] is one approach that provides an explicit link between technology and business strategy:

Figure 5.8: Enterprise-wide Information Management

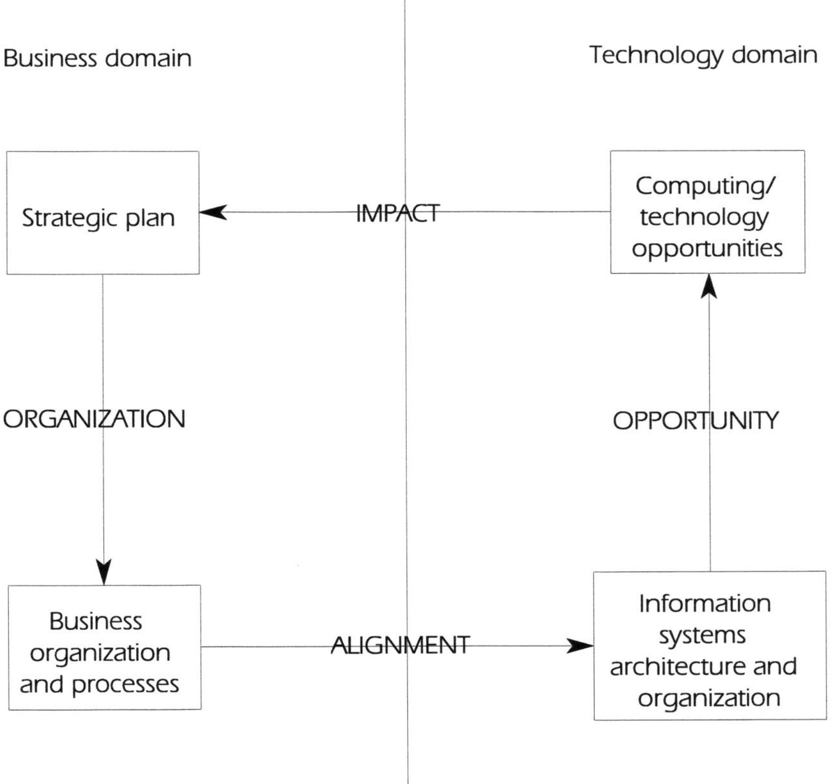

This includes four planning activities:

- Impact. Changing the business strategic plan in response to technology opportunities;
- Opportunity. Determining how to deploy current and future information systems resources;
- Alignment. Generating an information systems master plan to satisfy the needs of the business;
- Organization. Defining the organizational form necessary to carry out the business strategic plan.

22 MM Parker and RJ Benson *Information Economics* (Prentice Hall 1988) page 59

Maturity

We discussed a model for assessing the maturity of the corporate strategy process earlier in the chapter. There is a corresponding model for assessing the maturity of the information strategy process[23]:

- Adhocracy. There is an internal IT focus. The IS/IT function relates more closely to IT suppliers than to the business;
- Starting the foundations. The IS/IT function focuses on technology and is often seriously misaligned with the business;
- Centralized dictatorship. The IS/IT function becomes defensive and takes a gatekeeper role in response to business concerns over spending levels and delivery performance. (We discuss gatekeeping later in this chapter);
- Democratic dialectic and cooperation. The IS/IT function recognizes the need to cooperate with the business but continues to expect the business to accept IT's values;
- Entrepreneurial opportunity. The business recognizes the potential of IT to deliver strategic benefits but the IS/IT function is heavily committed to legacy work and struggles to deliver;
- Integrated harmonious relationship. This is rarely accomplished due to the difficulties of reconciling differing values!

The term 'legacy' is used to describe older systems, often dating from previous generations of IT and using obsolete technology. Legacy systems are often essential to the organization's operations and represent a very large investment, but they are expensive to maintain and difficult to change to meet the organization's changing needs.

Effective strategic information planning requires[24]:

- The search for competitive advantage through the application of IS and IT;
- A broader scope for planning, which incorporates a wider spectrum of technologies than the traditional data processing;
- The need to unite technologies as they emerge and with the installed base;
- The development of information, systems and technology architectures to guide the introduction and integration of new and existing technologies;
- A shift away from traditional, formal structured plans produced from an inflexible planning process towards more flexible approaches, whose aims are to find and implement the most important initiatives for the benefit of the business and epitomized by:

23 RD Galliers and AR Sutherland 'Information systems management and strategy management and strategy formulation – the stages of growth model revisited' *Journal of Information Systems* 1 (1) 1991

24 CH Sullivan 'An evolutionary new logic redefines strategic systems planning' *Information Management: The Executive's Journal* 1986

- Responsiveness, in being able to shift resources to where they are needed;
- Creative use of IT by the business;
- Ability to evaluate options;
- Use of benchmarking to establish standards of performance relative to external and competitve organizations.

Components of the Information Strategy

Information strategy development takes place in a context set by the external environment, the corporate strategy and the internal structure and capabilities of the organization[25]:

Figure 5.9: Strategic Impact of IS and IT

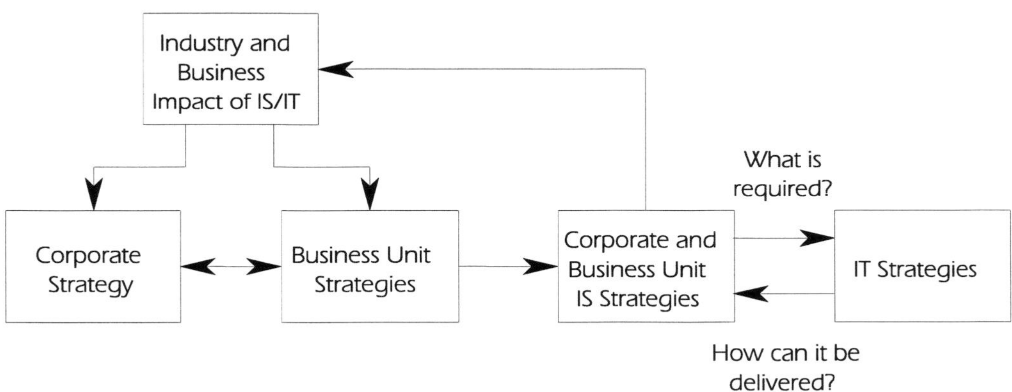

The organization's internal structure is reflected in the breakdown into Strategic Business Units (SBUs). One important issue is whether the information strategy should be developed at corporate level or at SBU level, and an important study[26] from the 1980s suggested that SBU level was the most appropriate. Financial services organizations may be different in that the possibility of substitution in financial services – discussed in Chapter 1 – means that the boundaries between SBUs may be looser and subject to a greater rate of change than in other types of organization.

We can focus on the IS/IT planning process[27] (Figure 5.10 opposite).

One result of this is the systems and information architecture. This describes how our current portfolio of applications relates to the organizations' activities and information needs.

25 J Ward and P Griffiths *Strategic Planning for Information Systems* (John Wiley 1996) page 541

26 Strategic Planning Institute *Management productivity and information technology* Overview report 1984

27 J Ward and P Griffiths *Strategic Planning for Information Systems* (John Wiley 1996) page 137

Figure 5.10: IS/IT Planning Process

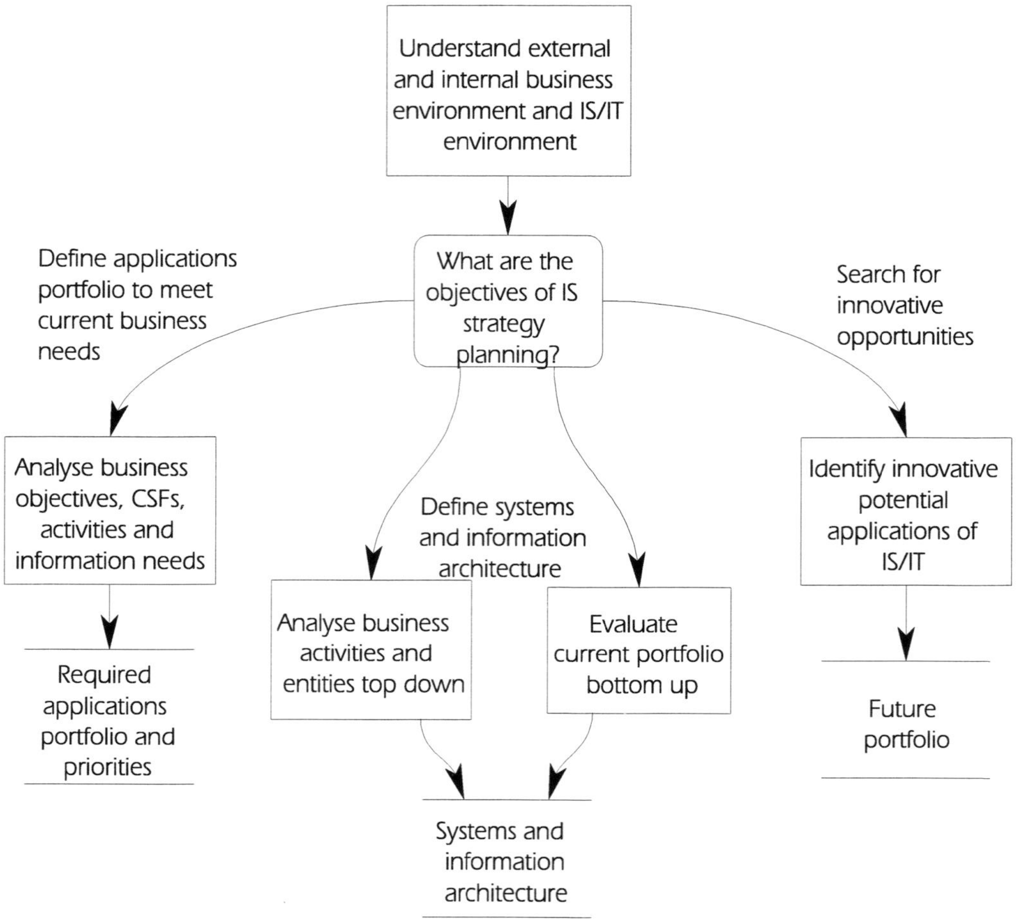

Understand external and internal business environment and IS/IT environment

What are the objectives of IS strategy planning?

Define applications portfolio to meet current business needs

Search for innovative opportunities

Analyse business objectives, CSFs, activities and information needs

Define systems and information architecture

Identify innovative potential applications of IS/IT

Analyse business activities and entities top down

Evaluate current portfolio bottom up

Required applications portfolio and priorities

Future portfolio

Systems and information architecture

The architecture includes the existing hardware, telecommunications, system software and applications software. The various components within this architecture represent an investment by the organization and are interrelated.

Information Technology Strategy

IT strategy will affect the IT architecture but is also affected by it. Major changes in the architecture would be expensive and, because of the interrelationships, would affect other components. It is usual to make such changes when the particular component is close to the end of its economic life but other factors such as competition or changes in relations with a major supplier may force such changes.

IT strategy is concerned with 'infrastructure'. This includes:

- Development environment. This includes the methodologies and CASE tools we use for developing systems;

- System software. This includes operating systems and databases. A particular issue is whether to adopt 'open' or 'proprietary' software;
- Hardware. This includes computers and peripheral devices;
- Telecommunications. This includes networks and telecommunications devices such as modems. The use of leased lines, packet-switched networks or value-added networks is also part of the telecommunications strategy.

One way of classifying technologies is as follows[28]:

- Emerging
- Pacing
- Key
- Base
- Obsolete.

Emerging technologies are at a very early stage of development. These evolve into pacing technologies, which are still at an early stage but which are seen as a potential future source of competitive advantage. Key technologies are mature and are sources of competitive advantage. Base technologies are well established and critical to the industry, but all organizations have access to them and they are a 'price of entry' rather than a source of competitive advantage. Obsolete technologies have been overtaken by later technological developments.

The main driver of technology strategy is value – the ability to make the maximum resources available to meet business requirements at the lowest unit cost.

Information Systems Strategy

An information systems strategy can be defined as 'a plan for the development of systems towards some future vision of the role of information systems in the organization'[29]. An information systems strategy is required for the effective alignment of the business and information strategy.

One approach uses the idea of visioning. This is a strategic planning technique that develops a vision or 'desired future state' – a detailed statement of where the organization would like to be at a future point.

This can be used as a starting point for the development of the information strategy by identifying the business and technology implications of the vision[30]:

28 JP Martino 'Technology audit: key to technology planning' *IEEE Proceedings of the National Aerospace and Electronics Conference* Vol.2 1994

29 TD Wilson 'The implementation of information systems strategies in UK companies: aims and barriers to success' *International Journal of Information Management* 9 1989

30 PD Metz 'Integrating Technology Planning with Business Planning' *IEEE Engineering Management Review*, Winter 1996 volume 24 number 4 page 119 (reprinted from *Research Technology Management*, May-June 1996 volume 39 number 3 pages 19-22)

Figure 5.11: Visioning

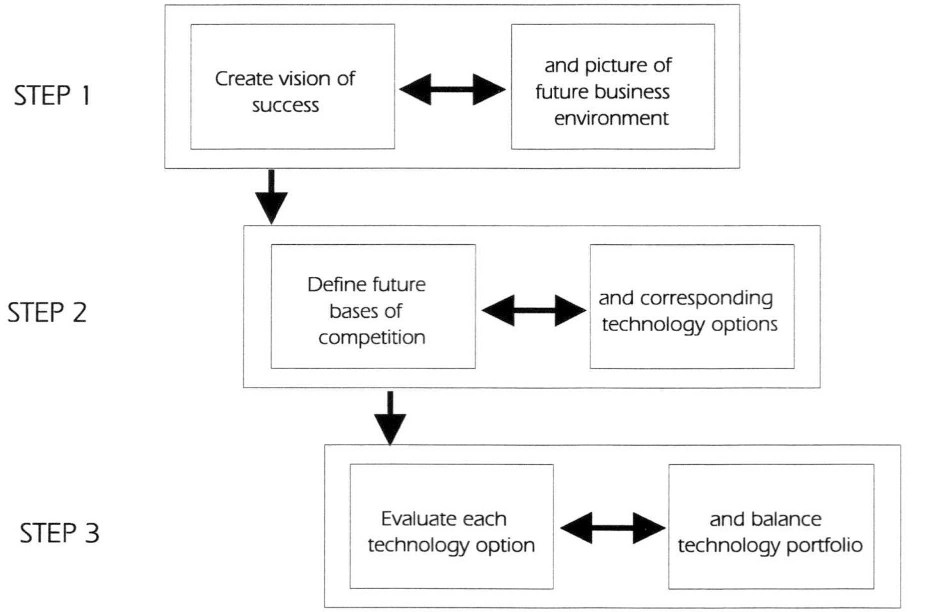

An important feature of this approach is the focus on the future competitive environment and the technology options for gaining competitive advantage in step 2.

One approach widely used for the strategic planning of information technology is structured information systems planning. This involves the following activities[31]:

- Consider organizational goals and strategies and the business and IT aims;
- Assess the current set of information systems;
- Identify information needs of business processes;
- Evaluate the external competitive environment;
- Assess the external technological environment;
- Agree system priorities concerning old and new systems and systems under development;
- Provide individual project planning;
- Involve users in the planning process;
- Gain top management support and commitment.

31 DJ Flynn and E Goleniewska 'A survey of the use of strategic information systems planning approaches in UK organisations' *Journal of Strategic Information Systems* volume 2 number 4 December 1993 page 294

Portfolio Management

Our information systems strategy determines how we are going to invest to support the business. The objective is to develop and manage the portfolio of applications that contributes most effectively to meeting the overall objectives of the business.

One approach[32] classifies applications as:

- High potential. These are applications that may be important to support future success;
- Strategic. These are 'mission critical' applications which must be delivered to support future business strategy;
- Key operational. These are applications on which the organization currently depends for success;
- Support. These are applications that are valuable but not critical.

There is an obvious overlap with the product lifecycle, with high potential applications corresponding to the introduction stage, strategic corresponding to growth, key operational corresponding to maturity and support corresponding to decline.

We can also relate these classifications to the technology classifications we discussed earlier:

Figure 5.12: Technology classifications

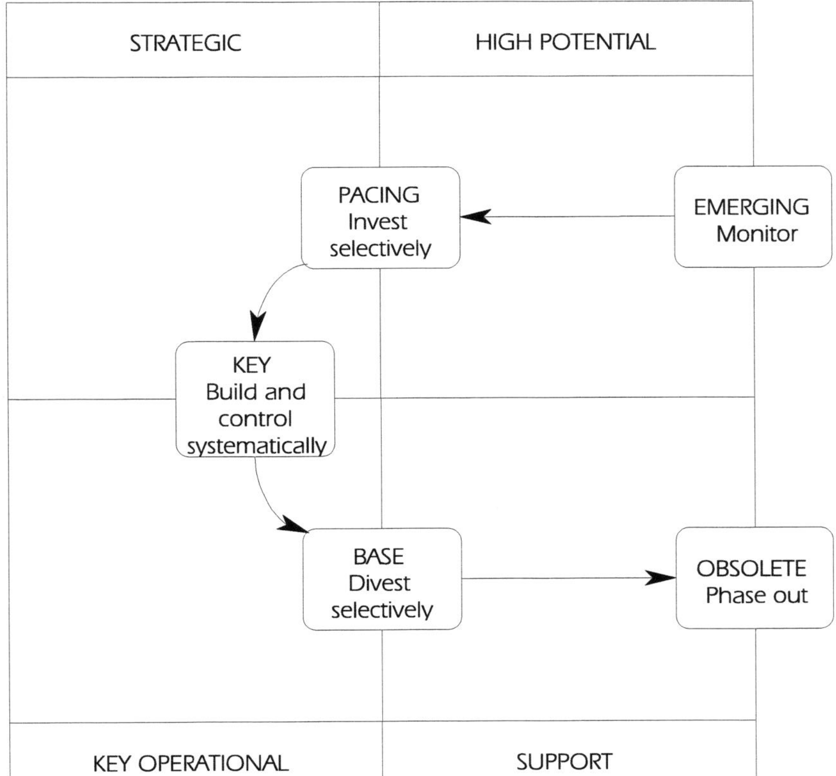

32 FW McFarlan 'Information technology changes the way you compete' *Harvard Business Review* May/June 1984

Emerging technologies must be monitored and emerging technologies that show promise should be introduced experimentally, in high potential applications. As the technology matures, it may become a *pacing* technology we will selectively invest in these technologies and deploy them in strategic applications.

The technology will mature further to become a *key* technology and will be used more widely in key operational applications. As the technology matures to become a *base* technology, new technologies will emerge. The base technology will be used more in support of legacy applications and the organization will start to reduce its investment. Finally, the technology will become *obsolete* and be phased out – although the rate of this will depend on the size of the organization's investment in the technology and it may take many years before has been completely replaced.

Another approach looks at applications in terms of *infusion* and *diffusion*[33]. Infusion is the extent to which the organization is dependent on information technology to carry out core business functions. Diffusion is the extent to which control over information technology is decentralized through the organization. The combination of infusion and diffusion lead to four strategies:

Table 5.3

	Low infusion	High infusion
High Diffusion	Opportunistic	Complex
Low Diffusion	Traditional	Backbone

Infusion tends to be driven by external competitive pressures. As these increase the business becomes more dependent on information technology to deliver competitive advantage. Diffusion tends to be driven by internal organizational pressure. Business units increasingly want to take control of the information technology they use.

Therefore there is a gradual evolution from a 'traditional' application portfolio through either 'opportunistic' or 'backbone' portfolios into a 'complex' portfolio.

5 Strategic Alignment and the Strategic Disconnect

Strategic alignment occurs when the goals and activities of the business are in harmony with the information systems that support them[34].

33 CH Sullivan 'Systems planning in the information age' *Sloan Management Review* Winter 1985
34 Roger Woolfe 'The Path to Strategic Alignment' *Indications* volume 9 number 2 1992

If this harmony does not occur, this leads to the strategic disconnect which Charles Wang defines as 'a conflict... that has misaligned the objectives of executives and impairs or prevents organizations from obtaining a cost-effective return on their investment in IT'[35].

Strategic alignment can be seen simply as ensuring that IT strategy is aligned with the business strategy – the 'business-driven' approach. If this is used the contribution of the technology strategy development process to business strategy becomes purely descriptive – providing a model of the business[36] which executive management are free to review but are under no obligation so to do.

We have already highlighted lack of top management awareness of the impact of IS and IT as a barrier to effective implementation strategy. The business-driven approach does not address this, although it is possible to use techniques such as executive management workshops to influence business strategy by promoting executive management awareness of technology trends and possibilities.

The partnership approach requires the integration of business and technology strategy, ss shown in the 'strategic triangle'[38]. This is a clear articulation of and tight linkage between Technology Strategy, Business Strategy and Organizational Change Strategy:

Figure 5.13: Strategic Triangle

35 Charles Wang *Technovision II* (McGraw-Hill 1997)
36 GW Laware 'Strategic Business Planning: Aligning Business Goals with Technology' *Information Systems Management* Fall 1991 pages 46-48
37 N Goldsmith 'Linking IT Planning to Business Strategy' *Long Range Planning* Volume 24 Number 6 1991 pages 69-76
38 LR Bruss and HT Roos 'Operations, Readiness, and Culture: Don't Reengineer Without Considering Them' *Inform* April 1993 pages 61-62

The failure to build the strategic triangle results in the automation of existing patterns of operation that have evolved over time[39]. These are inherently inefficient and do not exploit the potential of technology.

6 Strategic Positioning and Innovation

Strategic Positioning

Organizations must decide how closely they are going to follow the leading edge of technology. This is called strategic positioning. There are three options:

- Leader. Leaders position themselves at the leading edge of technology;
- Fast follower. Fast followers position themselves just behind the leading edge;
- Laggard. Laggards use only well-established and proven technology.

The advantage of adopting a leader strategy is the possibility of developing a 'killer application' – a system which gives such a large competitive advantage that it will take competitors many years to catch up. The disadvantages are the high cost and the risk that a competitor will be able to 'leapfrog' the organization by introducing the same technology once it has been proven, without the high start-up costs. The leading edge is sometimes called the 'bleeding edge', reflecting the very high costs involved and the effect on the organization's cashflow.

Many financial organizations try to position themselves as fast followers. They try to ensure that their technology is not so far behind that they would be unable to meet the challenge posed by new developments, but they avoid the costs and risks of technological innovation.

Some financial organizations use only fully proven technology. Quite often this is by default – the result of not having an IT strategy. This can be successful if the organization is able to exploit a market niche that does not require much use of IT.

The competitive environment is very important. Organizations cannot generally afford to fall too far behind their competitors' systems and technology. Also, an awareness that a competitor is actively looking at a particular area of technology can stimulate an organization to investigate that area, to avoid the risk of a killer application being developed.

Consider First Direct as an example. First Direct was not the first telephone banking service, but it did stimulate those banks and building societies that did not offer telephone banking to do so. We have seen similar development in Internet banking, where Royal Bank of Scotland's introduction of full service Internet banking stimulated its competitors to follow suit.

Technology Development and Diffusion

The development and spread of new technology follow a well-defined path. The overall shape is that on an 'S-curve' – similar to the product lifecycle curve discussed earlier. There

39 GP Hackett 'Investment in Technology - The Service Sector Sinkhole?' *Sloan Management Review* Winter 1990.

is an initial period when development proceeds very slowly, then there is a rapid period of development as the initial challenges have been largely solved, and finally there is a period where innovation slows down as only the most intractable problems remain.

Another feature of technology development is the emergence of a number of different approaches to solving the problem, all of which may be based on the same original idea. Each of these follows a similar S-curve shape, producing an overlapping set of S-curves. This is called a technological trajectory and follows the same overall S-curve shape as do the individual approaches.

Eventually, one of these approaches will become the 'dominant design'. This will not necessarily be the best technical solution but will be the solution that best meets the needs of the customers. Once a technology becomes dominant, competitors will be forced to adopt that technology or to operate in niche markets.

Perhaps the best known example is the videotape, where VHS emerged as the dominant design after fierce competition with the technically superior Betamax format. Similar struggles have taken place with personal computers, mobile telephones and compact discs.

When a technology has established itself, it may spread as a crossover or a hybrid technology. Crossover technologies are those that are well established in one industry and are introduced into another. Hybrid technologies are combinations of established technologies to create a new and innovative technological solution.

Technology convergence occurs as different branches of technology come together and adopt a single dominant technology. The technology adopted may be the result of a crossover or may be a hybrid – this process is also called technology fusion.

The Internet provides a good example of technology convergence between telecommunications and computing. This resulted from the crossover of digital computer technologies into the analogue telecommunications industry. There has been a more general convergence between the TIME (telecommunications, information, media and entertainment) industries based around the Internet.

Technology Acquisition

The emergence of new technology presents many challenges. In the last chapter we discussed the rate of change of technology, Moore's Law and Meredith's Law. At the start of this chapter we discussed the opportunistic strategy and the need to respond to opportunities as they emerge. How can we acquire the new technology to adapt to changing circumstances?

A critical role in technology acquisition is the gatekeeper role. Gatekeepers determine what technology will come into the organization. If the IT function carries out the gatekeeper role, the policy may be too restrictive and limit technology acquisition to what IT can control. If the gatekeeper role is decentralized from the business, this may result in the acquisition of a range of incompatible technologies that cannot be used together. The requirement is to strike a balance. Some organizations create a specific role, reporting to the Board but with no operational IT responsibility, to act as gatekeeper.

The stages in the technology acquisition process are:

- Identification. The identification of technologies of potential benefit. Sources of information include research and development, customers, competitors and scientific information such as articles in journals;
- Selection. The evaluation of potential technologies and the selection of the most suitable. Organizations must take account of their own capabilities and the fit with their strategies;
- Acquisition. The acquisition of the technology. Organizations may acquire technology through a partnership with or the acquisition of another organization with access to the technology, or may buy in the technology;
- Exploitation. The development of products and processes to exploit the technology, and their introduction into the market;
- Protection. The protection of the technology and of the application of the technology by the use of patents and by asserting copyright and design rights. Effective protection of the technology delays the transition from key technology to base technology.

The relationship between these may be shown as follows[40]:

Figure 5.14: Technology Acquisition – 1

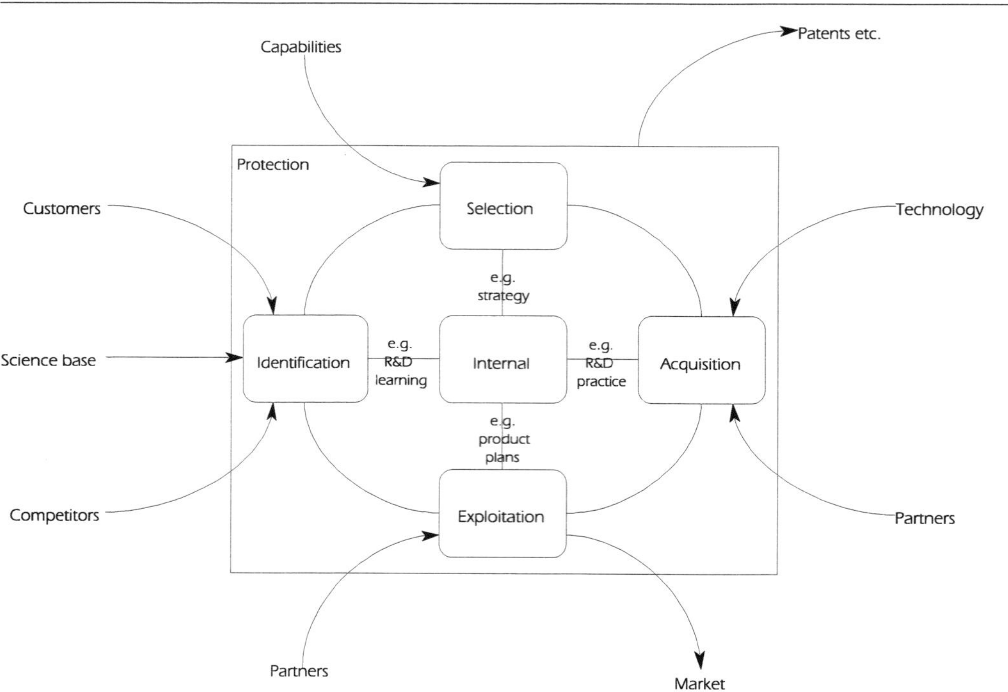

40 Adapted from MJ Gregory 'Technology management: a process approach' *Proceedings of the Institute of Mechanical Engineers* Part B Issue B5 1995

An alternative model views this as a four-stage process[41]:

- Identification and initial investment. The emphasis is on learning. Decision making is often in the hands of technicians rather than the business. Poor initial results may result in the potential being overlooked. Stagnation may occur as a result;
- Experimentation, learning and adaption. There is an awareness of the potential and the development of the technical skills to support the technology. The main dangers are that the pilot will be limited to an excessively narrow area or that there may be too many pilots with no coherent overall development plan. Speed is important here to minimize opportunity costs and avoid potential users becoming frustrated;
- Rationalization and management control. The objective is to develop the necessary skills and to control the rate of release of the technology, to limit risks and to avoid excessive expenditure with little real return. The emphasis is on deploying the technology where it is appropriate. The main danger is that the controls will be excessive, slowing development and degrading the skills learned;
- Widespread technology transfer. The new technology is made generally available. Controls and guidance are still needed and scarce resources must be managed effectively. The main danger is inadequate resources leading to a focus on the short term. This is a particular problem if expertise is localized in a user department, which has to provide a service to other departments impacting its main role.

We can show this as a diagram (see Figure 5.15).

41 JL McKenny and FW McFarlan 'The information archipelago – maps and bridges' *Harvard Business Review* September/October 1982

Figure 5.15: Technology Acquisition – 2

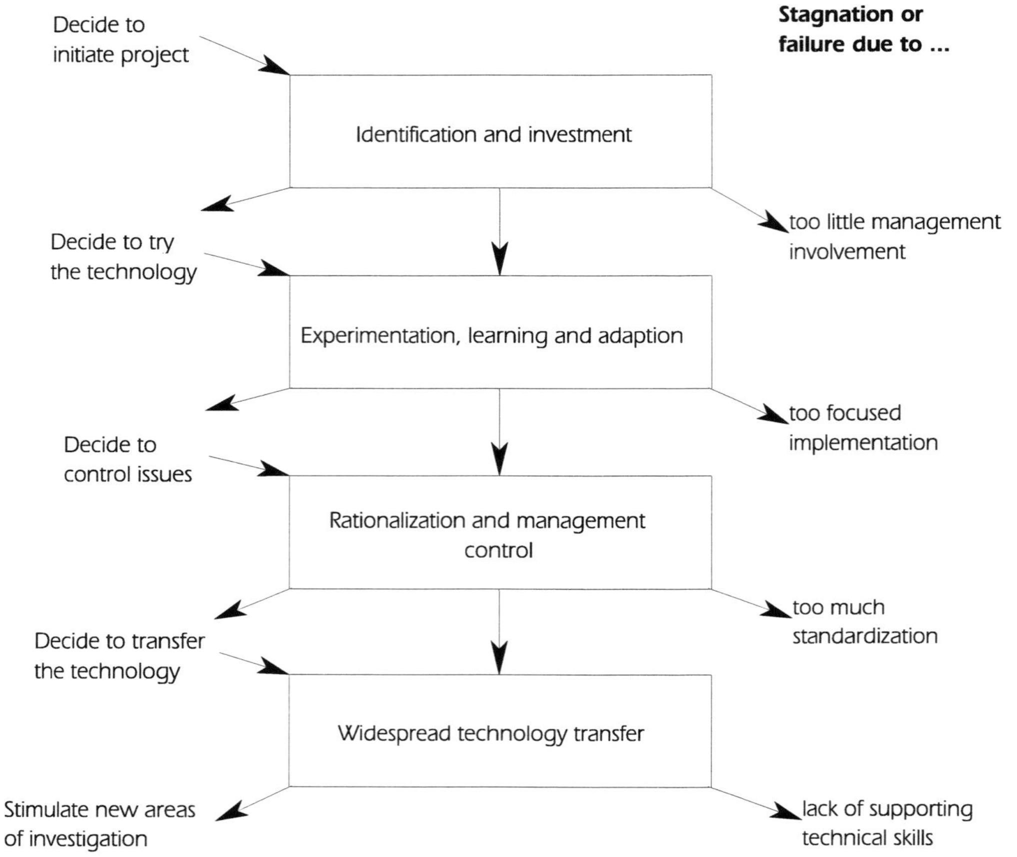

Stagnation or failure due to ...

Decide to initiate project

Identification and investment

too little management involvement

Decide to try the technology

Experimentation, learning and adaption

too focused implementation

Decide to control issues

Rationalization and management control

too much standardization

Decide to transfer the technology

Widespread technology transfer

Stimulate new areas of investigation

lack of supporting technical skills

Innovation

Innovation is the introduction of new technology into the organization. Although innovation has been very successful as a source of competitive advantage in manufacturing, the link between business results and technology innovation has been very difficult to establish in the financial services industry and the credibility of IT in the financial services organizations has suffered as a result. This is partly because of the different innovation processes typical of manufacturing (the 'producer goods cycle') and services (the 'reverse product cycle').

The producer goods cycle is as follows[42]:

42 JM Utterback and WJ Abernathy 'A dynamic model of process and product innovation' *Omega* volume 3 number 6 Elsevier Science Ltd. 1975.

Figure 5.16: Producer Goods Cycle

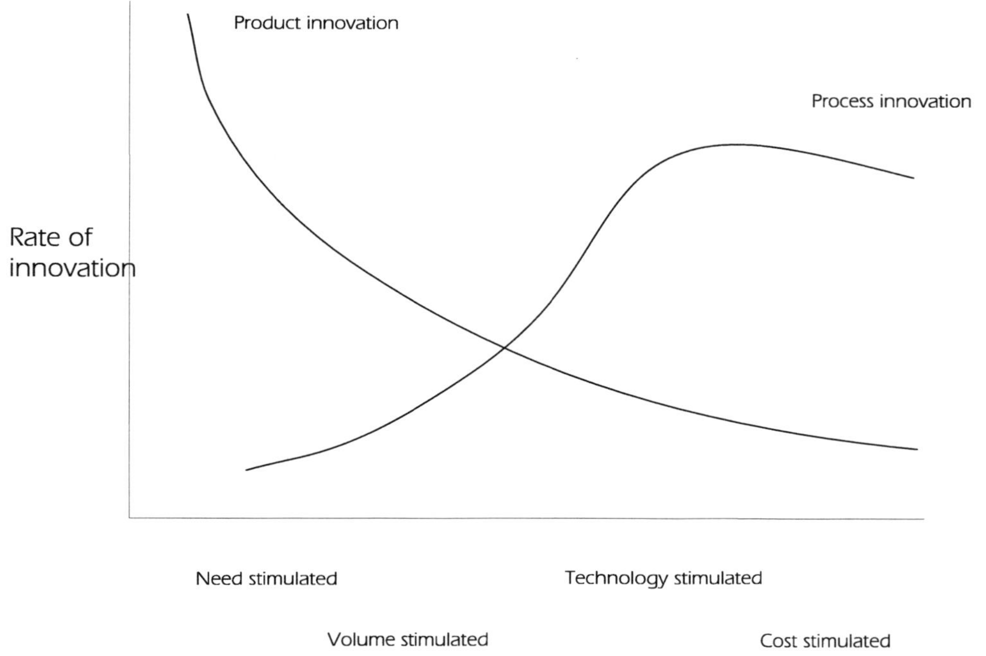

The relationship between the producer goods cycle and profitability is easy to establish. If we compare the producer goods cycle with the standard product lifecycle:

Table 5.4

Producer goods cycle stage	Product lifecycle stage	Profitability
Needs stimulated	Introduction	Negative
Volume stimulated	Growth	Improving
Technology stimulated	Maturity	Depends on market position
Cost stimulated	Decline	Depends on market position

The producer goods cycle starts with a 'needs stimulated' stage of product innovation which corresponds closely to the introduction stage of the product lifecycle. Profitability is negative due to the initial investment in the product (the 'wild cat' stage of the Boston Matrix).

As the product goes through its growth stage, demand increases leading to a 'volume stimulated' stage of product and process innovation as producers gear up production. Profitability improves over this period but is affected by the marketing cost incurred to build a strong competitive position (the 'star' stage).

As the product reaches maturity the producer goods cycle enters a 'technology stimulated' stage with some product innovation (e.g. adding technology features to the product to stimulate demand as 'mid-life kickers') but mainly process innovation. Profitability will depend on market position, with market leaders able to benefit from higher volumes as well as commanding premium prices (the 'cash cow' stage). Products with lower market share (the 'dog' stage) will not necessarily be unprofitable (because marketing costs will be low) but will not be produce very high profits.

Finally the product enters the stage of decline and the associated price wars lead to a 'cost stimulated' stage of process innovation. Profitability will again depend on market share (whether the product is a 'cash cow' or a 'dog'). Even during decline, 'dogs' will not necessarily be unprofitable as competitors withdraw from the market.

This clear link between the innovation process and the product lifecycle is not true of the reverse product cycle that predominates in service industries[43]. The reverse product cycle includes three stages:

- An incremental process innovation stage. Organizations seek to cut costs through small-scale changes to the processes. The organization is dependent on IT suppliers for the technology used;
- A radical process innovation stage. As organizations reach the limits of cost cutting, they look for more radical innovations which are typically driven by the desire to improve quality;
- A product innovation stage. Organizations use their experience of innovation to improve their products. Unlike the first stage in the process, the organization, rather than the suppliers, provides the technology direction.

The evidence[44] suggests that the incremental use of technology to support existing processes produces little if any benefit. Another problem is that this first stage is dominated by suppliers, which makes it is difficult to protect any competitive advantage because the supplier will want to profit from the technology by widening the market.

The cost savings from the second stage will result in from the simplification and standardization of processes (business process re-engineering). The role of technology as an 'enabler' to allow these savings to be realized is frequently overlooked.

43 R Barras 'Interactive Innovation in Financial and Business Services: the Vanguard of the Service Revolution' *Research Policy* 19 1990.

44 GP Hackett 'Investment in Technology - The Service Sector Sinkhole?' *Sloan Management Review* Winter 1990.

The role of technology in delivering competitive advantage in the third stage is more obvious and the classic service industry examples (the Sabre airline reservation system and Merrill Lynch's Cash Management Account) provide a clear demonstration of this. However, the development of new products may reduce overall earnings as customers switch from existing, high price products to new and cheaper alternatives.

Although the second and third stages may well produce competitive advantage it is difficult to differentiate between the contribution made by technology and other factors. This is a factor in producing the credibility gap we discussed earlier.

6

PROJECTS AND PROJECT MANAGEMENT

Objectives

After studying this chapter, you should be able to:

- define a project and a programme, and distinguish these from each other and from 'business as usual' work;
- understand and be able to describe the role of the project manager;
- understand and be able to describe the deliverables which define the project, in particular:
  - the terms of reference
  - the business case – including the types of cost and benefit, and the methods of cost justification that can be used;
- understand and be able to explain the project planning process, the main stages in the process and the deliverables from it;
- understand and be able to explain the importance of project control, and be able to describe the main techniques for controlling time, cost and quality;
- understand the role project management software can play in project planning and control;
- understand the activities associated with project closure;
- understand and be able to distinguish between the project manager's line and functional responsibilities;
- understand and be able to describe how a project may be organized and structured;
- understand and be able to discuss the role of stakeholders and the issue of project governance.

1 Introduction

We usually talk of activities such as developing a computer system as a 'project'. Definitions of a project include:

- A group of connected activities with a defined starting point, a defined finish and a need for a central intelligence to direct it, carried out in order to achieve a business objective.

  and

- A discrete undertaking with defined objectives often including time, cost and quality (performance) goals. All projects evolve through a similar 'lifecycle' sequence during which there should be recognized start and finish points. The project objectives may be defined in a number of ways, the important point being that the goals are defined and the project is finite[1].

Features of projects include:

- They have defined start and finish points;
- Each project is unique;
- There is a 'contract' between the project manager and the business sponsor;
- The project organization is temporary and may change during the project;
- There is an element of risk and uncertainty;
- The project team may need to interact with other groups within and outside the organization.

It is worth noting that this is different to the way in which most of us work. Most work in financial services organizations is driven by the customer – we do not start the day with the specific objective of serving exactly 500 customers before the branch closes! Nor is there any obvious relationship between tasks such as cashing a cheque, looking up an account balance and amending a standing order.

However, there is a recent trend for 'business as usual' to be run on a project basis. This has always been true for activities such as marketing campaigns, new branch openings and product launches. Events of this type are becoming more common and project management techniques are being applied to new activities requiring organizational change. Therefore it is likely that there will be a greater transfer of project management responsibility into the business over time.

2 Programme Management

In the introduction to this part, we showed how project management must be seen in the

1 Association for Project Management *Body of Knowledge*

context of an overall strategy layer. We discussed the ideas of strategic alignment and portfolio management in Chapter 5, but we have not yet discussed programme management.

A programme has been defined as 'a specific undertaking to achieve a number of objectives. The most common examples of programmes are development programmes or large single-purpose undertakings consisting of a series of interdependent projects.'

The second of these definitions – a series of interdependent projects to achieve a single business objective – is the most significant for this book.

So how does this differ from a project? Differences include:

- A programme does not necessarily have a defined end point;
- Programmes usually have more complex objectives than projects;
- Programmes are usually larger than projects.

These may seem to be differences of degree rather than substance, but in practice programme management is very different to project management. Programmes are usually organized as a number of projects and the programme manager's role is to manage the *relationships* between these projects. The programme manager is not responsible for the individual projects.

3 Project Management

Project management is 'the planning, organization, monitoring and control of all aspects of a project and the motivation of all involved to achieve the project objectives safely and within agreed time, cost and performance criteria'[2].

Project management includes the following stages:

- Agree the project objectives and define the project manager's role;
- Plan the project;
- Monitor and control the project;
- Close the project.

Objectives and Role

We have said that one difference between projects and other types of work is the 'contractual' nature of projects. Because each project is unique, the project objectives and project manager's role will vary and must be specified in some form of contractual document. The most important documents are:

- The project terms of reference;
- The business case.

2 Association for Project Management *Body of Knowledge*

Terms of Reference

Terms of reference are the contract between the project sponsor and the project manager. They are essential because:

- They set the sponsor's expectations for the project;
- They define the project manager's mandate and authority;
- They provide a framework for the development process.

The acronym BOSCARDI is sometimes used for the contents of the terms of reference. This stands for:

- Background
- Objectives
- Scope
- Constraints
- Assumptions
- Reporting
- Deliverables
- Issues.

Background is the background to the project.

Objectives says what the project is trying to achieve. The objectives section of the terms of reference will be used to assess the overall success of the project and they need to be SMART (specific, measurable, achievable, relevant and timebound).

Scope says what the project will and will not consider. The scope may relate to a business process or a functional area. One approach that is sometimes used is to draw up a table of what is and is not included in the scope.

Constraints are any restrictions within which the project team must operate. The most common constraints are project cost and time taken.

Assumptions document any assumptions made by the project team. Common assumptions include access to senior management within the organization.

Reporting defines to whom the project team reports. This is discussed later in this chapter under project organization and accountability.

Deliverables define what the project team is expected to produce. The terms of reference will specify only the key deliverables that are subject to sign off. This is discussed later in this chapter under project control.

Issues include anything that still needs to be resolved. All issues should be resolved before the terms of reference are finally signed off. The general topic of issues and issue management is discussed in Chapter 10.

Terms of reference for IT projects will usually cover the entire project up to implementation. They may need to be revised during the development as conditions change. Alternatively, separate terms of reference may be produced for individual stages within the development.

Business Case (Cost Benefit Analysis)

The business case is the financial justification for the project. It considers the costs and benefits of the project and uses accounting techniques to determine whether the project should go ahead.

We can classify costs as one off or recurring. One-off costs can be classified as capital or development costs. Recurring costs can be classified as maintenance or operating costs:

- Capital costs. These include the cost of new hardware (processing power, storage and peripherals) and telecommunications links such as installing new lines. They may also include the costs of additional office equipment. Additional space might be needed (for example to house a new computer) and the associated property costs would be included;
- Development costs. These include the costs of the staff involved in building the new system. They may also include overhead costs for managing the project and for non-IT staff (for example the user department or internal audit staff). They include one-off costs associated with any new software licences that may be needed;
- Maintenance costs. Where new software or hardware is purchased these will be specified in the contract. There will be an allowance (typically 10% of the development costs) for changes and improvements to the system;
- Operating costs. These include the cost of additional resources required to run the system – for example, the annual cost of any additional processing or storage requirements. They will also include any annual licensing costs for new software or hardware. They will include the predicted costs for 'consumables' such as additional telecommunications line charges, paper, floppy disks etc.

We can classify benefits as tangible or intangible. Tangible benefits result in a direct financial return, for example in reduced costs or increased income. Intangible benefits are less easy to quantify. Common sources of tangible benefits include:

- Benefits due to cost savings. These include any projected savings due to being able to use fewer staff or lower-graded staff, together with any associated premises cost savings. They may include one-off cost savings through not renewing equipment leases or contracts with suppliers;
- Benefits due to cost avoidance. Organizations may carry out projects to avoid costs that they would otherwise incur – for example to replace equipment that is expensive to operate with equipment with lower operating costs;
- Benefits due to increased earnings. These usually arise when the new system provides an additional business opportunity. For example, EFTPOS not only saves financial

organizations the high cost of processing cheques, it also provides opportunities to earn fees from the retailers for processing EFTPOS transactions;

- Benefits due to income protection. These may arise when organizations have to respond to the actions of competitors to avoid the loss of market share.

Common sources of intangible benefits include:

- Benefits due to better quality. In principle, better quality can improve customer loyalty and market share, reduce the costs associated with correcting mistakes and lead to better decisions. In practice it can be difficult to quantify these in money terms;
- Benefits due to reduced risks. Reduced risks can reduce the costs needed to manage those risks. These are usually intangible but calculations such as the Annualized Loss Expectancy (discussed in Chapter 9) can be used to get an indicative saving;
- Benefits due to improved information. These can improve management decision making or the ability to identify business opportunities. In practice these are very difficult to quantify.

In assessing the business case for a project, we need to apply two tests. First, is it a good investment? We need to estimate all the costs and all the benefits from the solution in money terms and use an investment appraisal technique in order to decide whether spending money on this particular solution is a good investment. Second, is it within the overall projects budget? Many organizations limit their overall budget for projects to prevent costs growing faster than the overall growth in earnings. If the cost of an investment is greater than the available budget it will be approved only under exceptional circumstances – for example, if it is necessary to meet a legal obligation or if the return on the investment is exceptionally high.

Cost benefit analysis uses standard accounting techniques to decide whether the investment in the project will be justified. The most important of these are:

- Net present value. This looks at the amounts that will be spent (costs) or earned (benefits) over the expected life of the project. These are discounted by a notional 'interest rate' to allow for the fact that interest needs to be paid on money spent now, so future earnings need to be at least as great as the lost interest if the project is to be financially justified. The value of all the discounted costs and benefits are added up to find out what the total would be now – the 'net present value'. If this is greater than zero, the amount the project will earn is more than the amount of lost interest and the project is financially justified;
- Internal rate of return. This works on the same principle as the net present value calculation (this principle is called 'discounted cashflow' or DCF). However, instead of setting a rate for discounting cashflows, it calculates the actual rate required to produce a net present value of zero – the 'internal rate of return'. If this is greater than the organization's target rate for return on investments the project is financially justified;
- Payback. This works by comparing at the project's initial costs (capital costs plus

development costs, less any one-off savings due to sale of surplus equipment or premises) with the future earnings (benefits less maintenance and operating costs). The amount of time that will be needed before the benefits pay back the initial investment is calculated and compared with a target. If the investment will be paid back in less than the target the project is justified;

- Economic value added. This works by estimating the operating revenue after tax due to the investment and subtracting a funding charge for the capital employed (the amount of capital multiplied by the organization's cost of capital). One benefit of economic value added is that it relates directly to market value added – the net impact of the investment on market value. According to financial theory, the market value added is the net present value of the economic value added;
- Total cost of ownership. This is usually used to compare hardware investments. Total cost of ownership calculations take account of a wide range of costs including management costs and the costs of keeping software up-to-date;
- Option pricing. The techniques of option pricing are outside the scope of this book. The principle is that an investment in technology gives the organization the right but not the obligation to make further investments to exploit the technology. In effect, the organization has purchased a call option on the exploitation of that technology and it has the option of allowing this to lapse or investing further.

  Let us consider an example. Project A requires an investment of £4.5 million and has a negative net present value of £460,000. Project B can take place only if we go ahead with project A. It requires an investment of £9 million and has a net present value of £4.5 million. There is a high level of uncertainty associated with project B and the decision whether to go ahead with project B will take place in three years.

  Under option pricing, project B is a 3-year call option on an asset with a value of £4.5 million and an exercise price of £9 million. The value of such an option may be £500,000. If we adjust the net present value for project A to take account of the option value, we end up with a positive net present value of £40,000 and the investment is cost justified.

DCF calculations rely on a notional interest rate, which in theory is the cost of capital for the organization. In practice financial services organizations often use 'hurdle rates' which compare the investment with the opportunity cost of using the capital elsewhere. International comparisons show a higher rate of return is expected in the UK than in countries such as Germany and Japan, and this has been suggested as a reason for the relatively low level of technology investment in the UK.

Net present value is generally accepted as the best of the established techniques, but internal rate of return and payback are widely used. Internal rate of return is often used to compare projects but this can be slightly misleading (for reasons of interest to those studying accountancy, which we shall not go into here). Payback is a very crude technique which has the benefit of providing a simple way of assessing risk – the longer the payback period the more likely it is that changes in the nature of the business or in technology will make the system obsolete.

Economic value added, total cost of ownership and option pricing are newer techniques. Economic value added is the most common of these, reflecting the financial services industry's adoption of the ideas of shareholder value theory, but is open to the objection that it is too complex. Total cost of ownership is a simpler measure usually used to compare the cost of computer equipment. Option pricing is particularly useful for strategic, long-term investment decisions.

Both research and practical experience suggest that business cases often overstate the value of benefits. One piece of research[3] indicates that although cost reduction benefits are usually greater than expected (110% of forecast), sales expansion benefits (60% of forecast) and new product benefits (10% of forecast) are much lower than expected. Studies suggest that management has little confidence in benefits estimates for IT projects, but there is an increasing trend towards monitoring the extent to which claimed benefits are realized in practice[4].

In spite of this, organizations continue to invest in technology and organizations failing to invest are less successful than those that do. One possible reason for this is suggested by research into the introduction of computer-aided design (CAD)[5]. Although the short-term benefits were lower and the costs higher than expected, organizations realized long-term benefits both through business process re-engineering (discussed in Chapter 8) and by linking CAD with computer-aided manufacturing (CAM) technology. Similarly, financial services organizations which invested in the development of Internet expertise are looking to benefit from developments in e-commerce.

Project Planning

Project managers try to balance what is to be delivered, when it is to be delivered and how much is will cost – function, time and cost. The project terms of reference will define what is to be delivered and may set some limits on time and cost, but the project manager must produce a plan identifying the likely time and cost.

The project planning process involves the following:

- Work breakdown structure
- Milestone plan
- Logic network
- Critical path analysis
- Gantt chart

3 JL Bower 'Capital Budgeting as a General Management Problem' *Managing the Resource Allocation Process* Harvard Business School 1970

4 Gartner Group *TCO Conference* 1998 and 1999

5 Peter Senker 'Implications of CAD/CAM for Management' *Omega* 12(3) Pergamon Press 1984

- Resource histogram.

Another technique is the Programme Evaluation and Review Technique (PERT).

Work Breakdown Structure

Project planning starts by breaking the project down into its component tasks and activities. Project management specialists draw a distinction between tasks and activities, but we shall use the word activities to cover both. We can simply show the result of the breakdown as a hierarchy of activities. This is called a work breakdown structure and is a useful way of showing what needs to be done.

There are various ways in which we can break projects down. An engineering project might be broken down into the main sub-assemblies as a product breakdown structure. Projects might be broken down by time – the systems development cycle (discussed in Chapter 7) is an example of this – or by the department responsible.

Another approach is to break the project down into different types of work or 'workstreams'. As an example, let us consider the activities associated with opening a new branch. See Figure 6.1 opposite.

Each workstream represents a different type of work. Site selection is a marketing activity, lease negotiation is a procurement activity, structural work and installation of equipment and fittings are both project management activities but are likely to use different people and to require different skills.

The work breakdown structure is the starting point for the next stage of the planning process.

Milestone Plan

The next stage is to produce a milestone plan. A milestone is a significant event associated with the project or one of its workstreams. For example, signing the lease will be a milestone for the lease negotiation workstream.

Figure 6.1: Work Breakdown Structure

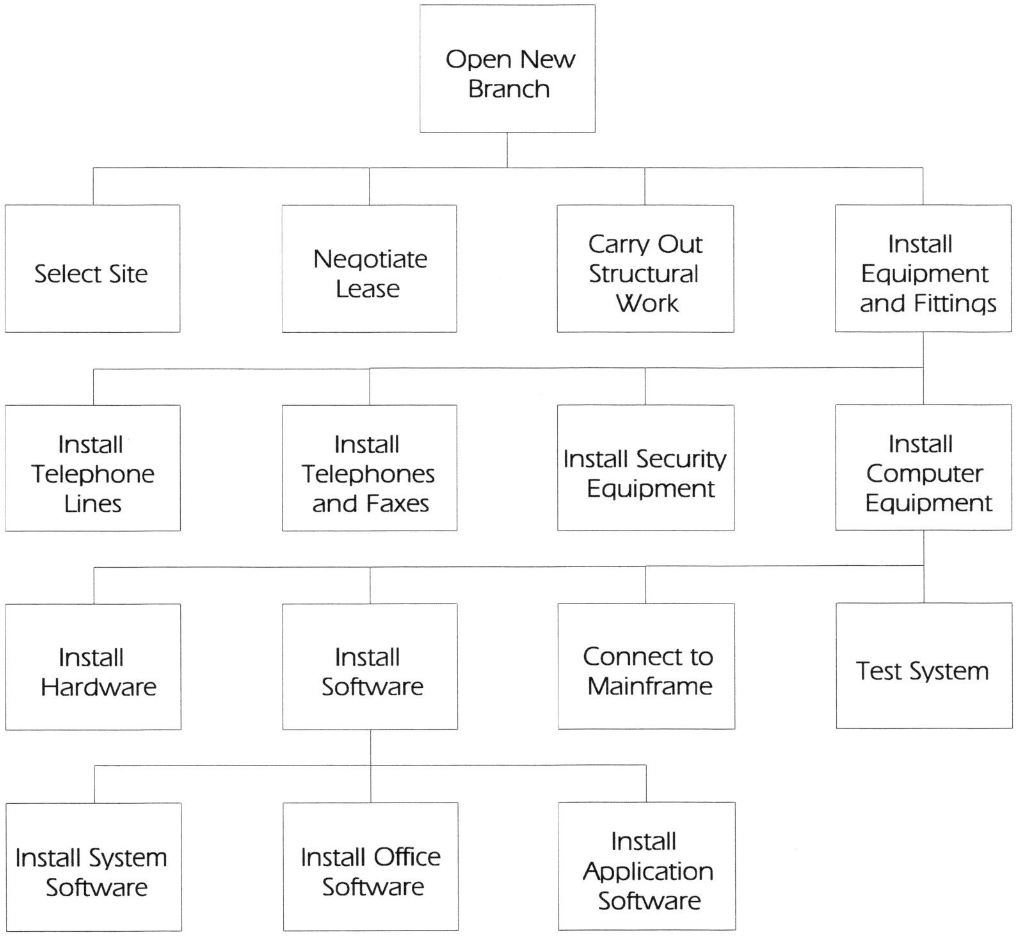

Milestones are physical outcomes or results that the project sponsor can see. By defining the milestones for a project, we are able to manage the sponsor's expectations and provide a basis for the sponsor to monitor the progress of the project.

We have already discussed how we break projects down into activities. Milestones result from the completion of activities. We also need to take account of the relationships (or 'dependencies') between activities – for example, where one activity must precede another. By considering these dependencies we are able to show the project milestones in a clearly-defined order.

This diagram demonstrates two dependencies which cross workstreams – from the installation of the telephone lines to the installation of the telephones and faxes and to the mainframe connection.

Figure 6.2: Milestone Plan

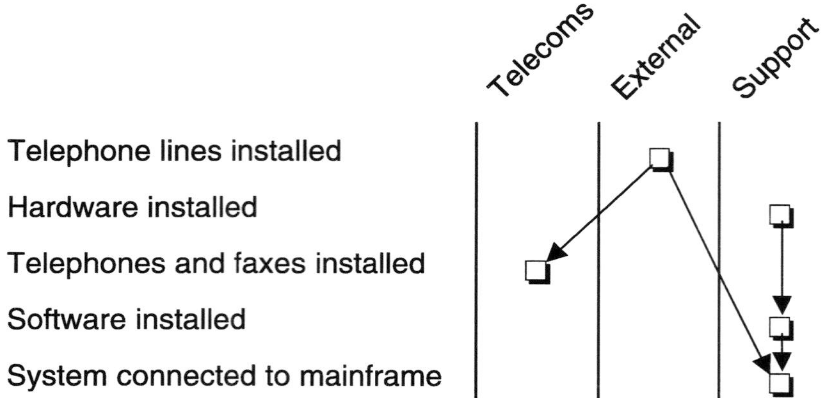

Logic Network

We can also show the activities and the dependencies between them as a logic network. This will have a start point (which shows when the first activity can start) and an end point (which is after the last activity has been completed). This is the basis for identifying how long the project is expected to take.

It might help to illustrate this with an example. Consider our computer equipment installation. The computer must be ordered and delivered before we can do anything. We then need to install the system software. After that we can connect the computer to the mainframe, install the office software and install the application software at the same time. When all of these have been completed we can test the computer.

Figure 6.3: Logic Network

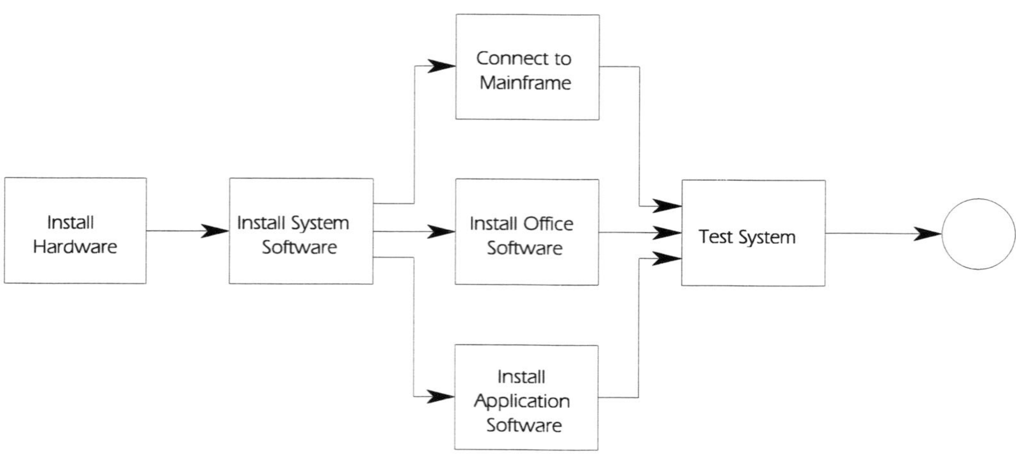

Estimating

From the work breakdown structure, the next stage is to estimate how long each activity will take. Various methods can be used for estimating. Three of the most common are:

- Factor analysis. We can analyse each task into various components and use this as a basis for estimating. An example of an estimating method based on factor analysis is Function Point Analysis (FPA). FPA takes account of factors such as the number of transactions and the amount of data to produce an estimate for the size of an activity in terms of 'function points'. We can then use productivity information about how long it takes to complete one function point to produce an estimate for the activity;
- Extrapolation. We can extrapolate how long the task will take, either from how long similar tasks have taken in the past or how long earlier phases of the development have taken;
- Delphi technique. We can ask experienced staff how long they think the task will take. If we ask a number of people and get broadly similar answers they are likely to be reasonably accurate.

Assume we have the following estimates for the activities identified above:

Ordering and delivery	7 days
System software installation	5 days
Mainframe connection	9 days
Office software installation	5 days
Application software installation	7 days
Testing	20 days

We can show these estimates on the logic network:

Figure 6.4: Logic Network with Estimates

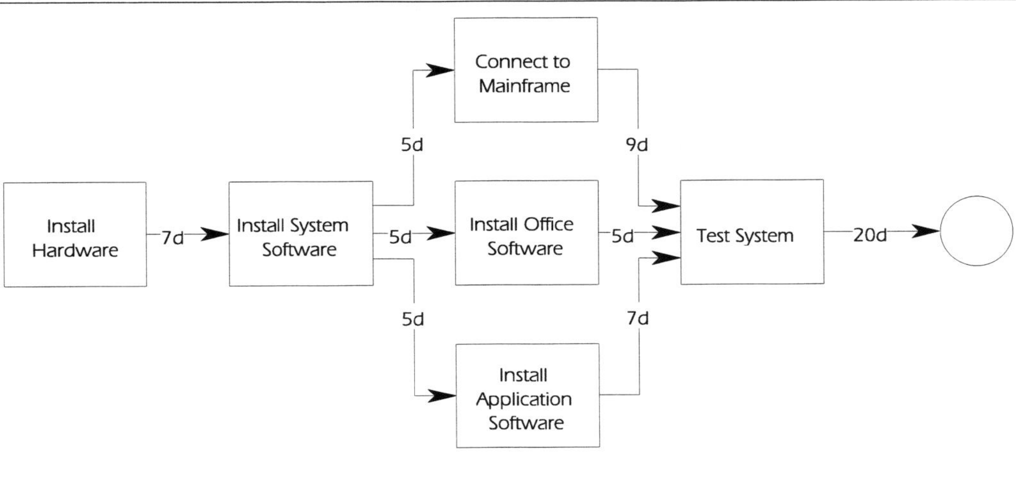

Estimates are shown in terms of effort – man-days or person-days. To convert this to elapsed time, we must take account of weekends and holidays.

Critical Path Analysis

The next stage is to estimate how long the project as a whole will take. The project manager works out the longest way through the logic network. This is called the 'critical path' and is the shortest time in which the project can be finished.

The longest path through this is 41 days (7 days + 5 days + 9 days + 20 days). Therefore the shortest time in which we can install the computer equipment is 41 days.

We cannot start testing until we have completed mainframe connection – 21 days after the start. However, if we start office software installation at the same time as mainframe connection we will have completed this 17 days after the start – 4 days before we can start testing. This 4 days is called the 'float'. This means we can delay the start of office software installation by up to 4 days without delaying the start of testing. Application software installation also has float, this time of 2 days.

This method of project planning is also called critical path analysis because the manager needs to find the project's critical path in order to estimate how long the project will take. The critical path activities are shown as shadowed on the diagram, and these activities have zero float:

Figure 6.5: Critical Path Analysis

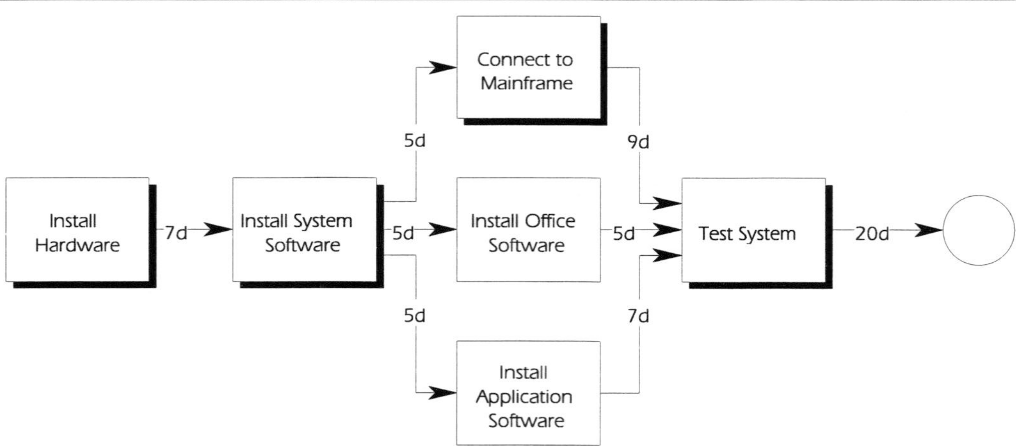

Gantt chart

A Gantt chart provides an alternative way of showing how long the project will take, and is also used by managers in deciding who will carry out the various activities. This is named after Henry Gantt (a management theorist from the last century) and shows the activities down the left side and the project dates across the top. Next to each activity, a line or bar is shown from the scheduled start date to the scheduled end date:

Figure 6.6: Gantt Chart

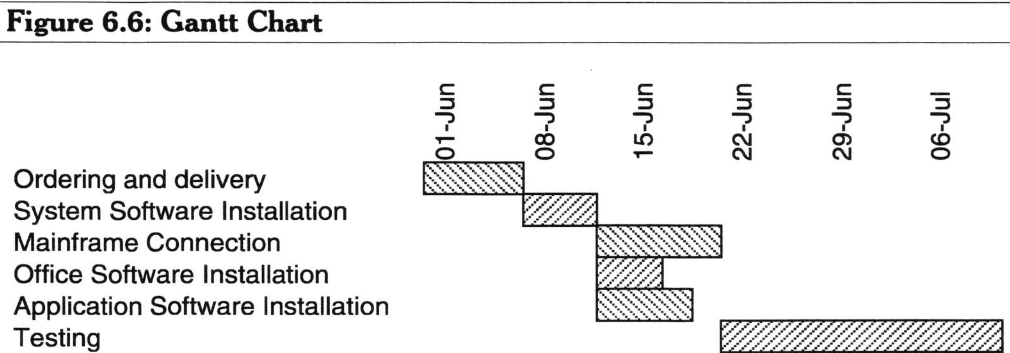

The manager will decide what skills are needed to carry out each activity, and put this on the Gantt chart. He or she can then look at the overall picture and see whether there are enough people available with the right skills at any one time. If not, the manager may need to reschedule or to bring in more people with the skills needed:

Figure 6.7: Gantt Chart with Resource Allocations

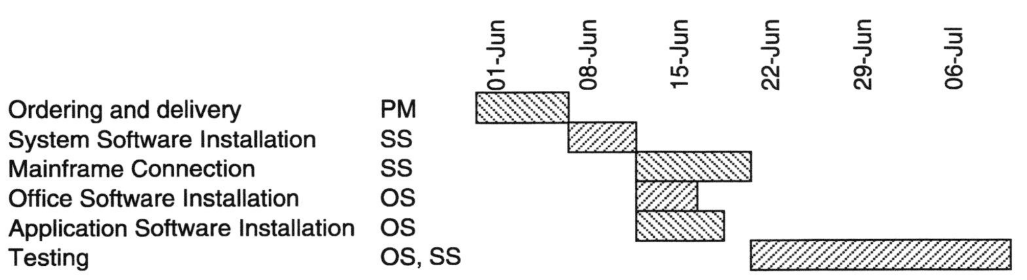

The skill sets required in this example are the project manager, system support and office support.

Resource Histogram

A more formal approach to deciding whether the right skills are available is a resource histogram.

The Gantt chart breaks the project down into time periods (usually weeks or months). It also lists the skills needed to work on each activity. We can draw a histogram showing the total amount of each skill required for each time period. By comparing this with the resources available, we can find out if we have too few people with the right skills available to complete the tasks, or if we will have people with insufficient work to do:

Figure 6.8: Resource Histogram

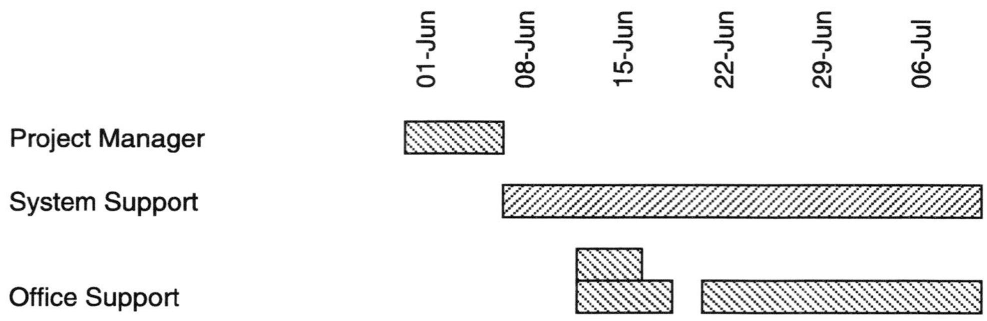

01-Jun 08-Jun 15-Jun 22-Jun 29-Jun 06-Jul

Project Manager

System Support

Office Support

The manager will then decide who will carry out each activity. He or she will need to keep in view that people working on activities on the critical path should not be given other activities at the same time – this will delay completion of the critical path activity and of the project as a whole.

Other Planning Techniques – PERT

There is another form of precedence planning which makes use of the idea of float. This was developed by the US Navy and is called Program Evaluation and Review Technique (PERT). A PERT chart shows a network of activities, in the same was as critical path analysis, but each activity has four dates associated with it. These are the 'early start', 'late start', 'early finish' and 'late finish' dates.

The early start date is the earliest date the activity can be planned to start – the start date of the project plus the amount of time needed to complete all preceding activities. The late start is the latest date the activity can be planned to start without delaying the project – this will be the early start date plus the amount of float for the activity. The early/late finish date will be the early/late start date plus the amount of time needed to complete the activity.

We can show this on a diagram:

Figure 6.9: PERT Diagram

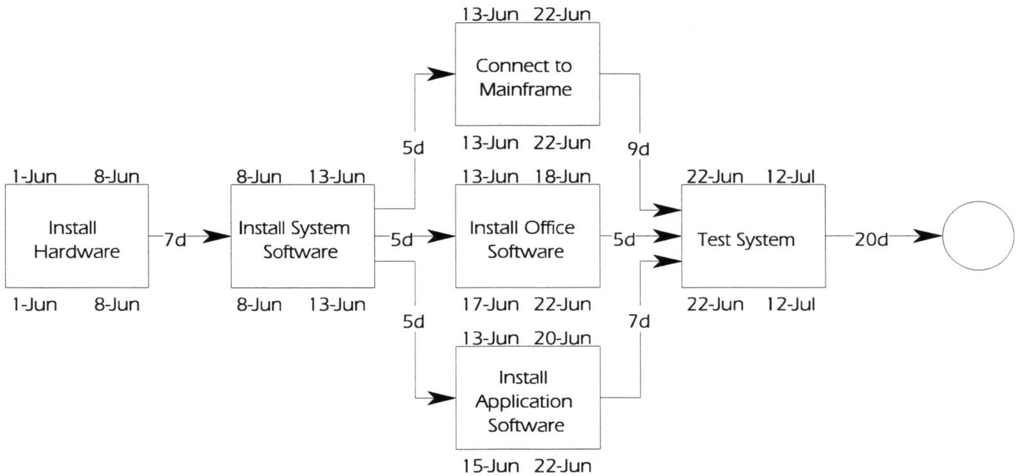

To keep the example simple weekends have been ignored. Note the difference between the early (above the task) and late (below the task) start and finish dates for office software installation and application software installation.

PERT charts can also be used to look at the effect of risk on a project. The estimates for individual activities are uncertain and it may be more accurate to estimate the effort required for 'mainframe connection' as being between 8 days and 10 days. This would give an early finish date for the activity of 21-Jun, which would also be the early start date for the successor activity (testing). The late finish date for mainframe connection would be 23-Jun.

Project Control

The project manager is responsible for monitoring and controlling the project. The areas of control include:

- Costs
- Timescales
- Quality.

The project manager's role involves balancing cost, time and quality to produce the best overall result for the business:

Figure 6.10: Balancing Time, Cost and Quality

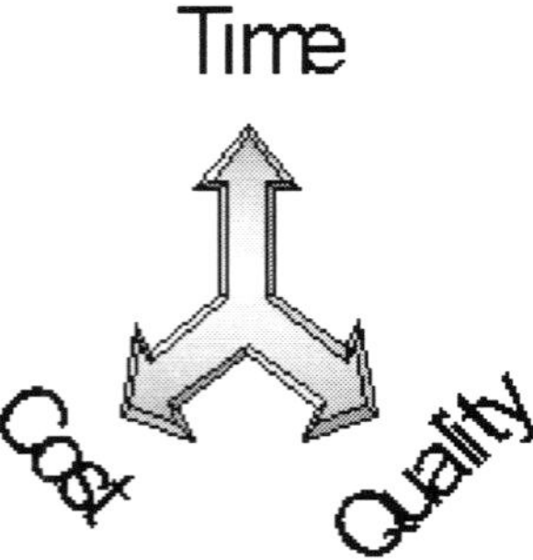

One example of balancing time and cost is 'crashing'. Project managers usually try to minimize total project cost, but crashing techniques allow projects to completed in a shorter time but at higher cost – for example, by building the use of overtime into the plan.

Controlling Cost

Techniques used for controlling project cost include:

- Budgets
- Timesheets
- Earned value analysis.

Budgets are a standard financial control technique. Project budgets can be set and monitored against actual expenditure.

For IT development projects in particular, staff time is the largest controllable cost item and using *timesheets* to monitor staff time is an effective alternative to using project budgets. This approach ignores non-staff costs because they are either relatively small (for example, travel expenses) or outside the project manager's control (for example, premises costs or equipment costs).

The problem with using budgets for cost control is that they show the costs incurred but they do not show the amount of work completed. *Earned value analysis* is a method of assessing this.

Let us consider the example we have been discussing. The total amount of effort required is 53 days (7 days + 5 days + 9 days + 7 days + 5 days + 20 days). If we assume our costs are £100-00 per day, we have a total budget of £5,300.

The first two tasks are planned to require 12 days (7 days + 5 days) effort and therefore should cost £1,200. If we have completed them while actually spending £1,100 we will be ahead of budget and if we actually spent £1,300 we are behind budget. We cannot get this information from budgets alone – these would continue to show the £5,300 budget cost.

In earned value analysis terminology, the planned cost of £1,200 is the Budgeted Cost of Work Performed or BCWP whereas an actual cost of (say) £1,300 is the Actual Cost of Work Performed or ACWP. The cost variance is £100 (£1,200 – £1,300) adverse or 8.33% (£100 as a percentage of the BCWP £1,200) adverse and the cost efficiency is the BCWP divided by the ACWP or 92.3% (£1,200 divided by £1,300, expressed as a percentage).

Earned value analysis can be used to provide a range of information about both costs and timescales and is becoming an important project control technique.

Controlling Time

Techniques used for controlling time include:

- Gantt charts
- Milestones
- Timeboxing.

We have discussed how *Gantt charts* are used for project planning, but they are also very useful for project control. A second line can be drawn next to each activity, from the actual start date to the actual end date, and this can be used to identify activities that have started late or taken longer than planned. By drawing a line down the chart the manager can identify all activities that are scheduled to be in progress and all activities that are scheduled to have been completed:

Figure 6.11: Gantt Charts for Project Control

Ordering and delivery
System Software Installation
Mainframe Connection
Office Software Installation
Application Software Installation
Testing

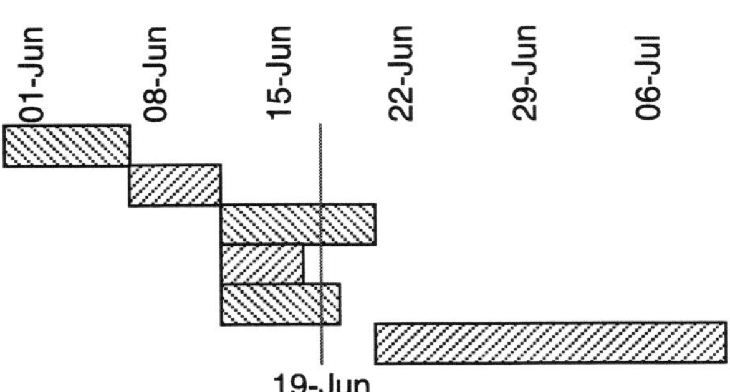

We have also discussed *milestones*. Milestones represent physical deliverables, the dates for which and have been agreed with the project sponsor. Therefore the ability to achieve milestone dates is a very visible measure of how well the project is meeting its planned timescales.

Timeboxing is a technique by which each piece of work is given a fixed time in which it must be completed. If it exceeds the time allowed, the piece of work is stopped. The Development Bank of Singapore provides an extreme example of this, where *all* projects must be completed in three 3-month timeboxes – limiting each project to a total of nine months.

Controlling Quality

Quality control is a major concern of all project managers. Activities poorly completed will generally cause later activities, which are dependent on them, to take longer. This will increase the project time and costs.

When we discuss managing quality, we are really discussing how we manage what functions we shall be delivering. The project manager may find it necessary to meet time and cost constraints by delivering slightly less than was originally planned, or the delivered system may need more manual work arounds.

It is worth thinking of this in engineering terms. Components are not made to a precise size, but to 'engineering tolerances'. For example, a part may be specified as having a diameter of 8.32 mm, but the engineering tolerances might allow it to be between 8.29 mm and 8.35 mm. Therefore the part is 'fit for purpose' provided its diameter falls within these limits. Similarly, systems can achieve their objectives quite adequately provided the functions they offer fall within acceptable limits.

Techniques used for controlling quality include:

- Statements of work
- Walkthroughs
- Inspections
- Testing
- Deliverable sign-off.

Some approaches to project management require a *statement of work* to be drawn up for each task. This is a precise definition of exactly what is required to complete the task and of the measures of quality which will be applied to the results. This may form the basis of a legal contract, especially if the task is to be sub-contracted to an outside organization.

A *walkthrough* is a meeting at which the developer presents his or her work to an audience which may include other members of the project, IT staff from other projects, business users and IT staff with relevant technical knowledge. The purpose of the meeting is to give the audience the opportunity to ask questions or make suggestions.

An *inspection* also takes the form of a meeting and has a very similar audience. However, proceedings are controlled by an independent inspector, instead of the developer. The inspector will usually either be a quality assurance specialist or an IT specialist and will have studied the developer's work carefully in advance of the meeting.

Inspections should be more thorough than walkthroughs, both because a second person has had the opportunity carefully to examine the work and because the inspector is accountable for any problems that are found.

Walkthroughs and inspections are usually carried out at the end of each stage of the systems development cycle before system testing. It is common to break large developments down into 'sub-projects' and to carry out separate walkthroughs or inspections on these.

Testing takes place during the development process and is discussed in more detail in Chapter 7. We can distinguish between:

- Unit testing takes place during the construction stage and checks that individual system components work as specified. Unit testing is carried out by the developer;
- System testing takes place as a separate stage and checks that the system works as a whole and that it will not adversely affect other systems. System testing is usually carried out by a designated system tester who may be independent of the project team.

One of the main forms of project control is *deliverable sign-off*. Deliverables which need to be signed off include the Terms of Reference and the key outcomes from the development stages. The lifecycle used in the systems development process may also say which deliverables should be produced and signed off for each development stage. This sometimes takes the form of a project deliverables catalogue or a project responsibility matrix.

Once a project has completed a development stage it should not continue until the deliverables have been signed off. Without sign off, the project team does not have the authority to continue. In practice this rule is sometime waived because it would lead to all work on the project being halted, but organizations must ensure that sign off takes place as quickly as possible.

Project Management Systems

Project management systems are computer programs that will assist the project manager. These allow the project to be planned using a number of common starting points, including the list of activities from the work breakdown structure and the logic diagram.

The program will identify the critical path and calculate the float and the early/late start and finish dates for each activity. It will identify whether resources have been overscheduled (sometimes presenting the results as a histogram). It can produce individual work plans for every member of the project team.

These programs are particularly useful for project control. They usually allow staff to enter their timesheets (often based on the individual work plans) and can apply 'charge-out rates' to calculate staff costs. Some programs can bill users for staff time if necessary.

They can be used to record when individual tasks are complete. If a task runs over schedule, they can forecast a new estimated completion date for the project as a whole. These programs generally also allow a 'percentage complete' figure to be entered against tasks in progress (although people's estimates of how much work remains to be done should usually be treated with extreme caution!).

Perhaps the greatest benefit of these programs is that they capture all the information about the project, including the initial plan, any revisions and the actual time and cost of the project. This information can be used to improve planning and estimating for future projects.

Project Closure

Project closure includes the following activities:

- Transferring the project into operations;
- The post development review (PDR);
- The post implementation review (PIR);
- Decommissioning the project environment;
- Maintenance may be covered for a period;
- Closing the project accounts;
- Releasing project resources.

Some of these are described in more detail in Chapter 7.

Transferring the project into operations involves handing the system over to operational management.

Closing the project accounts involves balancing and closing the accounts for the project.

Releasing project resources involves redeploying the resources used on the project – which may include equipment and premises as well as people – back into the business.

4 Project Organization and Accountability

Projects are an example of matrix management, with the project team having both 'line' and 'functional' responsibilities.

To illsutrate this, we shall start by considering an influence diagram, showing the project manager's lines of responsibility.

Figure 6.12: Influence Diagram

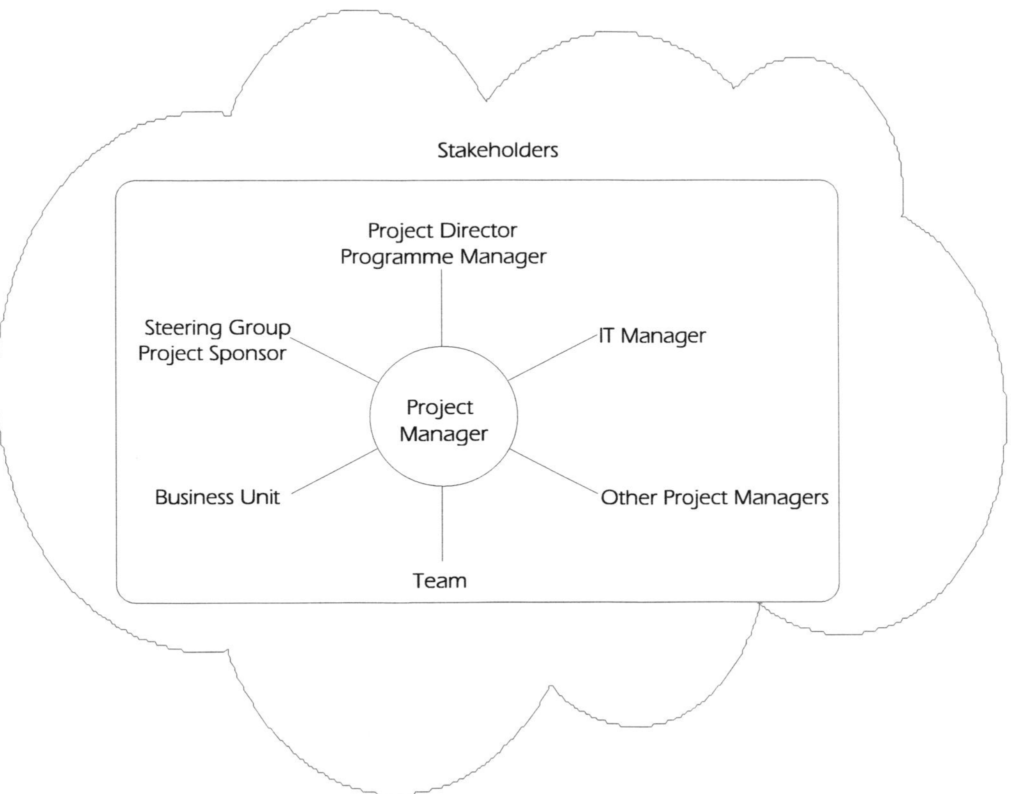

The project manager's functional responsibility is to the business, through the project sponsor and steering group. There may be a project director or a programme manager who will have an additional accountability to ensure the project achieves the business objectives. The project manager will also have a responsibility towards the business units with which he or she is working.

The project manager's line responsibility is to the IT manager, to other project managers and to the project team.

Project Organization

Projects are organized into project teams. There are two approaches to this:

- Matrix management
- Permanent project teams.

Matrix Management

Under matrix management, the organization would regard its people as a 'pool' of resources with various skills. When a project team needs to be formed, those people who are available and have the most suitable skills will be brought together. A project manager will be appointed from within the project team, who will not necessarily be the most senior member but who will be the person best able to manage the team. The key feature of matrix management is that project team members will report to the project manager for project work but will have a separate 'resource manager' for personnel matters such as salaries and appraisals.

Permanent Project Teams

An alternative is to operate permanent project teams, often specializing in particular areas of work. The size of the project team may vary, depending on the demand for work in which it specializes, but the core group will remain together.

Comparison of the Approaches

Matrix management uses resources more efficiently. Permanent project teams allow the development of 'centres of expertise' in particular areas. In practice, most organizations use a mixture of both approaches.

Multi-Disciplinary Teams

A project team includes people with a variety of skills (a 'multi-disciplinary team') who can contribute towards the current stage of the project. During the systems analysis stage, for example, the project team might include a business analyst (who has a good understanding of the business problem), some systems analysts (who can describe the processes needed to solve the problem in logical terms) and a data analyst (who understands how to describe the data in logical terms).

During the systems design stage this would change. Some of the systems analysts might be replaced by designers and the data analyst would be replaced by a database designer. These people's skills are in deciding how the logical description produced at the systems analysis stage should be turned into a physical system.

This raises the issue of continuity. As membership of the project team changes, how can we ensure that the project as implemented will meet the intentions from the problem definition? One approach is for the same people to occupy key roles such as project manager, project director and project sponsor throughout.

Project Structure

Functional Reporting

There will be a steering group for large projects and projects affecting different parts of the organization. The steering group will be drawn from senior business management and will be responsible for ensuring that the project meets the requirements of the stakeholders. The steering group will authorize changes to the project budget and will sign off major deliverables.

The project sponsor will commission the project and define its objectives. If there is no steering group the project sponsor will discharge its responsibilities. The project manager will report progress to the project sponsor, typically on a monthly basis.

For large projects there may be a project director. The project director will represent the interests of the business but will be involved on a much more regular basis than the project sponsor or steering group. The project director's job is to provide overall direction and to deal with issues and identify those which need to be escalated to the steering group.

The project manager also has a responsibility to the Business Unit that will use the outcomes from the project. The resulting system must be usable and of acceptable quality.

Line Reporting

The IT manager will have overall responsibility for providing IT resources for the project. The split of management responsibilities by which the project manager reports to the project sponsor for project issues and the IT manager for resources and staffing issues is an example of the use of matrix management in project work.

If the project forms part of a programme, the programme manager will coordinate the projects.

The project team will carry out the work necessary to complete the project. The project team reports to the project manager, who will plan and organize the work of the team and monitor progress.

The project manager has a responsibility to other project managers in the department to present a professional image and to share best practice.

The formal project structure may be as shown in Figure 6.13 over the page.

It is important to understand the difference between project management and project direction:

- Project management is concerned with *how* the project is managed on a day-to-day basis. Project management is a specialist skill and is completely different to 'business as usual' management in a functional organization. Project managers must be trained specialists and managers drawn from the business often find it difficult to make the transition to project management;
- Project direction is concerned with *what* the project is doing and whether this will meet business needs. Project direction should usually come from the business and there are a number of approaches including the appointment of a project director and/or a steering group. A business project manager is sometimes appointed, whose role will often be providing project direction rather than project management.

Stakeholders

In addition to the formal project structure, any project will have a number of 'stakeholders' who will be affected by its outcome. If we consider a large IT project within a financial services organization the stakeholders will include:

Figure 6.13: Formal Project Structure

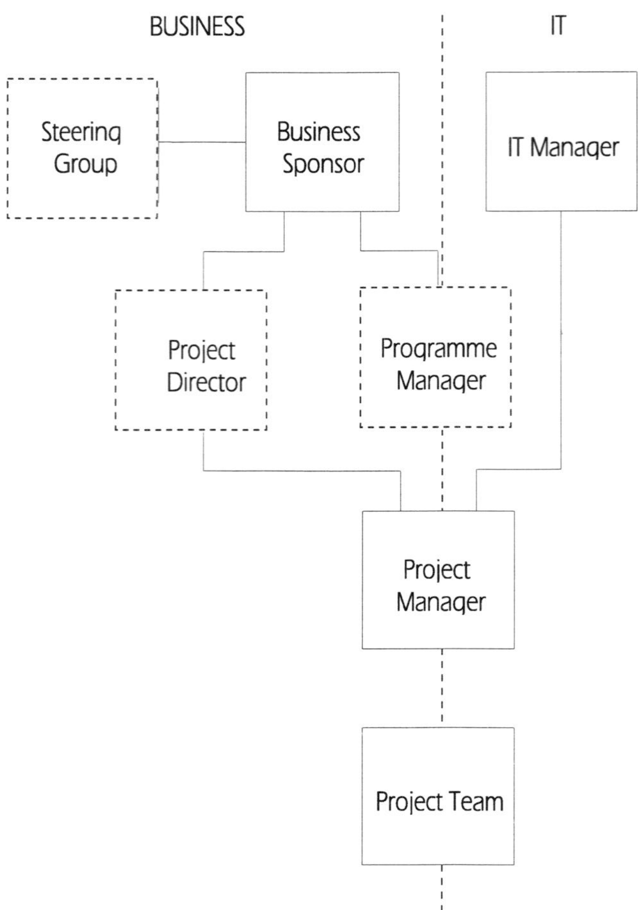

- Staff in other departments who will be affected by changes in the user department;
- The financial services organization's senior management;
- The financial services organization's shareholders;
- Those customers who may be affected by the changes;
- Finance Department;
- Inspection/Audit Department;
- Legal Department;
- Compliance Department;
- Those suppliers who may be affected by the changes;

- Those suppliers who are participating in the project.

Given the number of stakeholders, it is hardly surprising that project organization is very complex. The interests of stakeholders can be represented through:

- Formal involvement in the project;
- 'Sign off' of the relevant parts of the project;
- Participation at the implementation stage.

The method of representation varies but a typical pattern might be:

Table 6.1

	Formal involvement	**Sign off**	**Participation at implementation**
Other affected department staff			Yes
Senior management		Yes	
Shareholders			Yes
Customers			Yes
Finance Department		Yes	
Inspection/Audit Department		Yes	
Legal Department		Yes	
Compliance Department		Yes	
Affected suppliers			Yes
Participating suppliers	Yes		

It is worth noting how few of the stakeholders will usually have formal involvement in the project. In particular, it would be unusual for key stakeholders such as shareholders and customers to have any involvement prior to implementation.

Governance

Governance is the process of ensuring that the IT function produces what the business requires. The project director is responsible for governance at an individual project level, but governance across the organization as a whole depends greatly on the relationship between the business and the IT function. There are two main views of what this should be:

- One view is that the relationship is *contractual*. Systems development is a supplier like any other supplier and should be managed according to terms agreed in a contractual document;

- The alternative view is that the business and systems development should operate in *partnership*. Systems development is not a zero sum activity and both parties benefit by cooperating rather than competing.

Both approaches have their advantages and most financial services organizations fall somewhere between these, moving closer to one or the other as recent experience and management fashion dictate.

The main advantage of the contractual relationship is that of certainty. Both parties are committed to take certain actions and are liable should they fail so to do.

The main disadvantages of the contractual relationship are interpretation and the risk of the systems development function not going beyond the narrow view of the contract:

- Interpretation is a source of problems for all complex contracts. During the early stages of the systems development process it is often very difficult to define a precise contract because the objectives of the development and the method of work may be difficult to specify with any certainty;
- We have already shown that changes occur naturally during the course of a project. A contractual relationship needs to consider how such changes are accommodated and who will bear the cost. Contracts must specify how responsibility for changes is to be allocated;
- A contractual relationship implies that the systems development function will deliver exactly what is specified. This is a disincentive for systems developers to use their knowledge and experience to suggest improvements beyond the contracted minimum.

One approach that relies on a contractual relationship is to use an external supplier for systems development. This is called outsourcing. External suppliers can also be used for operating computer systems, where it is called facilities management.

The contractual relationship is the preferred approach for most financial organizations at the time of writing, and many are considering facilities management and outsourcing.

Outsourcing has the disadvantage that the organization loses control over its development process. If we regard information as a tradable commodity and source of competitive advantage (as discussed in Chapter 1) we can readily see the disadvantages of outsourcing. There are a number of examples of organizations outsourcing the systems development process and then buying this back to recover control. Further, studies show 80% of outsourcing contracts do *not* save the organization money – the usual rationale for outsourcing.

Facilities management does not have this disadvantage and the main issue with facilities management is security of supply – can the supplier guarantee the service levels the organization requires?

7

SYSTEMS DEVELOPMENT CYCLE

Objectives

After studying this chapter, you should be able to:

- understand the function of the systems development lifecycle and be able to describe lifecycles for:
  - waterfall development
  - package selection
  - outsourcing – including full outsourcing, turnkey development, partial outsourcing and facilities management
  - joint application development;
- understand and be able to describe the stages in these lifecycles, in particular:
  - the role of the business at each stage of the lifecycle
  - the outcomes and deliverables from each stage.

1 Introduction

The systems development cycle or lifecycle was developed by the National Computing Centre (NCC) in the 1960s. A lifecycle is a list of the stages we go through in developing an IT system.

There are various lifecycles in commercial use. The original NCC lifecycle included six stages and lifecycles typically have between five and ten stages.

There are four common approaches to developing IT systems:

- The traditional approach is called 'waterfall development'. This defines the development process as a series of stages through which the project moves. It is called waterfall development because it is not possible to go back up the waterfall – once a stage has started it is not possible to go back to an earlier stage, as shown in Figure 7.1:

Figure 7.1: Waterfall Development

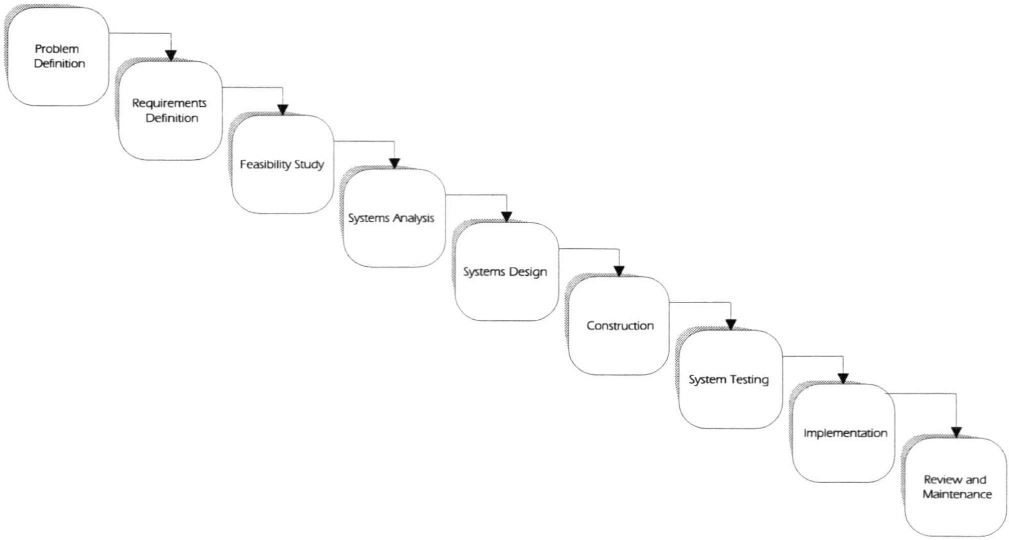

- A popular alternative is to buy a 'package' from an external vendor. Vendors can supply software ranging from full service packages covering industries such as banking and insurance to specialist niche packages covering areas such as payroll or derivatives trading;
- Another alternative is outsourcing. This uses an external vendor to meet some or all of the organization's requirements for systems. Again, this can range from full outsourcing of all systems provision to the more limited provision of 'turnkey' systems in niche or non-strategic business areas;
- Another approach is joint application development, also called prototyping or iterative development. Unlike waterfall development this does allow us to go back to earlier stages during the development process.

Each of these approaches may have its own lifecycle.

2 Waterfall Development

Developing a system using the waterfall approach involves going through a series of stages in order. Before we can go on to the next stage we must have completed the previous stage and had the deliverables signed off.

We shall use a ten stage lifecycle as a basis for considering waterfall development as follows:

- Problem Definition
- Requirements Definition
- Feasibility Study
- Systems Analysis
- Systems Design
- Construction
- System Testing
- Implementation
- Review
- Decommissioning.

Problem Definition

The problem definition stage answers the question, what problem are we trying to solve? Although this may seem obvious, it is common to find symptoms and possible solutions confused with the real problem. For example a manager may define the problem as 'I need this report on my desk at 8:30 every morning' when what is *really* needed is access to the information the manager requires to take decisions. This could be the report asked for, it could be a different report giving more relevant information, it could be on-line access to the information or it could be access to a decision support system.

It is the responsibility of the business user to define the problem clearly and correctly. This does raise two problems. First, the business user may take a parochial view – considering only the effect on the particular department and ignoring other possible users of the system. Second, the business user may not have the skills to analyse the root causes of the problem or the knowledge to understand what IT can achieve.

Business analysts – IT specialists with a good understanding of the business – can play a useful role here, bringing analytical skills and an understanding of what IT can (and cannot!) achieve to the problem definition. IT specialists may also need to be involved where solutions to the problem are likely to affect other systems or to involve a requirement for additional hardware, system software or telecommunications.

Others who may need to be involved could include organization and methods specialists and internal audit staff. External consultants may be able to advise on approaches other organizations have taken to the same problem.

A short conference or 'workshop' usually forms an important part of the problem definition stage, allowing all the relevant groups an opportunity to discuss the problem and its impact on them. The outcome of this stage will be a problem definition report which will be used as input to the feasibility study stage.

Requirements Definition

Requirements definition looks in detail at what the new system is expected to do. This will include the functions carried out by any existing systems (whether manual or on a computer) together with any new requirements.

Interviews and questionnaires are used to identify the requirements. New requirements may be identified using techniques such as brainstorming, workshops and throwaway prototyping (discussed later in this chapter under joint application development).

Observation and participation may be used to build up a description of the current system. Workflow within the office is documented and copies taken of forms and reports. Published documentation such as procedure manuals are an important source of information. Business analysts will sometimes work in the department for a period to observe and participate in the business processes. The current system is often documented using techniques such as process maps and flowcharts because these can be easily used in the later stages of the development.

The business analyst carries out the requirements definition, working closely with the business users. At this stage, additional IT staff – systems analysts who will work on the next stage – may also be involved.

The outcome of this stage is a requirements definition report containing a list of requirements and charts describing how the current physical system works. These are supported by examples of forms, copies of relevant documentation and statistics about the number of transactions carried out.

Other lifecycles use the term 'systems investigation' for this stage.

Feasibility Study

The feasibility study stage looks at possible solutions to the problem and considers whether they are feasible and how much they might cost. Feasibility includes:

- Technical feasibility – can the problem be solved given the current availability of technology?
- Fit with existing systems – how will the technology required fit with our existing systems? In particular, how do we get the information we need into and out of the various possible solutions?
- Fit with strategy – does solving the problem fit with the organization's business strategy? Does the technology fit with the organization's IT strategy?
- Technology risks – what risks are associated with the technology? How will the organization manage these risks? 'Leading edge' technology in particular is prone to risks, including whether it will work and the risk of obsolescence if it is overtaken by a different technology.
- Cost benefit – do the expected benefits offer a satisfactory return on the investment required? We discussed cost benefit analysis in Chapter 6.

The feasibility study starts by identifying different options for solving the problem. This will consider factors such as whether the problem can be solved using a package, how much of the solution should be delivered using technology and what technologies are available. This stage must also include the identification of evaluation criteria and the assessment of the options against these criteria.

The feasibility study stage is usually carried out by a business analyst. If additional hardware, telecommunications components and/or software forms part of the solution it is likely to involve discussions with potential suppliers and also with the technology strategists within the organization. Internal audit staff may be involved if there are any security issues.

The outcomes from this stage will include a feasibility study report (outlining options and making recommendations), a cost benefit analysis and (if outside suppliers are likely to be involved) a draft request for information.

A request for information describes the work the supplier will be required to do and asks for an estimate of time and costs – either on a fixed-price basis (once the tender is accepted the agreed price is fixed) or on a time and materials basis (the price may change if the supplier completes the work cheaper or more expensively than estimated). Requests for information are discussed in more detail later in this chapter.

Systems Analysis

The systems analysis stage produces a full description of *what* the system will need to do. This is based on the description of the current system and additional requirements developed during the requirements definition stage. It does not consider *how* the system will do it or the constraints under which the system will operate. This is described as a logical model of the system.

The analysis of an existing process usually starts by removing the constraints that affect the physical system. For example, physically it is usually impossible for two different people to work on the same document at the same time. This constraint would be ignored during analysis. The analysis of new requirements often starts by identifying how they fit into the existing process. A detailed discussion of systems analysis techniques is outside the scope of this book.

This stage is carried out by systems analysts, some of whom may have been involved in the requirements definition stage. The business analyst will usually continue to be involved and may work as a systems analyst – the skills required are similar. A specialist data analyst may be involved in producing a logical model of the data.

The business users will be involved in checking the analysis and confirming that the system would meet their requirements. The analysis stage usually involves specifying screen and report layouts and the business users would be involved in this.

The outcome from this stage will be a systems requirements definition containing models of the processes and data to be provided by the new system.

Systems Design

The systems design stage looks at how the system can actually be built – it produces a physical model of the required system. This will include deciding which processes will be carried out manually and which by the computer. This is called the 'man-machine boundary'. The manual component of the system will need to consider how staff will interact with the computer.

It also needs to identify the constraints under which the new system will operate. These are likely to be different from the constraints of the current system – for example an on-line system, where up-to-date information can be requested at any time will be less constrained than a batch system where information is available only as reports printed at the end of the previous day. These constraints are then applied to the logical model from the systems analysis stage to produce a new physical model.

Design of the computer system will depend greatly on technical factors – whether the system will be batch, on-line or real-time, whether a database will be used etc. It is important that the computer system design is efficient in the particular environment in which it will operate.

The systems design stage may be carried out by specialist system designers or by systems analysts carrying out a design function. The skills required are more technical than in the systems analysis stage, and a common approach is to have one or more specialist system designers working with the systems analysts who worked on the systems analysis stage. One area where a specialist designer is almost always required is database design.

Business users will have limited involvement in this stage, although they may be consulted about the 'user interface' – what the screens and reports will look like – if these were not fully defined during the systems analysis stage.

The outcome from the systems design stage will be an overall systems design report and possibly a set of program specifications. Alternatively, the program specifications may be written during the construction stage.

Construction

The construction stage involves writing the computer programs required. It also involves a certain amount of 'unit testing' to ensure that the programs work properly.

This stage is largely the responsibility of IT staff. Unless a prototyping approach is used, the business users' only involvement may be in producing documentation and forms and in preparation for testing the system.

The outcome of this stage is a set of computer programs.

System Testing

The system testing stage involves a far more thorough test than that carried out at the construction stage. Not only does it check that the programs work on their own, it also checks that they work together and that they do not cause any problems for other programs which may be running on the computer. This stage may include a number of tests:

- System testing, to check that all the system components work together;
- Regression testing, to check that the system works with other systems which may be running at the same time;
- Volume testing, to check that the system will handle the required numbers of transactions;
- Operational proving, to check that the system will run on the system for which it is intended and that the operating instructions are complete and accurate;
- Acceptance testing, to check that the system will meet the business requirement and that the user manual is complete and accurate.

Which of these tests are carried out depends on the nature of the system, but systems testing (always), operational proving (almost always) and acceptance testing (sometimes) are the most important.

IT staff are often responsible for all of these. Business users are involved in the acceptance test and, in some organizations, may have complete responsibility for it. Business users will be involved in drawing up 'test cases' to be system tested and in checking the results.

The outcomes from this stage will be a set of tested programs with operating instructions and user manuals. Many organizations retain the test cases and results to make it easier to test changes to the system or to regression test other systems.

Implementation

The implementation stage involves making the programs available for use. This will include designing any training programmes, writing manuals and designing forms for the users. There are four approaches to implementation:

- Big bang, in which the new system is implemented through the entire organization, all at once;
- Parallel run, in which the new system and the current system are allowed to run alongside each other for a period. The results from the two systems are compared to check the correctness of the new system;
- Pilot run, in which the whole of the new system is implemented in part of the organization – say 2-5% of the branch network for a large retail financial services organization. A pilot run requires different versions of the software to be used in different parts of the organization and the technique of allowing changes to be switched on and off is usually used.

  When the system has been proved in part of the organization, it will be 'rolled out' to the remainder. This roll out is often carried out in stages – for example, an initial roll out to 15% of the organization followed by three further roll outs covering the entire organization;
- Phased implementation, in which part of the new system is implemented in the whole of

the organization.

The decision as to which implementation strategy should be adopted is mainly that of the business user. However, IT staff should be involved and the decision may need to be approved by internal audit.

Review

Reviews are very important to allow the organization to learn from the development. There are two types of review

- Post development reviews;
- Post implementation reviews.

Post development reviews cover the *efficiency* of the development process and are carried out by IT staff. They are usually carried out by someone who was not involved in the original project team and look at whether all of the stages in the systems development cycle were completed correctly and what problems were encountered.

Post implementation reviews cover the *effectiveness* of the system and may be carried out by IT staff, business users or external consultants. They look at the original objectives of the project and determine how well the system meets these. They look at whether agreed service levels are being achieved. They also consider how easy the system is to use and issues such as cost overruns and late delivery.

Decommissioning

Some types of project have a formal decommissioning phase when the main project deliverable reaches the end of its economic life. Obvious examples include projects to build nuclear power stations and off-shore oil rigs where the cost of decommissioning has a substantial effect on the project's business case.

Although this is rare for information technology projects we must give consideration to when the system will be replaced. As systems get older they incur increasing costs:

- Maintenance costs increase. Changes to the system often have the effect of increasing maintenance costs and it may be expensive to support obsolete technology. We can use the analogy of an old car where it may be hard to find spare parts or find a mechanic who understands how to service it.
- The system may act as a constraint on the business. The limitations of the system may limit the business's ability to enter new markets. This will impose an opportunity cost in terms of lost business opportunity.
- Maintaining the system diverts scarce resources away from the development of new systems to meet business needs. We consider one solution to this – outsourcing system maintenance – later in this chapter.

For an information technology project it would be very unusual to include a specific decommissioning stage in the initial project plan. However, maintenance costs should be monitored and the decommissioning or replacement of the system should be considered when these get too high.

3 Using a Package

The decision to use a package does not mean that we can do without a structured approach to the process. We shall use a ten-stage lifecycle as a basis for package selection. The first three and last five stages are similar to the corresponding stages in the waterfall development lifecycle. The stages are as follows:

- Problem Definition (as for waterfall development);
- Requirements Definition (as for waterfall development);
- Feasibility Study (as for waterfall development);
- Request for Information and Vendor Shortlist;
- Invitation to Tender and Vendor Selection;
- Procurement;
- System Testing (regression testing, operational proving and acceptance testing);
- Implementation (as for waterfall development);
- Review (post-implementation review);
- Decommissioning (as for waterfall development).

During the feasibility study stage we will have used sources such as reference books, the computer press, consultants, competitor information and perhaps customers to identify that a package is a potential solution to our system requirements.

Request for Information and Vendor Shortlist

A request for information (RFI) is a document that typically contains:

- A brief description of the main requirements. This may be a summary of the requirements definition report;
- A statement of the constraints under which the system will need to operate. These might be quite specific (for example, a description of our hardware and telecommunications environment and a requirement that the package must operate within this environment) or they might be more general (for example a requirement to be able to analyse information using a spreadsheet – it will be the vendor's responsibility to determine how best to move the information from the package into a spreadsheet);
- A request for information about the company. This will include financial health and

standard terms of business including warranties and the availability of support and consultancy;

- An outline of the tender process, including the timescales and the form in which tender documents must be submitted.

The RFI may be produced during the feasibility study stage.

The next stage is to draw up a vendor shortlist from the requests for information, as follows:

- From the requirements definition and systems analysis stages, identify the criteria that will be used to assess the package. These will include the functions that the package needs to be able to perform and compatibility factors such as whether the package can run on existing hardware;
- For each of these criteria, decide whether it is 'must have' or 'nice to have'. An alternative classification takes the acronym MoSCoW from the initial letters of the classification must have, should have, could have, want. Give each of the criteria a 'weighting' which reflects its relative importance;
- Assess each package against the selection criteria. A common approach is to give a score from 1 (does not meet) to 5 (meets very well) against each criterion for each package;
- Calculate the total score for each package. For each criterion, multiply the weighting by the score. Add up the results to give a total;
- Draw up a shortlist of suitable packages. These will be the packages that:
    - Meet all of the 'must have' criteria – typically having a score of at least 3 for each criterion;
    - Represent good value to the organization, taking account of their cost and overall score.

Before embarking on this process organization have to be aware of the problems that might arise during selection. These include:

- There may be no package that adequately meets the selection criteria. In this event it may be necessary to consider bespoke development;
- Available packages may meet some of the selection criteria but some of the required functions may not be available. Here, bespoke development is an option or it may be possible to tailor the package.

The objective is to reduce the number of potential vendors to a manageable shortlist, usually of between three and six.

Invitation to Tender and Vendor Selection

The shortlisted vendors will be sent an invitation to tender (ITT) which may be prepared during the shortlisting process and will typically include:

- A list of specific questions about how the proposed solution will meet the requirements;
- Information about how any changes to the package will be implemented;
- Information about 'reference sites' – other organizations that already use the package;
- Specific proposals about costs, training, warranty, consultancy and support arrangements.

The next stage is to select the vendor:

- The shortlisted packages will be examined in more detail. Depending on the type of package, this may well involve talking to and possibly visiting reference sites;
- All of the shortlisted packages should provide the main functions required by the organization. The final selection will take more account of other factors such as:
    - Performance and response times;
    - Ability to handle required volumes;
    - Compatibility with existing hardware;
    - Compatibility with system software;
    - Quality of documentation;
    - Availability and quality of support;
    - Costs, including operating and maintenance costs;
    - Audit trails and security/control features;
    - Access to and cost of upgrades and enhancements;
    - Access to source code.

Procurement

The procurement stage is not usually the responsibility of the project team. Finance or a central purchasing function is usually responsible for this.

The objective of the procurement stage is to secure the package on the most favourable terms to the organization. This will not necessarily be at the lowest possible price because factors such as support, training and security of supply must be considered.

The procurement stage starts during the vendor selection process.

4 Outsourcing

Financial services organizations have several options for outsourcing IT:

- Full outsourcing of all systems functions;

- Turnkey development;
- Partial outsourcing;
- Facilities management.

Even where the organization is handing over responsibility for system development, we must still consider this in terms of a lifecycle. Some stages – Problem Definition and Requirements Definition – are common and similar to the waterfall development lifecycle. Also common are the stages required to select an external vendor. Others will depend on the type of outsourcing adopted.

The selection of an external vendor is similar to the selection of a vendor for a package solution, involving Request for Information (also called a Request for Proposal), Invitation to Tender and Procurement stages. The evaluation process will consider the ability of the vendor to meet the requirements, rather a specific solution.

Full Outsourcing

If a financial services organization fully outsources its IT, it transfers all responsibility to a vendor. This is rare in financial services, although it may happen when a financial services organization meets its needs by buying a package together with a maintenance and facilities management arrangement. Therefore the lifecycle we use for buying a package applies to this type of outsourcing.

Turnkey Development

Turnkey systems development involves the organization transferring responsibility for the development of some of its systems to an external vendor. Financial services organizations generally use turnkey development for systems that are not strategically important, for example administrative systems such as payroll and property management.

The Problem Definition and Requirements Definition stages are as for waterfall development. The systems resulting from turnkey development will be used alongside the organization's other systems. Therefore the later lifecycle stages are needed:

- System Testing (regression testing, operational proving and acceptance testing);
- Implementation (as for waterfall development);
- Review (post-implementation review only);
- Decommissioning (as for waterfall development).

The most important factor is ensuring that all of the requirements – including any methodologies or standards to be used – are clearly documented. Asking the supplier to make changes during the development will be expensive. The completed system, including any documentation, must also be carefully checked to ensure that it complies with the requirements before sign off.

Although we cannot ensure that the supplier uses our methodology, we can require that they document the system in a way consistent with it and with any other standards we use. An important issue here is who is going to maintain and support the system? If this is the supplier, it may not be necessary for the technical documentation to meet our standards. If we are, it is important that all the documentation is consistent with our own.

Standards are rules to be used in the development process. Standards include:

- Documentation standards. These define what documentation should be produced and in what format;
- Data naming standards. These define how data elements should be named;
- Operability standards. These define how the system should run in the data centre – for example what action the system should take if it cannot find a file it needs.

Partial Outsourcing

We have a number of options for partial outsourcing of the development process. Common approaches include:

- Using contract staff as part of the development process;
- Outsourcing the construction stage;
- Outsourcing the maintenance stage.

None of these approaches has a significant effect on the lifecycle.

The reasons for using contract staff as part of the development process include securing access to skills and knowledge that are scarce within the organization and coping with temporary peaks in demand for developers.

The reason for outsourcing the construction stage is that it is largely independent of the other stages. One option is to outsource this to another country where computer programmers are cheaper, and countries such as India have developed major software industries through this.

Maintenance typically uses up to 80% of an organization's total spending on information systems and outsourcing this frees resources to use on the development of new systems. The main disadvantage of outsourcing maintenance is that it requires expertise and knowledge of the organization's existing systems which an external vendor will need to develop.

Facilities Management

Facilities management involves the transfer to an external vendor of responsibility for some or all of the following:

- Operation of the organization's data centres and mainframe computers

  OR

Processing of the organization's work on the vendor's mainframe computers;

- Operation of the organization's telecommunications network

  OR

  Transmission of the organization's telecommunications traffic over the vendor's network;
- Support for the organization's telecommunications network;
- Support for the organization's 'desktop' – its PCs and terminals.

Facilities management is becoming increasingly important. A few financial services organizations have outsourced their data centres either by floating them as separate companies or by selling them (and transferring their staff) to an external vendor. Outsourcing the telecommunications network and desktop support are more common.

The advantages of facilities management are:

- The organization does not have to pay for upgrades to hardware and software except through the cost of the service. The vendor will be able to spread the cost over a number of clients and will receive discounts as a large user, so the cost of such upgrades is likely to be lower than the financial services organization would have been able to secure;
- The vendor may be able to operate the hardware and software at a lower cost, both because of economies of scale and because the vendor specializes in this type of operation and should be able to generate savings through process improvement.

The disadvantages of facilities management are:

- It may be expensive if the organization relies on unusual hardware or software. Because the vendor cannot easily spread the costs, the organization will not achieve any cost savings. This also limits the organization's ability to delay taking new releases of system software because the vendor may be willing to support older versions for only a limited period;
- The organization loses control over its systems. If a contractual dispute arises the organization's security of supply may be jeopardized if the vendor can withdraw the service offered.

It is important to note that financial services organizations are increasingly outsourcing non-IT operations functions such as cheque clearing.

5 Joint Application Development

Joint application development (JAD) involves a series of meetings or workshops between the developers and the business users to develop the system. This is an iterative process, with new requirements or changes being identified at each meeting and incorporated in a prototype or model of the system prior to the next meeting.

One approach used for JAD is the Rational Unified Process (RUP). This is a four-stage methodology including:

- Inception
- Elaboration
- Construction
- Transition.

The *inception* stage defines the scope and requirements through a 'vision' of the end product. This stage also considers the business case, priorities, risks and development process.

The *elaboration* stage defines elaborates the vision into an overall architecture. This emphasis on the early development of a robust architecture is the key feature of RUP. This stage also produces a firm project plan and ensures that all risks have been addressed.

The *construction* stage is broadly similar to the construction and testing stages in the waterfall development lifecycle.

The *transition* stage is broadly similar to the implementation stage in the waterfall development lifecycle.

An alternative is the Dynamic Systems Development Methodology (DSDM). This is a five-stage methodology including:

- Feasibility study;
- Business study;
- Functional model iteration;
- System design and build iteration;
- Implementation.

The *feasibility study* and *implementation* stages are broadly similar to the corresponding stages in the waterfall development lifecycle and the business study is equivalent to the requirements definition (system investigation) and systems analysis stages.

The *functional model iteration* stage involves several cycles of iteration in developing a functional model of the system. The objective of this stage is to work out exactly what the system has to do. The model can be developed using very simple tools – pen and paper can be used to develop prototypes – but will usually use tools such as databases and screen painters (to simulate computer screens).

The *system design and build iteration* stage again involves several cycles of iteration. The objective is to take the functional model developed in the previous stage and create a system that offers robust and efficient performance.

An important technique used in all JAD approaches is timeboxing, which we briefly described in Chapter 6. Each cycle of iteration is limited very strictly to a period of time. Timeboxing is important because it allows the development to be kept under control – without timeboxing developers might be tempted to keep including additional features without going back to the business user to confirm the requirement. Timeboxing can also be used in waterfall development to maintain control over phases such as requirements definition.

We may start JAD by choosing one clearly-defined business function within the system. We will use our prototype-building tools to develop a system which supports that business function. We can then choose another business function and prototype that, adding it to our original prototype.

When we have built a prototype that covers the entire system we will go through the prototype with the business user to identify which parts need further development. We will make the necessary changes and go through the prototype again. Only when the user is completely happy that the prototype meets the business requirement can the prototype be considered complete.

There are three things we can do with our prototype. We can implement the prototype as it is. We can throw it away and redevelop the system using waterfall methods. We can 'evolve' the prototype.

Implementing the prototype as it is seems obvious. However, there are disadvantages. The system will have been developed with a single user – will it be sufficiently robust to cope with a large number of users at the same time? Is the system efficient, or will it use very large amounts of computer resources? The system will not have been documented – how easy will it be to identify and correct faults or to make changes as the business requirements change?

Implementing the prototype is a common approach where the risks of failure are low – typically systems with a small number of users. Systems running on a large network or alongside other systems should not be implemented directly without considerable testing.

Throwaway prototyping may sound ridiculous but it is a common technique. We have used the prototype to design a system that meets the requirements of the business. This means that we have completed the most difficult stages of the systems development cycle. Further, we know that the system works. If we redevelop the system using waterfall methods and a third-generation language we will produce a robust and efficient system, usually at lower cost than if we had used other methods.

Throwing the prototype away is most common when the system will need to be implemented across a large network, where robustness and efficiency are critical factors.

Evolutionary prototyping involves 'tuning' the system to increase its efficiency and robustness. Important components may be rewritten if necessary, possibly using a third-generation language.

Evolutionary prototyping attempts to combine the benefits of implementation and throwaway prototyping. Its disadvantage is that the two parts of the system (the original prototype and the rewritten components) have been developed in different ways and may not fit together very well. One situation where this will not usually present a problem is in a client/server system, where the original prototype can be used for the 'client' component of the system and the 'server' component can be re-written for greater robustness and efficiency.

8

METHODOLOGIES AND TECHNIQUES

Objectives

After studying this chapter, you should be able to:

- be able to distinguish between a methodology and a lifecycle;
- be able to give examples of methodologies;
- understand business process re-engineering and be able to:
  - apply the process to organizational change
  - illustrate the process with examples;
- understand and be able to explain the main techniques for modelling processes, data and events;
- understand and be able to describe the main types of computer aided software engineering tool, and explain their role in the systems development process.

1 Introduction

In Chapter 7 we discussed lifecycles. A lifecycle is a checklist, telling us what stages we need to go through in developing a system and what we are trying to achieve in each of these stages. It tells us *what* to do during the systems development process.

The word 'methodology' really means the study of methods. In IT, we use this word to describe a comprehensive approach which covers *how* to develop systems as well as what must be done. The main characteristics of a methodology are:

- It covers the whole of the systems development process from the initial identification of the problem to the period after implementation;
- It includes its own lifecycle and it may allow alternative lifecycles to take account of the difference between types of project;
- It includes a set of techniques and it may have its own distinct 'notation' for describing

parts of the system. The same techniques will usually be used throughout the development process, with additional levels of detail being added during the later stages, and will form the basis for most of the documents produced during the development;

- It may include project management techniques and some methodologies, such as PRINCE (Projects In Controlled Environments), are mainly concerned with project management;
- It may include a set of computer-aided software engineering (CASE) tools specifically designed to support the methodology, possibly also including project management tools;
- Training and consultancy in using the methodology will usually be available.

We shall discuss some examples of methodologies. We shall then go on to look at two of the components of methodologies – techniques and CASE tools – in more detail.

We shall consider four examples of methodologies:

- Structured analysis;
- Information engineering;
- Projects in controlled environments (PRINCE);
- Business Process Re-engineering.

Structured Analysis

A number of methodologies follow the approach described as structured analysis. The important point about these methodologies is that they start by analysing the processes that are required. The data required by the system is defined by the data requirements of the processes within it.

Structured analysis methodologies are very effective for automation – improving existing processes using IT to make them more efficient. Their main disadvantage is that they consider only data used within the processes or defined as an input or output of the system. The value to management of collecting additional data is not considered.

Information Engineering

An alternative approach is adopted by methodologies following the principles of information engineering. These methodologies start by using conceptual data modelling to produce a data model. This ensures that the value of management information is taken into account. It also provides an overall framework (or architecture) for developing systems.

Information engineering methodologies are effective for developing systems that rely on data – for example management information systems. They also provide a good basis for developing an information systems strategy. Their disadvantage is that they are dependent on the quality of the data model they start with. Concern about costs may lead to too little senior management time being spent on conceptual modelling, resulting in a poor-quality data model.

PRINCE

PRINCE is a project management methodology and provides a management framework for systems development. It is designed to be used with the UK government's structured analysis methodology Structured Systems Analysis and Design Methodology (SSADM).

PRINCE has five major components:

- Organization
- Plans
- Controls
- Products
- Activities.

The organization component is concerned with the project structure and organization. The plans component provides a structure for preparing and managing project plans. The control component provides a control structure. Products are what we referred to as deliverables in Chapter 7 and are the outputs from the project. Activities includes management activities, technical activities and the quality process.

Business Process Re-engineering

We have discussed the process of developing IT systems to meet business requirements. But we need to avoid taking a narrow technical view of systems development. There are numerous examples of projects that were technical successes but which failed to deliver the expected benefits through a failure to consider other factors, and there are many examples where these wider factors made it impossible to produce an IT solution to a business problem.

The traditional approach to the use of IT in financial services is business process automation. The existing processes are taken as a starting point and IT is introduced at points in the process. There is no attempt to examine the process on an end-to-end basis or even to assess whether the process in necessary.

In July 1990, Management Consultant Michael Hammer wrote an article in the *Harvard Business Review* entitled 'Re-engineering Work: Don't Automate, Obliterate'. This article has launched a new management philosophy called Business Process Re-engineering (BPR), which is often portrayed as a panacea to financial organizations' long-standing IT problems of systems taking too long to develop and then being too inflexible to change. The term 're-engineering' is now used widely as a magic solution to business problems promising:

- Reduced costs
- Increased quality
- Improved customer satisfaction
- Increase in profitability.

The original definition of BPR from Hammer and Champy's 1993 book was 'the fundamental thinking, rethinking and radical redesign of business processes to achieve dramatic improvements in critical contemporary measures of performance, such as cost, quality, service and speed'. Other definitions extend this to include a focus on customers and on the marketplace.

Another feature of BPR is that it looks to make the most effective use of IT. Instead of adapting the existing processes, as in business process automation, BPR ignores the existing processes and considers how the results can be achieved while making the best use of IT.

It is possible to draw a distinction between business process re-engineering and business re-engineering. Business re-engineering involves a fundamental re-examination of the activities of the organization, considering whether it should operate certain lines of business at all. Our emphasis in this book will be on BPR.

Some consultancies and texts describe BPR using other terms, for example Business Process Redesign, Business Process Engineering and Business Process Transformation.

BPR can be broken down into seven stages:

- Identify the core business processes;
- Map and cost these core processes;
- Conduct detailed analysis of customer requirements to identify what the customer wants;
- Prioritize the core processes for BPR;
- Radically redesign the processes by simplifying and rationalizing;
- Manage the change to ensure benefits are achieved;
- Establish on-going measurement systems to ensure continuous improvement.

Core Processes

BPR focuses on the core business processes. These are the processes that are central to the business, as opposed to support or peripheral activities which should perhaps be outsourced.

Process Mapping

Process mapping is a technique for describing business processes. The process map provides a basis for examining and questioning the process.

The type of questions that should be asked at this stage are:

- The purpose of the process. What is being done? Why is it being done? What else could be done? What should be done?
- The place. Where is it being done? Why there? Where else could it be done? Where should it be done?
- The process timing. When is it done? Why then? When else could it be done? When

should it be done?

- The person. Who does it? Why that person? Who else might do it? Who should do it?
- The procedures. How is it done? Why that way? How else can it be done? How should it be done?

Customer Requirements Analysis

The customer is central to BPR. If a process does not add value for the customer, we need to question why it is being carried out at all. The purpose of customer requirements analysis is to establish what the customer needs from the process.

Prioritization

We need to apply some form of prioritization to ensure that we concentrate our re-engineering effort where we shall get the greatest benefit.

One method is Pareto analysis, also known as the 80:20 rule. Organizations will typically find that about 20% of their processes account for 80% of their costs. Prioritization will focus effort on the processes that account for the highest proportion of costs.

Another approach would be to focus on processes that are known to be unsatisfactory, perhaps from customer satisfaction measures or work measurement. An alternative is to use gap analysis and focus on the processes where there is the greatest gap between customer requirements and the actual outcomes of the process.

Redesign

Redesign involves simplifying and standardizing the processes, together with the creative use of IT.

Most processes have become more complicated than they need to. There are a number of reasons for this – the complications may be result of the physical layout of the office, or the process may have needed to provide reporting information that is no longer needed. Any step in the process that does not directly contribute to meeting customer requirements should be challenged.

Processes also often have a range of exceptions. This makes them excessively complicated. The choice is usually between removing the exceptions and splitting the complex process into two or more simple processes – one for the main process with the others dealing with the exceptions.

Most processes were originally developed as manual processes, with IT being introduced at a later stage. Therefore they contain steps relating to the physical movement of documents and restrictions such as two people being unable to work on a document at the same time. IT can be used to avoid these steps and restrictions and to produce a faster and simpler process.

Management of Change

We discuss the management of change in Chapter 10.

Work Measurement and Continuous Improvement

We discussed work measurement in Chapter 3. There is a general axiom to the effect 'we cannot improve what we cannot measure' and the measurement of results is essential to provide a basis for process improvement.

We discuss continuous improvement below under Total Quality Management.

Examples

The TSB mortgage process provides an example of the benefits of BPR.

Customer research identified the customer needs as:

- Fast decision;
- To be kept informed as the purchase proceeds;
- Simple application;
- Good advice on appropriate repayments and insurance.

The process mapping within TSB revealed that the average turnaround time from mortgage application to formal offer was 30 days, with less than one third achieved within 20 days. It took an average of four to five interviews with the customer to achieve completion, and there were five forms covering 167 questions of which only 24 were unique. For example, the customer's account number was required no less than seven times! There were two different processes with loans that were managed centrally and some that were managed within the branch. Four different computer systems were involved and five different functional areas.

Clearly the existing process was not only very inefficient but it failed to meet the customers' basic requirements.

Having built the process map TSB then looked at how their mortgage system could be radically changed using BPR. The redesigned process reduced the cost of processing by 25% and cut the time from application to formal offer to less than seven days. The customer was required to complete only one simplified form and was given a single contact point within the branch. This also enabled the computer systems to be rationalized.

Another example is the re-engineering of the branch back office.

Traditionally branches processed most of the work generated by their customers within the branch. This required the bulk of the space in the branch to be dedicated to this processing work leaving limited space for the customer and branch sales staff. For example, a typical branch layout might be:

Figure 8.1

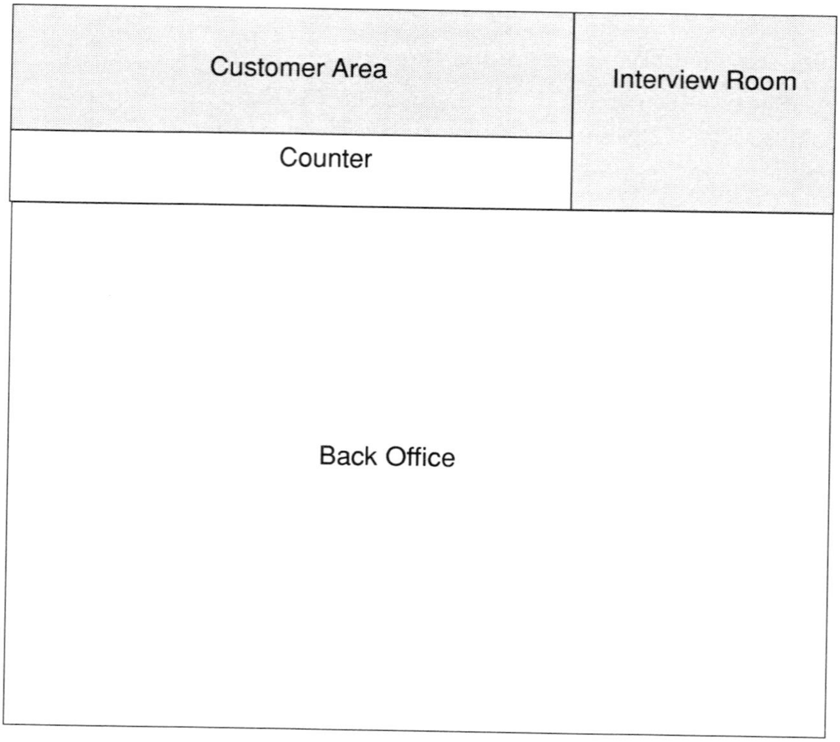

Clearly from a business point of view this was not a good use of prime retail space, (e.g. supermarkets and other retailers devote the maximum space to customers and products, keeping their 'back office' in warehouses on industrial estates).

Similarly all of the computer systems to support the branch have tended to be developed assuming that the processing would remain in the branch. Over the years the systems have improved branch efficiency but it is only in the last 5 or 10 years that banks have questioned the need or appropriateness of processing work within the branch.

BPR has been used to think radically about how back-office processing could be undertaken outside of the branch at either regional processing centres or automated completely, allowing branches to provide much more space for the customer. This leads to a layout such as:

Figure 8.2

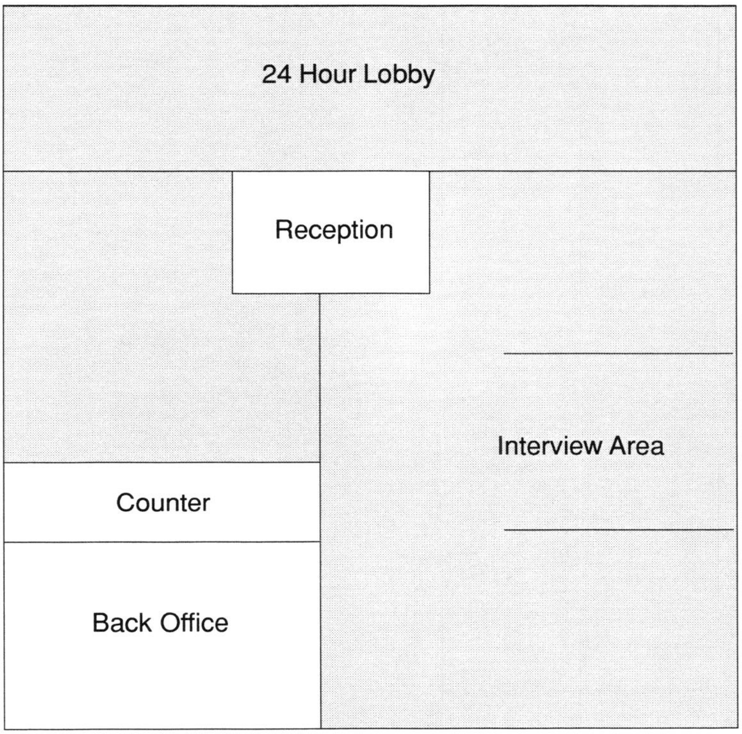

For example, in 1988 all cheque processing for Midland Bank was undertaken within the branches with each branch submitting its cheques to the bank's clearing house each day. This involved the sorting of cheques, their encoding and daily balancing of the work. Because the work was being undertaken in almost 2,000 different branches the quality varied enormously and each branch had to have sophisticated machines to read, sort and encode the cheques with magnetic ink. The volumes of cheques varied dramatically from branch to branch and there were many different ways that branches organized their staff to complete the work.

Customers required that their cheques were accurately processed and at a low cost. The existing process met neither of these requirements and so Midland used BPR to radically re-engineer the process. The result was to establish eight district processing centres to which all of the cheques and credits were delivered unprocessed. These centres would then use the latest very high-speed encoders and reader sorters to process the work using production line techniques taken from industry. The result was to dramatically reduce the cost of processing while reducing error levels from over 100 in a million to single figures. Space and time was freed up in branches and Midland achieved a competitive advantage in both processing costs and quality which it could use to obtain bulk cheque-processing work from major retailers.

2 Techniques

An important distinction between a lifecycle and a methodology is that the latter includes a set of techniques. There are different sets of techniques covering:

- Process modelling
- Data modelling
- Event modelling.

We describe systems using diagrams to make them easier to understand. People can see how a flow marked on a diagram corresponds to a physical movement of paper within an office. Stages in the process where several different things can happen are easier to show on a diagram than to explain clearly in words.

Process Modelling

The methods we use to describe processes have their origins in the second half of the 19th century. The theorists of the Scientific School of Management identified techniques for describing business processes, which later developed into 'work study' or 'Organization and Methods' (O&M).

These methods are still used to describe and improve business processes. An important technique here is process mapping, used as a basis for business process re-engineering or BPR. The same techniques have also been adapted to describe computer processes – the dataflow diagram to describe logical processes and the flowchart to describe physical processes.

All these techniques are mainly concerned with describing flows of information between processes. O&M considers physical flows – for example the movement of documents in an office or parts on a factory floor. Process mapping is concerned with the physical and logical flows of data within a business process. Dataflow diagrams are concerned with logical data flows. Flowcharts are concerned with the flow of physical data within a computer system.

We shall discuss the techniques used for modelling:

- Business processes
- Data flows
- Program control.

We usually present process models as a levelled set of diagrams. The top level contains one diagram that explains the entire process but with very little detail. The second level will contain one diagram for each process in the top level, broken down to give a further level of detail. There will then be a third and possibly a fourth level below these, allowing more detail to be shown. This is similar to the work breakdown structure discussed as a component of project planning in Chapter 6.

Business Processes

A business process describes an interaction with a customer or supplier. The business process describes the *entire* (also called end-to-end or E2E) interaction – this is an important difference between business processes and processes identified during systems development. Process mapping is an important technique for modelling business processes and is used as part of business process re-engineering, discussed above.

The first stage in process mapping is process decomposition – breaking the process down into a logical sequence of sub-processes. Each sub-process will involve some form of value-adding activity and if the sub-processes are taken together they form a 'value chain' showing how the inputs to the process are transformed into the corresponding outputs.

Identifying the processes and their inputs and ouputs, together with the timescales, can be a difficult task. A technique that is often used to map the value chain and understand the whole process is tagging.

In tagging, a form (the tag) is attached to each unit of work entering the process. For example if we wished to process map the account opening process in a branch then a tag form would be attached to the application form. Every person receiving that input form must complete the relevant details on the tag. The time taken in each stage of the process will be logged on the tagging form.

The tag must be simple, to ensure it is accurately completed without significantly impacting the workflow. There may be many products or processes involved in producing the final product – for example a cheque book and cheque card would have to be ordered for a new account. It is essential to identify and define each of these as products within the process map.

Each tag form should be sequentially numbered to ensure that all are returned, and missing tag forms should be investigated because these may reveal other parts of the process map.

An example of a tagging form is:

Date attached ________ Serial No. ________

Time attached ________

Department ________

Product ________

Processes ________ Actions ________

1. Pre Advice
2. Open Debit
3. Amend Debit
4. Blank Doc

1. Receive
2. File
3. Print
4. Check
5. Despatch
6. Open
7. Amend
8. Pay
9. Other

Desk Code	Time In	Action Taken	Time Out

Date Detagged
Time Detagged ________

For processes where volumes are fairly constant, tagging a process for one day may be all that is needed to produce an accurate process map. If there are large daily, weekly or seasonal variations in the volume of work handled, there may be corresponding wide fluctuations in the time taken or even the steps in the process. For example, during quiet periods counter staff may answer customers balance or other account enquiries but during busy periods such as lunch times refer customers to a specific enquiries desk. Tagging would need to cover an extended period and the process map would need to cover all of the variations.

Tagging will help to identify:

- The steps in the process;
- Average overall processing time taken;
- Delay between steps in the process;
- Process times at each stage;
- Incidence of holdover (work processed the following day or period);
- The workflow through the process;
- Sources of bottlenecks and underutilized resources.

The result of this analysis is a process map that can then help to identify whether the whole process needs radical re-engineering to achieve the customers' requirements or if only parts of the process need to be changed.

Data Flows

In Chapter 7, we identified a logical model – describing *what* the system does – as an outcome of the systems analysis stage. Dataflow diagrams are a technique used to describe the flow of data between the components of this logical model.

Dataflow diagrams have four components. Individual methodologies each use a different set of shapes (or 'notation') to represent these. We will keep things simple and use a single notation to describe all the techniques. This has four components:

Figure 8.3: Dataflow Diagram Notation

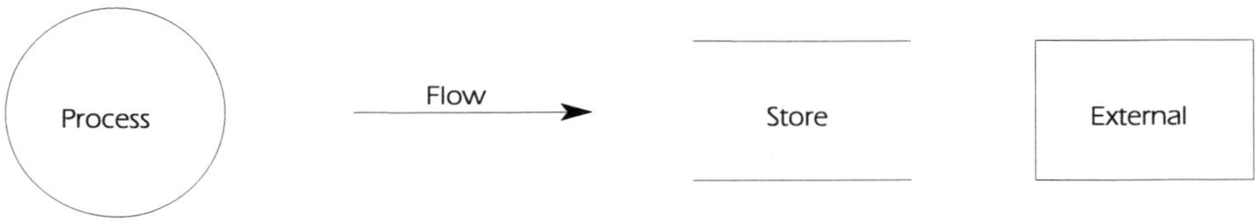

Process

Flow

Store

External

We defined processes above.

A flow is a movement of data. Flows take place between processes and other processes, stores and externals. Other flows might occur (between externals, for example) but these are outside the scope of the system we are describing and would not be shown on the diagram.

A store is a place where data or physical objects are held. In a data flow diagram, this is a logical data store or entity.

An external is something outside the system we are describing. A customer might be an external. Externals interact with the system but are not part of it.

We shall briefly describe another notation. This is the IDEF notation and processes are described as follows:

Figure 8.4: IDEF Notation

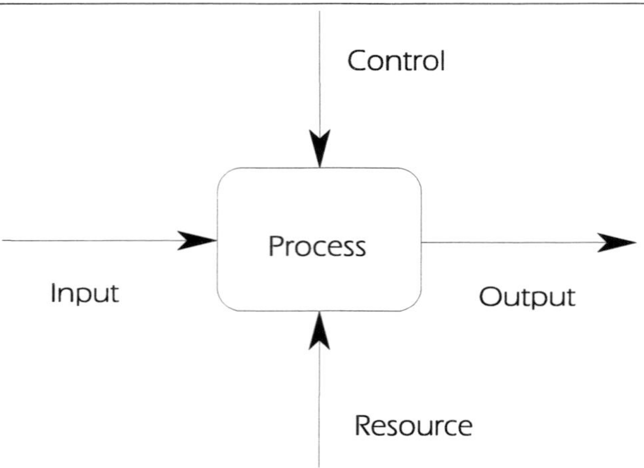

The ability to show controls and resources is an advantage of the IDEF notation.

Program Control

The system design stage transforms the logical model into a physical model, identifying what programs are required and *how* they work to satisfy the system requirements. Flowcharting is one of the most important techniques for describing the flows in the physical model.

In many ways a flowchart is similar to a dataflow diagram. There is one important difference – a flowchart needs to show control flows as well as data flows. When we draw flowcharts, we need one additional shape to represent decision points. The shape usually used for this is:

Figure 8.5: Flowchart Notation – Decision Point

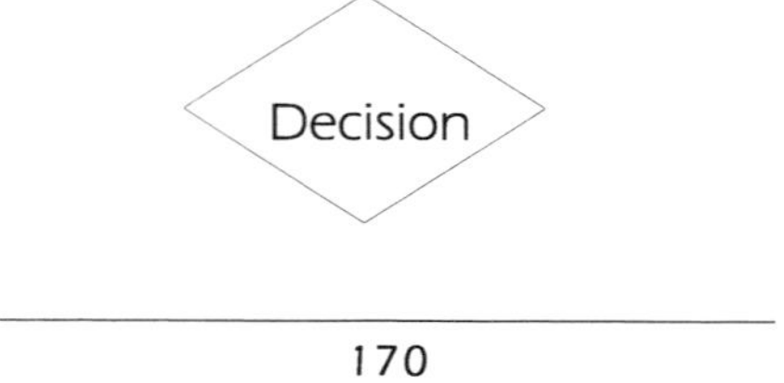

The other difference between dataflow diagrams and flowcharts is that the components have different meanings. For example, dataflow diagrams show processes and entities, whereas flowcharts show programs and databases.

Data Modelling

The methods used to describe data are of more recent origin. We describe data in terms of entities, relationships, attributes and keys.

An *entity* is anything that is important to the business and about which the business needs to hold information. Entities of interest to financial organizations include customers, accounts, cheques, bank giro credits etc.

A *relationship* describes direct relationships between entities. For example, there is a relationship between customers and accounts – one customer may hold many accounts.

An *attribute* is one of the pieces of information the business needs to hold. So the attributes we might hold about the customer entity would include date of birth, sex and address, among others.

A *key* is an attribute that we can use to identify a particular 'occurence' of an entity. For example, we can use an account number to identify one particular account.

Describing Logical Data

The two main approaches for describing logical data are conceptual data modelling and normalization. Both techniques produce an 'entity relationship diagram' – showing entities and the relationships between them – and other documents including definitions for entities and attributes, and lists of attributes and keys for each entity.

Again, individual methodologies use different notations for entity relationship diagrams. The one we shall use is:

Figure 8.6: Data Modelling Notation

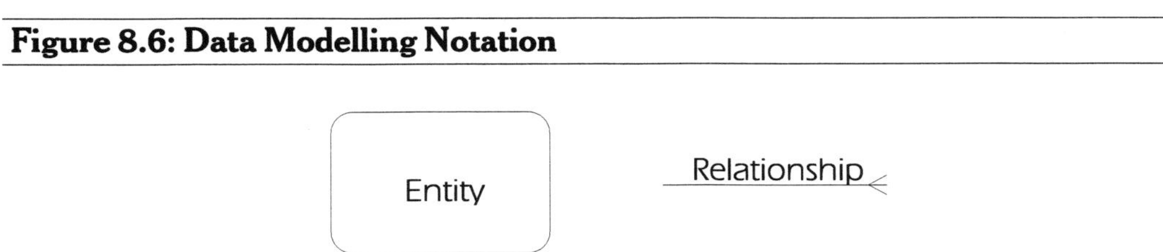

For example, we can show the relationship 'one customer holds many accounts' as an entity relationship diagram as follows:

Figure 8.7: Customer Account Relationship

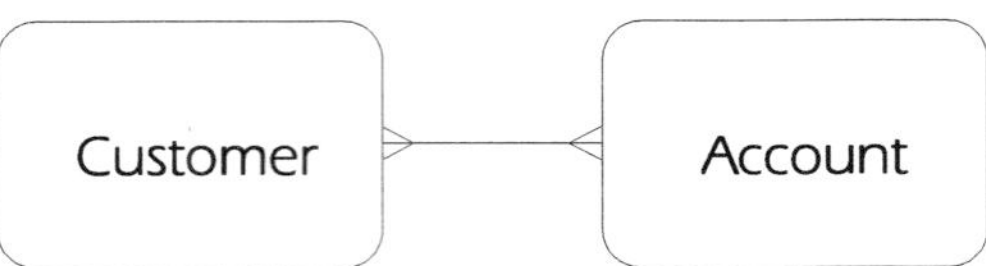

We can also describe the relationship on the entity relationship diagram, as follows:

Figure 8.8: Customer Account Relationship with Description

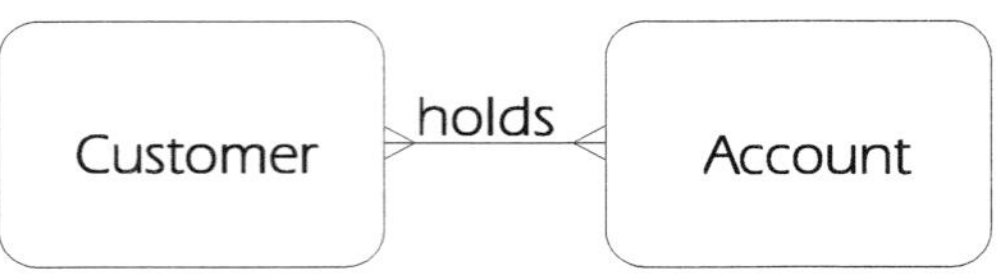

Strictly speaking, all relationships should be described in this way. However, this can make the diagrams cluttered and difficult to read and we will not do this for the purposes of this book. The only time that relationships should always be described is where more than one relationship can exist between two entities, for example:

Figure 8.9: Customer Loan Relationship

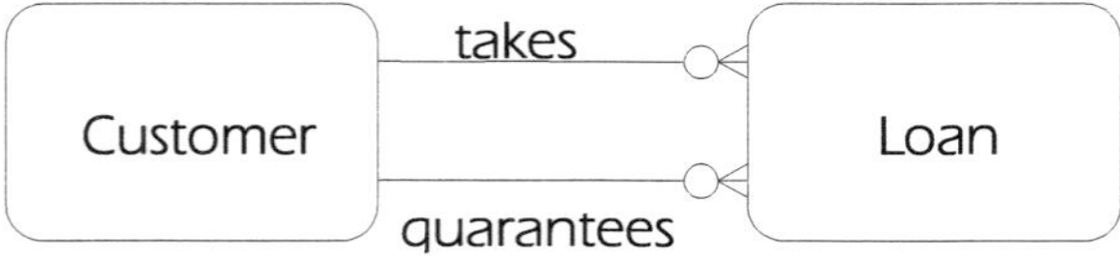

Indirect relationships are relationships where there is another entity involved. For example, there is an indirect relationship between customer and cheque through account. This is because customers have cheque books only because they hold accounts. Entity relationship diagrams only show these as the corresponding direct relationships:

Figure 8.10: Customer Cheque Relationship

The three lines on the right of the relationship are called 'crows feet' and show the 'cardinality' of the relationship. This is the number of occurences of one entity that go with the number of occurences of the second entity. For example:

- One account may have many cheques drawn on it. One cheque may be drawn on only one account. We say the cardinality of the relationship between account and cheque is one-to-many and the cardinality of the relationship between cheque and account is many-to-one;
- One customer may have a number of accounts. One account may be for more than one customer (e.g. joint accounts). We say the cardinality of the relationship between customer and account and the cardinality of the relationship between account and customer is many-to-many.

We can change the way we show the relationship to indicate the cardinality:

Figure 8.11: Cardinality

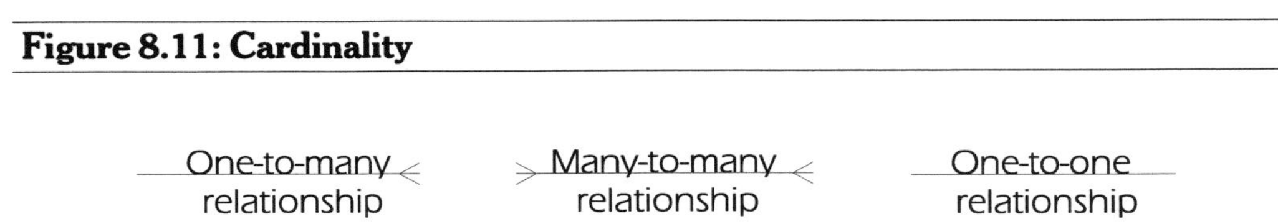

Relationships can also be optional. For example, an account need not have cheques (a deposit account or a savings account). We can show this by putting a circle on the relationship:

Figure 8.12: Optionality

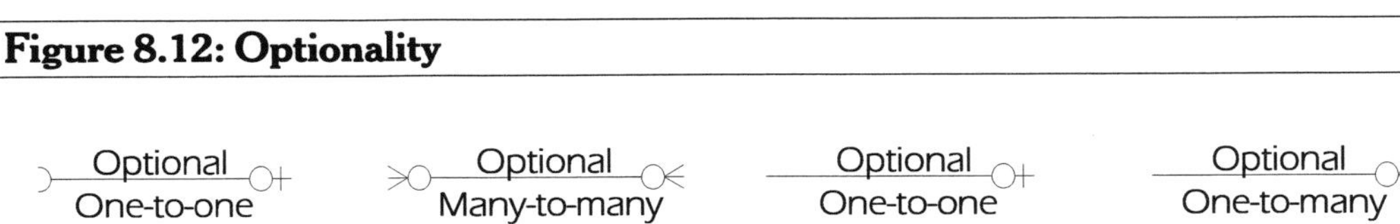

Note that relationships can be optional both ways (as in the first two examples) or only one way (as in the last two). Our cheque example demonstrates one way optionality – an account may have cheques but a cheque must be drawn on an account:

Table 8.13: Customer Cheque Relationship Optionality

Customer | Account | Cheque

Note on which end of the optional relationalship the circle appears. The relationship from

Account to Cheque is optional, and the circle appears on the far end of the relationship between the entities.

Attributes can be shown on the entity relationship diagram, although this often makes the diagram difficult to read and we shall not do this. We usually produce a separate list of the attributes for each entity. We shall use asterisks to indicate keys, for example:

ACCOUNT

** Account Number

* Customer Number

Indicates that the ACCOUNT entity has a primary key of Account Number and that Customer Number is a foreign key, linking the account to the CUSTOMER entity.

Describing Physical Data (computer)

Entity relationship diagramming can also be used to describe physical data held on documents, reports etc. Although the technique can be used to describe physical data held on computers, it is more usual to use different methods depending on how the data is stored – as files or on a database.

Conceptual Data Modelling

Conceptual data modelling starts by trying to identify entities. We have already defined an entity as something important to the business about which the business needs to hold information. This is usually enough to allow us to get an initial list.

We can check this list in various ways. An entity will usually either represent something physical (such as a customer or a branch) or something recorded on paper (such as an account or a contract). We can also try to decide whether items on the list are something we know – attributes – or something we know about – entities.

We then need to identify the relationships between the entities. Usually it should be fairly obvious which entities are related.

An alternative method of identifying the relationship between entities is called logical data association. We start by drawing up a grid showing the entities on both axes:

Customer	Account	Cheque	
			Customer
			Account
			Cheque

We then tick the squares in the grid where two related entities intersect:

Customer	Account	Cheque	
	✔	✔	Customer
		✔	Account
			Cheque

Finally we need to review the grid to ensure all the relationships are direct, deleting any which are not:

Customer	Account	Cheque	
	✔	~~✔~~	Customer
		✔	Account
			Cheque

One way of checking whether entities are related is to describe the relationship. If we cannot express the relationship in a simple form it is quite possible that the relationship is indirect.

It is possible that we are not able to identify any relationships for an entity. This could indicate several things:

- The entity may not really be an entity. We need to check it against our definition of an entity to see whether it should be included at all;
- We may have failed to identify a relationship. We need to check that the entity is not related to any of the other entities;
- We may have failed to identify an entity. We need to consider if the entity is related to any entities that we have omitted;
- The entity may be outside the scope of the system. We need to check why we have included the entity in our model.

Using conceptual data modelling it is unlikely that we shall be able to identify a full list of attributes. We should be able to identify a primary key for every entity and possibly some secondary keys.

We should be able to identify foreign keys. If two entities are related, the primary key of one should be a foreign key for the other. This gives us another check on the relationships – whether it is sensible for an attribute to be a foreign key.

We may also be able to identify some of the main attributes.

Normalization

Normalization is an alternative approach to identifying entities, relationships, attributes and keys. It is much more thorough than conceptual data modelling. Normalization usually involves three stages leading to a 'third normal form' (or 'TNF') entity relationship diagram. You will not need to know the stages of normalization for the exam but we shall briefly cover these to give you an overall understanding of the technique.

The first stage involves removing 'repeating groups'. Look at a bank statement. As well as the basic account details there are details of transactions that have passed over the account during the statement period. These transaction details are a repeating group and removing these gives us two entities – account and transaction. After this stage, we describe the data as being in 'first normal form':

Figure 8.14: First Normal Form

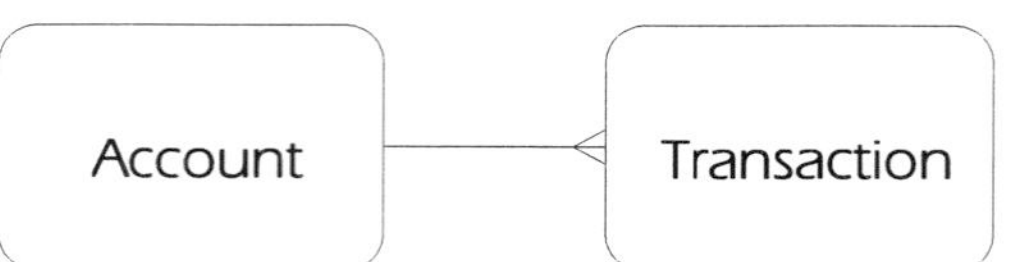

The second stage involves removing any 'part key dependencies'. The account details on the statement will include information about the branch – the sorting code, branch name and perhaps some telephone or address details. But the sorting code is enough to identify the branch. Instead of holding all the branch details with the account, we can hold the branch name, telephone and address details as a separate branch entity with a primary key of sorting code. We would hold sorting code as a foreign key on the account entity. This defines the relationship between account and branch. After this stage, we describe the data as being in 'second normal form':

Figure 8.15: Second Normal Form

The third stage involves removing any dependencies in the data. For example, the address may contain both a postcode and a mailsort code. But this data is related – the house number and postcode can be used to find the addresss and mailsort code. Instead of holding the full address with the account, we could hold house number as an attribute and postcode as a foreign key, holding the rest of the address on an address entity. After this stage, we describe the data as being in 'third normal form':

Figure 8.16: Third Normal Form

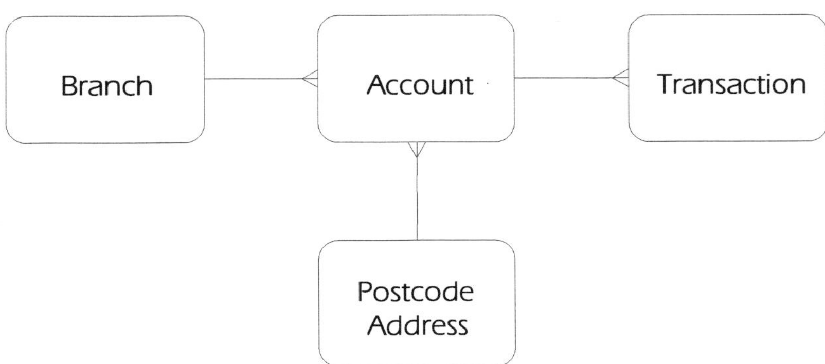

At least two further normalization stages may take place. These are outside the scope of this book.

Event Modelling

Event modelling considers how data is affected by processes. We shall consider:

- State transition diagrams;
- Entity life histories.

State Transition Diagrams

The example of a tagging form we showed earlier listed a number of activities such as receive, file and check. If the tagging form was attached to an application form (for example) these correspond to states the application form would go through.

A state transition diagram shows the states an input can take and the allowed transitions between these.

Let us consider an order as an example. The state transition diagram might look something like:

Figure 8.17: State Transition Diagram for Order

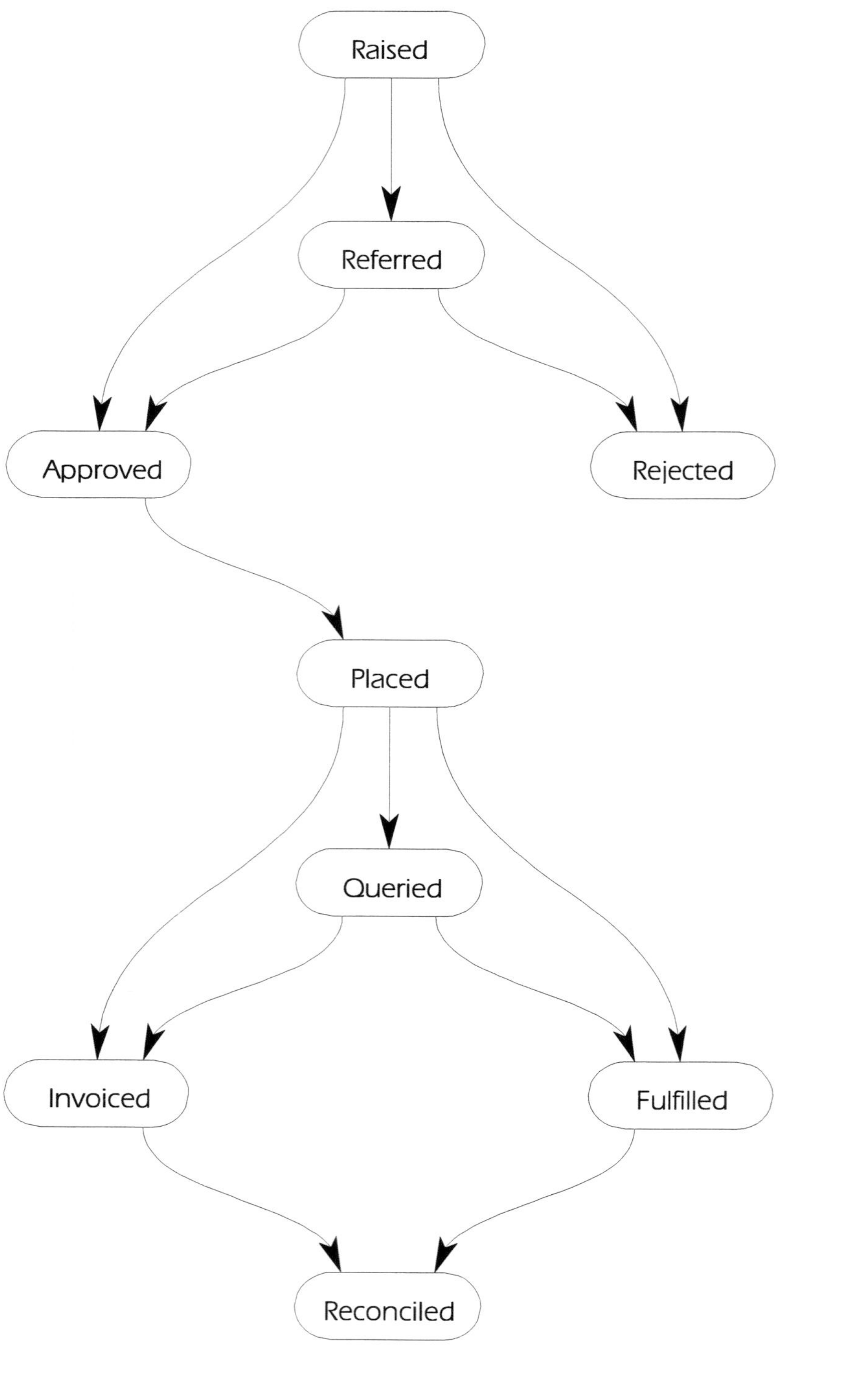

This shows that once an order has been raised, it can be approved, referred or rejected. It also shows us which transitions are not allowed – once an order has been fulfilled it cannot be queried, for example.

Entity Life Histories

The tagging form also shows activities such as open or amend. If tagging the form was attached to an application form for a loan (for example), these correspond to states the loan account would go through.

An entity life history is similar to a state transition diagram except that it considers the logical data – the entities – rather than the physical input forms. Again, the states and the allowed transitions between them are shown.

3 Computer-Aided Software Engineering

CASE is an acronym for computer-aided software engineering, and a CASE tool can be any computer program or system that can be used as an aid in the development of computer systems. There are a number of types of computer program that could be considered as CASE tools, for example:

- Data dictionaries
- Graphics systems.

Data Dictionaries

Data dictionaries record how and where data is held, both logically and physically. These are widely used in systems development, especially where we need to use or change data that is already held on the system. The investigation of how a proposed change will affect existing systems is called impact analysis.

Graphics Systems

Graphics systems can be used for the diagrams, which form an important part of the techniques used in systems development. General purpose graphics systems often have clipart 'templates' that support some of the most common notations, and there are also graphics systems specifically designed to produce systems development documentation.

Other Types of CASE Tool

In addition to these, there are a number of other CASE tools specifically designed to support the systems development process. These can be classified as:

- Workbenches
- Generators

- Environments
- Meta-CASE tools.

Workbenches

Workbenches are tools that support one part of the systems development process. The main types of workbench are designed to support:

- Systems analysis
- Data analysis
- Systems design
- Data design
- Construction (programming).

Systems analysis workbenches support the techniques required to describe and analyse logical processes. They provide a diagramming tool (which can also control the levels of diagram) and a glossary of process, flow, data store and external names. They sometimes include data analysis workbenches.

Data analysis workbenches provide similar features for data. They have a glossary which holds entity, relationship, attribute and key names. They can check the correctness of relationships from the keys.

Systems design workbenches can be used on their own or with systems analysis workbenches. Although they hold similar information, they present it in a way that allows it to be used as a 'first cut' design for the construction phase. In particular, they allow the system to be broken down into a hierarchy of programs and modules and show the flow of control between these. This first cut design can then be changed as needed to meet the particular requirements of the organization.

Data design workbenches are usually used with data analysis workbenches. They use the information about entities, relationships, attributes and keys together with information about the number of records expected and the order in which the entities will be accessed to develop a first cut database design. This can then be changed to meet the requirements of the organization.

Programmers' workbenches allow programmers to develop and carry out some testing on programs. The main benefit of these tools is in their testing facilities, because they allow programs written for mainframe computers or minicomputers to be tested on a microcomputer in a very interactive way. This is cheaper and easier than using the main computer for testing. When the program has been tested on the workbench it will still need to be tested on the main computer, but the majority of the errors should have been identified and corrected.

Generators include *program generators* and *application generators*.

A program generator uses an input source file similar to a fourth-generation computer language

(4GL) or a fifth-generation computer language (5GL). Whereas a 4GL or 5GL will either be run directly using an interpreter or compiled to give an object file, the program generator will convert the source file into a source file in another language – usually a third-generation computer language (3GL) such as COBOL or C. This can be used as a starting point and the programmer can make further changes to make the program do exactly what is required and to improve the program's efficiency.

An application generator takes this further, often using a systems analysis workbench to identify what is required. This will be translated into a working system, either written in a 4GL or using a program generator to produce a system written in a 3GL.

Environments

Environments include integrated CASE environments and component CASE environments. Both of these support the main stages of the systems development cycle (typically from systems analysis through to construction, although some may also include feasibility study, system investigation and maintenance). This means that they include all the types of workbench discussed above. It is also possible for organizations to use meta-CASE tools to build their own environments.

In an *integrated CASE environment*, all of these come from the same supplier (who will usually also supply a methodology, consultancy and training). This has the advantage that tools work well together. The disadvantage is that the individual workbench tools may not meet the organization's needs.

Component CASE environments attempt to overcome this disadvantage. A central repository (similar to a Data Dictionary but also including information about processes, computer programs and the computer itself) is used to coordinate information from different workbenches (which may come from different suppliers). The disadvantage of this approach is that it is technically quite difficult – workbenches designed to support Structured Analysis and Information Engineering will work quite differently, for example.

Meta-CASE tools can be used to build bespoke development environments, designed to fit exactly the methods used by the organization. This has the advantages of both the integrated CASE and component CASE approaches but the organization will incur costs in developing and maintaining such environments.

Both component CASE environments and meta-CASE tools need the ability to exchange information between CASE tools. Two methods of achieving this are the CASE Data Interchange Format (CDIF) and the Portable Common Tools Environment (PCTE).

Computer-Aided Software Testing

Computer-aided software testing (CAST) tools are a type of CASE tool designed specifically to support aspects of the testing process. The main types of CAST tool are:

- Capture and playback tools;

- Test scripting tools;
- Test data generation tools;
- Stress testing tools;
- Desktop testing tools;
- Test management tools.

Capture and playback tools allow us the 'capture' the keystrokes when we enter test data. If we need to rerun the test, we can 'play back' the recorded keystrokes rather than needing to re-enter the data. This saves considerable amounts of time and ensures consistency between the tests.

Test scripting tools allow test 'scripts' to be run automatically. These typically have features such as requesting external resources and handling errors that may occur during the test.

Test data generation tools allow large amounts of test data to be produced quickly and automatically.

Stress testing tools allow large volumes of transactions to be presented to the system. These are similar in function to some of the programs used for the 'denial of service' attacks discussed in Chapter 9.

Desktop testing tools allow some testing of mainframe systems on workstations.

Test management tools allow the testing process to be managed and controlled. They are similar in function to the project management tools discussed in Chapter 6 but are specific to testing.

We took a narrow view of testing in Chapter 7, only looking at testing during the construction and testing stages of the lifecycle. Test plan development can occur throughout the lifecycle and the quality control methods we discussed in Chapter 6 – walkthroughs and inspections – can also be regarded as part of the testing process. This is reflected in the following diagram:

Figure 8.18: Test Planning *v.* Systems Development Lifecycle

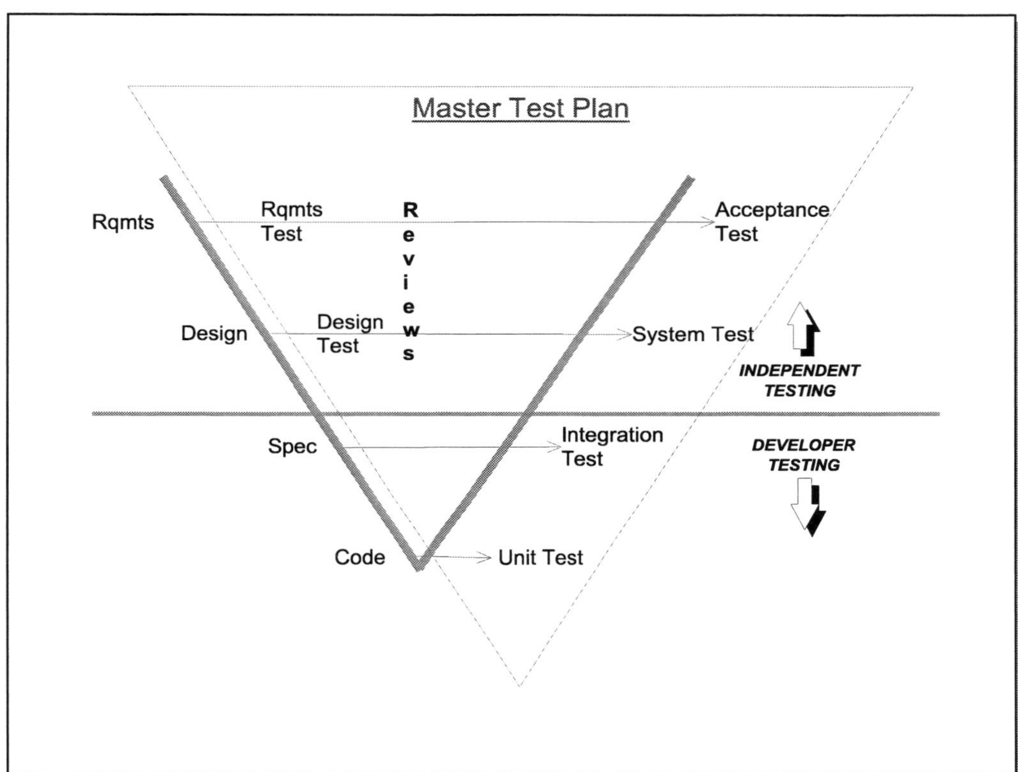

This defines the relationship between systems development lifecycle stages and testing stages:

- Acceptance testing must test the system against the requirements. Therefore the acceptance test plan can be drawn up as part of the requirements definition stage;
- System testing must ensure that all the system performs all the functions expected. Therefore the system test plan can be drawn up as part of the systems design stage;
- Integration testing. We did not discuss integration testing in Chapter 7, but this occurs late in the construction stage and involves testing the various computer programs together to ensure that they work as specified. Therefore the integration test plans can be drawn up when these programs are specified at the start of the construction stage;
- Unit testing is carried out by the programmer and provides his or her check that the program is working. Therefore the programmer will draw up the unit test plan in coding, during the construction stage.

9

RISK MANAGEMENT

Objectives

After studying this chapter, you should be able to:

- distinguish between a threat, a failure mode, a risk and an outcome;
- distinguish between business risk and project risk, and understand the particular uncertainty associated with the latter;
- distinguish between and describe data confidentiality, data availability and data integrity;
- understand and explain the main approaches for quantifying and managing risk;
- understand and be able to describe the main threats to data security:
  - threats due to malicious action
  - threats due to disaster
  - threats due to hardware or software failure;
- understand and be able to describe the main responses to these threats;
- understand how intellectual property can be protected;
- understand the issues associated with Internet security and the methods available to protect against threats on the Internet.

1 Introduction

Risk management is very important to the financial services industry. What is risk management? We shall start by drawing a distinction between a risk, a failure mode and a threat:

- A risk is an impact on the business. Therefore we can quantify risks – usually in terms of their financial impact, although safety risks are often quantified in terms of the likelihood of death or injury;
- A failure mode is a way in which something can go wrong;
- A threat is something that can cause failure – usually an external event that may or may

not happen. We can quantify threats in terms of probability – how likely they are to occur.

Let us illustrate this with an example:

- There is a risk that the authors will not complete this book in time. This has a quantifiable financial impact on the authors (who will not be paid) and on the Institute (who will need to commission another book);
- This could come about in various ways – the failure modes. For example, the authors may not have enough time, or they may suffer computer problems and lose their work;
- There are various threats that could cause failure. Insufficient time could be the result of additional work or changed family commitments (an external event), but it could also be the result of poor planning. Computer problems could be the result of hardware failure or a virus. We can assign probabilities to these (the probability of the authors being given additional work is close to 100%!).

We can also show this as a decision tree:

Figure 9.1: Risks, Failure Modes and Threats

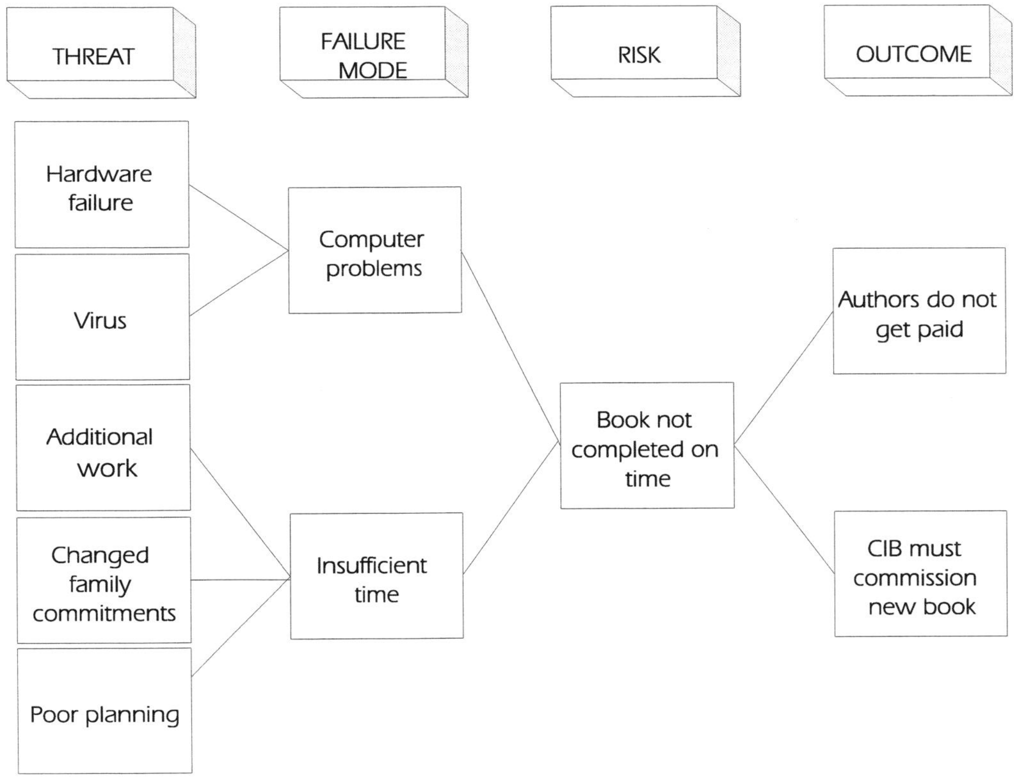

2 Business Risk and Project Risk

It is sometimes useful to draw a distinction between business risk and project risk.

Organizations have no choice about incurring risks in the normal course of business – it is the price of entry to the financial services industry. Projects are an investment and organizations must balance the risk against the expected reward before deciding whether to undertake the investment.

In addition, projects are very much more risky than normal business. There have been various studies on IT project success rates and these indicate the extent of the problem:

- Only 2% of projects are implemented without changes;
- Less than 16% of projects are implemented to time and budget;
- Only one third of projects are judged 'successful' by business management;
- 31% of projects are cancelled before completion;
- 15% of projects deliver absolutely nothing.

We must be careful not to read too much into these figures. Business requirements do change so we should expect projects to change or even to be cancelled to reflect this. However it does illustrate the uncertainties associated with projects.

We can think of normal business risk as having one dimension – we know what our business is but we do not know which of the various threats may materialize. With projects we have two additional dimensions:

- Process uncertainty. Each project is unique. Although the lifecycle gives us some guidance there is usually some uncertainty about the best way to do things;
- Control uncertainty. The control processes associated with projects are not always reliable. Whatever methods are used to ensure quality, it is impossible to be certain that the project will meet the requirement until it is implemented.

Risk management usually considers only the risk of failure, but sometimes the risk of success should also be considered. An example illustrating this is the launch of Egg, where the demand for access through the Internet was so great that the system was unable to cope.

Consultants Gartner Group have suggested a model for classifying project risk which looks at 'team risk' and 'technical risk'. Team risk looks at the knowledge and experience available within the project team. Technical risk looks at factors such as the size of the system and the familiarity of the project team with the technical environment for which in which the system will operate. A high level of uncertainty on both dimensions suggests a very high level of risk for a project.

3 Data Security

We discussed the financial services industry's responsibility for data security in Chapter 2, and this one of the most important aspects of risk management. We usually consider this under the headings:

- Data confidentiality (this is also called data privacy);
- Data availability;
- Data integrity.

We shall start by considering the threats to data security. How we manage these threats will depend of the potential loss or damage to the business – the risks associated with the threat. We also need to be aware of the particular threats posed by the nature of IT. IT allows:

- Much more information can be produced, which will need to be stored and disposed of securely;
- Information can be produced in a portable form, for example floppy disks, magnetic tapes and portable computers, which will need to be protected against theft;
- Transactions can be entered and enquiries made by anyone with access to a workstation attached to the computer network provided that he or she knows the passwords. Physical security is important to limit access to workstations and automated security checks such as passwords must be kept secret;
- Offices and branches are now almost totally dependent on IT to provide an acceptable level of customer service, so hardware, software and data needs to be protected against damage and plans need to be in place to restore service as soon as possible in the event of failure.

Quantifying Risk

To convert threats into risks we need to consider the probability of the threat being realized and the expected cost to the organization if it is. One method is Courtney risk analysis. The probability of the threat being realized in the next twelve months is multiplied by the expected cost to give an Annualized Loss Expectancy or ALE.

The expected cost itself depends on the possible consequences of the threat being realized and the cost of those consequences. Many threats have a range of possible consequences, some of which are very low risk because their financial implications are small or because the probability of that particular consequence is very small.

This assumes that both the probability and the cost can be quantified. This is often not the case and these must be estimated or alternatives must be used.

Scenario analysis can be used when it is difficult to estimate the probablility – often when a large number of factors are involved. The usual approach is to look at an 'optimistic' scenario, an 'expected' scenario and a 'pessimistic' scenario. The consequences of these scenarios are then estimated.

Scenario analysis does not give any absolute answers and much of the value of the technique comes from analysing how the organization might respond to the various threats.

Monte Carlo methods, also called stochastic analysis, can be used when it is difficult to estimate the cost. A model of the situation is set up and a large number of situations are put through it. A random number generator is used to change key variables. The results are averaged to give an estimated cost.

Another approach is called failure mode effect analysis (FMEA). This involves the following stages:

- Identify the potential failure modes;
- For each failure mode, identify the potential effects of failure;
- For each failure mode, identify the potential causes of failure. These are the threats;
- For each threat, identify how likely it is to occur. This is expressed as a number between 1 (low) and 10 (high);
- For each threat, identify how severe a problem it will cause if it does occur. This is expressed as a number between 1 (low) and 10 (high);
- For each threat, identify how likely it is that the threat will be detected. This is expressed as a number between 1 (high probability) and 10 (low probability);
- Multiply the likelihood of occurrence, the severity and the likelihood of detection to calculate a risk priority number (RPN). A high RPN indicates a major threat for which there must be countermeasures.

Managing Risk

Having quantified the risk, the next stage is to manage it. Lane defined four general approaches:

- Eliminate it
- Reduce it
- Ignore it
- Transfer it.

Eliminating the risk involves reducing to zero the probability that the threat will be realized. This is rarely possible, although some threats may materialize in a number of ways and it may be possible to eliminate some of these.

For example, we can eliminate the risk of computer viruses being introduced through infected floppy disks by using PCs that do not have floppy disk drives. It is still possible for computer viruses to be introduced over the network, however.

Reducing the risk involves either reducing the probability of the threat being realized or reducing the cost, or both. This is a common approach to risk management.

Ignoring the risk is feasible provided that the ALE is small and the cost is not excessive. This approach is common for small risks.

Risks can be transferred, either to a supplier or to an insurer. Should the risk be realized a supplier may have to put things right or pay compensation, or both. This approach is common, with suppliers being expected to provide warranty against failures.

Where a service is provided, for example where a supplier runs the financial services organization's computer systems (facilities management), service level agreements allow the risk of poor service to be transferred in much the same way.

Corporate assurance is similar to a warranty, except that a guarantor (rather than the supplier) provides the assurance. This is common where the supplier is a relatively small organization and the guarantor has a relationship with the supplier, for example in providing marketing support.

An insurer would simply pay the organization's loss. This is common, particularly where the probability of the risk being realized is low but the potential cost is high.

Another approach to managing risk is potential problem analysis. This builds on some of the ideas of FMEA and some of the stages are identical:

- Identify the potential problems (potential effects) of failure;
- For each potential problem, identify the possible causes of failure. We have described these as potential causes (FMEA) or threats;
- For each threat, identify how likely it is to occur. In potential problem analysis this is expressed as a number between 0.1 (low) and 1 (high);
- For each threat, identify how severe a problem it will cause if it does occur. This is expressed as a number between 1 (low) and 10 (high).

These are stage 2-5 in FMEA. The remaining stages in potential problem analysis are:

- Multiply the likelihood of occurrence by the severity to calculate a risk assessment. A high risk assessment indicates a major threat for which there must be countermeasures;
- For each threat, identify the possible preventative actions. Identify the cost of the preventative action;
- For each preventative action, identify the probability of its failing. This is expressed as a number between 0 (none – the preventative action is certain to succeed) and 1 (high);
- Multiply the risk assessment by the probability of the preventative action failing. If no preventative action has been identified the probability of its failing is 1;
- For threats where the risk assessment multiplied by the probability of failure is not zero, identify contingency plans to mitigate the effect of the threat. Identify the cost of contingency plans.

Potential problem analysis provides a structured framework for identifying preventative actions and contingency plans. However, the decision as to which actions and plans to put in place will depend also on the cost if the threat is realized.

Threats

We shall focus on three main categories of threat:

- Malicious action
- Disaster
- Hardware or software failure.

Malicious Action

Malicious action is carried out deliberately, either with the intention of doing damage or of committing another crime. The most important types of malicious action are:

- Hacking
- Introduction of a computer virus
- Fraud.

Other forms of malicious action are less common and include sabotage.

Hacking is unauthorized access to data or computer systems. The main types of hacking are:

- Use of the Internet to gain access to systems and data;
- Use of dial-up telecommunications links to gain access to systems and data;
- Electronic eavesdropping, including tapping telecommunications links;
- Internal hacking.

Most people would associate the word hacking with illegal access through the Internet and this is the most common form of external hacking.

With the increase in the use of the Internet, dial-up telecommunications links are perhaps less common than they used to be. They are still used to provide customers with access to PC banking services (although the Internet is increasingly taking a more prominent role). They are often used to provide a secondary communication link in case the main link fails. They are increasingly used to allow staff working outside the office to access organizations' systems and data through a cellular telephone link.

Hackers can use a 'demon dialler' to call telephone numbers randomly. When the response comes from a computer system the demon dialler stops and the hacker will attempt to gain access to the system, perhaps using a dictionary program to try passwords. Another approach is to try to cause an error in the system that will give the hacker access to the operating system. Once the hacker has identified a telephone number that gives access to a computer this may be shared with other hackers.

Electronic eavesdropping can use a wire tap on a telephone line. If wireless telecommunication or a cellular telephone link is used this can also be intercepted. The eavesdropper can listen to the message and potentially alter its content. A variant on this is to intercept the image of a computer screen. Computer screens emit radiation that can be detected using a tuneable monitor, which can recreate an image of the original screen.

A lot of hacking is internal. Staff access data and systems for which they are not authorized, either taking advantage of poor security systems or using stolen passwords. This is sometimes associated with fraud.

Although hacking is mainly seen as a threat to data confidentiality it can also threaten the integrity of the data. Hackers using the Internet or dial up connections are not always content just to look at the data but may also want to leave messages to announce what they have done. These messages may change the value of (or 'corrupt') data used by the system. Hackers may also change web sites.

Computer viruses are computer programs that can duplicate themselves. They 'infect' other programs by adding a copy of themselves to the end of the program. Some viruses are harmless but others can destroy data held on disk or even physically damage the computer. There are a number of different forms of virus, the most important of which are executable viruses, macro viruses and worms.

Executable viruses affect computer programs – for example .EXE and .COM files on PCs. These are the original and best-known type of computer virus.

Executable viruses work as follows:

- When an infected program is run, the program's first action is to write a copy of itself into memory. It will then go on to complete the program's normal functions;
- The copy of the virus in memory is actually a small computer program of a type called 'terminate and stay resident'. It does not do anything until another computer program starts;
- When another program starts, the virus will first check to see if it has already been infected. If it has, the virus will not do anything. If not, the virus will attach a copy of itself to the end of the program and will change the first instruction in the program so that the virus is run before the program does anything else. It will then write the program back to disk with the copy of the virus attached.

  Viruses check to see if the program has already been infected because they want to stay hidden for as long as possible. If a virus kept re-infecting the same program, the program size would increase (remember that viruses infect programs by adding a copy of themselves to the end) and it would soon be obvious by the increase in size that the program was infected.

  To see if programs have already been infected, viruses look for a 'signature'. This is a part of the virus that has an identifiable pattern. Some viruses (called 'polymorphic' viruses) continually change the pattern, which makes it harder for virus checker programs to identify them;
- Most viruses will not take any other action until a certain amount of time has passed or

until they have infected a number of other programs. This gives the virus the chance to spread as widely as possible. Once this has happened, the virus will wait for a trigger – usually a date, such as Frodo's birthday (September 22nd) for the Hobbit virus or Friday 13th for the virus of the same name;

- When the trigger arrives, the virus will take whatever action it is designed for. Despite the publicity attracted by viruses, many of them do little damage (the Hobbit virus simply displays the message 'Frodo Lives').

  Viruses such as this cause no damage to the data on the computer, or they may simply hide files (they are still stored on disk but the operator cannot see them). Other viruses delete files, but the operator can recover the data fairly simply provided he or she realizes what has happened. However, there are viruses that do more substantial damage, over-writing the contents of files with meaningless data or causing physical damage in some way.

Macro viruses affect the macros used with office automation software, especially word processors. They usually create an AutoOpen macro that will run automatically when the document is opened. The threat of macro viruses is growing faster than any other type of virus, because of the ease with which they can be spread using e-mail and because the older generation of virus checkers was unable to detect them.

In 1988, Robert T. Morris wrote a program – now referred to as the 'Internet Worm' – that crashed computers all over the USA. The program exploited several known security holes in the UNIX operating system, and gathered user and network information as it duplicated itself and spread from machine to machine. It also employed a dictionary of common and easily broken passwords to access user login accounts. The Worm also tried to hide its activity by changing its name to a common UNIX program, and even tried to erase any trace that it had penetrated the system in the first place. Estimates vary, but it was calculated that between 2,000 and 6,000 computers were infected by Morris' Worm program. Likewise, the financial cost was even harder to calculate, but figures quoted range between $1m and $100m. Morris was convicted in 1990 under the US 1986 Computer Fraud and Abuse Act, and was sentenced to 3 years probation, ordered to pay a $10,000 fine, forced to do 400 hours community service and even ordered to pay an additional $100 per month supervision costs during his probation period.

Worms affect networks. These used to be relatively rare, but the increasing popularity of e-mail has provided an effective method of spreading them. The virus is usually carried in an attachment to the e-mail and may be a macro virus or a computer program disguised as another type of file – for example, a word processor file, a picture or a music file. Opening the attachment activates the virus, which spreads by e-mailing copies of itself to people in the recipient's address book.

Worms are a particular threat. Because they spread directly, through the e-mail system, viruses can spread very rapidly and cause damage immediately. This also makes it difficult for anti-virus software to be introduced in time to combat the effects of the virus. The Love

Bug virus is estimated to have reached 45 million PCs on the first day and early estimates of the damage caused by the virus have been as high as £6 billion world-wide.

Trojans are programs that create security weaknesses. An example might be a program to steal passwords. Trojans are not viruses but are often spread by viruses – for example, the Love Bug virus installed password-stealing trojans on infected computers.

In most '*computer frauds*' the computer is used only to create the documentation – the fraud takes advantage of weaknesses in the organization's procedures and controls rather than in its computer systems. For example the computer can be used to record the receipt of false invoices, but this relies on a failure to reconcile invoices against orders and delivery notes.

Another type of fraud is the misuse of the organization's computer resources. Hugo Cornwall in 'Datatheft' gives the example of two employees who used their office computer to run a music rescoring business. They were using three-quarters of the available storage space before they were detected.

Disaster

Disaster includes various categories such as fire, smoke, flood and explosion.

The effects of fire are obvious and usually result in the complete loss of everything in the affected area – not only the computers but also magnetic disks, optical disks and magnetic tapes. Smoke can also produce damage over a much wider area, causing electrical short circuits and damaging magnetic disk drives.

Water also causes damage by short-circuiting electrical equipment. Water damage can be the result of flooding, burst pipes or sprinkler systems designed to combat fire. In many small office fires the threat of damage to computers from the sprinkler system is greater than the threat due to the fire!

Explosions can be due to gas leaks, chemical explosions, bombs or disasters such as air crashes. An explosion can cause great damage to computer equipment in the vicinity, warping disk drives and breaking circuit boards. Debris spread by the explosion as shrapnel may cause further damage. The explosion may be followed by a fire, resulting in additional damage due to the fire and smoke. Water damage may result from pipes fractured by the explosion and from sprinkler systems activated if there is a fire.

Hardware or Software Failure

The most common causes of hardware failure are wear and tear, and environmental factors such as variations in power supply. Wear and tear includes connections becoming loose, circuit boards cracking and disk drive read-write heads getting out of alignment. Variations in power supply include both electrical 'surges' and power cuts.

Peripheral equipment is equipment attached to the computer and is subject to a wide range of temporary failures including paper jams on printers and 'parity checks' on storage devices. Ionizing radiation (such as X-rays or ultraviolet radiation) or magnetic or electric fields can corrupt data held on magnetic storage devices such as disk or tape.

Telecommunications links are subject to various types of failure including lines being cut and electrical interference. Even if interference does not prevent messages being received the amount of 'noise' may make it impossible to interpret the signal correctly or the message received may not be the same as the message sent. Telecommunications components such as modems and multiplexors are also subject to the same causes of failure as other hardware devices.

Software failure is often the result of errors made when the software was written. The software may not have been designed to cope with a particular set of conditions and, when these occur, there will be an error. Alternatively the software may not work on the particular hardware (perhaps because there is insufficient storage space) or with other systems software components.

4 Risk Prevention

Before we look at specific responses to the types of threat we considered earlier, we need to consider the most important approaches to risk prevention. These are:

- Contingency sites;
- Fault tolerance;
- Backups and checkpoints;
- Passwords and access security;
- Encryption.

Two additional topics we will consider at this stage are business continuity planning and audit trails.

Contingency Sites

Contingency arrangements allow financial services organizations to use alternative computer equipment if they have a problem. Most such organizations have spare equipment of their own but it is also possible to make contingency arrangements with equipment suppliers or computer bureaux. There are two types of contingency arrangement, hot site and cold site.

Hot-site contingency means that the spare computer equipment is fully set up and loaded with the data needed to run the organization's systems. This may be up to date as at the start of the business day, or data may be copied to the contingency site on a regular basis. If the main computer system fails, the hot-site computer can be ready to take over.

This may not be immediate. Unless completed transactions are immediately copied to the contingency site there will be a need to re-process or re-enter data lost when the main system failed. Even so, it should be possible to restore access to systems and data within a relatively short time.

Cold-site contingency simply means that spare computer equipment is available. If the main computer system fails, the cold-site computer will need to be loaded with the programs and data required to run the organization's systems. Data lost when the main system failed will need to be re-processed or re-entered. This may take several hours.

Hot-site contingency is much more expensive than cold site. In effect the financial services organization needs to pay for two computers, only one of which will be fully used. Some organizations exploit this by splitting their workload between the two computers. If both are working neither is fully utilized, but they are able to carry out additional, lower-priority work. If one computer fails, all work is switched to the other and low-priority work is discontinued. Even if this approach is not used, some systems are so important that the extra cost of hot-site contingency can be justified. An example is a dealing system, where the organization could lose large amounts of money if it is unable to react to exchange rate changes.

Fault Tolerance

An alternative to contingency sites is the use of 'fault tolerant computers'. These are designed so that important components are duplicated – if the original fails the duplicate can take over. Fault tolerant computers are used where it is very important that computer systems do not break down, such as the payment systems CHAPS and SWIFT.

We can also apply the idea of fault tolerance to magnetic disk storage. RAID, which stands for a 'redundant array of inexpensive disks', can be used to store data. The data can be 'mirrored', with copies stored on two or more separate disks, so that the failure of one disk will not result in the data being lost. RAID allows data to be stored on cheap disks and to be at least as safe as data stored on more expensive, higher-quality disks.

An alternative to mirroring is 'striping'. Three disks are used, and the data is split between two of the drives. The data on the two drives is compared and the *difference* is written to the third drive. If one of the drives holding the data fails, this can be reconstructed from the other data drive and the drive holding the difference. Striping is possible because the computer can treat data as if it were a series of numbers and this is important for a number of risk-prevention techniques.

Backups and Checkpoints

Taking a backup involves copying data and programs to a removable storage medium such as magnetic tape, magnetic disk or optical disk. If the data or programs are later lost, the backup copies can be reloaded. This will not completely prevent the loss of data – transactions entered since the backup was taken will still have to be re-entered – but it will minimize the loss. All data and programs must be backed up regularly.

The usual approach is the three-generation (or 'grandfather-father-son') backup. Let us use this approach to see how we might take backups over a typical week:

- Monday's work will be processed. At the end of the day all data will be copied to magnetic tape (tape 1) and stored in a fireproof container;

- Tuesday's work will be processed and the data copied to tape 2 which will be stored in a fireproof container. Tape 1 will be sent to another location for safekeeping;
- Wednesday's work will be processed and the data copied to tape 3 which will be stored in a fireproof container. Tape 2 will be sent to another location for safekeeping. Tape 1 will be retrieved from storage and returned to the building;
- Thursday's work will be processed and the data copied to tape 1, overwriting Monday's work. Tape 1 will be stored in a fireproof container. Tape 3 will be sent to another location for safekeeping. Tape 2 will be retrieved from storage and returned to the building;
- Friday's work will be processed and the data copied to tape 2 which will be stored in a fireproof container. Tape 1 will be sent to another location for safekeeping. Tape 3 will be retrieved from storage and returned to the building.

If the data on the computer is found to be corrupt there are three backups available for recovery – the previous day's work (the 'son', stored on site in a fireproof container), the work from the day before that (the 'father', stored off site) and the work from the day before that (the 'grandfather', on site after retrieval from off-site storage). This allows for two types of problem:

- The backup tapes themselves may be corrupt. Three-generation backup provides three chances of finding a readable tape, although if the father or grandfather backups are used some data will have been lost and will have to be re-entered or re-processed;
- The problem may have arisen earlier in the week but may only just have been discovered. Three-generation backup allows the organization up to three days to discover any problems.

We have said that backups can be made to any removable storage medium. The choice of back-up medium depend on a number of factors, the most important of which are cost, robustness and the amount of programs and data which needs to be backed up.

- Cost. Cost can be expressed in terms of cost per megabyte (a megabyte is one million characters of information);
- Robustness. Robustness is the probability of the backup medium getting corrupted, so that the stored information cannot be read. Robustness can be expressed as the mean time between failures (MTBF) – the average number of hours usage before the medium fails;
- Amount of programs and data. This is also called volume and is the storage capacity of the medium.

Magnetic tape is one of the oldest media used for backup and is still one of the most important. It is very cheap, quite robust and can store very high volumes.

During the first and second generations of IT, magnetic tape was usually in the form of a reel of tape which had to be loaded manually and was suitable only for mainframe and minicomputers. This has now largely been replaced by magnetic tape cartridges, similar to video cartridges, and a smaller version is used for backing up personal computers. More recently, digital audio tape (DAT) has been introduced.

The main disadvantages of magnetic tape are that reloading backed-up data is slow and that data stored on magnetic tape can be corrupted, especially when the tape itself is heavily used. However, low cost and high capacity still make magnetic tape the most important medium for long-term storage of backed up information.

An important alternative is optical disk. This can be 'write only', which is cheaper and can hold more information, or rewritable. The price of optical disk has fallen greatly over recent years and it is now little more expensive that magnetic tape. It is robust and can store very high volumes.

A major advantage of optical disk is that it can be read randomly, like magnetic disk, and reloading backed-up information is much faster than for magnetic tape. Optical disk backup is often provided through 'jukeboxes' having a number of optical disk drives and a mechanism allowing optical disks to be loaded into the drives from an expansion rack.

Integrated storage units are becoming increasingly important. They will usually store current information on magnetic disk, older information to which access is still needed on optical disk and information for which access is rarely needed on magnetic tape. A particular feature of these units is that the user does not need to know where the information is stored to get access to it – the information can be requested using the standard database access language SQL and the unit will work out where it is stored and will retrieve it.

Removable magnetic disk storage is still often used, especially for personal computers. Floppy disks have been used for many years but their capacity is too low to be used for backing up significant amounts of information. More common is the 'zipdrive', a high-capacity floppy disk unit which uses data compression to allow it to store large amounts of data.

Data compression uses patterns in the data to reduce the amount that needs to be stored. The phrase 'the cat sat on the mat' contains 22 characters. If we replace 'the ' with '*' and 'at ' with '#', we can store this phrase as '*c#s#on *mat', which contains 12 characters (note that we have to put 'mat' rather than 'm#' because there is no final space). We have reduced the amount of storage needed by almost 50%.

Removable hard disk is also found, especially in the form of PC cards designed to fit into slots in portable computers. This is usually too expensive to be effective as backup and its main benefit is the ability for individuals to hold personal data and transfer this to any computer to which they have access.

Magnetic disk storage is generally more expensive than magnetic tape and only zipdrives offer cost or capacity comparable to optical disk. It is also less robust than the major alternatives. Information backed up onto floppy disk or removable hard disk can be read directly, with no delay while the data is reloaded, and this can be of benefit.

In spite of their low capacity, floppy disks continue to be used for backup because:

- Floppy disk drives are installed as standard in personal computers and can be used to back up programs and data at no additional cost;
- Data compression software such as WinZip allows them to be used for backup provided the amount of information to be stored is not too large. Note that the capacity of a floppy disk with data compression is still much lower than that of a zipdrive;
- Differential backup, which backs up only the program and data files that have changed, can be used to reduce the amount of storage required. The disadvantage of differential backup is that reloading the computer requires every differential backup to be applied in turn – a very time-consuming process and vulnerable to corruption affecting any backup in the series.

  A more sophisticated version of the differential backup, which is used on mainframe computers, is checkpointing. Instead of copying the whole of a data file, only the items of data that have changed are copied. This is much faster than copying the entire file and checkpointing can be used to recover from errors while processing individual transactions.

  Compare this with other forms of backup, where we have to recover from the start of the business day (or a previous business day if differential backup is used or there is a problem with the most recent backup). This would mean that almost an entire day's work might need to be re-entered if there was a problem towards the end of the business day. Checkpointing avoids this problem.

Passwords and Access Security

We can restrict access to systems by asking for a code to gain access. Each user will typically have a 'user ID' (which defines who the user is) and a 'password'.

The user ID is not necessarily secret. John Smith, employee number 12345678, may have a user ID of JohnSmith, SmithJ, SmithJ1 (if there is another J Smith in the organization) or 12345678. The user ID will not change and its long-term secrecy cannot be guaranteed.

The password must be kept secret. The user chooses a password and must change it regularly, usually on a monthly basis. The password must typically include between six and thirty two characters and the system may check to see that the new password is not too similar to the previous password. To gain access, the user must enter both the user ID and the current password correctly. To protect the secrecy of the password, the system will not show the characters of the password on the screen but will usually show a character such as '*' instead to prevent onlookers from identifying the password.

If the password is wrong the user will usually be allowed to enter it again, but many systems allow a maximum number of tries (typically three) and may prevent the user ID, the workstation itself or both being used after this maximum has been reached.

For each user ID, the system will store a security profile saying what the user can do and what data he or she can access. This usually gives a level of authority. For example, branch staff may be classified as tellers (who can only make enquiries), clerks (who can enter transactions or make changes), supervisors (who *cannot* enter transactions but *can* authorize them) and a manager (who can do anything, including change security profiles).

Variations on passwords include test keys, as used in telex messages, and code books. The code book can be used to validate messages sent over a network. Each branch has a unique list of codes. Whenever the manager wants to send a message he or she will use the next code in the list. The computer processing the message has a copy of the list of codes and will check that the correct code has been used for the branch. The code book itself is kept securely under lock and key.

Passwords can also be used to restrict access to hardware, for example workstations or terminals. Most personal computers have a 'power on password' which must be entered correctly to use the PC. Power on passwords apply to the computer itself and are not specific to a user or associated with a user ID. Workstations or terminals can have a security profile, for example to restrict which terminals can enter certain types of transaction. This is useful for ensuring that transactions such as money transfers can only be entered in secure areas. We can combine terminal profiles with individual profiles to provide a further level of security.

It is common automatically to 'log off' terminals from any systems to which they are attached if a period of time passes without anything being entered. This ensures that staff do not leave terminals in a position to enter transactions when they go to lunch or go home, for example. We can also restrict who is allowed to use certain terminals by checking the terminal against a list of valid user IDs.

An alternative is to use screensaver passwords. Screensavers are computer programs that put some form of moving pattern on the computer screen when it is not used for a period. The purpose of the screensaver is to protect the screen – if the same image remains on the screen for too long it will leave a permanent imprint. A password can be assigned to the screensaver and this will protect the system if it is left unattended.

Alternatives to user IDs and passwords include badges and biometrics. Badges can be required in order to activate terminals – this could be combined with a system where staff need badges to gain access to the premises. The badge is usually a magnetic stripe card which is swiped through or placed in a reader attached to the terminal. Smart cards can also be used and another alternative is the active badge or radio badge, which activates the terminal when it is within a certain distance of a sensor attached to the terminal.

A variation on this is often used for office banking. The customer uses a smart card which not only proves his or her identity to the system but also provides a key for coding and decoding messages sent to and from the bank. A new smart card is sent to the customer on a regular basis, changing the key used for encrypting messages.

Biometrics have started to gain acceptance as a means of identification. The most important methods currently are fingerprint recognition, iris recognition and voice recognition:

- Fingerprint recognition relies on the pattern of a fingerprint or thumbprint. Personal computer manufacturer Compaq now sells a fingerprint reader as an optional attachment.

This is perhaps the most likely approach to using biometrics for identifying individuals in an office environment;

- Iris recognition photographs the pattern of the iris. This has largely replaced the older method which used a laser to scan the pattern of blood vessels on the back of the retina. Nationwide Building Society has used iris recognition in an automated branch pilot in Swindon since mid-1998, and surveys suggest that 94% of customers would recommend its use. Three other European banks have plans to trial this technology;
- Voice recognition can be used in telephone banking and recognizes the pattern of the voice. Do not confuse voice recognition with speech recognition (which interprets speech) or voice response (which recognizes the tones from a touch tone telephone). Voice recognition systems achieve an accuracy of about 95% and are less reliable than fingerprint or iris recognition.

Encryption

Encryption is used to encode messages or data and is another technique that relies on the computer's ability to treat data as a series of numbers. When the computer encrypts data, it carries out a mathematical operation using the data and an encryption key.

The mathematical operation usually used is the 'exclusive OR' (XOR), but we can illustrate the principles using multiplication. If our encryption key is 67 and the data we wish to encrypt is 12345 we can multiply these to get 827115. It is impossible to get back to the original data without knowing the key.

In practice encryption keys are much larger than 67! 'Weak' encryption uses a key of 40 binary digits – allowing numbers of over one *million* million to be used. 'Strong' encryption starts at 56 binary digits – 72 thousand million million – and systems used to encrypt financial transactions may use 128 binary digits – three hundred million million million million million million.

Financial services organizations have two main requirements for encryption:

- To encode data held on portable computers. This is important because staff increasingly use portable computers when visiting customers' premises, to store information about both the customer relationship and any new business. This protects sensitive information if the portable computer is lost or stolen;
- To encode messages containing confidential information or carrying instructions for the transfer of value.

The example we have used is an example of symmetric or secret key encryption. We use the same key to encrypt and to decrypt the data. Therefore we must ensure that the encryption key is kept secret. The Data Encryption Standard (DES) is a symmetric key encryption standard.

The difficulty with using encryption to encode messages is that the sender needs to have access to the encryption key. If a financial services organization provides thousands of its customers with the key, how can this be kept confidential?

One possibility, which we have already discussed, is the use of smart cards to provide customers with encryption keys. However, issuing new smart cards every month is too expensive to be practical for the retail market. Other methods – using the telephone, post or e-mail – carry a risk of interception.

An alternative approach is to use different keys for encoding and decoding the message. The key used for encoding is called the 'public key' and the key used for decoding is called the 'private key'. Together the public and private keys are called the 'key pair' and there is a mathematical relationship between them. This is called asymmetric or public key encryption. Asymmetric encryption was developed by Rivest, Shamir and Adleman, after whom RSA encryption is named.

Asymmetric encryption is slower than symmetric encryption but provides better security. If someone wants to send a message to us, they will encrypt it using our public key. We then use our private key to decrypt it. If we want to reply, we use the other person's public key to encrypt the message and they will use their private key to decrypt it.

We can encrypt data using either hardware or software. Hardware encryption uses a special computer chip that automatically carries out the encryption process. It is faster than software encryption and is used where large amounts of data need to be encrypted. Software encryption is more flexible, and keys and algorithms (the method of encrypting the data) can more easily be changed.

There is also a form of encryption called steganography, in which the encoded message is hidden in a picture file. This is makes it difficult to detect whether an e-mail contains a coded message at all.

Business Continuity Planning

Business continuity planning attempts to answer the question, if any part of our IT systems fails what will we do? It is also called contingency planning, disaster planning or recovery planning.

The answer will depend to a large extent on the likely cost of the failure to the organization. There is no point in making elaborate plans to recover from systems failure if these cost more than the failure would. Techniques such as Courtney risk analysis are important to quantify the various risks and to identify how much should be spent on countermeasures.

Organizations need to be aware of the time value of different types of information. For example the loss of information about the organization's foreign exchange position, even for a few minutes, can be very expensive if rates change. The loss of information about customer balances for a very short period would generally be less expensive.

Most organizations will have recovery plans that cover a large-scale failure, perhaps the loss of a data centre or of a major part of the organization's telecommunications network. There is ample evidence that companies that suffer catastrophic failure such as fire can go out of business if they do not have adequate recovery plans.

Organizations may not bring the same level of planning to more localized failures. Offices and branches are often left to make their own plans for the failure of local components such as workstations and even LAN file servers. Although this approach is valid (a centrally imposed plan may be costly to develop and inflexible to implement) there do need to be checks to ensure that offices and branches have drawn up adequate plans. Although the immediate financial costs of failure within a branch may be small, the effect on customer service and satisfaction needs to be considered.

Audit Trails

Audit trails keep a record of everything which happens in the course of processing a transaction. The most common form of audit trail is a system 'log' which records all attempts to access systems and data. Attempts that are unsuccessful may well be shown on a separate security report for later investigation.

In addition to the system log, most systems in financial services organizations maintain their own audit trails. These systems usually require different people to enter and authorize transactions and maintain an audit trail by recording who entered and authorized each transaction, when it was entered and authorized and sometimes the terminals on which it was entered and authorized.

Audit trails do not prevent breaches of data protection, but they make it easier to detect and to identify who is responsible. Audit trails may also be needed to comply with the Police and Criminal Evidence Act 1984 and the Civil Evidence Act 1995.

5 Specific Responses to Threats

Let us return to our three main categories of threats:

- Malicious action
- Disaster
- Hardware or software failure.

How can we apply the risk prevention methods we have discussed to these, and what other methods can we use?

Malicious Action

Some of the approaches to risk prevention we have discussed above apply to the threats due to malicious action. For example:

- Backups allow programs and data to be recovered to their state before the malicious action took place;

- Passwords and access security prevent access to systems by hackers or by those intending to introduce a computer virus;
- Encryption prevents hackers from intercepting messages, either to breach data confidentiality or to alter the message with the intention of committing fraud. Encryption also prevents thieves from reading the data stored on a stolen portable computer.

In addition to these general measures, there are some specific measures financial services organizations can take to protect themselves against malicious action. These include:

- Eavesdropping detection
- Virus protection measures
- Authorization.

Electronic eavesdropping on telecommunications links can sometimes be detected, either because the signal received is not as strong as normal or because of increased static on the line. If either of these happen, the message can be delayed or switched to another line. As well as helping to counter eavesdropping, this ensures that messages are sent over the clearest possible line which reduces the chances of message corruption. This does not apply to wireless links because there is no loss of signal.

The Tempest standard defines the shielding required to ensure the radiation from a screen cannot be picked up on a tuneable monitor.

Virus protection measures include restrictions on sources of software, controls over microcomputer floppy disk drives, firewalls and virus-checking programs.

Restrictions on sources of software usually require that all software is obtained from reputable sources and is still sealed in its original packaging when it is delivered. Cheaper sources of software such as shareware are sometimes infected with computer viruses. If software media are not sealed in their original packaging there is a risk that they will have been used on a computer infected with a virus and will have picked up an infection that way (there are also licensing implications, as we discussed in Chapter 2).

A common source of virus infection is the use of floppy disks containing infected files. We can prevent this entirely by using workstations that do not have floppy disk drives. A more common but slightly less effective approach is to lock the floppy disk drives.

Firewalls are used to reduce the risk of infection over networks, especially the Internet.

There are two main types of virus-checking program:

- One type looks for the signatures of known viruses. This has the advantage of allowing a virus to be detected before the program is run, but it cannot detect new viruses (where the signature is not known to the virus checker) and it usually cannot detect polymorphic viruses, which change their signatures.

  All new microcomputer software should be checked using this type of program;

- The other type records information about all the programs on the computer. When it is run, it will check that the programs have not changed (remember that the virus adds a copy of itself to the end of the program).

  We cannot use the change in file size to identify virus infection. Viruses can change the information held about the file to hide the change in size. Instead we again rely on the ability of the computer to treat a computer program as a number. The virus checking program carries out mathematical calculations to produce a distinctive 'checksum' which is then stored in a file. The next time the virus checking program is run the checksum is recalculated and the value compared with that stored. If they are not the same this suggests a virus infection.

Another approach is to prevent any data being written to the area where computer programs are stored. This may take the form of setting up a separate area on the hard disk for software and preventing any changes to this data, or at least warning if such an attempt is made. This approach is often used to protect programs stored on the file servers of local area network.

Methods that rely on preventing or detecting changes in files are effective only against executable viruses. We want to be able to change word processor or spreadsheet files and templates, and we are forced to rely on signature detection to detect macro viruses.

Authorization involves another person – often a supervisor – checking the data back to the original input instructions and authorizing it. Authorization is used for transactions such as payments and new accounts where an error could be expensive for the organization.

Disaster

Some of the approaches to risk prevention we have discussed above apply to the threats due to disaster. For example:

- Contingency sites allow rapid recovery of the most important systems and data in the event of disaster;
- Backups allow programs and data to be recovered to their state before the disaster took place.

In addition to these general measures, there are some specific measures financial services organizations can take to protect themselves against disaster. These include:

- Fire prevention
- Flood prevention.

Fire prevention measures include the use of smoke detectors, fire alarms and fire doors. Fire extinguishers should be available and should use carbon dioxide or powder instead of water-based foam. Copies of back-up data stored on site should be kept in firesafes or fire-resistant cabinets.

Sprinkler systems should not be used near computer equipment because the water will cause damage. 'Halon gas' systems, which spray gas to smother a fire, are usually used near mainframe computer equipment.

Flood prevention measures include the use of false floors provided with drainage to allow small amounts of water (for example from a burst pipe) to drain away. Computer facilities such as data centres should not be sited where they are likely to be subject to flooding.

Hardware or Software Failure

Some of the approaches to risk prevention we have discussed above apply to the threats due to hardware or software failure. For example:

- Fault tolerance allows hardware to continue to operate even if some components fail;
- Backups and checkpoints allow programs and data to be recovered to their state before the failure took place.

In addition to these general measures, there are some specific measures financial services organizations can take to protect themselves against hardware or software failure. These include:

- Uninterruptable power supplies;
- Preventative maintenance;
- Parity checking and data correction.

Computers are very sensitive to variations in power. Some of the most sensitive equipment is protected by capacitors. In the event of power failure these supply power for long enough for the equipment to close down safely, preventing any damage. Another method is the use of surge protectors to prevent a power surge causing damage.

Uninterruptable power supplies are more sophisticated and can be used to ensure that voltage does not go outside the range acceptable to the computer. Large data centres will usually also have a standby generator, allowing rapid restoration of power in the event of power loss.

Computers, like cars, need regular maintenance to detect and sort out problems. This is called *preventative maintenance* because it helps to prevent the computer from failing when it is processing the organization's work.

Parity checking is used to identify corruption in data read from magnetic disk or tape, or received over a telecommunications link. It again relies on the ability of the computer to carry out mathematical operations on data. The results of these operations are stored as additional characters with the data. When the data is read or received, the computer repeats the calculations to see if it gets the same answer. If not this shows that the data has been corrupted.

Errors in data sent over telecommunications links can be corrected automatically. When the receiving device gets a block of data it checks the parity. If this is correct it will send an acknowledgement (ACK) back to the sending device. If the parity is incorrect it will send a negative acknowledgement (NAK) back, and the sending device will send the block again. A system of this type is called an Automatic Repeat Request (ARQ) system.

6 Protecting Intellectual Property

Software producers can protect themselves against illegal software copying in two main ways. The first is to make the user run a special computer program to install the software before using it. This can include a number of measures against copying:

- It can show the registered user's name whenever the software is used. This does not stop further copying but it makes it easier to identify software that has been illegally copied;
- It can keep a count of the number of times the software is installed. For a piece of software designed to be used by one person, two copies are usually allowed (one copy is for backup, in case the main copy is destroyed) and the install program cannot be run more than twice;
- It can record some information about the machine on which it is installed which makes it impossible to install the software on any other machine.

The second method is to make the user run the software with either a 'key disk' or a 'dongle'. A key disk is a floppy disk that contains information about the software. When the software is run it will check to see if the key disk is there and, if not, it will stop. A dongle is a small device that is attached to the back of the computer (where a printer would be attached). Again, if there is no dongle the software will not run.

The most common method is a requirement to install the software. Software pirates commonly use 'clone' programs in an attempt to copy floppy disks and CD-ROMs prior to installation, but these can be made difficult to copy exactly. Dongles are usually only found with special-purpose software.

Internet Security

It has been said that the problem with the Internet is 'security, security and security'. Why is this and how can we overcome it?

The problem is that the Internet is an open network. Anyone can connect to the Internet and the standards and protocols are widely published.

Another effect of the open nature of the Internet is that it can be (and is) used by criminals, terrorists and those opposed to their governments. Therefore, governments have been reluctant to allow the export of encryption technology and have attempted to secure control over encryption keys.

Examples of Security Breaches

There are many (in)famous cases of Internet security breaches, which demonstrate the problems faced by companies who enter cyberspace with their eyes firmly closed, or who underestimate the threat of internal or external hacking.

In 1993, Paul Bedworth, then a student at Edinburgh University, was acquitted of charges relating to unauthorized access to several computer systems worldwide. Bedworth's case was the first major trial brought under the newly introduced Computer Misuse Act 1990, which legislated against hacking in the UK. Bedworth was alleged to have used a dial-up account to gain access into a local university, and from there obtained unauthorized access to various high-profile computer networks and systems including British Telecom, Lloyds Bank and an EC computer system in Luxembourg. Bedworth's lawyer submitted a plea of 'computer addiction', stressing that Bedworth was not responsible for his own actions. The plea was successful, and Bedworth was subsequently acquitted (interestingly, Bedworth's co-accused pleaded guilty and was duly sentenced).

Another famous cases of Internet security attack is that directed at Cliff Stoll's computer network at Lawrence Berkeley Laboratory. Stoll spent a year tracking down his hacker, and the plot involved the CIA, FBI, foreign governments, the Strategic Defence Initiative (the so-called 'Star Wars' project) and the KGB. Stoll eventually tracked his attacker to West Germany – the hacker was eventually prosecuted and charged with espionage. Stoll later wrote about his experience in the book 'The Cuckoo's Egg'. It should be noted that Stoll only embarked on this epic manhunt because he noticed a difference in an accounting budget of only 75 cents, and was curious as to the cause!

There are also many groups who actively publish information on how to hack into computer systems, networks and other on-line resources such as web sites. One such organization is the Chaos Club based in Germany. In February 1997, members of the Club went on live German TV to demonstrate an ActiveX hacking program that allowed them to transfer money between bank accounts using the Quicken financial package developed by the company Intuit – and to transfer this money without having to provide the usual passwords required by the Quicken security system.

Another web site can be found at http://www.2600.com, which has 'before' and 'after' versions of famous web sites that have been hacked. These include web sites belonging to the UK Labour Party, the Conservative Party, the CIA (the group changed references of 'Central Intelligence Agency' to the 'Central Stupidity Agency'), NASA, the US Department of Justice, the Church of Christ and even the Spice Girls' web site. Another hacking organization is the Anti-Online Group which has a similar web site at: http://www.antionline.com.

How do security incidents occur? Security breaches are usually a result of weak links, weak services or internal threats.

- Weak links. Breaches are normally attributable to several factors occurring individually – but when they all occur together then mayhem usually ensues. For example, an easily-broken user password can let in a would-be hacker to cause damage, and if this user account is held on a computer system with known security holes (that have not been corrected) then the problem is easily compounded – even more so if the compromised account is the root or system administrator's account.
- Weak services. Internet services themselves are not 100% secure – they were never designed to be so. They were originally developed for the rapid exchange of information,

not to prevent hostile attacks. However, Internet services can be made secure easily enough in a number of ways; e.g. integrating a security module, using encryption, understanding the weaknesses, deploying best practice, staff training and education, etc.

- Internal threats. By far the biggest threat to computer systems is not, as one might first think, from an external hacker lurking somewhere on the Internet, possibly on the other side of the world. In fact, the biggest threat to computer and network security comes from staff internal to an organization. It is estimated that over 80% of security breaches originate from a company's own personnel. These staff members usually have the biggest motivation for causing such damage: they may have been ignored for a pay rise or job promotion, or may not get on well with their boss, or may have social or personal problems that increase the chance of them causing vicious or hostile damage to a corporation's valuable resources. They also have the best opportunity – staff are already inside the organization and do not need to gain physical access to the data and resources.

The main security weaknesses are in services, data and communications:

- Services. In theory, all Internet services are under possible threat or attack. This includes internal and external e-mail, company web sites, file transfer facilities, remote logins, networked (shared) file resources, etc. Although all these services have the ability to introduce loopholes, careful deployment of the technologies, and a firm understanding of their limitations, should ensure all is relatively risk-free;
- Data. Corporate information and data is probably the greatest company asset, and it should therefore be protected. However, it can still be compromised; a troublesome staff member may decide to copy, destroy, sell or otherwise tamper with this information. Such actions should be planned for and suitable countermeasures introduced;
- Communications. This same corporate data could also be intercepted as it travels from one computer to another (either on the same Local Area Network or over the Internet). Software applications and hardware devices are available that allow such 'sniffing' or 'snooping' of information when its in transit. One possible solution to this problem is to encrypt all data as it travels across the internal network as well as out onto the Internet.

There are many types of attack that can be used and directed towards computers, networks and other resources. Perhaps the four most common are:

- Denial of service. This type of attack involves a user or intruder taking up so much of a system resource that none is left for other legitimate users. The attack itself can take several forms: destructive attacks (re-formatting hard disks, deletion of system-critical files, cutting power or network cables etc.); overload attacks (continually querying a server so that it cannot process valid requests etc.); file system attacks (filling up all available disk space thus not allowing others to save data/files etc.).

  Denial of service attacks over the Internet are sometimes called cracking. Trojans are planted on innocent systems that will, on activation, query the target server. This makes the source of these attacks very difficult to identify;

- Spoofing/impersonation. Both computers and individuals can be impersonated and forged. Computers can easily be configured with fake or forged IP addresses that can subsequently allow access to specific networks, resources and information. Similarly, individuals can use 'social engineering' techniques to try to obtain privileged information. The classic example is someone telephoning the technical support desk and saying: 'Hi. This is Fred over in Accounts. I've forgotten the password to access the payroll data. Can you let me have it please?'
- System intrusion. If corporate resources have succumbed to an attack, then it is likely that an intruder will be able to wander around the networked systems and resources. What they do while they are on their 'electronic stroll' is open to question depending on how they feel at that particular time. They may be kind and leave everything untouched, or they may be particularly nasty and delete files, tamper with user accounts, crash machines, leave backdoors to gain future (unnoticed) access, send fake e-mails, corrupt web sites – the list is endless;
- Data corruption and disclosure. Corporate data is valuable and must be safeguarded and protected – otherwise it may well be destroyed and/or duplicated by an intruder. The integrity of the data will come under question – how can the organization be sure that it was not edited, tampered with, or changed in some other way? How can the organization now control who gets to see it? Will it be sold to a corporate competitor?

Public Key Infrastructure

A particular problem with carrying out a transaction electronically is, how to identify the parties?

This is similar in some ways to the problem of 'card not present' credit card transactions. Cardholders receive a measure of protection in these transactions through indemnities, rules on delivering goods to the cardholder's registered address and expert systems that can identify attempted fraud. These measures are not generally available for electronic transactions.

One approach is to use a digital signature. This allows an individual to establish that he or she sent the message – provided the recipient knows the sender. In many cases the recipient will not know the sender personally.

An alternative is to use a Public Key Infrastructure. This allows the sender to be issued with a digital certificate to establish his or her identity.

Digital Signatures

With asymmetric encryption the message is encoded using the recipient's public key, with the recipient using the private key to decode it on receipt. A digital signature works the other way round – the sender uses his or her *private* key to encrypt the signature information. The recipient will use the *public* key to decode it. This proves the identity of the sender, as the only person to know the private key. We call this the signature key pair to distinguish it from the encryption key pair.

Digital Certificates

A digital certificate is an electronic identity document issued by a certification authority and corresponding to a physical identity document such as a driver's licence or passport used to identify the parties in a physical transaction. A digital certificate may contain information such as:

- Identification information (for example name and address) for the certificate holder;
- The certificate holder's public key;
- Information about the certificate (for example serial number and validity dates);
- Identification information about the certification authority who issues the certificate;
- The certification authority's digital signature. This allows the parties to the transaction to authenticate the digital certificate.

The certificate must be issued through a 'trusted third party' in which all parties to the transaction have confidence. There will be a 'certification hierarchy' by which a certification authority of undoubted probity can certify others to issue digital certificates. Financial services organizations could act as certification authorities or trusted third parties.

The integrity of the certificate-issuing process must be clear. Certification authorities must issue certificates only to parties of whose identities they are certain and must have systems for tracking certificates in issue. There must be a certificate revocation list to identify unauthorized and expired certificates.

Digital certificates are generally issued as software at present. This creates a potential security weakness and the security of the digital certificate can be compromised if the keys are known. In future it is likely that smart cards will be used to store digital certificates, providing additional security.

Digital Envelopes

Another security device is a digital envelope. This combines symmetric and asymmetric encryption. The system generates a random symmetric key that is encrypted using the recipient's public key and sent to the recipient. The message is encoded using the symmetric key before being sent with the encoded key in the digital envelope. This provides an additional level of security.

Secure Electronic Transaction Standard

The Secure Electronic Transaction standard (SET) was developed by Visa and MasterCard as a method of protecting financial transactions over the Internet. It makes use of encryption and digital certificates. As SET is restricted purely to financial transactions it is not subject to the US government restrictions on the export of encryption technology. SET also allows brand differentiation between the Visa and MasterCard payment networks.

SET meets five major business requirements:

- It ensures the integrity of the data;
- It protects the confidentiality of payment and other information forming part of the transaction;
- It provides authentication of the cardholder's identity and status as a legitimate user of a payment card account;
- It provides authentication of a merchant's identity and ability to accept payment card transactions through an acquiring financial institution;
- It creates a set of rules that is independent of the security mechanisms used.

Integrity is ensured through a 'message digest'. This operates on the same principle as the checksum we described above. The message digest is encrypted using the signature key, allowing any recipient to make sure that the message has not been altered.

Confidentiality is preserved through encryption. We may want different parts of the transaction to be accessed by different parties – for example we may want a financial services organization to have access to the payment details and the counterparty to have access to the commercial details. SET allows a 'dual signature' by which different parts of a message can be kept confidential. There is one dual signature that covers both parts of the message. This includes the message digests, allowing the parties to have confidence that the messages have not been altered.

Digital certificates are used to authenticate the identity of all parties to the transaction. As well as the purchaser and merchant, these will include the payment gateway and the acquirer. The certification hierarchy is used to verify these certificates.

Although the account number is needed to validate the cardholder's certificate, the account number is not held on the certificate and cannot be calculated from it.

An alternative approach, which also uses both public key encryption and digital signatures, is the Secure Sockets Layer (SSL) developed by Netscape. One advantage of SSL is that the SSL client is included as standard in Netscape's Navigator browser so customers do not need any additional software. SSL is widely used in the USA for e-commerce.

Firewalls

A firewall includes software and sometimes hardware and protects the organization from viruses and other forms of malicious action. If the firewall does not have its own hardware it is installed on a router. There are two types of firewall:

- Filtering firewalls. A filtering firewall allows only specified types of data through. For example, a filtering firewall can be set to allow Internet access for e-mail only;

- Proxies. A proxy is more sophisticated. Instead of allowing data through the proxy 'pretends' to be the organization's systems to anyone trying to access them externally and pretends to be the external network (for example the Internet) to anyone trying to access it from inside the organization.

  This allows the proxy to examine the data much more thoroughly than with a filter firewall and proxies are better at detecting and eliminating attacks such as viruses.

In practice most firewalls combine both approaches.

Firewalls also provide other services including:

- Providing an audit trail of all data passing through the firewall;
- Providing an alarm about apparent attempted security breaches;
- Supporting network address translation (NAT). NAT allows us to use different addresses within and outside the organization. This is very important if we want people to be able to send e-mail over the Internet to people within the organization – it hides the real address and also allows us to register a single IP address rather than one for each server;
- Some firewalls allow authentication of security devices such as smart cards;
- Some firewalls can operate a virtual private network (VPN). A VPN uses public links but messages are wrapped in a digital envelope to provide a very high level of security.

Handshakes

Handshaking allows two computing devices to recognize each other. This involves an exchange of information between the devices before any sensitive information is sent. The concept is similar to that of a digital certificate but it identifies devices rather than individuals.

This was used in ATM networks operating on a remote batch basis to ensure that the ATM was connected to the financial services organization's mainframe before sending details of any ATM transactions.

It is also used in the Mondex system. Mondex only allows e-cash to be transferred between Mondex cards, and the cards go through a handshaking routine before any transfer. This could also be used in transferring e-cash across the Internet.

Cookies

A cookie is a small text file stored on the PC's hard disk. When we access a web page it may update the cookie file.

Cookies are used to store identification information about the PC. This is similar in principle to handshaking but is for convenience rather than security. It can be helpful because the web site will not need to ask again for information it already has. Cookies are particularly useful for holding registration information because the web site will know that the user is already registered the next time it is accessed.

Cookies are text files and cannot carry viruses. A cookie can be accessed only by the web site that created it and cannot be used to trawl for information about what sites the PC has accessed. Current versions of browsers allow users to request a warning before cookies are created or to refuse to accept all cookies.

10

Quality Management and Organizational Change

Objectives

After studying this chapter, you should be able to understand and to describe:

- quality management;
- issue management;
- change management;
- configuration management;
- service management;
- problem management;
- management of benefits;
- management of expectations;
- management of change;
- Total Quality Management.

1 Introduction

This chapter considers the other disciplines that support the development process, including quality management, the operations management disciplines (issue management, change management, configuration management, service management and problem management) and the organizational change disciplines (benefits management, expectations management and management of change).

2 Quality Management

The concept of quality is poorly understood. It may help to start with four definitions:

- Quality is defined as 'fitness for purpose' – how good something is at doing the job for which it is intended. If we want a family runabout, we buy a Ford Mondeo in preference to a Rolls Royce. For this particular purpose, the Ford Mondeo is the 'quality' car;

- Quality assurance (QA) is concerned with ensuring that all the checks in a defined process have been completed. The Systems Development Lifecycle, for example, usually has checks at the end of each stage and QA ensures that these have been carried out;
- Quality control (QC) is concerned that the tasks in the process are carried out to standard. This is measured by the checks built into the process. Quality control is discussed in Chapter 6;
- Total Quality Management (TQM) brings together QA and QC into an approach for managing quality throughout a process or an organization.

QA can be validated externally and quality standards such as BS5750 and ISO9000 are QA standards.

3 Operations Disciplines

Issue Management

An issue is anything that arises during the project which needs to be resolved before project completion. Issues may include items such as:

- Possible new legislation that could have an impact on the project;
- Changes to the organization's strategy that could change the project's priority;
- Competitor activity to which the project may need to respond.

The distinctive feature of issues is that they cannot be resolved by the project team or the sponsor alone. They will usually require a decision from executive management and may require outside opinion – for example, from the Inland Revenue, regulatory bodies or legal opinion from counsel.

The issue management process is as follows:

- Record the issue on an issues log;
- Identify the impact of the issue and the date by which it must be resolved;
- Identify the appropriate escalation route and allocate responsibility for resolution;
- If necessary, seek the sponsor's approval for any budget required (e.g. for external legal opinion);
- Escalate the issue;
- Monitor the issue resolution process and, if necessary, follow the issue up to ensure that it is resolved in time.

Change Management

Changes can arise during the development process as a result of:

- Changing business requirements. Major changes to market activity will affect the system and competitive activity, or customer pressure may well change the functional requirements;
- The issue management process. Resolution of issues may change the scope of the project;
- Problems encountered during the development process. A common example of this is where a system component from an external vendor does not work in the way expected. The system may need to be changed to use a different component or to perform additional tasks to remedy deficiencies in the component. More rarely, the component may have capabilities beyond those anticipated allowing it to perform tasks that the system itself would otherwise have to perform;
- Changing technology. Changing technology during a project is not usually recommended but it may be necessary. One example is where the intended technology is becoming obsolete. The project team may have to choose between changing technology and proceeding in the knowledge that competitors will be able to leapfrog them by using the new technology.

Change can also arise after the system has been implemented as a result of either changes in business requirements or problems with the system.

The change management process starts when a change request is raised. The stages are as follows:

- Record the change request;
- Link the change request to any corresponding issue or problem record;
- Analyse the impact of the requested change;
- Review the change. This is usually carried out by a Change Control Board of senior managers who will decide whether the change will go ahead and allocate a priority to it. Small changes can sometimes be approved under a small changes budget without approval by the Change Control Board;
- Schedule the change;
- Small changes will often be bundled together into a software 'release' to avoid staff being subject to constant minor system changes. Large changes such as the implementation of a new system will usually form a release on their own.

Release management is a part of change management. Releases are often designed so that small changes can be individually switched on or off, allowing them to be switched off if we want to go back to the previous version.

Configuration Management

When we make changes to a system, we do not simply replace the old system component with a new one. Instead we create a new version of the system component and change the system to use the new version rather than the old one. There are two main reasons for this:

- We may want to go back to the old version. The new version may not work, or may cause problems with another part of the system or we may find that the change does not achieve our objectives. Creating a new version and keeping the old one makes it easier to go back;
- We want to keep an audit trail of changes to the system. If we did not do this, it would be easy to commit fraud by changing the system, putting through a fraudulent transaction and then changing the system back again.

Configuration management involves the following:

- If a system component is to be changed it needs to be 'checked out'. This avoids problems where several people are trying to change the same system component simultaneously;
- The change is made and tested;
- The system component is 'checked in', assigned a new version number and scheduled for release into the production environment.

Software library management tools can be used to control access to software components, including check in/check out and version control.

Service Management

Service management controls the performance of the system. This is specified in a service level agreement and a failure to meet the agreed level of service may be reported as a fault. Service level agreements cover aspects such as response times to enquiries entered through the screen, when the service will be available for use and the proportion of time the system should be working. Service level agreements may also cover fault correction, setting maximum times for the investigation and correction of faults by type and priority.

Problem Management

Problem management starts with a problem report (fault report) being raised and allows users to report perceived problems for resolution. The user will also indicate the priority allocated to its correction. The stages in the problem management process are:

- Record the problem and allocate responsibility for dealing with it;
- Check that it is a problem. Problem reports are sometimes raised because the user is not fully trained in the use of the system or has not consulted the system documentation;
- Analyse the causes of the problem and identify what changes need to be made to rectify it;
- Progress the changes through the relevant stages of the change control process;

- When the problem has been rectified, mark the problem report as closed.

4 Organizational Change Disciplines

Managing Benefits

Managing benefits is an increasingly important part of systems development. Benefits management involves:

- Identify anticipated benefits as part of the initial business case;
- Identify how to measure whether the benefits have been achieved and allocate responsibility for realizing each benefit to the relevant senior manager in the business;
- Ensure that the information required to assess the achievement of the benefits is collected and monitor progress towards it;
- Assess whether the benefits have been achieved as part of the post-implementation review.

An alternative approach is[1]:

Figure 10.1: Benefits Management

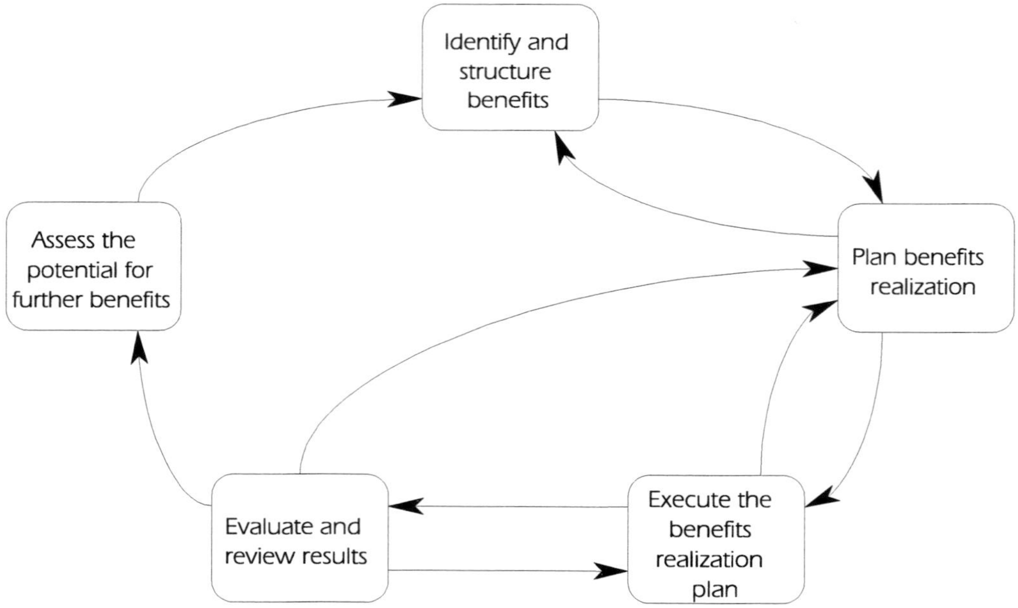

These are best practice and many organizations still make little systematic attempt to assess whether the benefits anticipated are realized in practice. Note that measures such as number

1 J. Ward and P. Griffiths *Strategic Planning for Information Systems* (John Wiley 1996)

of staff employed are not good for benefits measurement because they are affected by other factors such as changes in business volumes.

Managing Expectations

One reason why project sponsors are often disappointed by the results of systems development is a failure to manage expectations. Business cases may present an optimistic assessment which may not be realized in practice.

One way of investigating this is to compare the actual NPV of benefits realized with the NPV forecast by the business case. For projects intended to produce cost savings the benefits realized are 110% of the benefits forecast. For projects intended to produce increased sales the benefits are 60% of forecast. For new products they are only 10% of forecast.

Stakeholders may also develop unrealistic expectations. The development process involves finding out what the business wants. This may create the expectation that all the requirements identified will be satisfied.

Those involved in systems development must set realistic expectations and manage these actively. This includes:

- A clear distinction between the 'vision' of what is expected in the long term and what will be delivered initially;
- A focus on the 'must have' requirements rather than those that are less important;
- Open acknowledgement that not everything that is requested will be delivered;
- A means of 'parking' requirements that are identified as important but which fall outside the scope of the development.

Managing Change

In this context, managing change is concerned with organizational change and not with change control. We can look at managing change through the transition curve:

Figure 10.2: The Transition Curve

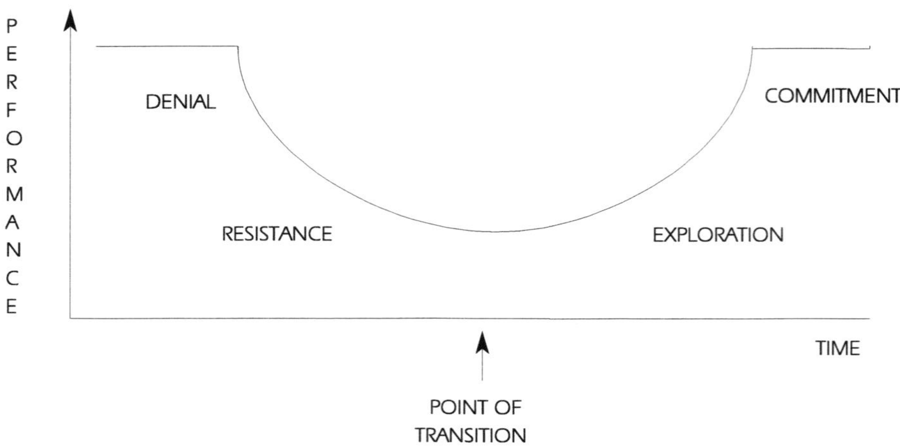

The stages are:

- Denial. The first stage is a denial that the change will happen, or that the change will affect the individual;
- Resistance. The second stage is resistance to the change which often takes the form of non-cooperation with those implementing the change;
- Exploration. The third stage is an acceptance that the change is going to happen and exploration of its possible consequences for the individual;
- Commitment. The fourth stage is the individual's commitment to the change.

The objective of managing change is to ensure that fastest possible progression through the stages to commitment.

Managing change is a complex subject deserving of a book of its own. Two important models of change are:

- The force field model. This looks at change as a balance of driving forces and restraining forces. Change will occur only if the driving forces are stronger than the restraining forces. This can be achieved by strengthening the driving forces or weakening the restraining forces.

Figure 10.3: The Force Field Model

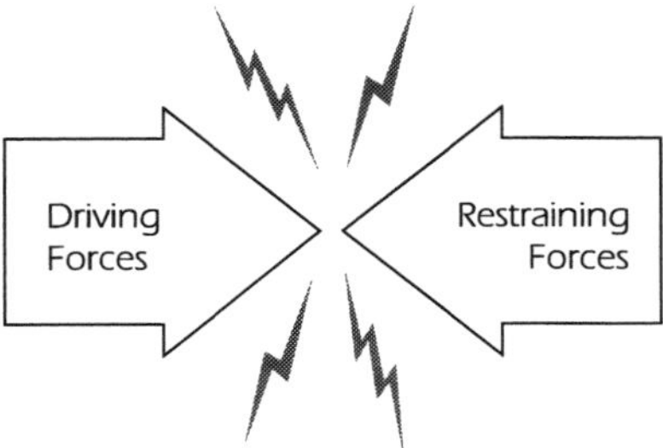

- The unfreeze-change-refreeze model. This looks at the process of change. The first stage is to 'unfreeze' the current situation. This includes making people aware that change is inevitable. The second stage is to make the change. The third stage is to 'refreeze' the situation into the new pattern. This includes reinforcing the change and making sure that people do not revert to their old pattern of behaviour.

In the context of information management the key processes are:

- Communication. The project team should communicate with all stakeholders throughout the process.

  Communication is essential to manage expectations. If this does not take place, stakeholders will be influenced by the grapevine and 'fear, uncertainty and doubt' (FUD). Communication helps to weaken the restraining forces and is important both in unfreezing the current situation and refreezing the changed situation;

- Consultation. As far as is possible, all affected stakeholders should be consulted and involved in the process. Some groups, such as the trade unions, may need a formal consultation structure.

  Consultation gives a sense of ownership of the change. Those consulted may also be able to identify possible problems with the change and suggest improvements. Consultation helps to weaken the restraining forces and can improve the quality of the change;

- Training. Those expected to work with the system will need to be trained in its use.

  We discuss the benefits of training in Chapter 11. Training is critical to the refreezing process;

- Support. Those affected by the change need both technical and personal support.

  Technical support usually takes the form of helplines. Personal support may be provided through counselling and assistance, especially to those whose jobs will be adversely affected by the change. Even where people are not directly affected they may still need support – 'survivor syndrome' is a bereavement reaction found in organizations where large numbers of staff have been made redundant. Support is important to the refreezing process;

- Continuous improvement. Major changes are rarely perfect when they are first implemented and a programme of continuous improvement is of benefit in eliminating any problems. It has the further benefit of transferring ownership of the new system to those who are using it.

  Continuous improvement is part of the refreezing process. It is likely to produce further changes to the system to support or implement the changes made and weakens the restraining forces for these subsequent changes. The idea of continuous improvement is strongly associated with the Total Quality Management ideas of W Edwards Deming.

Total Quality Management

We defined quality as 'fitness for purpose'. Another way of expressing this might be to define quality as 'conformance to the customer's requirements through setting and monitoring standards and ensuring value for money by avoiding extra checking, reworking and servicing' or 'giving customers what they want when and where they want it at the right price without mistakes'.

Quality in this context does not mean luxury (e.g. a Rolls Royce may not be a quality product if it does not provide what the customer wanted, equally a MacDonald's hamburger while being a low-cost item may be a quality product if it fulfils the customer's requirement).

Many companies set service levels and define acceptable levels of service, a company may for example consider that an error rate of 1% is acceptable. On the face of it a 99% success rate may be considered reasonable but would you fly with an airline that considered this failure rate acceptable?

Total Quality Management is a philosophy where the objective is to conform fully, without error, to the customers' requirements.

TQM is focused on the requirements of the customer. A satisfied customer will return, an unhappy or dissatisfied customer will not.

It is generally agreed that TQM originated in Japan after World War II. American Dr W Edwards Deming, working with the US Army in Japan, convinced Japanese industrialists that the production of reliable goods at lower prices was the way to take on, and to beat, the Western manufacturers. Deming was a statistician and his approach to quality control was based on his experience of consumer research and analysis. Instead of designing a product and then trying to stimulate a demand for that product, his approach was based first of all on the identification of the needs of the consumer and then developing and manufacturing products to meet those needs, to the required standards, at the lowest prices.

Financial services is about long-term customer value. Customers are encouraged to stay with a bank for their entire life and therefore repeat business is critical to the success of a financial services organization.

Research has shown, however, that financial services organizations are not always very good at maintaining customers in the long term, for example an analysis of why customers close their accounts shows:

- 40% close because of poor service;
- 13% because of unhelpful staff;
- 11% consider banks impersonal.

It is also considered to cost six times as much to acquire a new account as to retain an existing account.

Dr Joseph Juran regards the commitment of management to quality as the first and most important factor in successfully achieving a TQM programme. In his book, *Planning for Quality* (Free Press 1988), Juran defines an approach in three stages:

- Quality planning
- Quality control
- Quality improvement.

Juran explains this approach in his 'quality planning roadmap', the key elements of which are:

- Who are the customers?
- What are their needs?
- How are those needs best described?
- Develop a product that meets those needs;
- Design the product to meet our needs as well as the needs of our customers;
- Develop the means to make the product;
- Design the most favourable method of making the product;
- Prove that the method can produce the product successfully under actual operating conditions;
- Transfer the process to operations.

11

USABILITY AND TRAINING

Objectives

After studying this chapter, you should be able to understand:

- the importance of the user interface and how good user interface design can improve usability;
- and be able to discuss different views of the role of training;
- and be able to discuss the training process;
- and be able to discuss the relationship between training and learning;
- and be able to discuss the relationship between training and information technology;
- and be able to describe and compare:
  - on-the-job training methods
  - off-the-job training methods.

1 Introduction

If we are to benefit from a computer system we need to be able to use it. This chapter considers usability as a general topic as well as the more specific topic of training.

2 Designing the User Interface

The part of the computer system we interact with is called the user interface. It has always been important to design the user interface so it is easy to use, but with systems used by an ever increasing number of people this is more important than ever. The recent trends towards outsourcing to the customer and multi-channel banking are other factors influencing user interface design.

Graphical User Interfaces are one way of improving the ease of use – usability – of computers. Usability is very important for employees (where improving usability reduces training costs and can reduce errors and rework) and where customers have to use the systems directly.

GUIs provide a very easy way for users to give instructions to the computer. The advantages of using GUIs rather than 'character based' user interfaces are:

- Without GUIs, users would need to learn a complicated language in order to tell the computer what to do;
- GUIs can be used for communicating with any computer program. This makes it quicker to train people because GUIs are so easy to use. It also makes it much easier to train people to use different computer programs because systems which use GUIs look very similar to the user.

There are a number of rules for improving usability:

- Clear screen design. In particular, good contrast between foreground and background colours. Screens should not contain too much (a screen that is too cluttered is described as 'busy');
- Screens should follow the natural order of the transaction as far as possible. If data is entered into the screen from a form, the design of the screen and the form should be similar. If data is entered directly during an interview or over the telephone the screen design should be in the order of the conversation;
- Navigation. If there is more than one screen, the screens should be in a logical order and the movement from one to the next (the navigation) should be obvious. It should usually be possible to go back to previous screens to change or add information. It should usually be possible to leave the screens simply – it should not be possible to get lost;
- Information about what the system is doing. If the system is doing something this should be obvious (PCs usually show an 'hourglass' symbol). If the system is waiting for the user to enter something this should be obvious (systems often show the cursor flashing in the field in which data is to be entered).

Other ways of improving usability include help screens. These can either offer an index for the user to look up the topics required or can provide help about what the user is trying to do (context sensitive help). A variant on context sensitive help is cue cards – as the cursor is moved around the screen cue cards appear telling the user what to do. Assistants are very similar to cue cards.

Electronic Product Support Systems (EPSS) include help screens, reference material, training material and 'field notes', allowing users to report on problems or to give hints and tips that might be useful to others.

Some systems can 'learn' the preferences of their users. This is called intuitiveness.

3 Training

Training is very important if we are to realize the benefits IT offers. Staff need training to understand how to use and get the best out of the systems available to them. Training is also important as a motivator. It increases employees' skills and represents a real and obvious investment by the employer in the employee. This has become more important as career expectations have changed. The traditional 'job for life' expected by financial organizations' employees has been replaced by greater uncertainty.

Training is 'a planned process to modify attitude, knowledge or skill behaviour through learning experience to achieve effective performance in an activity or range of activities. Its purpose, in the work situation, is to develop the abilities of the individual and to satisfy the current and future manpower needs of the organization'[1].

Training is often seen only in terms of the training methods used – attending a course, for example. This is a very narrow view and training should be seen as:

- A planned activity;
- An investment;
- Part of the personal development process;
- Part of the learning process.

IT has also introduced new training methods and new ways of delivering established training methods. An example of the latter is the proposal to introduce a 'University of the Internet' in which lectures will be broadcast around the world using Internet technology.

Training as a Planned Activity

We can view training as a six-stage process[2]:

- Identify the learning requirement;
- Set learning objectives;
- Determine training strategy;
- Design and plan the training;
- Implement the training;
- Evaluate the training.

Identify the Learning Requirement

One way to identify training needs is to look at the 'skills gap'. This is the gap between what the employee can do and the needs of the job. You should not only consider what the job is now, but also how the job is going to change (for example, through the introduction of new technology) and the employee's next job.

1 Manpower Services Commission *Glossary of Training Terms* 1981

2 John Kenney and Margaret Reid *Training Interventions* (Institute of Personnel Management 1988)

An alternative approach is to look at 'competencies'. These are underlying characteristics that affect an employee's ability to do the job. An example of a competency might be written and verbal communication. Assessment of competencies is often used for identifying long-term career development needs.

Set Learning Objectives

You need to set training objectives that will meet the training requirement. You cannot always do this directly – there are some needs which cannot be fully met by training. Lending is an example of this – you can teach the basic techniques but the character judgement which is a key part of it needs to be developed by experience.

Training objectives need to be 'SMART' – specific, measurable, achievable, relevant and timebound.

Determine Training Strategy

The training strategy is the overall approach – in particular the mix of on-the-job training, off-the-job training and planned experience. The decision is based on the learning objectives, effectiveness, resources and factors specific to the trainee, such as learning style.

Design and Plan the Training

Scheduling training is very important. In general, training should be given shortly before the new skills are needed, perhaps with refresher training a few weeks or months later. If training is given too early, the trainee will forget important parts before he or she gets the chance to use them. If training is given too late, the trainee will not have time fully to understand the training.

In addition, training materials must be developed and the trainers must be briefed.

Implement the Training

The training must be delivered.

Evaluate the Training

Evaluation includes two processes – validation and evaluation.

Validating the training means checking that it has worked – after completing the training programme, can the trainee meet all the training objectives? Note that the training can only be validated if SMART objectives were set initially.

Evaluating the training means checking that it is value for money. Is the value to the organization of meeting the training objectives greater than the cost of the training programme? This is not usually a problem for IT training because people need to know how to use the system in order to take advantage of the facilities it offers them. Evaluating training is also useful for comparing different training methods – is it worth using a cheaper method that gives slightly less thorough training?

Training as an Investment

Training should be regarded as an investment. Organizations investing in training must have a clear understanding of the costs and expected benefits of the training process, and should monitor the benefits to ensure they are achieved.

Some organizations take account of this by including an assessment of future value when selecting staff for training. This may consider length of service (on the basis that this reflects loyalty) and the individual's potential for further development. Age may be a factor, although younger staff are more likely to leave the organization. Formal techniques such as human asset accounting can be used.

The Investors in People standard requires that training should be treated as an investment.

Training and Development

Training is part of a wider learning system. Other components of that system include development and education[3]:

- Development is 'the growth or realization of a person's ability, through conscious or unconscious learning. Development programmes usually include elements of planned study and experience, and are frequently supported by a coaching or counselling facility'.
- Education is 'activities which aim at developing the knowledge, skills, moral values and understanding required in all aspects of life rather than a knowledge and skill relating to only a limited field of activity. ...Education...involves...the acquisition of ...skills which are basic to learning, personal development, creativity and communication'.

Training tends to focus on skills that can be applied immediately in the workplace. Development and education are broader and seek to develop a wider range of skills and abilities.

Training and Learning

Training, development and education are all learning activities. Kolb, Rubin and McIntyre described the learning process in terms of a learning cycle[4]:

3 Manpower Services Commission *Glossary of Training Terms* 1981

4 DA Kolb, IM Rubin, JM McIntyre *Organisational Psychology: A Book of Readings* 2nd edition (Prentice Hall NJ 1974)

Figure 11.1: Learning Cycle

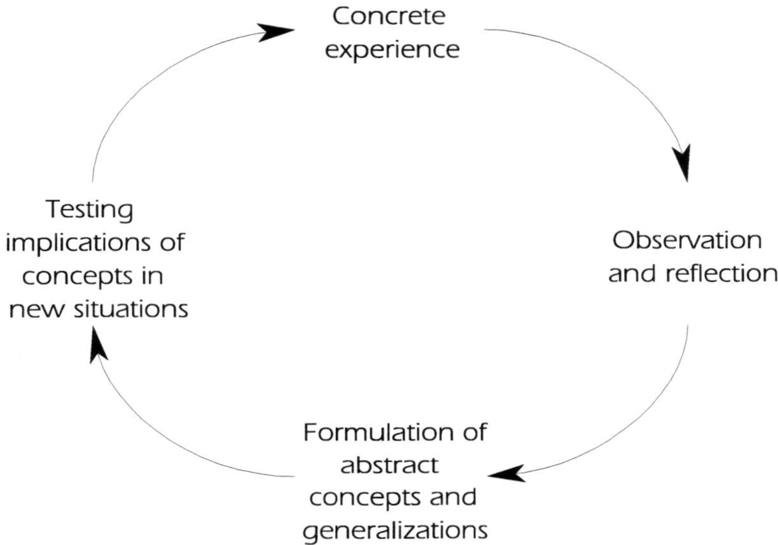

The stages within this cycle are:

- Concrete experience. This is the stage of applying learning to a situation;
- Observations and reflections. This is the stage of observing how something is done, and of thinking about (reflecting on) the best approach;
- Formulation of abstract concepts and generalizations. This is the stage of understanding the theory and the concepts behind it;
- Testing implications of concepts in new situations. This is the stage of trying out the ideas in new situations.

This is a cycle and an individual must go through all the stages before the learning process is complete.

However, individuals tend to have a preference for one or more stages of the process, and Honey and Mumford used this in developing the idea of learning styles. There are four learning styles, each of which corresponds to a stage in the cycle:

- Theorist. This corresponds to the formulation of abstract concepts and generalizations stage. Theorists like to start by having a detailed understanding of theory;
- Activist. This corresponds to the testing implications of concepts in new situations stage. Activists prefer a 'learning by doing' approach;
- Reflector. This corresponds to the observations and reflections stage. Reflectors like to develop understanding by observing the practice;

- Pragmatist. This corresponds to the concrete experience stage. Pragmatists focus on what is of practical value to them.

This was based on the work of Kolb, Rubin and McIntyre, who developed a different classification:

- Converger. This combines the theorist and activist styles;
- Diverger. This combines the pragmatist and reflector styles;
- Assimilator. This combines the theorist and reflector styles;
- Accommodator. This combines the pragmatist and activist styles.

Although Kolb, Rubin and McIntyre originated the idea of learning styles and developed the popular learning styles inventory (LSI), which allows people to identify their own preferred learning style, Honey and Mumford's classification is the more common.

One of the benefits of using IT to deliver training is the ability to match the training provision to the learning style. For example, let us consider how training in office software can be delivered:

- Manuals and helpfiles provide the theorist with detailed information to understand the product. The 'Quick Tour' offered by some products provides context both for the theorist and for the reflector;
- Hands-on tutorials allow the activist to experiment without risk. Context-sensitive help and bubble help are available to support both the activist and the pragmatist.

4 Training for Information Technology

Training has always been important, but the increase in the use of IT has had a major impact on the demand for training. Reasons for this include:

- As we discussed in Chapter 5, IT is a major investment. Financial services organizations can only maximize their return on this investment by ensuring that employees have sufficient training to use IT as effectively as possible;
- As we discussed in Chapter 4, the rate of change of technology is very high. This creates a demand for constant changes and improvements to IT systems, creating a corresponding demand for training;
- As we discussed in Chapter 3, the use of IT creates a demand for the development of new, IT-related skills;
- More generally, IT acts as an enabler to support changes in the nature of work. This creates a constant demand for employees to learn new skills and for retraining for employees whose skills are in declining demand.

5 Training Using Information Technology

IT has also had a direct impact on the training process. We shall consider this impact in terms of:

- Training methods
- Training delivery.

We shall discuss the various training methods below. Some of these, such as computer-based training and interactive videodisk, are clearly dependent on technology. Even the more traditional methods such as lectures have been affected by technology and it is not uncommon for multi-media presentations to form part of a lecture.

The impact on training delivery has also been considerable. Trainees can now have on-line access to training material over the Internet or intranet, or access to material in an easily-distributed form such as a CD-ROM. This makes it practical to deliver training directly to the trainee's own desk to an extent that has not previously been possible.

6 Training Methods

Training methods describe how we deliver the training. Various training methods can be used. We can split these into on-the-job methods, where training is carried out in the work environment, and off-the-job methods.

On-the-Job Training

On-the-job training is delivered in the workplace, either at scheduled times during the working day or during less busy periods. Some of the methods can be used either on-the-job or off-the-job. The main on-the-job training methods are:

- Coaching
- Computer-based training
- Videos
- Training database
- Books and manuals
- Circulars.

On-the-job training methods are generally seen as cheap, because employees do not have to be taken away from the workplace. However there are often hidden costs, because the trainees call on other employees for advice and support, and these reduce the cost advantage of these methods.

Coaching

Coaching is also called 'sitting next to Nellie' and involves an experienced member of staff sitting next to the trainee and showing him or her what to do.

The advantages are that this method is cheap, because it does not require specially produced training material, and it makes good use of staff knowledge.

The disadvantages are that the trainee may learn bad habits, that the training may not cover all situations and that it disrupts the work of the experienced staff member.

Computer-Based Training

Computer-based training (CBT) uses a computer program that takes the trainee through the training material, with exercises to assess progress.

The advantages are that this method is cheap to deliver and that the CBT can cover all situations.

The disadvantages are that CBT is expensive to develop and update with changes, and that it may not be seen as relevant to work.

Videos

Training material may be distributed on video. This may also include exercises. Videos are often used with a workbook.

The advantages are that this method is cheap to develop and deliver and can cover all situations (especially when used with a workbook).

The disadvantages are that the communication is one way – the trainee does not receive feedback – and that the trainee may get bored.

Training Database

A training database is a separate database used only for training. This allows trainees to try out computer system facilities without affecting the 'real' database.

The advantages are that this method is cheap to develop and deliver and is usually cheap to update.

The disadvantage is that this does not give the trainee any guidance or feedback, unless it is supplemented with CBT.

Books and Manuals

Books and manuals are published training material, written by a teacher or a 'technical writer'.

The advantages are that this method is cheap to deliver, it covers everything and it can also be used for reference.

The disadvantages are that the trainee may get bored, and books and manuals have poor visual impact.

Circulars

Circulars are information circulated by the employer containing updating information.

The advantages are that this method is very cheap to deliver and is quick to produce, ensuring it can be up-to-date.

The disadvantage is that it is not good for large amounts of information.

Off-the-Job Training

Off-the-job training cannot be delivered in the workplace. The main off-to-job training methods are:

- Lectures
- Briefings
- Seminars
- Interactive videodisk
- Business games.

Lectures

Lectures are also called 'talk and chalk' and are delivered by a lecturer standing in front of a class and talking.

The advantages are that this method is good for large amounts of information and that the lecture notes provide reference material.

The disadvantages are that trainees may get bored, the lecturer cannot easily adjust the pace to meet individual needs and the quality of feedback depends on the lecturer's knowledge.

Briefings

Briefings are similar to lectures but are less formal – they usually present only a summary of the material.

The advantage is that this method is good for updates on very recent material.

The disadvantages are that briefings lack depth and may be incomplete or biased.

Seminars

Seminars usually involve a seminar leader making a presentation, followed by discussion in small groups.

The advantage is that this method allows for detailed discussion, improving trainees' understanding.

The disadvantage is that seminars are time consuming, and therefore expensive.

Interactive Videodisk

Interactive videodisk (IVD) uses a multimedia 12-inch optical disk containing case study material. The trainee follows the case and may choose different courses of action. The results of the action chosen are shown.

The advantage is that this method allows the consequences of mistakes to be shown, reinforcing learning.

The disadvantages are that it is expensive to develop and update and that it requires special equipment, making it expensive to deliver.

Business Games

Business games are simulations of business situations, usually played against other people and often using a computer system as 'referee'.

The advantages are that this method keeps trainees interest and provides the opportunity to practise techniques.

The disadvantages are that the competitive element may take precedence over learning and that they may be seen as irrelevant.

Comparison of Methods

Generally, on-the-job methods are cheaper than off-the-job methods. Not only are the methods themselves often cheaper, staff do not have to be taken away from work (which increases costs because these absences need to be covered). On-the-job methods can also be scheduled to fit in with the normal working day – using CBT during quiet periods, for example.

Against this, on-the-job methods can often be disruptive – trainees asking questions, for example. On-the-job methods such as coaching can result in the trainee picking up bad habits from the coach. Off-the-job methods are much better for training complicated skills because there are no distractions and because the trainer can be an expert in the subject. Off-the-job methods are also often better for new skills, where there is no-one in the workplace who could answer questions and the trainee might feel lost if on-the-job methods are used.

Part 3

Knowledge Management

This part of the book considers how information can be organized and understood in order to create value for an organization.

It provides insight into the development and use of customer-based databases and how to build and implement Customer Relationship Management Systems (CRM).

Chapter 12: Explains the types of information and how external research and segmentation approaches can be used to give insight into future customer behaviour.

Chapter 13: Describes the components that make up a CRM system and how this links together to form an integrated customer-driven approach to customer management.

Chapter 14: Provides an overview of how CRM systems are implemented and links to the underlying technology required.

Chapter 15: Shows how information systems are developed to provide support at strategic, tactical and operational level within a financial services organization.

12

Customer Knowledge Management

Objectives

After studying this chapter, you should be able to:

- understand the external forces and demographic changes affecting financial services organization customers;
- understand and be able to describe the sources of qualitative research information;
- understand and be able to describe the categories of behavioural information;
- understand and be able to distinguish customer differentiation and customer segmentation;
- understand and be able to explain customer value.

1 Introduction

Most financial institutions would list their top three assets appearing in their balance sheet as:

- Employees;
- Physical network of branches, call centres and processing centres;
- Investment in technology.

There is, however, another asset that does not (at least currently) appear in the financial assessment of an organization, the value of the customer information the organization holds and its ability to use this information to enhance the customer experience and create value. This is the essence of Customer Knowledge Management: it is insufficient to just hold information it must be structured and connected to enable its use for the benefit of both the customer and the organization.

Customer knowledge management brings together external macro-economic research and links it to demographics with the goal of applying this insight with individual customer behaviour to predict likely future needs of each individual customer.

Figure 12.1

2 Understanding External Forces

Figure 12.2: Understanding Customer Needs in a Restructuring Financial World

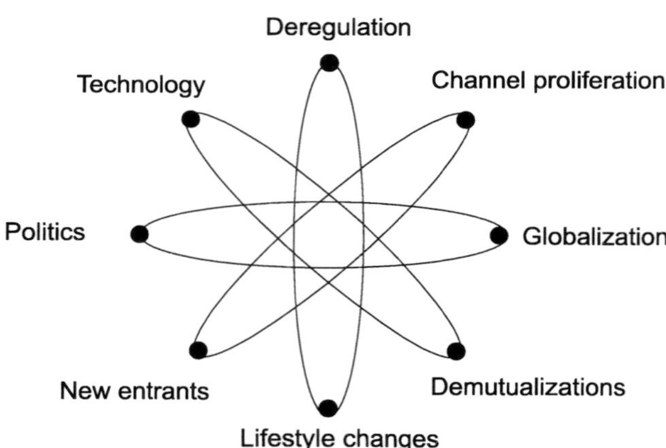

The types of external forces and agents of change, which form the backdrop to effective knowledge management, are shown in the diagram above.

Deregulation

The increasing desire of governments to create a level competitive playing field to encourage active competition while creating a mix of self and statutory regulatory bodies.

Channel Proliferation

The growth in the number of different ways in which a businesses and consumers can interact, the removal of geographic boundaries through 'virtual' channels such as the telephone and Internet.

Globalization

Virtual channels and increasing desire to exploit economies of scale is leading to businesses (and individuals) thinking and acting beyond traditional borders.

Demutualization

The need for the ability to move quickly and dynamically to embrace opportunities is making some corporate structures such as mutuality appear cumbersome. This is further fuelled by the desire for short-term returns and 'financial windfalls' for members on conversion.

Lifestyle Changes

Traditional life patterns are changing rapidly with increasing mass wealth giving access to more consumer goods and lifestyle options.

New Entrants

Financial services products are in most cases virtual rather than physical and, with the removal of barriers to entry (such as Branch network) together with increasing demand and good historic margins, new players are appearing almost daily.

Politics

Growth in desire (from all major political parties) for individuals to take on more personal responsibility for their lives and financial well being, the gradual reduction of the state 'safety nets' to a basic level.

Technology

Development and innovation created by the merging of computers with communications and multi-media, challenging traditional methods of delivery.

3 Demographics

Demographic information enables financial organizations to understand how the population of customers will change over time and therefore predict likely needs and consumer demand for products and services.

Ageing, maturing – Demography of the UK

There will be more elderly people and fewer young people in the population of 2010.

Increased longevity – the outcome of better nutrition, greater health awareness and improved health care – is a prime indicator of our success as a society of relative plenty, prosperity and protection. On current evidence, there will be substantial increases in the older age groups – with the 85+ age group growing the most. The shifts by age group from 1991 to 2011 are shown in the chart:

Figure 12.3: Changing Age Structure (1991-2011) (UK)

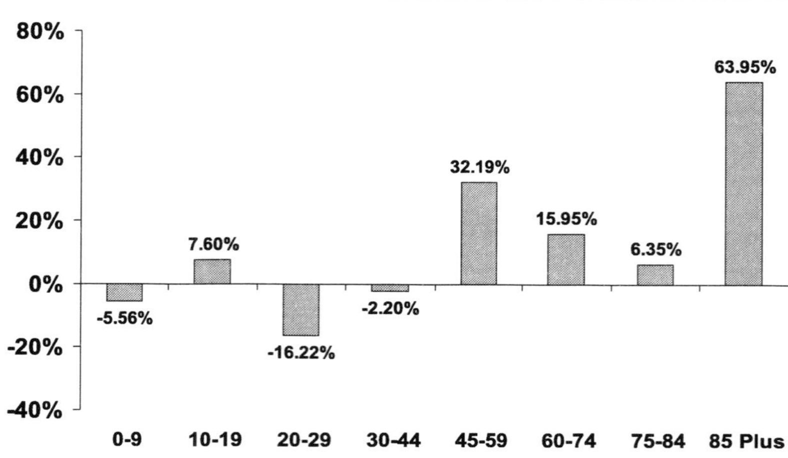

Source: Government Actuary/The Future Foundation © *future foundation*

Some medical commentators are predicting life expectancy of 130 years for children born in the first years of the new Millennium... which means that the pensioners of 2060 might have a further 70 years of active life to fill and to finance. Of course, by 2060 retirement may well have changed so radically in form and function that the idea of it being a quiet 'twilight time' is far from relevant. But looking towards a nearer horizon, the future foundation group estimate there could well be 5 million healthy and active 65+ year-olds in 2010 – half the total of this age group.

This information alone is likely to lead to increasing demand for:

- Medical and life care insurance
- Pensions
- Flexible investment plans
- Home visits
- Easy access to services (increased proportion of population with disability).

and decreasing demand for:

- Personal loans (most taken out by 20-29 age group)
- Mortgages for first-time buyers
- Starter homes.

Changing Household Composition

Reduction in married couples and growth in the single-person forecast will change the demand for housing provision and design, probably fewer bedrooms and more flexible living space to accommodate home working etc. As the Internet plays a greater role in serving domestic consumers it is anticipated that a modern-day version of the traditional neighbourhood milkman could re-emerge as part of the social fabric and informal support structure of communities. Delivery agencies, for example, may be charged with alerting health services if a single or elderly clients fails to open the door at a pre-agreed delivery time.

Figure 12.4: Forecast Changes in Household Composition

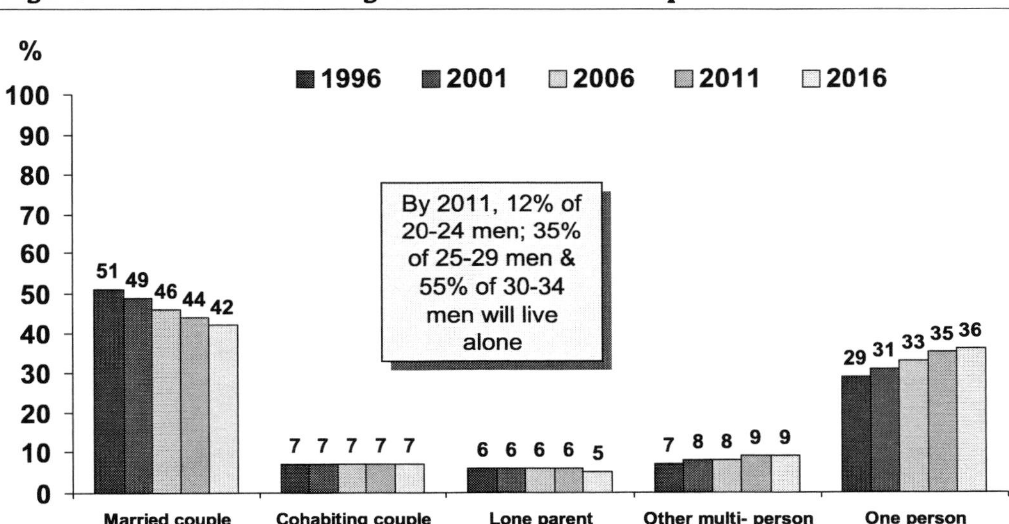

Source: Department of the Environment – © the future foundation

Impact of Technology in Education

It is now 20 years since information technology was first parachuted into schools and there has clearly been an appreciable and accelerating growth in technological confidence among young people. There is no doubt that new communications technologies have already had a revolutionizing impact on the way information is accessed and shared, as well as on working and learning methods.

Students are the group of the population with greatest exposure to new media and new communications technology. Today's school students can have experience of creative play, networking and remote contact and collaboration in, for example, virtual school exchanges. They can also learn how to plan and manage their time, using real-time and deferred contact, through e-mail, multi-player game play etc. This raises questions about how this generation will respond to directed work in the future and what value will be placed on communications in the Global Networked Society.

Taking the forecasts for numbers of young people together with trends in access and usage of the Internet and new media, Future Foundation group estimate that by 2010 there will be a technologically literate population of 40 million in the UK.

Some 30% of these will be 'functionally literate' – that is, they will be capable of finding readily accessible public domain information and shopping via simplified games console-type digital TV interfaces. This group will typically be those who have adopted new technology in adulthood. A further 60% will have grown up regarding new media as today's middle-aged would the TV – these will tend to be younger people. While not experts in information technology, they will be adept at using it for all types of transactions, for games, for networking and as the 'default medium' for contact with their family and peers. They will naturally gravitate towards jobs in the service sector which can capitalize on their familiarity with communications technology. A further much smaller group will be expert users, including developers, engineers and architects of integrated systems.

4 Integrating Traditional Research

Many financial organizations undertake their own (or are partners in) bespoke research. This is either quantitative where the objective is to achieve a statistically acceptable number of responses to specific questions, e.g. 75% of UK population will have access to a mobile phone by end of 2000, or qualitative where the research explores the reasons why consumers have an opinion or have made a decision.

An example of quantitative research:

Figure 12.5: On-line Searching for Financial Products

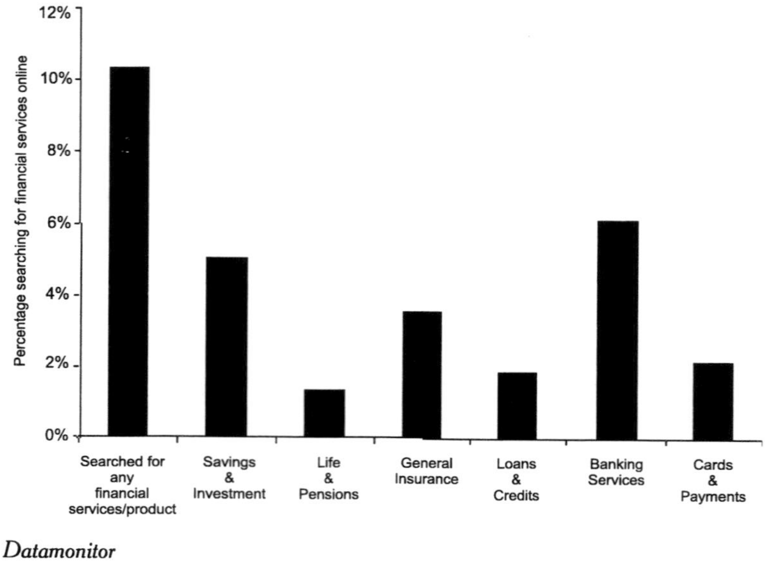

Source: Datamonitor

An example of qualitative research is shown in Figure 12.6:

Figure 12.6: The Customer's View

Customers want	Banks are
• An 'adult-to-adult relationship'	• Self-serving, rip you off
• To be known and valued	• Act as if they can survive without you
• Intelligent proactivity	• Uninterested in the customer
• Qualified, accountable staff	• Under pressure to sell
• A 'sense of trust'	• Seeing customer as 'guilty until proven innocent'
	• Lacking personal touch

Source: 'Banking is useful, Bank's are not' CIOB Cambridge Seminar 1999

5 Understanding Individual Customer Behaviour

The external forces and market research gives a good picture of how groups of customers or segments may behave. There is however another rich source of customer knowledge which can be drawn from the information held by financial organizations on individuals or purchased at individual or household level from data brokers (e.g. Claritas, Experian, Axiom).

The information falls into five broad categories:

Transactional

This includes all basic product purchases or transactions on accounts. For example a bank will have access to all transactions on the current account or credit card; this information can give a very clear insight into the lifestyle of the customer. The timing, amount and payee enable a picture of the customer's life to be established – for example, payments to a garage indicate vehicle ownership.

Personal

Facts about the individual, age, address, income, sex etc. These can be enhanced by linking the individual to a household (through address and postcode) to help assess socio-economic class, life stage and lifestyle.

Attitudinal

This is normally obtained through individual customer survey which can either be at an attributable individual level (i.e. consumer gives his or her name) or at a segment level where the attitudes are attached to a type of customer, e.g. customers over 85+ much prefer access to a branch than through e-mail.

Channel Usage

Understanding which delivery channels customers use and for what type of transactions. This can be obtained through transactional information and tracking the types of delivery channels customers have access to (e.g. home has access to digital TV). Understanding this information not only gives a view on how customers prefer to contact an organization, it can aslo give an insight into how the organization should contact the customer. It will also provide insight into how the customer undertakes complex transactions. For example, in purchasing a mortgage the customer may go to the Internet first to obtain some quotes but will then want to visit a branch to complete the transaction with a financial planning manager.

Figure 12.7

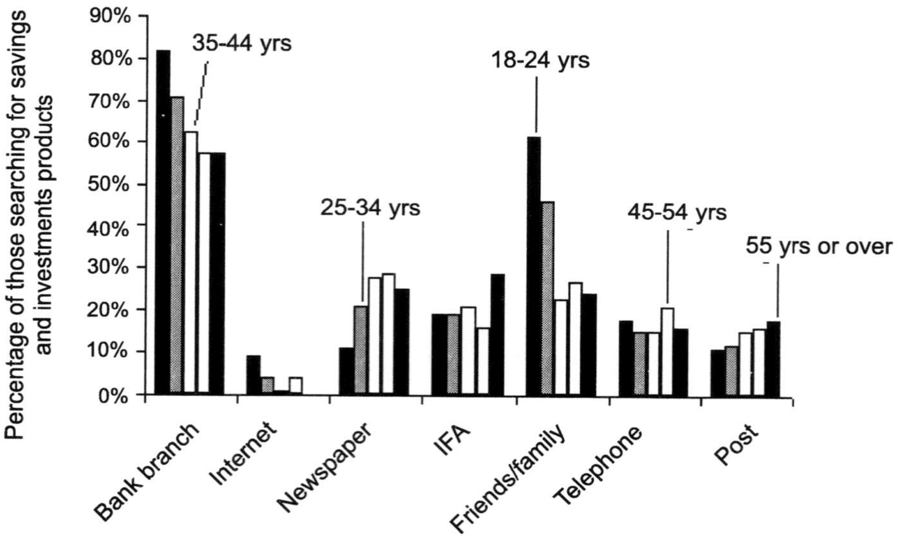

Source: Datamonitor: Customers preference for obtaining information on savings & investments

Risk Assessment

Assessing probability of default is a key factor in agreeing and pricing risk products such as loans and overdrafts. Information on individuals' risk history can be built up internally from previous lending successfully repaid and externally from credit reference agencies (e.g. Experian).

6 Customer Differention and Segmentation

In the previous section we examined the sources of customer information and how this could be combined to provide a powerful knowledge base for understanding and predicting customer behaviour. Ideally this can be then applied in a 1:1 interaction with the customer to help to identify the correct needs and solutions.

However most organizations still make use of customer segmentation models which look to collect customers into groups that will have common needs. It is important that these common needs exist or the segmentation grouping is useless.

Types of Segmentation

By Product

This is the most traditional analysis method where each product is managed independently and the analysis takes a product (rather than customer) view of the portfolio. For example a bank's personal loan portfolio could be segmented by:

- Purpose of loan
- Length of loan
- Amount of loan
- Interest rate applied etc.
- Age of loan
- Loans in default.

By Geography

This is a customer approach where customers are segmented by geography. It is useful in the assessment of areas for the building of branches or their redesign to match the types of customer the organization wishes to attract in an area. Companies such as GMAP and Experian specialize in this type of segmentation to assess:

- Type of housing by postcode
- Customer demographics by postcode
- Transport routes
- Competitor branch locations.

Lloyds Bank used this type of segmentation analysis in assessing the viability of its merger with TSB.

By Socio-economic Grouping

By segmenting customers by their socio-economic grouping, where A is the most affluent and E the least. Depending on the type of customer the organization wished to contact this analysis will help, for example if you wished to attract AB customers for an investment product then the Datamonitor research would imply that marketing through the branch and newspapers was likely to be the most successful.

Figure 12.8

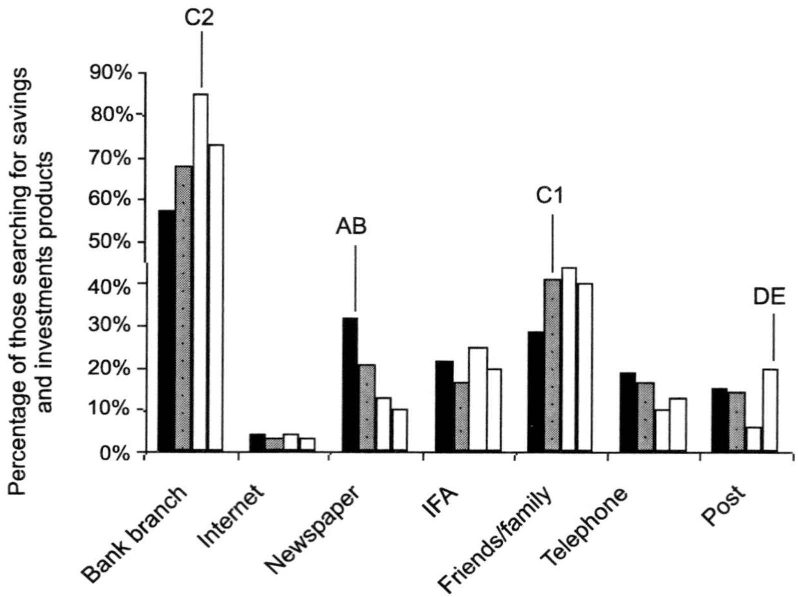

Source: Datamonitor

By Lifestage

Customer's age has been used widely as the single best predictor of likely financial needs. However the changes in lifepath resulting from the changes in society mean that this is a less reliable segmentation method. Many retail organizations are now moving to 'lifestage' segmentation where they try to place each customer in a lifestage e.g. young single, young worker, family former, family with older children. This method offers the flexibility that matches changes in society where a person may get married, get divorced and then remarry to create a second family. Each lifestage will carry high propensities for certain financial needs, for example:

Figure 12.9: Segmentation by Socio-economic Group and Lifestage

Socio-economic Group
- Professional & Managerial (AB)
- Junior Managers & Non-manual (C1)
- Skilled Manual (C2)
- Semi-skilled & Unskilled (DE)

Lifestage
- Young Singles
- Pre-family
- Family Formers
- Older Families
- Older Singles & Child-free Couples
- Empty Nesters
- Retired

Lifestage: Young Single (18-24)
- Credit card = High propensity
- Personal loan (for transport) = High propensity
- Investment in equities = Low propensity
- Pension = Low Propensity
- Short-term savings = High propensity
- Saving for house deposit = Medium propensity
- Internet-based current account = High propensity
- Cash machine access = High propensity

By Customer Value

This is the opposite type of approach to product segmentation. Here the total product holdings a customer has with an organization are used to assess the customer's value. Most organizations are keen to move to this type of segmentation but it does require detailed information on all of the customer's products and a robust customer database. In the 1990s some banks and credit card providers started to do this analysis and were shocked to find that their initial assessments indicated that 80% of their income streams were being generated by less than 20% of their customers. Further refinements by banks such as Citicorp have shown that, having taken costs into account, the top 20% of customers generate over 100% of income, the next 50% contribute about 30% and the bottom 30% lose or 'destroy' value of about 30%.

This type of segmentation, although very powerful, does have risks. Financial organizations need to retain customers over a long period to maximize return, and customers may be loss-making in the early years (e.g. students, customers with 'special offer' discounted mortgages) but they will offer significant future potential.

The most sophisticated segmentation by customer value is now made up of many dimensions for example:

- Customer risk: short-term probability of default;
- Current value: calculation of actual customer profitability based on current products and services used;
- Future value: an estimate of future potential based on analysis of customer lifestage, previous history, socio-economic group and size of 'wallet' or wealth.

By Customer Attitudinal or Behavioural Segmentation

This is another fairly recent approach to segmentation and it again requires an in-depth knowledge of the customer. Here customers are grouped by their common attitudes and behaviours. For example 'early adopters' of technology, indicating that these customers will be more receptive to (or even demand) access to the latest technology. Firstdirect has a high proportion of 'early adopters' who joined the bank when it was created as the first telephone-based 24x7x365 Bank. Because of this their customers are much more likely to want Internet, WAP and other new delivery channels compared to say the customer base of a small building society or a traditional High Street bank. This type of segmentation has led to a number of companies offering to group customers into 'pen portraits' or 'stereo types' with some amazing names like 'Lemons', 'Oranges'.

Attitudinal segmentation can be very important in understanding the buying preferences of customers, for example it can be used to discover which type of customers would prefer a traditional relationship with a member of staff and those who would prefer to make decisions on their own.

Example of analysis based on customer behaviour:

Figure 12.10: Next Purchase Intention

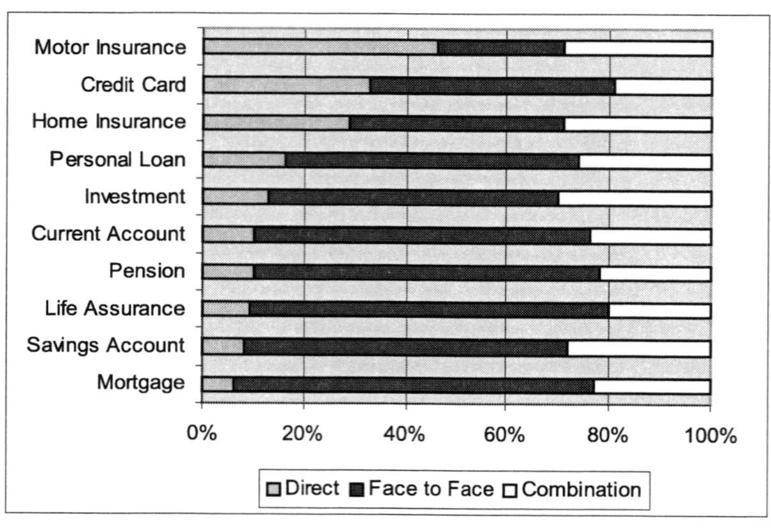

Source: Prospektus June 1999

Which Segmentation to Choose?

No single segmentation method will provide all of the answers required – this is one of the reasons why financial organizations have built large databases, pulling together external and internal information to provide insight into customer behaviour.

Each of the above segmentations (and there are many more) provides a way of helping to answer a particular set of business questions. For example product segmentation is vital in understanding the profitability and dynamics of a product portfolio. Whereas channel usage segmentation will help to understand which customer is likely to want to buy a product through which channel.

In Chapter 15 the use and application of information is covered in more detail.

13

Customer Relationship Management

Objectives

After studying this chapter, you should be able to:

- define and explain the purpose of customer relationship management;
- describe the customer relationship management process;
- understand and be able to explain the concept of mass relationship management;
- understand the types of customer and customer relationship;
- understand the four-stage approach to customer relationship management and be able to use this to analyse customer interactions;
- understand and be able to explain the benefits of customer relationship management.

1 Introduction

Customer Relationship Management (CRM) is a key initiative in many financial organizations today. Proliferation of delivery channels such as the Internet, TV and mobile phone together with increased competition and customer sophistication continue to increase the competitive pressures on financial institutions. Such pressures have revolutionized the way we do business and nowhere is this more apparent then in the need to understand customers as individuals and draw as much value as possible from the information generated during every interaction.

CRM is corporate glue, as custodians of customers' information banks are obligated to use this information wisely and to make it available when and where they need it and to help customers understand and solve their financial needs.'

Today, organizations are finding that they no longer have the initiative. Customers are now empowered by ready access to information and have greater access to businesses than ever before. According to Peter Soraparu, managing director for Retail Financial Services at the Bank Administration Institute 'CRM is a passé concept. It assumes customers can be managed. That is no longer the case. It is the customers who are managing their own financial services'.

Customers are demanding access and treatment on their terms, not the bank's. More than ever it is essential for a company to excel at each customer contact point, be it in the field with a mobile sales force, traditional face-to-face interaction at branches, or in the contact centre by phone, fax, and e-mail correspondence. The acceptance of the web has further changed this landscape as customers and channel partners increasingly interact in a self-service environment. Businesses are faced with adapting to this new reality or becoming irrelevant.

A Definition of CRM

> *CRM is the intelligent use of information to identify, predict and learn from customer behaviour and contact in order to initiate appropriate action to achieve commercial benefit.*

2 Single-Customer View

Businesses need to form a single view of customer information to enable relationship building. A single view of information helps a business to identify its most valuable customers and understand the value they get from the business. When a business understands its customers, it can show customers that it cares about them and their needs.

CRM helps to address this challenge by connecting delivery channels to the hub of a CRM plan. Additionally, the focus moves from viewing the various transactions that occur with customers as single transactions to viewing all of the transactions as a continuing dialogue with each customer.

New and integrated access channels are required to meet the needs of customers. Channel 'etiquette' must also be understood. Businesses must also realize that different channels require different etiquette. For example, people tend to be more informal with e-mail than they would ever be by telephone or written letter. Businesses need to consider all of the dynamics of new access channels. CRM can address the need to find and integrate access channels. Additionally, CRM can help businesses to capture information about consumers at all access channels.

Many finance companies are organized along the lines of various functions, such as marketing, customer service, or by product line, rather than along customer lines. Too often the various vertically organized departments have different measurements and objects. For example, learning about customers and what they need and want is a task assigned to marketing but creating the things customers need and want falls to the product managers. Customers are brought into a company by marketing, but the area that is charged with keeping the customer happy is the branches.

Every time information about a customer transaction moves from one department to another, it runs the risk of being lost in the process. There are several inefficiencies in the process:

- Strategies and plans are developed by each department independently;

- Information sharing and joint problem solving are limited;
- Accounting, measurement, and reward systems are separate and unsynchronized;
- Customer relationship is fragmented.

The result of this process is that customers are often frustrated and always looking for a better deal from another provider. CRM should help companies to create seamless customer experiences so that no matter where customers interact with the company – on the Internet, through the telephone, or in person – they receive the same experience. Additionally, all departments are working towards common goals, sharing information and viewing the same information. The result (hoped for!) is that if companies create a seamless customer experience, customers will want to do business with them on a continual basis.

3 Linking CRM to Corporate Objectives

In essence any organization with customers is trying to achieve an optimal mix of the following:

Customer Acquisition

Which customers do we wish to acquire?

What do they need?

How should we go about it?

How much is it worth spending to achieve the acquisition?

What is the predicted return?

Customer Growth

Which customers offer the best prospects for cross-sales?

What do they need?

How should we contact them to achieve this with maximum return on investment?

How do we build the product and delivery to suit the customer?

Customer Control

Which customers are (or are likely to) destroy value (e.g. potential bad debts or negative customer value)?

What actions should we take to minimize this risk?

Which customers do we wish to lose?

How do we lose them with minimal damage to brand and reputation?

Customer Migration

Which customers are going through (or about to go through) a life event (e.g. student to graduate, single to family former, working to retired etc.)?

What do they need?

How should we contact them to achieve this with maximum return on investment?

How do we build the product and delivery to suit the customer?

Customer Retention

Which customers are we vulnerable to losing?

What actions should we take to minimize this risk?

How should we contact them to retain our return on investment?

Obviously the best way to answer these questions is to forge a strong relationship with a customer at an individual level. This is essence of CRM and 1:1 marketing.

Figure 13.1: Using Customer Knowledge

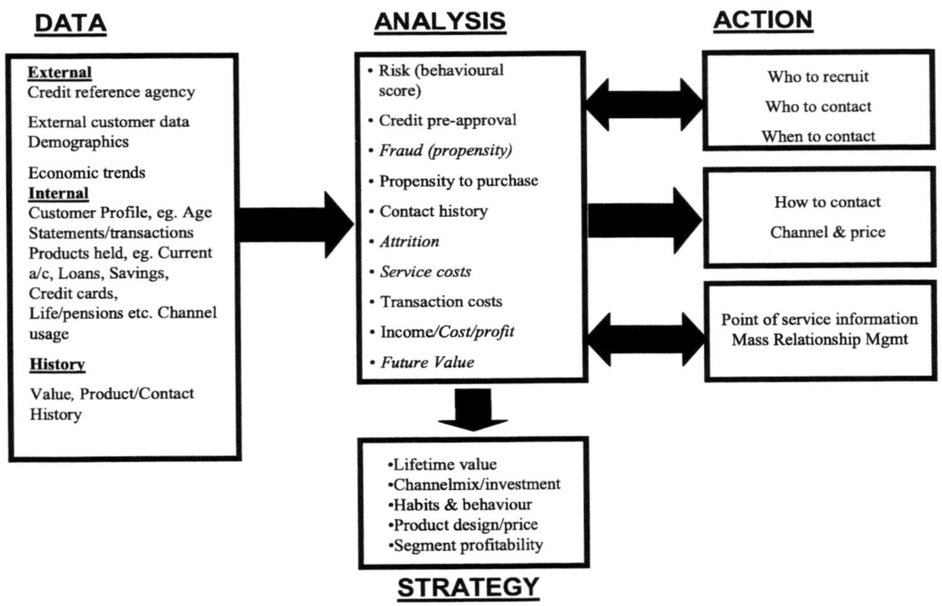

The above diagram gives an overview of how the interaction between data from internal and external sources can be linked, with insight gained from individual customer interaction, to provide an analysis of the business and answer some of the questions above.

4 Relationship Management as a Process

The term 'relationship management' is used to cover a wide variety of activities. Figure 13.2 tries to rationalize these into a process which helps to understand how a traditional relationship manager (e.g. Branch Manager or Account Manager) undertakes his role.

For example, consider a Branch Manager of a bank in the 1950s. All of the knowledge of interactions with the customer would be kept either in the manager's memory or on paper in the form of interview notes or correspondence.

Before meeting the customer the manager would review this information and then try to predict the likely needs of the customer and therefore the products and services to introduce.

The meeting would then take place and the manager would listen to the customer's needs (refining and matching this to previous knowledge) and then propose some solutions.

Figure 13.2: Role of a Relationship Manager

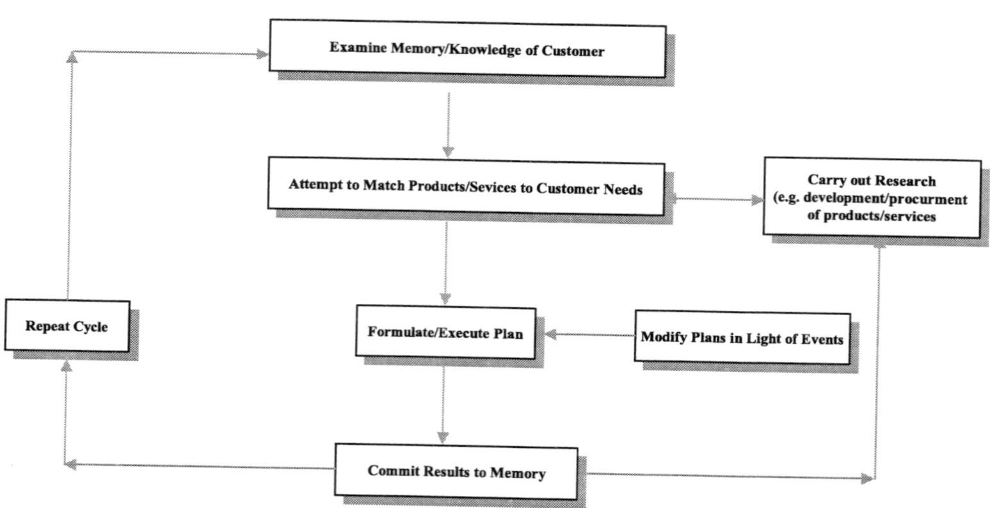

An agreement would then be reached and the appropriate actions taken to provide the products and services.

The manager would then update the customer's file with any new customer knowledge.

The cycle would then repeat.

Traditionally FSOs have offered this method of relationship management to a few customers. However the massive expansion in customers needing (and able to afford) financial services together with a highly competitive market with consequent reduction in margins have challenged the viability of this model.

To make matters worse the ability to understand the customer through contact has been made increasingly complex with the ever-increasing number of delivery channels and the relentless drive towards 24x7x365 service. In short, organizations cannot afford to deploy the traditional human relationship manager unless the value and complexity of the customer relationship warrants it.

5 Creating the 'Virtual' Relationship Manager

Having understood the process it is easy to see how the simple relationship management model described can be automated either in its entirety or in part. This 'virtual' style of relationship management offers the 'holy grail' to industries where high levels of customer interaction are required to understand and provide service. This approach is also sometimes referred to as 'Mass Relationship Management'.

If we now re-run the previous example today then the interaction may go as follows:

- Customer accesses bank through internet and browses some product and services;
- The system tracks his passage through the website and matches this to knowledge already held in the central customer database;
- System prompts and guides the customer through his needs to some appropriate solutions;
- Customer either completes transaction or requests to speak to someone in the bank's call centre or arranges an interview in a local branch;
- Database records are updated accordingly.

The underlying process is the same as in our 1950s example but the relationship management responsibilities are spread across different channels (e.g. Internet, call centre and branch), the CRM system providing the 'corporate glue' to hold the customer experience together.

6 Defining a Customer

In structuring information the key is to understand who your customer is. This may sound obvious, but defining a customer does require an organization to make some fundamental decisions. For example, a person holds a personal account and a business account with a bank, how many customers are there? Logic would lead you to believe there was one customer; however many banks would define this as two customers despite there being only one legal entity. Reasons for this may be that the bank wishes to hold separate behavioural and attitudinal information in order to aid segmentation or business reporting. However, frequently it is because either the commercial and personal systems are separate or incapable of holding two addresses (i.e. one for the business and one for the person). If the customer was a director of a limited company then would the answer be different? Obviously in law we now have two separate legal entities; the bank's systems must reflect this for accounting purposes but what about for marketing and analysis purposes?

Similarly joint accounts can give a problem. You have two customers sharing a product but if either also holds a sole account then the other party to the account has no right of access to information on the other's sole account unless specifically granted through a mandate from that customer.

7 Customer Types and Relationships

Most organizations resolve the above dilemmas by defining certain customer types and then defining relationships that can link customer types together. For example:

Table 13.1

Customer Types	
Personal	Personal customer (who has or has held a product or service with the organization)
Personal Prospect	Customer who has no products with the bank but has been targeted or received a marketing approach (e.g. direct mail)
Business Customer	Sole trader or other unincorporated business
Incorporated Business	Separate legal entity
Relationship types	
Parent/Child	Linking a parent to a child
Personal/Business	Linking personal customer to a business
Partner/Partner	Husband/Wife
Household Member	Live at the same house

But even here problems can occur and restrictions exist in data protection as to the use banks can make of such links. For example poor credit history on member of a household cannot be used in the assessment of creditworthiness of another member of the household.

8 Structured Approach to CRM and 1:1 Marketing

Peppars and Rogers in their book *Field Guide to 1:1 Marketing* defined a four-stage approach to understanding customers and enabling a 1:1 marketing approach.

Stage 1: Identify

It may seem obvious but if you are unable to identify a customer as a customer and understand the products, services and interactions the customer has with your organization then tailoring that experience is going to be very difficult.

It is therefore vital that the first stage in the development of CRM is to answer the question:

> Who are my customers?

In most organizations this involves the pulling together of data from so-called legacy product systems and to create a customer- (rather than product-) driven view of the world. Obviously in start-up situations such as 'Egg' or 'Virgin One' this is easier because the systems architecture can be built from this viewpoint, but equally they start with little or no data. Traditional organizations have basically two options. They can either re-engineer their systems totally (as in the case of Woolwich [see case study]) or connect and evolve their existing systems into an integrated CRM system (HSBC Bank plc have followed this approach). The decision on which (or any) approach to follow will involve an assessment and balancing of the following:

- Risk: does revolution or evolution offer the lower risk to the business?
- Functionality: is it a better investment to build on existing (often rich) functionality or better to start from scratch (or buy a package)?
- Development cost: can the organization fund the development in terms of skills and resources required?
- Financial cost: can the organization afford the investment?
- Executive sponsorship: is the commitment there to develop CRM?

The basic structure of the customer database could be as outlined in the diagram below:

Figure 13.3: Database Structure

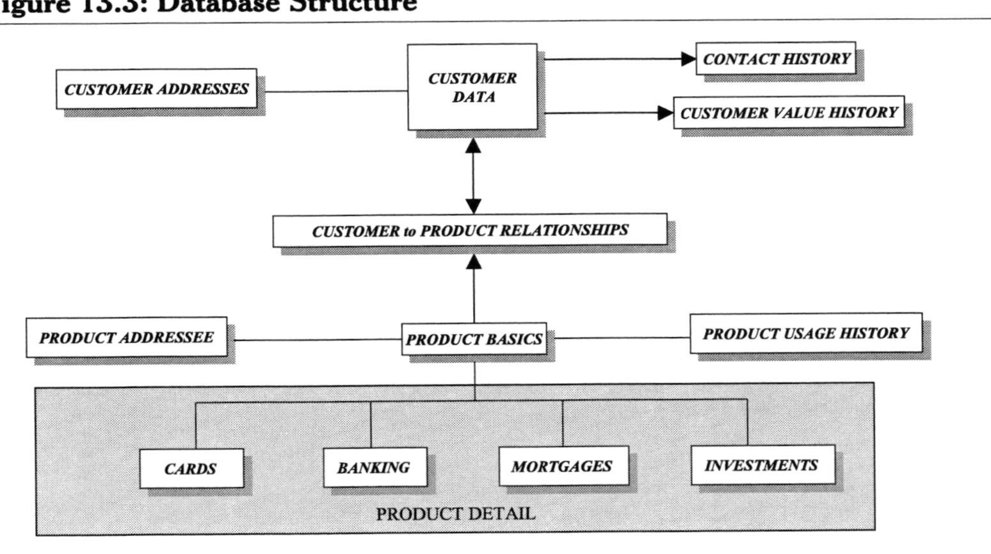

In the above example the customer database pulls together information on the customer (e.g. name, address, age, income, customer value, customer preference, propensity to purchase and channel/contact history) which is then linked to the product holdings (e.g. type, balances, transactions, interest rates etc.).

The detailed structure of building data warehouses is covered in Chapter 14.

Stage 2: Differentiation

Having established a single-customer level view it is then possible to analyse and interrogate the database (tools for doing this are explained in Chapter 14) to understand what customers have in common and how they differ.

For most established mass retail organizations such as banks and building societies that have been used to a 'one size fits all' approach with maybe some limited segmentation (such as a special youth or first-time home buyer packages), this analysis can come as a shock.

Figure 13.4: Analysis of Customers by Individual Customer Value

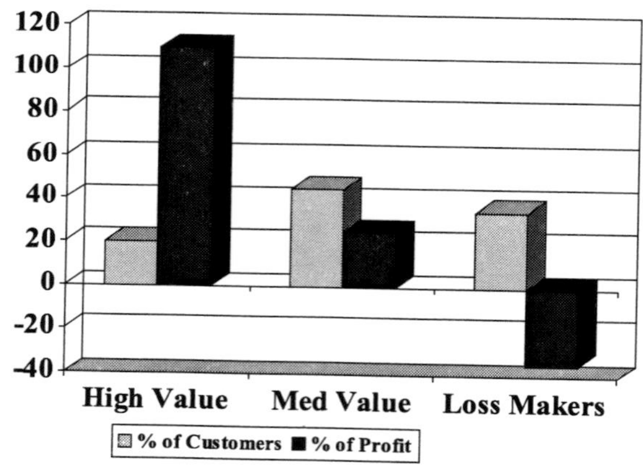

The above diagram is a typical analysis of customers by individual customer value that banks in the USA and Europe have discovered. Finding out that 20% of your customers generate over 80 -120% of your income and that 30% of your customers are currently destroying value (or losing you money) is not a message that many FSO CEOs are happy with!

At this stage the organization is not undertaking 1:1 marketing but can start to tailor its marketing and contact approach at a portfolio level. In other words you can identify a large number of customers with a similar profile and approach them with the appropriate product. This takes us on to stage 3.

Stage 3: Customer Contact

With an integrated single-customer view it is now possible to start to allocate inbound and outbound resources in alignment with the value and potential of each customer segment. To start with the segments are likely to be large.

Example 1: Outbound campaign

External research and internal database analysis indicate that 18-25-year-old males have a high propensity to purchase cars and motorcycles using credit.

Therefore mailing for a campaign would select: all creditworthy male customers who are in age group 18-25 identified for a personal loan mailing.

A crude selection criterion but significantly more effective then mailing all customers.

Example 2: Inbound campaign

Customer call centre decides to prioritize incoming calls in the queue not on a 'first in, first out' basis but on a 'most valuable customer' basis.

Therefore once the customer has identified himself, by keying in or through voice recognition, using the IVR (interactive voice response) system, the customer database identifies the market segment the customer is in. This can then be used to allocate a queue priority for answer by a call centre agent (more valuable/higher potential customers being answered more quickly).

This is a relatively sophisticated application where service levels are being determined by customer value.

Example 3: Allocation of commercial business managers

Bank wishes to allocate commercial customer portfolios by customer value and potential rather than just size of credit line.

Understanding customer value and future value/potential enables a bank to rank customers and allocate expensive resources such as business managers in line with income-generating customers. In this example the bank found that many of its best customers did not borrow at all and hence had not benefited from a dedicated business relationship manager; equally many of the borrowing customers were their best customers!

Stage 4: Customization of Relationship

Once you are able to understand the breadth and depth of the customer relationship with the organization and have this information available whenever and however the customer chooses to contact, you are in a position to start customizing the relationship. This is a view that is endorsed by Irene Dorner, General Manager Marketing at HSBC Bank plc: 'This is when it gets exciting; used wisely you can now start to build your bank around the customer'.

At this stage customer segment and portfolio analysis will primarily be used only for reporting purposes, customer interactions being tailored at a 1:1 level.

Example 1: Build your own credit card

Knowing a customer's risk profile, value and attitudes to finance it is possible to offer multiple options on a product such as a credit card and allow each individual customer to choose the options that best suit him.

Example 2: Tracking customer 'click streams'

Organization tracks how customer uses his web site and notices that customer has undertaken a series of self-quotes for mortgages. This information is combined with central customer knowledge and customer channel preference, resulting in the account manager contacting the customer to offer assistance.

Example 3: Customer transactions on credit card

These can indicate frequent overseas stays. FSO is able to offer travel protection and foreign exchange products.

9 An Alternative View of CRM

Figure 13.5: Customer Relationship Management Process

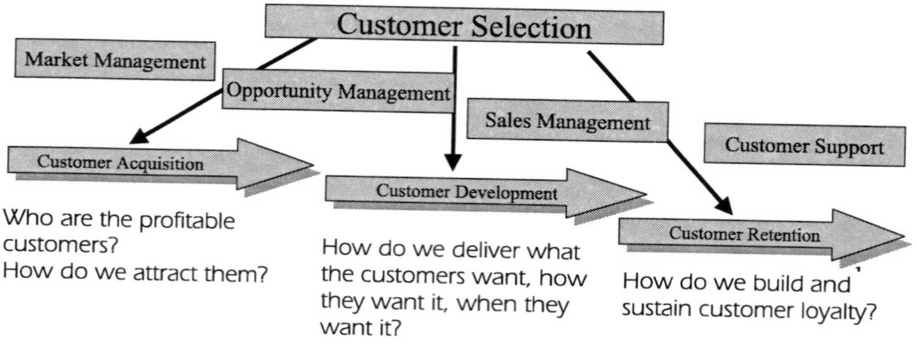

In this model traditional marketing functions such as market management and opportunity management are linked through the CRM system to the sales and customer support functions.

CRM encompasses the totality of the business processes that an organization performs to identify, select, acquire, develop and retain its customers. This is illustrated in the diagram above.

Customer relationship solutions have evolved to meet the increasing demands placed upon them. At first, CRM solutions automated specific customer interaction business processes. These included the automation of sales, service, marketing, and support functions. These original CRM solutions were directed at creating efficiencies in these specific business departments and are characterized as 'point solutions'. These 'point solutions' were stand-alone, non-integrated systems sold at the department, business-unit level.

As the benefits of a holistic customer view became more apparent, the need for integrated CRM solutions also grew. This meant the delivery of an integrated 'front-office' application suite (sales, service, marketing, support).

However, even the delivery of such integrated CRM suites still did not address the full spectrum of CRM capabilities and requirements. Increasingly, the e-business revolution is driving fundamental customer-lead business change. This is resulting in three compelling CRM trends:

- Existing CRM processes will be Internet-enabled. This clearly leads the market in demonstrated business value and ROI, and is expected to be the next business driver;
- Business survival will drive re-intermediation of firms with their customers. This will be accomplished in part through redefinition of business processes and access channels around discovery and satisfaction of individual customer needs;
- Delivery of unique customer value propositions will drive the need to integrate the entire business value chain;

As a result, the emphasis within CRM processes are changing:

Table 13.2: Emphasis within CRM Processes

Previous Emphasis	Evolving Emphasis
Call	Interaction
Point of complaints	Point of communication
Product focused	Customer focused
Cost-minimizing	Profit-maximizing
Fragmented	Integrated
Centralized	Virtual/Networked
Call centre	Contact centre - Voice -e-mail - Web -Kiosk...
Market segmentation/Business intelligence	1:1 marketing
Moments of truth/Transaction driven	Sustained dialogues/Relationship driven
Personalization	Personalized customer value

10 Integrated CRM System: Closing the Loop

Table 13.6: CRM Learning and Action Loop

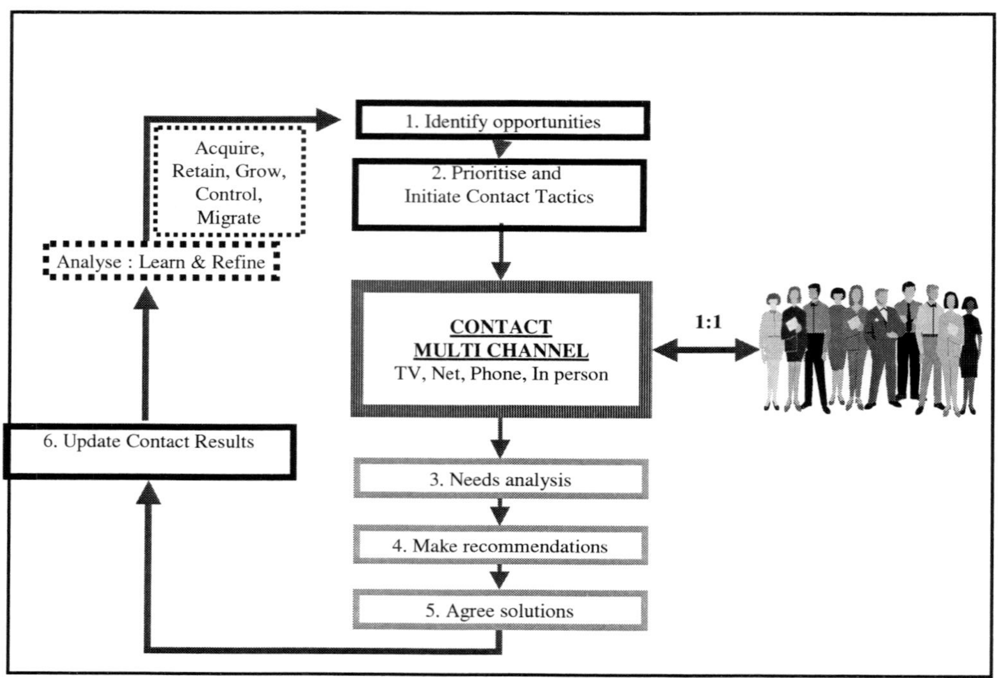

The above diagram provides an overview of how an integrated CRM system enables an organization to translate strategic objectives of customer acquisition, growth, control and lifestage migration into action.

1. The central data warehouse is used to synthesize customer transactions and behavioural information to identify opportunities.
2. These opportunities are then prioritized and a series of contact tactics created based on knowledge of the customer's channel preferences.
3. Contact takes place (either initiated by the customer or the organization) and the customer's needs are matched with the existing customer knowledge.
4. This generates product and service solutions.
5. Agreement or rejection of the offers.
6. The central data warehouse is updated with the results of the contact and 'learns'. This then enables the process to start again using refined knowledge and rules based on experience.

11 Benefits of CRM

CRM is intended to directly affect the bottom line of organizations. Although the use of software associated with CRM strategy enables productivity gains, the biggest benefits of CRM arise from business expansion – doing more of the right things. This is in contrast to the focus of many organizations, which has been on doing more things right.

Business expansion is made possible by CRM because a holistic view of customers enables the organization to:

- develop the most attractive products and services according to customers' needs and requirements;
- market and sell to a smaller, but better qualified group of prospects;
- retain profitable customers

CRM entails taking a long-term view – to pay more attention to the lifetime value of a customer than to the value of each transaction. It is this emphasis that makes one holistic view of the customer necessary. Firstly, it enables profitability analysis. Secondly, it is only possible to continue to do business with a customer who is satisfied with all aspects of his interaction with a company.

Customer satisfaction is a good thing in its own right, but it is also important in the context of CRM because it is crucial to retaining customers. Even a small increase in retention can have spectacular effects on profitability.

There have been a number of studies in and around the subject of customer retention. *The Loyalty Effect* by Fredrick Reichheld shows that it costs six times as much to acquire a new customer as it does to keep a customer. He went on to show that loyal customers refer new prospects to the business, which then tend to be more loyal.[1]

It is normal for a company to experience a certain amount of churn in its customer base. Reichheld's study indicates that where churn is reduced by x%, the cost of winning new business to replace lost customers is decreased by 6x. These savings have two effects:

- they decrease cost of sales directly;
- they free resources to expand the business. Rather than spending time and effort replacing lost customers to maintain revenues, that time and effort can be spent either increasing the number of customers overall or increasing the value of sales to existing customers – hence the business grows.

Another effect of customer satisfaction is preventative. Dissatisfied customers do not just leave, they also tell their family and friends about their negative experience. This further increases the cost of winning new customers.

Software employed in the pursuit of CRM directly contributes to customer satisfaction by:

1 Source: Zero Defections: Quality Comes to Services+, *by Frederick R. Reichheld and W. Earl Sasser, Jr., September, 1999*

- using business intelligence tools to discover what is required and therefore targeting customer needs more directly;
- its ability to provide all employees with all information that is required to service the customer. This means that needs can be more easily met at interaction time.

Customer retention and satisfaction leads to loyalty. Loyalty not only means that the customer prefers to do business with a company, it also means that the customer may not even consider other options. This has two effects on margins:

- customers are less price-sensitive, so having a higher price than the competition's is still considered good value for money if the service provided is better;
- the cost of winning more business from existing customers is less. Hence, profitability can be greater at a price that is equal to, or even less than, competitors' prices.

A holistic view of the customer makes it possible to not only retain customers and win business that might otherwise have gone to competitors, but also to increase the value of business with each customer through cross-selling and up-selling.

This can be achieved in two ways:

- opportunistically, where in every interaction with a customer, a holistic view provides information that aids selling activity. This includes customer-specific data, such as previous transactions, service history preferences and interests. Other types of information are also useful both to employees serving customers and to customers directly – for example, information about the company's products and services, competitors' products and services, pricing lists, delivery schedules, discounting policy and other related information as appropriate;
- by planning, where cross-selling and up-selling information are discovered by performing analysis to determine what product and service combinations will be attractive to customers.

In Chapter 14 we shall explore the tools needed to implement the CRM system.

14

Creating the CRM System: An Integrated Knowledge System

Objectives

After studying this chapter, you should be able to:

- understand the requirement for integration across channels and sources;
- understand and be able to describe the main technologies including:
  - datawarehouse
  - datamart
  - data mining
  - data transformation
  - campaign management;
- understand and be able to explain the data management issues associated with customer relationship management;
- understand and be able to explain database marketing.

1 Introduction

In this chapter we explore the components of a CRM system and how they link to the customer contact or delivery channels.

Figure 14.1: An Integrated CRM system

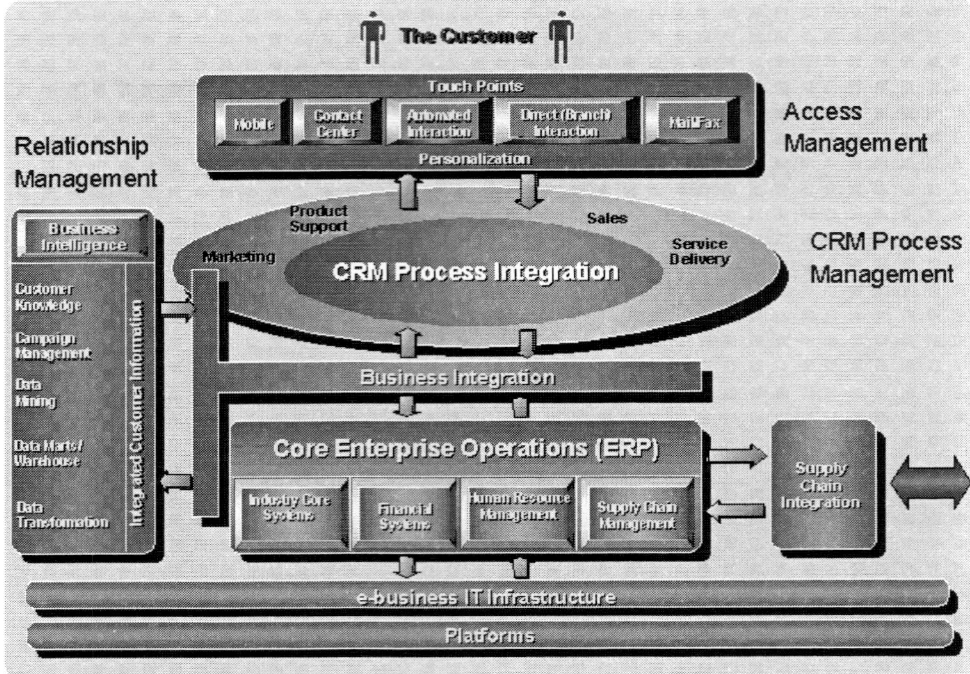

Source: IBM

The above diagram draws together all of the components that together provide an 'end-to-end' delivery system for deploying CRM.

2 Business Intelligence

This is the integrated customer information system which will comprise of:

- Customer Knowledge: Raw data and information drawn from customer interactions, product and transaction systems;
- Campaign Management: The system for launching, controlling and monitoring customer contact strategies;
- Data Mining: The tools to analyse data, identify patterns and correlations to infer actions;
- Data Warehouse: The database repository for the customer knowledge;
- Data Transformation: Tools for absorbing and matching data from product and other third party systems.

3 Customer Knowledge: Creating the Corporate Memory

Data Warehouse

Definition: Database and data warehouse tend to be used interchangeably. The primary difference is the assumption of scale and integration that is implied in a data warehouse, i.e. it is a large database pulling together information from other product and transaction systems. At its simplest, a data warehouse is a very large database which is used for the long-term storage of data likely to be of continuing value to the organization. As with any warehouse, the data is only of value if it can be accessed when it is needed and so the other aspect of a data warehouse is some form of query language.

Data warehouses have been made possible by two main developments:

- Improvements in the size, performance and cost of storage devices and relational databases.

  An example is the development of tiered storage. This allows the most frequently used data to be stored on hard disk, and less frequently used data to be stored on optical disk or tape cartridge. The user does not need to know where the data is stored and can use a single instruction to access the data irrespective of its physical location.

  We can show this as a diagram:

Figure 14.2: Data Warehouse

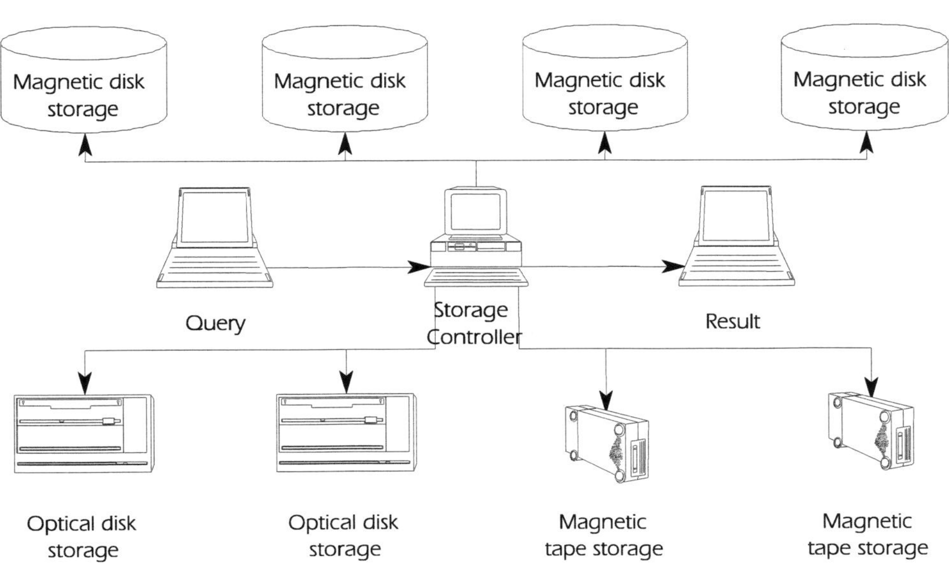

- Improvements in the technology available to access data. This includes developments in computer hardware and software.

An example is the database machine. This spreads the data over a number of different storage devices, each of which has its own processor. This allows very rapid access to data because each processor will look for the data requested on its own storage device. In simple terms, if there are a hundred processors the database machine will find the data one hundred times quicker than a conventional computer.

We can show this as a diagram:

Figure 14.3: Database Machine

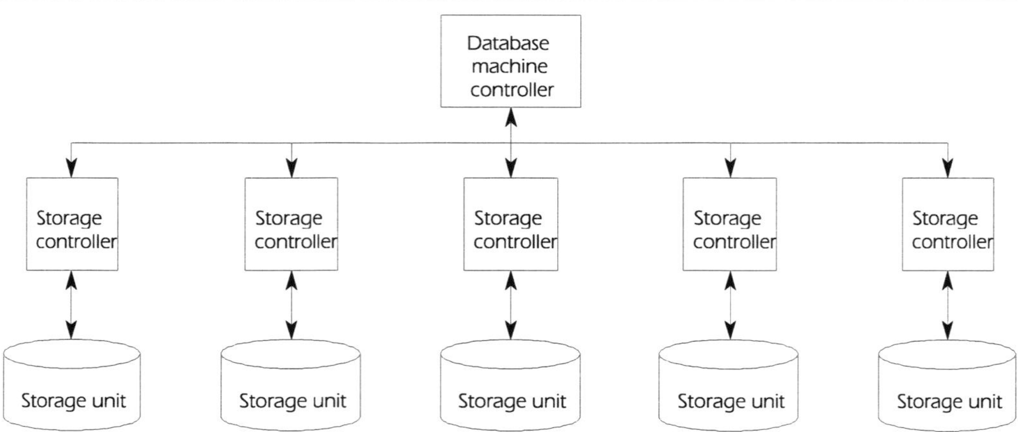

There are three things we can do with our data warehouse:

- We can run enquiries against the data. We can use a standard query language but there are also a number of query languages designed to be used in a data warehouse environment. It is also possible to use software such as spreadsheets and electronic office databases and link these to the data warehouse using database connectivity tools – these are discussed in Chapter 13;
- We can extract some of the data into one or more datamarts. These are discussed in the next section;
- We can analyse the data. This is discussed below under On-Line Analytical Processing (OLAP).

Datamarts

A datamart differs from a data warehouse in that it includes only the data relevant to a specific function – often a single department or line of business. The advantage of a datamart is that it is much easier for the business users to find the information they need as, by definition, the datamart only contains the data relevant to them and can be organized in the way that best suits their needs. The users can retrieve this information using a query language or database connectivity.

In contrast, the traditional approach to management information took a series of data extracts from the operational system databases and loaded this into isolated databases for each function within the organization The problem with this was that the data could be inconsistent between the various users. Different functions (e.g. Finance, Credit and Risk, Marketing) with access to different information could take different and even contradictory decisions.

If a data warehouse is used, all data is first loaded into the data warehouse. Extracts are then carried out against the data warehouse to load the individual datamarts:

Figure 14.4: Data Warehouse and Datamarts

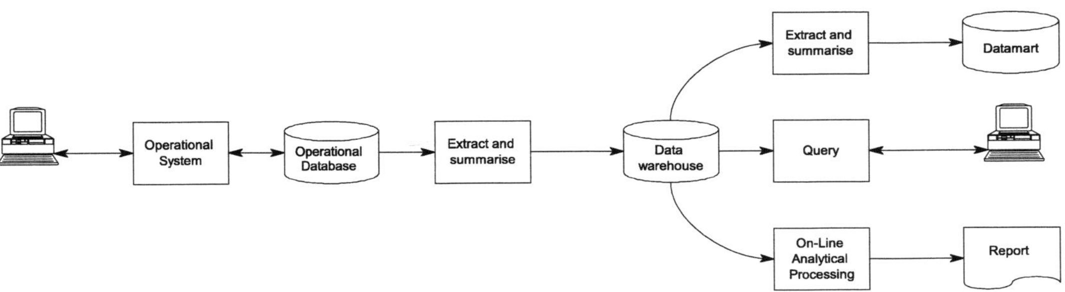

The data warehouse presents a 'single image of business reality' and helps to ensure consistency between the various sources of management information. Datamarts are designed round the needs of their business users, presenting the data needed in the format needed but because the information is drawn from a single source it is consistent and comparable.

4 Building the Data Warehouse

First-Generation Warehouses – Batch Orientation

First-generation data warehouses batch-process data useful for supporting decisions about pricing, market positioning, business development, and so on. For example, a first-generation data warehouse implementation might be to perform list selection and extracts for direct mail and telemarketing campaigns. However, these list pulls are largely initiated by human intervention or predefined scheduling criteria that are largely independent of individual customer events.

Next-Generation Warehouses – One-to-One Relationship Orientation

The next generation of data warehouse implementations support real-time analytics to assist in managing the customer relationship at any and all touch points and in understanding the customer as an individual. This approach is particularly important in light of the impending tidal wave of e-commerce. Conducting business over the web will eliminate traditional channels of relationship building. The self-service model of e-commerce reduces operational costs of customer service.

However, marketing organizations in astute corporations are already grappling with the impact of losing direct contact with the customer.

Thus, the trend toward integrating the data warehouse with customer interactions will be adopted even more aggressively and evolve towards more sophisticated use of information as corporations explore ways of developing a customer relationship management strategy such as event-based triggering for conducting business in the face of e-commerce. An overview of a simple customer data warehouse structure is:

Figure 14.5: Database structure

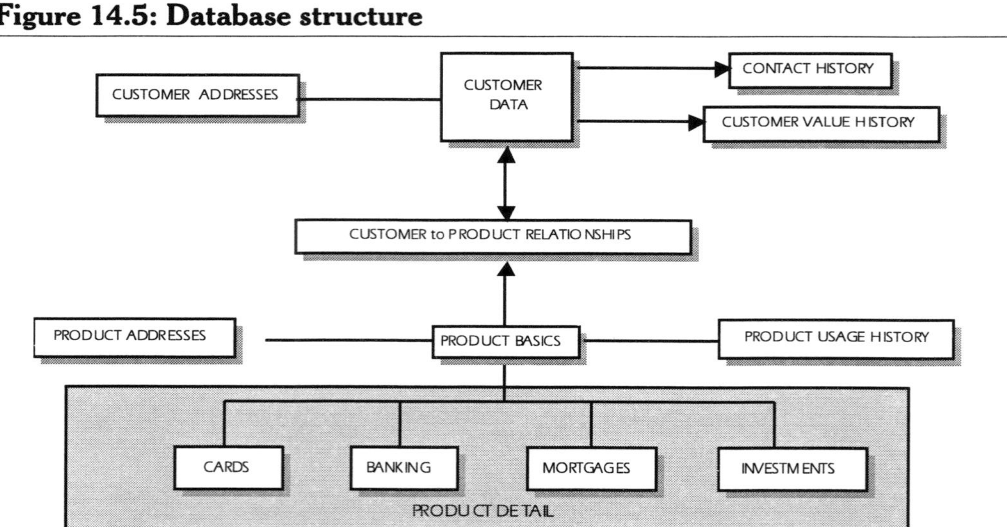

Data Management: Obtaining and integrating data in the warehouse

The process of identifying and cleaning data is fundamental to creating a usable data warehouse and is often the most challenging part of creating the CRM system; keeping data up-to-date together with data integrity is a continuous and major endeavour.

Tasks include:

- Data parsing – Extracting specific data items from a mixed domain field. For example, extracting multiple names from mailing labels or removing product codes from a comment field;
- Data conditioning and domain integrity – Modifying data when values are missing or in error. Changing data from one set of codes to another ensures that values of specified fields fall properly within defined ranges;

- Attaining entity integrity and data integration – Ensuring that only one set of attributes reference a particular entity and that only one occurrence of each key entity exists. Data integration resolves character-level anomalies such as spelling errors, abbreviations, and conflicting data;
- Data conflict resolution – Finding multiple records that refer to the same entity, but possess conflicting attributes – for example, customer records that list the same name and address, but have different social security numbers;
- Data enrichment – Adding data from external data sources;
- Data moving and routing – Moving legacy data to their proper locations within relational tables;
- Data-rule embedding – Embedding business rules to influence how data is integrated, moved, changed or filed.

Products such as Integrity from IBM provide an automated means to transform imperfect data from multiple legacy and external sources into a consolidated view of the business across systems, departments, and business lines.

5 Campaign Management System (CMS): The System for Launching, Controlling and Monitoring Customer Contact Strategies

The customer database provides the central corporate 'glue' for holding together a record of a customer's interaction with an organization. The campaign management system helps to turn this knowledge into proactive customer contact with the aim of increasing net customer value.

Database marketing – A definition

The use of information technology and analytical techniques to facilitate customer relationship management and the on-going development, implementation and monitoring of marketing strategy.

NB. Those who are able to use information with superiority and cleverness are certain to achieve great results. This is the essence of strategy. (Sun Tzu – ***The Art of Strategy****)*

In Chapter 13 we introduced the concept of closed loop marketing. The campaign management system consists basically of three components that align with stages of 1, 2 and 6 of the process:

1. Opportunity spotting: detecting the right customer to contact at the right time with the right product or service;
2. Campaign prioritization and delivery: which opportunity to pursue and through which delivery channel or combination of channels;
6. Contact management: what was the result of the contact and how should that influence future contact?

Figure 14.6: CRM Loop

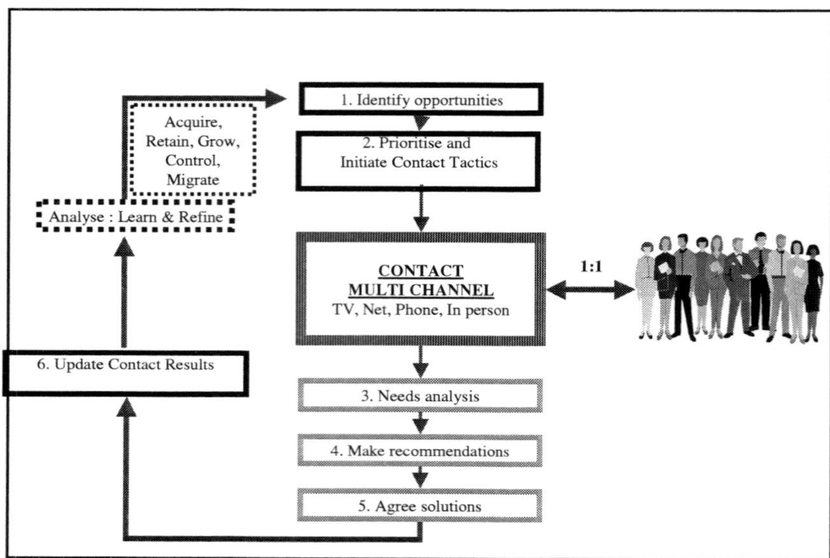

The strategy is to gain and secure customers' confidence via targeted communication that relays a coordinated single-source entity. The organization will contact customers only when there is a perceived 'need' to be filled. The coordinated effort encompasses the different customer touch points, centralized direct marketing (direct mail, telemarketing, Internet, mobile phone, call centre), and localized efforts (branch telephone, direct mail, walk in, ATMs etc.). This includes taking advantage of the information available and combining it with a contact and campaign management strategy.

CMS is a tool to coordinate and synchronize the central and branch 'push' marketing process, suppressing or de-duplicating customer lists and automating the process of running event-driven campaigns. In a centralized marketing context, the 'automated leads' and 'individual solutions' can become simultaneous campaigns that will need to be coordinated and synchronized (central and branch) to ensure customers do not acquire 'contact fatigue' (over contacted). Campaign response and impact can be assessed with results fed back to the data warehouse to assist future campaigns. The introduction of continuous event-driven and large numbers of simultaneous campaigns mean that an integrated system is required.

How is this coordinated to the customer is such a way that the customer perceives the organization as a single touch point and not a series of disjoint channels and contacts?

This is achieved by keeping a perpetual history of customer contact and using this information in a coordinated effort between centralized and local efforts.

Figure 14.7: Database Marketing System – Components

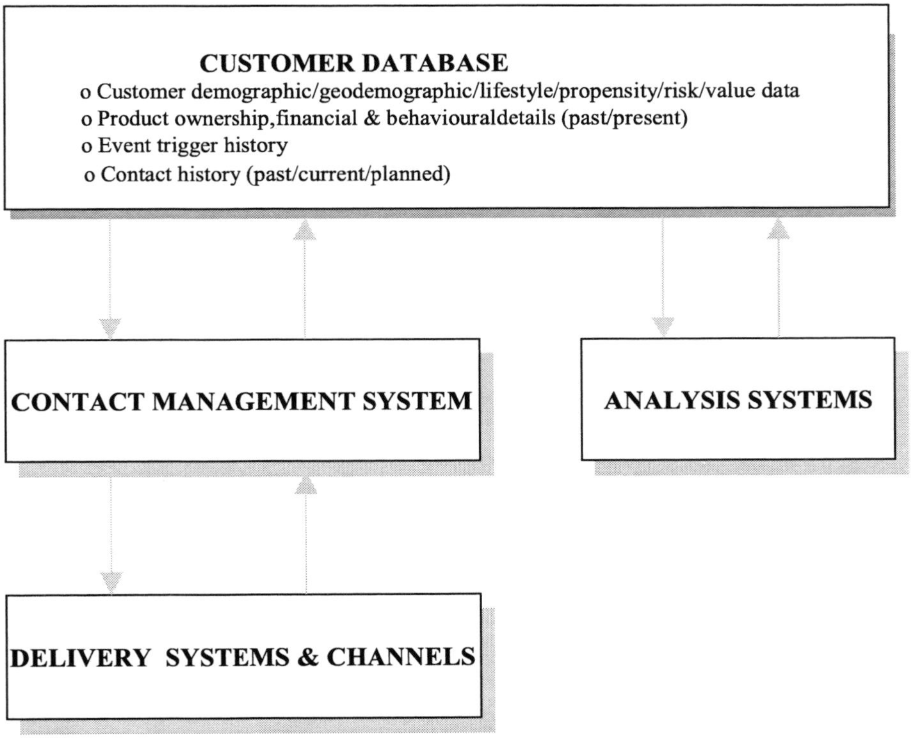

6 Analysis Systems: Identifying the Opportunity

Data Mining

This is the technique using software tools to automatically detect unique patterns or trends in data. This is accomplished by sifting through large amounts of data to create data-dependent relationships.

Data mining identifies hidden relationships, new trends and previously undetected patterns hidden within data. It helps decision makers to make intuitive, yet strategic, decisions regarding customer contact. An example is IBM's Intelligent Miner product.

To fully exploit the data warehouse, an automated analysis tool, which can rigorously interrogate the data is used. Typical data-mining questions that could be answered are:

- What product categories or groups of products do our customers most commonly own?
- What products or product categories are owned by specific customer segments (customers with similar characteristics)?
- What are the characteristics that delineate this purchasing segment from segments that do not purchase?
- What are the product propensities for the segments?
- What is the attrition (churn) of certain products for specific segments?

In addition to answering specific business questions as outlined above, the overall goal of data mining is to improve marketing, sales, and customer support operations via a more complete and better understanding of the customer. This is accomplished by detecting meaningful and relevant behavioural patterns through automated exploration and analyses of large quantities of data.

A simple example of a behaviour pattern would be 'customers with children purchase savings plans whereas customers without choose a different type of mutual fund'. Data mining encompasses the ability to evaluate customer information either automatically or semi-automatically. This knowledge discovery consists of pattern recognition. The explanation of these patterns is used to explain past events and to predict future events.

The process of DIRECTED knowledge discovery includes selecting specific variables or fields and explaining the relationships in data. This process consists of searching large volumes of data and looking for current behaviour patterns that can accurately predict future behaviour in customers. This can be accomplished by using OLAP tools with/without statistical tools. The objective is to confirm a hypothesis, i.e. that a relationship exists between the predetermined variable(s) and the results

Instead of manually choosing and assessing variables that may be predictive, data mining can go through UNDIRECTED knowledge discovery where no prior assumptions are made and the data speaks for itself. This type of knowledge discovery consists of 'recognizing' relationships in data instead of 'explaining' the relationships. This will require a statistician to interpret the findings and confirm whether the relationships are viable, i.e. the key component is a good understanding of the data and the statistical significance of end reports and analysis produced by the data-mining tool. Although not always intuitive, the relationships identified by the data-mining tool helps marketing to improve its understanding of customer behaviour. This in turn allows it to target marketing campaigns more accurately and to align campaigns more closely with the needs of the customers.

Front End Analysis (targeting/querying)

Incorporates the functions that result in the derivation of targeted lists of customers from the data warehouse, i.e. identification of the targets. These functions include generating target customer counts, producing standard reports to profile the targets, and developing statistical models to assess the probabilities of response, creating actionable targeting tools to assist in sales and evaluation of the customers/clients, e.g. customer relationship scores, product propensities etc.

List Processing (list creation) and Execution

Incorporates the functions that follow once the decision has been made to make the list selections, i.e. processing the final criteria, scoring statistical models, pulling list, list suppression/de-duplication, creation of contact groups (cells), sales procedure integration (coordination of follow-up or stages), quality checks, data security and execution (shipping of mail tape).

In addition to standard or traditional direct marketing, the contact/campaign management system must support the automation of complex, multi-stage, multi-channel program/campaigns, using any media. Specifically, it should have the ability to create program/campaigns based on the following types of marketing methodologies:

Event-Driven Marketing is based on calculated recognition of key events affecting customers – e.g. a lease that comes due; an upcoming birthday; a major holiday. The marketers must have the ability to define significant events, the marketing response, and then automate the execution of those efforts.

Velocity Marketing is based on the rate of change in customer/household/account activity. Marketers must have the ability to effectively respond to gradual or sudden shifts in customer behaviour, and to compare changes over multiple periods of time.

Longitudinal Marketing combines within the same or a series of program/campaigns multi-stage marketing efforts with event-triggered marketing to support continuous, multi-stage programs in which each stage is customized (or governed) by the customer's response to the previous marketing initiative.

Threshold Marketing establishes absolute or relative thresholds or parameters that govern marketing communication strategies. A relative threshold methodology would simply alert marketers when certain boundaries are breached (e.g. balance exceeds a certain amount).

Liquid Marketing is the evolution to 'real-time 1:1 marketing'. With liquid marketing, a specific offer, promotion, or program/campaign is created on-the-fly for a specific customer/household/account, based on certain pre-defined rules and parameters. The offer might exist for a very brief period of time and, in fact, might never be recreated in the same way for another customer.

7 Contact Management

Campaign Prioritization

Having selected a customer for potentially multiple contacts/campaigns the CMS will then use rules to establish the order and priority of execution. Clearly just initiating all campaigns for a customer simultaneously is likely to cause customer confusion and very probably dissatisfaction!

Techniques for prioritization include:

Organizational need: this is where the organization is in need of a certain business mix (e.g. it needs more loans) and therefore priority is given to campaigns that will generate this mix. This is not a customer-centric approach and is often linked to organizations with a product-push target-led culture.

Value added: this is where the likely value of the product or service prioritizes the contact. For example, the potential sale of a mortgage, being a high-income product, would take precedence over the potential sale of, say, car insurance.

Probability of success: this is where prioritization is based on the likely probability of the individual customer taking the product or service on offer. E.g. if probability of taking a personal loan is 65% and of taking a credit card 40%, the loan campaign would take priority for that customer. This is a more customer-centric approach.

In reality a combination of the above is normally used. Capital One Bank uses a combination of value added and probability of success as its prime prioritization methodology.

Campaign Delivery

Having identified and prioritized the contact, delivery can now take place. This will , ideally, take into account customer preference for channel (e.g. e-mail *v.* direct paper mail) and take into account appropriate cost of contact for the likely value to be generated from success.

For example, sending a relationship manager to see a customer at home with the hope of selling household insurance is not likely to be an economic proposition because the margin on the product would be outweighed by the cost of delivery.

This requires the organization's front office systems to be linked to the campaign and contact engines.

Contact History

Having undertaken the campaign the CRM system needs to collect the result and store this within the customer contact history for the customer. Capturing this information can be done in a number of ways:

Automatic contact history update: this is done normally as the result of a successful contact where the customer has taken the product or service; the physical taking of the offer generates a product opening within the product system which is then fed back to the data warehouse.

Manual contact history update: this requires a physical input to the customer contact history either by the customer directly (e.g. customer clicks 'no thanks' when offered an increased credit card limit over the internet) or by staff following a conversation with the customer. In order to achieve this it is vital that the customer contact system is available and integrated with front-office processes.

15

Decision Support Systems & Customer Behavioural Tracking

Objectives

After studying this chapter, you should be able to:

- understand and be able to describe the characteristics of information and the features of:
  - a management information system
  - an executive information system
  - on-line analytical processing
  - statistical models
  - scoring systems
  - expert systems;
- understand the different types of information user and be able to discuss their differing requirements for information.

1 Introduction: Strategic, Tactical and Operational Information

Information has some important characteristics:

- It must be relevant to its purpose. Strategic information about market share should not include information about production costs, for example, because this might distract or even confuse the manager using it;
- It must be sufficiently timely for its purpose. This means that the manager needs to get the information in time to take some action. There is no point in telling the manager that his or her costs will be over budget after the end of the financial year;

- It must be sufficiently accurate for its purpose. The accuracy needed varies depending how the information is going to be used. Balance sheets are usually shown in thousands of pounds and this is sufficiently accurate for this purpose. If you are going to calculate rates of return on products you need much more accurate balances because a small difference in the rate might have a big effect on how the bank or building society markets the product;
- It must be presented in the right way and to the right person. Information for senior management should generally be presented as charts, perhaps showing trends over time or market share. The lower the level of management receiving the information, the more detail should generally be shown;
- Information should not cost more to produce than its value to the business.

2 Management Information Systems

Management Information Systems (MISs) are databases that are designed to be used by managers to select and cross-reference data. An MIS consists of a relational database holding the data of interest and a user interface that allows managers to specify the data they want to extract.

Figure 15.1

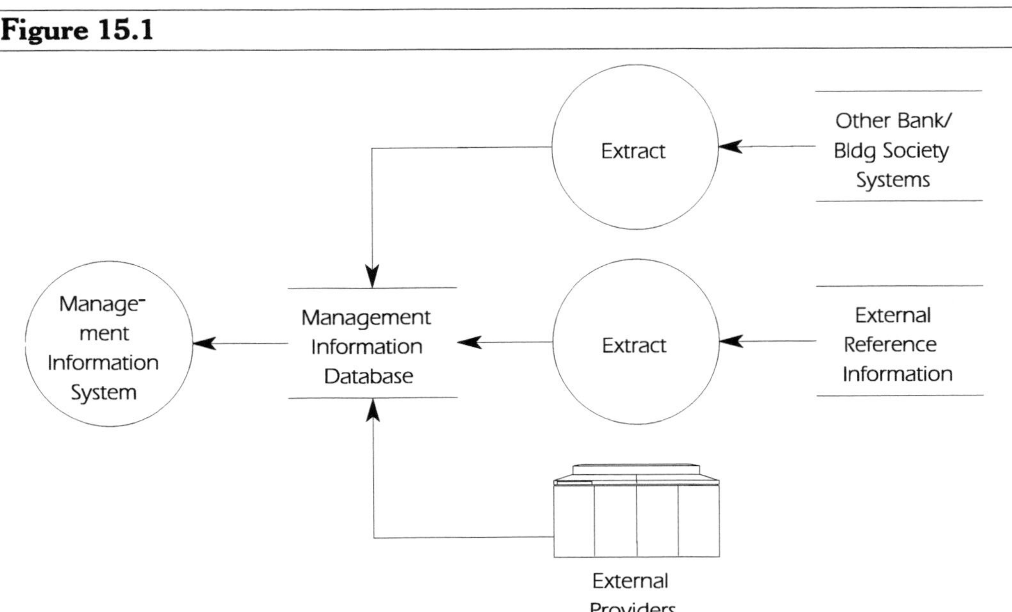

Different managerial levels need different types of information. We usually distinguish between:

- Strategic information, used by senior management;
- Tactical information, used by middle management;

- Operational information, used by first-line management and supervisors.

The differences between these types of information is summarized in Table 15.1.

Management information systems will often provide only strategic and tactical management information. Operational management information is often taken from the processing system

There are usually differences between the information held in an MIS and that held in the corresponding operational database. Reasons for this include:

- Need for history. Managers need to monitor what is happening over a period of time – for example, monthly sales figures for the past eighteen months. Operational systems usually need data for much shorter periods;
- Operational systems may include physical data related to transactions, such as delivery instructions. This information is usually of little relevance to managers;
- Scope. Managers often need to compare data from a number of different operational systems and external data sources to get an overall picture.

Table 15.1

	STRATEGIC INFORMATION	TACTICAL INFORMATION	OPERATIONAL INFORMATION
Used by	Senior Managers	Middle Managers	First-line Managers
Time horizon	1-10 years	3-18 months	Up to 1 month
Sources of data	External and strategic management information systems	Operational and tactical management information systems	Operational systems
Internal or external	Internal and external	Mainly internal	Entirely internal
Frequency of decision	Infrequent and at irregular intervals	Weekly, monthly, quarterly or yearly	Very frequent during the day
Basis for decisions	Facts, projections and judgements	Facts and projections	Facts
Type of decision	Unprogrammed – each decision is unique	Programmed – follows overall policies and precedents	Prescriptive – follows defined rules and procedures
Presentation	Summaries and trends	Summaries and supporting detail	Usually detailed
Examples	Market share and product profitability	Actual costs and revenues *v.* budgets	Customer financial histories

Because of these differences, MISs are usually built up over time from data extracted from the operational database systems. Much of this data is in summary form.

Data held in an MIS is a copy of data taken from operational systems. This means that it will usually be out of date when the data is accessed. This is rarely important for management information but it does limit the uses to which it can be put. Data warehouses and datamarts also contain copies of operational data.

The data for an MIS is taken from the operational systems and external sources as shown in the Figure 15.2:

Figure 15.2

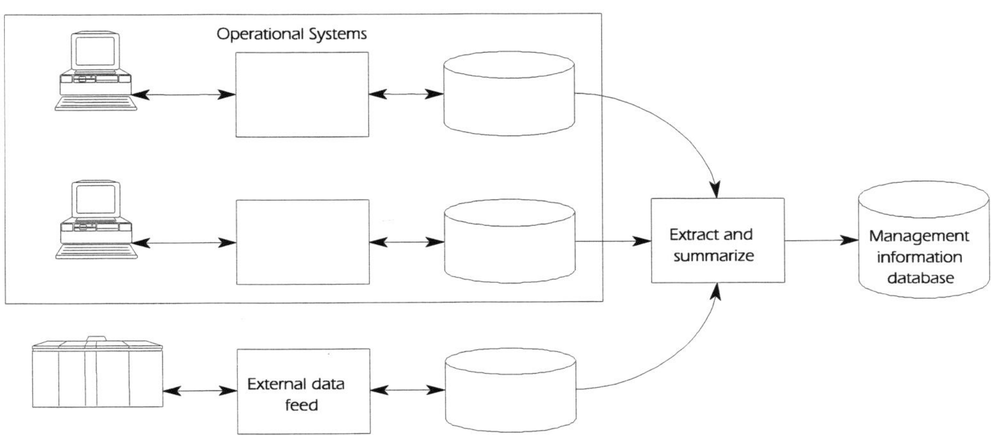

The features of an MIS include:

- Either a query language or a number of standard queries into which the manager can enter parameters.

  'Canned queries' are a feature of older MISs whose query language capabilities were often limited. A series of basic queries was set up into which managers could enter parameters such as date ranges, market segments and minimum and maximum amounts.

  Modern query languages are easier to use and include functions such as 'query by example'. This allows managers to show the system what information they require and allow the query language to work out how to get it;

- Interfaces to electronic office products such as spreadsheets. The simplest way to achieve this is extract data from the MIS into a data file and import this into the electronic office product, and this approach is used in some older MISs. It is also possible to extract data from the MIS in the required form – for example as a spreadsheet file – or to create a link between the MIS and the electronic office product. Database connectivity, discussed in Chapter 13, can also be used and this allows the electronic office product to request the data directly from the DBMS;

- Standard calculations such as cost and profitability calculations. The MIS allows executive management to compare information from across the organization and standard calculations are needed to make sure the values being compared have the same meaning;
- Most MISs hold some data in summary form. An example might be transaction posting data where the amount of data is very large but the individual postings are not needed because management information and monthly summaries can be used instead.

The ability of managers to enter queries is an example of 'end-user computing'. Providing end users with the tools to get the information they need directly, without having to go through the IT function, increases the benefit of IT to the organization. However end-user computing is less efficient than producing a report to provide the same information and the additional costs must be balanced against the benefits.

We introduced the idea of power users in Chapter 5. The problem with end-user computing is that it uses computer resources very heavily and often inefficiently. We can improve the efficiency by using a powerful computer language such as SQL, but these are not designed to be used without training. Power users have the training and knowledge to use these languages. This knowledge equips power users to act as a bridge between business users and systems developers because they understand the problems of both sides.

3 Executive Information Systems

Executive information systems (EISs) provide a way of presenting information to senior management. An EIS works in much the same way as an MIS except that it is usually less powerful at retrieving information but better at presenting it.

The main features of an EIS are:

- It presents information in a way that is very easy to understand. It can highlight figures that are particularly good or bad (green is usually used for above target, yellow for below target and red for well below target). It allows information to be shown as either a chart or a table and to be switched between these presentations in a very simple way;
- It can 'drill down'. For example, if a region is shown as well below target the manager can see how the area figures contributed to that. If one of the areas is well below target he or she can go down to the individual branches.

For example, an EIS system and its links to its data sources might look like this:

Figure 15.3: An EIS System and its Links

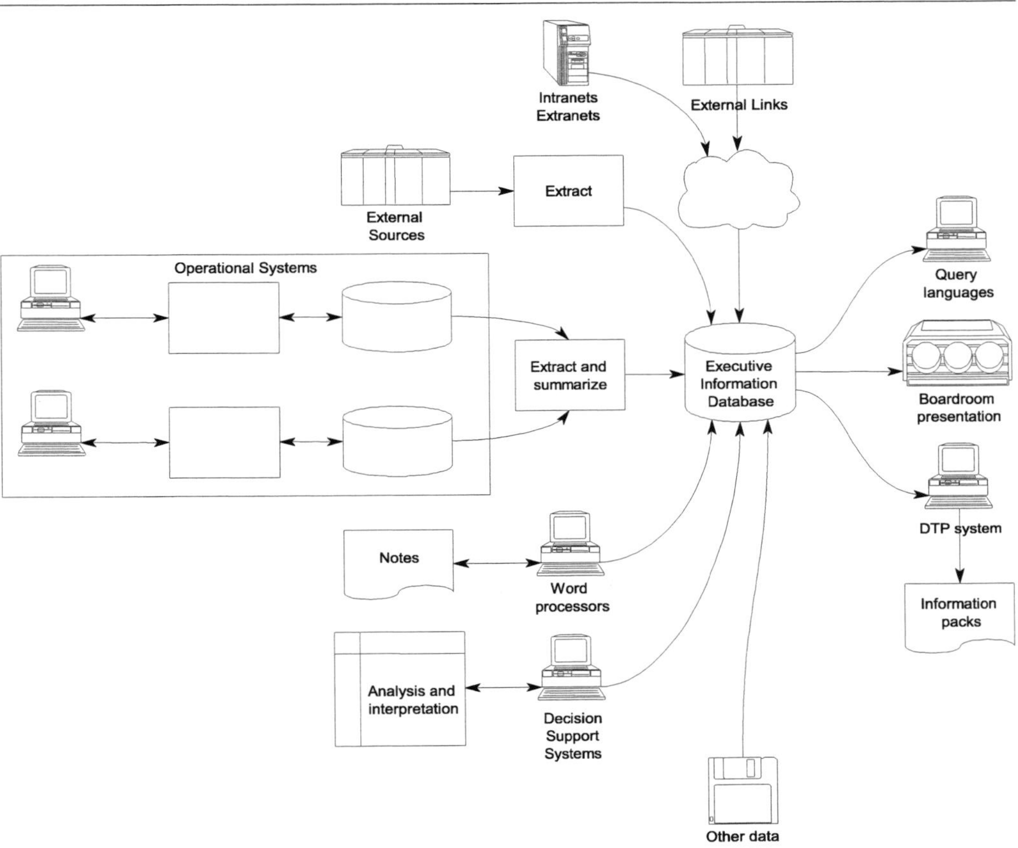

Before being able to decide which software or combination of software would be most beneficial to an organization we must look into the usage and the users' needs. This means finding out the types of users available at each site and what their needs and expertise would be. The business intelligence community has outlined descriptions of different information users.

Table 15.2

User Categories	User Types	Objectives/ Functions	Knowledge	Perspective of World	Usage Pattern
Tourists (Generalists)	Executives, Managers, Casual users	Broad business perspective Executives, in particular, need basic information to assess the overall health of their companies	Cover a breadth of material quickly but in little depth Aware of the data, information and knowledge that the business produces	In terms of business function	Unpredict-able
Operators (Focused)	Customer support, Inventory Control, Manufacturing	Use intelligence derived by explorers/farmers to improve business Primary source of feedback into the information process	Provide pressure on information source in terms of availability, data freshness and query performance	In terms of process	Fairly predictable
Farmers (Clear)	Sales Analysts, Financial Analysts, Marketing Campaign Managers, Accounting Analysts	Monitors the effect of decisions on the business by tracking key performance metrics Provide explorers with feedback on effectiveness of predictions	Know what data they want, and how they want it displayed, when they want it and in what media Understand value of integrated, cleansed data	In terms of dimensions (time, product, geography) and metrics (usage, revenue, counts, costs)	Fairly predictable
Explorers (Innovative)	Marketing Analyst, Actuaries, Process Control Engineers	Endeavour to understand what makes the business work by looking for hidden meaning in the data Strive to predict the future based on past events	Very knowledgeable about content of data within and outside of business Have little or no idea of what to expect prior to query execution	In terms of data and data relationships	Unpredictable
Miners (Thorough)	Statisticians, Expert Marketers, Risk Controllers, Logistics Specialists	Scan large amounts of detailed data to confirm hypothesis or suspected	patterns Good idea of what to expect prior to query execution	Operate on a base of very flat, highly de-normalized data that has been pre-conditioned for analysis	Reasonably predictable

Source: GartnerGroup, Bill Inmon

Once the users have been designated as belonging to one of the above categories, a simple analysis can be performed. This analysis is two part, i.e. what quantity of users are there in each category and, from this, which software should be implemented to acquire the biggest return (with respect to number of users and action ability)? In short, the software required will be based on the business user data needs and the sophistication of these users.

The easiest way in assessing the software needs is to look within your user community and identify the number of 'data' or information users and the categories that these users fall into. As an example, if there were 20 users that are all branch managers and /or executives, this would suggest all the users are 'tourists'. The tourists' 'needs' can be met with an EIS or On Line Analytical Processing (OLAP) tool.

If however, there are 20 users and 15 are marketing experts and analysts and the remaining 5 are executives, it will be more appropriate to forego the EIS and concentrate on OLAP, statistical tools and a campaign management tool. The statistical tools will allow the users to group the customer into similar segments, while the campaign management tool would be key in an environment where there are numerous campaigns. This tool would be used to coordinate multiple campaigns from multiple customer touch points.

The user types and categories are important in deciding the appropriate software to meet the users' needs.

Table 15.3

User Categories	User Types	EIS (Executive Information System)	OLAP (Query/ reporting)	Statistical Language or Decision Support	Campaign Management	Data Mining
Tourists (Generalists)	Executives, Managers, Casual users	X	X	X	X	X
Operators (Focused)	Customer support, Inventory Control, Manufacturing	–	**X**	**X**	**X**	**X**
Farmers (Clear)	Sales Analysts, Financial Analysts, Marketing Campaign Managers, Accounting Analysts	X	X	X	X	X

Table 15.3 (continued)

User Categories	User Types	EIS (Executive Information System)	OLAP (Query/ reporting)	Statistical Language or Decision Support	Campaign Management	Data Mining
Explorers (Innovative)	Marketing Analyst, Actuaries, Process Control Engineers	–	X	X	X	X
Tourists (Generalists)	Statisticians, Expert Marketers, Risk Controllers, Logistics Specialists	–	–	X	X	X

4 Tactical and Operational Management Information Systems

Predictive techniques in Customer Contact Management

The main techniques used to predict customer behavior are:

- On Line Analytical Processing Tools (OLAP)
- Campaign Management
- Statistical Models and Scoring
- Datamining
- Expert Systems
- Credit Scoring Systems

OLAP (On Line Analytical Processing Querying and Reporting Tool)

OLAP is a development of Decision Support Systems (DSSs). Like a DSS, an OLAP system holds data in a multi-dimensional form. The features of an OLAP system include:

- Usability. Speed – an OLAP system should respond to an on-line query in real time. 'Intuitiveness' – business users should be able to make queries by taking simple, obvious actions. Flexible presentation – the ability to present the results of a query in a number of different formats to suit the user's needs;

- Database and 'reach through' features. Reach through is the ability of the OLAP system to identify when it does not have the data required to answer a query and to retrieve missing data from a data warehouse or from the operational systems. This is related to transparency – the business user does not need to know where the data is physically stored. Other database features include data security and integrity;
- Analysis features. The ability to produce standard reports based on parameters (this is similar to the idea of canned queries described for MISs). The ability to 'slice and dice' data – looking at different subsets of the data, similar to the idea of 'views' discussed under workgroup computing in Chapter 10. This is usually supported by 'drill down', which is discussed later in this chapter. The ability to support goal-seeking and 'what if' analysis;
- Multi-dimensional features. Rotation – the ability to switch easily from one view of the data into a different view. For example, the ability to switch between a product and a market view of revenues. Auto-consolidation – the ability automatically to consolidate data in a hierarchy. For example, the ability to consolidate data from branch level to area level, and from area level to regional level, without significant effort.

Business users need to have flexible access to CRM data in order to convert information to knowledge (i.e. develop customer insights) that will prompt value-added actions. There needs to be a capability to 'slice and dice' (cross tabulation) information from the data warehouse or datamart to facilitate the appropriate perspectives required in reporting and analysis. Standard reporting will cover the central and distributed access to information needed to support the business whereas ad-hoc querying will normally be a centralized facility with appropriate controls over its use for security purposes. An example of an ad-hoc query would be the production of customer listings to support centralized direct marketing activities (mailings, telemarketing, etc.). These ad hoc queries are specific to an individual user's interests and requirements. This can be accomplished by writing specific selection criteria to extract information to estimate how many customers meet the pre-defined specifications. The resulting counts would allow the centralized business user to estimate the potential sales that can be acquired from the contact.

There are various ways in which this can be applied.

Initial Counts

Provides the ability to analyse summarized and aggregated information along a series of dimensions (time, product, geography etc.). The user starts by writing selection criteria against the data warehouse or datamart to find out how many customers meet user-specified conditions. Counts give the user a general idea to the potential size of the campaign. For example, a user may wish to find out that certain age groups are interested in certain products, with the result that would assist in tailoring cross-sell strategy accordingly. The user supplies criteria, i.e. the variables (age and product type), and the system generates an answer, being the range of products mapped to age of current customers.

Standard and Ad-hoc Reports

After generating initial customer counts, the user may wish to dig deeper into the selected populations. One short-hand way is to use standard reports when available. These are pre-formatted reports, which provide profiling statistics – such as age, geographic location, status, gender, demographics, etc. on any population the user selects.

OLAPs facilitate ad-hoc analysis of customers, products, branches – i.e. planning, trending and forecasting. This allows data pivoting, slicing and dicing (which encompasses rotating the view of data by different dimensions – i.e. branch, regional manager, relationship manager, bank, etc.) and the ability to drill down (move from an aggregated or higher perspective to a lower more detailed level of information).

Basic Statistics

The user may want to go a step further by generating more detailed analyses on selected target customers, such as frequency distributions, averages, sums, etc. If marketing does not have the skills, this may initially require the help of a database analyst to help to set up the query using the OLAP tools. After a period of time, the analyst or 'explorer' can set up a 'template' for similar analytical requests, to alleviate the need to recreate the query for each individual request. These templates could be used to monitor effectiveness of different initiatives or to assess where the opportunities are:

Identify cross sell/sales opportunities by querying product combinations across other variables (i.e. age, marital status, etc.) to assess the supplementary or next-best product, e.g. current account and savings account for a customer < 25 years of age will need a ATM card.

Identify if there is a retention issue (i.e. comparing previous month/quarter customer information with current customer information).

Sampling

Often the user may want an unbiased representation or 'sample' of a specific group of customers from the datamart or warehouse. This is most common for predictive or statistical modelling purposes. Predictive models do NOT require information on all the customers to predict future behaviour. They do, however, require unbiased samples. The easiest way to acquire an unbiased sample is to select every X record, i.e. there must be ability to choose every 'nth' customer (i.e. every 2nd, 5th, 10th, etc. customer) to make up the full sample. Campaign management systems (CMS) are described in Chapter 14, section 5.

Statistical Models and Scoring

Subjective reporting and extraction from the database is limiting in its ability to meet certain business objectives. Statistical techniques are needed to process the information available, and to produce models and scores that help business processes. Some of the common modelling applications include:

- Product acquisition propensity models to improve sales targeting and effectiveness for cross-selling;
- Segmentation models to split customers into groups with similar product behaviour characteristics;
- Attrition models to estimate and predict customer's fund movement behaviour and likelihood of fund attrition or defection due to other changes (e.g. fee change);
- Relationship management (individual solutions) model that provides a recommended course of action for each customer based on balances information, product usage, propensity scores, demographic data, and segment indicator;
- Credit risk models to assess and contain risk at customer level. Examples of these are behavioural and credit scoring packages.

The statistical and data mining techniques needed to develop these scores and models are normally very complicated and require specialist skills.

Although the analytic OLAP approaches (counts, reports, business statistics) can yield powerful customer understanding, even deeper understanding can be provided through the development and application of models from the data warehouse. Models can find underlying relationships that other analysis can miss. Details of models are as follows.

RFM Models

When interrogating the data warehouse (or more normally a datamart) for targets for a proposed campaign, the most important data available is customer behaviour data (such as purchase history). Such information can be used for 'RFM' models. RFM models target customer based on:

- Recency – how recently a customer has purchased or transacted a product or service;
- Frequency – how often a customer has purchased or accessed a product or service;
- Monetary Value – how much a customer has spent on products or services (could be based on the transaction amounts).

RFM models are attractive to direct marketers because they do not require statistical knowledge to build and are fairly straightforward to implement. Essentially, the RFM attributes of the customer database are grouped into ranges predetermined by the analyst. For example, 'Monetary Value' might be represented by a breakdown of 'less than £500', '£500 to £1,999', '£2,000 to £4,999', '£5,000 to £9,999', and '£10,000+'. If 'Recency' and 'Frequency' are also broken down to ranges, then a matrix is created where each customer is in one of the cells defined by the combination of the dimensions. For example, if each dimension had 5 this would give 5 x 5 x 5 = 125 cells. Many different RFMs can be run on selected populations.

The arbitrary nature of the ranges coupled with the non-inclusion of potentially relevant customer data (such as age and income) limit the usefulness of RFM, particularly with the availability of the more analytically rigorous approaches used in predictive modelling. However, RFM can still be a valuable 'first cut' alternative in understanding customer behaviour, and can be implemented faster than statistical models.

Statistical Models

Eventually, the large amounts of customer information can be unworkable for the user who wishes to know what the customer's needs are with respect to the relationships of other customer variables. OLAP will answer specific questions and 'what if' scenarios.

Statistical analyses are generally used for two main reasons: predictive modelling and behavioural segmentation.

Predictive Models (or Propensity Score Cards)

Predictive models are used in identifying individual customers or prospects who are most likely to respond to a marketing programme (such as cross-selling offers) or most likely to perform in a particular way (such as renewing).

Modellers use a variety of statistical techniques to identify customers to target for cross sell, acquisition and retention. However the process in developing a model remains the same:

- Marketer defines sample subset(s) of the data warehouse or datamart for the statistician;
- Statistician builds model and tests on validation ('control') sample;
- Model implemented across data warehouse to 'score' customer records;
- Scores are stored on data warehouse as customer attribute;
- Customers selectable by score or range of score;
- Process runs in real time or more frequently batch to refresh scores as customer data changes.

A predictive model can fine-tune a campaign by ranking customers, e.g., from highest product propensity to lowest propensity (as in the case of a cross-selling program) or from most likely to cancel ('attrite') to least likely to cancel. Customers are rank ordered and therefore both effort and money can be saved since it can focus on only those customers most likely to need a product promoted in a specific program. In short this means the entire population need not be contacted for a promotion. But, instead maybe the top 5% to 10% of customers, as predicted by the model.

Behavioural Segmentation

The best way to understand the customer needs is to observe customer behaviour. The goal is to eventually observe each customer's behaviour and offer products and services that are appropriate to match the needs demonstrated by the behaviour. The more we can differentiate the treatment of that customer, the more we can affect his reaction. The next step in working towards the ultimate goal of 1 to 1 marketing is the development of groups or segments based on behaviour. This involves using transactional behaviour to group customers into behavioural segments.

Complex data interrelationships may require statistical analysis to uncover them. So the experienced user may move from OLAP and RFM to data mining, to predictive models and behavioural segmentation. For example, an organization may decide to use data mining to find the predictive factors for product acquisition, and the data mining tool might determine that males older than 45 were likely responders. But the data mining might also discover something else, e.g. change of address and percent of mutual funds in investment mix were also elements of response, i.e. something that may not have been intuitive.

Applying this newfound knowledge to customers in the data warehouse is a dynamic process. As the market conditions change, so do the customer perceptions and the need for specific products or bundles of products. As a result, the process of segmenting and modelling becomes a dynamic process.

Data mining is covered in detail in Chapter 14.

5 Examples of Business Intelligence Tools

For example, IBM provides a suite of products called the IBM Data Information Factory. These consist of three products, all of which can be linked to form a seamless reporting environment:

Ad Hoc Query and Reporting – IBM has partnered with Business Objects to provide this function. Business Objects products provide non-technical business users with access to information stored in data warehouses, data marts, and packaged business applications. Business Objects provides a complete suite of decision support tools offering ad hoc query and reporting capabilities as well as integrated analysis functionality, for both client/server and internet environments.

OLAP- DB2 OLAP Server – is an enterprise-scale, on-line analytical processing system for a wide range of multidimensional reporting, analysis, modelling, and planning applications. DB2 OLAP Server is based on Hyperion's Essbase OLAP Server.

DB2 OLAP Server can be used for a wide range of applications:

- Management and reporting
- Planning and modelling
- Sales analysis
- Profitability
- Market share
- Supplier analysis
- Executive information system (EIS)

- Financial consolidations
- Budgeting
- Forecasting.

Expert systems

The most common are knowledge-based systems. An expert in a particular field describes the process he or she goes through to assess something. The steps are coded as 'rules' and entered into a 'knowledge base'. Someone with less expertise can consult the system, which will ask a series of questions. Depending on the responses to those questions, the expert system's 'inference engine' will use the information in the knowledge base to decide the most likely answer to the question. Some systems have a self-learning capability – they can adjust the rules depending on the results of their decisions.

We can show a knowledge-based system as a diagram:

Figure 15.4: Knowledge-based System

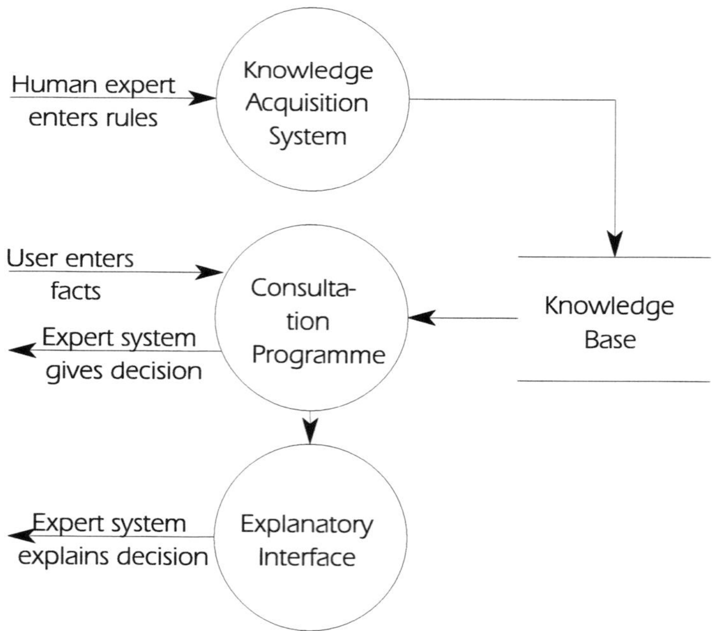

A typical approach to building an expert system might be as follows:

- A human expert would define a set of rules, working with an IT expert systems specialist or possibly directly with the computer. These would be entered into the system's knowledge base;
- The system would be tested and the rules adjusted depending on the results. This

process would be automatic if a neural network or a self-learning program were used;

- A user would be able to consult the system, by answering questions or by supplying data. The inferencing engine will compare the information against the rules in the knowledge base and reach a conclusion. This may be a single statement or it may be a range of possibilities, each with a percentage probability (expert systems used for medical diagnosis often work this way);
- If the user does not understand or does not agree with the conclusion, he or she can ask the explanatory interface how it has been reached. This will show which rules were applied and how the conclusion was reached.

Limitations of Expert Systems

There is nothing magical about expert systems. They are only as effective as the rules entered into them. They are used for fraud detection for credit cards and for some loan assessment and portfolio management systems.

Knowledge-based systems, without a self-learning capability, are the most common form of expert system used in financial services organizations. Their main advantage is that they give consistent answers, unlike the other systems where the answer will be affected by what the system has learnt from recent experience.

The disadvantage of knowledge-based systems is that they assume that the rules stay the same. Although this is generally true in retail finance it is not the case for the wholesale markets and neural networks and genetic algorithms are widely used in, for example, securities trading. Neural networks and genetic algorithms are also used in fraud detection.

Case-based reasoning is used to some extent in the credit assessment of small business customers. It allows customers to be ranked against other firms in the same line of business. This is more common in the USA where information about industry segments is available through the bankers' trade association.

Neural Networks

Neural networks are becoming increasingly important. These learn in much the same way as the human brain. They contain a large network of inter-connected processors. Information fed into this chooses its own path through the network, based on rules that have been entered and on past experience. If a particular path has been successful under a set of circumstances, it is more likely that the same path will be chosen if the circumstances are similar. By running a large number of cases through the neural network, it learns and improves its rate of success.

Genetic Algorithms

Another relatively new approach is the genetic algorithm. These 'evolve', with the less successful in each generation becoming extinct while the more successful go through forced mutation to form the next generation. As with neural networks, feeding a large number of cases through the genetic algorithm allows it to learn and improve its rate of success. An important difference between neural networks and genetic algorithms is that the latter only require software and can be run on a standard PC.

Case-Based Reasoning

Case-based reasoning is a different approach. This relies on a large library of similar cases with known results. Every problem that is presented is compared with the cases in the library and the most similar cases are identified. The result of the new case can be predicted on the basis of the results of similar past cases.

Credit-Scoring Systems

Credit-scoring systems attempt to predict how likely a borrower is to repay a loan from a combination of demographic information (age, occupation, residential status etc.) and past account behaviour. They carry out the functions of expert systems, although they are not generally developed using expert systems technology.

Demographic scorecards give loan applicants a 'score' depending on their answers to the questions on the application form. For example, a residential status of owner occupier might be worth 20 points whereas a status of tenant might only be worth 5.

Behavioural scorecards work in the same way but use account history information. For example, if the customer has not gone over limit at all in the last 18 months this might be worth 20 points, one or two limit excesses might be worth 5 points and three or more limit excesses might be worth -10 points.

Credit-scoring systems also include policy rules. These are conditions under which the loan will automatically be refused, for example if there are county court judgements outstanding against the applicant.

The scores for all the questions are added up and compared against a cut-off. If the total score is below this the loan will be refused. If the score is above the cut-off and all the policy rules are satisfied the loan will be granted.

Credit Reference Agencies

Credit-scoring systems often include links to external credit reference agencies. These match applicant's against records such as the electoral roll, county court judgements and information drawn from applicants' credit history. This may include both 'black' (late or missed repayments) and 'white' (good credit record) information, although not all credit providers look at white information.

Advantages

Credit-scoring systems have three main advantages for the banks and building societies:

- They ensure that customers are treated in the same way throughout the branch network.

By automating the system they avoid situations where the same loan application would be treated differently by different managers;

- They allow lending decisions to be made by less experienced (and therefore cheaper) staff;
- The bank or building society can adjust the cut-off score and policy rules depending on its overall strategy. If the organization is trying to build market share it can lower the cut-off score, accepting more business. If it is trying to cut loan losses it can raise the cut-off score. This is much easier than changing the lending behaviour of hundreds of individual managers.

Part 4

DELIVERY CHANNELS AND e-COMMERCE

This part of the book considers how financial services organizations deliver their services to customers and link this to their back office and fulfilment processes.

Chapter 16: Explains how computer networks operate.

Chapter 17: Provides an overview of the different types of delivery channel and the technology required to implement and operate them.

Chapter 18: Explores the challenges facing organizations as they try to integrate this growing range of channels into a coehisive distribution strategy providing a quality customer experience.

Chapter 19: Gives an overview of the implications of all of these channels on back-office operation and the drive towards applying Business Process Re-engineering to provide seamless Straight Through Processing. (STP).

Chapter 20: Concentrates on the Internet and its use for e-commerce.

Chapter 21: Provides a discussion framework for the some key future trends and gives two brief case studies covering CRM and Channel Integration.

16

COMPUTER SYSTEMS AND NETWORKS

Objectives

After studying this chapter, you should be able to:

- be able to describe and distinguish the different types of computer;
- understand and be able to describe the function of servers and routers;
- understand and be able to describe the function of standards and protocols;
- be able to describe the main local area network topologies and be able to explain how they work;
- be able to trace the evolution of wide area networks and be able to describe their main components;
- understand and be able to describe the technology behind the Internet;
- understand emerging data communications technologies such as Bluetooth and the mobile telephone technologies.

1 Introduction

This chapter describes some of the technical components of computer systems and networks.

2 Computer Hardware

Types of Computer

We usually talk about three different types of computer: mainframe computers, minicomputers and microcomputers.

- Mainframe computers are very large and powerful. Hundreds of people can use the same mainframe computer at the same time. They are kept in special 'data centres' where the environment – temperature, humidity, dust – is carefully controlled. Specialist 'computer operators' are needed to run them.

- Minicomputers are much smaller, but can still by used by large numbers of people at the same time – although the maximum number is usually fewer than 100. They can be used in an office environment provided it has good air conditioning and is reasonably free of dust. They can be operated by office staff after training.
- Microcomputers are small enough to fit on an office desk. They are usually used by one person at a time. They are very robust and will put up with higher temperatures and more dust than larger computers. The most modern microcomputers can be used by anybody with almost no need for training.

Two other common terms are personal computer (or PC) and workstation. Both of these are alternative ways to describe microcomputers.

- The term PC is most often used for a microcomputer that is not attached to a computer network. However, the term is very widely used simply as an alternative to microcomputer.
- The term workstation can be used in two senses. It can be used for a microcomputer attached to a computer network – it is usually used in this sense in this book. Or it can be used for a particularly powerful type of microcomputer, often used for a job that needs a lot of computer power.

Developments in microcomputers have been one of the main technological drivers of the past decade. A modern microcomputer has far more computing power than a mainframe computer of 10-15 years ago and the ability to network microcomputers increases this power enormously. One effect has been to reduce the importance of the minicomputer.

Historically, minicomputers were used by organizations too small to need the power of a mainframe computer. Now, powerful workstations and networked microcomputers can meet such organizations' needs. Another role for the minicomputer was to combine data-processing applications (traditionally run on mainframe computers) with electronic office applications. However, attempts to combine these applications were not always effective and the alternative (using networked microcomputers to run electronic office applications, linked to a mainframe computer or workstation which is used to run data-processing applications) is now generally preferred.

Minicomputers are still widely used, but we need to be aware of their reduced importance.

Servers and Routers

We have discussed servers in the context of client server. Servers are important in local area networks (LANs) and have an extremely important role to play in the Internet, where service providers and content providers operate 'server farms' with a large number of servers. Servers are powerful microcomputers.

Another important component of the Internet and LANs is the router. In the context of the

Internet, routers are computers or computer software that look at the destination of information and determine how best to get it to this destination.

The Internet uses a packet switched network to send data. Instead of relying on a permanent link between the terminal and the mainframe computer, the message can 'switch' across a number of routers or exchanges. The link is set up only when the message is sent.

Compare this to making a long-distance phone call. When we dial, the exchange to which our telephone is connected will take the call. It will use the dialling code to find the right exchange for the person we are trying to call, and it will set up the connection. It may have to go through intermediate exchanges to do this, especially if we are telephoning abroad.

Packet switching works in exactly the same way. The message is broken up into 'packets', the first of which contains address information (like the dialling code and number). When the first packet is sent, the router or exchange will work out how to get the message to its destination.

Routers have another function in that they allow a LAN to be connected to a LAN of a different type or, in some cases, to a wide area network (WAN). Other devices that can perform similar functions include:

- Gateways or communications servers, the most important function of which is to connect LANs to WANs. They can also be used to connect a LAN to a different type of LAN;
- Repeaters, which are used to extend the maximum length of a LAN. An important limitation on the length of a LAN is that the signal gets weaker as it travels over longer distances. The repeater boosts the signal – in effect it acts as an amplifier;
- Bridges, which are the main method of connecting LANs of the same type to each other. Bridges allow all the resources on the LANs to be shared – users of one LAN can access software or data stored on another, for example – under the control of the network operating system.

The difference between gateways, bridges and routers is very technical (it depends on the level of the Open Systems Interconnection – OSI – protocol at which they operate).

Standards and Protocols

If we want to connect different types of computer in a network, we need to have a set of rules to make sure the computers can understand each other. This is called a 'prototcol' and controls the format, timing, order and error control for messages sent over a network. As long as one computer speaks the same protocol as another computer then they should be able to communicate with each other.

We have briefly touched on one example of a protocol – the Open Systems Interconnection (OSI) model developed by the International Standards Organization. This model has seven 'layers'. Whereas the lowest of the layers supports only the physical transmission of messages, the highest allows users of one computer to run application software on another (interoperability).

Another example is the TCP/IP protocol used by the Internet. TCP/IP stands for Transmission Control Protocol/Internet Protocol and is really two separate protocols. TCP's task is to break down the information into packets at the sender side, and to re-assemble these packets in the correct sequence at the receiving end. IP's task is to ensure that each individual packet of information is sent to the correct destination.

Every computer that connects to the Internet must be able to process and handle TCP/IP, and to do this it needs special software called a socket or TCP/IP stack. On a PC this software is called Winsock, and for a Macintosh the software is referred to as MacTCP. In either case, the software acts as 'middleware' between the computer and the Internet, processing and handling all TCP/IP operations seamlessly.

Computer Addresses

One feature of TCP/IP is the IP address. This is a number of the form 234.56.78.012 and provides a unique address for each computer on the network.

Fortunately we do not need to remember the IP address to use the Internet! The form of address that we will use is the Uniform Resource Locator (URL), which will usually be of the form http://www.cib.org.uk. This may be made up of a number of elements:

- The protocol
- The host name
- The port number
- The directory
- The filename.

The protocol specifies what communication mechanism (or protocol) the browser should use to retrieve the information from the relevant web site.

There are several possible protocols available today, but the most common by far is 'http', an abbreviation for HyperText Transfer Protocol. Other protocols available include ftp, gopher, news, telnet, etc. If ftp is specified then an ftp (file transfer protocol) connection is made between the browser and the server. If telnet is specified, a remote login connection is made, and so on.

The host name specifies the individual computer host name (e.g., www.scotent.co.uk) where the web resource is located. An IP address can also be used instead here, such as 146.176.160.236, which uniquely identifies the computer host name. The 'www' prefix refers to the world-wide web. The high-suffixes 'co' and 'uk' show that the organization is a company based in the UK. Suffixes of this type are called domains and other high-level domains include '.com' for companies, '.org' for organizations and '.net' for networks.

An optional port number can also be specified in a URL – a port number can be thought of as a communications channel on the web site computer. This port number, if present, tells the web browser which channel is actually running the web server on the remote machine. Most web servers by default run on port 80, so this can usually be dropped in URLs.

However, if a single computer is running more than one web server then each server must be allocated a different port number. Convention dictates that additional web servers start at port 8000 (8080 is a common choice). Hence, the URL to access a different web server on the same above computer may be: http://www.scotent.co.uk:8080/sectors/software/softnet.html.

The directory specifies the directory pathname where the web resource (i.e. the HTML file) is actually located within the remote machine. In the above example, this directory path is given as: '/sectors/software/softnet/'. Hence, this directory must exist for the resource to be successfully returned and displayed within the user's web browser – the user must also have permission to retrieve the specified web page or object.

The filename represents the actual HTML filename (or any other web resource) that should be retrieved and displayed within the user's web browser (or played back if it is an audio or video file, etc.), for example 'index.html'.

All IP addresses and URLs must be unique and must be registered with the Internet Assigned Names and Numbers Authority. A central database is used to translate URLs into IP addresses.

The HyperText Transfer Protocol

HTTP is an abbreviation for HyperText Transfer Protocol, and is the fundamental communication mechanism for the transfer of information on the web. When we visit a web site (such as http://www.ecommerce-scotland.org/) we shall be using HTTP as the mechanism for requesting and receiving information from that site.

Most web browsers by default will assume an HTTP connection, which means we may not have to specify the 'http://' in the URLs you type and we could just use, for example, www.scotent.co.uk.

There are four main stages involved when we click a hyperlink to retrieve information from a web server (whether it be an html file, a graphical image, a video clip, a sound file, etc.). These four stages form the 'handshaking' procedures executed between the web browser and web server that together make up an http connection.

These four stages are: Connect, Request, Respond and Disconnect.

- Connect. The connection between the web client (browser) and the web server (site) is made.
- Request. The web browser requests an object from the web server, such as an html file, graphic (e.g., gif, jpeg), etc.

- Respond. The web server responds to this request – e.g., by sending the required object, or returning an error message if the object was not found, or asking for more information (such as a username and password if authentication is required), etc.
- Disconnect. The connection between the web browser and web server is closed.

Note that a separate connection must be made for each and every object retrieved from a web server. For example, if we wish to download a web page that contains five individual graphical images, then a total of six separate connections must be made to retrieve all the desired items.

The first connection retrieves the web page itself (the text in the HTML file), followed by five additional connections to download each one of the remaining five graphics. This can sometimes be seen occurring in the bottom left-hand corner of a browser (e.g., on Netscape), when it displays a status report indicating how much of each graphical image has been downloaded so far, such as '25% of 12k', '68% of 33k', '48% of 5k', etc.

Cookies

HTTP is sometimes referred to as a 'stateless' protocol; the reason for this is due to the fact that no information is maintained across a series of connections between the web browser and the web server.

Every time we connect to a web server to retrieve information, the server has no way of recognizing that we have already made previous connections, or indeed that we may make future connections. The web server does not remember anything about a query after its responded to that query.

One method of reducing this potential problem is to use 'cookies', which are simple files placed on the local computer by a web server. This file contains information that can be used by the web server should the computer return to the same web site at some future point. The information stored in a cookie file normally has an expiration date associated with it, after which time the web server will ignore the information it contains.

How is this cookie information used? Well, should we return to a previously visited web site, and cookie information has been placed on our computer by that web server, then we may find that information displayed to you has been personalized in some way, such as 'Welcome back, Steve. Good to see you again!' or 'Angela, since your last visit we have added two new products that may be of interest to you'. These are simple examples – there may be more sophisticated customizations in progress depending on what information was stored in the cookie file and what web sites were visited.

There are privacy issues associated with cookies. In theory, each cookie is available only to the server that set it up. Some people do not have confidence in this. Advertising banners represent a particular problem because they may be set up by a third party. Organizations such as Doubleclick, which provide a lot of advertising banners, can collect a wide range of information about individuals' use of the Internet.

Most web browsers allow us to specify how we want to handle cookies sent to our computer. There are generally three options: to accept all cookies that are sent to the machine, to prompt when a cookie is sent so that the computer user can decide whether or not to accept it, or refuse to accept all cookies.

3 Local and Wide Area Networks

Local Area Networks

Local Area Networks (LANs) were originally introduced to allow computer resources such as storage devices and printers to be shared, usually within a single department.

A LAN usually includes the following:

- A file server which stores files and computer programs for the LAN;
- A print server, attached to one or more printers;
- A number of microcomputer workstations;
- Often, a gateway which connects the LAN to a WAN;
- Sometimes, repeaters to extend the length of the LAN;
- Sometimes, bridges and routers which connect the LAN to other LANs.

We discussed gateways, repeaters, bridges and routers earlier.

File servers store the software that runs on the LAN, including the network operating system that controls the LAN. Software designed for use on a LAN is sold on the basis that only a certain number of users can use it at the same time, and the software usually has controls to count the number of users and ensure these limits are met.

File servers can also be used to store data created or used by users of the LAN. Data that needs to be shared – accessed by different LAN users – should always be stored on the file server. Some storage devices, called network attached storage, can be attached directly to the network to provide additional storage capacity at a lower cost.

Software and data stored on the file server can be more tightly controlled than software and data held on workstations. Physical access to the file server is usually controlled (e.g. by placing the file server in a locked room). Software upgrading – updating software whenever a new version comes out – is easier if it is stored on the LAN because the upgrade needs only to be made in one place. Back-ups – copying software and data to another storage medium in case of fire or other damage – is easier if the software and data is stored on the LAN, again because this needs only to be done in one place.

Print servers are usually workstations attached to one or more printers. Data for printing is 'spooled' – copied to disk – and a print request is sent to the print server. This schedules the printing with requests received from other workstations and prints it when a printer is available. The order in which print requests will be dealt with may be changed or print requests may be removed from the schedule. Some printers can be attached directly to the LAN.

Microcomputer workstations allow users to access the LAN. They can themselves store software and data, and they can even be connected directly to a printer (this is useful where one LAN user needs to use an unusual type of printer – for example a colour printer or a plotter).

A LAN can be arranged in different ways (or topologies), of which the three most important are the 'bus LAN', the 'star LAN' or the 'ring LAN'.

Bus LANs

A bus LAN uses a continuous communications cable to which the servers and workstations are attached. This type of LAN is sometimes called an Ethernet LAN (after one of the most important early suppliers) or a Carrier Sense Multiple Access with Collision Detect (CSMA/CD – after the way in which the LAN works) LAN.

Each device 'listens' to the LAN at all times (this is 'Carrier Sense'). If a device wants to send a message, it will wait until the LAN is quiet and then try to send its message. If another device wants to send a message at the same time ('Multiple Access'), the device will identify this ('Collision Detect') and both messages will be ignored (this stops them getting mixed up).

Instead, the two servers or workstations will wait for a short period and try again. A system of random numbers determines how long the devices wait (this is to stop them trying to send at the same time again) and they will listen to the LAN to make sure it is quiet before trying again.

Bus LANs are cheap to set up and repeaters can be used, allowing very large LANs. Their main disadvantage is that their performance deteriorates badly when the LAN gets busy – more messages mean more collisions.

A bus LAN looks like this:

Figure 16.1: Bus LAN

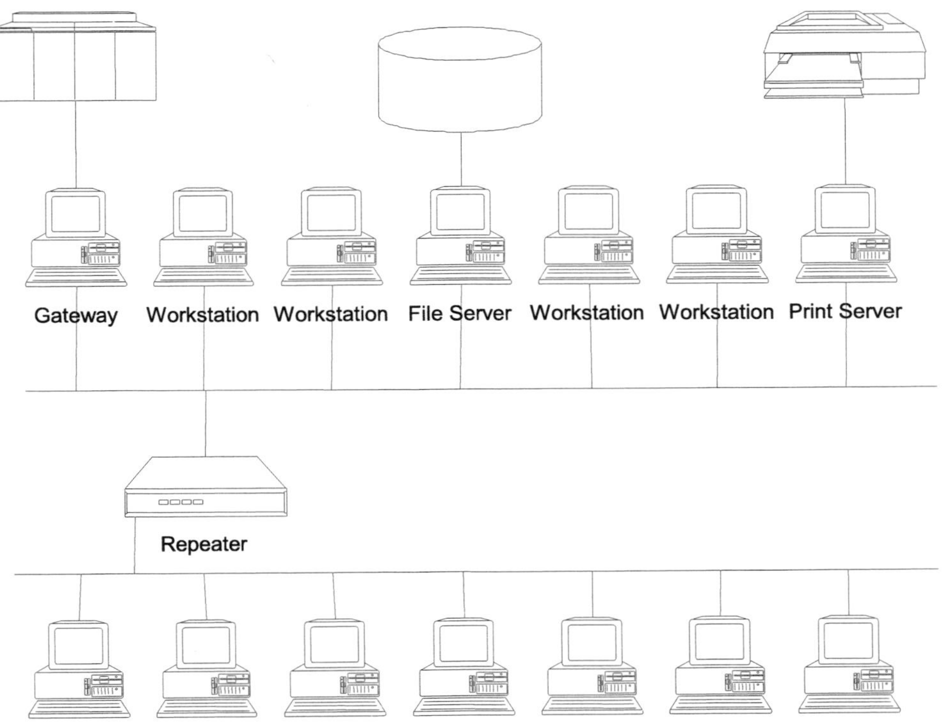

Star LANs

A star LAN works in much the same way as a WAN. The file server is at the centre of the star, with all the workstations connected to it. Workstations can send messages to each other, but only through the file server.

The file server polls each workstation in turn, sending a message to it to check if the workstation wants to send or is due to receive any messages.

The advantage of a star LAN is that it gives a consistent level of performance, not greatly affected by any increase in the number of messages sent.

A star LAN looks like:

Figure 16.2: Star LAN

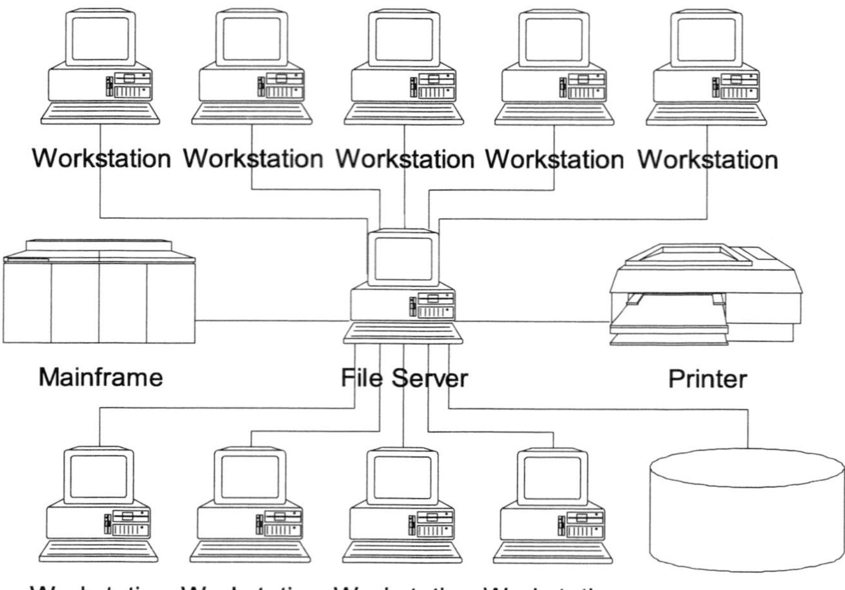

Ring LANs

In a ring LAN, the servers and workstations are arranged as a continuous ring. They are usually attached through a Multi-station Access Unit or MAU. The main purpose of the MAU is to prevent the ring from being broken in the event that the workstation or server is not switched on or does not work – if an MAU is not used and this happens, the LAN will not work.

Another purpose of the MAU is that additional devices can be attached to it. In effect, the MAU can act as the hub of a star LAN containing up to seven devices, all attached at a single point on the ring LAN.

The most common form of ring LAN is the token ring. A special message called the 'token' is passed round the ring. When a server or workstation receives the token, it must first check whether the token is marked as 'busy'. If not, the device can send a message (by marking the token as busy and attaching the address and message). If the token is busy, the device cannot send a message but must check to see if the message the token is carrying is addressed to it.

The token will then pass round the ring until it reaches the destination device, which will take the message. The token will still be marked as busy and will pass round the ring until it returns to the server or workstation which sent the message. Only then will the device remove the address and message, and mark the token as free.

The performance of a ring LAN depends on the number of messages sent. Unlike the bus LAN, the deterioration in performance is proportional to the increase in the number of messages. The main limitation of ring LANs is the maximum distance between workstations (100 metres) which makes the topology unsuitable for large LANs.

A ring LAN looks like:

Figure 16.3: Ring LAN

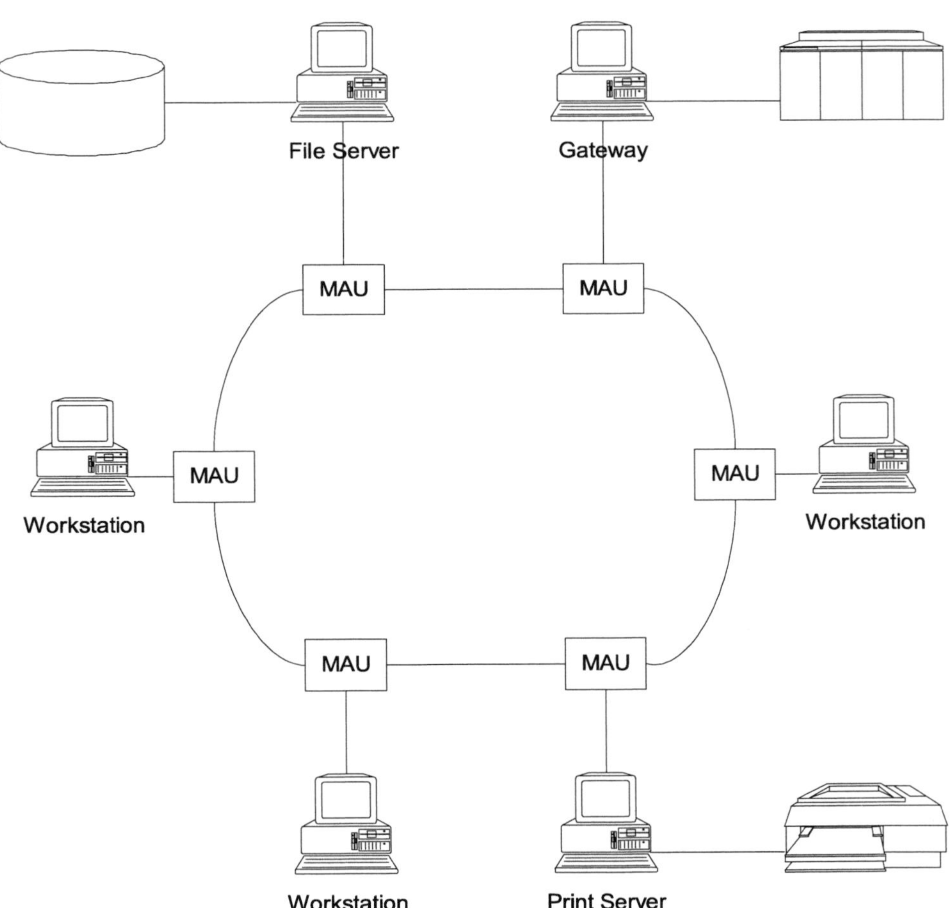

Wide Area Networks

Simple WANs

The simplest way to design a wide area network (WAN) is to have a central mainframe computer with a number of terminal computers (or 'terminals') attached directly to it. The terminals do not need to do any processing (this is carried out on the mainframe) so they are made up of little more than a computer screen and a keyboard. The terminals are usually linked to the mainframe over ordinary telephone lines. These may be leased from the telecommunications provider or they may be 'dial-up' connected lines through the normal exchange network.

We do need one extra piece of equipment and this is called a 'modem' (short for modulator-demodulator). This is needed because computers and telephone lines carry information in different ways.

Computers carry information digitally – as if it were a series of 0s and 1s. This can be compared to a digital clock – the numbers only change every minute or second. Signals in the computer are made up of two different frequencies, and might look like this:

Figure 16.4: Digital Signal

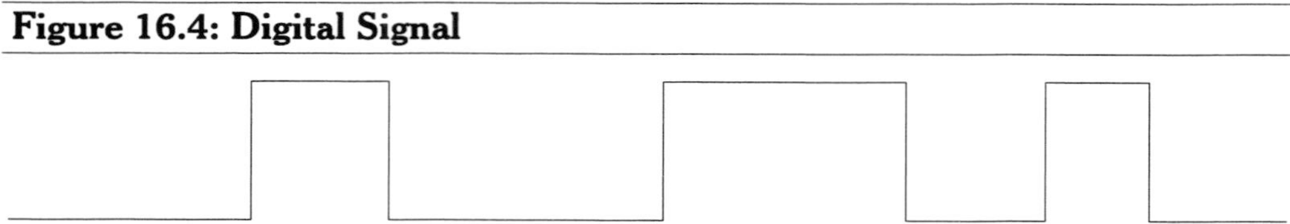

Most telephone lines use analogue transmission – carrying information as a continuously varying signal. This can be compared with an analogue clock face – the hands go round continuously. Signals sent over analogue telephone lines are of a range of frequencies that vary continuously (the 'carrier') with the information being carried as a small distortion to the carrier. The carrier wave might look like this:

Figure 16.5: Analogue Signal – Carrier Wave

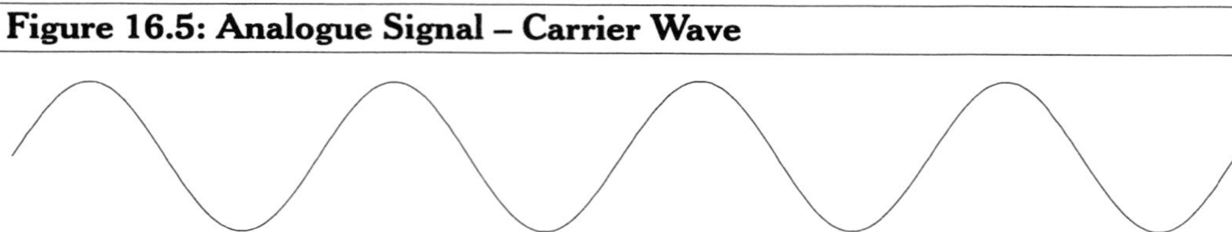

The distortion can take two forms. In amplitude modulation, the amplitude or height of the waves is changed. In frequency modulation, the frequency of the waves or the distance between the peaks is changed.

The modem converts (or 'modulates') a digital signal from a computer into an analogue signal which can be sent over a telephone line. At the other end, a second modem demodulates the analogue signal back into digital form for the computer.

Some telephone lines can carry signals digitally. British Telecom offers a national network of digital lines called ISDN (Integrated Services Digital Network) and is introducing a new technology called Asynchronous Digital Subscriber Line (ADSL). These have a number of advantages:

- A modem is not needed;
- The lines can carry more information;
- Messages can be corrected automatically and so are more likely to be received correctly.

Digital lines are more expensive than analogue lines, but their use is becoming increasingly common, especially where large amounts of data needs to be transferred at high speed.

So our simple WAN will consist of terminals, each of which is attached to a modem. These modulate the digital signal from the terminal into an analogue signal, which is then transmitted over the telephone line to another modem. This modem demodulates the analogue signal into a digital signal, which goes to the mainframe computer:

Figure 16.6: Simple WAN

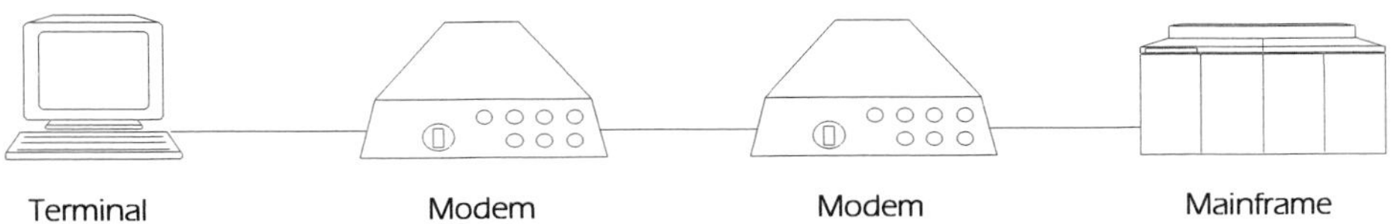

Mutiplexed WANs

This very simple type of WAN is becoming less common. It requires a very powerful mainframe computer just to handle the number of separate terminal connections. Also, the cost of having a separate telephone line for each terminal is very high. One way to improve this is to use a multiplexor.

A multiplexor allows several terminals to share the same telephone line. We could, for example, connect five terminals to the multiplexor. The multiplexor would then be connected to one modem and messages from all five terminals would be sent over a single telephone line. Again, there would be one modem at the other end and the messages would go to another multiplexor. This would separate ('demultiplex') the messages into five sets of messages – one from each terminal – for processing by the mainframe computer. Using a multiplexor allows us to reduce the number of telephone lines we need, but the mainframe computer still needs to be able to handle one connection for each terminal.

There are two types of multiplexor, frequency division multiplexors and time division multiplexors.

Frequency division is the oldest type of multiplexing. This works by splitting the 'bandwidth' of the telephone line into 'logical channels'. The bandwidth is the range of frequencies that the telephone line can carry without distortion. A typical voice-grade telephone line has a bandwidth of 96,000 hertz.

A frequency division multiplexor will split this into 24 logical channels. Each channel will have a bandwidth of 3,000 hertz for the signal with another 500 hertz on each side being left free to make sure signals do not overlap – in effect, each channel has a total bandwidth of 4,000 hertz.

The disadvantage of frequency division multiplexing is that signals sometimes interfere with each other, despite the gap between the logical channels. It has now largely been replaced by time division multiplexing.

Time division multiplexing works by allocating separate time slots to each signal. Before describing the methods used, we need to consider the difference between synchronous data transmission and asynchronous data transmission.

Using synchronous data transmission, data is sent in blocks and is accompanied by timing information – two or more 'synchronization characters' at the start of the message. These are of a standard format known to the receiving modem, which will measure how long it takes to receive them. From this, the receiving modem knows how long it will take to receive any other characters and can demodulate the message correctly.

Using asynchronous transmission, data is sent a character at a time. Each character has a 'start bit' attached to the front and one or two 'stop bits' at then end. The start bit tells the receiving modem that it is going to receive some data and also tells it how long it will take to receive each individual bit of that data.

Synchronous data transmission is more efficient when large amounts of data need to be sent. The signal is also less likely to contain errors. Asynchronous data transmission is better for small amounts of data and is usually used by microcomputers.

Three methods of time division multiplexing can be used for synchronous transmission. These are:

- Polling, where the multiplexor sends a message to each device in turn. We described this under local area networks (star networks) above;
- Clocking, where each device has a fixed schedule for sending or receiving messages. The multiplexor and the devices attached to it synchronize their clocks to ensure that messages are sent when expected by the receiving device;
- A system by which a device with a message to send can reserve a time slot. This prevents time slots being wasted by polling or clocking devices that do not have messages to send.

Time division multiplexing for asynchronous transmission usually relies on Carrier Sense Multiple Access/Collision Detect (CSMA/CD), which we described under local area networks (bus networks) above.

A multiplexed network might look like this:

Figure 16.7: Multiplexed Network

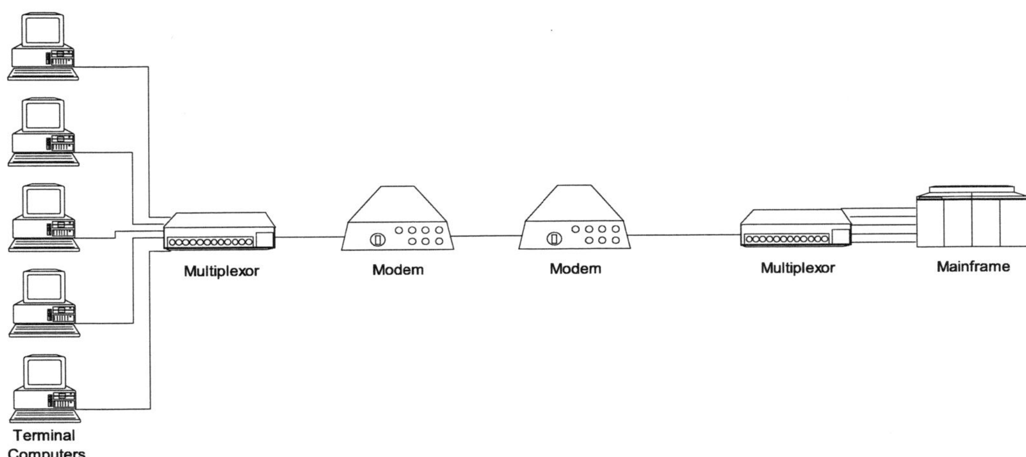

Packet Switched Networks

We have discussed packet switching in the context of the Internet, but packet switching can also be used for other forms of WAN and BT offers a packet-switching service called the Global Network Service (GNS).

With the Internet, each package may be sent by a different route (the 'connectionless' approach). Services such as GNS set up a 'virtual circuit' between the sending computer and the receiving computer that will stay open until the last packet has been sent.

Messages first need to be sent to a 'Packet Assembler/Disassembler' or PAD. The PAD will add header information (e.g. the address to which the message is being sent), break the message down into packets of standard size and add a tail which contains additional information allowing the message to be checked.

From the PAD, the message goes to the Packet Switching Exchange or PSE. The PSE sets up the virtual circuit through other PSEs to the final destination.

At the final PSE, the message is passed to another PAD that rebuilds and checks it before passing it to the receiving device.

Some devices are described as supporting the 'X.25 interface'. This is the standard for packet switching networks and these devices can be directly connected to a PSE, without requiring a PAD.

The following diagram shows a typical packet-switched network:

Figure 16.8: Packet Switched Network

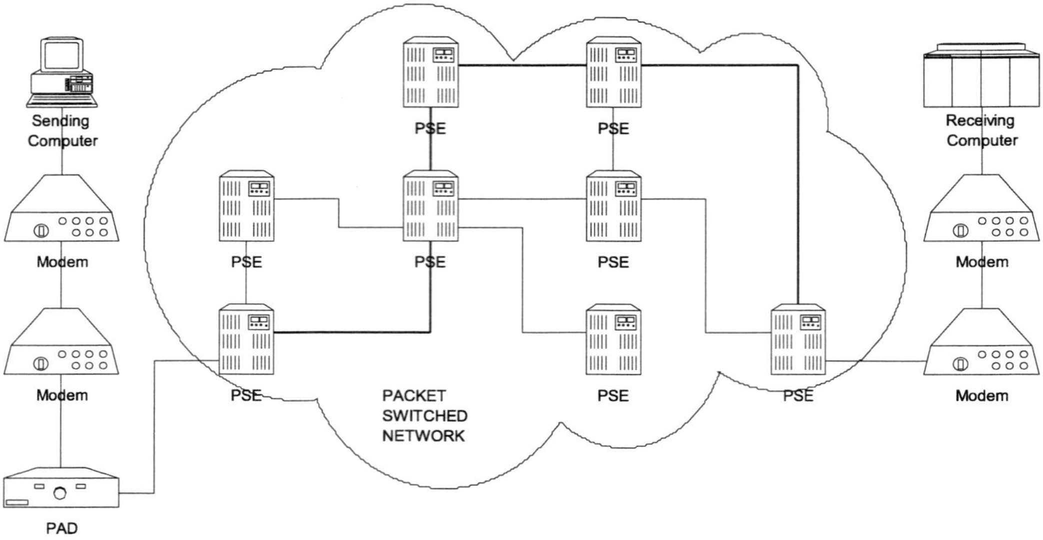

The thicker lines in the diagram show the virtual circuit through the packet switched network.

Gateways

Another approach is to use microcomputer workstations instead of terminals. The microcomputer workstations can be arranged as a LAN and a 'gateway' can be used to connect the LAN through the WAN to the mainframe computer. This is becoming a lot more common.

The advantages include:

- Only a single telephone line is needed and the mainframe computer needs only to be able to handle one connection for each LAN irrespective of the number of workstations attached to the LAN;
- An additional microcomputer workstation can be added to the LAN without making any changes to the mainframe computer – this makes it faster and cheaper to add new workstations;
- Microcomputers not being used to process transaction over the WAN can be used for other purposes – e.g. word processing or spreadsheets;
- The microcomputer workstation can carry out a certain amount of processing itself. This can save work for the mainframe computer and reduce the number of messages sent over the telecommunications links, resulting in some cost savings.

Complex Networks

We have discussed the various types and components of networks, and introduced the use of gateways to link these together. How a financial services organization uses these in practice defines its 'network architecture'.

A number of factors affect this architecture. Workstations in a large branch network will not be linked directly to the organization's main computers. Modems and analogue telecommunications will not be used where large amounts of data need to be transmitted. Contingency arrangements will exist in case of hardware or telecommunications failure.

The network architecture for a financial organization may be along the lines of the following:

Figure 16.9: Network Architecture

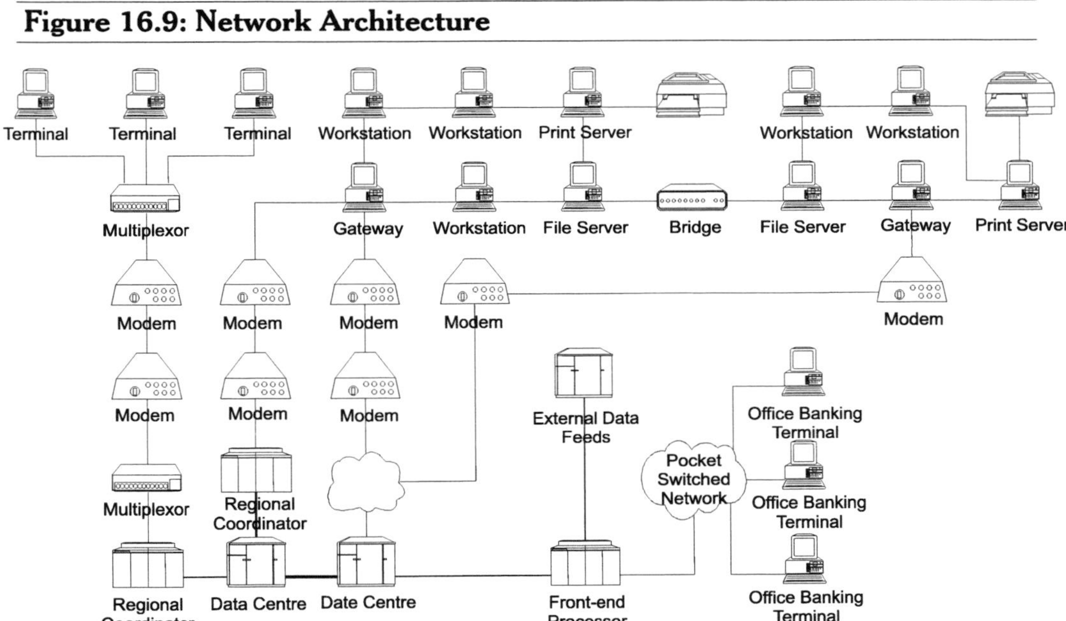

There will usually be a minimum of two data centres. High-speed links will allow the rapid transfer of data between them and there will be sufficient spare processing capacity to allow the network to continue operating even if one data centre fails (although there may be a reduced level of service).

The branch network will be linked to the data centres through regional concentrators. There may be several levels of regional concentrator between the branch and the data centre. Regional concentrators collect messages sent from a number of branches and send them to the data centre over high-speed links.

The advantage of this is that cheap, low-speed telecommunications links can be used for the branches. The regional concentrator allows the most efficient use to be made of expensive, high-speed links into the data centre. In a sense the regional concentrator is being used as a multiplexor, but with the added ability to store messages when the links are busy and send them when they are quiet.

The branches will usually be connected to the regional concentrator through a gateway on the branch LAN. Some branches may be linked, bridges or routers being used to connect their LANs through a single gateway. Some branches may not have LANs, in which case a multiplexor may be used.

Connections between data centres and from regional concentrators to data centres will be digital. Large branches will also have digital links but smaller branches may use modems and analogue links. Digital or analogue, the main network will use telephone lines leased from the telecommunications supplier.

Contingency arrangements should allow every branch at least two routes into two different data centres. These will often use dial-up lines, by which the branch simply dials into the public switched telephone network (or 'PSTN') using a modem and low-speed analogue line to connect to the packet-switched network. The data centres, regional concentrators and possibly some branches may have direct X.25 links to the packet-switched network.

Customers (office banking), external information services and external networks (e.g. ATM networks, EFTPOS and EDI) will be connected to the data centres. A front-end processor will usually be used to handle any differences in standards and, especially for office banking, to provide additional security features such as authentication and encryption. Firewalls may also be used to prevent hacking.

4 Client Server

A network can be described as client/server if work can be shared between the various computers on the network. The distinctive feature of client/server systems is that the minimum necessary data is sent over the network.

A 'client' is a computer that, instead of carrying out a function itself, requests another computer to provide this as a service. The 'server' is the computer providing the service.

We have already discussed three types of server. File servers provide file storage as a service for clients on a LAN. Print servers provide printing as a service. Communications servers provide telecommunications as a service.

The client computer will normally be a workstation, attached to a LAN or a WAN. However, in a true client/server environment *any* computer can be a client or a server. The client and server can also be different programs on the same computer.

Client/server systems have the following benefits for the organization:

- Reduced telecommunications costs. Because the client/server approach involves sending the *minimum* data over the network, the amount of data to be sent is reduced as are the associated costs;
- Improved response times. Sending data over the network takes time. As less data is sent, there are fewer delays and response times are improved;

- Reduced processing costs. The cost of processing on a microcomputer is typically 10% of the cost of processing on a mainframe. Client/server systems allow processing to be split between microcomputer workstations and minicomputers or mainframe computers;
- Reduced impact of system failure. If one component of the system fails, it may be possible to continue work using a client workstation on its own.

5 The Internet

There are a number of common elements that define Internet technology. We have already discussed the TCP/IP communications protocol and packet switching. Two other elements are hypertext mark-up language and Java or ActiveX.

Hypertext Mark-up Language

We have already said that hypertext mark-up language (HTML) was developed by Tim Berners-Lee and is the basis of the web. What is HTML?

The word 'hypertext' means that the information can include links. We can click on a link to go from one page of information to a different page (which may well be on a different computer – possibly in another country). Or we can use the link to load more information onto the page – perhaps a picture or a video clip.

Apart from its ability to include links, HTML is similar to normal text. The new generation of word processors are able to produce HTML documents directly, allowing word-processed documentation to be put on an Intranet with little or no formal IT involvement, and Microsoft's Office 2000 products can store all data as HTML and XML (extended mark-up language) files.

Java and ActiveX

Java is a programming language developed by SUN Microsystems and is designed to work on any computer. The computer's software must be modified to include what is called a Java 'virtual machine' which translates the Java language into the language used by the computer.

Java is not a mark-up code like HTML, but a programming language designed to be interpreted by any computer. Netscape Navigator and Internet Explorer have in-built Java interpreters, so visitors do not need extra software to view it.

Java is an object-oriented programming (OOP) language. It shares a few similarities with other programming languages such as C and C++. However, Java was developed to be a programming language in its own right, and is now a very popular language used not only on the Internet and World Wide Web, but is also being adopted in many 'conventional' areas of banking usually associated with other well-established programming languages such a C+. Java is a standard language for developing software for smartcards.

Object-Oriented Programming is a very powerful method of constructing software applications. In OOP, the computer program consists of several objects interacting with each other that pass messages between themselves. There are rules that describe how such interactions and communications are created, and for dictating what specific actions objects perform when requested by other objects.

For example, in a Java science fiction game there may be a 'Hero' object fighting a number of 'AlienLifeForms' objects. The 'Hero' object may retrieve bullets from the 'AmmunitionsArsenal' object to fight the aliens. Another 'HelperSpirit' object may check the arsenal content and call the 'MotherShip' object for further assistance when ammunition supplies run low. Object classes can easily be created, with new 'sub-objects' inheriting properties (or not) from their parent objects.

Java can run on any machine. Java's ability to run on any computer platform brings it considerable advantage over other programming languages, especially within systems that, by necessity, must run across different platforms. Java is platform-independent at both the source and machine levels.

Therefore, after a Java program has been compiled (transformed from plain text files into machine-level files), it can be executed on a different platform without the need to recompile the Java source code for that new platform.

Compare this with compiling a program written in a conventional programming language. The computer creates a machine, or processor level, binary instruction file. The contents of this binary file are specific to the type of processor used on the compiling computer. For example, programs compiled on a Windows PC will not run on a Macintosh – it will only run on other Windows machines. To execute the same programs on a Macintosh involves obtaining the original source code, getting a compiler for the Macintosh environment, and then re-compiling the code. The same argument applies for other platforms, such as UNIX.

To combat this problem, Java uses a program called a 'Bytecode Interpreter' – it is this interpreter that actually runs the Java program. Most web browsers have this interpreter built into their software, so there is no need to specifically install it (unless perhaps you want to develop your own Java applications and applets).

It is this extra layer introduced by the bytecode interpreter that allows Java to run across any computer platform as long as the interpreter is installed on that machine. Perhaps the biggest problem with bytecodes is that the speed of program execution is dramatically reduced. Instead of offering an application tailored to a specific processor or platform, bytecodes are handled by the interpreter, which is not an optimal situation. This reduced speed, however, is normally barely noticeable and if really required, there are solutions available to speed up Java program execution, but these invariably mean that platform independence is sacrificed.

Java offers a secure, platform-independent method of running software code on the World Wide Web. However, Java also offers features such as:

- Increased interaction. These features breathed much-needed life into the Internet/Web during its early days by providing an interactive facility to a mainly passive or one-way communications channel. Early examples of such interaction were crossword puzzles that allowed users to type in answers into a graphical crossword just like those in newspapers and magazines. Such interaction would not be possible – or would be very difficult – without the Java language;

- Graphics. Java also allows the easy display and manipulation of graphics within web pages. Early examples of this included web sites that let visitors drag and drop images within their browser window by use of the mouse (again adding increased interaction to a web site);
- Reduced server load. In the early days of the web much of the hard work in processing requests from a user was done by the web server. However, to reduce the load on servers (which are extremely valuable resources), there has been a shift of moving processing activity from the server over to the clients, or web browsers. This shift started with the development of client-side image maps that moved responsibility from the web server to the web browser when checking and retrieving URLs associated with imagemap 'hotspots'. Java also helps to reduce server load by allowing web browsers to run their own local copies of specific Java applets that would otherwise eat up valuable server time, especially at the busier web sites.

Java Applets

An applet is a Java program written for inclusion on a web page. Applets are usually interactive and dynamic, and can cover a wide range of processing tasks.

The main differences between a Java application and a Java applet are that an application can be viewed as a stand-alone system that has a 'main' calling program or unit. Such applications can have unrestricted access to the host machine running the program. An applet, however, is usually executed within a web browser and has a strictly controlled access to the host machine – e.g., an applet cannot normally read or write files on local host machines, but a full-blown application may well have such privileges.

JavaScript

Confusion often arises between Java and JavaScript – it is very easy to assume they both offer the same services, facilities and capabilities, which is not true. JavaScript was developed by Netscape as a powerful scripting language that offers object-based features capable easily embedded within HTML pages.

JavaScript, like Java, offers interactive, dynamic web-based applications that can be executed within web browsers, but that is effectively where the similarities end. JavaScript and Java use a similar syntax – of sorts – and both provide dynamic executable content in web pages, but the two languages are completely different.

JavaBeans – Re-Usable Components

With the increased interest in Java as a programming language, there has also been a similar drive to create re-usable component technology to add support for the Java language and

Java developers. Re-usable software components are not new, and Java's success prompted SUN to create a business unit with SUN solely devoted to the Java language – this was named JavaSoft. One of JavaSoft's early targets was the creation of a comprehensive software technology, or re-usable library, for the Java language. The basic approach is to create a small software module which, once tested and verified, can be re-used time and time again in several, much larger, applications.

Applications Programmer Interface (API)
This is where JavaBeans comes in: it offers both a platform-independent as well as an architecture-independent Applications Programmer Interface (API) for the creation, management and deployment of Java software modules.

ActiveX
Although Microsoft supports Java, it also has an alternative product called ActiveX that provides the same functions.

Computer Viruses
One disadvantage of both Java and ActiveX is that they can be used to write viruses. The Chaos Computer Club of Germany demonstrated a virus that could have used ActiveX to transfer funds fraudulently out of on-line bank accounts linked to the personal financial management product Quicken (this virus was never used and was intended purely to illustrate potential risks).

6 Other Devices

Networks are not confined to computers. Mobile telephones can be used to access the Internet and a technology called Bluetooth allows a wide range of other devices to communicate with each other and, ultimately, with the Internet.

Mobile Telephones

The mobile telephone is widely predicted to become the most important device for accessing the Internet. Much of the excitement has surrounded the launch of the wireless application protocol (WAP). How significant is WAP?

Internet access by mobile telephone has been available for a number of years. One common approach has been to use the short messaging service (SMS), which allows text messages to be sent and received on mobile telephones. SMS is part of the GSM (global standard for mobile) standard, the most widely used standard for mobile telephony.

Perhaps the most widely used service is offered by Japanese mobile telephone operator NTT DoCoMo. This is called i-Mode and was expected to have 5 million subscribers by the end of 2000. The handset has a portal with links to over 300 websites and there are a further 4,000-5,000 web pages created by individuals.

The advantages of i-Mode include mobility and simplicity. The main disadvantage is that web pages must be designed specifically for it – i-Mode cannot be used to access every website.

The great benefit of WAP is that it provides a simple way of stripping the complex graphics out of a web page and sending the page to a mobile telephone. Therefore a WAP telephone will be able to access a much wider range of web pages. Several banks already offer services based on WAP telephones, and surveys suggest that 45% of banks are intending to offer such services in the future.

The main practical problem with WAP at present is that the data transfer rate is very slow. Services such as BT Cellnet's Genie deliver information at 9,600 bits per second – almost six times slower than a typical 56.6KB modem installed in a PC.

A new technology called general packet radio services (GPRS) is being developed and will increase data transfer rates ten-fold. The benefits of WAP may be limited until GPRS is introduced.

WAP may be overtaken by third generation (3G or G3) telephony. The UK government has recently auctioned the radio spectrum to allow the provision of G3 services and there will be commercial pressure to bring these services into use as soon as possible, to start to recover the very high costs of the auction.

G3 will be able to transfer data twice as fast as GPRS. G3 would be 'always switched on', allowing continuous updating of information such as sports scores. G3 would also allow the development of 'location aware' services – for example, the ability to ask for the location of the nearest restaurant or hotel. G3 mobile telephones will also be able to use Bluetooth technology – outlined below – as an alternative to the Internet for short distance communication.

One issue with using mobile telephones for Internet access is control of the portal. Changing the portal on a PC is simple – it is much harder on a mobile telephone. This gives mobile telephone operators a lot of control over the portal and there are competition issues with this.

Bluetooth

Bluetooth is a technology that allows computing devices to communicate without wires over relatively short distances – typically up to ten metres. Bluetooth operates at very low emission levels and is not thought to be a danger to health. Bluetooth also supports encryption (although it is not considered sufficiently secure for financial transactions without additional encryption layers) and can be used to send quite large amounts of information.

Much of the interest surrounding Bluetooth has been centred on the idea of the 'wired house' – the refrigerator telling the oven what is for dinner, in simplistic terms. Bill Gates discusses some of the possibilities of this in *The Road Ahead*. However, Bluetooth also has major commercial applications.

The most important alternative technology is the use of infrared. Although this is quite well-established, Bluetooth avoids restrictions such as a requirement for a line of sight and in considered a superior technology. Alternatives such as power line technology – using the mains electricity system for communication – have had limited success in spite of considerable investment in research.

17

DELIVERY CHANNELS AND CUSTOMER CONTACT

Objectives

After studying this chapter, you should be able to:

- understand the impact of multiple channels on distribution strategy;
- understand the functions and technology of the available delivery and communication channels including:
    - full service branches
    - tailored branches
    - mobile salesforce
    - Automated Teller Machines (ATMs)
    - kiosks
    - telephone banking
    - mobile telephone banking
    - Internet banking
    - interactive digital television
    - Electronic Funds Transfer at Point of Sale (EFTPOS)
    - electronic purse
    - mail and email.

1 Introduction to Delivery Channels

A hundred years ago there were basically two ways in which a customer could interact with a financial services organization, by physically visiting a branch to talk to someone or by using the postal service. The mass adoption of the telephone created the first 'real-time' remote delivery channel where a customer could interact with banker without both being physically in the same location. Banks embraced the telephone slowly with concerns over identification and confidentiality, diminishing (initially) the power of this channel.

The mass automation of basic accounting functions in the 1960s fuelled by the developments and integration of telecommunication and information technology has now lead to an explosion of delivery channels, culminating in the Internet and the capability of creating a virtual bank with no physical branches.

Each new channel has its own characteristics and, like the atomic bomb, they cannot be dis-invented or ignored.

FSOs therefore – either through choice, customer demand or competitive pressure – are compelled to examine and embrace each one. It is often claimed that many of these new channels offer the dream of reducing costs while increasing customer access, satisfaction and sales. In this chapter we shall examine the technology required for each channel and the channel's contribution to the distribution capability of the organization.

Figure 17.1: Across Multiple Channels

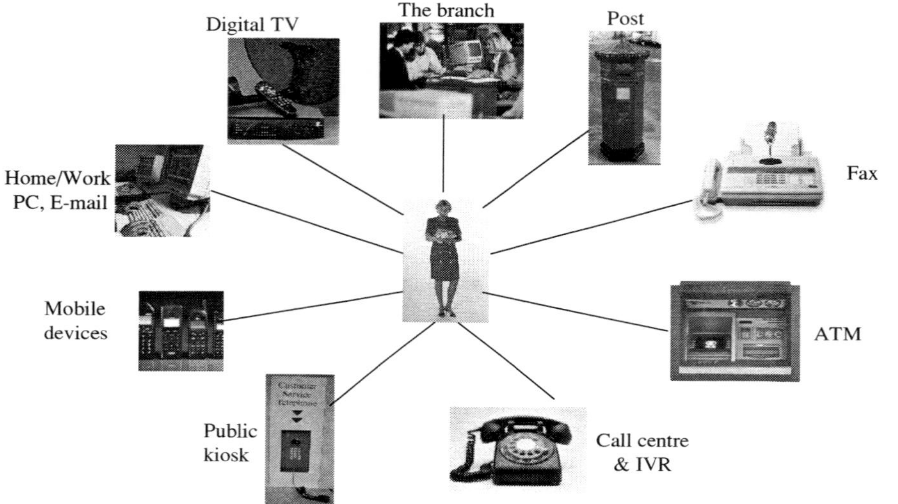

2 Distribution Strategy

With these multitude of channels an organization is faced with a number of strategic questions:

- How do our customers wish to access our services and buy our products?
- How is customer behaviour and channel usage mix likely to change over time?
- Can we afford to offer a universal (all-channel) service and, if so, to all customers?
- How do we provide an integrated back office to support multiple channels?
- How do we ensure a consistent brand and customer experience across all channels?
- How do we compete with the mono-channel and mono-product providers?

Physical Branch Network

Despite all of the predictions of the rapid demise of branch networks, customer behaviour still indicates they have an important role to play in both service and sales. However the design and functions carried out by the branch is changing. The Branch is no longer at the centre of the customer relationship for all customers and this implies that information can no longer reside in the branch alone but must be held electronically and available, as appropriate, to all channels.

Figure 17.2: Where Do You Find Out About Banking Products?

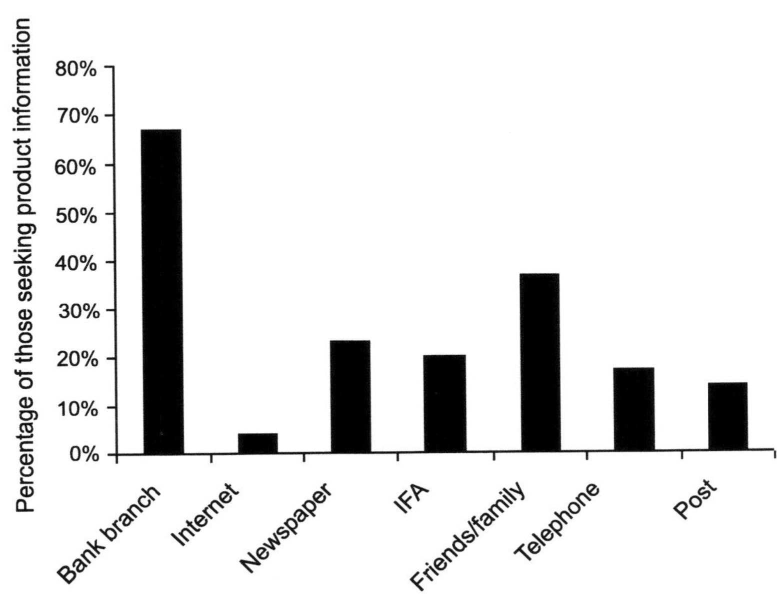

Where do you find out about Banking products? Source: HSBC 1999

The functions of a full-service branch normally consist of:

- Transaction capability: Pay-in/Pay-out
- Sale of products: (e.g. accounts, insurance, investments)
- Customer needs analysis (e.g. financial planning)
- Servicing (e.g. Enquiries, problem resolution)
- Sanctioning and control of lending (though this may be physically managed at a central site)
- Relationship management for a portfolio of customers.

Technology used:

Hardware:

- LAN connected to WAN giving mainframe access
- ATM and other self-service devices

- Workstations
- Counter terminals
- Multi-media terminals.

Applications:

- Internet
- Intranet
- Customer Relationship Management (CRM) (single customer view etc.)
- Customer Needs Systems (financial planning and advice)
- Product opening
- Transaction processing.

The application of technology together with the removal of back-office processing to central sites or automated has enabled the branch to be re-engineered, freeing up space for customer service.

Tailored Service Branch

By understanding the customer profile and potential of an area many banks are now tailoring their physical proposition to match. For example, if the demographics indicate a high population of students (say a branch near a campus), design components may emphasize Internet access and automated equipment with little demand for a traditional counter. In a retirement area with low commercial traffic the branch could include easy access stock market information to encourage investments and dealing. Indeed some branches are being designed exclusively for the use of a high-value customer segment (e.g. HSBC Premier, Barclay's Premier). Branches can be either 'attended' (with staff present some or all of the time) or unattended, relying on automation with perhaps the support telephone, Internet or video link.

Mobile Salesforce

Functionality

Many customers prefer home visits and therefore many banks now have mobile salesforces which have evolved from their insurance and investment sales teams. Typically the mobile salesforce undertakes the following functions:

Relationship Management

Increasingly the manager's role is more mobile, particulary for commercial customers where visting the offices and factories to discuss requirements is a key customer requirement. This is now extended to high-value individuals to reflect the growth in High Net Worth (HNW) individual through the expansion in 'Private Banking'.

Investment Management (Financial Advice)

For many customers financial planning is considered complex and their preference is to discuss their requirements with a specialist at home or place of work.

Technology

Technology used:

Hardware:

- Lap-tops or personal digital assistants (PDAs)
- Modem or wireless access to central databases
- Mobile phones and WAP technologies.

Applications:

- Internet
- Intranet
- Customer relationship management (CRM) (single customer view etc.)
- Customer needs systems (financial planning and advice)
- What-if modeling
- Portfolio management
- Risk assessment.

Automated Teller Machines

Automated Teller Machines (ATMs) are widely used for basic services such as cash withdrawals and balance enquiries. Customer Activated Terminals (CATs) are similar to ATMs but provide additional facilities.

An ATM includes a reader for a magnetic strip card, a computer screen and a keypad which the customer can use to give instructions to the ATM. ATMs in some countries (such as France and Japan) will read smart cards as well as magnetic strip cards. The ATM is connected to the financial services organization through telecommunications links.

When a customer wants to use an ATM to withdraw cash, he or she will put a magnetic strip card in the reader. The computer in the ATM will check that the card is valid and will ask the customer to enter a personal identification number (PIN) to prove that it is his or her card. The computer will check the PIN against information held on the card and against information held on the financial services organization's computer. It will also check the account balance and any withdrawals made the same day. If everything is in order the ATM will issue the cash and will update both the magnetic strip on the card and the financial services organization's computer.

Most bank ATMs are on-line processing systems. The transaction is recorded on the bank's mainframe computer but the account balance is not updated until the end of the day. Many building societies and a few banks have real-time systems, where the account balance is updated immediately. Remote batch systems – where the ATM carries out its checking against the information held on the magnetic strip and stores transactions itself to load to the mainframe computer at the end of the day – are no longer used in the UK because of the risk of fraud.

All of the major banks and building societies use ATMs to offer cash withdrawal, balance enquiries and facilities such as ordering statements and cheque books. Although they have their own ATM networks, they have built links between these and there are now three combined networks:

- MINT (HSBC, National Westminster, Lloyds TSB);
- Four Banks (Barclays, Lloyds TSB, Royal Bank of Scotland, Bank of Scotland);
- Link.

The Link network originally included the building societies and former building societies, together with some smaller banks. The High Street banks have now joined the network, which may eventually become the sole UK ATM network.

Bank and building society customers can use the ATMs of other organizations in the same network. The banks and building societies monitor withdrawals made by their partners' customers and make 'reciprocity charges' if more use is made of their machines by their partners' customers than the other way round. To date the banks generally have not passed these charges on to their customers, although Link rules permit this. Recent consumer and media pressure has forced banks into removing the bulk of direct usage charges.

Most financial organizations' ATMs are also linked to either the Visa or the Mastercard network, providing an international ATM network. Other international networks include Cirrus and Europay. ATMs are also linked within the HSBC group, providing a global network.

One innovative application of technology to ATMs its use to image cheques. The cheque image is printed on the receipt to provide proof of deposit. This has been developed by the Citizens Federal Bank of Dayton in the USA.

Figure 17.3: Kiosks

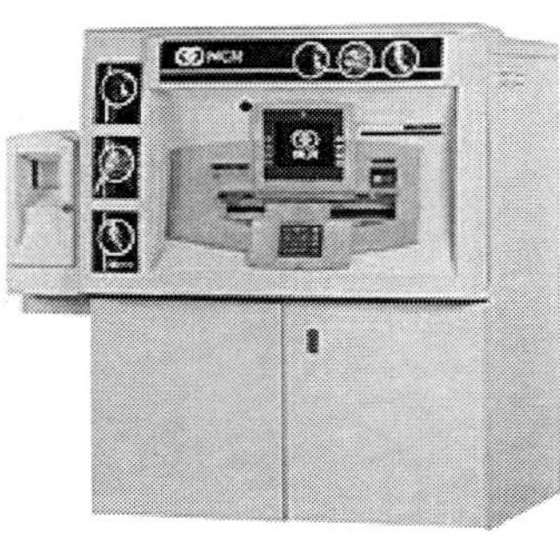

Drive through ATM

Internal ATM

Kiosks

ATMs can offer a broad range of services, some even offering a kiosk-type environment with interactive video links to call centres. The linking to the Internet and provision of browser-based applications further enhances their capabilities for providing financial information (e.g. stock prices) and product sales (e.g. travel insurance).

Example: Lloyds TSB use kiosks with touchscreens and video links to provide customers with an easy and effective way to buy insurance. The kiosk also provides off-line information about the insurance products.

The potential of the kiosk lies in its ability to put the customer in direct touch with an expert at the touch of a button. This is important for Lloyds TSB as the largest distributor of personal lines insurance in the UK.

The kiosk can operate in stand-alone mode for some insurance types and uses an ISDN video conferencing link for others. The link allows a customer/client to contact a 'remote expert', an insurance sales consultant located in a call centre.

For products that can be purchased with the kiosk in off-line mode, the customer enters necessary data (name, address and bank details) on the touchscreen to allow the kiosk to print out a personalized insurance quotation and application forms.

For products requiring the remote expert, the customer requests a quote and the kiosk establishes a video link with the call centre. Any data that is required is entered by the remote expert, who will also display data at the kiosk end for inspection/approval by the customer.

The customer accepts a quotation simply by signing the application form (a direct debit mandate) and posting it back into the kiosk with immediate cover being provided there and then.

Technology required:

Hardware:

- LANs and WANs
- Secure communication lines
- Satellite links for remote access ATMs
- Video links to call centre.

Applications:

- Internet
- Intranet
- Customer relationship management (CRM) (single customer view etc.)
- Customer needs systems (financial planning and advice)
- What if modeling
- Product opening.

Telephone Banking: The Growth of the Call Centre

The most popular form of direct banking remains telephone banking. Most banks and some building societies now offer telephone banking via call centres for personal customers. An effective telephone banking system relies heavily on the use of IT to get customer information as quickly as possible – delays that may be acceptable when the customer is standing at a branch counter are not acceptable on the telephone.

An automatic call distribution system (ACD) is used to route calls to free agents. The ACD also allows calls to be transferred between agents and provides statistics such as the average length of call.

Computer telephony integration (CTI) allows an ACD to be linked to a computer system. When a telephone call is transferred to another agent the details on the screen are transferred as well. This saves time when transfers are made and also allows 'blind transfers' where a call can be transferred to an agent who is unaware of the caller's identity – this is useful for taking password changes over the telephone because the agent handling the change does not know the caller to whom it relates.

CTI can also be used with caller line identification (CLI). This allows the caller's telephone number to be identified and the agent can be presented with a list of possible callers on the screen when he or she takes the call. It can also be used in conjunction with skills-based routing (SBR) so that once a customer has been identified the call can be routed and given appropriate priority based on the customer's value and predicted reason for contact. Capital One make use of CLI and SBR to reduce call duration, handovers and increase cross-sales.

Some telephone banking systems use interactive voice response (IVR), which recognizes the 'tone' – the sound made by pressing a number on a touch-tone telephone. For customers without touch-tone telephones, we can get the same effect by giving them a tone-pad. This approach is taken by the Alliance and Leicester and Nationwide systems.

An alternative is to use a speech recognition unit. This recognizes a limited number of words and phrases, allowing the customer to give instructions directly to the computer. This is more complicated than a voice response system because the computer needs to recognize words spoken by people who may have colds or strong accents. This type of system is good for handling a relatively small number of standard transactions and enquiries. This approach is taken by the National Westminster Bank and Lloyds TSB systems.

The market leader in telephone banking is the HSBC subsidiary First Direct. First Direct has chosen to use human operators instead of voice response or speech recognition. This is slightly more expensive but it makes the customer feel more comfortable and allows First Direct to use the telephone contact to try to sell extra services to the customer. A similar approach can be used to sell other financial products such as insurance (e.g. Direct Line) and mortgages.

3 Banking on the Mobile Phone: Mobile Telephony

Financial services providers have embraced the Internet and PC banking as channels to market, but it is the mobile phone, with its benefits of ubiquity, reach and convenience, that looks set to become one of the most powerful distribution devices in the 21st century.

The potential of the mobile phone as a delivery channel may have been vastly underestimated by retail financial services providers.

Figure 17.4

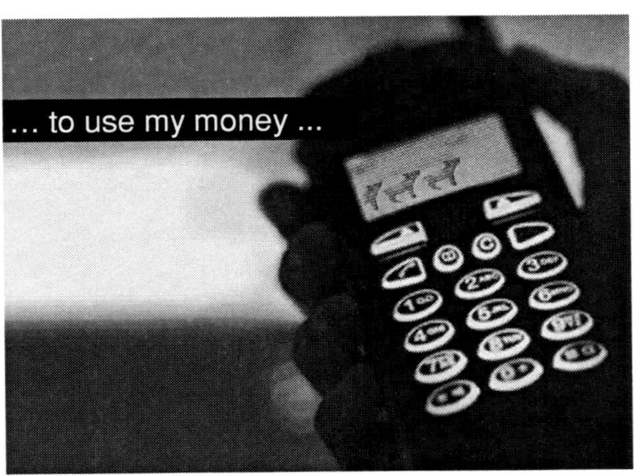

Mobile Phones – The Technology

Today's mobile phones are still based on the Global System for Mobile Phones (GSM) standard which is established in over 80 countries and has attracted millions of subscribers, but a number of major advances are just around the corner. Mobile phones use in the UK is expected to reach 75% penetration of households by the beginning of 2001.

Figure 17.5: UK Mobile Phone Ownership

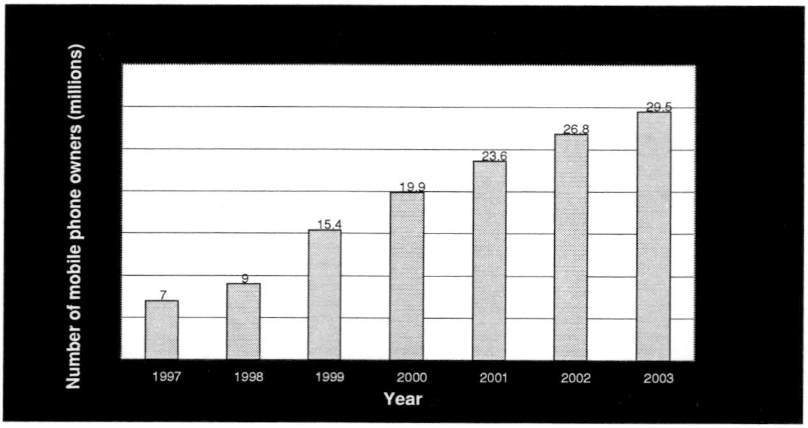

Source: Cellnet (1999)

At present, the main function of GSM is to provide a telephony service, but it can also be used to send and receive data. It also offers a practical service known as SMS (short message service) for the delivery of short text messages, and this has formed the backbone of today's mobile phone banking services.

However, this technology is now taking giant steps forward with the emergence of new, advanced mobile phone standards.

Wireless Applications Protocol (WAP)

Wireless application protocol (WAP) standard allows the complete integration of equally powerful voice and data transmission capabilities in one device.

Effectively, WAP brings a whole host of HTML-type functions to the mobile phone, turning it into an all-round communications medium which allows users to access the Internet, send e-mails and even create web pages, as well as make telephone calls. However the data transmission rates of the 1st generation of WAP phones is slow (typically 9,600 Baud), making their use cumbersome and unreliable. Early indications are that adoption in the UK will be slow, with customers feeling the marketing message of 'surf the net with your phone' as being over-hyped.

Figure 17.6: Wireless Applications Protocol (WAP)

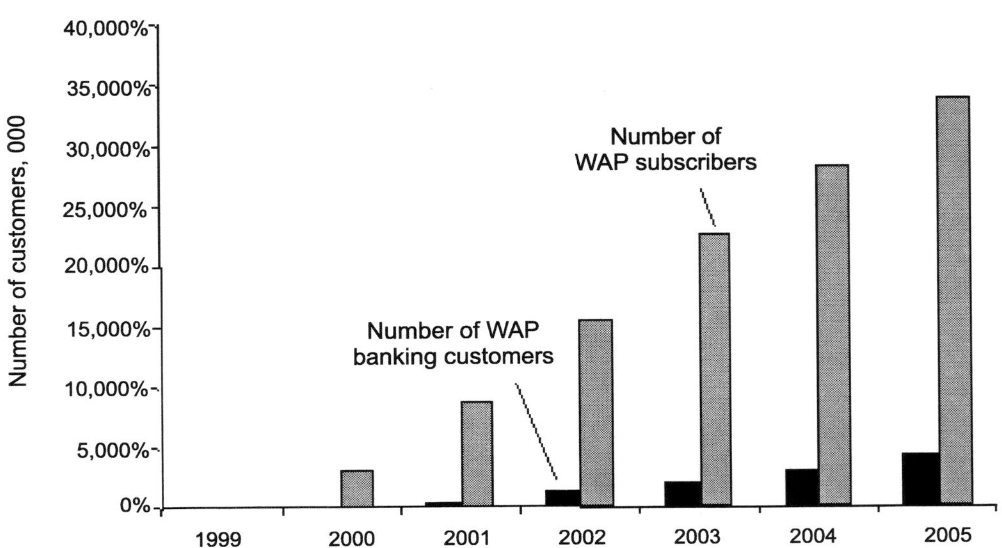

Two new technologies are in the pipe line for improving the bandwidth and hence speed and usability of the mobile phone.

GPRS: launches in 2000 will give 56k bps access (similar performance to most PC connection speeds using a modem). However, that capacity is shared with other users of the cell you are transmitting from. GPRS will also provide an 'always connected' facility where e-mails etc. can be 'trickled' down to the phone.

UMTS (Universal Mobile Telephone Standard) (or GSM2): will offer much larger bandwidth giving 384k+ access speeds, allowing users to watch video over their phone device. Prototypes based on this standard have already been developed and GSM2 is expected to become a market reality by 2001/2. Indeed the mobile licences to have channel access have raised £20+ billion in the recent UK auctions, indicating the telcos belief in this as a delivery channel for more than voice.

MOBILE PHONE = 'A Credit/Debit Card with an Aerial'

The mobile phone with its SIM card offers the capability of an integrated payment mechanism and this is already a reality in some of the Nordic countries. Coca Cola has developed a prototype drinks dispenser that is activated by a phone call, the cost of the drink appearing on your phone bill.

The mobile phone's potential as a convenient distribution channel for bank statements, bank balance information, credit card information and other financial details is already being well exploited outside the UK.

The Mori research has also revealed that the largest proportional uptake of mobile phones would be in the 16-24 age bracket (34%) and in the DE social class bracket (22%). The availability of new payment options, such as pre-payment and pay-as-you-go, has clearly made mobile phones more affordable to a greater segment of the population.

In Hungary, for example, Interbank Europa has been offering mobile phone banking services since 1995. Features of its service include account balance details and day-end closing balances as well as receipt of transfers.

And in France, three leading banks have established their own mobile phone banking services which enable customers to choose the banking information they would like to receive via their mobile phones and when they receive it.

Interested customers can subscribe to any mobile phone operator and use any handset as long as it is SMS (short message service) compatible.

Finally, in the Netherlands, ABN AMRO is currently testing the benefits of this medium by offering free mobile phone banking to 5,000 established, active customers.

The UK Experience

In the UK, three financial providers have already experienced significant success with mobile phone banking.

First Direct recently responded to its customers' demands for mobile phone banking.

It developed a new service in conjunction with ICL which enables customers to receive mini statements detailing the last five bank transactions they made and also informing them of their balance on two of three types of account – savings, cheque or visa via SMS messaging.

First Direct is now extending the service's functionality by allowing customers to personalize it to receive alert messages. This effectively means that customers can program their mobile phones to inform them of specific events, such as when their salary is paid or when they are within £100 of their overdraft limit.

Barclays Bank also offers mobile phone banking services in the UK. It offers an integrated mobile phone and smart card package which allows for the future possibility of downloading electronic cash via a mobile phone. Customers can use this service to access Barclaycard and Barclays Bank accounts, and the features available include mini statements, credit card limit enquiries, balance enquiries and payment due enquiries.

The Woolwich has integrated WAP-enabled phones within its Open Plan banking concept.

From a banking perspective, ultimately, the mobile phone could evolve into the 'ubiquitous device', the portal used by consumers to manage their access to financial information – not only to receive transactional informationl – but also to make online purchases.

4 The Internet

The growth in use and access to the Internet has created the framework for a whole new delivery channel for financial services organizations. (Operation and use of Internet is covered in depth in Chapter 19.)

Figure 17.7: If You Build It They Will Come

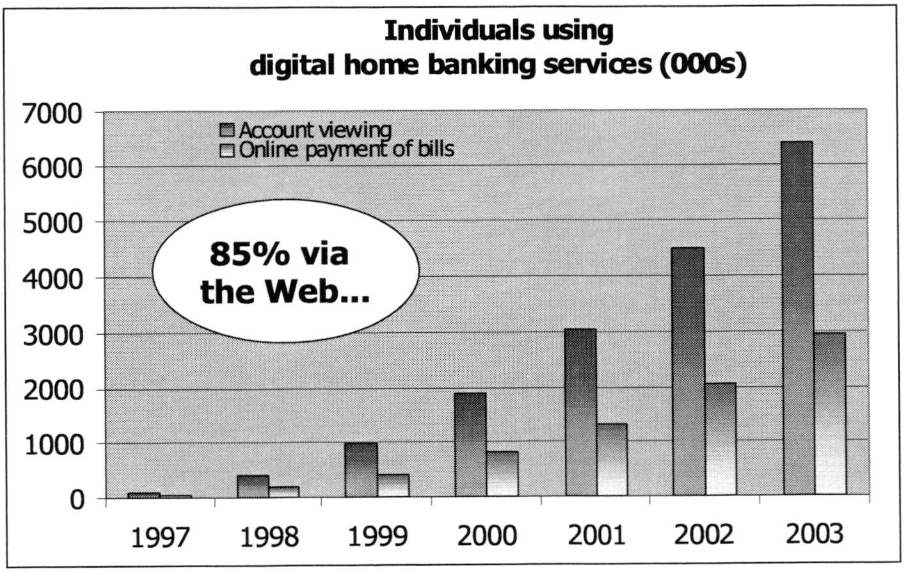

Source: HSBC UK: Use of digital via PC or TV

Currently 75% of UK households have some form of access to the Internet and all of the major banks have some form of Internet-based service. Development of this channel can be broken down into four generations.

First Generation

First-generation Internet sites offered little more than information on the organization and their products. In most cases you could at best order a brochure on line or identify a telephone number.

Second Generation

Second-generation sites offer access to bank accounts for balances and some limited transactions. Typically some limited quotations can be requested prior to brochure ordering.

Third Generation

Third-generation sites offer true interaction with the ability to open accounts and products, buy and sell shares etc. The site offers very similar services to a traditional service branch.

Fourth Generation

Fourth-generation sites offer full customer customization where the CRM tools described in Chapter 14 enable the system to respond in a seemingly intelligent way to the individual customer's needs and preferences. This can range from simple screen organization (always show me the value of my portfolio and favourite share prices) to undertaking share deals automatically based on my attitude to risk and preferred investment strategies.

Intelligent Agents

Intelligent agents are software programs that gather customer information for financial providers.

Such agents are hosted by distribution channels – Internet, ATMs, kiosks and even the TV – and can be used to advise customers on their finances. At the same time, they gather information about individual customers which can then be used to build profiles and offer customers appropriate products and services.

The current agent set includes: life planning agents, retirement planning agents, pension product finders, house moving agents, authentication and general insurance product renewal agents.

For example Epicenter's TIA (Trusted Internet Advisor) provides human-like interaction with the user by personalizing the online experience and assisting in locating the user's requests as well as providing information about products and services to introduce additional sales.

TIA can address users by their first name and remember the user's name in subsequent visits. TIA's intelligent deduction engine can 'learn' from each visit by a user and make recommendations to the user based on previous patterns and past history. For example, TIA can greet the user, assist the user in browsing, and recommend sale or promotional items of interest to the user.

TIA can also recommend product upgrades. For example, if a user is browsing a toy grouping such as Star Wars action figures Darth Maul, Obi-Wan Kinobi, and Qui-Gon Jinn, TIA can recognize the user's interest and recommend that those figures also come in a play set featuring the Battle at Naboo Hangar. TIA may also suggest that the play set is currently on special and if purchased now, shipping is free.

TIA can carry on a conversation with the user, much as if TIA were a real person. Additionally, TIA is fully integrated with the natural language search interface and the 3-D Navigator. Currently, TIA is a human-like high resolution animated female.

TIA personalizes the user's on-line experience and actually serves as an on-line sales representative or helpful store clerk.

Advice Agents

Advice agent technology focuses on the use of animated characters to give financial advice and information to consumers via a range of channels, including TV, the Internet, kiosks and even compact discs.

Effectively, advice agents are expert systems which take in the knowledge of human financial advisers and then use this to give advice via an image or animation to the financial consumer. The use of natural language processing enables the consumer to converse with the animation, and ask it questions, either by speaking directly to it or by typing into a keyboard.

Advice agents will become a very cost-effective way of offering advice on personal pensions and other financial products in the future.

An example of an advice agents is the ICL Virtual Adviser, a 3D financial adviser, which exploits opportunities to deliver financial services to consumers in the home.

Figure 17.8: ICL Virtual Adviser

This technology takes consumers for 'a car journey' down the 'road of life'– an arcade game style interface – and presents them with information and key-event scenarios such as marriage and moving house. During this period, the consumers reveal their aspirations and the adviser helps them to plan for them.

Internet Investment Adviser

Similarly an investment advisor is an Internet-based system that offers advice on the purchase and sale of a wide range of investments and can handle the entire transaction process.

For example, the system monitors the performance of stock market shares and advises on which ones to buy, with criteria ranging from best performance to lowest risk. It also offers consumers advice on a range of investments which include ISAs, Peps and even derivatives.

When allocated a sum of money and criteria to follow, an internet investment adviser can handle the entire portfolio management process for the customer, including the purchase and sale of investments.

Interactive Digital TV

Digital terrestrial and digital satellite television can not only carry signals from the broadcaster to the subscriber's television but can also be linked (typically by a phone line) to carry signals back again. This connection can be used to make telephone calls, and makes possible interactive services such as home shopping and banking.

With the help of a set-top box with a phone line connected to the TV, we can overlay TV programmes, such as financial programmes, with financial advice or information derived from the Internet. The strength of this approach is that consumers can actually order information or even buy financial products, while watching a TV programme.

Figure 17.9

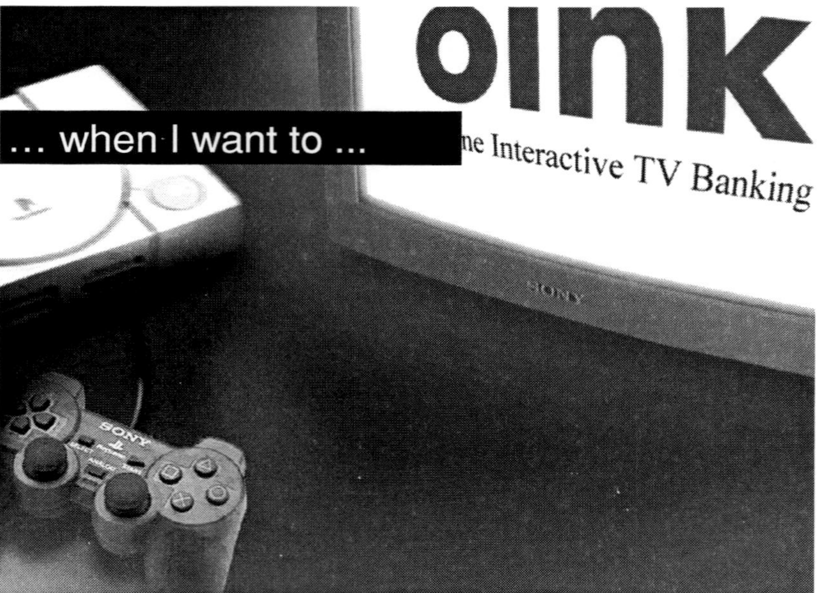

The development of this type of service has been pioneered by OPEN in the UK, which is now part of the Sky broadcasting service.

Figure 17.10: UK Household Digital TV Penetration

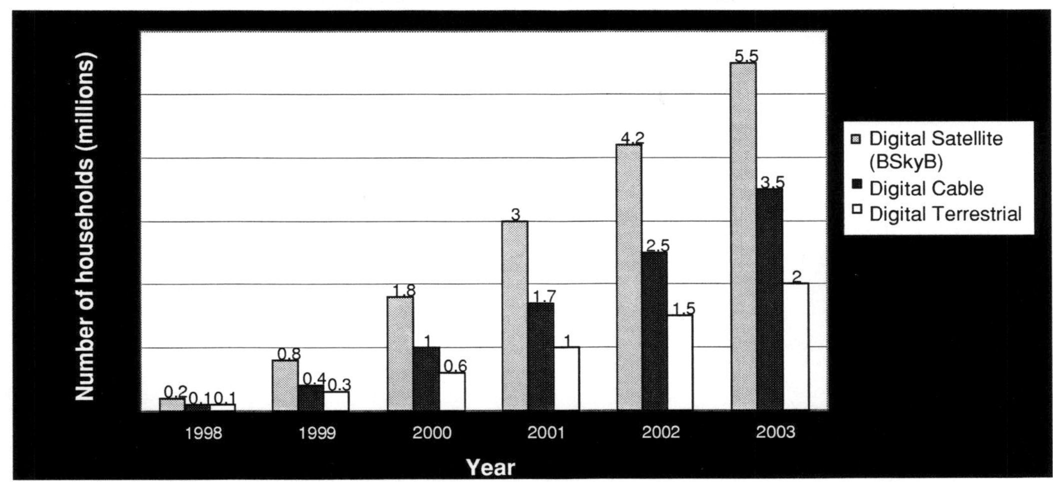

Source: Dresdener Kleinwort Benson estimates (1998)

Primarily OPEN provides three types of interactive service:

Link to TV Advert/Programme

Customer selects interactive icon during a TV advert and this launches the OPEN application and takes the user to a fulfillment screen, where he or she can select the product or service. At this point the user will go on-line, with the set-top box making a connection to the OPEN mainframe via the user's telephone line.

Open 'Shop'

Customer selects 'interactive' button on remote control and this launches the OPEN application, allowing customers to select from information already downloaded into the set-top box or sent in cycles (similar to teletext) with the television signal. Basic calculations, quotations and ordering can all be done off-line. However to place the order or undertake functions the user will log on to the appropriate service through OPEN. For example, HSBC's shop enables you to obtain quotes for a personal loan off-line and then to go on-line to apply for the loan.

Open 'Banking'

Banks such as the Woolwich, Abbey National and HSBC all offer access to customers' banking accounts through the OPEN service. The customer selects the 'interactive' button on the remote control and then selects the appropriate banking service. Connection is made via the phone line and the customer is taken through security and given access to his accounts. HSBC currently offers the broadest range of services, enabling bill payment, transfers, product ordering and statements.

5 Card-Based (Magnetic Strip and Smartcard) Delivery: EFTPOS

EFTPOS stands for Electronic Funds Transfer at Point of Sale. EFTPOS systems use magnetic strip cards and both debit cards and credit cards can be processed. Smart card systems such as the Mondex 'electronic wallet' are starting to be introduced, but these work in a slightly different way and will be considered later in this chapter.

How EFTPOS works

EFTPOS is a bit more complicated than ATMs, with up to six different parties involved – the customer, the customer's bank, the card issuer, the retailer, the merchant acquirer (who processes the transaction for the retailer) and the network that links these together.

The retailer needs a magnetic card reader attached to a point of sale terminal. When the customer offers his or her card for payment it is 'swiped' through the reader to read the information recorded on the magnetic strip. The computer in the point of sale terminal first checks that the card is valid. It may also check a local 'hot card' file, which records cards reported lost or stolen. This will be held on the point of sale terminal's computer and updated on a daily basis.

The retailer will have a 'floor limit' and transactions up to that limit do not need further authorization. If the transaction is above that limit the point of sale terminal will send a message to the computer controlling the network. This will check that the card is not recorded on its own hot file (which is updated as cards are reported lost or stolen) and will send a message to the card issuer to check the balance or limit.

The card issuer may be the customer's bank or building society or an organization such as Access/MasterCard or Visa. If the transaction is in order, the card issuer will 'earmark' the amount of the transaction to prevent the customer drawing out funds that would make him or her overdrawn or overlimit and will send an authorization message back through the network to the retailer.

If the computer controlling the network or the card issuer's computer rejects the transaction, a rejection message will be sent to the retailer. If the transaction is valid, the point of sale terminal will print out a slip for the customer to sign to authorize the card issuer to debit his or her account. The retailer keeps these slips in case the customer disputes the transaction.

If payment was made by credit card, the retailer gets paid immediately. Debit card transactions were originally settled three days later (the same as a cheque) but they are now often settled earlier – next-day settlement is usual for very large retailers. Settlement is made between the retailer's bank and the customer's bank or building society using the Bankers Automated Clearing System (BACS), which credits the retailer's account and debits the customer's account.

6 Electronic Purse (Example: Mondex Card)

What is Mondex?

Mondex is 'cash on a card' or an 'electronic purse'. The Mondex application is held on a chip which is embedded in a conventionally sized plastic card. This chip, effectively a microprocessor, holds the 'purse' application holding Mondex electronic cash and has the ability to record and process information and communicate with other Mondex purses.

Cardholders can load electronic cash onto their cards through a variety of Mondex devices, including cash machines, telephones and Mondex Service Points. They can also receive Mondex direct from other cardholders. This 'cash' can then be spent in Mondex-accepting retailers and service providers or in a variety of specially adapted unattended points of sale.

The entire process is built on the ability of one Mondex chip to recognize and communicate with another to complete Mondex value transfers between them in a secure fashion. Mondex enables payments between individuals or organizations to be made through a variety of telecommunication channels, including fixed and mobile telephones, the Internet and set-top boxes used in conjunction with your television at home.

Wherever one Mondex purse is put in contact with another through one of the interface devices, whether it is bank-to-cardholder, cardholder-to-cardholder, cardholder-to-retailer or retailer-to-bank, Mondex electronic cash passes between the participants, just like physical cash.

The chip-to-chip communication to enable value transfer is a highly secure process that is claimed to be resistant to attack, hacking and emulation. It also provides an environment in which the cost of a transaction is virtually zero, allowing retailers to receive low-value payments cost effectively. The Mondex card is a 'stored value' card and needs to be loaded with money before it can be used. The customer can load the card through an ATM or over the telephone – either a modified BT payphone or an adapted home phone. A Mondex card can only transfer value to another Mondex card. When the customer pays for goods, value is transferred from the customer's card to the retailer's card. The value on the customer's card is immediately reduced and the value on the retailer's card is increased.

E-cash is issued by loading Mondex 'bullion' cards held by the Mondex-issuing banks. Mondex International loads the bullion cards under the supervision of the Bank of England. When the customer loads his or her card, value is transferred from the bullion card to the customer's card, debiting the customer's account. The retailer 'banks' the takings by transferring value from the retailer card to the bullion card, crediting the retailer's account.

The Mondex card, unlike the rival Visacash card, is 'non-accounted'. This means that there is no central record of transactions made. The only record is on the card, where the customer can look at the last ten transactions carried out. This makes security very important because there would be no way of identifying whether e-cash on a Mondex card was forged.

Mondex security takes three forms:

- Handshaking. The two Mondex cards will 'talk' to each other to ensure that they are both valid Mondex cards before any value is transferred;
- Encryption. All messages to load cards or bank takings are encrypted to ensure that they cannot be read or altered during transmission;
- PIN. Each Mondex card has a personal identification number (PIN) which can be used to lock it – preventing it being used for payment.

Mondex customers can unlock their cards at special 'unlocking points' provided by the retailers. Note that there is no authorization process at the point of sale and cards *cannot* be unlocked at the till. The customer will unlock the card using the device before going to the till. He or she will pay using the card and will use the unlocking device to lock the card again before leaving the premises. The customer will also be able to lock and unlock the card using a special wallet or an adapted telephone.

The Mondex card is multi-currency in that it can store values in up to five currencies. Each currency will have a separate issuer and they can be exchanged only through a bank account. This is different from the position with credit or debit cards where the customer can pay a bill in (say) US dollars, with his or her account being debited in (say) sterling.

HSBC is also taking part in the UK and Hong Kong trials of Mondex. Mondex is now owned by MasterCard.

MasterCard, Visa and Europay have developed an accounted system (the Europay MasterCard Visa or EMV system) in which there will be a central record of transactions. MasterCard's involvement in this consortium preceded its take-over of Mondex and EMV has become a standard to which Mondex partly complies.

The Technology behind Mondex

The Mondex Card is an integrated circuit card (ICC), a 'smart' card – a normal plastic card with a small microcomputer 'chip' embedded in it. The card takes the form of an ISO 7816 integrated circuit card – the international standard for IC cards.

This microcomputer has been programmed to function as an 'electronic purse'. The electronic purse can be loaded with value, where it is stored until it is used as payment for goods or services at retailers or service outlets or transferred to another Mondex Card, by inserting the card into a card reader.

The electronic purse can also be locked using a personal code so that only the card's owner can access the value on it. Mondex chips have been designed to withstand normal extremes of cold and heat, damp, X-rays or electrical interference.

The key components of a Mondex chip are:

- The contact plate, which provides electronic access to the chip itself;
- The chip, connected to the contact plate by interconnect wires, has an 8-bit CPU, a 16K ROM, 512bytes of RAM (and 8K EEPROM for data storage). Compared to

a PC which typically can run at above 500Mhz, the Mondex chip has a clock speed of up to 10Mhz and is less than 20mm square;

- The packaging material is an epoxy-based resin to bind the chip, contact plate and interconnections together;
- The card body is made of PVC or similar plastic material and holds all of these components.

The first of the product development specifications for Mondex, was issued in April 1994 – with updates appearing in June 1995 and May 1996 following close consultation with manufacturers involved in developing products. Currently more than 450 companies in over 40 countries are working with these specifications.

The specifications are designed to enable manufacturers to develop Mondex-compatible products such as point-of-sale terminal equipment for retailers and bank cash machines.

The specifications also allow the more general production of other Mondex devices such as the Mondex electronic wallet and the Mondex personal balance reader – or their integration with manufacturers' existing products.

What is MULTOS?

MULTOS is a high-security, multi-application operating system for smart cards. It enables a number of different applications or products to be held on the same smart card, separately and securely. This means that applications such as electronic cash, credit, debit, loyalty, travel tickets etc., which previously needed separate cards, can be carried on a single card.

MULTOS was originally developed by Mondex International. An independent consortium, called MAOSCO, has been created from a group of the world's leading players in the smart card industry to develop MULTOS as an open industry standard. Consortium members are: Mondex International, American Express, Dai Nippon Printing, Discover/Novus, Europay, Fujitsu/ICL/Amdahl, Giesecke & Devrient, Hitachi, Keycorp, MasterCard and Siemens.

MULTOS' open approach means that anyone (individual or company) can take an application development licence and develop applications.

MULTOS ensures the security and integrity of each business service on the card through the use of firewalls between applications. It also allows the controlled addition or removal of applications via PC, Internet, telephone or network while the card is still in the hands of the consumer.

7 Paper Communication

Bank Statements

Even the humble bank statement is being developed as a customized delivery channel. It is being used to provide consolidated financial information bringing together all of the accounts and products held by the customer. It is also being used to provide individualized statement messages offering tailored messages and advice together with financial diary reminders – e.g. house insurance due for renewal, tax-free savings allowances not used yet.

Paper Mail

Increasingly paper mail is being redirected to central processing sites either physically or through imaging and workflow technology. Some organizations such as HSBC, Standard Chartered and American Express are using imaging technology to transport work beyond country borders to processing centres in other countries where labour costs are less.

8 e-mail

One of the major challenges facing financial service organizations is how to deal with e-mail. Customers will wish to send 'free format' messages and expect a quick response (faster than paper mail). Handling the likely volumes and complexity of requests is a huge logistics problem. Two types of solution are emerging, the first is to use automatic e-mail responders, the second is to introduce structured e-mail templates to enable automatic routing of requests to the appropriate processing function.

e-mail responder

This is designed to take away the labour-intensive task of reading and replying to the many different types of e-mail which a financial organization may receive. It reads incoming mails, segregates the type of message, auto-responds to those which it can and, where it cannot respond to an e-mail, passes it on to a human operator.

e-mail responder claims to respond to about 75% of the e-mails which a financial organization receives automatically and can easily take away simple tasks, such as requests for information and forms, thereby freeing up staff to deal with the complex value generating requests.

18

Channel Integration and Customer Experience

The Economist
JUNE 7TH - 13TH 1997

British banks

Blood on the high streets

Commercial banks in Britain haven't had it so good for easy riches may be drawing to an end

IT IS hard to believe that a mere five years ago British banks were awash in losses from reckless boom-time lending. The change in their fortunes has been breath-

Britain, its marke billion, makes it l tional institutio NatWest.

'For most people, banks are an awkward stop on the way to the shop, in a street where parking is impossible.'

Distribution Management *Briefing April 1999*

Objectives

After studying this chapter, you should be able to:

- understand the customer and competitive pressure towards channel integration;
- understand the impact of changes on the customer experience;
- understand what is required if financial services organizations are to use the new channels successfully.

1 Delivery Channels: Anytime, Anyhow, Anywhere

Introduction

'Banking is useful, banks are not...they are dinosaurs' – Bill Gates' statement publicly threw down a challenge to banks and questioned the traditions that have underpinned banking for many years. The emergence of new delivery channels is stretching the ability of banks to adapt even further, bringing greater competition and threats to survival.

It is the customer's experience of delivery channels – this will be the critical battle ground for all players. This chapter covers:

- the experience customers will want in the future and the challenges this poses for financial organizations;
- what successful practitioners will be doing to meet this, and finally;
- establish some basic principles upon which banking differentiation and competitive advantage can be based.

Major changes in the provision of retail financial services in the UK have left the traditional retail banking fraternity with little room for complacency. The proliferation of methods of distribution (or delivery channels) requires the development of an integrated channel management strategy supported by a sophisticated customer relationship management (CRM) system.

Retail banks today are having to come to grips with the fact that they must rethink how they manage their business and look carefully at the proposition they put before their customers. This means that they must escape from the confines of legacy systems and be prepared to harness and exploit a growing range of new ways to interact with customers.

The drive for change in the retail banking sector stems from three main factors. In the first instance, banks are coming under greater pressure to increase their profits and improve shareholder value. This is against a backdrop of the removal of the traditional barriers to entry such as a physical network and increased margin pressure from the new 'virtual' network players. The result has called for a focus on cost reduction through improved efficiency in the way they manage their business, and consequently, the way in which they use the technologies available.

At the same time, banks are becoming increasingly aware of the importance of customer loyalty. Although new customer acquisition continues to be seen as a means of increasing business and enhancing profits, banks are becoming more wary of the need to retain existing customers and maximize their profitability by understanding (and predicting) their customers' financial needs.

2 Customer Demand for Accessibility

Consumers themselves are also becoming much more sophisticated and exacting in terms of the products and services they expect from their financial provider. Changes in lifestyles – more women working, longer commuting hours and longer working hours – have led them to expect a higher quality of service and they are looking much more closely at what they are getting for their money. Indeed, one of the key trends identified by a recent ICL/MORI survey is that customers today want more availability and choice when handling their financial affairs. They are no longer content to wait until branch opening times to pay bills or withdraw and deposit cash, and are looking for providers who can guarantee them an 'anytime, anyhow, anywhere' service.

Historic loyalties are consequently becoming threatened. As the research revealed, 28% of consumers would be happy to switch providers if there was a more convenient way of handling their finances.

3 Competition

With this in mind, it is hardly surprising that the third main change-inducing factor is the increasing competition in the financial services marketplace as a whole. Recent years have not only witnessed greater rivalry for custom among traditional players, but also a wave of new entrants to the sector, as well as a surge in interest from foreign banks, all of which are staking their claim to a slice of the action.

The new entrants, led by well-known names such as Virgin, Tesco and Sainsbury's, or new brands from traditional players such a First Direct (HSBC), Egg (Prudential) or IF (Halifax) pose a particular threat with aggressive marketing and advertising campaigns; grasp of new technologies; innovation; and commitment to meeting customer needs.

Such innovation and responsiveness have also been witnessed among foreign banks such as Citibank, which offers a telephone and Internet banking service geared exclusively at the needs of AB business people who are busy and on the move. The consumer orientation of these players at a time when financial customers are becoming all the more demanding clearly means they are ready to mount a major challenge to traditional providers. In fact, the situation can be, perhaps, best summarized by a comment in a recent conference speech by KPMG: 'Banks are no longer able to exist in the way they do now. If they don't address their customers – the retailers will take them away.'

4 Channel Integration

So what solutions should traditional providers of retail banking now be pursuing to ensure their futures? On the one hand, they need to react to customers' requirements for an 'anytime, anyhow, anywhere' service and work towards offering products through a wider range of distribution channels – ATMs, kiosks, call centre, Internet, interactive TV, mobile phones and personal digital assistants.

Figure 18.1: ...where everything is connected ...

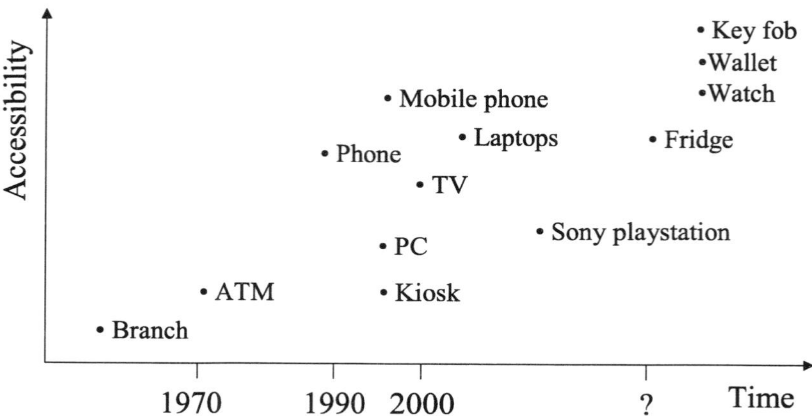

The proliferation of new delivery channels is shown in the above diagram. Indeed NCR at their research and development labs have connected microwave cookers and fridges to the Internet!

Financial organizations are looking towards embracing one-to-one marketing techniques and targeting individual customers with appropriate products at the right time.

This can be achieved only through an integrated approach to channel management, with CRM providing the 'corporate glue' to hold the customer relationship together across channels.

Figure 18.2: Channels Akin to Animals in a Zoo

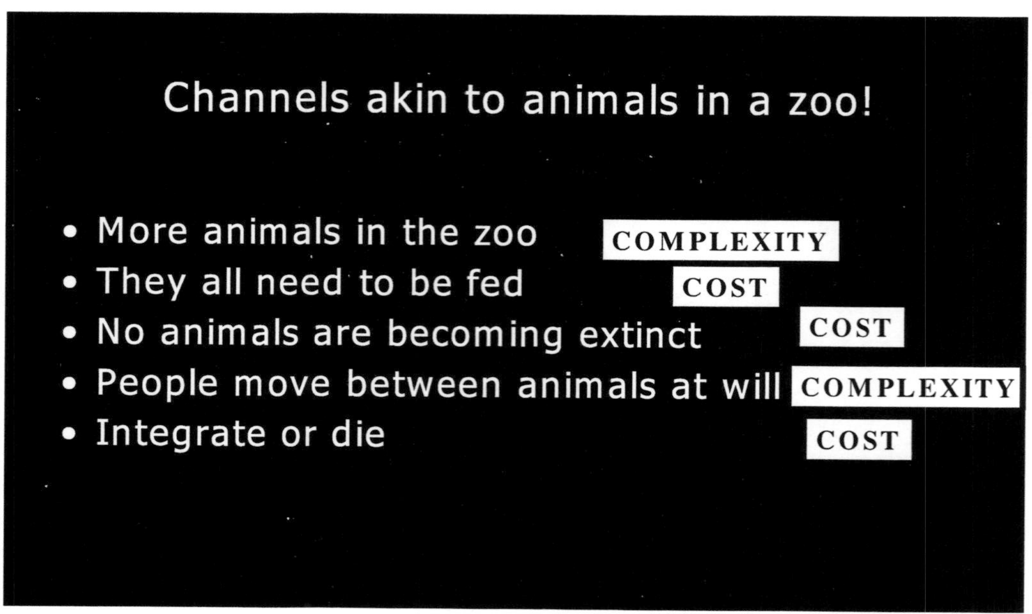

Multiple delivery channels may create opportunities, but also involve drawbacks. Each investment in new channels is akin to putting a new animal in a zoo – it requires its own specialists to look after it, its own technical environment and creates its own customer experience together with an ongoing lust for resources.

Just creating channels in a 'me too' environment without understanding how they integrate to provide the right customer experience can be at the very least expensive and reputationally damaging and at the worst organizational death.

An organization's reputation and brand will be created by the customer experience in the weakest of their channels.

Additionally, at a time of pressure for profits, new channels to market represents a major cost implication, a cost that must be weighed up against the effectiveness of each channel in terms of usage and the profitability of customers attracted to it. The key to success will be determined by the ability of organizations to integrate these channels to reflect how customers want to buy and receive service.

A third key concern is how to embrace one-to-one marketing techniques when servicing customers through a variety of distribution channels. A greater number of channels means that the customer data used for analysis has to be captured at a variety of locations; it then has to be collated, stored and made sense of in order to be used to full advantage.

Figure 18.3: Traditional 'Product-Led' Distribution Model

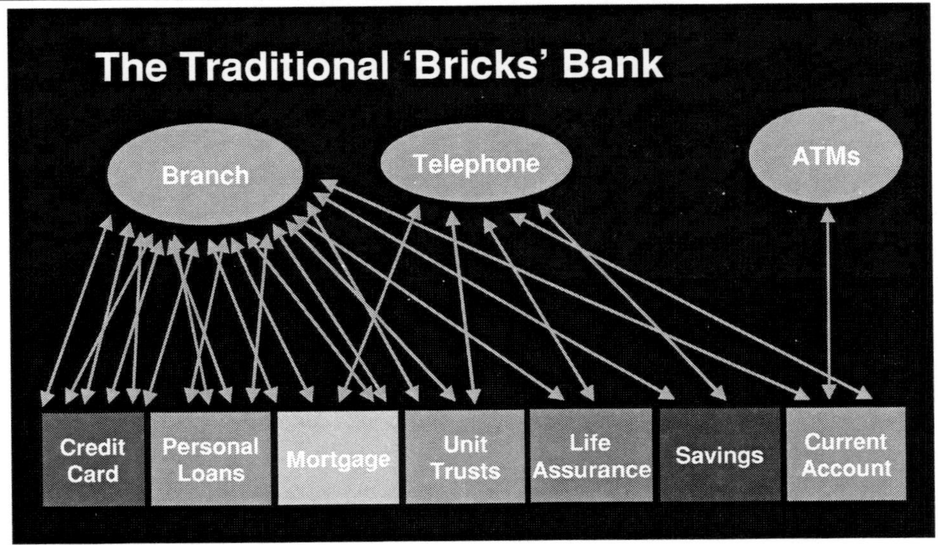

Figure 18.4: Channel Integrated Model

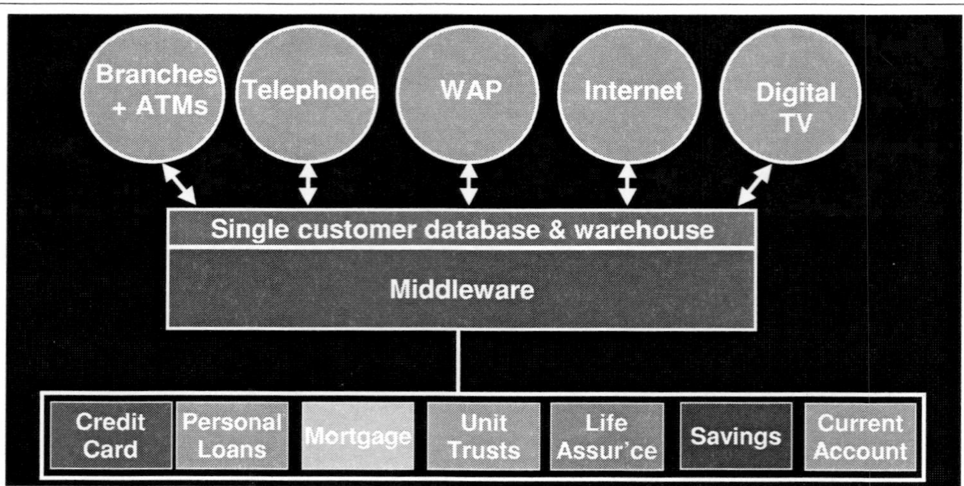

Source: Woolwich

5 Branches: A Costly Anachronism?

For many people, bank branches are now an inconvenient stop on the way to the shop, in a street where car parking is impossible. Once, their physical presence was a prerequisite to garner deposits or lend. They offered reassurance of those more intangible elements of trust, permanence and fidelity. News of the death of branches is very premature for most personal and business customers. Yet they, or newer channels, no longer offer such reassurance of future success and profitability.

This shift in attitudes in recent years has been accentuated by the massive influx of new players following deregulation, to an already congested, but clearly an attractive, marketplace. Society has changed as well, with new forms of relationships, working patterns, jobs and attitudes to lifestyles. New competitors see a gap in what the market offers, or how it is offered and they have an interest in drawing attention to it. This has helped lead to:

- Emergence of new brands and competition;
- Faster market entry for new services;
- Erosion of margins and price commoditization;
- Enhanced consumer choice;
- Much greater complexity and confusion;
- Rising customer power and demands for value, individualism and equality.

Paradoxically, the older UK banks in the mid to late-1990s have achieved some of the best returns on capital, increases in profitability and share values ever. Are the new entrants wrong, or has the market changed so much that looking backwards is not a good approach to walking forwards?

In the future it is clear that consumers, be it personal or business, will insist on using *their* money and select *their* banking services on *their* terms. They are becoming more aware, banking is becoming demystified and choice abounds. The explosion in new channels of delivery has highlighted the opportunities and threats facing banks. The range is endless – PC, TV, Internet, microwave, watches, palm tops, telephone. Everyone is peddling his delivery channel with the claim that this is **the** virtual High Street of the future in which bankers must reside if they are to survive.

6 Customer Experience: Understanding How the Customer Feels

Yet with all this rapid change and technology complexity, how does the consumer feel?

- '*You have given me more ways to talk*': originally the branch, then an ATM, then at the telephone, now PC and right now TV.
- '*You have made it easier*': most banking is now 24 hours a day, with 'Bank Holidays' soon to become a misnomer.
- '*You are great for transactions*': automated balances, enquiries, payments, credit cards are all available.

BUT:

- '*You have put distance between us*': 40% now do not go into their branch (or any branch);
- '*Your competitors have also made it easier*': there are now more entrants entering through new delivery channels obviating the need for a visit to the High Street;
- '*You have not invested in our relationship*': customers do not believe that banks act in the customer's interest – banks are self serving and do not understand what customers want;
- '*You are not interested in me*': research consistently shows that customers want to be treated more as individuals, whereas banks are perceived as offering only services they want to sell, how they want to, when they want to.

Are these new automated 'cold' delivery channels in danger of increasing the utility feel of financial services?

Alan Hughes, CEO First Direct, summed up the problem '...So having increased accessibility for transactions (rational services) and therefore increased cost bases, traditional banks have reduced their accessibility for relationships (emotional services)? Are traditional banks playing into the hands of the new entrant and making it less likely that we will be able to broaden and deepen relationships with customers, just when we need to?'

What does the consumer really want from his or her bank? Financial services, yes, but more than that. Buying financial services is a chore, it is only a means to an end. Most customers want reassurance and simplicity. Bank branches knew that once. When it comes to it, the requirements are simple:

- Recognize my value to you;
- Know me and treat me as an individual;
- Provide expertise I can get at;
- Be on my side;
- Leave me in control;
- Be my trusted adviser (editor of choice).

Yet financial organizations have made it harder to provide these basic needs consistently across an expanding confusion of delivery channels.

How then do banks replicate those essential elements of a relationship when they are no longer face-to-face and handling the whole of that customer's banking arrangements? How do they create and establish a new multi-channel banking experience?

Only by providing a better and more consistently rewarding banking experience, based on meeting these needs. It is recognizing that technology alone is not sufficient – it is the fusion of many elements including systems, culture, brand and staff behaviour. Building a better experience will be the cornerstone of sustainable competitive advantage. Knowing this is one thing, achieving it is quite another.

7 The Challenges

Where do we start from in this challenge?

Firstly, unlike many industries, banks are still vertically integrated. They research, design, manufacture, promote, distribute and service most of their key products and services. It was upon this paradigm that IBM operated until the advent of PCs radically upset the computer industry. The major food manufacturers likewise dominated the food industry until retailers realized that they commanded the essential element of the chain – the link with the consumer. The advent of new channels is challenging the banking model in the same way. Prudential's 'Egg' aims to become the consumer's trusted adviser and first point of contact for financial services on the Internet. They source their services across a range of companies, not just in-house. It is a brand and organization designed for that purpose.

Secondly, there are organizational schisms with overlapping channel and product silo mentalities. Customers want a consistent experience no matter where they touch the organization. The internal barriers created in separate product areas hamper achievement of this. Customers want to be treated holistically for their overall relationship with their bank and have their value respected in dealings wherever they be.

Thirdly, IT backlogs. The impact of Year 2000 systems and potential ramifications of a single currency have taken considerable resources. Add to this legacy systems, separate company IT purchase decisions, skill shortages and increasingly sophisticated technology that allows almost immediate leap-frogging of competitors. Compare this with the competitive lead that new financial service providers have on entering the market. They own new flexible systems that are designed for multi-channel access and managing customer contact.

Finally, the proliferation of channels. This has led to increased infrastructure costs (what channel has ever closed?), higher opportunities for customer promiscuity through choice and easier access for new players, without the need for traditional outlets. Moreover, just building new channels does not solve the problem.

8 If You Build It, They will Come: M25 Effect of Channels

Experience from First Direct illustrates this. It had 150,000 (1999) customers using PC banking. It is interesting to see how they used the new channel. Customers have substituted their basic transactional calls with on-line enquiries – self-service in effect. Yet requests for advice have remained constant. It shows that customers will tailor their use of these new services according to their needs – they will channel hop and expect the bank to know, anticipate and deliver that consistency of contact and understanding across all channels, any time, anywhere.

To say customers are more demanding in their expectations of banks is a cliché. But like most clichés, it is also true and often overlooked. Banking requires a high level of consideration and on-line efficiency, more than any other service. This reflects the complexity of the service, but also the importance placed by customers on having reassurance, from trusted advice, from brand and from their experience. Any successful on-line service needs to give the customer the ability to communicate with experienced advisers. Without this, customers will purchase on basic criteria such as price. Remember: a brand is only as good as the experience the customer had the last time he or she interacted with it.

9 Issues with More Channels

Providing more channels poses issues for banks and their shareholders.

- More channels mean increased management complexity and greater need to integrate into existing delivery media.
- Set-up costs are high with lengthy paybacks and uncertain attribution of income (are they retaining, winning or just substituting income?).

- Channels rarely fade away neatly to allow costs to be reduced.
- Customers move between channels at will with consequential requirements for consistency, immediacy of knowledge and value: they are demanding integrated channel management.
- Some new channels (telephone) may be a transitional phase (why call someone else to look at a screen you can be in control of on your own TV?); how much should banks continue to invest now?
- New players do not have the same cost overheads or issues over pricing discrimination between channels that existing players face.
- Customers will consume more information before coming to a purchase decision and will be more knowledgeable: there will be more pressure on margins, greater expectations of service.

Overall, customers will want to see more value in return for their banking relationship.

10 Role Models – Cyber Heroes

What can we learn of role models in the new channels? There are some key messages and lessons to be learnt already of how to win in the new High Street.

Individualization	Dell computers allow people to customize their buying experience, choosing the best for them.
Intermediation	Expedia, operating in the travel business, act as an on-line search agent linking customers directly to their holidays, dis-intermediating the airline and the customer.

Figure 18.5: Expedia

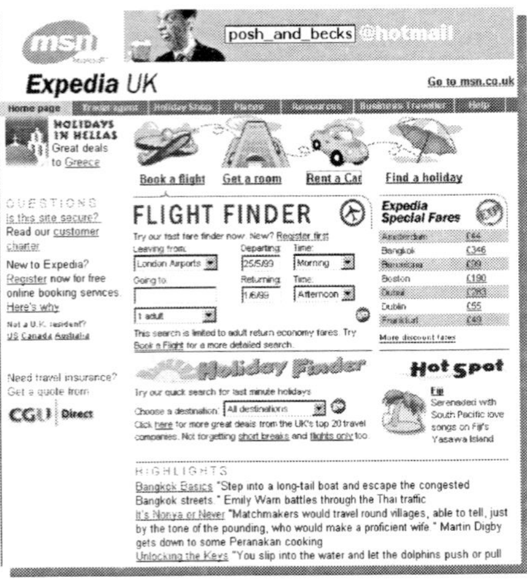

Relationship Marketing	Amazon.com develop a profile of each customer, their likes and dislikes, build trust and then broaden their offering accordingly.
Trusted Adviser	Autobytel, operating in the car purchase sector, offer their expertise to negotiate on your behalf or just let you make comparisons and self-select. The customer again chooses and can access expertise as he or she needs it.
Integration	Tesco are now building their on-line services as part of their total proposition, leveraging the High Street traffic and brand halo.

Figure 18.6: Tesco

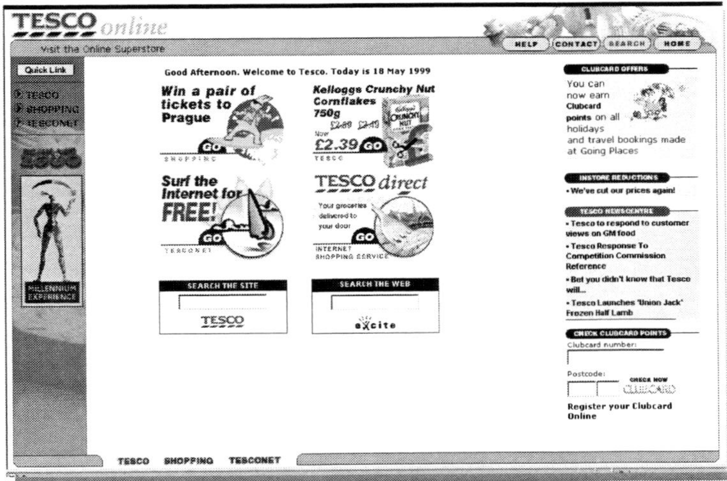

All these players are exploiting technology plus a brand name to give consumers both the value and the confidence they require, while at the same time in some cases integrating the new channels into existing ones. They are also redefining the way customers can purchase and setting principles others will have to follow.

11 Lessons of New Channels

Gates is correct, banks have no right to survive unchanged if new options better meet customers' practical AND emotional needs. There seem to be several important lessons, if any are new.

1. The customer is in charge

> *If you have an unhappy customer on the Internet, he doesn't tell his six friends, he tells 6,000 friends*
>
> *Jeff Bezos, CEO Amazon.com*

On-line service means outsourcing to the customers – they become more confident, more demanding, more value conscious, potentially more promiscuous. Customers expect better treatment and understanding: a segment of one, which in a retail environment is hard to attain, suddenly becomes possible. Worse, customers will demand it and penalize you if they do not receive it. The development of new brands and services is fast – look at the growth of Amazon. To achieve adoption, customers need to see tangible benefits compared to their existing physical world experiences. Amazon did this based on a combination of benefits – not least choice, speed and reliability of delivery and advice as well as the early taster of price...**and it does not matter if these 'dot.coms' survive or not, they have changed the rules of customer engagement.**

2. Grow your customer

Develop and foster customer relationships that are profitable. Tomorrow's portals will be price-sensitive agents and intermediaries. As a result, brand alone will not be enough unless customers feel that they derive benefit from the relationship – the equivalent of mutuality. As recruitment costs decline, but attrition rises, increased emphasis will focus on retaining the profitable relationships and the post-purchase experience.

3. Contact your customer

By 2001 it has been estimated that 25% of all customer contact will originate through e-mail and web-based forms. Can our structures cope with this new form of communication? Where does it sit – in the branch or a central site? Who handles it? How do we use the information to respond to the customer's needs? How do we encourage customers to purchase our services? Information on the customer must be harnessed quickly and deployed to enable staff to take action. Our contact strategies must allow customer choice and preference to influence our approach: costs and price will play a part but ultimately the customer will win. More interaction can be good or bad. More staff must be able to handle more contacts with confidence, authority and discretion in a consistent way – a real challenge for a command and control hierarchy. How the customer felt about the last contact will be at least as important as what it achieved.

4. Do not fragment: integrate

Customers will expect the new channels to talk with one another. A common brand across channels may help but equally can be damaged if there is not consistency and integration. Fragmentation will increase costs and inefficiency. Worse, it will lower customer satisfaction as internal messages get garbled or go unactioned. The key is to behave like the consumer – sample your services and see where a hand-over works or not.

Customers will search on one channel and buy on another. Every new channel adds an order of magnitude to organizational complexity. Our mortgage service is available simultaneously in the branch, at the telephone, on the PC, on the TV. Yet most customers elect to take quotes remotely and then sign up with an adviser. It combines their need for information when they want it, with access to a trusted adviser. The customer decides.

5. Stay flexible

To succeed, banks need open data platforms that allow rapid deployment to meet new emerging channels. A consistent picture of the customer is required wherever and whenever they touch the organization. Equally the level of service the customer experiences must be consistent across channels and commensurate with their value. The power of networks means that the web platform is growing faster than all others are. As technology platforms converge, integrated customer service becomes attainable. However, so does the risk of over-servicing less profitable customers at the expense of other more profitable but more traditional users. Knowledge of the customer will become more key to avoid inappropriate channel and customer investment.

6. Protect your brand

Customers, faced with a multitude of choices and criteria will, in time, look for trusted and familiar names. Yet the brand does not equate to the size of the advertising budget – it is effected most of all by the customer's experience, feelings and satisfaction. New channels not only add to costs, but allow new players to build their brands at much lower cost. Customers will judge brands not only by attractiveness on the web, but also at the phone, downtime at ATMs, length of the queue in their nearby branch and perhaps most by the tone of voice and initiative or 'humanity' shown by the last person they spoke to. It is the total experience that counts.

12 What Will Customers Do Next?

As customers become more familiar and confident with the new channels, their knowledge and therefore their expectations will increase. Customers will:

- Search, become informed and channel hop at will;
- Buy from people they trust and who gave a good experience last time;
- Want speed and ease as prime hygiene factors: make it hard for them and they will go elsewhere;
- Expect their needs and preferences to be anticipated (and then met);
- Want to enjoy the experience.

Evolve or Die

Over the last decade we have had a golden age of banking where customers bought what the banks chose to sell them. Increasingly customers will expect banks to tailor their products to their individual needs. In the future, use of these new channels and intelligent search engines will enable customers to dictate to banks what they wish to buy, how they wish buy it and when they want it. Evolution will be driven by customer expectation, government intervention (e.g. Cruickshank, OFT investigation into Business Banking, Social Exclusion) and competition.

In the future worry about three things:

1. Channel integration
2. Customer management
3. Brand – the customer's experience

In effect: *'it is how you make me feel'*.

The mantra of retailing has been location, location, and location. As banks have just begun to understand those implications it has changed again. In the future it will be experience, experience and experience. Customers want the same things today as they did in the past: trust, confidence and good value. Marble pillars may have been replaced but the feeling must be the same or customers will go elsewhere.

19

THE ELECTRONIC BACK OFFICE

Objectives

After studying this chapter, you should be able to:

- understand and be able to explain straight through processing;
- describe document image processing and explain the technology and its use by financial services organizations;
- describe workflow automation and explain the technology, its use by financial services organizations and the Workflow Management Coalition architecture;
- understand and be able to describe workgroup computing;
- understand and be able to describe the intranet and knowledge management.

1 Introduction

Financial services organizations have increasingly moved 'back-office' processing away from branches. Where has this work gone?

Much work has moved into service centres – for example, the HSBC District Service Centres. These are large 'factory' environments carrying out work for several hundred branches. Service centres may also carry out work for direct channels, but a preferred method is automated fulfilment or 'straight-through processing'.

2 Straight-through Processing

We use the term straight-through processing to describe an environment in which transactions are processed without any manual intervention by financial services organization staff. Examples of straight-through processing include ATM withdrawals and EFTPOS transactions.

The increase in direct banking and in the use of service centres have contributed to the increased interest in straight-through processing. Direct banking channels such as the Internet are ideal for straight-through processing – as the customer enters the information, no manual intervention is needed provided the computer systems can process the transaction.

Other technologies that support straight-through processing include interactive voice response, intelligent speech recognition and optical character recognition. We shall discuss optical character recognition later, under document image processing.

Interactive voice response and intelligent speech recognition can be used in call centres to filter incoming calls. A high proportion of calls are simple balance enquiries which can be dealt with automatically.

The issue with straight-through processing is how to balance the cost savings provided by automated processing with the cost, risk and inconvenience of providing it:

- Cost. The cost of developing a system to support straight-through processing depends largely on the complexity of the transaction. Simple transactions such as balance enquiries can be developed at low cost. One particular problem with straight-through processing is what to do about errors – if we want to avoid manual intervention, we may not be able to refer the problem to a member of staff to sort out;
- Risk. There is a risk that the transaction may be fraudulent or that an error may have been made – for example, the customer asking to make a payment of £5,000 instead of £50.00. Straight-through processing systems need effective controls;
- Inconvenience. The term 'voice mail jail' is sometimes used for interactive voice response systems that lock the customer into a long series of questions and answers to carry out a transaction. These are particularly irritating if they do not give the customer an opportunity to correct mistakes. As we attempt to process more transactions on a straight-through basis, we need to ask the customer more questions to identify which transaction is required.

If we cannot process a transaction on a straight-through basis, we want to minimize the amount of manual involvement. In a call-centre environment we can achieve this by ensuring our agents can carry out as wide a range of transactions as possible without needing to refer to other people.

Again, there is a cost issue. To provide agents with the training and IT systems to support our entire product range is expensive. Therefore we concentrate our effort on the simpler and more common transactions. The agent will refer more complex transactions to a supervisor or a specialist adviser.

3 Document Image Processing

Document image processing (DIP) uses a scanner to record the image of documents coming into the system. Instead of physically moving the document between different processes, its electronic image is transmitted over the computer network.

The features available on DIP systems include:

- Data storage and retrieval features. Documents are usually stored on a database held on an optical disk 'jukebox' attached to a mainframe computer. The document must be indexed to identify the customer, the date received and the type of document. Bar codes are sometimes used to identify the document type. The ability rapidly to retrieve any document on information such as customer, document type and date is required;

- Concurrent working. As the document is held as an image, several different people can work on it at the same time.

A DIP system might be as shown in the following diagram:

Figure 19.1: Document Image Processing System

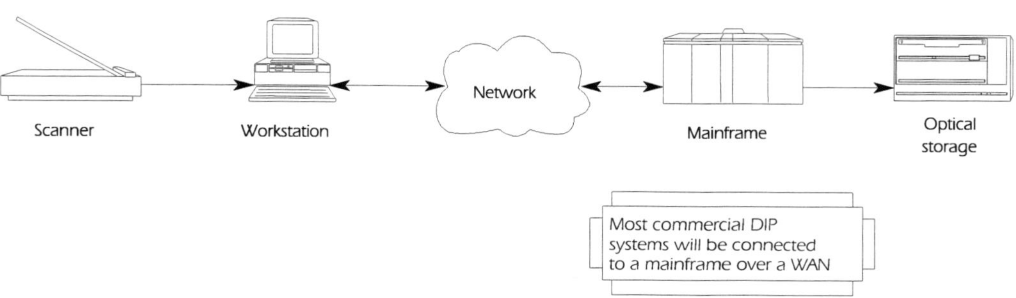

One advantage of DIP is that documents can be scanned and stored in one location and processed in another. This can save valuable office space and reduce costs.

DIP can be used on its own or with an optical character recognition (OCR) or optical mark recognition (OMR) system. OCR allows typed or printed characters to be interpreted. Some OCR systems can interpret handwriting, especially block capitals. OMR can be used to recognize ticked boxes on forms, and also to identify whether the form contains information such as notes or signatures.

OCR and OMR can be used to support straight-through processing in service centres. The document is scanned and OCR and OMR technology are used to interpret it. Tolerances can be set to allow the document to be rejected if there is any doubt about the interpretation of a field – different tolerances can be set to allow stricter checks to be made on fields such as amounts and account numbers, as opposed to fields such as names. If a document is referred, it will go to an operator who will confirm or correct the interpretation as described under workflow below.

DIP can also be used as part of a workflow automation system.

4 Workflow Automation

Most computer systems are designed to automate a single process (for example opening an account). The overall workflow of the organization – how the application is received, what checks are carried out, where documentation is filed – remains largely manual.

Workflow automation systems automate everything from the initial receipt of the document through to final archiving or disposal. Instead of the operator deciding what to do and using the computer to support individual processes, the computer controls the sequence of events.

Telemarketing and telephone banking systems also make use of workflow automation. They rely on scripting to tell the agent exactly what action to take during the call. They also use the statistics produced by the system to monitor the agents' work. These systems are described in Chapter 17.

The features available in workflow automation systems include:

- Identification and routing features. The ability to identify the type of document and to send (route) it to an operator with the appropriate skills;
- Queue management features. The ability to monitor the number of items of each type in a 'queue' waiting to be processed. This allows work to be switched to different operators to ensure that priority items are completed and to avoid large backlogs of one type of work. Problems and errors are also handled using queues – if an operator is uncertain what to do or makes an error, the work item can be routed to a supervisor for resolution;
- Modelling features. The ability to describe the transaction in terms of a process model. Some workflow automation systems allow the flow of work through the process model to be simulated, which allows inefficiencies and bottlenecks to be identified. These models are used in business process re-engineering, as we discussed in Chapter 7.

Workflow automation is often used in conjunction with DIP. Processing will typically go through the following stages:

- Scanning
- Indexing
- Routing
- Processing
- Checking
- Filing.

Documents are *scanned* as near as possible to the point at which they are received. Scanning stations may be adjacent to or even in the post room. We discussed scanning earlier.

Indexing identifies the type of work and sometimes the customer.

In some cases the type of work may be identified from the form type. Forms may be marked with some form of identifier. This could be a bar code, similar to those used to identify goods in supermarkets, or optical character recognition could be used or the system could be designed to recognize a part of the form. When the document is scanned the identifier is used to identify the document type.

It is not always possible to index the document automatically. It may not be possible to identify the work type, for example if the same form is used for more than one work type. The form may also include notes that will need to be read before it can be processed.

Indexing may also identify the customer. It is rarely possible to automate this, although optical character recognition can sometimes be used to recognize a customer or account number. Customers are sometimes sent pre-printed forms that already contain their details, and the customer can be automatically identified on these forms.

Indexing is very important, because documents that are wrongly indexed will not be routed correctly. The need to re-index and re-route such documents will increase cost and time.

Workflow is used to *route* the document to an operator who has the appropriate skills to process the work type. This is called skills-based routing. Each operator has an individual work queue. The workflow system has a profile for each operator, identifying the work types for which the operator is trained. It decides to which queue it will add the work item depending on the length of the work queues, the work type and the operator profiles.

The operator will *process* the document. OCR and OMR may be used to recognize as much of the information on the document as possible. This minimizes the amount of keying required of the operator.

The operator will enter information that has not been recognized automatically. Workflow systems often use a split screen, showing an image of the document on one half of the screen and a partially completed input form on the other half. The operator can read from the image and type the information into the input form.

Some documents may contain more than one work type. For example, a form might include written instructions to carry out a different type of transaction. The instruction may be processed by the same operator, but will often be routed to a different operator who is currently dealing with this work type.

Operators in service centres will typically be trained to deal with up to six work types. If we compare this with the many different types of work back-office staff would have been traditionally expected to process we can see that service centre operators have the opportunity to develop a very high level of skills.

Many workflow systems operate as remote batch systems. The processed documents are placed in a queue and sent to the mainframe computer by software 'robots'. There are two reasons for this:

- Processing on the mainframe computer can cause a delay while the operator waits for a response (this is called the response time). Workflow is used to maximize throughput – the number of items that can be processed – and such delays are unwelcome;
- Dealing with errors breaks the operator's working rhythm, and there are some errors that the operator may be unable to resolve. It is often better to present errors as a fresh work item.

The input is then *checked*. The mainframe computer system provides one level of validation. If it detects errors, the item is sent back and may be added to the original operator's work queue or may go to a separate error queue to be dealt with by a supervisor. The approach to be adopted may depend on the type of error – simple data input errors will often go back to the original operator, whereas more complex errors might go to an error queue.

Depending on the work type, a proportion of items may need verification. The work item is routed to a second operator who will enter only the most important fields – for example account numbers and amounts. Workflow systems can apply complex rules for verification – for example, to verify all payments in excess of £50-00, 50% of payments between £20-00 and £50-00 and 10% of payments below £20-00. These rules can also take account of the operator, allowing a higher proportion of items to be verified for less experienced operators.

Verification is mainly a risk management technique, but sampling combines risk management and performance measurement. A proportion – usually between 1% and 5%, but up to 100% for trainee operators – of an operator's work is sampled and routed to a supervisor's queue for checking. This is a purely visual check – data is not normally re-keyed – but any errors may be marked and routed back to the operator's work queue for correction.

Both the original document and the image must be *filed*. Ideally the document should be filed immediately after it is scanned. Some form of document reference number is allocated to each document and attached to the image, allowing the original document to be retrieved if necessary.

Another option is to destroy the original documents and rely on the Civil Evidence Act 1995. If the original has been destroyed, the image becomes 'best evidence' and is admissible in legal proceedings provided the scanning process complies with the British Standard. This approach leads to significant cost savings for the organization but tends to be used for only a limited range of documents.

The most expensive option for the organization is to file the document with other customer documentation. The documents will need to be held until they are indexed. The indexer will identify the customer and the document can then be filed.

The image will be filed on a database. The work type and customer number should be stored with the image. Images need a lot of storage and are usually stored on optical disk 'jukeboxes'. Tiered storage systems are sometimes used, with the most recent images stored on magnetic disk, optical disk used for older images and magnetic tape used for long-term storage.

Performance measurement is a critical feature of service-centre environments. Possible measurements include the number of items processed, the number of errors and the amount of time the operator is working. Workflow automation systems can record this information automatically.

One technique that is used is statistical process control (SPC). This is a total quality management technique that relies on probability.

Assume we have a form that normally takes 60 seconds to enter. This is the average (or the 'mean' in statistical terms) and the actual amount of time will vary depending what is on the form and on other factors such as the individual operator. We can measure the amount of variation to get a statistical amount called the 'standard deviation'. Assume the standard deviation is 4 seconds.

Statistics tells us that 95% of forms will be processed in the mean ± two standard deviations – between 52 seconds and 68 seconds in our example. 98% of forms will be processed in the mean ± three standard deviations – between 48 and 72 seconds in our example. If we use SPC, we can set an 'upper control limit, at either 68 or 72 seconds and a 'lower control limit' as either 52 or 48 seconds.

Why do we do this? What we are trying to achieve is a distinction between variations in processing time that fall within the normal range and variations that identify possible problems. So if the processing time stays broadly between the upper and lower control limits, this suggests that this is normal. If the time starts to go outside these limits, this suggests the process should be looked at to identify possible problems.

SPC can also be used to look at error rates.

Another feature of service centres is an emphasis on continuous improvement. Because operators deal with a relatively small number of work types, they are in a good position to identify how to improve the processes. Continuous improvement techniques such as quality circles can be very effective in a service-centre environment.

A system combining workflow with DIP might be as shown in the following diagram:

Figure 19.2: Workflow Combined with DIP

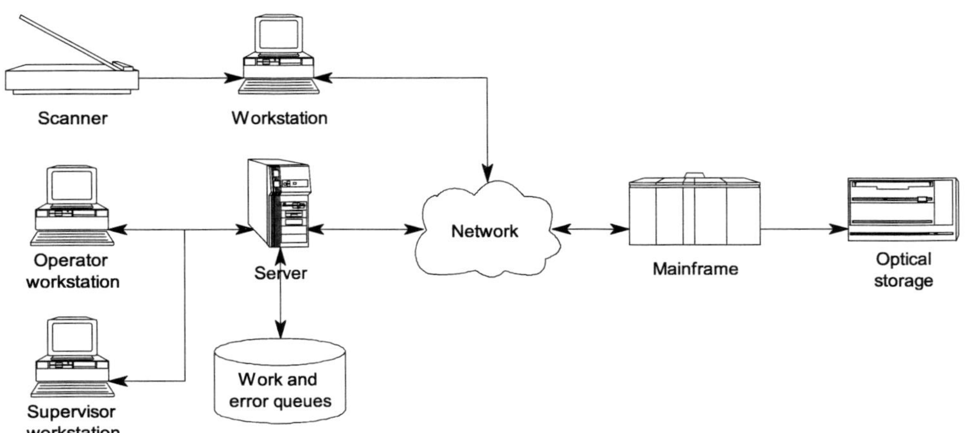

Workflow Architecture

The Workflow Management Coalition (WfMC) includes vendors and users of workflow automation software. The WfMC has defined the following architecture for workflow systems.

Figure 19.3: Workflow Management Coalition Architecture

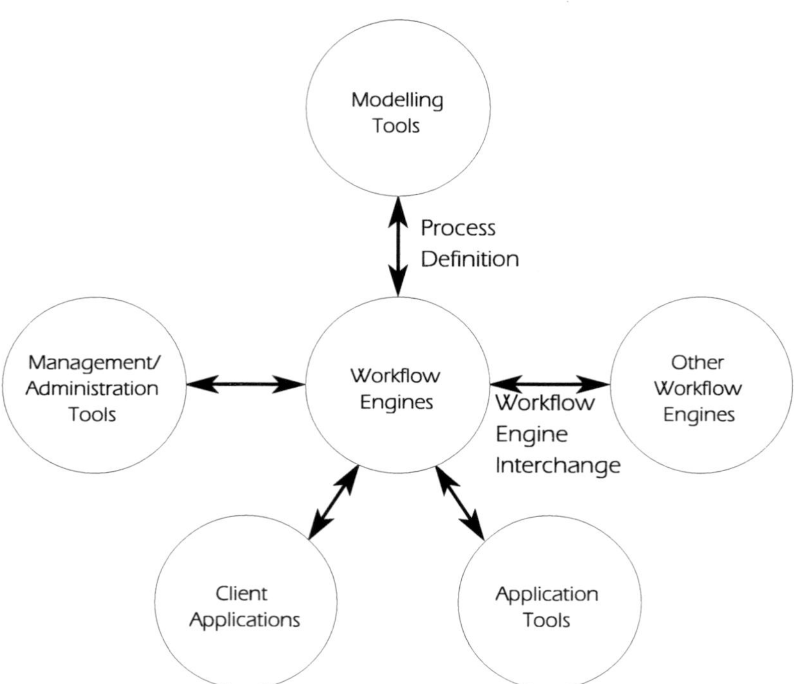

The components of this architecture are as follows:

- Workflow Engines. These are the systems that actually control the workflow;
- Modelling Tools. These are used to describe the business processes to the workflow engines. Business processes are often re-engineered before workflow is implemented, and the models produced from the re-engineering process can be used for the workflow;
- Management and Administration Tools. These are used to provide managers and administrators with information about the system – e.g. the performance statistics described earlier;
- Other Workflow Engines. There may be other workflow systems operating, possibly developed using different workflow automation software, with which 'our' workflow engine needs to communicate. For example, a workflow engine managing the lending process may need to communicate with a workflow engine for debt recovery;
- Client Applications. These are the systems used by the business, either to enter information or to respond to the workflow management system;
- Application Tools. These are the other tools that might be used. They might include

word processors and document image retrieval and handling systems.

These components are linked using application programmer interfaces or 'APIs'. APIs in software serve much the same purpose as protocols in data communications – they define standards for linking different components. All the components in the architecture are linked through their APIs to the workflow engines:

- The Process Description API provides a standard method for Modelling Tools to describe workflow processes;
- The Workflow Engine Interchange API provides the ability for two workflow engines to exchange data and may also provide 'interoperability' – the ability for one workflow engine to give instructions to another workflow engine;
- The API to the Management and Administration Tools provides a standard method for producing information;
- The API to the Client Applications provides a standard method both for passing information from the client applications to the workflow engine and for passing information and instructions from the engine to the client applications;
- The API to the Application Tools provides a standard method for invoking the use of tools. Note that application tools may be invoked only through the workflow engine – client applications would need to go through the engine to invoke them. This ensures that the workflow engine remains in control of the workflow.

5 Workgroup Computing

Workgroup computing allows people to work together in groups, even if they are in different physical locations. It uses computer systems and telecommunications networks to allow people to communicate and to coordinate their work.

An example of a workgroup computing system is Lotus Notes. This is a text database and differs from relational databases in that the information in the database is held as large blocks of text rather than in fields. Lotus Notes does have fields but these are used mainly for keys.

The features available in workgroup computing systems include:

- File, navigation and editing features similar to those available in word processors;
- Database features. The ability to define keys which can be used to present the information in the database as a series of 'views' allows users to see the data in the order most relevant to their needs. The ability to produce forms to enter data is also a feature;
- Audit trail features. The ability to record who has proposed changes to documents and what has happened to them. An approach taken in products such as Lotus Notes is to record proposed changes as 'responses' to the original document and comments on these proposals as 'responses to responses';

- Knowledge management features such as search engines. The ability of the workgroup computer system to act as a 'corporate memory' to record management experience;
- Replication. The ability to change copies of the database held on different computers and to reconcile these changes at a later stage. This allows workgroup computing systems to be used on portable computers and any changes to be added to a central database when the portable computer is next linked to a telecommunications network.

Some features have also been incorporated into word processors, for example the ability to collect comments from different reviewers and to combine them with the original document.

6 The Intranet

Intranets use Internet technology over an internal wide area network. Web browsers are used to access the intranet.

Intranets can be used for a number of purposes. They can be used to replace the organization's wide area network by distributing application software. They can be used to distribute information. They can be used for e-mail, although this is unusual.

One of the most important uses of an intranet is for collaborative working. We have discussed workgroup computing. Many of the features of workgroup computing systems are now available using intranet software, and tools such as Lotus Notes can be used to share information over an intranet.

The intranet can also be used for knowledge sharing and knowledge management.

7 Knowledge Management

An organization's own know-how is a valuable resource. Some studies have suggested that 20%-30% of an organization's total costs are the result of solving problems for which the organization already knows the solution. Knowledge management provides a series of tools and techniques to allow the organization to exploit this know-how.

Knowledge management has been defined as 'codifying the knowledge your company creates and disseminating it to the people who need it – when they need it'. The key words are 'codifying' and 'disseminating':

- Codifying includes both capturing and categorizing information;
- Disseminating includes both accessing information that is relevant and delivering it to the people who need it when they need it.

Categorization is perhaps the most important and the most difficult of these processes. Knowledge is information that can be applied to a valued purpose. We need to categorize all the information we capture in a way that allows us to identify its relevance to the various purposes we may have for information dissemination. Therefore we first need to develop a system of classification – sometimes called an ontology – that meets the needs of the business.

The categorization process can be carried out manually, often by attaching keywords to each piece of information. This is time-consuming and will need to be reviewed whenever new keywords are added. There are a number of approaches to automatic categorization:

- The simplest is to automatically search for all occurrences of important words in information. These can then be used to build an index. This can be made slightly more sophisticated by also looking for synonyms – for example we might want to categorize both 'loan' and 'advance' under loan;

  There are some disadvantages to this. For example the word 'credit' could refer to a loan or to a payment received;
- A variation on this is to look at the 'keyword in context'. The index is based on keywords but the words immediately surrounding the keyword are also shown. This is useful for identifying how the keyword is used;
- More advanced approaches attempt to identify similar pieces of information based on other words. For example, information containing the word 'credit' might be categorized differently depending on whether it also includes the word 'card' or the word 'account'. Search engines such as Excite use this approach.

Determining what information is relevant depends on our ability to express our needs in a way that matches the way the information classified. We have discussed a number of ways to do this in Chapter 15 including 'canned queries' and query by example. An approach that is attracting an increasing amount of attention is natural language queries, in which the query is expressed as if it were a piece of spoken English, and the 'assistants' supplied with the latest versions of office automation products and some Internet search engines such as Askjeeves make use of this.

Some of the most important applications of knowledge management techniques are:

- Best practice databases
- Summarization and abstraction
- Knowledge discovery.

Best practice databases record the organization's experience of the best way to do things. Best practice databases such as Ford's 'Things Gone Right Things Gone Wrong' act as the organization's memory and help to avoid the cost of rediscovering knowledge the organization already possesses.

A new application for knowledge management is in summarization and abstraction. This allows text information to be automatically summarized without losing any important information. This helps to reduce the amount of information people have to deal with.

Knowledge discovery is the 'non-trivial extraction of implicit, previously unknown and potentially useful information from data'. Data mining is an example of knowledge discovery.

Knowledge discovery examines data to look for:

- Correlations. These may be events that usually happen together or items of data that are often found together. A trivial example of the latter might be if households that have two cars are more likely to take foreign holidays – this might be useful in suggesting that holiday insurance could be advertised in car magazines;
- Forecasts. These are events that form a predictable sequence. An obvious example is that a rise in interest rates precedes a rise in bad debts. Note that the use of data mining to identify forecasts does not require any causal relationship between the events and data mining is perhaps most useful where it identifies relationships that do not have any obvious relationship but which do seem to be valid;
- Classifications. These are different ways of classifying data items. For example it may be possible to classify groups of customers who will behave in a certain way from data held about them.

20

INTERNET AND e-COMMERCE

Objectives

After studying this chapter, you should be able to:

- understand and be able to explain the alternative visions of 'networked world' and 'privacy world';
- evaluate two case studies – Capital One and Woolwich Open Plan – in the context of the material in the course.

1 Introduction

Definition of e-commerce

The ability to trade electronically is known as 'e-commerce'. It covers both trade between businesses (known a 'B to B'), between business and consumer (B to C) and between consumers C to C. The majority of e-commerce is now carried out over the Internet.

Examples:

B to B: Manufacturer to supplier

B to C: Bank to customer

C to C: Swap shops, personal auctions and 'classifieds'

How does the Internet work?

The Internet is referred to as a 'packet-switched' network. This means that information sent over the Internet is not done so via a direct, unbroken connection between sender and receiver. Instead, the information is broken up into smaller 'chunks' or packets, and then sent over many different routes where it is finally re-assembled at the receiving end.

This packet-switching mechanism is handled by the two fundamental Internet protocols; Transmission Control Protocol (TCP) and Internet Protocol (IP), and are generally referred to collectively as TCP/IP. TCP's task is to break down the information into packets at the sender side, and to re-assemble these packets in the correct sequence at the receiving end. IP's task is to ensure that each individual packet of information is sent to the correct destination.

Every computer that connects to the Internet must be able to process and handle TCP/IP, and to do this it needs special software called a socket or TCP/IP stack. On a PC this software is called Winsock, and for a Macintosh the software is referred to as MacTCP. In either case, the software acts as 'middleware' between the computer and the Internet, processing and handling all TCP/IP operations seamlessly.

2 Connecting to the Internet

There are several ways of connecting to the Internet, each with its own associated costs and tariffs.

Dial-up account

At the simplest level there's a dial-up account. For this you will need a computer, a modem, a telephone line and an account with an Internet Service Provider (or ISP). To access the Internet your own PC dials into the ISP network using the telephone line and, after successfully connecting, you will then be able to access and use most – or all – of the Internet's services.

The dial-up number is usually charged at local rate or some suppliers offer free access at off-peak or as part of a telephone service package The number of ISPs offering free (or local call charge) Internet access is gathering pace; as is the number of 'non-Internet' companies who become ISPs. These companies have realized the increasing importance of e-commerce, and are positioning themselves in the Internet field to gain a large user base and become 'Portal' owners controlling the access to the web. Freeserve (created by Dixons) is the largest of this new breed with a 2 million users.

Leased-line connection

It is also possible, at the other end of the spectrum, to connect to the Internet via a leased line. These are permanent connections to the Internet, and usually allow much faster Internet access rates – anything from 128k to several Megabits. Costs for a leased-line service vary among ISPs, but expect to pay several thousand pounds a year for a 128k leased line. Every line upgrade thereafter (e.g., to 512k, 1024k, etc) will cost a few thousand pounds increment each time. Leased lines are usually charged at an annual flat rate, so there are no running charges for actually using the leased line on a daily basis.

ISDN

Somewhere between these two extremes are several other methods of accessing the Internet, most notably ISDN (Integrated Services Digital Network), offered by most telecommunications providers. ISDN has been around for years, and at the basic level offers speeds of 64k and 128k, and can even let you surf the Internet while simultaneously making conventional telephone calls. ISDN also needs an ISDN modem – although it is actually referred to as a terminal adapter, which lets you send and receive digital signals through the

ISDN lines. There is a one-off installation cost, and a monthly line rental of approximately £30-50. There will also be the usual connection charges every time you use the ISDN service.

ADSL

ADSL is an abbreviation for Asymmetric Digital Subscriber Line, which is currently being rolled out to a number of cities in the UK. ADSL will turn an ordinary telephone line into a high-speed digital connection offering communications speeds between 10 and 40 times the speed of a conventional modem. British Telecom plan to upgrade 600 exchanges in 2000. More information can be found at: http://www.bt.com/adsl.

Wholesale prices will range from £40 to £100 per month to service providers for every customer they wish to connect. Actual retail prices, and services offered, will be determined by the service providers.

One important benefit of ADSL is that service is 'always switched on' to provide customers fast, convenient and constant access to their service provider.

3 Functions of the Internet

Internet as an information source

The Internet can be viewed in many different ways; it is a collection of information and resources – this is reflected, for example, with the vast number of web sites that currently exist, and seem to be springing up in large numbers every day, with each site providing access to vast quantities of information on widely differing subjects. These resources may be brochures, documents, printed material, databases, images, video clips, sound files, company catalogues, software, CD-ROMs, music clips, organization directories, and increasingly as a medium to conduct electronic commerce (or e-commerce), etc.

Internet as a collection of networked computers

The Internet can also be viewed as an amalgam of thousands of individual telecommunication networks (Local Area Networks, Wide Area Networks, Metropolitan Area Networks, Dial-Up Networks, ISDN, etc.), each speaking internally using its own proprietary language, but all speaking together using a common language or protocol called 'Transfer Control Protocol/Internet Protocol', or TCP/IP.

Each of these networks will have its own collection of computers (simple PCs, server machines, database systems, etc.) and other resources contained within the network; and each network will have a gateway (a link from the internal network to the outside world – e.g.,the Internet).

Internet as a collection of individuals and organizations

The Internet can also be viewed as a collection of individuals, departments, companies, cities, countries, etc., that communicate with each other using the Internet's underlying mechanism, including facilities to send and receive electronic mail (e-mail), the World Wide Web (WWW), Internet telephony, Internet Relay Chat, File Transfers, Usenet Newsgroups, etc.

Internet as a tool to link business to business

While business-to-consumer activities do indeed make up a large percentage of e-commerce traffic, 'business-to-business' activities are set to overtake and escalate enormously by 2002. Companies not e-commerce-enabled at that time will be at a serious competitive disadvantage unless steps are taken now. The costs may not be that prohibitive – some vendors offer e-commerce services for as little as £40 or £50 per month. This may or may not suit specific requirements, but companies should be encouraged to investigate and evaluate how adoption of ICT and e-commerce technologies can provide considerable competitive advantage.

Internet as a tool to link business to consumer

Much of the current e-commerce focus has been on 'business-to-consumer' activities. Companies such as Amazon and Dell have opened up their web sites to visitors who are able to buy their respective products – greatly discounted books in the case of Amazon, and computers and related services in the case of Dell. These activities are centered on business-to-consumer transactions, but business-to-business activity is set to explode over the coming years.

Electronic mail (e-mail)

e-mail is by far the most popular service used on the Internet, and is similar in nature to conventional land mail (or 'snail mail' as it is often called because it is usually considerably slower than e-mail). Electronic mail (or e-mail) lets you exchange information, sometimes almost instantaneously, with someone else anywhere on the Internet – and therefore anywhere in the world. The types of information available for exchange via e-mail is immense: simple text, graphical images, sound files, video clips, word-processing documents, spreadsheets, voice messages, etc. – and the list is growing.

To use e-mail you must first have a few basic items: a connection to the Internet, an e-mail program (client) to send and receive the e-mail, and an actual e-mail address. Internet Service Providers (ISPs) will usually give you a collection of e-mail addresses when you subscribe with them, normally about 5 or 10 addresses.

Your e-mail address can be viewed as your own little space on the Internet, and if people know your e-mail address, then they can send you e-mails (likewise, if you know their e-mail address then you can send them e-mails).

There are many programs available for sending and receiving e-mails (such programs are sometimes referred to as e-mail 'clients'). These e-mail programs cover most hardware platforms (PC, Apple Mac and UNIX), and are either freeware (no charge to use them), or must be purchased from a commercial organization. Popular stand-alone e-mail packages include Eudora, Pegasus and Outlook, but basic e-mail packages already come bundled-up with the two leading Web browsers – 'Netscape' and 'Internet Explorer'.

4 e-commerce

Until recently, most businesses thought of their web site as a novel extension to their business activities.This normally translated into '...letting others know who we were and what we did...'. However, within the last few years more and more businesses are realizing the business benefits of embracing Information and Communications Technology (ICT), and in particular how adopting these technologies can 'e-commerce enable' their own organizations.

Government legislation

E-commerce is set to have a major impact on global economies over the coming years, with various governments releasing legislative bills to try to create the correct infrastructure for e-commerce to flourish. Global competitiveness underpins commercial success, a theme echoed in the UK Government's 1998 Competitiveness White Paper, as well as in other publications and directives, most notably the recent e-commerce Act.

Creating an e-commerce website

There are four stages to establishing an e-commerce capability on the world wide web:

1. Registering a domain name. A domain name is not just an address on the Internet, it is also the e-business brand name e.g. HSBC.COM, AMAZON.COM;
2. Somewhere to host the site. Most businesses use a third party 'Web host' to provide the connectivity, processing power and disk space for the site;
3. Join a payments system to provide the capability to receive and make payments;
4. Obtain web software to enable creation of the site and ordering facilities.

Things to consider in creating an e-business.

- Set goals – know what is to be achieved and who the audience is.
- Be realistic – consider whether the product or service will work online. Generally the web works for things that already sell well directly or via catalogues, or niche products such as those that customers cannot find locally.
- Be committed – be prepared to update the site on a regular basis to encourage customers to revisit. This requires time and the resources to support and maintain the site.
- Be responsive – the site should be made as interactive as possible, in order to capitalize on customer feedback.
- Keep it relevant – do not simply put the contents of a company brochure onto the net.

Information should be short, sharp and easy to understand, like a conversation not a lecture.

- Think like a consumer – under-design it and they will think it is unprofessional. Over-design it with unnecessary wizzy graphics and gizmos (slowing performance) and customers will quickly loose patience and leave.
- Make it enjoyable – make it easy to navigate, easy to understand and easy on the eye. Interactivity makes a visit much more interesting.

Creating Content

The home page is the main advert. As such it should offer visitors a clear and simple benefit, or they will go elsewhere. The expression 'a picture paints a thousand words' is especially true of the net. It is important to establish a careful balance between attractiveness and download times. Download times can vary depending on size and colours of images used.

There are two ways of producing images to place on a Web site:

- *Digital Camera*

These are ideal for taking good-quality photos of products, premises and so on. The images can then be transferred directly to PC. They are already in JPEG format, which is just right for use on web sites

- *Scanner*

Scanners are good for people who already have business material printed. To get a better quality image the scan should be at 150 dpi and the size of the image reduced.

Image files

Image files can be large and therefore take a long time to download. It is important to compress any graphics to use on a web site into JPEG or GIF format. There are plenty of web sites offering free software that compress image files.

Plug-ins

If the site is interactive or animated, visitors may not have the appropriate plug-ins. This can be overcome by giving them the ability to download plug-ins such as Flash, Shockwave and Adobe Acrobat by placing links to the relevant web sites.

Maximizing awareness

When people log onto search engines, they type in key words to find what they are looking for. A list should be made of the words that best describe the business to be put on the Net.

When registering with a directory or search engine, they generally ask for a one-line description of the business. This should be prepared in advance by looking at the competition and then improving on it. There are tags that make it easier for the search engine to find the home page.

Page tags
Search engines seek out the words in the title bar at the top of your screen known as the 'title tags'. A short phrase in the title bar describes the business. For example, an independent financial adviser may have 'Premier Finance – financial planning, independent financial advice, investment adviser'.

Metatags
These are HTML codes that affect how search engines index a site, which are very often hidden from the web site visitor.

There are two types of metatags:

- Meta description – allows you to write a 15 – 20 word summary of your page;
- Meta keywords – tags that let you specify a number of key words which the search engine will give preference to when searching your page.

There are a number of web sites that offer free Metatag creators. A piece of coding is simply copied and pasted into a website.

Tracking visitors – to find out who is looking at a site and what browser they are using to view it there are free tracking applications on the Internet.

FTP (File Transfer Protocol) is the process of transferring HTML files and graphics files (such as GIF & JPEG) from a computer to the computer that hosts the web site. It is the most popular way to transfer files across the Internet. Having designed web pages, they will then need to be FTP'd to the Web space.

Typical costs are as follows:

- To rent space with an ISP – approximately £8-£20 for 50Mb per month;
- To rent space with a web host – approximately £100-£300 per year for an average package;
- To register a web site address – approximately £30-£100;
- To design site pages – free using a text editor (basic word processing software supplied free with every computer). More user-friendly basic web design programs start from approximately £60. Web designers or multimedia consultancy starts at approximately £200 a day.

Targeting

Before even beginning to start setting up on-line, it is wise to carry out some research and find out exactly what else is out there. Who else is targeting the same customers on-line? Review competitors' sites, as well as high-revenue sites (not necessarily related to the same business), to get ideas for this site's content and features. A lot can be learnt from browsing through other sites.

Choosing software

There are a number of software packages available which enable products to be sold on-line. Basically, there are three options for businesses wanting to set up on-line:

1. To buy a ready-made e-commerce solution;
2. To rent space in a network-based e-commerce solution;
3. To build a system from scratch with components and parts.

All of these solutions have pros and cons. A ready-made solution could be bought and, depending on budget, some additional options configured. But this is a short-term solution and will soon become outdated.

Alternatively, space could be rented within existing network-based e-commerce solutions. This option does not give the flexibility to personalize a web site but if budget is allocated to build a web site from scratch, it will require expertise, time and energy to coordinate the project.

Although it is tempting to pick an off-the-shelf software package, consideration should first be made as to what kind of experience is to be delivered to on-line customers, and where the on-line business is aiming to be in one, two, five, even ten years from now. If it is set up correctly now, when the company grows and expands add-ons can be attached to the original foundation without wasting previous efforts.

There are two components to consider when selecting the right set up for e-business:

1. Software to help to manage products, promotions, customers, and their orders;
2. Additional programs to handle the tax, shipping, and payment processing of the orders.

It is now possible to create a 'virtual shop' on a web site using specialist software. This will enable customers to:

- browse through stock;
- place items in a 'virtual shopping basket';
- search for specific items, e.g. a specific DVD, video or CD.

Once the customer has decided on the product to buy the program should then:

- total the cost of the purchases;
- let him or her choose a payment method;
- give an automatic order reference;
- enable the customer to pay in any currency;
- calculate tax rates if required.

These programs can be linked to a company's existing databases and stock-control systems, and perhaps most importantly help to build a profile of customers and their interests.

Payment Types

Many payment options are available such as credit cards, cybercash, debit cards, procurement cards, purchase orders, corporate credit accounts, pay-on-arrival, cheques, invoice and cash.

Authentication

Checks should be put in place to guard against fraud.

Payments – Off Line and On Line

Most customers will expect to pay by credit or charge card. To facilitate this a merchant account will need to be set up. If a company already has merchant status it will still need to receive authorization from its bank to accept charges over the Internet.

Customers' credit card details can be received via a secure e-mail transmission. The sale can then be transacted off line using normal transaction facilities (manual or electronic machine). This is known as off-line payment processing. This is a low-cost solution for those who already have a merchant services agreement, but note that the company will have full access to the card details and therefore responsibility for them.

On-line processing involves a secure, real-time, on-line credit and debit card transaction, authorization and clearance service. The security and privacy of all card details are maintained and transactions can be authorized within seconds. All transactions are then cleared through an acquiring bank at the end of the day.

Online Credit Card processing follows three steps:

- Authentication – ensures that the card(s) have authentic numbers, have actually been issued and have not been reported stolen;
- Authorization – a check to see if the funds are available for purchase. If they are the funds are reserved, but the actual money is not transferred as yet;
- Settlement – once the products are shipped to the customer the company will advise the bank. The bank then releases the reserved funds, and the money makes its way through various intermediaries to the company account. The customer's card should not be debited until the products are shipped or delivered. In the mail-order business, technically the merchant is not allowed to move money immediately unless the product is delivered or shipped *on the same day*.

Order Processing

To process orders effectively, the following will need to be considered:

- Inventory – is the company willing to supply only items in stock or can it afford to order items from a supplier?
- Out of stock – When should the customer be informed if an item is out of stock or likely to take extra delivery time?

- Back orders – When should visitors be notified of a back order? When they are checking out? After they have placed an order? Or should an alternative solution be recommended?
- Controls – If an inventory is at a minimum, should a banner be put up to say products cannot be offered? Will this policy apply to all products or be different for different products?
- Partial sales – How will the company deal with returns of part of an order?
- Fulfilment – In most cases, consumers will buy products from e-businesses that offer a secure and reliable service. Managing customers' expectations is vital if they are not to be disappointed. There are various issues related to delivery such as timing, updating of orders and customer service which play a vital part in making sure the first customers become loyal customers. Never promise next day delivery unless you are sure you can deliver and your customers are willing to pay the price.
- Delivery charges – It is important to remember that the cost of sending out a product is not necessarily the same as what the customer will be charged. A page of the web site should be devoted to explaining delivery charges. There is nothing worse than for a customer to go through the whole ordering process only to see a shocking delivery charge added to the cost of the goods.
- International delivery – If you international delivery is offered, different carriers may need to be utilized for different delivery zones.
- Timing – If customers order late in the day, consider the chances of being able to reach the post in time. Talk to the local post office or couriers before deciding on a cut-off time.
- Customer service – When problems arise, customers will want to telephone to find out what is going on. Make sure a Help Number is clearly advertised.
- Updating orders – Should the fulfilment centre inform the system when an order has been shipped? Is there a shipping number to be attached to an order number? Does shipping status require updating, and if so how often?
- Order status – Should there be a customer facility to look up shipping status on-line? If there are any changes to the customer order, should he or she be e-mailed in advance? When accepting an order will confirmation be sent?
- Technical support – Will additional customer support be available with products?
- Local support – If the business is carried out on a world-wide scale, consideration needs to be made as to language, currencies and regional pricing structures.
- Security – Because the Internet is a public network, anyone can access it, which is why some customers can be nervous about giving their credit card details over the Internet. However, there are several ways around this:

- Most modern browsers now have security built-in so that unauthorized persons cannot read, forge or intercept and on-line transaction;
- ISPs host secure transactions, supported by encryption standards like SSL (Secure Sockets Layer) and SET (Secure Electronic Transaction);
- If you publish information so that your customers are likely to visit your site several times you can set up subscriptions to your site which require password access;
- If your customers are still nervous, you can take most of their order on your web site, then call them back for their credit card details, or allow them to pay by post.

Encryption technology scrambles a message so that only recipients can unscramble it. To implement this kind of technology you or your ISP will need to enable SSL on your web server. But this will work only with other SSL-friendly servers. Today, most servers do support SSL.

Customer Concerns over Security

Many people are wary of shopping on-line and therefore good e-commerce sites highlight the security measures taken such as:

- Encryption;
- Firewall protection;
- Feature secure site symbols (a complete key on Explorer, a locked padlock on Navigator);
- Membership of a digital signature scheme;
- Guarantee of refund.

Establishing Terms of Business

e-businesses need to consider these questions:

- What policies and disclaimers must be made available to customers?
- What are the terms and conditions of sale?
- What is the return goods policy?
- Offer guarantees or limited warranties?
- Are there any locations where the products cannot legally be sold by a retailer?

Promoting the Site

It is essential to the success of any site to register with the leading search and list engines. These are free and are the most commonly used method for potential customers buying things over the Internet. There are currently over 1,000 of these.

Search engines and directories are the places that matter because they drive up to 98% of new traffic to sites. What is more the quality of this traffic, in terms of conversion rates, is considerably higher than that achieved through banner advertising. Why? Because search engine users are actively looking for specific information. To build targeted search engine traffic, high scorings under the relevant keywords are essential (i.e. to appear in the first two pages of a search result).

To get the best out of crawler type 'search engines', sites need to ensure that it makes good use of the appropriate metatags – Description and Keyword – so that the site is appropriately cross-referenced and the search result is meaningful to a viewer.

Some ISPs automatically register sites with a number of search engines.

It is also vital to register the site in small directories that cater to the appropriate business market. For instance, if you are selling stationery it may be useful to be featured in a directory of stationery suppliers, suppliers in an area, trade associations for printers etc. These are particularly useful for generating quality leads.

Newsgroups are another way of publicizing your web sites. There are thousands of newsgroups on the web, each dedicated to a specific topic.

Advertising through banners carefully on established, high-traffic sites (e.g. AOL financial pages) that cater to the target audience. Cost is a function of the number of times the advertisement is served, otherwise known as an impression. Costs start at approximately £20 for about 1,000 impressions a month.

Partnering

Egg, Virgin and HSBC have all created financial 'supermarkets' where they are palcing the sale of their own products alongside that of other brands where they act as an introducer. Similarly many FSO's promote links to other businesses in order to 'lock in' the customer to the website. For example, a car supermarket may offer links to many banks for personal loans or a bank may offer links to removal firms and solicitors as part of a 'moving home' site. There is a danger of brand association so it is important to ensure the associated company has a complimentary image and service quality level with that of the introducing business.

5 Creating a Web Site

A web site can be viewed as one's own little publishing space on the WWW, where 'one' can mean an individual, company, charity, government, academic institution or research establishment.

This web site will be hosted on a computer – normally abbreviated to 'host machine' or simply a 'host' – that is permanently connected to the Internet so that other people surfing the web can visit the site.

Web pages and HTML

The web site itself will consist of a number of web pages written in a language called HTML, which is an abbreviation for 'HyperText Markup Language'. The format and structure of a web page is usually very straightforward (although there are exceptions), and HTML can usually be mastered after a few hours toying with it to construct simple web pages.

These web pages can contain several types of information, including simple text, graphical images, audio and video files/clips, database search facilities, online form fill-in, customer survey information, games – the list is endless, and as more and more information is added to the WWW, the type of data available can only increase.

Hyperlinks

However, perhaps the most important element of a web page is an item called a hyperlink. These are mouse-clickable areas of a web page that, once selected, take you to another web page. What is important to note here is that this new web page can be located anywhere on the WWW; it can be another section or paragraph of the same web page, a completely new web page in your own web site or it can be a web page on a completely different web site located anywhere in the world. These hyperlinks, like web pages themselves, can be constructed from a number of different sources. For example, a hyperlink could be a simple word in your document; it could be a simple clickable image; it could be a complex graphical image containing several different hyperlinks (an imagemap), etc.

Hence, the WWW can be viewed as a continually evolving, distributed, inter-woven collection of information resources, scattered throughout the world, similar in structure to a spider's web (hence the name!), with a web site located at each node in this web. New sites added to the WWW extend the coverage and information available to the world's web surfers.

Website structure

The pages in a web site can be arranged in a number of ways, and the hyperlinks between these pages designed to reflect the underlying information structure, such as grid, hierarchical, table of contents, linear, etc. Some formats may be better suited for specific web sites and the type of information they contain, but more often than not a web site will use a combination of one or more of these formats.

Website hosting

This latter activity will involve contracting the services of a suitable Internet Service Provider (ISP) that will be able to host your web site, preferably on a fast Internet line, and provide you with sufficient technical assistance and backup to ensure your web site runs smoothly and efficiently. Costs for this service vary greatly, depending on how big your site is, how much traffic you expect, what backup facilities you require, whether you want to incorporate advanced processing facilities on your site (so-called 'Common Gateway Interface', or CGI, programs), the speed of the ISP's connection to the Internet, whether you want your own dedicated host machine (as oppose to sharing a machine with several other company web sites), etc. As a rough guideline, expect to pay anywhere between a few hundred pounds per annum right up to several thousand.

Web browser

A web browser is a software application that incorporates the features necessary to browse the information and resources available on the WWW. There are several such web browser applications available, but by far the two most popular are those offered by Netscape and Microsoft. There is really not much to choose between the two browsers, and it boils down to a simple choice of taste or preference. Both offer a range of services, including the ability to send and receive e-mail, access to the Internet's 45,000 or so Usenet discussion groups, management of your 'bookmarks' (a file containing your favourite or most regularly visited web sites), inclusion of an in-built HTML editor to create your very own web pages, the ability to video (and audio) conference with someone else on the Internet, Java development utilities, etc.

URLs

URL is an abbreviation for Uniform Resource Locator (also referred to as a Universal Resource Locator), and is used to specify the location of a resource on the WWW, much like a conventional address does for a home, company, university, etc. In essence, a URL tells other people on the Internet where to go to visit a particular web site.

If you did not know a specific URL then it would be very difficult for you to quickly find the information and resources you require. A URL means you can type this web address into your browser window and tell it go straight to the web site represented by the URL.

Hostname

This specifies the individual computer hostname (e.g., www.bigbank.co.uk) where the web resource is located. An IP address can also be used instead here, such as 146.176.160.236, which uniquely identifies the computer hostname.

Directory

This specifies the directory pathname where the web resource (i.e., HTML file) is actually located within the remote machine.

Filename

This represents the actual HTML filename (or any other web resource) that should be retrieved and displayed within the user's web browser (or played back if it is an audio or video file, etc), for example 'index.html'.

HTTP

HTTP is an abbreviation for HyperText Transfer Protocol, and is the fundamental communication mechanism for the transfer of information on the web. When you visit a web site (such as http://www.ecommerce.co,uk/) then you will be using HTTP as the mechanism for requesting and receiving information from that site.

There are four main stages involved when you click a hyperlink to retrieve information from a web server (whether it be an html file, a graphical image, a video clip, a sound file, etc.). These four stages form the 'handshaking' procedures executed between the web browser and web server that together make up an http connection. These four stages are: Connect, Request, Respond and Disconnect.

CONNECT: The connection between the web client (browser) and the web server (site) is made.

REQUEST: The web browser requests an object from the web server, such as an html file, graphic (e.g., gif, jpeg), etc.

RESPOND: The web server responds to this request – e.g., by sending the required object, or returning an error message if the object was not found, or asking for more information (such as a username and password if authentication is required), etc.

DISCONNECT: The connection between the web browser and web server is closed.

Cookies

Stateless Protocols

One often hears HTTP referred to as a 'stateless' protocol; the reason is that no information is maintained across a series of connections between the web browser and the web server. Every time you connect to a web server to retrieve information, the server has no way of recognizing that you have already made previous connections, or indeed that you may make future connections – that is, there is no way of maintaining state information. Or simply, the web server does not remember anything about a query after its responded to that query.

Description

Cookies reduce this potential problem; 'cookies' are simple files placed on your computer by a web server. This file contains information that can be used by the web server should you return to the same web site at some future point. The information stored in a cookie file normally has an expiration date associated with it, after which time the web server will ignore the information it contains.

Cookies are used should you return to a previously visited web site, when the cookie is used to help the site personalize it in some way, such as 'Welcome back, Graham. Good to see you again!' or 'Phil, since your last visit we have added two new products that may be of interest to you'. These are but simple examples – however cookies are not a method for achieving security.

Privacy issues

Some consider the use of cookies as an invasion of privacy because web sites (and therefore the companies owning these web sites) have the potential to view your cookie file to see where you have been previously surfing on the Internet – information you may not wish a third party to view and inspect. Most web browsers let you specify how you want to handle cookies sent to your computer. There are generally three options: (1) accept all cookies that are sent to your machine, (2) prompt you when a cookie is sent so that you can decide whether or not to accept it, or (3) refuse to accept all cookies.

Hits *v.* Visits

One often hears companies say that their web site had '10,000 hits this week', or '...we reached 250,000 hits in February...'. The term 'hit' can have different meanings for different people, and is often misused to exaggerate a web site's popularity or its visitor numbers. A 'hit' can be defined as an individual object that is accessed from a web server. Hence, a single web page that contains, say, 10 graphical images, will generate a total of 11 'hits'; one for the web page itself, and a further 10 for each of the individual images stored on that web page. Note that any resource accessed will generate an individual 'hit', whether it be a html page, a graphics image file, a CGI program, an audio file, a video file, etc.

This means that 10 individual users visiting the same web site, and downloading this same web page, will generate a total of 110 hits; this figure is dramatically higher than that actual number of visitors to the site itself – a mere 10.

Also remember that a visitor returning to your home page during the same browsing session will again increase the hit rate even though it is the same visitor who, for example, may just be using that web page to navigate through your site. Or looking at it another way, two individual web sites may have the same number of visitors, but have two vastly different hit rates depending on how the information is presented.

6 Search Engines

Robots and spiders

A search engine is a web site that uses its own software, sometimes referred to as 'intelligent robots', 'web spiders' or 'web robots', that roam, catalogue, index and compile references to as many web sites as they possibly can. They follow hyperlinks contained in each web page they encounter, and continue this process from web site to web site, building up libraries of information as they progress. This indexed information is then stored on very large databases at the search engine's own web site. Visitors to this site can then interactively query this database to obtain results to their specific search queries.

Robot search rules

Each search engine uses its own proprietary software as it roams, with each robot using its own set of rules to guide how it searches and indexes the web – for instance, some locate every link on a home page, and then examine those links in turn to search for more information.

Some search engines are programmed not to locate graphics, sound or video files, and may not search specific Internet and web resources, such as databases, etc. Other spiders are instructed to index and catalogue only the most popular web sites. This is why it is a good idea to try a different search engine if you have no luck finding the information you need. What may be missed by one search engine may well be picked up by another at a different web site – and vice versa.

Cataloguing information

While these spiders locate and store these URLs, other software modules are busy downloading the actual web document the URL refers to – these are then sent to the main indexing software that analyses the web document in more detail, and stores information about that document on the search engine database. It is this database that is queried to obtain the information you require when you visit the search engine web site.

Indexing methods

These search engines build up their indexes in very different ways – which is why each search engine returns different results when provided with the same query. Some search engines give more weighting to a word or phrase if it appears as a section title (as oppose to just appearing in a paragraph); other search engines give more weighting if a word or phrase appears more than once in a web document, and they may even take the size of the document into consideration when assigning the weighting.

Most search engines will present the results to you in a ranked list – that is, the higher a web site appears on the result list, the more relevant it will be to your query. Again, you need to check how the search engines rank each query to decide how appropriate the references are for yourself.

The most popular search engines on the Internet can be found at: www.yahoo.com, www.infoseek.com, www.lycos.com, www.excite.com, www.google.com, www and www.hotbot.com.

Meta search engines

There are also so-called 'meta search engines' that can be queried just like conventional search engines. The main difference with meta engines is that, after you submit your query, the meta search engine forwards this query to a number of the other search engines and awaits a response from each of them. When all responses have been received back, the meta search engine collates and displays this information for your perusal.

This mechanism is something of a best-of-all-worlds scenario, but be warned – your average meta search engine can sometimes be quite slow, not just because they have to wait to collate the responses from the queried search engine resources, but also because they are very popular with Internet users, and so you will probably have to wait your turn to access their web site, e.g. www.savvysearch.com, www.onesearch.com, www.1blink.com, www.askjeeves.com

There is an alternative method of finding information on the Internet – these are the web directories. These differ from search engines in that people have to submit their own web addresses to the directories so that visitors can browse the directory for information, much the same way as they would a phone book. These web directories are usually arranged in a tree-like structure with general categories being available at the top of the tree, and more specific categories appearing as you delve deeper into the hierarchy. These web sites – and others – can be found at: www.yell.co.uk, www.isleuth.com, www.whatson.com, www.elibrary.com,www.ukonline.com.

7 Security

One of the most neglected issues in Internet technology is that of computer and network security. Companies are eager to get themselves onto the Internet to promote their profile, products, services, personnel, etc., but ignore the safety aspects of preserving their corporate data, knowledge and image; all of which could easily be compromised if the simplest of security steps are not implemented.

There are many (in)famous cases of Internet security breaches, all of which demonstrate the problems faced by companies who underestimate the threat of internal or external hacking.

Barclays Internet

31 July 2000: Barclays is forced to shutdown Internet service to 1.2m customers after an upgrade allowed users access to other peoples' account details.

Powergen

Powergen, the electricity and gas supplier, is forced to compensate 2,500 customers after their banking details were accessed through the website by a hacker.

The Internet Worm

In 1988, Robert T. Morris wrote a program – now referred to as the 'Internet Worm' – that crashed computers all over the USA. The program exploited several known security holes in the UNIX operating system, and gathered user and network information as it duplicated itself and spread from machine to machine. It also employed a dictionary of common and easily broken passwords to access user login accounts. The Worm also tried to hide its activity by changing its name to a common UNIX program, and even tried to erase any trace that it had penetrated the system in the first place.

Estimates vary, but it was calculated that between 2,000 and 6,000 computers were infected by Morris' Worm program. Likewise, the financial cost was even harder to calculate, but figures quoted range between $1m and $100m. Morris was convicted in 1990 under the US 1986 Computer Fraud and Abuse Act, and was sentenced to three years probation, ordered to pay a $10,000 fine, forced to do 400 hours community service and even ordered to pay an additional $100 per month supervision costs during his probation period.

2600.com

Another web site can be found at http://www.2600.com, which has 'before' and 'after' versions of famous web sites that have been hacked. These include web sites belonging to the UK Labour Party, the Conservative Party, the CIA (the group changed references of 'Central Intelligence Agency' to the 'Central Stupidity Agency'), NASA, the US Department of Justice, the Church of Christ and even the Spice Girls' web site. Another hacking organization is the Anti-Online Group who have a similar web site at: http://www.antionline.com.

How Do Security Incidents Occur?

In theory, all Internet services are under possible threat or attack. This includes internal and external e-mail, your company web site, file transfer facilities, remote logins, networked (shared) file resources, etc. While all these services have the ability to introduce loopholes, careful deployment of the technologies, and a firm understanding of their limitations should ensure all is relatively risk-free.

Weak Links

The simple answer to this is that it is normally attributable to several factors occurring individually; but when they all occur together mayhem usually ensues. For example, an easily-broken user password can let in a would-be hacker to cause damage, and if this user account is held on a computer system with known security holes (that have not been corrected) then the problem is easily compounded – even more so if the compromised account is the root or system administrator's account.

Also, Internet services themselves are not 100% secure – they were never designed to be so – they were originally developed for the rapid exchange of information, not to prevent hostile attacks. However, Internet services can be made secure easily enough in a number of ways – e.g., integrating a security module, using encryption, deploying best practice, staff training and education, etc.

Corporate data can also be intercepted as it travels from one computer to another (either on the same local area network or over the Internet). Software applications and hardware devices are available that allow such 'sniffing' or 'snooping' of information when it is in transit. One possible solution to this problem is to encrypt all data as it travels across your own network as well as out onto the Internet.

Internal Threats

However, by far the biggest threat to computer systems is not, as one might first think, from an external hacker lurking out there somewhere on the Internet, possibly on the other side of the world. In fact, the biggest threat to computer and network security comes from staff internal to an organization.

Perhaps the biggest security threat for any organization rests with its own staff. It is estimated that over 80% of security breaches originate from a company's own personnel and not, say, from an outside hacker using a computer in their bedroom located somewhere on the other side of the world. Why is this figure so high? There are several reasons: staff are already inside the organization (no need to gain physical access to the data and resources); staff may have a serious grudge with the company (missed a promotion, social interaction problems, conflict with line managers, disagrees with company's environmental policies, etc.); staff may be leaving the organization and wish to create as much mayhem as possible over the last few days, etc.

8 What Are the Types of Security Threat?

There are many types of attack that can be used and directed towards your computers, networks and other resources. Perhaps the four most common are:

Denial of Service

This type of attack involves a user (intruder?) taking up so much of a system resource that none of that resource is left for other legitimate users. The attack itself can take several forms: destructive attacks (e.g., re-formatting hard disks, deletion of system-critical files, cutting power/network cables, etc.); overload attacks (e.g., continually querying a server so that it cannot process valid requests, etc.); file system attacks (e.g., filling up all available disk space thus not allowing others to save data/files, etc.).

Spoofing/Impersonation

Both computers and individuals can be impersonated and forged. Computers can easily be configured with fake or forged IP addresses that can subsequently allow access to specific networks, resources and information. Similarly, individuals can use 'social engineering' techniques to try to obtain privileged information. A classic example is someone telephoning the technical support desk and saying: 'Hi. This is Fred over in Accounts. I've forgotten the password to access the payroll data. Can you let me have it please?'

System Intrusion

If your corporate resources have succumbed to an attack, then it is likely that an intruder will be able to wander around your networked systems and resources. What they do while they are on their 'electronic stroll' is open to question depending on how they feel at that particular time. They may be kind and leave everything untouched, or they may be particularly nasty and delete files, tamper with user accounts, crash machines, leave backdoors to gain future (unnoticed) access, send fake e-mails, corrupt your web site – the list is endless.

Data corruption and integrity

If your corporate data is valuable (which is particularly true for financial organizations) then it has to be safeguarded and protected otherwise it may well be destroyed and/or duplicated by an intruder. The integrity of your data will come under question – how can you be sure that it was not edited, tampered with, or changed in some other way? How can you now control who gets to see it (it may have been there on a 'need to know' basis)? Will it be sold to your main corporate competitor?

9 Private Key Encryption

Shared Key

Private key encryption – also referred to as 'symmetric key' encryption – uses the same key to encode and decode the information or document. With this type of encryption, both the sender and recipient of a message share the same key. For example, if I wish to send Sarah a secure document, I could use a private key algorithm and use the password (or passphrase) 'verity' to encrypt the document. For Sarah to decrypt that same document she must know the password ('verity') that I used to encode the original information.

The main problem with using private key encryption is ensuring the key is kept secret. In the above example, how do I tell Sarah the password? –telephone her (someone may eavesdrop our conversation), write to her (postman may intercept the letter), e-mail her the password (someone else may read her e-mail), etc.

Public Key Encryption: Two keys

Public key encryption – also known as 'asymmetric key' encryption – uses two keys: one to encrypt the information and the other to decrypt it. Each key can be thought of as the components of a unique two-piece jigsaw. The terminology used to describe each piece can, however, be slightly confusing. In public key encryption everyone owns a unique pair of keys; one key is referred to as the 'public key', and should be disseminated to as many people as possible. The other is referred to as the 'private key' and should be held and kept secret by the key owner.

Should someone wish to send you a secure message, they obtain your public key, encrypt the message with your public key and then send the encoded message to you. This encrypted message can only be decrypted with the corresponding private key – which only you possess.

Alternatively, if I wanted to send an encrypted message, encrypt it first with my own private key and then send the encoded message. The recipient would then use my public key (which I make freely available to as many as possible) to decrypt my message. If the message is decrypted successfully, then the recipient knows that it was indeed sent by me (because I am the only person who has the corresponding private key).

21

FUTURE VISIONS AND CASE STUDIES

Objectives

After studying this chapter, you should be able to:

- understand and be able to describe the various categories of electronic commerce (e-commerce);
- understand how to create and promote an e-commerce website.

1 Introduction

In this chapter we explore two possible extremes of where the information revolution is heading. The first vision we call 'Networked World' and the second 'Privacy World'. Neither, we suspect, will come true but they give an extrapolation of two extremes of current trends.

In the second part we look at two case studies of financial organizations, Capital One and the Woolwich. Capital One is a market leader in its use of information within a CRM architecture and Woolwich is market leader in channel integration through its 'open plan' strategy.

2 Future Vision 1 – Networked World

There are a number of social, technological trends which together lead to a world where everything is connected and networked.

Invisible computers

Increasing use of embedded chips in things ranging from things that 'look like computers' to mobile phones, washing machines, toys, even things you wear. The falling cost of basic microprocessors will make them ubiquitous; you will have computers built into your clothes to indicate when they need cleaning or to actually control the heat retention characteristics of the material. Your key ring will have the ability to know where you are by linking itself to the global positioning satellites and be able to know where your car is, weather etc. etc.

Internet everywhere

The increasing use of satellites linked to the standardization of communication protocols such as WAP, UMTS and Bluetooth will continue to reduce the cost of data transmission. In the past costs have been related to distance (e.g. long-distance phone calls cost more than local calls) but the internet makes such calculations and methods of charging illogical; distance is no longer a function of cost. Cost of moving information and staying connected to the network will therefore continue to reduce until it is negligible or zero.

Metcalfe's law

Metcalfe's law: $p^{(n)} = n^{-2}$ i.e. the power and value of a network increases exponentially with number of users. In other words the more people who are connected to the web the more important it is to be a member. Internet membership becomes a mandatory requirement to do business.

Consumer power

A connected world offers power to the consumer. Instead of sellers dominating the design, pricing and availability of products, consumers will be able to band together in a virtual consortium to negogiate bulk deals. E.g. Letsbuyit.com where if, say, 50 people want a 32" wide screen TV then they connect via the site who then negotiate with potential suppliers for a best price.

Similarly the ability to spread rumour ('word of mouse') or establish lobby groups is dramatically amplified through a connected world. Chat rooms, bulletin boards and specific software plug-ins such as '3rd wave' all enable consumers to take control of the agenda. Sites such make-it-for-me.com enable customers to tailor order products such as computers and holidays to their specification.

Things communicating with things

In an increasingly time pressured society we will increasingly hand over responsibility to 'intelligent agents' to carry out either boring or mundane tasks or simply those that do not interest us. You will trust private information to these agents but with so much free information available and limited data protection legislation almost everything you do will leave a trail.

This has already started with PDAs and ISPs offering automatic diaries to remember (and even send birthday cards and presents), money management agents which will continually scan the web and look for the best deal; the next generation will actually carry out the deal for you!

Your car will be connected to the web via wireless connections, it will negotiate with local garages to book your car in for a service having highlighted items required. Your washing machine will negotiate with the power suppliers for the best price to buy power for the next wash!

That's just the way it is

Familiarity with computers, networks and 'intelligent devices' will have the same acceptance as using electricity. The current generation of children accept and expect such devices to enable instant 24x7x365 access to everything.

Overview

An interesting world with a global perspective causing a breakdown in most economic barriers. Financial organizations will polarize to either product manufacturers or information brokers/ intelligent agents.

3 Future Vision 2 - Privacy World

The technological advances described in Future Vision 1 continue but social acceptance of a 'free information' world is challenged.

National boundaries make a come-back

The lack of effective international agreements on data management, integrity and privacy makes the net an increasingly difficult and dangerous medium for business. Although security and encryption continues to develop and offer safety, well publicized breakdowns and errors create a public perception of insecurity. Rogue states offer little or no regulation of information processed or stored on servers within their physical bondaries. Information or information disruption becomes a new economic weapon of war.

Relationship technologies are rejected

The consumer's perception aligns with George Orwell's predictions in his book *Nineteen Eighty Four* and the feeling that individual privacy is now impossible with 'big brother' watching every move and analysing every piece of information. CRM technologies become misused and consumers start to deliberately break information links and provide incorrect data. The consumer rights lobby demands greater privacy and rejects the benefits of free information exchange.

Economic instability as markets seek real-time perfection

The whole basis of economics assumes that there is no perfect information flows, enabling markets to exploit short-term differences. In a world of connected information businesses could be destroyed in minutes if not seconds with work moving across time zones and countries in an attempt to reduce costs and survive in a 'super competitive' global virtual marketplace. Government taxation and social plans will be thrown into disarray culminating, maybe, in a return to the trade protectionism of the 1800s.

Overview

A world where either there is drive to create data protectionism or trade protectionism as consumers and governments fail to manage the effective flow of information and services in a global virtual economy.

4 Case Study 1: Capital One

Capital One is a major credit card provider which has focused its development on the analysis of customer information to test and refine its products and their delivery. It has now extended its product offering well beyond the traditional credit card.

Top-10 bank card issuer in United States

- Born as spin-off from Signet in 1994
- Today, $20.2 billion in loans
- Five consecutive years of earnings growth greater than 20%
- 23.7 million accounts in USA and UK, adding 5+ million each year.

While at Signet, founders invented 'teaser rate' and 'balance transfer' option.

Today, Cap One growth comes from learning, remembering and *anticipating* individual customer needs; 1.5 million customers call in each week.

Figure 21.1: Capital One

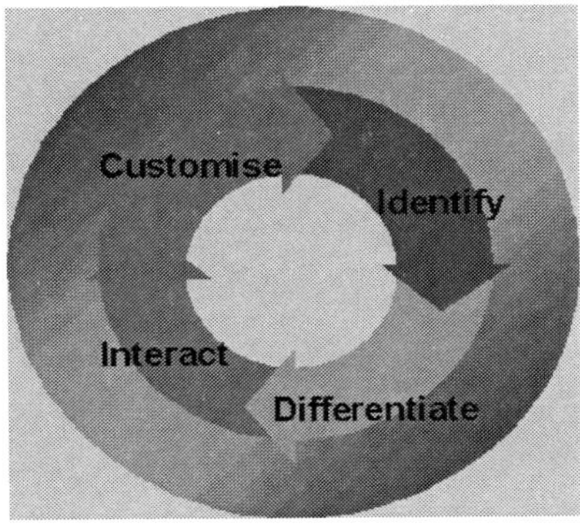

Mission

- Right product
- Right price
- To right consumer

- Customer prepares to ask, "what is my balance?"
- Capital One begins predicting John's needs, before the telephone rings.

Figure 21.2: The Customer Call

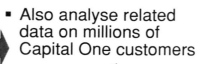

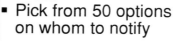

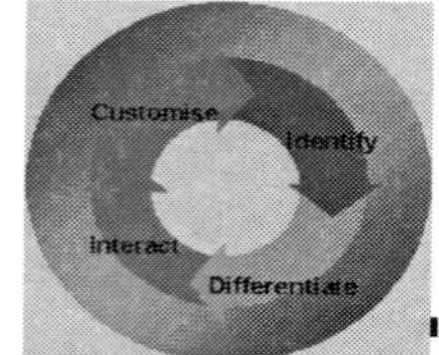
Customise
Identify
Interact
Differentiate

▪ Analyse data on 7M households
▪ Also analyse related data on millions of Capital One customers
▪ Pick from 50 options on whom to notify
▪ Remember and pass along 25 pieces of info related to this particular customer

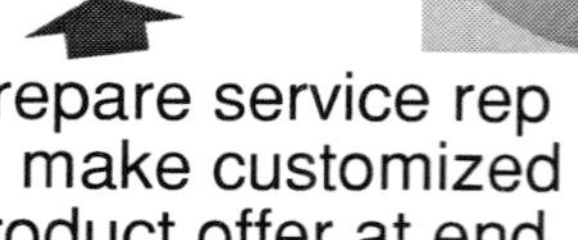
▪ Prepare service rep to make customized product offer at end of call

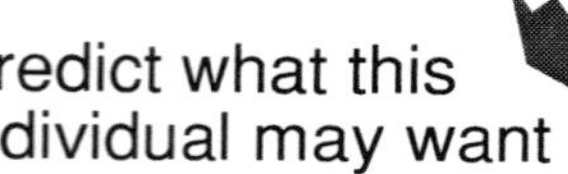
▪ Predict what this individual may want

Time-to-learning relationship: *0.1 second*

- Customized offer is prepared before the service rep picks up the call
- Based on enough consumer data to fill 200,000 personal computers
- Supported by ongoing feedback
- A scientific method for testing

Capital One receives 4.5 million calls a month. In 1997, bank found that calls were simply taking too long. Problem: wrong need, handled by wrong rep.

Company tried options . . .

Example:

Some customers called more than 5 times a year:

- Capital One sent a letter saying,

  'please don't call'
- Misfire: If you want people to call you,

  send a letter saying not to!

Analysis shows 90% of inbound calls fall into 1 of 10 categories

- Rates up, customer does not like it

- New card needs activation, etc.
- And a few fresh insights ...

You know the customer's number *and* this customer calls each month to check his balance...So make that *his* first option! 'Anticipation' success rate:

- 40% in first few months, 60-70% accurate now;
- Best reps sell to 15% of incoming callers with problems.

'Choice' is not the same thing as customization...

Capital One *customizes*, based on individual needs:

Incoming call: "I want to close my account"

- Data profile says there is an unspoken need: "I want a better deal"
- Service rep says, "I could lower your rate"
- Result: Service rep receives bonus for retaining high-value customer
- Capital One maintains revenue stream from customer

Incoming angry call: "What is this coupon fee on my new card?"

- Silver card has $59 annual fee
- $20 higher than previous card, but includes...
- Coupons good for car rentals or hotels
- Service rep says, "Use one coupon and you'll more than offset the service fee"
- Service rep then offers additional catalogue product — at exact point of customer interest

5 Woolwich: Open Plan: Channel Integration

Background

Review of Woolwich strategy post-conversion needed to address:

- Pressure on margins
- Competition based on price
- New entrants.

Increased customer profitability will be achieved by:

- Attracting new customers with a compelling proposition;
- Replacing wide margin solus product relationships with narrower margin multi-product relationships;

- Increasing customer retention through depth of relationship and service.

Open Plan achieve cross-sales by providing customized banking:

- Personal planning and advice;
- An integrated set of products;
- Greater accessibility for customers;
- Helping customers to see the whole financial picture;
- Customer relationship management;
- High-quality service delivery.

Figure 21.3

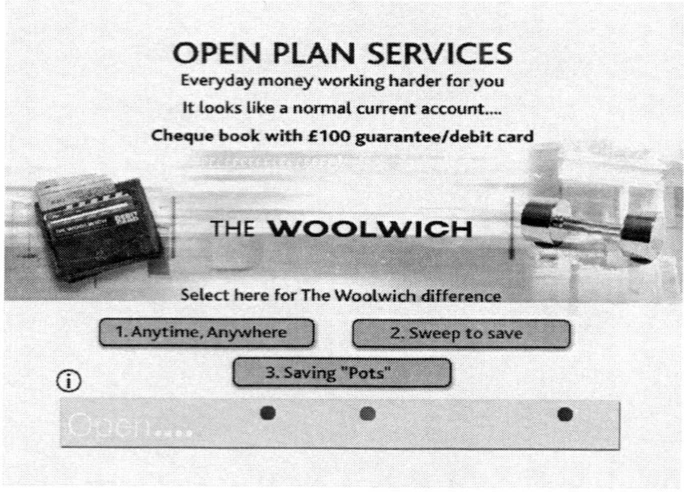

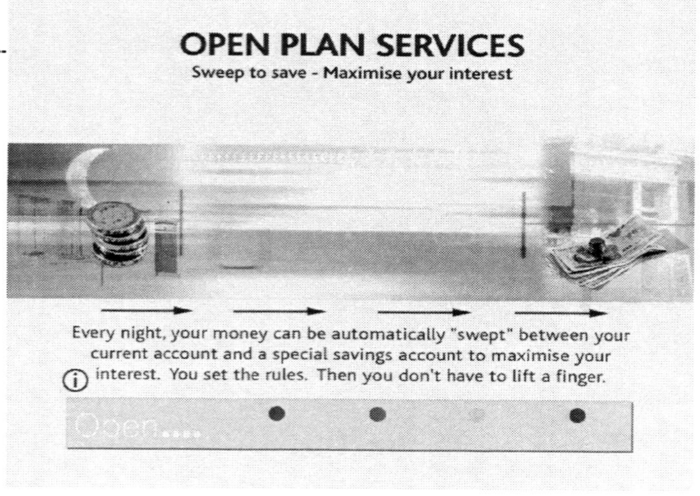

Offering integrated accounts with automatic sweeps between.

Compare this to:

Figure 21.4: The Traditional 'Bricks' Bank

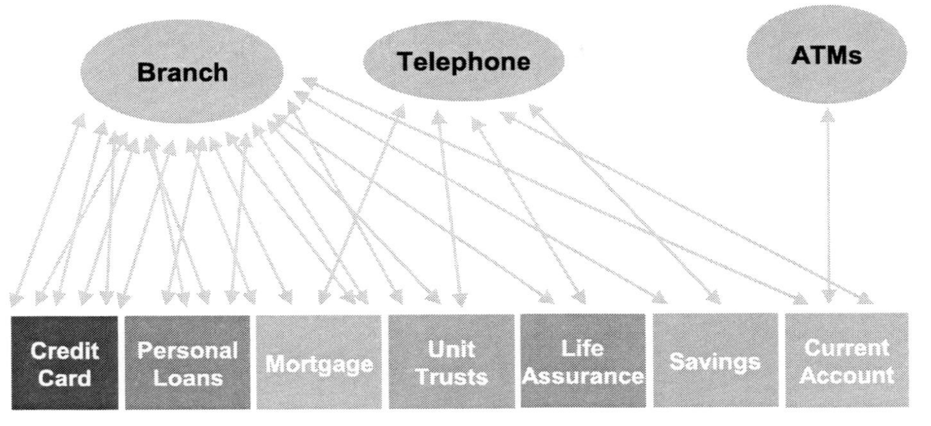

Confused points of contact with 'product silo' approach or a stand-alone Internet Bank:

Figure 21.5: Stand-alone Internet Bank

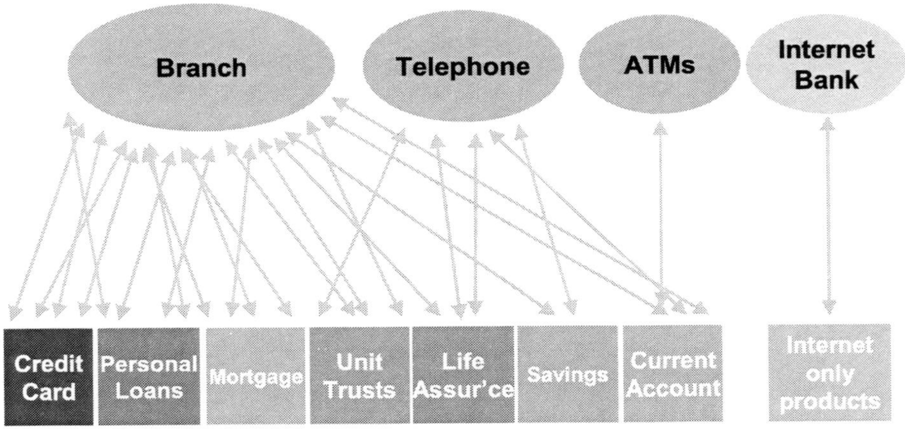

No access to traditional channels, can only deliver Internet based products.

Figure 21.6: Bricks and Clicks

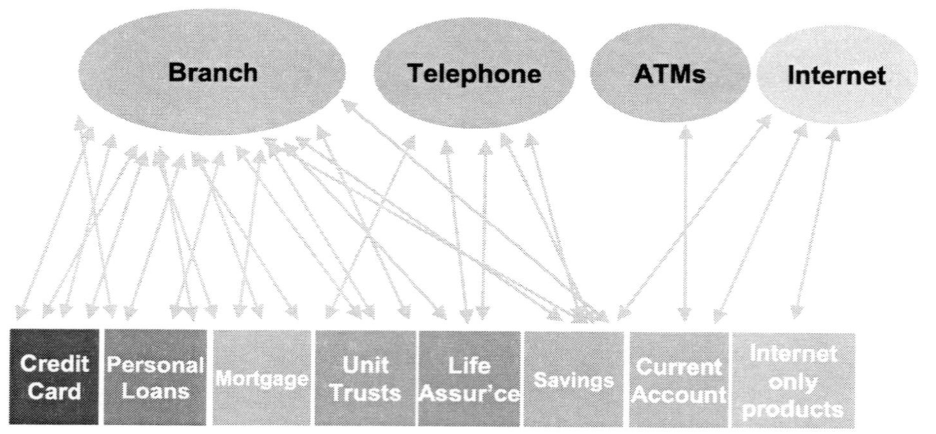

Confused mixture of channels with 'Internet' an add-on.

Figure 21.7: Complete integration – open plan

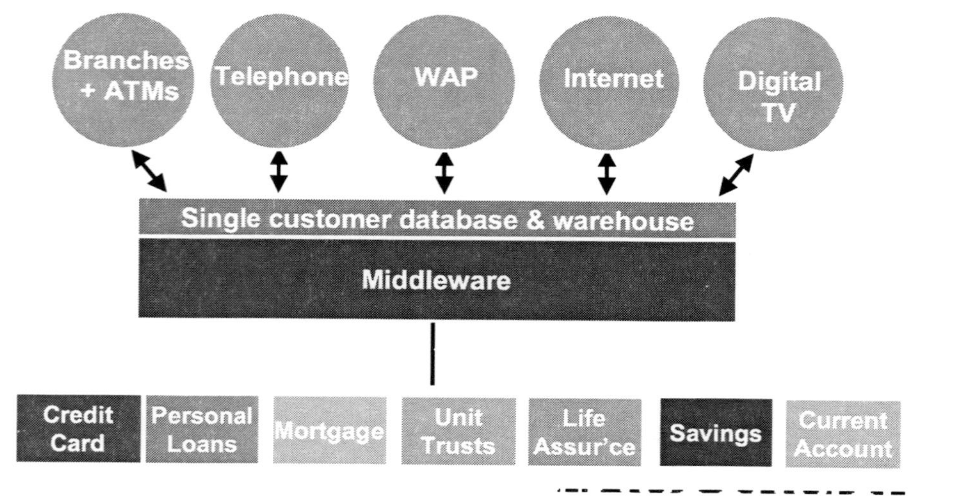

Using middleware, products are mapped onto channels in a 'martini' approach of anytime, anywhere, anyhow. Woolwich architecture provides a totally integrated channel approach.

INDEX

E

F

Q

R

S

T

Honey & Co.

The Baking Book

Sarit Packer &
Itamar Srulovich

Honey & Co.

The Baking Book

Photography by Patricia Niven

With all my love and admiration to my amazing parents (Hazel and Jeff). You inspire me – Sarit

---

To my mum (Eilat) for her love and all the sweetness in life – Itamar

---

'I got hunger.' – Alice Russell

Honey & Co.
Food From the Middle East

Contents

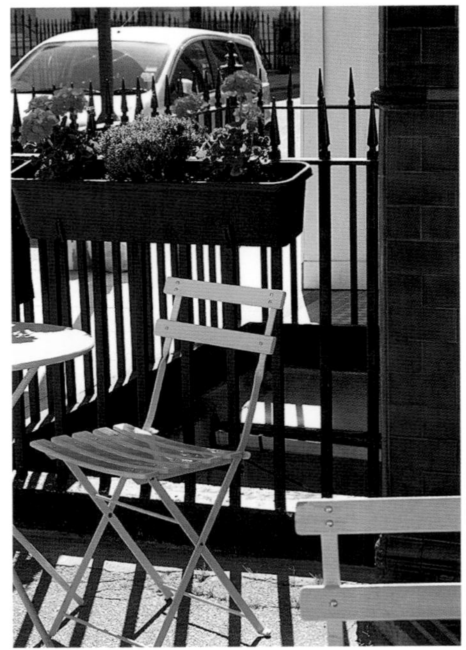

105 Mid-morning: Elevenses

235 After dark: Traditional desserts

Sarit Packer &
Itamar Srulovich
Honey & Co.
Food
From
the
Middle
East

Welcome

A restaurant, even a small one like ours, is a watering hole, a crossroads where people meet (by chance or design), to rest, to replenish. Dozens of people from all walks of life in London's mad parade pass through our doors every day, all through the day. From the quiet early-morning coffee and Fitzrovia bun for the road, through the manic, slightly crazed rush of lunch, to the last licked dessertspoon of dinner, our ten tables will be set, cleared, cleaned and set again constantly. An endless stream of suppliers and delivery men fill our stores and fridges with produce from all over the world: British berries, French wine, Lebanese spice, nuts from California, chocolate and vanilla from the African shores, Indian rice, cut flowers from Holland – all find space under our tiny roof, for the pleasure of our customers and ourselves.

A restaurant can have a life of its own. It can grow so quickly, seemingly unaided; at first it was just the two of us, doing everything, but now there are many of us working in Honey & Co. As I write this we have three pastry chefs and five chefs in the kitchen, three kitchen porters running up and down the stairs, seven waiters and shift managers working the floor upstairs, Louisa in the office and the two of us, trying to find a bit of space to work.

A restaurant is a machine with many moving parts. In order for things to fall into place time and again, it needs to have a culture, a routine, and at the heart of our routine is our baking. Even though it is only a part of what we do, the pastry section is the backbone of the operation, the driving force and the powerhouse. What baking requires represents everything we want our staff to have and our customers to feel – consideration, concentration, experience and patience, of course, but also a lot of passion, greed, an eagerness to please on an industrial scale and a great big heart. Our days are governed now by the rhythm of the pastry: weighing, mixing, kneading, shaping, baking, chilling, glazing, serving.

A restaurant takes the shape of the people in it, customers and staff. We never planned to have such an elaborate pastry offering – I originally thought we would do only one type of bread – but the selection grew rapidly. The cakes came about because we wanted something tempting in the window to lure people in, the desserts happened because of a friend's remark, the breakfast bakes because we needed to bring the morning trade to life. It all seemed gradual, almost accidental, but with hindsight I can say that the growth of our pastry was inevitable. I am a complete sweet tooth, always dreaming of new cakes and sweet things, while my wife has been baking all her life, and has a great passion and talent for it. You could almost say that baking is her favourite form of interaction with the world. I don't think I'm biased in considering her one of the best bakers in the world (although of course I am),

Zerbinati
www.zerbinatiagricoltura.it
S.Leone

and all of us at Honey & Co, employees and patrons alike, are united in our admiration and love for her gift. And the rest of the team are just as sugar-mad as we are – Giorgia, our pastry chef, lights up most when she talks about cakes; Julia and HD are always snuffling up the sweet offcuts; the girls upstairs argue constantly about which cake is their favourite, and each tries to convince our customers that their choice is best.

A purple plastic folder sits on the shelf in the pastry section. In it are neat spread-sheets containing pastry recipes that my wife has collected throughout her baking life. It has been with us for years now, since long before we opened our restaurant. It is divided into categories – sponges, mousses, biscuits etc. – and each recipe has a note about its origin – from famous patisseries to 'Barry's mom', busy brasseries to Michelin-starred kitchens – and another note about the end result, things like 'freezes well', 'not too sweet' or just plain 'delicious'.

This book has our favourite recipes from it, and the best of all of us.

Itamar Srulovich
London, 2015

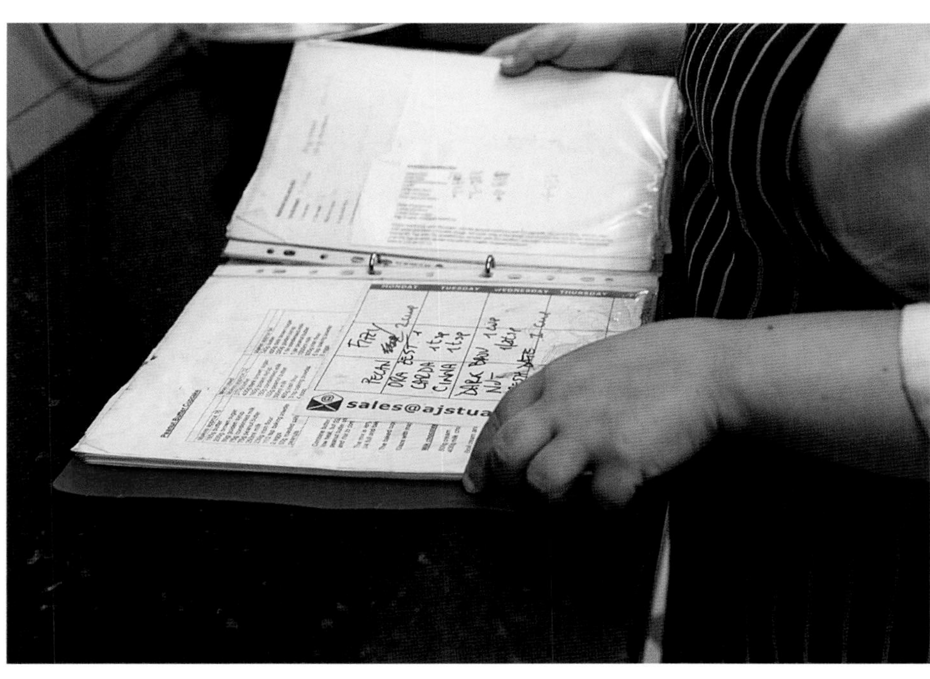

I have a really bad memory: old school friends, people I have worked with – I often draw a complete blank. My mum still has to text me to remind me of all my nieces' and nephews' birthdays. My dear husband says that if I put my mind to it, I would remember everything. He may well be right, because there are memories that are etched on my brain. I remember mincing meat with my mum when I was a child, and picking chicken off the bone to make a chicken pie. I remember the first cake I baked for my sister's birthday (the white chocolate cheesecake), and the first meal Itamar and I had in London at the Orrery when I returned there with him on holiday. And I remember the cakes, cookies, bars, ice creams and many other sweet confections that have been a part of my life, both personal and professional.

As a child I used to roll ginger cookies with my mum and I can still feel the silky warm dough forming into balls that we would bake to the crispiest cookies. On field trips we would make flat breads on a makeshift taboon, forming the dough into uneven lumpy shapes filled with the sand from our dirty palms (they tasted great). We were allowed to mess around in the kitchen from a very young age but I think I started baking seriously when I was eleven or twelve. My sister brought home an amazing pastry book on classic French desserts by one of Israel's most famous food writers and I was hooked. I wanted to try everything.

I started by making crème brûlée (my mum's favourite to this day). The book said to use a vanilla pod, which I assumed was the same as a cinnamon stick. It said to open it up and scrape out the black seeds. I didn't find any – I decided the writer was crazy – and my crème brûlées had a distinct whiff of cinnamon. It took years for me to discover my mistake. I went on to make tarts: fresh fruit tart, classic apple tart, rich chocolate ganache tart. Then cheesecakes became an obsession and I baked them whenever I could. I got more and more adventurous.

At eighteen I came to the conclusion that this was what I wanted to do for a living, and as soon as my compulsory army service was over, I decided it was time to learn the art of cooking properly. My parents had a few misgivings, so I resolved to earn my own money to pay for cookery school and at the same time enrolled in a French language class because I felt that France was the best place to learn about patisserie. It probably is, but I never got there, because after working for a year as a PA and part-time caterer for anyone who would hire me, I had earned enough to make a move and opted for London instead. I spoke the language, I had the passport and even had some family there, so I packed my bags, enrolled at catering college and never looked back. Everything about it was amazing, from cooking at The Apprentice (the college restaurant designed to give

us true-to-life experience) to discovering how to make ice creams with a balsamic reduction, how to bake my very own profiteroles and madeleines, and how to use a piping bag the correct way. After graduating I started work at the Orrery, and after six months I moved to their pastry section. There I learnt how to make jellies, opera cakes, ice creams, parfaits, caramels and soufflés. It was fine dining at the highest level.

After my time at the Orrery I headed back to Israel, eventually starting a catering company with a colleague. We thought being self-employed would mean that we could cook what we wanted, but nothing went to plan and we ended up in a converted chicken shed, running a pastry kitchen selling baked goods to cafés and restaurants. I baked cheesecakes by the dozens, babkas with millions of different fillings and cookies for the various holiday seasons. I made crazy, constructed mousse-cakes (they were all the rage at the time), loaf cakes, jams and savoury bakes. People came to our kitchen to buy a couple of cakes for the weekend, then some cookies for the week and a specialty cake for an occasion. It was a mad time. The old chicken shed was hotter than hell in summer and colder than the Arctic in winter, and we had to do everything ourselves, from cleaning to invoicing.

By this time I had met and moved in with Itamar, but we had no free time to spend together and we were running out of money, fast. After a year of living on Itamar's salary it was time to admit I needed to get a 'proper' job. It broke my heart, but what I had learnt made me stronger and smarter.

In each place I have worked since then, I have learnt more and more: ways to get things right; ways to improve quality and speed; how to teach other people to work with me, and how to trust them. When we moved to London I became sous-chef in charge of a large team of pastry chefs in the brasserie and restaurant at the OXO Tower. Penny, the head pastry chef, really taught me about mass production; we would feed over 800 people a day between the two venues. Itamar worked with me there, and when he left to work at Ottolenghi, he told Yotam all about me. I still remember our first meeting – I was late (as always) and way too cocky, but Yotam still decided to give me a chance.

When I saw the cake display at Ottolenghi, I was a little disappointed: no crazy sugar work, no colour, no French finesse. But when I got into the kitchen and started tasting things, it was a revelation – here it was all about flavour. Weekly pastry meetings with Yotam and Helen were inspiring and creative, and managing four separate pastry kitchens and a bakery was an exciting challenge. Ottolenghi was truly a turning point for me, but after four years I couldn't face baking another oversized

meringue and I wanted a change. I started by joining the team creating NOPI, but eventually Itamar and I decided it was time for our own place.

Our original business plan for Honey & Co didn't contain a single cake. I told Itamar I needed the place to be about chopping vegetables, roasting meats and grilling fish. But when we saw 25a Warren Street and its beautiful big front window, I knew that cakes would have to be a part of what we were going to do. We set about creating our own cake identity. Itamar suggested fruit and lots of colour, so that it would look like a Middle Eastern marketplace and I started with that. Then he suggested spice and coffee and honey, and I added them to the mix. This is how we work together: we develop, we taste, we get excited and angry and occasionally disappointed when something fails. But it is by far the most creative environment I have ever worked in. Those of you who have read our previous book will know that Itamar loves his cakes and sweets, and that he is my biggest inspiration. He dreams of cakes and I try my best to fulfil his dreams. Sometimes I hate his ideas and we argue, but at other times what he wants makes perfect sense to me. Sometimes I make something that I love and he hates (or thinks is too sweet, or not sweet enough, or too ugly, or too pretty) and I get really offended. I take it personally, for a while... But then we let our staff taste it and give their opinions, and we fix the things that have gone wrong and together we create something special. There is nothing quite like it.

Much of the above is by way of explaining that none of the recipes in this book are purely my inventions. They are always based on something. They may have been inspired by another recipe, or another method, or perhaps by a flavour combination that struck me as a revelation. In essence pastry is a combination of a few staples – butter, sugar, eggs, flour and occasionally nuts, chocolate and fruit. It is how you combine them and the proportions you use that create the huge variety. This book is inspired by my memories of my baking life, of all the people I have cooked with and the places I have worked; by recipes I found in a book when I was an eager teenage baker; and by amazing cakes baked by friends. In the same way that you learn from people about their cakes and methods, you teach others about yours. There is always another recipe to discover, or a trick you had never heard about. It is the search that is the best part.

Sarit Packer
London, 2015

How to be good at baking

General notes

I can't understand people who say they are not good at baking, or that they are scared of it. In my experience it is simple: you find a good recipe, follow the method and get great results. But in order to be able to do that, you need to understand the instructions. The following guidelines should help, so if you feel you need some assistance, have a read through and get to grips with the basics (according to me).

The golden rule

I will repeat this again and again throughout the book: **always** read the entire recipe before you start and make sure you understand it. Whenever possible, I strongly advise setting out all your ingredients in advance too; that way, there is less chance of forgetting something. I tend to weigh all my ingredients, including the liquids, as I find it a more effective and precise method, so I have listed both gram and millilitre measurements for liquids throughout the book.

Chocolate

The main types of chocolate I use in baking are:

- bitter dark chocolate with a cocoa content of 62% and over
- dark chocolate with between 42% and 54%
- milk chocolate
- white chocolate

Use a brand you like (my rule is that if I don't want to steal a piece, I shouldn't be baking with it) and check the cocoa mass. Be aware that you can't substitute a bitter dark chocolate with one that contains a much lower percentage of cocoa as it simply won't perform in the same way. However, you can be more flexible with milk and white chocolate varieties.

How to melt chocolate

Make sure you are using dry utensils and bowls (even a little water can ruin an entire batch). Break or chop the chocolate into even-sized pieces before you start melting it. Then you can use one of two methods.

• Place the chocolate pieces in a dry microwave-safe bowl and set on high for a minute. Remove and stir. Return to the microwave for another 30 seconds, then remove and stir again. If it still isn't fully melted, put it back in for additional bursts of 10 seconds, stirring in between each one, until it is completely liquid. Do note that microwaves vary in strength and chocolate is very easy to burn, so you will need to be cautious.

• The better method, I find, is to use a small pan and a bowl that fits snugly on top, so that there is no space up the sides for steam to escape. Pour some water into the pan. Place the bowl on top and check that it doesn't touch the water (if it does, tip some out). Set on the heat, bring to the boil, then remove from the heat again. Put the chocolate into the bowl. Allow to melt for 2–3 minutes before stirring, then mix to a smooth paste. If this doesn't prove sufficient to melt all the chocolate, you can return the pan and bowl to the stove on a very low heat for 2–3 minutes, but do watch it and take care not to overheat it or you will burn the chocolate.

When a recipe calls for melted butter and chocolate, I always start with the butter on its own. Use one of the methods above to melt it. Once the butter is warm and fully liquid, add the chocolate and stir until it dissolves.

When melting chocolate with a liquid, always bring the liquid to the boil first. Remove from the heat, pour over the chocolate pieces in a bowl and leave for 2–3 minutes. Place a whisk in the centre of the bowl and whisk in small circular movements in the middle until you have created a shiny liquid core. Then whisk carefully until the chocolate and liquid are fully combined.

Chocolate sets and hardens as it cools, so if the recipe calls for melted chocolate, don't melt it until you are ready to use it. Each recipe varies as to how and when to add the chocolate, so read the method carefully.

Sugars & caramels

The main types of sugar we use are:

- caster sugar
- light brown soft sugar
- dark brown soft sugar
- icing sugar
- demerara sugar
- granulated sugar (occasionally)

Each imparts a different texture and flavour and can affect the end result of your baking. You can swap them around a little, but you must make sure to dissolve the grainier sugars well if you want to achieve good results.

You can very easily turn granulated sugar into caster sugar by blitzing it in a blender for 15 seconds. You can even make it into icing sugar if you use a fine grinder, like a spice grinder. When I was growing up in Israel, grinding sugar ourselves was the only option, but luckily caster and icing sugar can be purchased easily these days, so I don't usually have to bother.

How to make caramel

There are two main types of caramel.

- **Wet caramel:** This is used mostly for sauces and bases that require additional liquid. Place the sugar in a small, clean (ideally heavy-bottomed) pan. Turn on the cold water tap to a very light trickle. Hold the pan under the tap, moving it around so that water pours around the edges only, leaving the centre of the sugar still dry. Remove from under the tap and use the tip of your finger or a spoon to stir very gently to moisten the sugar in the centre, taking care not to get it up the sides of the pan. If you do, moisten your finger or a brush with some water and run it around the sides of the pan to clean away any sugar crystals. You should have a white paste in the base of the pan. Set it on the stove on the highest setting and bring to a rapid boil. Don't stir it, but if you feel the urge, you can very gently swivel the pan in circular motions. Once the colour deepens to a light golden caramel, remove from the heat and add your liquids or butter. Be careful as the caramel may spit and seize. If it does, return it to a low heat and continue cooking until it liquefies.

- **Dry caramel:** This is mostly used for decoration work or making brittles. Set a heavy-bottomed pan on a high heat. Once the pan is hot, sprinkle the sugar in a thin layer over the base; it should start to melt almost immediately. Stir with a wooden or heatproof spoon. Once the first layer of sugar has melted, add another layer and repeat the process. Continue until all the sugar has been dissolved and the colour deepens to a lovely amber, then remove from the heat. At this stage you can:
  - cool it (by dipping the bottom of the pan into cold water), if you are making decorations, or
  - add butter and nuts, if you are making brittle, or
  - simply pour it onto a sheet of baking parchment and allow to cool before breaking it up.

Flour

I am not wedded to specific brands but do like to make sure my flour is fresh. Check the 'best before' / 'use by' date and try to use it up before then, rather than letting it sit forgotten in your cupboard. If you have a large freezer, store it there for a longer shelf life.

I use a few different types of flour in my baking. Each recipe will state which one is needed.

- **Plain:** I use this for most of my cake baking and some of the cookies. It is the generic, standard flour sold everywhere.

- **Strong white bread flour:** This is used in all my bread and yeast-based baking, and for cookies or biscuits that call for a very crisp end result.

- **Self-raising:** This is simply flour that has been activated with baking powder (very well mixed through). This gives a nice even rise to cakes. Sometimes I prefer the results you get using this flour to those you get by adding baking powder or baking soda by hand. If you don't have any self-raising flour, you can substitute pre-mixed baking powder and plain flour (use a teaspoon of baking powder for every 100g of flour).

Eggs

The freshness and flavour of eggs can greatly affect many desserts, especially ones that aren't baked, like mousses and creams. I tend to use free-range medium eggs for baking, and the best eggs I can find for desserts that aren't cooked through (and for eating generally). In the UK the tastiest eggs I have tried are from Cotswold Legbar and Burford Brown hens.

The best way to test if an egg is fresh (apart from the date stamped on it) is to dunk it in a bowl of cold water. If it sinks to the bottom, it is fresh; if it floats, it's best not to use it.

I store eggs in the fridge to keep them fresher for longer but always let them come up to room temperature before using, as cold eggs can give very different results compared to warm ones, especially when whisking.

Sabayon is a general term used in many recipes containing eggs. It is created by whisking eggs, usually with sugar (which is sometimes heated to a syrup). You should ideally use an electric whisk to give you more power. There are a few stages to the process (the same stages apply whether whisking whole eggs or egg yolks) and I specify which one you need to reach in each recipe. The three stages that I refer to in this book are:

- **foam:** Whisking combines the eggs and dissolves the sugar, making the mixture foamy (like bubble bath), while remaining quite yellow. Reaching 'foam' stage simply ensures that you have dissolved the sugar properly and added some volume to the eggs.

- **ribbon:** Whisked eggs at 'ribbon' stage should look almost velvety, with a light yellow colour. The larger bubbles present at 'foam' stage condense as you continue to whisk, and after a while the ripples caused by the whisk start to hold their shape. Mixture trailed from the whisk onto the remainder will sit on the surface for a little while, resembling a ribbon (hence the name), before sinking back in.

- **strong sabayon:** This has a very pale colour and more than three times the volume of the unbeaten eggs. A 'strong' sabayon should have a nice firm texture, similar to whipped cream.

Meringue (as a term, rather than the crisp-baked sugar sweets) is reached by whisking egg whites (on their own or with sugar) and has its own stages. The main points to remember are:

- use eggs at room temperature or even warm, as cold eggs will take twice as long to whisk and will have a denser texture.

- always start whisking on a slow speed, then increase the speed slowly once the first bubbles appear. This will help you achieve a strong texture.

- add any sugar according to the recipe instructions.

- **soft meringue** stage is when the mixture coming off the whisk leaves a trace of 'ribbon' on top of the rest of the egg whites; this will slowly sink back down (it is similar to 'ribbon' stage when making a sabayon).

- **strong** or **peaky meringue** stage means that when you pull the whisk out, the egg whites hold their shape in a little peak that doesn't sink back into the mixture.

Cream

I use double cream (42% fat) in the recipes in this book, unless something else is specified. You can often substitute a cream with a lower fat content, but the end result will be less rich. Do remember that you can't whip single cream, so it isn't a suitable alternative in recipes that call for whipping.

When whipping cream, always use a whisk (it doesn't matter if it's manual or electric). There are four main stages to whipped cream:

- **soft ribbon:** The whisk just starts to create shapes that, if left alone, sink back into the cream.
- **strong ribbon:** If you lift the whisk slightly above the bowl, the trail of cream falling off it should leave a visible mark on the cream still in the bowl.
- **soft whipped:** The cream doubles in volume and starts to hold the shapes created by the whisk.
- **fully whipped:** The cream holds in little peaks when the whisk is pulled out. I would only whip cream to this stage when I intend serving it.

Butter & other fats

I tend to use unsalted butter in my recipes (I will always mention when there is an exception) and I use a good one. My rule for butter (which is similar to my rule for chocolate) is that if I wouldn't spread it on my toast, then I shouldn't use it in a cake.

Burnt butter, or beurre noisette as it is called in French, is made by heating butter in a saucepan until the water boils off and the milk particles turn a dark golden colour and develop a lovely nutty flavour.

I occasionally use other types of fat, like margarine or shortening. This is usually in very traditional recipes where I have tried using butter instead, but have ended up deciding that the original was better.

Some recipes use oil as the fat. I sometimes specify a particular type of oil when I think that its richer flavour works well in that recipe, but the oils used are all interchangeable with a nice plain vegetable oil (e.g. sunflower).

Don't use olive oil as a substitute as it has a very strong flavour and density. In fact, unless olive oil is specifically called for in a recipe, don't bake with it.

Vanilla

I generally only cook with the vanilla seeds and use the leftover pods to make my own vanilla sugar. Vanilla pods are pricey and you need to treat them with respect so that you don't waste them. The best way to store them is in the fridge in an airtight jar or ziplock bag.

When you want to use a pod, run it between your thumb and index finger to flatten it, then lay it on a chopping board. Use the tip of a knife to slit it all the way along its length. If the recipe calls for only half a pod, put the other half back in the container in the fridge. Hold the curly tip of the pod with one hand and use the blunt side of the knife to scrape along the inside of the pod so the little black seeds accumulate on the back of the knife. Use the seeds in your recipe, then place the empty pod in a jar of caster sugar and shake about to infuse (see the vanilla sugar recipe on page 51).

Gelatine

Gelatine is a tricky one as there are so many forms. The pig stuff (God help us) comes in several different grades of thickness, so it is best to check the instructions on the packet for the recommended leaf to liquid ratio. The guidelines on the gelatines that I use advise one leaf for every 100g/ml of liquid. You can also use a vegetarian gelatine substitute, but you will have to figure out the appropriate amount yourself.

Whatever type of gelatine you use, I think it is best to have a soft-ish jelly. Definitely don't add too much, as a hard or rubbery full-set jelly is horrible to eat.

Do note that you need to adjust the amount of gelatine depending on whether you are making individual jellies or one large bowlful. As a general guideline, when using a recipe for a large jelly, I deduct one leaf of gelatine for every 500g/ml of liquid if I decide to make it in a number of small moulds instead. Similarly, if you take a recipe that makes individual portions but decide to set it all in one large bowl, add a leaf for every 500g/ml of liquid.

Nuts, seeds & roasting

I buy most of our nuts and seeds fresh, whole and already shelled, and roast them when I need them. Only almonds are bought in other forms – ground, flaked, nibbed and slivered – to use in specific recipes, as commercial machinery can achieve a better texture than I can by chopping or grinding.

I use the following table as a guideline for roasting times. Always lay the nuts or seeds in a single layer on a flat tray for best results.

Nuts / seeds	Temperature	Roasting time
Whole almonds, skin on	180°C/160°C fan/ gas mark 4 (nice and low to roast through without burning)	15–18 minutes
Flaked, nibbed or slivered almonds	190°C/170°C fan/ gas mark 5	10–12 minutes
Pine nuts, sunflower seeds, pumpkin seeds or sesame seeds	200°C/180°C fan/ gas mark 6	5 minutes, shake the tray, then a further 5–8 minutes till golden
Pistachios, walnuts and pecans	200°C/180°C fan/ gas mark 6	10–12 minutes
Hazelnuts	180°C/160°C fan/ gas mark 4 (nice and low to roast through without burning)	14–16 minutes

General baking terms

Creaming: This term is used to describe combining fat with sugar in vigorous circular motions to dissolve the sugar. Usually done with a paddle attachment (if using a mixer) or a firm spatula or wooden spoon (if working by hand). There are a couple of levels to creaming:

- **light creaming** dissolves the sugar without adding too much air and so keeps the fat quite dense. The fat will have lightened in colour and doubled in volume.

- **strong creaming** adds much more air while dissolving the sugar. The fat will be very fluffy and tripled in volume.

Folding: This generally involves gently working two mixtures together, usually one lighter and one heavier. The aim is to retain as much air in the mixture as you can. This is done with a spatula and a very light hand, scooping carefully and repeatedly up from the bottom of the bowl in the same direction each time (using either a circular or a figure-of-eight motion) until the mixtures combine.

Piping: I almost always use a disposable piping bag cut to the required size to fill tins with cake batter, as I find it cleaner and more controlled than using spoons. However, if you are a little clumsy with a piping bag, or think piping is more work than it is worth, then use two spoons, one to scoop and the other to push the batter off and into the tin. You will see that I also like to weigh the amount going into each tin when baking individual portions so that they will all be the same size and take the same amount of time to bake, but you don't have to do this if you think it is a step too far.

Dead of night

Store cupboard

25a Warren Street was a family home for decades, owned by an Italian couple who raised their kids upstairs and ran a business on the ground floor. They lived there all their lives and their children are now our landlords. After the parents passed away, the ground-floor café was rented out for a while, then stood empty for about a year before we took the lease. When the two of us first walked into the kitchen, it had a bit of a strange feel to it. Not unwelcoming; more the slight eeriness of a room rocked into life after being unused for a while. It seemed spacious and huge, and slightly empty. As we set about readying the kitchen for work, conditioning the equipment and getting comfortable in the space, we started hearing a strange sound, like someone strumming a harp. At first each of us thought we were imagining it, but when we started hearing it together, we realised that it wasn't a figment of our imagination. People came in to visit and they heard it as well, but we had enough on our plate with opening the restaurant, so we just called it a friendly ghost and went about our business, occasionally to the sound of heavenly harps.

We later discovered it was the old-fashioned freezer making that noise. The cooling unit consisted of very fine strings, and when the door was opened or closed, they would tremble and produce the sound we had come to like so much.

As the restaurant got busier and busier, our once huge, empty kitchen became smaller, fuller and much hotter. We were battling to find bench space for preparation and fighting over access to the hobs, and all the delicate doughs we needed to shape every day were struggling with the heat, so when our friend Bridget offered to do a few night shifts a week, it was the perfect solution for all of us. The delicate doughs would not melt in the heat, the jams would have space on the stoves and the spices would be ready, roasted and ground, for us to use in the morning. Best of all, Bridget would get to spend the day with Elizabeth and Freya (her two gorgeous girls) and we would get to see Bridget in the mornings, which for us is almost like having a social life.

When the ghostly freezer eventually died on us, we replaced it with a newer model. Sadly the new one doesn't sing, and if there is a sound from the basement when the restaurant is closed, it is only Bridget with her pots and pans. She does claim to have seen the spectre of a friendly little girl from time to time, but we hope it is just the time spent with her daughters and the long hours at work that are making her see things.

Jams

I love making jams. I got bitten by the bug as a child, when my family went to visit some friends from Canada who were staying at their grandma's house. She was a great cook and served the most lovely strawberry jam for breakfast. I was always a greedy kid and sweet things would make my day, but I wasn't sure I wanted to eat her jam, as I was used to smooth, jelly-like spreads. As always, in the end my sweet tooth got the better of me, and as soon as I had eaten the first strawberry, I was hooked. The jar on the table emptied all too quickly. Later that day, when I went to use the bathroom, I discovered a small door. Being nosy, I opened it, to discover a pantry with rows of glistening jars, all sealed, labelled and ready to eat. I was too young to read but could recognise strawberries (my favourite) and attacked a jar with my fingers, picking the whole fruits out of the rich syrup. I was amazed by the discovery that this was something you could make at home and have strawberries all year round.

When I think of this story, I am appalled. And I have never told anyone until now. What must this poor grandma have thought when she finally came to use that jar and saw half of it had gone, and the remainder no doubt spoiled (I had used my grubby little fingers to fish the strawberries out).

I was slightly too young to start boiling sugar straight away, but I kept the thought of that texture in my mind, and never did go back to favouring smooth jelly spreads. When I started making jams, I discovered my own ways to produce that wonderful soft-set with huge pieces of fruit suspended in it, vibrant with colour and freshness. Now our shelves at Honey & Co are laden with jars of glistening jam, neatly labelled and ready to eat – my tribute and my apology to that grandma's pantry.

General notes on jam-making (these apply to all the jam recipes in this book)

- **Try to use nice fruit. I am not saying** it needs to look perfect, but it does need to taste good and be in season (no amount of sugar will make up for tasteless fruit). It should be ripe but not overripe, as that can cause the jam to ferment and taste a little wine-y.

- **Wash the fruit briefly, but don't leave** it in water for long as this can saturate the fruit and dilute the flavour. If you can get hold of organic produce, then by all means use that, but check carefully for worms, caterpillars and insects.

- **Prepare your fruit to the size you** want for the finished jam. I like chunky jams, so I always try to buy small fruit that can be cooked whole or halved. You can cut it smaller if you wish, but try to keep all the pieces the same size so that they cook at the same speed.

- **I use caster sugar and never add** artificial pectin. You can add a halved apple (core and all) to the mix if you like a firmer set; just remove it before bottling. The set really depends on which fruit you are cooking; some naturally contain high amounts of pectin (apples, quince, black-currants) and don't need any more; others, like strawberries and peaches, are very low in pectin, so I add lemon juice or whole citrus fruits to assist the setting.

- **I cook jam in smallish batches** (about 1.5–2kg fruit to make 4–7 jars). It seems a bit pointless to make less and

Honey & Co.
Turkish Fig

a bit laborious to make more, but if you want to reduce or increase the quantities, you must take into account that cooking times will change too. And be aware that if you use double the amount of fruit and sugar, you should only increase the spices by 50%, or their flavour will be too strong.

• **Put all the ingredients in a large** cooking pan and mix well to moisten the fruit. It is best to use a jam pan or other heavy-bottomed pan. It should only be up to three-quarters full and no higher, as jams tend to boil over and therefore need space.

• **Before you start cooking the jam,** set a couple of small saucers or dishes in the fridge or freezer to cool – I find they serve best for testing the consistency.

• **Bring to the boil on a high heat,** stirring occasionally to avoid burning. A high heat is the secret to keeping the colour and flavour vibrant. If you cook jam slowly at a low heat, you tend to caramelise it and the end result is a very dark treacly jam which tastes more of sugar than of fruit.

• **Skim as much as you can and as often** as you care to. Use a slotted spoon to lift off the foam or dip a ladle in the top of the liquid so that the foam trickles into it. The more you skim, the clearer the resulting jam will be.

• **Once the bubbles change texture –** this will be very obvious, as they become larger and somewhat volcanic – it is time to test the jam for the first time. Take one of your cold saucers out and place a spoonful of hot jam in the centre, then count to 10. Start by looking at it. If there is runny liquid dripping away to the sides, looking thinner than the rest, continue cooking. If it stays in one blob, run your finger through the middle of it. If the jam closes over the line you traced, continue cooking; if it leaves a distinct track, it is time to bottle up.

• **Pour the hot jam into sterilised jars** and seal straight away. You can top each one with a circle of waxed parchment, but I don't bother. I just make sure to store them upright from the moment of bottling to the moment of consumption.

• **There are a couple of ways I use to** sterilise jars. The easiest is to wash the jars and lids well in hot soapy water, then rinse and drain. When your jam is ready, boil some water and fill the jars to the rim. Empty one at a time to fill with the hot jam and seal immediately. Alternatively, you can wash the jars in hot soapy water, then place them upright in the oven at 140°C/120°C fan/gas mark 1 for 10 minutes. Remove from the oven one by one when required to fill them while still hot. However you sterilise the jars, once they are sealed, leave to cool entirely before opening.

• **I always use a ladle to transfer the** hot jam carefully into a heat-resistant jug, then guide the jam into the jar with a spoon. If you are more comfortable with a jam funnel, use that.

• **Jam sealed this way should keep well** for over 6 months at room temperature, but once opened you should refrigerate and use up within a month. I find that the jam keeps longer if you use clean spoons to remove it from the jar, although in my experience it always disappears long before its use-by date.

Spiced plum jam

Makes about 1.4kg or 4 small jars

Takes about 1 hour

1.5kg red plums
1 cinnamon stick
2 star anise
1 orange, halved
800g caster sugar

Wash the plums under cold running water, then cut each one into 6–8 large wedges (depending on the size of the fruit) and discard the stones. Place in a large jam pan and add the spices, sugar and the halved orange. Stir to combine and allow to sit for 15 minutes – this will help draw moisture out of the plums.

Stir again, then place on a high heat and bring to the boil, stirring occasionally.

Once the mixture is boiling you can reduce the heat to medium and skim any foam that comes to the top. As plums vary greatly it is hard to give an accurate estimate as to how long this will take, but it will need to cook at a constant simmer for at least an hour until the fruit has mostly broken down and the syrup has thickened. You can check it by removing a piece of fruit and some of the syrup to a little bowl to taste (once it has cooled) to see whether the fruit is soft and sweet. If so, remove the jam from the stove, squeeze out the orange skins and discard them, transfer to sterilised jars (see notes on page 28).

Raspberry & lime jam

Makes about 1.8kg or 5 small jars

Takes about 45 minutes

1.5kg fresh raspberries
2 fresh limes
3 dried limes
900g caster sugar

Place the raspberries in a large pan. Zest the fresh limes and then juice them on top of the raspberries. Place the dried limes in the pan and finally top with the sugar. Stir well to combine and set on a high heat until the mixture comes to the boil. This starts off as a very loose mixture that will bubble violently but don't worry; just keep the heat high and skim the foam. Continue cooking on a high heat to keep the vibrant red colour and stir occasionally, making sure to reach all the way to the bottom, as the raspberries tend to break up and while there is still a lot of liquid the pulp tends to sink and can occasionally stick to the bottom.

You will see when the texture changes: the mixture will come together to form a thick mass of boiling lava. It gets really hot, so be careful. Once it has thickened (after about 40–45 minutes), check it on a small dish. If the jam stays as one without any thinner liquid spilling to the sides, it is ready to transfer to sterilised jars (see notes on page 28). Fish around to find the dried limes and remove them. It will set once cold, so don't worry if it still looks a little liquid when pouring into the jars.

Store cupboard.

Strawberry & rose jam

Makes about 2kg or 5–6 small jars

Takes about 1 hour

2kg strawberries (to end up with about 1.9kg once stems are removed)
1.1kg caster sugar
2 lemons
2 tbsp dried rose petals (or petals of 2 fresh unsprayed roses)
2 tsp rose water

Remove the green leaves and stems from the strawberries. If they are tiny keep them whole, but otherwise cut in half, or even quarters if they are massive. Place in a large bowl, cover with cold water, count to 5, then drain. Don't leave them for longer or they may become waterlogged and your jam will be too runny.

Transfer the strawberries to a large jam pan and add the sugar. Zest the lemons with a rough zester or a special strip zester (also called a channelling knife), and then halve and juice them. Put the zest and juice in the pan. Finally add the rose petals. Mix everything together to moisten but don't over mix, as you don't want to squash the strawberries.

Set the pan on a very high heat and bring to the boil. Make sure to stir every now and then, reaching all the way down to the bottom of the pan to make sure there is no residue of sugar that could burn. Once the first bubbles appear, remove the initial foam, then allow the mixture to boil for 5 minutes before you skim any more of the foam.

I like to continue cooking this jam on a high heat throughout as this helps maintain a good red colour and allows for more liquid evaporation. This can be a tricky method, as you need to keep a close eye on the jam and skim whenever there is an accumulation of foam, and make sure to stir on a regular basis so it doesn't burn, but it is worth it to achieve the bright red, fresh-tasting result. It will take between 40 minutes and an hour to achieve the correct consistency; the timing varies depending on the water content in the strawberries. You should see the shape of the bubbles start to change: they will appear larger and resemble volcanic eruptions. This is the time to add the rose water, then test the jam. When it is cooked, transfer to sterilised jars (see notes on page 28).

Black fig, cardamom & orange jam

Makes about 2.5kg or 6–7 small jars

Takes about 45 minutes

2kg black figs
1.35kg caster sugar
1 whole orange
1 vanilla pod (or 2 de-seeded pods, if you have used the seeds for other recipes like the one on page 186)
8 cardamom pods

For the best results use ripe soft figs. If you use dry thick-skinned ones you will end up with a leathery jam. Remove the tip of each fig and cut into quarters (if they are really soft you can just tear them in half). Place the figs in a large jam pan and add the sugar. Use a peeler to create wide strips of orange peel, then halve the orange and juice it. Put the strips and juice in the pan. Slit the vanilla pod in half and add as well. Finally, crack open the cardamom pods and place the cracked pods in the pan. Mix everything together to moisten – I get my hands in there and squash the fruit (use disposable gloves if you have them).

Now set on a very high heat and bring to the boil. Make sure to stir quite often until the first bubbles start to appear – there is a real chance of it burning at this early stage since this is a heavy fruit that takes a while to produce liquid. Once the first bubbles appear, remove the initial foam, and reduce the temperature until the jam is at a medium boil. Make sure to stir on a regular basis so the jam doesn't burn and continue skimming the foam that accumulates on top. This jam really doesn't take long to cook when using ripe figs: 30–40 minutes will achieve a thick gloopy texture with a deep coloured syrup and pieces of fruit still visible... and that is exactly the way I like it. Check the jam and when it's ready, transfer to sterilised jars (see notes on page 28).

Pear & ginger jam

This is a very soft-set jam that has lovely pieces of fruit and slivers of ginger and lemon suspended in thick syrup. It is Itamar's favourite from his days at Orna and Ella in Tel Aviv, and I make it especially for him.

Makes about 1.4kg or 4 small jars

Takes about 50 minutes

2kg (about 12) whole pears, peeled and cored (1.6kg)
3 lemons
80g fresh ginger, peeled (about 60g)
800g caster sugar

Cut the peeled pears into thin slices and place in a large jam pan. Use a strip zester to create lovely long threads of lemon peel or peel the lemons with a vegetable peeler and slice the peel into thin strips. Juice the lemons and add the zest and juice to the pears. Chop the peeled ginger into thin matchsticks and add to the pan. Finally add the sugar and stir to combine.

Place the pan on a high heat. Allow the mixture to come to the boil and skim the foam that accumulates on the top. Cook for 10 minutes on high before reducing the heat to medium, then continue cooking for 30 minutes, stirring occasionally. Check that the pear pieces are soft, then reduce the heat to the minimum setting and cook for a final 10 minutes. Transfer the jam to sterilised jars (see notes on page 28), seal and allow to rest for at least a day before opening.

Apricot & elderflower jam

We love making this as a very chunky jam with large pieces so we just halve the apricots, but if you prefer a less chunky version you can dice them and reduce the cooking time by 10 minutes.

Makes about 2.4kg or 6–7 small jars

Takes about 40 minutes

1.8kg apricots, halved and pitted
1kg caster sugar

For the elderflower
300g/ml elderflower cordial
juice of 1 lemon
or (in season) use
6 elderflower blossoms
150g caster sugar
zest and juice of 2 lemons

Place the apricot halves in a large jam pan and cover with cold water, then drain, leaving the apricots in the pan. This washes the apricots and adds a touch of moisture, which helps the jam along. Cover with the sugar, then add the elderflower cordial and lemon juice or (if you are making this in season) add the blossoms, additional sugar and lemon juice and zest. Mix everything really well to moisten the fruit.

Set the pan on a medium heat to start dissolving the sugar and cooking the fruit. Stir occasionally and bring to a slow boil, skimming as you go. This is a very quick jam and will only take about 30 minutes from boiling to cook down, but make sure to stir regularly as it can burn easily. I keep it on the medium heat for the duration and only check it once the bubbles change in consistency and become big, thick and gloopy. I go for a very soft texture but if you want a thicker jelly-like consistency, reduce the heat to low and cook for a further 20–30 minutes until really thick. Once it is the consistency you want, transfer to sterilised jars (see notes on page 28).

Store cupboard.

Quince jam

Makes about 1.5kg or 4 small jars

Takes about 1½ hours

1kg (about 3–4) quince, peeled and cored (750g), keeping hold of the peel and cores
1 lemon
1 litre water
500g caster sugar
1 cinnamon stick (if you like, it's delicious with or without)

Wrap the quince peel and cores in some gauze or in an infusion bag and tie to seal. Chop the peeled quince into a chunky dice and place in a large jam pan. Halve and squeeze the lemon over, then add the squeezed lemon halves to the pan as well. Place the bag of peels and cores in with the quince dice, lemon juice and lemon skins and cover with the water. Set the pan on a high heat to bring to the boil. Skim away any foam that comes to the top and keep at a steady boil on a medium heat for about 30 minutes, or until the quince is soft when you pierce it with the tip of a knife.

Now remove the pan from the stove and, using a large slotted spoon or tongs, carefully remove the bag of peel and cores and the skins of lemon. Squeeze them into the pan to release any excess liquid, then discard. Add the sugar to the quince mixture and stir to dissolve it. The fruit should still be covered with liquid (if too much has evaporated, add a little water to just cover the fruit). If you wish to add the cinnamon stick, do so now. Return the pan to a medium heat to cook for another 30 minutes at a steady simmer.

Remove from the heat and use a stick blender or a potato ricer to mash up about half the fruit to a rough purée, and keep the rest in nice dice. Return to the heat and continue cooking for a further 30 minutes before transferring to sterilised jars (see notes on page 28). The jam should be a dark orange by now and will set solid when cold.

Blueberry & apple jam

Makes about 1.5kg or 4–5 small jars

Takes about 50 minutes

600g apples (about 4–5 apples, ideally sour ones like Granny Smiths)
zest and juice of 2 lemons
1kg blueberries
700g caster sugar

Peel the apples and remove the cores. Chop into small dice (about twice the size of a blueberry), tip into a bowl and douse with the lemon juice, then add the zest. Put the blueberries and sugar in a large jam pan and top with the diced apple.

Set on a high heat and allow to cook for 5 minutes. This should blast heat into the blueberries and explode them. Use a large wooden spoon to mix everything together to combine. Allow the mixture to come to the boil and then skim the foam that accumulates on the top. Continue to cook on high for 10 minutes, then reduce the heat to medium-low and cook for 20 minutes, stirring occasionally.

Check that the apple pieces are soft. By now the mixture should be nice and thick with a strong purple colour. Reduce the heat to as low as you can and cook for another 10 minutes. That should be sufficient, but if you test it and it seems runny, cook for a further 10 minutes. Transfer the jam to sterilised jars (see notes on page 28) and allow to rest for at least a day before opening. This will allow the pectin to set so you should get a firm jelly-like consistency around the pieces of fruit.

Citrus jams

Citrus jams are a personal favourite, and have always been a staple in our household. Whenever we go on holiday my thrifty wife empties the fridge and kitchen cupboards so that no fresh food goes to waste. This has brought about some amazing discoveries, like soba noodle and pea omelette (has to be tasted to be believed), and some less happy ones, like cabbage and rice casserole (memorable for all the wrong reasons). As we always have lemons and oranges in our fruit bowl, marmalade is a constant in her waste-not-want-not campaign, and the smell of citrus and sugar cooking is forever linked in my mind to the excitement before a trip – clothes and suitcases everywhere, last-minute phone calls and emails, the sudden panic of 'where are the passports?' and a pan of marmalade bubbling in the background, a complete antithesis to the mayhem around.

These are our most successful attempts. Worth making even if you are not planning on going anywhere.

Orange, thyme & cardamom marmalade

Makes about 1kg or 3 small jars

Takes about 1¼ hours

3 large oranges (about 750g)
1 litre water
4 cardamom pods, split in half
4 sprigs of thyme, picked (1 tsp picked leaves)
750g caster sugar

Wash the oranges well with soapy water and rinse, or use organic unwaxed ones if you can find them. Remove the stem stump and halve the oranges. Remove the white pithy centre and any seeds you can see, then slice as thinly as you can. Place in a medium-large pan and cover with the water.

Bring to a rapid boil, then skim well and add the split cardamom pods and the thyme leaves. Boil for 30 minutes, then start adding the sugar gradually, stirring after each addition to make sure it dissolves properly.

Bring back to the boil and skim again. Boil on a medium-high heat for another 30 minutes or so until the look of the bubbles changes and the jam looks thick and syrupy, then transfer to sterilised jars and seal while hot (see notes on page 28).

Whole lemon &/or orange marmalade

Makes about 2.2kg or 5–6 small jars

Takes about 1 hour

8 lemons or oranges (or 50:50)
1kg caster sugar
500g/ml water

Place the whole fruit in a large pan and cover with plenty of water. Bring to the boil and cook for 45 minutes on a medium heat. Test the fruit by inserting the tip of your knife into the skin; if it goes in easily, remove the pan from the heat and drain. If there is still some resistance, cook for another 10–15 minutes. You may need to top up the water a little as you go to ensure that the fruit stays covered.

Once the drained fruit is cool enough to handle, pick it up and remove the hard stalk stump. Rip the fruit apart. Feel with your fingertips for any seeds and remove them. If there is a large white pithy bit, you can discard that as well. Then place the fruit in the food processor with a blade attachment (or use a large mincer disc) and blitz in pulses to create a thick, chunky purée with visible pieces of fruit and peel running all the way through. You should end up with about 1kg of purée. Don't worry if it is less or more, as the ratio is very simple – just add an equal weight of sugar and half that amount of water (e.g. if you have 1.2kg of purée, add 1.2kg of sugar and 600g/ml of water).

Place the purée, sugar and water in a large jam pan and stir well to combine. Bring to the boil on a high heat, stirring occasionally. Once the jam has boiled you need to be very diligent. Both oranges and lemons are high in pectin, so the marmalade will set quickly, but you want to develop the sweetness and cook the fruit skins so that they are delicious. Set a timer for 5–6 minutes and stir every time the alarm goes off, making sure to scrape the bottom of the pan. At the early stages the pulp will sink to the bottom, but later on it will become more homogenised. The mixture will start to erupt in big bubbles and the colour will deepen a little. This is the time to check the marmalade on a cold plate and, once you are happy with the consistency, pour it into sterilised jars (see notes on page 28).

Amalfi lemon & rosemary marmalade

Every time we make a batch of this jam, I know to put aside a couple of jars. They will end up in South Africa with our friend Nikki's dad, who needs a steady supply.

Makes about 1kg or 3 small jars

Takes about 40 minutes

4 unwaxed Amalfi lemons (about 700g)
1 litre water
1 sprig rosemary
500g caster sugar

Halve the lemons and cut out the core to remove the seeds and white pith in the centre. Slice as thinly as you can and place in a medium saucepan. Cover with the water, add the rosemary sprig and set on maximum heat. Bring to the boil, then skim any foam that comes to the top. Boil for 15–20 minutes, skimming away foam every time you remember, then take out a slice to check that the skin has softened.

If it has, start adding the sugar, a little at a time, stirring to dissolve after every addition. Once the sugar has all been added and dissolved, remove the sprig of rosemary (most of the little green needles will have fallen off into the jam by now).

Bring the mixture back to the boil, skim again and boil for 10 minutes before transferring to sterilised jars and sealing (see notes on page 28). Allow to rest unmoved overnight before opening, to allow the jelly-like texture to set.

Store cupboard.

Candied & crystallised fruits

Another great way to use up a glut of fruit and an afternoon. Candied fruit done well carries something of the fresh fruit, but with a character all of its own. A true cupboard hero, it can be used to top buttered toast or porridge in the morning, to add fruity sweetness to a stew or salad, or as accompaniment for dessert or after-dinner cheese. We use candied fruits in cakes and as a sweet treat when there is nothing else around, and they also look lovely and make a great gift. The following fruits will keep well in a sterilised jar for up to 3 months, but once opened they should be kept in the fridge and consumed within a month.

Candied quince

Makes 4 small jars of ruby-red quince segments

1kg quince (try to find 4 small ones, rather than 3 large, to make perfect segments)
2 lemons, halved
1.2kg caster sugar (3 x 400g)

Halve the quince, then cut each half into four segments. Remove the core but leave the peel on. Place the segments in a large pan, cover with water, then drain. This rinses the quince and washes away any loose seeds.

Pour in enough fresh water to just cover the fruit, add the lemon halves and 400g of the sugar and set on a low heat to slowly dissolve the sugar and start cooking the quince. Leave it untouched to cook for 30 minutes before adding another 400g of sugar. Very carefully shake the pan to help the sugar dissolve and then leave to cook slowly for another 30 minutes.

Now add the remaining 400g of sugar and cover the surface of the liquid with a round piece of baking parchment, cut to the same diameter as the pan. This will help keep the fruit submerged under the liquid as well as limit the amount of evaporation. Cook for another 30–40 minutes until the colour is deep ruby red. Transfer the segments to sterilised jars, cover with the syrup and seal while hot (see notes on page 28).

Candied orange peel

Treat this recipe as a guideline. Eat some oranges, save the skins in the fridge in a sealed container and, when you are ready, candy them. Simply adapt the amount of water and sugar to suit the amount of peel you have (the ratio is 3:3:1 for the sugar, water and peel – so if you have 250g peel, you'll need 750g caster sugar and 750g/ml water). If you are eager to make these, juice a batch of oranges, drink the juice and then you'll have a batch of skins to make candy. That is what we do at Honey & Co.

Makes as much as you want

500g orange peel (from about 12 oranges)
1.5 litres water (3 x 500g/ml)
1.5kg caster sugar (3 x 500g)

Clean any fruit residue from the orange skins: I use a small knife to cut away any flesh until I am left with the orange skin and the white pith, but nothing else. Cover with the first 500g/ml of water and bring to the boil. Drain the hot water away, then cover the peel with the second 500g/ml of water. Bring to the boil again, then drain again.

Pour in the final 500g/ml of water and bring to the boil once more. Once it is boiling, add the first 500g of sugar and reduce the heat to low. Cook really slowly on a low heat for 30 minutes. Add the next 500g of sugar, stir carefully to dissolve and cook for an hour on the lowest simmer you can. Finally add the last batch of sugar (don't stir this time) and cook for another hour, keeping the heat low.

Transfer the peel and poaching liquid to a heat-resistant plastic container or sterilised jar (see notes on page 28), seal and leave to cool entirely. Use as and when you wish but make sure to use a clean spoon or tongs when taking the skins out of the syrup, so as not to contaminate the rest of the batch.

Crystallised coconut strips

These are a perfect nibble or topping for a cake (as on page 214), and make a great addition to your breakfast granola.

1 coconut in its shell
100g granulated sugar to coat

Start by cracking the coconut. Go outside and throw it onto the pavement or a hard surface to crack the shell in a few places. It may take a couple of attempts.

Pull the shell apart to expose the white flesh. Slowly insert a spoon between the flesh and the hard shell and jig it about to loosen and release some of the coconut from the side. Once you have a few decent pieces, leave the rest for someone else to wrestle with and use a peeler to make the pieces into long shards of coconut. I like to keep the thin brown membrane on the flesh as it gives a lovely colour contrast.

Toss the shards in the sugar and lay them flat on a tray. Allow to dry and crisp at room temperature for 24 hours or, if you are rushed, in a very low oven (around 120°C/100°C fan/gas mark ½) for 2 hours, stirring or shaking the tray occasionally to stop the shards sticking together. These will keep in an airtight container for at least 2 weeks.

Preserved apricots

Makes
3 x 250ml jars

1kg apricots
1 vanilla pod, halved lengthways
3 sprigs of thyme
strips of peel from 1 lemon (use a peeler)
juice of 2 lemons (the one you peeled plus one other)
700g caster sugar

Heat your oven to 190°C/170°C fan/gas mark 5.

Halve the apricots, remove the stones and lay them on a baking tray. Add the vanilla pod, thyme sprigs and lemon peel to the tray and sprinkle everything with the lemon juice and sugar. Place in the oven for 5 minutes, then reduce the heat to 170°C/150°C fan/gas mark 3–4 and cook for a further 15 minutes.

Carefully remove from the oven. All the sugar should have dissolved into a syrup by now – use a spoon to baste the apricots with it and return to the oven. Reduce the heat to 140°C/120°C fan/gas mark 1 and cook for a further 20 minutes. Baste again and continue cooking for another 10 minutes. While the apricots are cooking for the final 10 minutes, wash your jars and then place them in the oven to sterilise (see notes on page 28).

Once the time is up remove the apricots and the jars from the oven. Very carefully transfer the apricot halves to the jars and cover with the syrup.

Spice mixes & flavoured sugar

We opened our restaurant on the tightest of budgets, looking for freebies wherever we could. Our old employers at Ottolenghi, with their typical generosity and kindness, rummaged around for any unused equipment they could spare and we ended up with a coffee grinder. We had already inherited one from the previous owners of 25a Warren Street, but we took what we could get. We soon realised we could use it to grind spices. We were quite a small outfit then and a domestic spice grinder would have sufficed for our needs, but now that we are so much busier and consume large amounts of freshly ground spices, we would not be able to cope without our second grinder. It does as much work as the one upstairs, providing fragrant spice mixes for the kitchen and for our customers, who buy them in little jars.

Do take the time to roast and grind your own spices – it is so little work and so satisfying on many levels, not least that it makes your kitchen smell wonderful.

Sweet spice mix

We mostly use this mix for cakes and baked goods, but it is also great in dishes that require a lighter touch.

10 cardamom pods
6 cloves
½ nutmeg
1 tsp whole fennel seeds
2 tsp whole mahleb seeds
3 tsp ground ginger
4 tsp ground cinnamon

Preheat the oven to 190°C/170°C fan/ gas mark 5. Roast the cardamom pods, cloves and nutmeg on a baking tray for 5 minutes, then add the fennel and mahleb seeds and roast for another 5 minutes.

Remove from the oven and allow to cool completely before grinding and then mixing with the ginger and cinnamon. Store any that you don't use straight away in a jar or other airtight container. This will keep for up to 6 months, but I always think you should try to use it within 2 months to get the flavour at its best.

Savoury spice mix (aka baharat)

1 dried chilli
3 tsp coriander seeds
4 tsp cumin seeds
2 tsp ground pimento
1 tsp ground white pepper
½ tsp ground turmeric
2 tsp sweet spice mix (see opposite)

Preheat your oven to 190°C/170°C fan/ gas mark 5. Crack the dried chilli open and shake out the seeds. Place the deseeded chilli on a baking tray with the coriander and cumin seeds and roast for 6 minutes. Remove from the oven and leave to cool completely on the tray.

Crumble the chilli between your fingers, then grind to a powder with the roasted coriander and cumin. Mix with the other spices and store in an airtight container. It will keep for up to 6 months, but ideally use within 2 months for the full effect.

Flavoured sugars

Vanilla sugar

You can use this in place of vanilla and sugar in recipes that call for both, or simply add it whenever a sweet hit is required. You can also just open the jar occasionally to get a whiff of vanilla and be happy.

used vanilla pods
caster sugar

Whenever you prepare a recipe using the fresh vanilla seeds, make sure to retain the used black pod as it contains loads of flavour (and most of the time you only use the seeds).

Pop the used pod in a jar containing 150g of caster sugar (I find that a ratio of 1 pod to 150g sugar works best). Shake it about and allow at least a day for the flavour to infuse. After that, each time you use another pod, add it to the jar and top up the sugar. You can store this jar for as long as you wish.

Spice sugars

We use a lot of mixed spice sugars, and some tried-and-tested combinations appear in recipes in this book (e.g. Fitzrovia buns, page 60). However, we also make flavoured sugar simply to add something special to a fruit salad, or to sprinkle over pancakes or French toast.

To make your own, just use one teaspoon of ground spice for every 150g of sugar and mix well. Keep the same ratio of spice to sugar whether you are using a single spice or a mixture. Fennel seeds, cardamom, mahleb, cinnamon and star anise all work amazingly well either individually or together.

Citrus sugars

These are great if you want to give your sugar a zesty finish. Spread the citrus fruit zest (lemon, orange, lime and mandarin all work well) on a tray lined with baking parchment. Place in a warm place for 12–14 hours to dry a little, then mix with 150g of sugar for every teaspoon of dried zest. Store in an airtight container.

First light

Sweet breakfasts

Every weekday at 8am someone (usually Rachael) opens the front door to 25a Warren Street to welcome our first customers of the day. This seemingly simple act is the culmination of our early-morning routine, the last of dozens of acts, all of which are necessary to get our little machine up and running for the day.

It starts with a baker – as all good things do – who comes in at 6am to do the morning bake. This is a very delicate dance of man (or woman) and dough; it requires great skill and experience to know when the dough is proved, when it is baked, when to sprinkle or brush, how much syrup to use, and how to arrange it all nicely on display. Then a cleaner will arrive. If it is David, he will put some music on; the harsh, violent beats of his favourite song, 'Futile Colossus Decapitated', lend him the energy to give the shop its first clean of the day. Then he puts out the tables and adjusts their feet so they don't wobble, before heading downstairs to squeeze plenty of oranges to fill our big white jug with juice for breakfast. The girls arrive at 7.30am. Our floor staff is almost always made up of girls. We have tried very hard to introduce boys to the system, but have never managed to get one to stick. (Sarit would insert a note here about multi-tasking and attention to detail, but I shall not, in the interest of gender equality.) The girls have a lot to do and not long to do it in. They need to stock up the bar, open the till, season the coffee machine, write little signs for the cakes, set the tables inside and out so everything looks inviting, and (most importantly) make coffees for the sleepy chefs arriving for their morning shifts, so that we actually have something to serve come lunchtime. And all this culminates in the quiet gesture of opening our front door with its cracked glass pane.

The first customers trickle in slowly. We don't know everyone, but we have got to know many, including when they'll arrive and what they'll want. Jo comes in shortly before the 8.30am rush. As soon as we see her, we get to work on her regular coffee, and would she like a milk bun today? Chris appears at 8.50am, just as the shop is busiest. Never mind, he will find a table somewhere. A single espresso is brought as soon as he sits down; we make it the moment we see his quiet smile as he comes through the door. Igor and his crowd sit outside, even on the coldest days, smoking cigars and playing with their dogs. And if we haven't seen Fran by 11am, we get worried: is she ill, or away?

Between 8am and 12 noon the neighbourhood comes to us. As people come and go, they become as much a part of our routine as we are of theirs. When our days meet, a little bond is created. They are our customers and we are here to serve, but these people are also a very pleasant part of our lives, as we hope we are of theirs.

Basic bun dough

With this basic dough one can create hundreds of fillings and variations; we've included some of our favourites in this chapter.

Here are a few guidelines to working with this dough:

- **Allow at least 2 hours to refrigerate** it before shaping, as it can be very soft when freshly made. Ideally, if you plan ahead, make the dough the day before, place it in a large bowl, cover and refrigerate overnight.

- **Try to work it with as little additional** flour as you dare. The end product will benefit greatly.

- **Work on a cool surface in a cool** kitchen, as the dough will soften quickly once out of the fridge.

- **Have all your fillings ready before** you start on the dough. It also helps if you have your tray lined in advance.

- **If you are going to bake after shaping,** leave the buns at room temperature to prove. If you are preparing in advance, freeze the unbaked buns as soon as they are shaped (to preserve as much yeast activity as possible when you send it to sleep in the freezer).

- **You can shape the buns in the** evening, place them on the baking tray and pop them in the fridge to prove slowly overnight and bake first thing in the morning (a good way of making your partner or guests indebted to you for the rest of the day/week/year).

- **Filled doughs will keep for up to a** week in the freezer but after that they start to deteriorate and lose their plumpness.

- **Always freeze unbaked dough** uncovered on a tray, then (once frozen) you can transfer to a container or freezer bag or wrap the tray with cling film. When you are ready to bake, thaw overnight in the fridge before taking out to prove in the morning (or if you only sleep 5–6 hours, simply leave them out at room temperature, and when you wake they should be ready to bake).

- **Most of the following recipes make** 6–9 individual pieces, depending on how big you like your buns. I would advise sticking as closely to my measurements as possible, as I have tested them to give you the best ratio of filling to dough and the correct yield from every recipe. You can of course improvise, but I take no responsibility for the results!

For the dough

70g unsalted butter, diced and at room temperature
20g fresh yeast or 1½ tsp dried yeast
1 whole egg
30g caster sugar
80–100g/ml milk
300g strong white bread flour
a pinch of table salt

Place the butter, yeast, egg, sugar and 80g/ml of the milk in a large mixing bowl, then top with the flour and salt. Use the dough attachment on your mixer or your hands to bring it all together to a smooth, shiny dough, adding the remaining 20g/ml of milk if it looks dry. Don't worry too much if you still have some whole flecks of butter running through the dough; they will make your final bun super-light.

Once the dough has a nice texture to it (after about 2–3 minutes with an electric mixer or 5–6 minutes working by hand), wrap the bowl in cling film and place in the fridge to chill for at least 2 hours. You can leave it there for up to 12 hours, but not much longer or it will start to prove.

Egg wash

I always use the same egg wash (unless I specify something else in the recipe) made from a whole egg beaten with a pinch of table salt, which helps break down the structure of the egg and allows you to brush it on evenly. Any left over can be added to scrambled eggs or used in a cake.

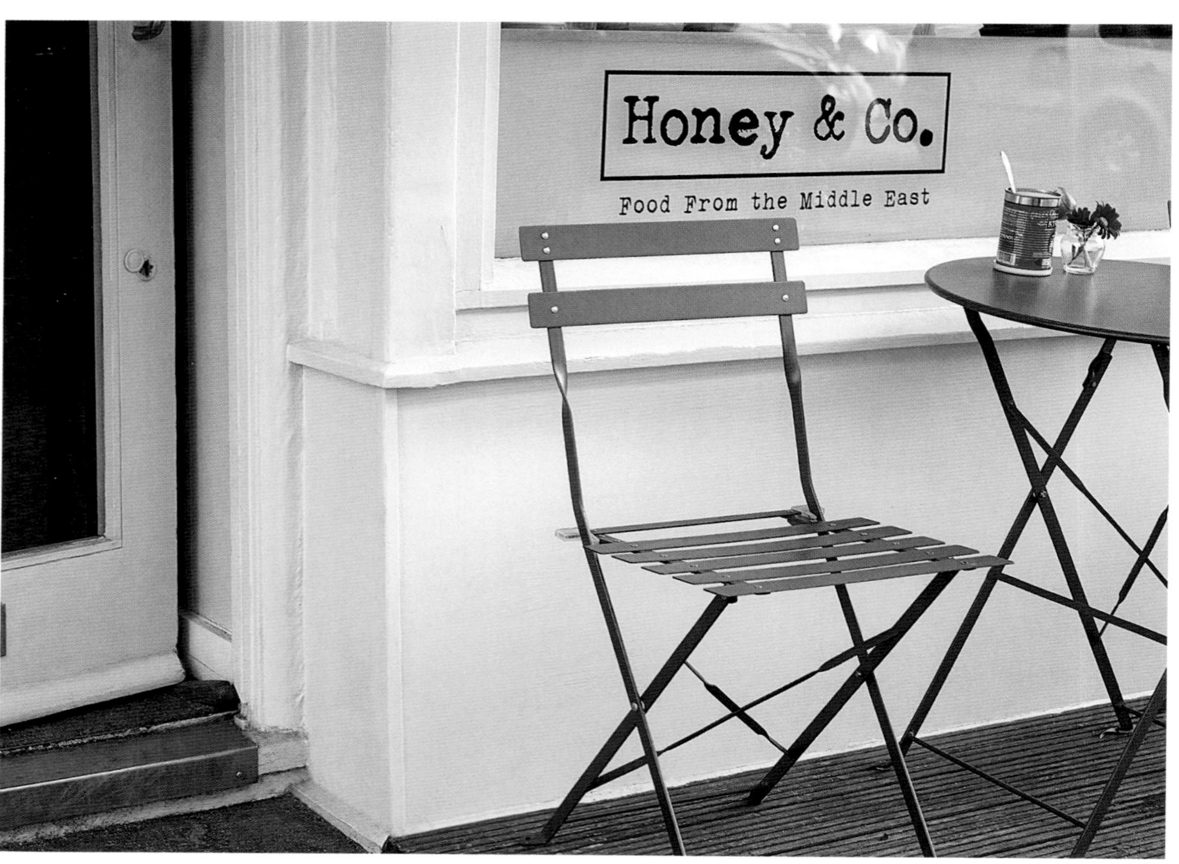
Honey & Co.
Food From the Middle East

Base sugar syrup

I like to brush most sweet baked goods with sugar syrup while they are hot out of the oven. It helps them keep moist, gives them a lovely shiny gloss and simply makes them tastier. You can of course eat them without it, but the dough is somewhere between sweet and savoury and I think it benefits from the addition of the base sugar syrup.

I use this syrup in other ways too: making iced teas or syrup cakes, or simply on fruit that needs a little love if it isn't at its prime. I tend to make ten times the amount in this recipe, using a litre of water, and store it in a bottle in the fridge, ready to use when needed (it'll keep for a while). However, the amount here will be good for the recipes in this chapter.

Makes 200g/ml syrup (enough to soak up to 9 buns)

100g/ml water
100g caster sugar
1 tbsp glucose or honey

Place all the ingredients in a small pan and stir to dissolve the sugar. Bring to the boil, skim off any foam that comes to the top and remove from the heat. If you are making a larger quantity (a litre or more), bring to the boil, skim and cook for 3–4 minutes, then allow to cool. You can make this syrup in advance – just keep it in a jar or bottle in the fridge for up to 2 weeks.

Seed buns

For simple, slightly sweet bread rolls that work well with light fillings such as egg salad, cream cheese and salmon, labaneh and cucumber and the like.

Makes 8 buns

Make a batch of basic bun dough (page 56) and set in the fridge for a minimum of 2 hours. Line a flat baking tray with some baking parchment.

Divide the dough into eight pieces. Roll each one between your palm and the work surface until the dough forms a tight, round, shiny ball. Place on the baking tray, leaving about 6–8cm between each one to allow them space to prove (no need to cover, as you want them to form a light crust).

Preheat the oven to 220°C/200°C fan/ gas mark 7. Once the buns have doubled in size, brush with egg wash (1 egg beaten with a pinch of table salt) and sprinkle with whatever seeds you have lying around – sesame, poppy, sunflower and nigella seeds all work well individually, or together if you want a funkier look. Sprinkle on some sea salt flakes too and place the buns in the centre of the oven for 8–10 minutes. They should have a lovely golden colour once baked.

Fitzrovia buns

We are great fans of a good Chelsea bun. A spiral of rich dough crammed full of currants and butter, it's been a staple of British baking for the last three centuries, spreading beyond the borders of its neighbourhood of origin and bringing it much pride. This is our humble tribute to it, and to the part of London that is such a happy home for us. In our more deluded moments we imagine how, 300 years from now, it'll make Fitzrovia as famous as Chelsea, since these buns are just as good as their ancestors. If you can get hold of mahleb, you are in for a truly exotic treat – it marries so well with the pistachios and cherries (if you can't get hold of it, use ground cinnamon instead – they'll still be delicious).

1 batch basic bun dough (page 56)

Makes 6–8 buns

For the filling
- *100g light brown soft sugar*
- *2 tsp ground mahleb*
- *seeds from ½ vanilla pod or 1 tbsp vanilla sugar*
- *50g very soft butter*
- *80g dried sour cherries*
- *60g chopped pistachios, plus 1 tbsp for decoration*

egg wash (1 egg beaten with a pinch of table salt)
1 batch base sugar syrup (page 59)

Mix the sugar with the mahleb and vanilla so it is well combined.

Remove the dough from the fridge and roll out with a rolling pin on a very lightly floured workbench to a rectangle about 30cm x 20cm. You may need to flip the dough over once or twice to get an even, smooth sheet, but try to work with as little flour as you can so as not to dry the dough out.

Lay the rectangle lengthways in front of you and spread the butter in a thin layer all over. Sprinkle the spiced sugar over the dough, all the way to the edges, then sprinkle the cherries and pistachios at regular intervals on top, so that each bite will contain a bit of everything.

Lift the long edge of the dough closest to you and start rolling it up away from you, keeping it nice and tight without stretching the dough, until you end up with a sausage about 30cm long. If it comes out a little longer, push it in from both ends to condense it a little; if it comes out shorter, then use your hands to roll it out a little until it reaches 30cm. Cut into six, seven or eight even-sized slices, depending on how many buns you want.

Line a baking tin with a piece of baking parchment so that it comes up the sides in one piece, and lay the buns flat on the base, spiral facing upwards. I like to use a long thin tart tin (12 x 35cm), but you can use any tin big enough to contain the buns with a little space in between them, as they will grow as they prove. This is the time to freeze the buns if you want to bake them at a later date; otherwise leave them in a warm place to prove.

After 15–20 minutes, preheat the oven to 220°C/200°C fan/gas mark 7. Allow the buns to continue proving until they look about ready to explode (another 20 minutes or so). The dough should have expanded to fill the gaps and it should be shiny and taut. Brush with the egg wash and sprinkle the remaining pistachios over the top.

Place in the centre of the oven for 10 minutes, then turn the tin for an even bake and reduce the oven temperature to 200°C/180°C fan/gas mark 6. Bake for another 8 minutes, then remove from the oven and pour over the sugar syrup. Allow to cool slightly before devouring.

Pistachio, rose & strawberry buns

Every morning rows and rows of fresh fruit greet us as soon as we leave Warren Street tube station. The fruit sellers are there come sun or dreadful rain, making our morning that much nicer and giving our day a colourful start, with mounds of apples and pears, persimmons and mandarins in autumn; British berries in the spring; and all kinds of peaches in the summer. Even on our most rushed mornings we stop to check the produce. Sometimes we may grab a good-looking avocado for Rachael. Or are surprised to see punnets of prickly pears and grab a couple to try them on a special for lunch, to see if they work well with feta (almost everything does). And if we see great strawberries for a great price, we buy all they have to make jam, depriving the late-coming commuters of their strawberries for that day.

1 batch basic bun dough (page 56)

Makes 8 large muffin-sized buns

For the pistachio cream
- *80g pistachios*
- *80g unsalted butter, at room temperature*
- *80g caster sugar*
- *1 egg*
- *1 tbsp plain flour*

8 tsp strawberry jam (you can use the recipe on page 33)
1 batch base sugar syrup (page 59)
1 tbsp rose water

Put the pistachios in a food processor and blitz until they resemble breadcrumbs, then add all the other pistachio cream ingredients and pulse until they are well combined to form a paste. Lightly butter an eight-hole muffin tin or eight individual pudding moulds.

Remove the dough from the fridge and roll out with a rolling pin on a very lightly floured workbench to a rectangle of 40cm x 20cm. You may need to flip the dough over once or twice to create a smooth, even rectangle, but try to work with as little flour as you can so as not to dry the dough out.

Use a sharp knife or pizza slice to cut a 2 x 4 grid into the dough so that you end up with eight squares of 10cm x 10cm.

Lift each square into a pudding mould or cup of the muffin tin and push it all the way down. Allow the excess dough to hang over the sides. Divide the pistachio cream between the squares to fill them, then top each with a teaspoon of strawberry jam. Fold the corners over lightly to cover the filling, but don't push them down. You can now freeze these if you want to save the baking for another day, but if you are ready to bake today, preheat the oven to 200°C/180°C fan/gas mark 6.

Allow the little buns to prove in the muffin tin / moulds (this will take 30–40 minutes). You can tell they are proved when the little dough triangles on the top have thickened and started poking up. Place in the centre of the oven and bake for 10 minutes, then turn them to bake evenly. Reduce the oven temperature to 180°C/160°C fan/gas mark 4 and bake for another 10 minutes, then remove from the oven. Brush generously with the sugar syrup that has been laced with rose water and allow to cool slightly in the tin or moulds before removing and serving.

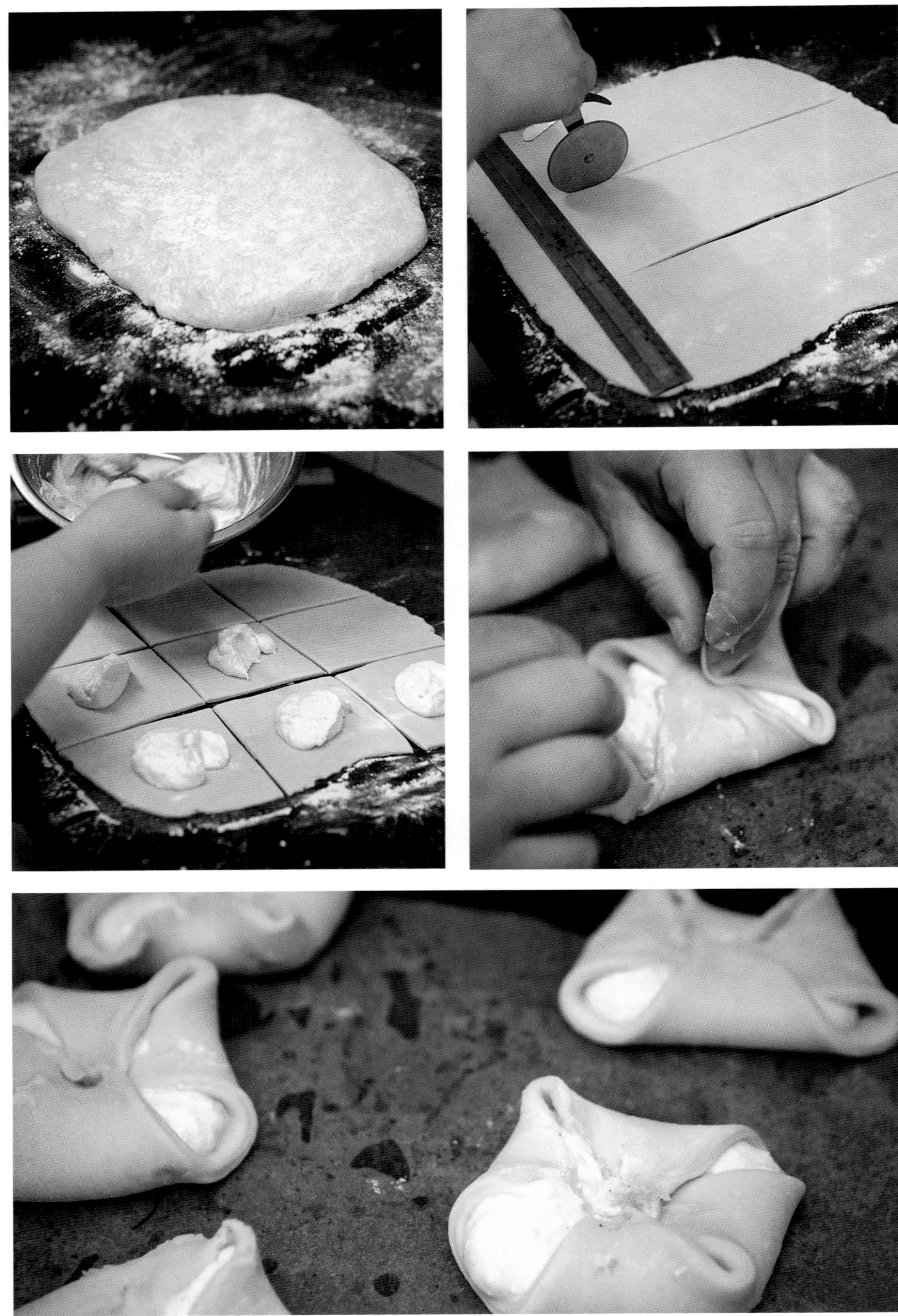

Sweet cheese buns (aka gviniyot)

When I was a kid, Friday was bakery day. It was the only day my mum didn't work, so she would pick us up from school, then we would go around the corner to collect the mail from the postbox in the village centre and buy the weekend papers. Then we would go to the local bakery. She would let me pick out the burekas that we would later have for lunch. There was always a potato one for me, a cheese one for my sister, a pizza one for my brother and a mushroom one for my mum (my dad still worked on Fridays and doesn't really like burekas anyway). Then I could choose the sweet ones, and again the same ritual: always a cinnamon one for my sister, a plain butter one for my mum, a chocolate rugelach for my brother and a sweet soft cheese one for me.

1 batch basic bun dough (page 56)

Makes 9 buns

For the sweet cheese filling
- *250g ricotta cheese*
- *1 egg*
- *3 tbsp icing sugar*
- *1 tbsp cornflour*
- *zest of 1 orange*
- *seeds from ½ vanilla pod*

egg wash (1 egg beaten with a pinch of table salt)
1 batch base sugar syrup (page 59)
1 tbsp orange blossom water

Mix the filling ingredients together until well combined.

Remove the dough from the fridge and roll out with a rolling pin on a very lightly floured workbench to a square of 36cm x 36cm. You may need to flip the dough over once or twice to achieve a nice and smooth square, but try to work with as little flour as you can so as not to dry the dough out.

Use a sharp knife or pizza slice to cut a 3 x 3 grid into the dough so that you end up with nine squares, each one about 12cm x 12cm. Divide the filling between the squares, placing it in the centre of each one. Take one square and fold two opposite corners into the centre. Fold the other two corners in and use your finger to press down on the point where all four corners meet until you feel the work surface underneath. This will give you a filled envelope of cheesy goodness. Don't worry if the sides are slightly open and the filling is showing; that is the effect you are looking for. Repeat with the other squares.

Place the filled envelopes on a baking sheet, allowing a fair amount of space (about 6–8cm) between them, as they need room to prove without touching. This is the time to freeze them if they are for future baking, otherwise set aside to prove until they have almost doubled in size and the dough is shiny and taut (30–40 minutes, depending on the temperature of the room). While they are proving, preheat the oven to 220°C/200°C fan/gas mark 7.

Carefully brush egg wash on all the dough surfaces you can see, leaving any cheese that is peeking out unglazed. Place in the centre of the oven for 10 minutes, then turn the tray for an even bake. Reduce the oven temperature to 200°C/180°C fan/gas mark 6, bake for another 6 minutes, then remove from the oven.

Put the sugar syrup and orange blossom water in a bowl. Use a pair of tongs to dip the buns carefully in the syrup before setting them back on the tray, or brush the buns very generously all over with the syrup, using it all up. Allow the buns to cool a little before eating, but don't let them sit there too long as they are delicious while the filling is still warm.

Salty-sweet orange & tahini pretzels

Our chef Juice is a man of great contrasts: he has a Masters in History but left academia for the kitchen, and is doing really well in ours. A big tall guy – charismatic, forceful, creative – his gentler side is most obvious in his cooking. We are always surprised when we look at the pretty, delicate plates he sends out. How can these massive sausage fingers have such a lightness of touch? Probably his piano playing helps, and also his fiancée's catchphrase: 'A little less ogre, a little more finesse.' These pretzels require a bit of dexterity, but they are quite easy to make even if you don't have piano training. If you do find making the pretzels too taxing on your fingers, just roll them into sticks – they will taste just as good.

Makes 8 pretzels

200g strong white bread flour
150g plain flour
½ tsp table salt
40g icing sugar
140g/ml milk
50g fresh yeast or 4½ tsp dried yeast
zest of 1 orange
50g date molasses or a strong dark honey (e.g. chestnut)
80g tahini paste
50g unsalted butter, diced and at room temperature

For the tops
egg wash (1 egg yolk beaten with a pinch of sugar)
sea salt to sprinkle

To dip (if you like)
3 tbsp tahini paste
3 tbsp date molasses

Put the flours, salt and icing sugar in a bowl and stir to combine. You can use a mixer with a dough hook attachment, but it is just as easy to work this by hand.

Warm the milk to blood temperature (i.e. when you touch it it feels just right, not hot or cold), add the yeast, orange zest and molasses and stir to dissolve. Add the liquid to the flour and knead together to form a ball. Slowly mix in the tahini and then the butter until everything has been incorporated into the dough. Cover the bowl and allow to rest for at least 1 hour at room temperature or in the fridge for up to 12 hours.

Line two trays with baking parchment. Place the dough on an unfloured work surface and divide into eight pieces of about 90g each. Roll a piece into a snake about 40–45cm long. Take one end of the dough snake in each hand and lift them towards you and off the surface a little, leaving the rest in a half-moon on the table. Twist the dough strands around each other about 4cm from the ends. Lower the dough to the table again so that the ends sit on the half-moon, with the twisted section in the centre of the pretzel. Press gently to attach the ends to the half-moon and carefully lift the pretzel. Flip it onto one of the baking sheets so the ends of the dough are on the underside. Repeat with the other pieces of dough. By the eighth one, you should know exactly what you are doing (and don't worry, as the ugly ones will taste just as nice as the pretty ones). Allow about 2–3 cm between each pretzel – they won't grow too much – and leave to prove for about 1½ hours.

Preheat the oven to 220°C/200°C fan/gas mark 7. Brush the pretzels with the egg wash, then sprinkle with a little sea salt. Bake for 10–12 minutes until they have a dark golden brown crust. They are delicious just as they are, but if you fancy a treat, serve them with a dish of tahini paste mixed with an equal amount of date molasses.

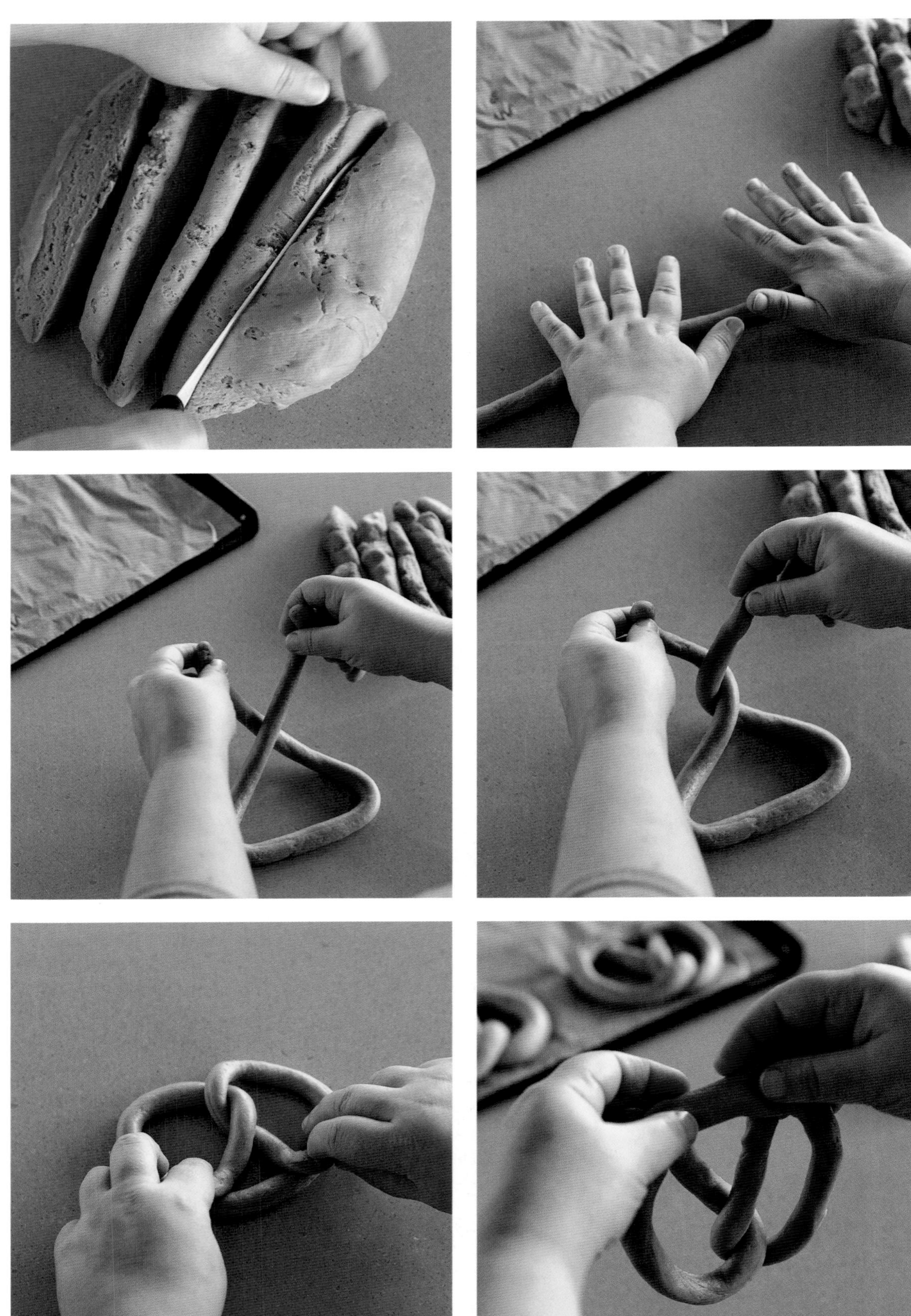

Baked doughnuts filled with lime & lemon curd

Fried doughnuts are delicious, but only for a few minutes when they come out of the oil; after that they become greasy and doughy. This recipe allows the dough to bake at the correct temperature and develop a light, airy crumb. Then, to tick the naughty box, we roll them in warm butter and sugar, and fill them with curd – the fresh citrus flavour works like a dream with all that richness. Not fried, but not for the faint-hearted.

Makes 8 doughnuts

For the dough
- *3 eggs*
- *15g fresh yeast or 1 heaped tsp dried yeast*
- *1 tbsp caster sugar*
- *1 tsp table salt*
- *300g strong white bread flour*
- *25g/ml milk*
- *125g cold butter, diced very small*

For the lime & lemon curd
- *75g unsalted butter*
- *120g caster sugar*
- *50g/ml lime juice*
- *80g/ml lemon juice*
- *2 whole eggs*
- *3 egg yolks*

For dipping
- *160g unsalted butter*

For rolling
- *100g granulated sugar*
- *zest of 1 lime*

Place all the dough ingredients apart from the butter in a mixer and combine with a dough hook at low speed. If you are using dried yeast, dissolve it in the milk before adding to the flour. Once the dough has formed into a ball, increase the speed to medium-high and start adding the butter little by little until fully combined. This takes some time (about 6–7 minutes) and the dough will soften quite a bit in the process, but don't worry, this is normal. The speed will work the gluten and give the doughnuts a great texture. Don't fret if there are some small flecks of butter in the dough, as they will melt during baking and lighten the texture. Cover the bowl and allow the dough to rest and set in the fridge for at least 4 hours (ideally overnight).

Place the chilled dough on a lightly floured surface and divide into eight (about 80g each). Roll each one in circular motions between your palm and the work surface until the dough forms a tight ball, then set on a baking tray, allowing about 5cm between each one. This would be the time to freeze them for future baking, if this is what you intend, but do note that this dough only freezes well for 3–4 days. Otherwise allow the doughnuts to prove and almost double in size (this will take about 40 minutes). After about 20 minutes, preheat the oven to 230°C/210°C fan/gas mark 8.

Put the butter, sugar, lime and lemon juices in a medium pan on a high heat. Stir until the sugar dissolves and the butter is fully melted. Mix the whole eggs and egg yolks together in a bowl. Once the liquid in the pan is just starting to boil, remove it from the heat. Slowly pour the egg mixture into the pan while whisking well, then return it to the heat, whisking all the time, until the curd thickens and the first bubbles start to appear. Carefully pour through a sieve into a clean bowl to remove any egg threads that may have developed. Lay cling film or greaseproof paper directly on the surface of the curd to cover it and avoid a skin forming, then cool in the fridge. This recipe makes a little more curd than you need here, but it is so tasty spread on toast or mixed into yogurt that it is worth making the whole amount. It keeps well for up to 2 weeks in a sealed container in the fridge.

Bake the doughnuts in the oven for 8 minutes. In the meantime, melt the butter in a small bowl, and mix the granulated sugar with the lime zest in a separate bowl. Once 8 minutes is up, check to see whether the dough is a lovely golden brown – if not, bake for another 2 minutes, but no longer.

Remove the doughnuts from the oven and quickly brush very generously with the melted butter until it has all been absorbed. Alternatively, use tongs to dip the doughnuts into the melted butter, being very careful not to break or crush them. Allow the doughnuts to rest on the tray for 3–4 minutes, then roll them in the sugar mixed with the lime zest.

Use a piping bag with a long nozzle to fill the centre of each doughnut with curd, or simply cut each one in half and spread thickly. These are nice eaten warm. They keep well for a few hours, but are best eaten on the day of baking. Make sure not to store them in the fridge, as that would ruin their texture.

Porridge & cereals

Hummus is traditionally a breakfast food in the Middle East. The old hummus shops in east Jerusalem and Acre still keep a pot of chickpeas cooking low and slow through the night, to be prepared early in the morning and served to hungry breakfasters with fresh pitta and onion wedges. The shops close when the hummus is finished, usually around noon. It may sound like a strange notion, as nowadays we expect hummus to be served as a nibble before or with a meal, but in essence it is not that different from a bowl of porridge. A helping of something mellow in flavour, warm and sustaining, is a great way to begin the day. It makes perfect sense wherever you are in the world... although we accept that most people prefer to start with their breath smelling of mint rather than onion. Here are a few alternatives. They tick the 'warm-and-sustaining' box and the 'Middle Eastern' box without involving cumin, lemon or onion. Eat them for a breakfast that will take you through to dinner or (in smaller portions) as dessert to a savoury breakfast. What an excellent way of adding dessert to yet another meal.

Semolina pudding with strawberry & cardamom compote

This used to be my favourite winter breakfast, a great alternative to oats and very comforting. Eating it makes me feel instantly like a child again, in a good way.

Makes a good breakfast for 4

For the semolina

- *500g/ml milk*
- *100g/ml double cream*
- *2 tbsp caster sugar*
- *zest of 1 lemon*
- *100g semolina*

For the compote

- *200g strawberries*
- *2 cardamom pods*
- *a pinch of freshly ground black pepper*
- *juice of 1 lemon*
- *80g caster sugar*

Remove the green stems from the strawberries and cut into quarters. Mix the strawberries with the cardamom, pepper, lemon juice and sugar, place in a pan on a high heat and bring to a rapid boil. Allow to cook for 6–8 minutes until the mixture looks thicker, then remove from the heat.

Put the milk, cream, sugar and lemon zest in a pan on a high heat and bring to the boil. Whisk in the semolina and stir until thickened; this will only take a few minutes. Divide between four serving bowls and top with the strawberry compote. Eat while it is still warm.

Israeli couscous & almond milk pudding

This is a great porridge-type dish for vegans and those with a dairy allergy – as well as for everyone else, as the nuttiness of the almond milk works so well with the Israeli couscous. I like to top this with fresh seasonal fruit, then drizzle with a little date molasses or honey. Of course you can buy almond milk and prepare this pudding in 5 minutes, but making your own almond milk is such a nifty trick to have under your belt, it's worth giving it a go at least once.

Makes a good breakfast for 2 or 3

For the almond milk (makes 1 litre)
- *400g whole almonds (skin on)*
- *600g/ml + 200g/ml water*

For the couscous
- *1 kg/litre almond milk*
- *250g Israeli couscous*
- *a pinch of table salt*
- *3–4 tbsp date molasses or honey*

fresh fruit of your choice (I like peaches, strawberries or blueberries)

Soak the almonds in 600g/ml of water overnight. In the morning, transfer the almonds and water to a blender or food processor and blend. Strain through a cheesecloth or a very fine sieve into a large pan. Return the drained pulp to the blender with the additional 200g/ml of water and blitz again. Strain this into the pan too, then squeeze the pulp to wring out any remaining liquid (after this, you can discard the pulp).

Place the pan of almond milk on a high heat and bring to the boil. Add the Israeli couscous and cook until it softens and absorbs most of the liquid, stirring occasionally so that it doesn't stick. This will take 10–14 minutes. Add the salt, then stir in 3 tablespoons of date molasses or honey.

Transfer to serving bowls, top with fresh fruit, drizzle with the remaining date molasses or honey and serve.

Puffed rice & dried fruit granola

This light and crunchy granola is an excellent one for those with gluten allergies. You can of course make it using other grains and dried fruits; this is simply a base to build upon until you find the combination you like best.

Makes a large cereal container full of this great breakfast treat

Gluten-free

75g unsalted butter
100g date molasses (or a rich dark honey, e.g. chestnut)
100g light brown soft sugar
175g puffed rice
70g walnuts, roughly chopped
70g pecans, roughly chopped
70g dried figs, diced
70g dried apricots, diced
70g raisins
1 tsp ground ginger

Preheat the oven to 190°C/170°C fan/ gas mark 5 and line a large, flat baking tray with baking parchment.

Combine the butter, molasses and sugar in a small pan and bring to the boil. Stir the puffed rice and nuts together in a large bowl or on a tray and carefully pour over the boiling syrup. Use a large spoon to mix well, making sure to coat all the rice puffs with syrup. Transfer to the baking tray and flatten out a little so that there is an even layer.

Bake in the centre of the oven for 10 minutes, then remove and allow to cool on the tray for 6–8 minutes. Add the dried fruit. Sprinkle with the ground ginger and stir to combine, allowing some larger clusters to remain, as they are the best bits.

Once the cereal is cold, transfer to an airtight container. This will keep for up to 2 weeks.

Honey & Co.
Food From the Middle East

Ashura cereal

Ashura is a traditional Turkish dessert also known as Noah's Ark pudding. The legend goes that, running low on supplies in the Ark, Noah boiled together everything they had – dried wheat, beans, fruit, nuts, spices and honey. The whole store cupboard. The result is a very substantial dessert; a meal in itself, really. We use the same ingredients (minus the beans), but instead of boiling them we roast them to make a great alternative to granola. The puffed wheat keeps it light and is easier on your jaw than crunchy oats. We have served this for breakfast with yogurt, jam and fresh fruit since we opened the restaurant, but it's great with just milk or even on its own as an addictive nibble (as many of our customers have discovered).

Makes a cereal container full of nutty crunchy goodness

85g/95ml vegetable oil (e.g. rapeseed or sunflower)
110g honey
110g dark brown soft sugar
1 tsp table salt
1 tsp ground cinnamon
½ tsp ground mahleb seeds
½ tsp ground cardamom pods
1 packet of puffed wheat (160g)
85g pecans, halved
40g sunflower seeds
50g pumpkin seeds
30g sesame seeds
85g almonds, very roughly chopped

Preheat the oven to 190°C/170°C fan/ gas mark 5 and line a couple of large flat baking trays with baking parchment.

Combine the oil, honey and sugar in a medium pan and set on a high heat. Mix well and bring to the boil, stirring occasionally to avoid it burning on the base. Put the rest of the ingredients in a large bowl and mix well. Once the honey syrup is bubbling, carefully pour it over the dry ingredients in the bowl. Use a large spoon to stir, turning the contents of the bowl over a few times until everything is well coated with the syrup. Transfer the mixture to the baking trays and flatten it out a little so that there is an even layer of cereal.

Place in the centre of the oven and bake for 10 minutes. Carefully remove one tray at a time and mix the cereal around to make sure everything is getting roasted and crispy. Return the trays to the oven for an additional 5–6 minutes, then remove and leave the ashura to cool entirely on the trays before breaking into large clusters.

Once the cereal is cold, transfer it to an airtight container. This keeps for well over 2 weeks, if you don't get addicted and eat it all long before then.

Savoury breakfasts

Breakfast seems to be the time when even the most adventurous palate craves familiar, traditional flavours. You may welcome a tray of sushi for lunch, but the notion of eating rice and fish before noon makes most of us shudder. Growing up in Israel, breakfast would consist of eggs, bread, soft cheese or yogurt, and a very finely chopped salad of tomato, cucumber, onion and whatever other vegetables we had kicking around, all generously seasoned with lemon and oil. If we couldn't be bothered with all the chopping, just a sliced fresh tomato would do. As a result, the notion of the 'great' English breakfast was truly strange to us. We could not fathom having sausages in the morning; eating baked beans then did not make much more sense; and the mere thought of black pudding made me gag at any time of day. Added to which, the only vegetable in sight was a warm, watery tomato.

After ten years in England I have learnt to love the English breakfast more than any other meal. If the ingredients are good and well prepared, I find the combination of bacon, sausage, beans, egg and toast completely irresistible. Mushrooms are a lovely addition and I always get an extra serving of black pudding if it's on offer.

When we started serving breakfast at Honey & Co, the reaction from our mostly British crowd to our Israeli breakfast was quite similar to our reaction when first faced with the British one. Raw vegetables and hummus for breakfast did not go down well. We have found a good solution to the problem with these savoury bakes, which are traditional in the Middle East and at the same time acceptable in this country, because no one can resist a freshly baked pastry. Although they are still considered somewhat exotic, they have gained popularity with our breakfast crowd. We serve them with a small dish of sliced tomatoes, olives and pickles, and tahini or yogurt. We notice that although the pastry always gets eaten, the little dish of olives and tomatoes occasionally remains untouched, but we would not dream of serving them without it.

Only on Saturday mornings do we indulge ourselves in cooking and serving a proper Israeli breakfast feast to our die-hard Middle Eastern food aficionados: hummus, pickles, fresh salad, yogurt, cereal and jam, followed by eggs cooked however you like them. The restaurant is full to bursting from the minute we open the doors. Saturday morning breakfast may be the craziest, hardest service of the entire week, as the eggs cook fast, and overcook even faster. For the longest time it was only Sarit who was able to do this service well. She earned the title 'kitchen ninja' for her amazing ability to produce plate after immaculate plate of food at incredible speed, seemingly without moving. Saturday morning service is now a rite of passage for all our chefs, and a point of pride for them if and when they pull it off (although Sarit is still the best at it).

Eggs in the nest

A good dish for a good beginning, and a great one to win hearts. My father used to make this for us when we were kids, and I make it for Sarit as a breakfast treat when we have a day off together, or as a midnight snack after a long shift. I made it for her nephew and niece and became an instant hero, and served it to Rachael as our first Honey & Co staff lunch ever (Rachael is still with us, and hopefully will be for a long time to come). The kids still make these eggs and have named them after me – the glory! Sarit still asks me to make them for her when she's in need of comfort (or just of a meal) and every time I do, I think of my father. Made with four main ingredients – bread, butter, eggs and salt – this can be whipped up almost any time, and has such universal appeal that it is guaranteed to win the heart of any child, and most adults.

Makes breakfast for a loved one

2 tbsp butter
2 slices of crusty sourdough bread
1 tbsp vegetable oil
2 lovely eggs, the best you can find
a sprinkling of salt and pepper

Butter the bread well on both sides. Use a small glass or a round biscuit cutter to cut the centre out of each slice (make sure to keep the centre).

Heat a large flat-based frying pan on the hob and add the oil. Place the bread and the cut-out discs flat in the pan and crack an egg into the central hole in each slice. Season with salt and pepper and fry for a minute or so until you can see the egg white starting to set where it meets the bread. Use a spatula carefully to lift a slice at a time and flip them (don't forget to flip the little discs too). Cook for 1 minute on the flip-side, then transfer to a serving plate. Use the little crispy bread discs as the best egg soldiers in the world.

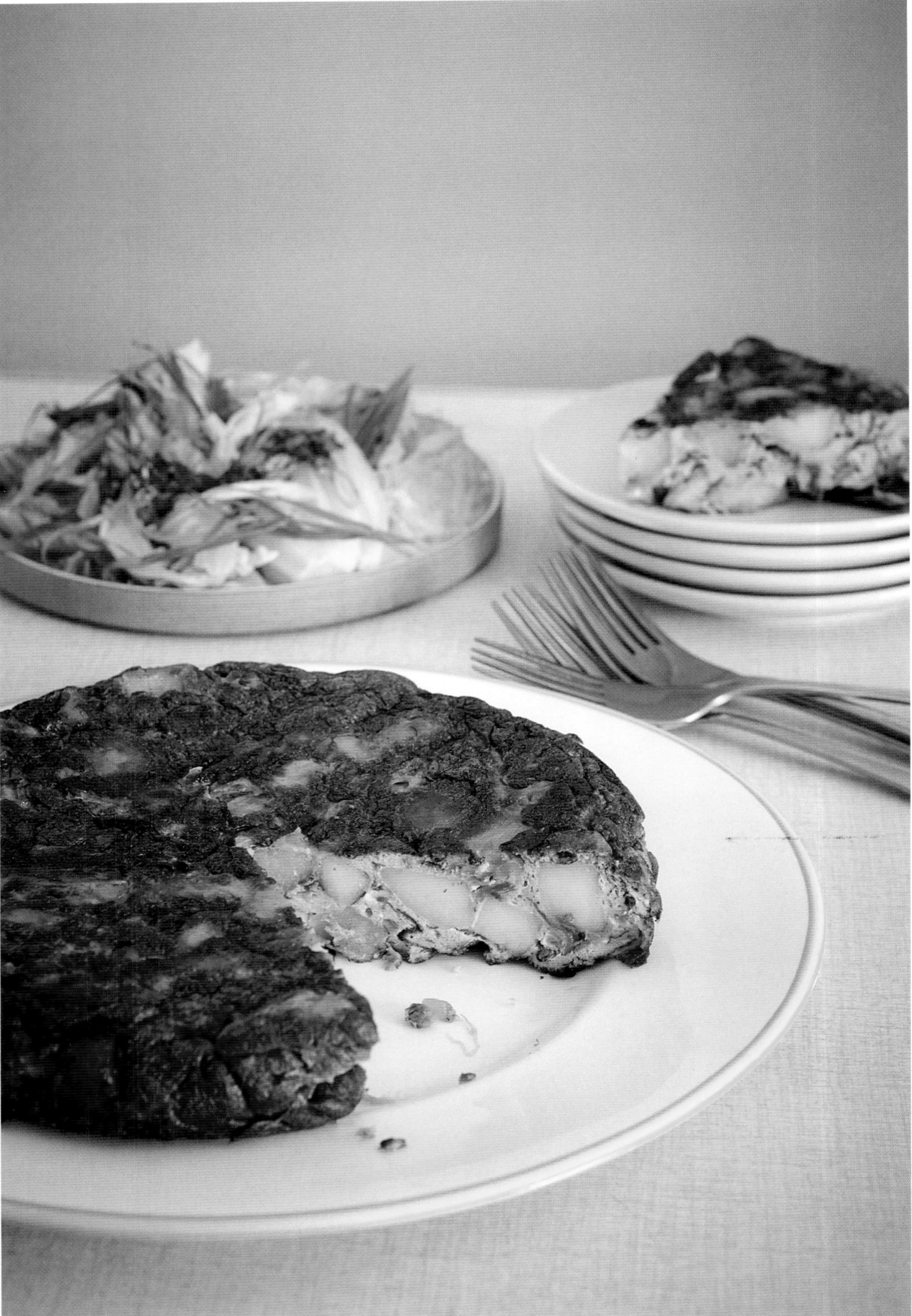

Maakouda

A traditional dish for Tunisian Jews, this is usually made by cooking the potatoes and onions in a pot of oil, then pouring the eggs in and placing the whole thing in the oven with a tray underneath to catch the oil overflow. While the original tastes gorgeous, we could not justify making it that way. We offer this lighter (but no less gorgeous) version.

Fills an 18–20cm (7–8 inch) frying pan

Enough for breakfast for 4 hungry or 6 modest guests

2 potatoes, peeled and cut in 2cm dice (about 300g)
½ tsp + ½ tsp table salt
50g unsalted butter
1 tbsp olive oil
2 onions, peeled and sliced (about 200g)
8 eggs
100g/ml double cream
2 tsp ras el hanut spice mix
2 tbsp capers
1 small bunch of parsley, leaves picked and chopped
a pinch of freshly ground black pepper

Place the potatoes in a pan containing 500g/ml of water seasoned with the first half-teaspoon of salt. Boil for 5 minutes, then drain.

Melt the butter and oil together in a good non-stick frying pan. Add the onions and fry on a medium heat until they soften entirely (this will take about 8–10 minutes). Now add the cooked diced potatoes and continue frying for a further 6–8 minutes. In the meantime whisk all the remaining ingredients together in a bowl.

Increase the heat to high and pour in the egg mixture. Allow 1 minute for the eggs to start cooking around the rim, then use a heatproof spatula or wooden spoon to push the mixture from the sides into the centre, all around the pan. Leave to cook for another minute, then repeat.

Now smooth the top and reduce the heat to low. Cover and cook for 2 minutes, then use the lid and pan combined to flip the maakouda. Carefully slide it back into the pan to finish cooking on a low heat for 5 minutes before transferring to a plate to serve. You can eat this hot, but it also keeps well for a packed lunch or picnic and is just as delicious cold as it is hot.

Shakshuka

We get a surprising number of calls to the restaurant asking if we serve shakshuka. This North African egg dish seems to be the one that most people conjure up when they think of a Middle Eastern breakfast. The appeal is obvious to me: fiery tomato sauce with eggs poached in it, the whites just set and the yolks still runny, oozing into the sauce as you pierce them with your spoon or, better yet, with a piece of bread. We do serve shakshuka, but only on Saturdays. I suspect if we served it all week, we would make nothing else.

Serves 4 for breakfast

2 tsp sweet smoked paprika
½ tsp cayenne pepper (or a touch more, if spicy is your thing)
2 tsp ground cumin
1 tsp ground cinnamon
2½ tsp caraway seeds, roughly ground or chopped
3 tbsp vegetable oil
15 cloves of garlic (this is no mistake, I do mean 15), crushed
200g tomato purée
50g/ml lemon juice (juice of 1 large lemon)
550g/ml water
1 tsp table salt
2 tbsp caster sugar
8 eggs
1 small bunch of coriander, chopped
some bread to serve

Mix the spices together in a small bowl. Put the oil and crushed garlic in a large, wide frying pan, set on a high heat and fry the garlic, stirring constantly, until a fragrant smell emerges. This will take about 2 minutes. Add the spices, mix well and cook for 1 minute. Stir in the tomato purée and continue stirring as it cooks for 2 minutes or until the purée starts to stick to the bottom of the pan.

Add the lemon juice in one go; it will sizzle a little, so watch out. Stir to combine and then add the water. Stir again and reduce the heat to medium-low. Cook for 10 minutes before mixing in the salt and sugar. Taste to see if you want to add another pinch of cayenne pepper or a little squeeze of lemon – this sauce should hit all the right notes: sweet, sour, salty and spicy.

Once you are happy with the sauce, break the eggs directly into it, leaving a little space between each one, so that you can later pick out one egg at a time without breaking the yolk of any of the others. Season with a little salt and pepper. Cover with a lid and leave to cook for 3 minutes until the whites are fully set but the yolks are still runny and soft. Remove the lid, sprinkle with chopped coriander and serve with the bread.

You can make shakshuka for a smaller number if you are feeding one, two or three. We always allow two eggs per person. You can also make the sauce in advance and store it in an airtight container in the fridge for 3–4 days. It freezes well too, so you could make a large batch and freeze it for future use; just remember to re-boil the sauce before you add the eggs.

Ijjeh (herb frittata)

You can buy these green-tinted omelettes, stuffed in pitta with labaneh and chopped salad, from roadside stands and falafel shops throughout Israel. We used to call them 'Popeye', as everything green was instantly associated with that cartoon. We later learnt they are called ijjeh, and are made with herbs rather than spinach. You can add any soft herb you like, and as much of it as you want; there really isn't such a thing as too much for this. At the restaurant we serve ijjeh hot for breakfast. Any leftovers end up in some pitta with labaneh and salad, as staff lunch.

Fills an 18cm (7 inch) frying pan

Breakfast for a hungry 4

2 leeks (about 300g)
½ tsp + ½ tsp table salt
50g unsalted butter
1 tbsp olive oil
8 eggs
100g/ml double cream
1 large bunch of parsley, roughly chopped (about 40g)
3–4 sprigs of mint, leaves picked and chopped
½ tsp freshly ground black pepper
80g feta cheese

Slice the leeks finely and wash them in plenty of water to get rid of any grit. Drain well, then place in a good non-stick frying pan with the first half-teaspoon of salt. Add the butter and oil and fry on a medium heat until the leeks soften entirely. This will take about 8–10 minutes. In the meantime put the eggs, cream, parsley, mint, black pepper and remaining salt in a bowl and whisk to combine.

Increase the heat to high and pour in the egg mixture. Allow 1 minute for the eggs to start cooking around the rim, then use a heatproof spatula or wooden spoon to push the mixture from the sides into the centre, all around the pan. Leave to cook for another minute, then repeat.

Crumble the feta into rough pieces and push them into the soft egg, then smooth the top and reduce the heat to low. Cover and cook for 2 minutes, then use the lid and pan combined to flip the ijjeh. Carefully slide it back into the pan to finish cooking on a low heat for 5 minutes before transferring to a plate to serve. You can eat this hot, but it also keeps well for a packed lunch or picnic and is just as delicious cold as it is hot.

Lahma base dough

Turkish lahmacun has a thin, almost cracker-like base; the Palestinian version is softer and more supple; and there are many other variations throughout the Middle East. What they have in common is the topping, which always includes spiced meat (the name means 'meat with dough'), often minced lamb. Although we do offer this version (page 90), many of our customers find the notion of lamb before lunch a bit tricky, so we came up with other toppings with a wider breakfast appeal. My fave is spinach, egg and yogurt – delicious and so good-looking; our girls' choice is roasted peppers and feta. These versions sell out early with no problem at all.

This dough is very similar to pitta but has a little more sugar and oil to enrich it. I prefer to prepare it a day in advance and let it slow-prove in the fridge overnight. This allows the flavours to develop, as well as letting me sleep for an extra hour, since I bake these for breakfast. You can make the dough with a pre-ferment or 'mother dough' starter if you happen to be feeding one in the fridge and the flavour will be even better, but even if you prepare the dough on the same day as baking, I still think you will be happy with the results. I mean, it is the Middle East's answer to pizza, and makes for a great breakfast (or lunch on the go) – what's not to like?

Makes 6 rounds

350g strong white bread flour
1 tsp table salt
2 tbsp caster sugar
20g fresh yeast (or 1 tbsp dried yeast)
about 180g/ml lukewarm water
4 tbsp olive oil, plus extra for shaping

Put the flour and salt in a mixing bowl. Separately stir the sugar, yeast and 100g/ml of the water together to dissolve. Add the yeast mixture to the flour and combine, adding enough of the remaining water to create a nice, soft dough. Then pour in the oil while kneading continuously. It will take a bit of work to get the dough to incorporate with the oil, but keep at it. Use a mixer with a dough hook if you have one, to make life easier. Once it is all combined and the dough is smooth, silky and soft (this will take at least 5 minutes of kneading), transfer it to a very large bowl – at least three times the size of the dough, as it will rise. Cover and place in the fridge to prove slowly overnight (or, if you want to bake it on the same day, leave it at room temperature to prove more quickly).

In the morning (or once it has doubled in size), place the dough on your workbench and divide into six pieces (about 90–100g each). Roll into balls, rub them all over with a generous amount of oil and allow to rest on the workbench for 20–30 minutes until they puff up again.

Preheat the oven to a very high setting (250°C/230°C fan/gas mark 9, or even 260°C/240°C/gas mark 10, if it goes that high) and set a flat baking tray in it to heat up. Now oil your hands and shape the dough balls. Push your fingers into the centre of each one and prod and stretch it out to form a disc about 14cm in diameter, leaving a thicker edge around a flatter centre, so it looks like a saucer or starter plate with a chunky rim. Cover with one of our suggested toppings (pages 89–90) or make up your own.

Now the only tricky part is to get the lahmas onto the preheated tray. The best way is to take it out of the oven first. Use a spatula to lift them one at a time and slide them carefully onto the hot tray (or you can lift them by hand and place them on the tray if you prefer). Return the tray to the oven and bake the lahma bases for 8–10 minutes or until golden brown all over.

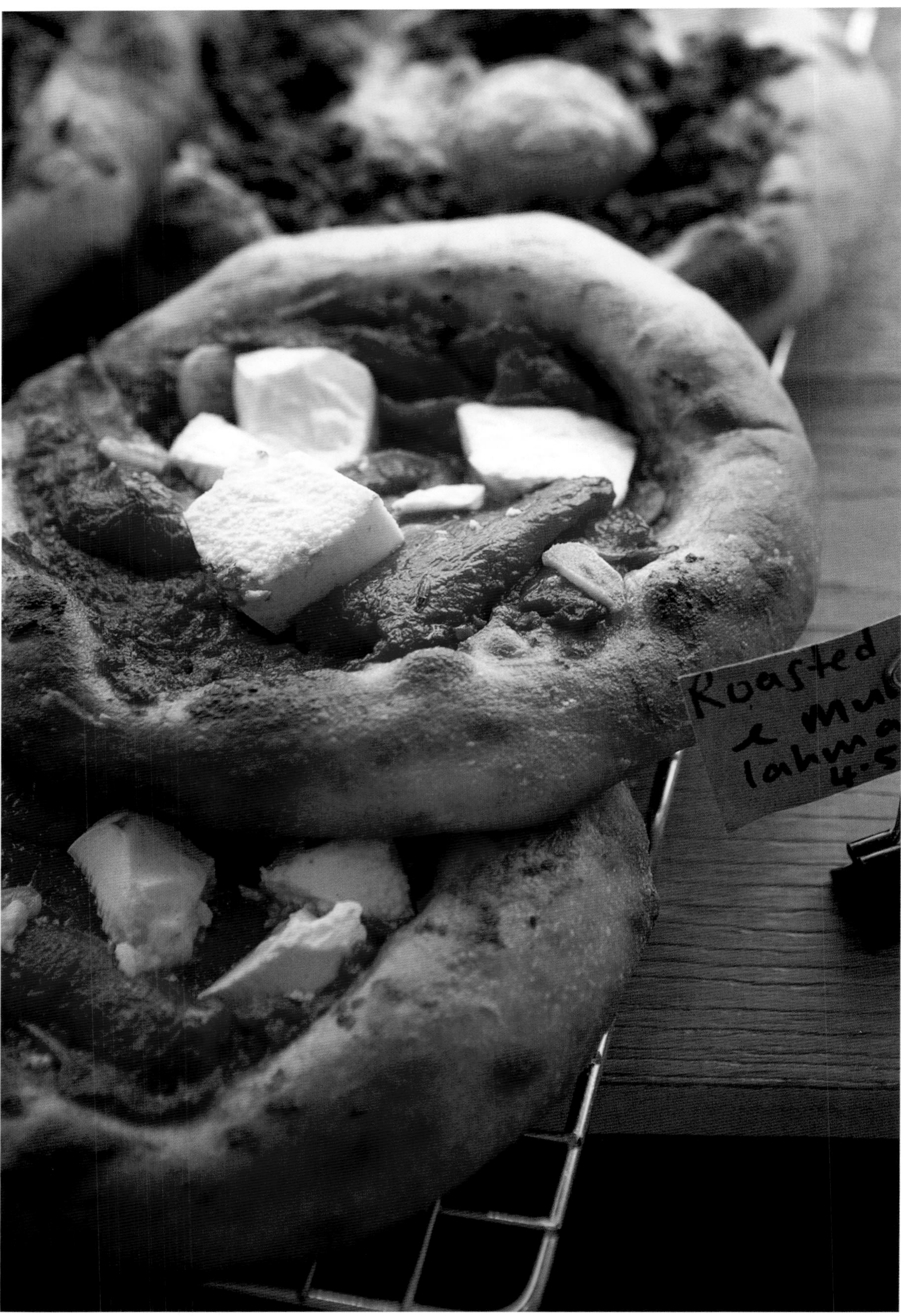
Roasted

Spinach lahma with egg

30g unsalted butter
400g baby spinach, washed
½ tsp table salt, plus more to taste
a pinch of freshly ground black pepper
1 small bunch of dill, chopped
1 small bunch of parsley, chopped
olive oil to smooth over the bases
240g thick plain yogurt
6 egg yolks

Heat a large pan, put the butter in it, and top with the spinach, salt and pepper. Cover with a lid and wilt the spinach – it should only take 2–3 minutes. Transfer to a sieve to drain and press down on the spinach with a spoon to really squeeze the water out. Once it has cooled a little, mix in the chopped dill and parsley, and season to taste (sometimes too much salt drains out with the water).

Smooth oil over the surface of the dough discs, then place a spoonful of yogurt (about 40g) in the centre of each one. Top with the spinach, dividing it between the six rounds. Carefully lift each one onto the preheated tray and bake for 6 minutes. Remove from the oven, place an egg yolk in the centre of each one and top with a pinch of sea salt. Return to the oven for a final 3–4 minutes. If you prefer your eggs well-done, bake these with the yolk in place from the start.

We like to serve these warm, with the yolk still oozy, and some goats' yogurt on the side.

Roasted pepper lahma with feta

3 large red peppers
2 tbsp olive oil
1 clove of garlic, crushed
3 sprigs of thyme
50g tomato purée
50g harissa paste
a pinch of table salt
a pinch of sugar
150g feta cheese

Preheat the oven to 250°C/230°C fan/ gas mark 9 or, if you have a grill setting, set it on the highest heat. Use a small knife to cut around the green stem of each pepper and pull it out, then remove the seeds with your fingers or a teaspoon. Place the peppers in the hot oven until the skin chars (this should take about 30–35 minutes). Remove carefully to a bowl and cover it with cling film. Allow the peppers to cool enough that you can handle them, then peel them (but don't wash them, as you want to keep the flavour of charring).

Once all the peppers are peeled, cut into thick strips and season with salt and pepper. Add the olive oil, garlic and thyme, and stir to combine the flavours (you could make this a day in advance – store in the fridge until needed).

Mix the tomato purée and harissa paste and season with the pinch of salt and sugar. Divide the harissa mixture between the dough discs and spread it around the flattened centres, leaving the rims clear. Top with the roasted peppers, then crumble on the feta. Carefully lift each one onto the preheated tray and bake for 8–10 minutes before serving. These keep well to eat cold later in the day, and make a great packed lunch.

Lamb lahma with pine nuts & cherry tomatoes

2 tbsp olive oil
2 onions, peeled and diced
500g lamb mince
2 tbsp baharat spice mix (page 49)
2 tbsp tomato purée
60g tahini paste
50g/ml water
a pinch of table salt
10 cherry tomatoes, quartered
50g pine nuts

Heat the olive oil in a large frying pan on a high heat, then add the diced onions. Sauté until they are soft and starting to colour (this will take about 8–10 minutes), then add the minced meat. Keep the heat high and mix the meat around vigorously to break it into little pieces. Season with salt and pepper, stir in the spice mix and continue cooking until the meat has browned (this should take about 5–6 minutes). Stir in the tomato purée and cook for another 2–3 minutes. Taste and adjust the seasoning as necessary, then remove to a bowl to cool a little.

Mix the tahini paste with the water and the salt, whisking it until it becomes smooth. Place a spoonful of tahini in the centre of each dough disc and spread it around a little. Cover with the cooked lamb, then top with the cherry tomatoes and pine nuts.

Carefully lift each lahma onto the pre-heated tray and bake for 8–10 minutes. We like to serve this with extra tahini dip and a fresh tomato salad.

Burekas

Made throughout the Balkans, burekas are savoury pastry parcels with different fillings, often potato, cheese or meat. The pastry varies as well, from short and crumbly to layered and crunchy, like filo or puff, or even doughy, more like bread rolls. For home baking I have found none better than this, the pastry dough that will change your baking life – our famed 'dough number 4'. It is easy to make, fail-safe and extremely tasty. At Honey & Co we use this for a few of our breakfast bakes, and it is great for canapés and pies. Alternatively, you could buy ready-made puff pastry and just make the fillings. It is cheating but the burekas will still be delicious, and no one need know. You can prepare your burekas in advance and freeze them; just remember they need to be thawed before baking so that the filling is nice and hot by the time the pastry is cooked. The fillings here are a few tried-and-tested suggestions. If you experiment with different fillings, be sure to over-season slightly, to make up for the fact that they will be wrapped in pastry.

'Dough number 4'

This recipe makes twice the amount you need for a single batch of burekas, but it is a versatile dough that freezes well, so it is worth making the full amount and keeping some for another day. If you prefer, you can halve the quantities; the only problem you face is halving an egg. The best way is to crack it into a little dish, whisk well and then use half. Use the remaining beaten egg to glaze the pastry before baking. Waste not, want not.

Makes about 1kg

500g plain flour
½ tsp caster sugar
1½ tsp table salt
1 tsp baking powder
250g cold unsalted butter, diced
125g full fat cream cheese
1 egg
125g/ml double cream

Place all the ingredients in a mixer bowl with a paddle attachment or in a food processor and work them together to form a nice smooth dough. (You could of course do this by hand, in which case you will need to rub the butter into the flour and other dry ingredients before mixing in the cream cheese, egg and double cream.) The idea is to keep everything cold and not to overwork the dough – you want some flecks of butter running through, as this will result in a lovely flaky texture once baked. Form the dough into a ball, press down to flatten it, wrap in cling film and chill in the fridge for at least 1 hour. You can prepare the dough up to 3 days in advance of baking – just keep it wrapped in cling film in the fridge until you need it.

If you are making a full batch but only need half for now, divide it in two, wrap both pieces in cling film, then put one in the fridge and the other in the freezer. It keeps well for up to a month; simply thaw before rolling and filling.

Potato & oregano burekas

Makes 8 carb-on-carb pockets of bliss

For the filling

- *3 large whole potatoes (about 500–600g)*
- *80g pecorino or Parmesan cheese, finely grated*
- *200g feta cheese, crumbled*
- *1 egg*
- *2 tbsp soured cream*
- *3 sprigs of oregano, leaves picked and roughly chopped*
- *½ tsp table salt, plus more to taste*
- *½ tsp freshly ground black pepper, plus more to taste*

For the pastry

- *½ batch 'dough number 4' (page 91) or 500g ready-made puff pastry*
- *1 egg mixed with a pinch of table salt, to glaze*
- *poppy seeds to sprinkle (if you like)*

Preheat the oven to 240°C/220°C fan/ gas mark 9. Place the potatoes on a rack in the centre of the oven and bake for 40–50 minutes, or until you can insert a knife without meeting any resistance. Leave to cool. Meanwhile, mix all the other filling ingredients together.

Once the potatoes are cool enough to handle, slit them in half and scoop the flesh into a bowl. Smash it a little, then combine with the filling ingredients. Taste and adjust the seasoning as necessary. Remember that because the filling gets encased in pastry, it needs to be very well seasoned.

Dust your workbench with a sprinkling of flour to stop the dough sticking (I try to use as little as I can). Roll the dough into a rectangle roughly 30cm x 60cm. Cut it in half lengthways and divide each strip into four, giving you eight squares roughly 15cm x 15cm.

Divide the filling between the squares. Slightly moisten the edges of the dough with a little water and fold the squares in half to create filled rectangles. Pinch the edges to seal or use a fork to press them together. Place on a tray lined with baking parchment. If you want to freeze the burekas this would be the time. Freeze them flat on the tray and, once they are frozen, transfer to a sealed container or freezer bag.

When you are ready to bake, heat the oven to 200°C/180°C fan/gas mark 6. Brush egg wash all over the top of the burekas and sprinkle them with poppy seeds if using. Place in the centre of the oven and bake for 20–25 minutes, turning the tray around halfway through, until they are golden and fully cooked.

Burnt aubergine burekas

Makes 8 large ones

For the filling

3 long purple-black aubergines (if you can, get Italian ones; they are amazing)
1 clove of garlic, crushed
150g feta cheese, crumbled
50g pecorino or Parmesan cheese, finely grated
½ tsp table salt
a generous pinch of freshly ground black pepper
1 small bunch of parsley, leaves chopped
1 egg

For the pastry

½ batch 'dough number 4' (page 91) or 500g ready-made puff pastry
1 egg mixed with a pinch of table salt, to glaze
sesame seeds to sprinkle (if you wish)

Start by burning the aubergines. I usually do this on the flame of a gas hob until the skin is burnt all over and the flesh is completely soft. If you don't have a gas hob, you can char them on a griddle pan (this will take longer than an open flame, about 20–30 minutes) or you can set them under the grill on its highest setting and turn them every 6–8 minutes until they feel very soft.

Remove them to a colander to cool and drain any excess liquid. In the meantime mix the remaining filling ingredients together. Once the aubergines are at a temperature you can handle, slit them in half and scoop out the flesh with a spoon. Combine with the other filling ingredients, then taste and adjust the seasoning as necessary. Remember that as this gets encased in pastry, the filling needs to be very well seasoned.

Dust your workbench with a sprinkling of flour to stop the dough sticking (I try to use as little as I can). Roll the dough into a large rectangle of about 30cm x 60cm. Cut in half lengthways and divide each strip into four, to give you eight squares of roughly 15cm x 15cm.

Divide the aubergine mixture between the dough squares. Slightly moisten the edges of the dough with a little water and fold the squares in half from corner to corner to create filled triangles. Pinch the edges to seal or use a fork to press them together. Place on a tray lined with baking parchment. If you want to freeze these, this would be the time. Freeze flat on the tray, then, once they are frozen, transfer to an airtight container or bag. Allow to thaw completely before baking.

When you are ready to bake, preheat the oven to 200°C/180°C fan/gas mark 6. Brush egg wash all over the top of the pastries and sprinkle with sesame seeds, if using. Place in the centre of the oven and bake for 20–25 minutes, turning the tray around halfway through, until they are golden and fully cooked.

Merguez sausage rolls

Brian delivers the meat from our excellent butcher, Godfreys in London's Islington. He is the sweetest man and everyone in the kitchen is happy to see him, especially HD, one of our chefs – the two of them seem to take special pleasure in slightly lewd banter. Every morning Brian comes in the kitchen with the same lame joke, 'Here's your order: sausages, bacon, black pudding...' as he unpacks our wonderful lamb, beef and chicken. The Moroccan lamb sausages he brings us are heavily spiced with cumin and chilli, and work a dream nestled in this pastry – lambs in a blanket.

Makes 8 rolls

For the filling

1 tbsp olive oil
2 cloves of garlic, peeled and finely chopped
80g tomato purée
2 tbsp harissa paste
1 tsp caster sugar
a pinch of table salt
125g/ml water
juice of ½ lemon
16 thin merguez sausages

For the pastry

½ batch 'dough number 4' (page 91) or 500g ready-made puff pastry
1 egg mixed with a pinch of table salt, to glaze
nigella seeds to sprinkle (if you wish)

Heat the oil in a medium-sized pan over a medium-high heat, then add the garlic and stir around until it starts to smell fragrant and stick to the bottom of the pan (roughly 2 minutes). Add the tomato purée, harissa paste, sugar and salt and mix together. Stir in the water and cook on a low heat for 5 minutes, then mix in the lemon juice and cook for a further 2 minutes. Set aside to cool.

Dust your workbench with a sprinkling of flour to stop the dough sticking (I try to use as little as I can). Roll the dough into a large rectangle of about 30cm x 60cm. Cut in half lengthways and divide each strip into four, to give you eight squares of roughly 15cm x 15cm.

Divide the tomato sauce between the dough squares, about 2 tablespoons per square, and top each with two sausages. Dampen the edges of the dough with a touch of water and fold over to encase the sausages so that only their ends are peeking out. Place seam-side down on a tray lined with baking parchment. If you want to freeze these, this would be the time. Freeze flat on the tray, then, once they are frozen, transfer to an airtight container or bag. Allow to thaw completely before baking.

When you are ready to bake, heat the oven to 200°C/180°C fan/gas mark 6. Brush egg wash all over the top of the rolls and sprinkle with nigella seeds, if using. Place in the centre of the oven and bake for 20–25 minutes, turning the tray around halfway through, until they are golden and fully cooked.

Three strange Yemeni breads

My grandmother was Egyptian by origin, but after she married into a Yemeni family she learnt to master Yemeni food, which has three essentials – the soup, the bread and the relish. Most Yemeni meals are based around a soup, of which there are a tremendous number, with grains, pulses, vegetables or meat, and always fragrant with hawayej, a traditional spice mix. The relishes are zehug, a mixture of fresh coriander and chillies spiced with cardamom (page 103), and hilbe, ground fenugreek seeds which have been soaked overnight. These are always on the table and are such an important part of the seasoning for every meal that Yemeni people have been known to carry a jar of each when they travel abroad. The bread is probably the most important part, and the most varied. There are so many types and so many regional, even familial, variants on each that I do not know them all. Some breads are simple and ubiquitous, and can be served at any time of day. Others are elaborate and, frankly, so strange that they are an acquired taste. The three below are the ones I grew up with, and are very easy to love.

Kubaneh

This Yemeni breakfast bread was the pride of my grandmother's table, and has the flavour of my fondest childhood memories – of all the family gathered for the holidays and my grandmother's oven producing the most heavenly smell as it opened to reveal simple aluminium pots, the contents of which would bring so much joy... and occasional anguish, as we would always squabble over the last piece.

Makes a classic metal bread pot or a 20cm (8 inch) cake tin of the strangest bread you can imagine

For the dough

- *60g light brown soft sugar*
- *15g fresh yeast or 1 heaped tsp dried yeast*
- *300–350g/ml warm water*
- *250g strong white bread flour*
- *250g plain white flour*
- *1 tsp table salt*

For shaping

- *3 tbsp vegetable oil*
- *100g unsalted butter (or, more traditionally, margarine) at room temperature*
- *1 tbsp honey*

Mix the sugar with the yeast and 200g/ml of the water in a small jug until the yeast is dissolved. Set aside for about 10 minutes until it starts bubble up a little.

Place the flours and salt in a mixing bowl (you can use an electric mixer with a dough hook or just work this by hand). Pour in the yeasted water while mixing, then slowly mix in the additional water until you have a very wet, smooth dough. Continue kneading until it has a supple and shiny texture; it gets very sticky, but the wetter, the better. Cover the bowl with cling film or a damp towel and set in a warm place to double in size (about 2 hours). Alternatively, let it slow-prove overnight in the fridge for a better flavour. Once proved, it should look all bubbly and happy and jumpy – that's a good sign.

Prepare your baking vessel. We use a traditional lidded aluminium pot, but you can use any ovenproof medium-sized pan with a tight-fitting lid, or a 20cm cake tin with a solid bottom and a home-made lid of aluminium foil. Brush some butter ›››

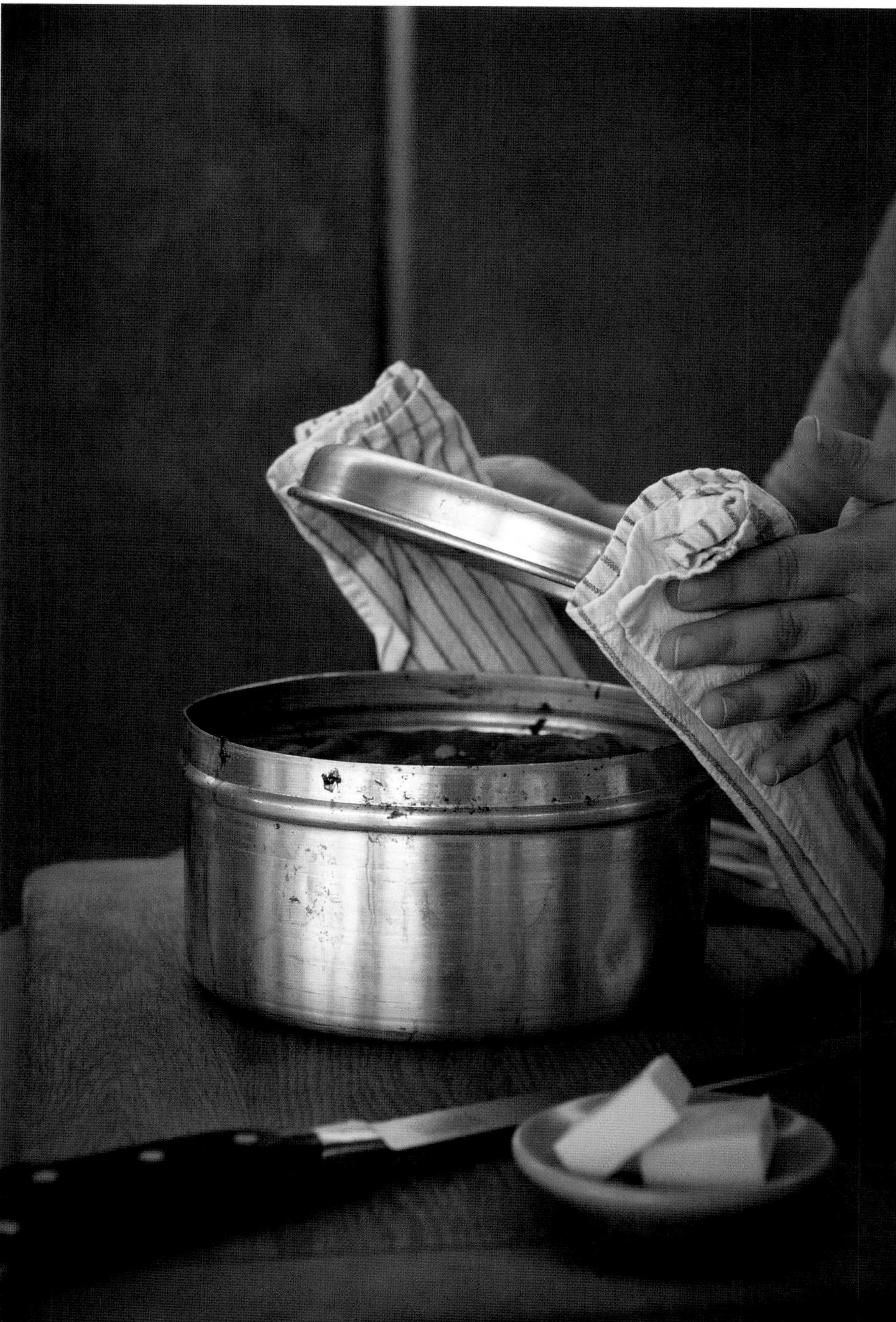

generously over the base and sides of the tin or pan, and inside the lid or foil.

Now here's the strange bit, so pay attention: you moisten your palms with water and flip the dough about in the bowl to knock it back. Repeat this process three times, moistening your hands between each flip.

Pour the oil onto a small tray. Divide the very wet, sticky dough into seven or eight pieces, and place them on it. Pat your hands in the oil and pick up a piece of dough. Stretch it a little, then place some soft butter in the centre. Spread slightly, then fold the dough around it and shape into a rough ball. Place in the centre of the tin. Repeat with the rest of the dough, placing the butter-filled balls around the central one to cover the base. The dough shouldn't come much higher than two-thirds of the way up the sides of the tin or pan, or it will overflow when baked.

Once all the dough balls are in, top with any remaining butter (don't worry if there isn't any) and drizzle with the honey. Cover the pot or tin with the lid or aluminium foil, and leave to prove for about an hour until the dough almost reaches the top. Preheat the oven to 220°C/200°C fan/gas mark 7.

Place the covered tin or pan in the centre of the oven and bake for 30 minutes. Turn it around 180 degrees so that it bakes evenly, then reduce the heat to 200°C/180°C fan/gas mark 6 and bake for a further 30 minutes. Finally, reduce the heat to 180°C/160°C fan/gas mark 4 and bake for another 30 minutes (1½ hours' baking in total). Turn the oven off and leave the bread inside for at least an hour. Keep in a warm place until you are ready to eat.

This bread is great on its own for breakfast, but in my grandmother's house we would have it with thick slices of butter. The best part is the darkly caramelised crust, the bit we would all fight over.

Jahnoon

You can halve the recipe if you are feeding fewer people, but honestly, while you are at it, make it all and eat what you will... which will probably be more than you think. Freeze the rest, as it defrosts well.

Love for this morning pastry has spread from the Yemeni community to the entirety of Israel. On Saturday mornings you can smell it baking in ovens all over the country. You can buy it frozen and ready-to-bake from the supermarket, and those who can't be bothered to bake it themselves can buy it from roadside stands, where they serve grated tomatoes and slow-cooked eggs to go with it – the traditional accompaniment.

When we first moved in together, Sarit decided to make it for me for breakfast as a treat. She was kneading and stretching, brushing and rolling. We finally went to bed with the oven glowing in the darkened flat, and promises of waking up to a pastry-scented home and a glorious breakfast. We woke up extra early, stomachs rumbling and mouths watering with expectation, but soon realised we couldn't smell anything. We rushed to the kitchen to see the oven still glowing, and the jahnoon pot sitting there, just near it, on the cold kitchen counter.

The timing is key in this recipe. If you want it for breakfast, you need to make the dough sometime between 4pm and 7pm and then put it in the oven to bake about three hours later, depending on how early you want to wake up. That way it will have enough time to bake while you are sleeping, but not so much time that it dries out (about eight or nine hours is ideal). Once it is baked, just turn off the oven and leave it there until you are ready to eat – it'll stay warm. But do remember to put it into the oven before you go to sleep.

Makes 14 logs, which will feed 7

For the dough

500g strong white bread flour
500g plain flour
100g caster sugar
1 tbsp table salt
1 tsp bicarbonate of soda
400g/ml water, plus maybe a little more
200g/ml vegetable oil
250g unsalted butter
60g honey

To serve (if you like)

1–2 eggs per person
1 tomato per person
chilli paste or zehug (page 103)

Mix all the dry ingredients for the dough in a bowl. You can use an electric mixer with a dough hook, or simply use your hands. Add the water in a constant fast stream while mixing to form a nice supple dough. If you are using a mixer, you can work on quite a high speed to develop a lovely shine. If you are hand-kneading, get some action going and go to town – you want the end result to be supple, soft and shiny.

Once you feel the dough is as lovely as it can be, divide into 14 pieces of about 110g–120g each. Roll each into a tight ball between your palm and the work surface. Take a large cake tin or a tray with a rim and pour the vegetable oil in. Roll each ball in the oil and then leave to sit in it (with a bit of space between each one) for 30 minutes. This is an important stage as it allows the dough time to relax. You can leave it for up to an hour, but ideally no longer.

Preheat the oven to 200°C/180°C fan/gas mark 6. Melt the butter. Choose a pan ››› with a tight-fitting lid (or improvise one with plenty of foil). Line the base with a large piece of baking parchment that comes right up the sides, leaving plenty of overhang so that when everything is baked you can simply pull the whole thing out in one piece.

Moisten your hands with some of the oil in the tin or tray containing the dough balls. Pick up a ball and place it on the work surface with the really oily part on top. Then use your palms to spread the dough out as thinly as you can to create a large sheet. You should see the work surface through the dough. If you want to be accurate about it, then try to create a rectangle of 18cm x 35cm. Brush the dough sheet all over with melted butter and roll into a tight log from one of the shorter ends, so you end up with an 18cm-long log of rolled pastry, like an old scroll. Place the log in the bottom of the lined pan, as close to the edge as you can. Repeat the process with the remaining dough balls – the first ones may look a bit manky, but after you've done a few you should have mastered the process. Place each one as close as possible to the one before and continue in a single layer until the base of the pan is full. Lay the next layer at a 90 degree angle to the first, so that the two layers are at right angles.

Once all your logs are in the pan, mix the honey with whatever butter you have left and drizzle all over the top. Cover the surface directly with greaseproof paper so that it touches the dough logs. If you decide to cook eggs to go with the bread, this would be the time to place them in their shells on top of the greaseproof paper (no need to pre-cook). If not, simply seal the pot with its lid or lots of aluminium foil.

Place in the centre of the oven and bake for 20 minutes, then reduce the heat to 180°C/160°C fan/gas mark 4 for a further 20 minutes. Finally, reduce the heat to 130°C/110°C fan/gas mark ½–1 and leave for a minimum of 6 hours, or up to 9 hours for the fully caramelised version.

In the morning, simply grate your tomatoes, shell the baked eggs and serve with some chilli paste on the side, peeling away layer upon layer of buttery bread and asking yourself: how come this is the first time I've tried this dish?

Lahooh (Yemeni pancakes)

These strange pancakes resemble an English crumpet but they are thinner, more savoury and a real Yemeni staple, usually served with a soup or stew to sponge up the juices. At the restaurant we serve lahooh with meatballs on top, letting the savoury sauce soak through. I love them for breakfast with some zehug and curd cheese, or with butter and good honey, but anything goes really. Try them as part of a fry-up for an English–Yemeni fusion, or with smoked salmon and crème fraîche for something different altogether.

Makes about 8–10 pancakes using a 15cm (6 inch) frying pan

For the batter

½ stale pitta (40g)
250g plain flour
10g fresh yeast
1 tsp table salt
1 tbsp caster sugar
350g/ml water

about 50g/ml vegetable oil for frying

For the zehug paste (if you like)

2 large bunches of coriander (about 100g)
2 cloves of garlic, peeled
1 green chilli, sliced (leave the seeds in)
1 tomato, diced
¼ tsp ground cardamom pods
¼ tsp table salt
2 tbsp olive oil

Place the pitta in enough cold water to cover and soak until it is soft, then remove from the water and blitz to a purée in a food processor or with a stick blender. Transfer the purée to a large bowl (or a mixer with a paddle attachment), add all the other batter ingredients and mix to a loose consistency. Cover with cling film and leave to bubble up. This will take about 30 minutes in a warm room and a little longer in a cold one. Once bubbles have appeared, the dough is ready to fry.

Set a good non-stick frying pan on a medium heat. Place some oil in a little dish, dip a piece of kitchen paper or a heat-resistant brush in it and lightly coat the surface of the pan. Pour a ladleful of the batter into the pan and spread it around with the ladle to cover the base. Reduce the heat to minimum and cook until bubbles appear all over the surface. Use a lid (or plate) to cover for 1 minute, then remove the pancake from the pan without flipping. It should stay a very pale creamy-white colour. Repeat with the rest of the batter. You may need to cool the pan in between pancakes if they start to take on too much colour. Stack the pancakes on a plate and cover with a clean cloth until you are ready to eat. When you are, spoon some zehug over your lahooh and munch away. These taste great with curd cheese or yogurt too.

To make the zehug, discard the coriander stems and wash the leafy parts well; no need to pick the leaves off separately. Place the washed coriander, garlic, chilli and tomato in a food processor and pulse to a rough-chopped salsa. Remove to a small bowl, add the cardamom, salt and olive oil and mix well. Store in an airtight container in the fridge for a couple of days and use to add a little kick to all your food.

Mid-morning

Elevenses

We love it when HD does a morning shift. The tiny Colombian turns every room he enters into a party; laughing, chatting, dancing, and always playing salsa and Reggaeton through his phone, streaming live Colombian radio. We know its 11am when we hear the bugles and drums of the national anthem, which they play at the start of the day (the start of the day in Colombia, that is).

11am is a very important time in our kitchen. It is when we have to wrap up all the morning prep, clear the stoves and workbenches, and set up for lunch service, which generally starts at noon but can sometimes begin as early as 11.30am (hungry people). Before lunch starts, we need to chop all our herbs, dress all our salads, and taste and adjust the seasoning in all our sauces and dips. The service fridge needs to be nicely stocked, and the pass must be neatly arranged and full (any missing item can cause serious delays in the short, fast tempest that is our lunch service). The sound of the Colombian anthem played by a marching brass band brings a much-needed spring to our step as we rush to get ready.

Upstairs the girls are getting ready as well: checking we have enough menus, iced tea and lemonade; ensuring we have plenty of white wine chilling and enough chairs for everyone who has booked to come to eat with us. We try to level the feet on the tables so they don't wobble... although they will again by the time lunch finishes. Plus we need to find time to feed all our staff and send them on a break before noon.

This hectic rush behind the scenes is in stark contrast to the atmosphere among our customers at this time of the morning. The 11am crowd is made up of those who are having a lazy day and want a late breakfast; those who've been cooped up all morning and have come out for some air and something sweet; those who will skip lunch today but need some fortification; and those who have gained a magical half-hour between one appointment and the next and want to celebrate it with a slice of cake. The most laid-back crowd of the day.

Spiced cauliflower muffins

I was only working with Yara for a few weeks, handing over my job as head chef in a small café in Tel Aviv before we moved to London. I was meant to be teaching her the job, but in the end I picked up more than a few of her great recipes, among them a lovely broccoli loaf with the florets running through the centre, so that when you cut it, they looked like little trees. I've made several versions, this being my favourite, and I think about her whenever I make it – the life of a recipe. I recommend that you take the time to place the florets carefully upright in the moulds to make sure you get a little cauliflower 'tree' in the centre of each muffin, but even if you don't, you are still in for a tasty treat.

Makes 6 small muffins

1 small head of cauliflower
700g/ml water
1 tsp table salt

For the muffin batter
175g plain flour
40g caster sugar
½ tsp baking powder
2 tsp ground cumin
1 tsp ground coriander
¼ tsp turmeric
¼ tsp table salt
a pinch of white pepper
4 eggs
150g unsalted butter, melted

For topping (if you like)
3 tbsp pumpkin seeds
3 tbsp grated pecorino or Parmesan cheese

Break the cauliflower into florets, making sure there are at least six large 'trees'. (You will most likely have more than six; cook them all and save the unused florets to eat another time.) Put the water and salt in a large pan and boil the cauliflower in it until soft (this will take 5–10 minutes). Check to see whether it is done by inserting a knife tip into the stem; it should penetrate without resistance. Drain well and set aside.

Preheat the oven to 190°C/170°C fan/ gas mark 5 and butter six muffin moulds. Mix all the dry ingredients for the batter together. Add the eggs and use a spoon or spatula to mix until combined, then slowly mix in the melted butter and fold until it has all been incorporated.

Place a spoonful of batter in the centre of each mould and stand a whole floret stem-down in each. Cover with batter to fill the moulds to the top. Mix the pumpkin seeds and cheese, if using, sprinkle on the muffins and bake for 15 minutes. Remove from the tin and eat while still warm – they are best this way.

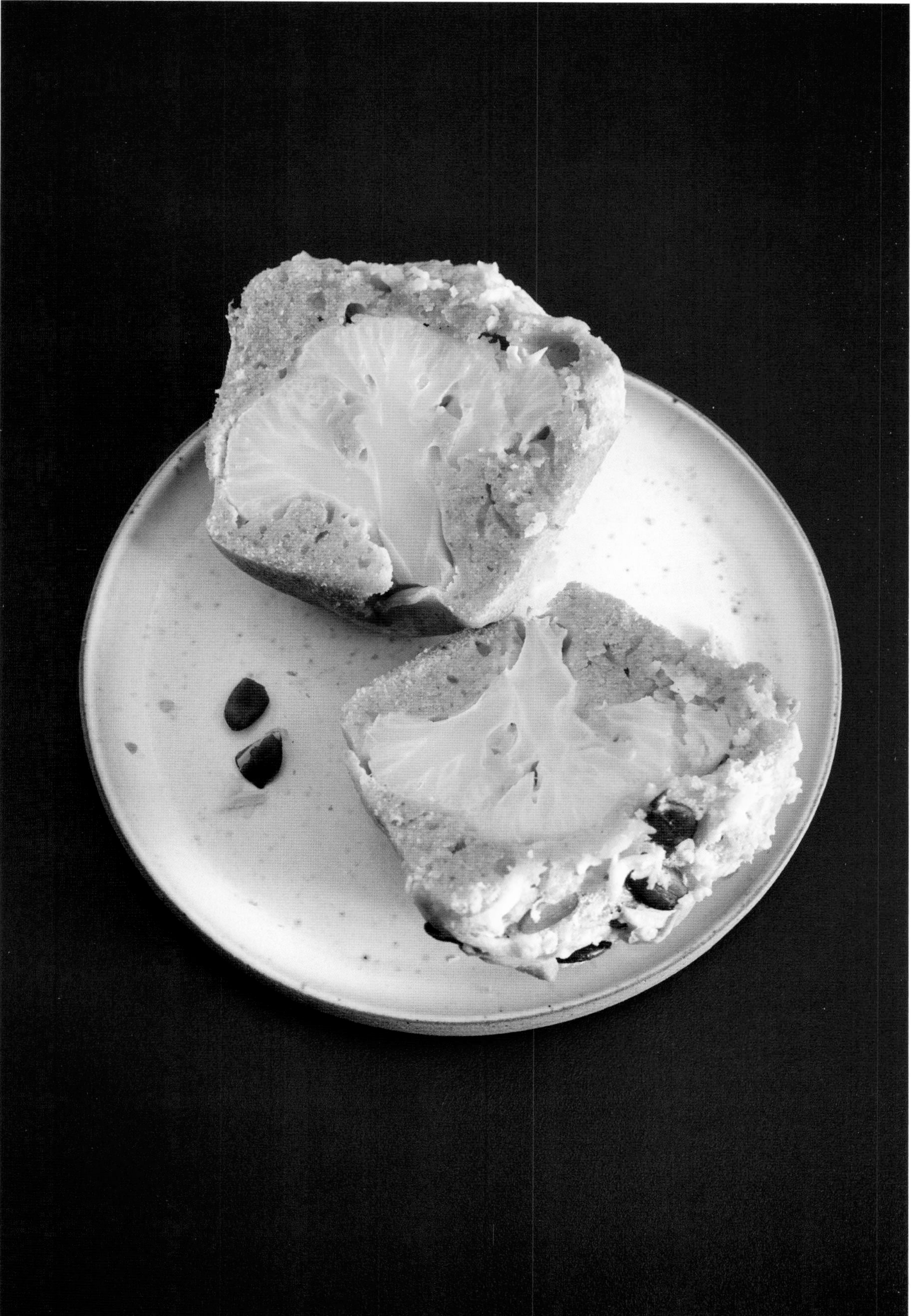

Feta & courgette muffins

Certain things should not happen: marzipan should not be in your main course and fish shouldn't feature in your pudding. We are not usually big on fusion, so if the term 'courgette muffin' makes you cringe and think of things that shouldn't be, we are with you. Perhaps we need to work on the title. However, these bakes are so delicious that any qualms you may have about their name will very soon be forgotten.

Makes 6

Bake in individual mini loaf tins or muffin moulds

300g courgettes
1 tsp table salt
200g self-raising flour
1 tsp baking powder
4 tsp za'atar
½ tsp freshly ground black pepper
50g black olives, chopped (Tassos or Kalamata work well)
100g feta cheese, crumbled
40g kashkaval or pecorino
1 tbsp fresh thyme, picked (or 1 tsp dried thyme)
3 eggs
80g grapeseed oil (or you can use olive oil)

Preheat the oven to 190°C/170°C fan/ gas mark 5. Grease the tins or muffin moulds with butter spray or brush with soft butter (or use paper muffin liners if you prefer).

Grate the courgette and mix with half the salt. Set in a colander over a bowl to extract some of the liquid. In the meantime place the remaining salt, flour, baking powder, za'atar, black pepper, chopped olives, feta, kashkaval and thyme in a large bowl. Stir lightly together to combine.

Squeeze the courgettes to remove as much liquid as you can and add to the other ingredients in the bowl. Top with the eggs and oil and stir with a wide spoon or spatula until just combined. Don't worry if there are a few lumps and don't overwork it, as you don't want the muffins to be dense. A light touch will help you achieve a light texture once baked.

Divide between the tins or moulds; there should be about 120–130g in each. Bake in the centre of the oven for 15 minutes, then turn the tray for an even bake. Leave for a further 10 minutes until the muffins feel springy to the touch. Remove from the tins to cool on a rack, or eat them hot with some yogurt or cream cheese.

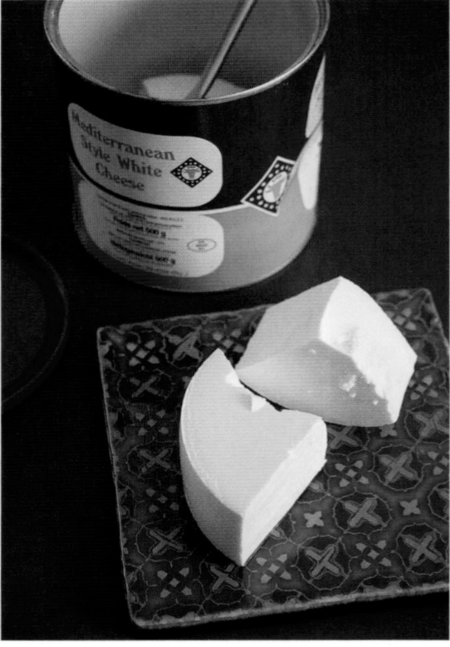

Abadi biscuits (aka ka'ach bilmalch)

Savoury snacks similar to these feature in many Middle Eastern cultures. In Israel the best and most famous brand is Abadi. They are so good that no one even thinks of making them at home – you just can't compete. We are not morning people, which is why the chef's life suits us so well. When we lived in Israel, we would get out of bed very late in the morning and buy a bag of these on our way to the beach, plus some yogurt to dip and a bottle of water. We would spend the warm early afternoon on the sand, playing backgammon, getting crumbs on the board and sand in the yogurt, whiling away the time till our evening shift started. Now we have neither the beach nor the hours to sit and play, and we have to make our own Abadi biscuits. These stand up to the original with pride. They taste quite simple when you first try them, but leave such a lovely aftertaste that you soon reach out for the next, and the next... So you might want to think twice before making this recipe, as it can lead to a lifelong addiction.

I like to use a mix of white and black sesame seeds, but you could sprinkle on whole spices to add a little something special; caraway seeds, fennel seeds or even cumin seeds would all work really well.

Makes 24 rings

250g strong white bread flour
½ tsp table salt
120g vegetable shortening, lard or margarine, cubed
½ tsp baking powder
½ tsp dried yeast
½ tsp caster sugar
90g/ml water
1 tbsp vegetable oil

To sprinkle (if you like)
black and white sesame seeds
sea salt

Place the flour, salt, cubed fat (shortening, lard or margarine) and baking powder in a bowl and rub together to a rough breadcrumb consistency. Put the yeast, sugar, water and oil in a smaller bowl and stir to dissolve the yeast. Combine the flour and yeast mixtures, either by hand or with a hook attachment in a mixer, and knead to a smooth, supple dough (about 5 minutes). Place in an oiled bowl, cover and allow to rest for 30–60 minutes at room temperature.

Preheat the oven to 200°C/180°C fan/gas mark 6 and line a couple of flat baking trays with baking parchment. If using, sprinkle some sesame seeds and sea salt onto a small flat plate. Cut the dough in 12 pieces of about 40g. Roll each piece into a snake of about 40cm long. This can be quite a tricky dough to roll, but don't worry about it too much – the rings may not look perfect, but they will still be delicious. Cut the dough snakes in half and form each piece into a ring, pinching the edges together to complete the circle. Dip each ring in the salted seeds to coat one surface, then place on the baking trays seeded-side uppermost, so that the sesame roasts nicely. Leave a little space between each one so that they don't stick together and allow to rest on the trays for 15 minutes.

Place the trays in the oven and bake for 15 minutes, then turn the tray so that it bakes evenly. Reduce the oven heat to 180°C/160°C fan/gas mark 4 for another 15 minutes until they are dark golden. Allow to cool entirely before eating. These should be really crispy and are great for scooping up hummus or labaneh, but are also nice just as a snack on their own. Store in an airtight container.

Oat, hazelnut & currant biscuits

Sometimes cheese is just an excuse for a biscuit. These are great with or without, and are really good to nibble when you get a little hungry before lunch. They feel inexplicably healthy, and the combination of nuts, dried fruit and oats makes you full and happy.

Makes about 40 biscuits

350g plain flour
80g light brown soft sugar
5g table salt
10g baking powder
50g oats
150g cold butter, diced
100–120g/ml milk
80g dried currants
80g roasted hazelnuts, roughly chopped
a sprinkling of sea salt (if you like)

Place the flour, sugar, table salt, baking powder and oats in a mixer with a paddle attachment (or in a large bowl that you can get your hands in easily). Add the diced butter and either rub between fingertips or use a slow speed on the mixer until you have a rough breadcrumb consistency. Use just enough of the milk to form a lovely dough and then mix in the dried fruit and nuts.

Divide the dough in half and roll each piece into a log about 20cm long. Wrap each in cling film and place in the fridge to set for at least an hour (or up to 48 hours, if you are making ahead).

When you are ready to bake, preheat the oven to 190°C/170°C fan/gas mark 5 and line a couple of flat baking sheets with baking parchment. Take the dough logs out of the fridge, remove the cling film and slice them into thin discs (about 1cm). You should get 18–20 biscuits from each log. Lay them flat on the baking trays, allowing 1–2cm between each (they won't change too much in size) and sprinkle with the sea salt, if using.

Bake for 10 minutes, then turn the trays around for an even bake and leave for another 5–10 minutes until the biscuits are golden all over. Lift one up carefully (they will be hot – as you would be if you had just sat in a hot oven for 15–20 minutes) and check the underside to make sure it is golden too. Don't worry if they seem a little soft now; they will crisp as they cool and the oats drink up any excess moisture.

Cool on a rack and, once cold, store in an airtight container. These last well for about a week, but I think you'll find they disappear way before then.

Breakfast bars

Not exactly cakes but not quite anything else either, these are great pick-me-ups that really come into their own when you just need a little something to bridge the gap till lunch.

Strawberry-hazelnut slice

We met Tim sitting at one of our pavement tables on a sunny morning. Our waitresses were hovering around, checking out his massive mop of curly hair and lovely eyes. We offered him a slice of our latest experiment and discussed what we should call it – Hazelberry? Strawbernut? He tried to convince us to come and make a TV pilot with him. We laughed out loud and said he was crazy. And that unless he could find a camera that would make instant Photoshop improvements, he had the wrong couple. So many things happen to us by accident and we never know what will be the next crazy idea to come through the door, but we do know it should always be considered over a slice of cake, and there is none better than this for clarity of mind and nourishment of soul. There are so many possible variations: you could use apple and blueberry; figs; pear and blackberry; currants and raspberries; or gooseberries. They would all work well, but I simply love strawberries.

Fills a 12cm x 35cm (or 20cm x 30cm) rectangular tin

Makes 8 bars

For the dough

- *150g unsalted butter*
- *115g caster sugar*
- *115g ground hazelnuts*
- *1 egg yolk*
- *150g plain flour*
- *1 tsp ground cinnamon*
- *a pinch of ground cloves (if you like, or use ground nutmeg instead)*

For the topping

- *200g strawberries, stems removed and cut into quarters*
- *1 tbsp cornflour*
- *1 tbsp caster sugar*
- *50g hazelnuts, roughly chopped*

Preheat the oven to 190°C/170°C fan/ gas mark 5 and line the tin with a piece of baking parchment that covers the base and comes a little way up the sides.

Cream the butter with the sugar, then add the ground hazelnuts and egg yolk and combine. Mix in the flour and spices to form a rough dough – it will bind but try not to overwork it, as you will be crumbling it. Set aside 100g of the dough and crumble the rest over the bottom of the tin. Top with the quartered strawberries, sprinkle with the cornflour and sugar and then crumble the remaining dough over the top in small clumps. Finally sprinkle with the roughly chopped hazelnuts.

Bake for 15 minutes. Turn the tray so that it bakes evenly and leave for another 10 minutes until the dough pieces on top are nicely browned. Allow to cool in the tin and only remove once it is completely cold. You can now cut the bar into eight thick fingers that are ready to eat or be packed in your lunch box. It is best to store these in the fridge, as they are made with fresh fruit so will not last longer than a day or so at room temperature (they will keep in the fridge for up to a week).

Coconut slice

Gluten, it seems, is public enemy No. 1 these days, on a par with smoking and drink-driving, and everyone is looking for recipes without it. In the eight days of Passover every (observant) Jew is required to avoid eating food made with flour, so over the centuries, we Jews have amassed plenty of flour-free (and therefore gluten-free) recipes. The two of us are not religious and cannot imagine a life without bread – not one that is worth living anyway. We enjoy this slice simply because it tastes great. It is a rich and nourishing bar that can easily be packed into your lunchbox for a late-morning energy boost, or cut into tiny cubes to eat as a small treat any time, no matter what your religion or opinion on gluten.

Fills a 23cm (9 inch) square tin

You can cut into whatever sized bar you want (we can never agree on the perfect size)

Gluten-free

100g dark chocolate (at least 56% cocoa solids)
150g caster sugar
200g desiccated coconut
50g dried sour cherries
50g pistachios, roughly chopped
50g whole almonds, roughly chopped
100g unsalted butter, melted
2 eggs

Line a 23cm x 23cm baking tin with a large piece of baking parchment to cover the base and about 5cm up the sides.

Melt the chocolate in a heatproof bowl over a pan of boiling water or in the microwave (see notes on page 12). Pour into the lined tin, spread around to cover the base entirely and chill in the fridge until the chocolate is completely set. In the meantime preheat the oven to 190°C/170°C fan/gas mark 5.

Mix the dry ingredients together in a bowl, pour the melted butter over and use a large spoon to combine. Add the eggs, stir thoroughly, then tip the mixture into the tin, on top of the set chocolate. Smooth out to create an even layer, but leave the surface a little messy.

Bake in the centre of the oven for 10 minutes. Turn the tray so it bakes evenly and leave for another 6–8 minutes or until the coconut is all golden on top. Remove from the oven and allow to sit for about 10–15 minutes before transferring the tin to the fridge to cool for at least 2 hours. Once fully cold, remove from the tin, peel off the layer of baking parchment and using a warmed sharp knife slice into whatever size pieces you fancy.

Oat slice with apricots & orange blossom

I use semi-dried apricots for this recipe to keep the bars moist, but if you can only find dried ones, simply soak them in hot water for 20 minutes and drain before chopping.

Makes 12 decent-sized bars

250g semi-dried apricots
100g pecans, roughly chopped
50g pine nuts
50g dried golden berries (physalis) or golden raisins
zest of 1 orange
300g rolled oats
1 tbsp orange blossom water
125g grapeseed oil (or another pure vegetable oil)
125g caster sugar
125g honey (orange blossom honey works best)
a pinch of saffron (if you like)

Preheat the oven to 190°C/170°C fan/ gas mark 5 and line a shallow tray or tin with baking parchment. I use a rectangular 20cm x 25cm tray, but if you don't have one, use a larger one and don't quite fill it – this is a firm mixture that will hold its shape. Just make sure that whatever you use is at least 5cm deep (the depth of the bars).

Roughly chop the apricots into thirds or quarters and mix in a large bowl with the pecans, pine nuts, berries or raisins, orange zest and rolled oats. Stir in the orange blossom water to combine.

Bring the oil, sugar, honey and a pinch of saffron (if using) to the boil in a large pan, mixing all the while with a long-handled spoon. Once the whole surface is bubbling and the ingredients look well combined, tip in the oat mixture. Stir thoroughly until the oats and fruit are coated in the syrup, taking care as this gets really hot.

Transfer to the lined tray. Lay a piece of baking parchment on the surface of the mixture and press down to flatten to an even depth of about 5cm. Remove the piece of baking parchment and bake for 15–20 minutes until golden all over. Allow to cool entirely in the tray before cutting in half lengthways and then in six across, to make 12 bars in total. These will keep in an airtight container for 3–4 days.

Soured cream, pecan & cinnamon mini loaves

This is an easy mix-and-bake number. It is not the star of the show, just the ultimate sidekick for your mid-morning coffee. It is best eaten warm (or dunked in your morning drink).

Not strictly a bar, this makes 8 small loaves (or bake in a 2kg loaf tin and slice)

1 vanilla pod
125g soft butter
zest of 1 orange
275g caster sugar
3 eggs
140g/ml soured cream
160g self-raising flour
a pinch of table salt

To sprinkle
50g dark brown soft sugar
½ tsp ground cinnamon
¼ tsp ground cardamom
90g roasted pecans, roughly chopped

Preheat the oven to 190°C/170°C fan/ gas mark 5. Grease eight small loaf tins with butter spray and, if you wish, line each with a strip of baking parchment to cover the base and long sides, allowing a little to overhang so that this can be used to help lift the loaves out later.

Scrape the seeds out of the vanilla pod (see notes on page 19). Beat the butter, vanilla seeds, orange zest and sugar until just combined. The mixture should come together in a ball but take care not to overbeat or cream. Add the eggs one at a time, incorporating each one fully so that the mixture is completely smooth before adding the next. Mix in the soured cream, then the flour and salt (if you are using a mixer, you can work at full speed for a few seconds at this stage to make sure everything is well combined).

Mix the sugar, spices and pecans together. Divide half the batter between the loaf tins and spread to cover the bases. Then divide half the nut mixture between the tins, sprinkling it over the batter. Divide the remaining batter between the tins and top with the rest of the sugar-and-spice nuts.

Bake for 10 minutes, then turn the tins for an even bake. Leave for a further 10 minutes before removing from the oven. (If you are baking this in one large loaf tin, you will need to leave it for another 15–20 minutes to cook through.) Eat warm.

Rich fruit loaves

I love a thick, sticky fruit cake. This is my English heritage talking, as there is no tradition of these heavily spiced fruit cakes in the Middle East. I think it is just too hot to eat them, but in the UK, with its cold grey weather, they really hit the spot. Here are my three variations on the fruit cake theme, each with a distinct character and slight Middle Eastern twist. We use the fruit and nut loaf (below) as our version of a Christmas cake. Once baked, we halve it and fill it with a layer of marzipan.

Fruit & nut loaf

My first kitchen job was at Orna and Ella, a café in Tel Aviv. I worked there on and off for five years, and if I know anything important about food and people, I learnt it there. Every year around September the pastry section would go into a frenzy, baking honey cakes for the Jewish new year. The smell of them would fill the entire street, and drive us mad in the kitchen. Containing every kind of spice, plus coffee, tea and (obviously) honey, these cakes were legend. We would give them away to our regular customers and to all our suppliers, and each of us got one (or three) with best wishes for a sweet year to come. At Honey & Co we kept the tradition but changed the cake and moved the baking frenzy to the end of December, so that each staff member leaves for their Christmas holiday with our best wishes, and our cake.

This is a rich loaf with very little cake batter and lots and lots of fruit. You need to soak the dried fruit in tea and brandy for at least an hour, or ideally overnight. I candy my own lemon or cedro (aka citron) and orange peel using the method on page 44, but you can use a shop-bought selection if you prefer. Similarly, the fruit and nuts here are my suggestion – use your favourite combination, but do keep the sour cherries, as they give a special tangy burst of flavour now and again which makes this loaf really special.

Makes
a 1kg (2lb) loaf

For the dried fruit (200g in total)

- *50g golden raisins*
- *50g dried currants*
- *50g dried cranberries*
- *50g dried sour cherries*
- *1 mug of strong black tea*
- *3 tbsp brandy, plus 1 tbsp*

For the nuts (200g in total; I use whole nuts with the skin on)

- *50g pistachios*
- *50g hazelnuts*
- *50g almonds*
- *50g walnuts*

For the candied fruit (150g in total)

- *50g candied orange peel, cut in thick strips*
- *50g candied ginger, cut in rough dice*
- *50g candied cedro or lemon peel, cut in thick strips*

For the cake batter

- *75g/ml whole milk*
- *75g/ml golden syrup*
- *25g unsalted butter*
- *50g caster sugar*
- *50g dark brown soft sugar*
- *140g self-raising flour*
- *1 tbsp sweet spice mix (page 48)*
- *a pinch of table salt*
- *1 egg*

Put the dried fruit in a large bowl and make a strong cup of tea (better still, make two cups, so that you can drink one while the fruit soaks in the other). Pour the tea and brandy over the fruit and leave to soak for at least one hour (or ideally overnight). While it is soaking, roast the nuts for 6 minutes at 190°C/170°C fan/gas mark 5 and prepare your other ingredients.

Drain the soaked fruit in a sieve over a large bowl. Retain the soaking liquid, add the extra tablespoon of brandy to it and set aside. Preheat the oven to 180°C/160°C fan/gas mark 4. Butter a 1kg (2lb) loaf tin and line with a sheet of baking parchment to cover the base and long sides, allowing a little overhang so that this can be used to help lift the loaf out later.

Warm the milk, golden syrup, butter, caster sugar and dark brown sugar together in a large saucepan until the sugars have dissolved and the mixture is just starting to boil. Remove from the heat and stir in the flour, spice and salt. Mix in the drained fruit, whole roasted nuts and candied fruit, then add the egg and combine thoroughly. Transfer to the lined tin and smooth the top.

Bake in the centre of the oven for about 30 minutes, then turn the tin around for an even bake and leave for another 20 minutes. At this stage it should feel nice and bouncy. If it still feels a little soft, bake for a further 10 minutes until it does feel bouncy.

Remove from the oven and use the retained soaking liquid to douse the cake all over (I prick the surface with a toothpick or skewer before dousing to help the syrup to sink all the way in). Allow to cool in the tin, then wrap in cling film and store at room temperature. This keeps well for 2 weeks and improves with time. If you are feeling Christmassy, you can cover it with marzipan and decorate (or do as we do: cut it in half and fill the middle with a layer of marzipan).

Ginger & date cake

This cake embodies the best of traditional British baking: it is dark and moist, glistens with molasses and is perfumed with all the spice of a Dickensian Christmas. But at the same time the flavours are Middle Eastern: ginger, cinnamon, cardamom and sweet dates. This perhaps is the happy meeting point for our country of origin and our adopted one.

Makes a 1kg (2lb) loaf

150g/ml double cream
150g date molasses (or black treacle), plus more to glaze (if you like)
50g unsalted butter
100g dark brown soft sugar
200g self-raising flour
2 tsp ground ginger
2 tsp ground cinnamon
½ tsp ground cardamom
½ tsp table salt
130g pitted dates, chopped
50g crystallised ginger, chopped, plus more to garnish (if you like)
1 egg

Preheat the oven to 180°C/160°C fan/ gas mark 4. Butter a 1kg (2lb) loaf tin and line with a sheet of baking parchment to cover the base and long sides, allowing a little overhang so that this can be used to help lift the cake out later.

Warm the cream, date molasses, butter and sugar together in a large saucepan until the sugar has dissolved and the mixture is just starting to boil. Remove from the heat and stir in the flour, spices and salt. Mix in the chopped dates and ginger, then add the egg and combine thoroughly before transferring the batter to the lined tin.

Bake in the centre of the oven for about 30 minutes, then turn the tin around for an even bake and leave for another 30 minutes. At this stage it should still be a little soft to the touch, but stable and with a lovely thick crust. You can't really test this cake with a toothpick as it has a gooey texture even when fully baked, but if you push down a little with the tip of your finger in the centre and it doesn't sink, remove from the oven. If you feel there is still quite a bit of softness there, bake for a further 10 minutes, but do take it out after that – you will just have to trust me that it will be fine once it has cooled. As soon as the cake comes out of the oven, brush it generously with the extra date molasses (if using) and leave to cool in the tin.

If you want to make this look really special, chop up some more crystallised ginger, toss it in caster sugar and sprinkle the pieces all over the sticky top. Don't worry if you can't be bothered; it is delicious just as it is. This is a cake that improves with age (within reason), so it is even better the day after baking, and lasts well for a couple of weeks in an airtight container.

Fig, orange & walnut loaf

This is the unsung hero of our cake counter. It is plain-looking compared to the others, and none of the ingredients has the sex appeal of chocolate, say, or fresh fruit, but if you eat it toasted with butter and whole orange marmalade (page 41), as we serve it, you will understand its popularity. Every so often we get a call asking us to reserve a whole loaf. We know who it is for: a friendly group of pensioners from a village in Devon (quite a posh village, I suspect) who had it once on a visit to London. Now, whenever one of them is in town, they pick up a loaf and a jar of marmalade for the rest of group. We love the thought of slices of our cake being passed around from house to house, like contraband, in a quaint village halfway across the land.

We got a lot of grief for not including this in our previous book, so here it is now, humble and glorious. The secret to its success is the use of candied orange peel. You can either candy it yourself (page 44) or, if you can't be bothered, use the best quality you can buy. Alternatively, just come to us before noon for a freshly toasted slice of this loaf; we promise always to have it on our menu.

Makes a 1kg (2lb) loaf

120g/ml whole milk
120g honey
40g unsalted butter
75g caster sugar
75g light brown soft sugar
230g self-raising flour
4 tsp sweet spice mix (page 48)
½ tsp table salt
75g walnuts, roughly chopped
75g dried figs, each cut in 4 pieces
75g candied orange peel (page 44 or shop-bought), cut in strips
1 egg
30g demerara sugar to sprinkle

Preheat the oven to 180°C/160°C fan/ gas mark 4. Butter a 1kg (2lb) loaf tin and line with a sheet of baking parchment to cover the base and long sides, allowing a little overhang so that this can be used to help lift the loaf out later.

Warm the milk, honey, butter, caster sugar and light brown sugar together in a large saucepan until the sugars have dissolved and the mixture is just starting to boil. Remove from the heat and stir in the flour, spice and salt. Mix in the walnuts, quartered figs and candied orange peel, then add the egg and combine thoroughly before transferring the batter to the lined tin. Smooth the top and sprinkle with the demerara sugar.

Bake in the centre of the oven for about 30 minutes, then turn the tin around for an even bake and leave for another 30 minutes. At this stage it should still be a little soft to the touch, but stable and with a lovely thick crust. You can't really test this cake with a toothpick as it contains so much fruit, but if you push down a little with the tip of your finger in the centre and it doesn't sink, remove from the oven. If you feel there is still quite a bit of softness there, bake for another 10 minutes, but do take it out after that. Allow to cool in the tin.

This is lovely just as it is, but at Honey & Co we serve thick slices with salty butter and orange marmalade. It keeps well for a couple of weeks in an airtight container and, once you think it is losing its lustre, simply toast it.

Vegan loaf cake

This was a revelation to me. How can a cake containing no eggs or dairy taste so good? Well, I have no idea, but it does. You can bake this as written, or use it as the base batter (with the necessary changes to spices and dried fruits) for any of the fruity loaf cakes (in the three previous recipes).

Makes a 450g (1lb) loaf

175g caster sugar
250g plain flour
a pinch of table salt
½ tsp bicarbonate of soda
1 tsp ground ginger
1 tsp ground cinnamon
100g water
100g date molasses
100g vegetable oil
40g demerara sugar to sprinkle

Preheat the oven to 190°C/170°C fan/ gas mark 5. Butter a 450g (1lb) loaf tin and line with a sheet of baking parchment to cover the base and long sides, allowing a little overhang so that this can be used to help lift the loaf cake out later. If you are making this as the base batter for one of the fruit variations on the previous pages, use a 1kg (2lb) loaf tin.

Combine the sugar, flour, salt, bicarbonate of soda and spices in a large bowl. Mix the water, molasses and oil in a small saucepan and bring to the boil, stirring so it doesn't burn. Once the first bubbles appear, pour the hot syrup over the dry ingredients and stir to combine. Transfer to the lined tin, smooth the top and sprinkle with the demerara sugar to create a crust.

Bake for 20 minutes, then turn the tin around for an even bake and leave for another 10–15 minutes. The cake should feel bouncy to the touch. Allow to cool entirely in the tin before removing and slicing. This keeps well for up to 5 days in an airtight container.

Selection
ARABICA 100%
Selection
NAJJAR
NAJJAR
Honey & Co.

3 versions of yeast cake (babka)

It is a brave soul who attempts these cakes, as there are so many processes involved: making the dough, filling it, rolling it, proving it, baking it... but it's the brave that get the glory. And although there are multiple processes, each is quite simple, and if you follow these instructions carefully, success is guaranteed. The pride you'll feel as the plaited loaf comes out of the oven; the particular joy of pouring the syrup on top, hearing it hiss and seeing it disappear as it soaks in; slicing into it and seeing the beautiful layers of filling and dough – pure joy and comfort; and, best of all, sitting down to enjoy that first taste with a cup of strong, dark coffee. Nothing you have baked before is likely to give more satisfaction on so many levels.

The filling variations are endless and there are many ways to shape the loaf too. At Honey & Co we mainly use these:

- **Plain closed plait:** This is by far the easiest. Two coils of rolled pastry are twisted around each other so all the filling is encased and stays nice and moist. Not the most impressive from the outside, but glorious once you cut into it.

- **Krantz:** Beautiful and inviting, this is my favourite shape, as it allows the filling to spill out a little and caramelise in the corners, adding a little something special. It is made by cutting the rolled filled dough in half lengthways, exposing the inner layers, then twisting the two halves together.

- **Roses:** The dough is initially filled and rolled as for a krantz cake, but instead of being halved lengthways, it is cut into 5cm slices which are arranged in a round baking tin. The filled spirals join together as they prove and bake to form a lovely cake that resembles a bunch of roses.

These cakes take a little practice, but even if your first attempts aren't very pretty, they will still taste great. They last well for 2–3 days at room temperature, but are best on the day of baking.

Yeast dough

This base dough is very butter-rich and needs to be cold when you work it, so don't take it out of the fridge until you are ready to fill and shape it.

Makes enough dough for one cake (about 620g)

20g fresh yeast (or 2 tsp dried yeast)
330g strong white bread flour
40g caster sugar
a pinch of table salt
1 whole egg
85g/ml milk
90g unsalted butter, at room temperature

Crumble the yeast into the flour, sugar and salt in a mixer bowl with a hook attachment and mix together. (If you are using dried yeast, dissolve it in the milk before adding to the flour.) Add the egg, milk and butter and combine to form a dough that comes together in a ball. This will take about 5–6 minutes on a medium speed. Cover the bowl and chill in the fridge for at least 6 hours or overnight.

Poppy seed roses

Every week I buy flowers for the restaurant at the stall outside Brixton tube; and every week I am surprised to find people on the tube smiling at me as I head to work with them. I am not sure if it is the blooms themselves that get the smiles or the comedy of a fat man trying to negotiate the Victoria line at rush hour with a massive bunch of flowers. My relationship with the stallholder was initially rather strange. Sometimes he would recognise me and be very friendly – have a chat, even throw in the occasional bunch for free; other times he'd act as if he'd never seen me before. I put it down to eccentricity until I saw the two of them together one day. Twins.

Makes a 23cm (9 inch) round cake

1 batch yeast dough (page 131)
a little egg wash (1 egg beaten with a pinch of table salt), if you like
200g/ml base sugar syrup (page 59)

For the filling
150g poppy seeds, ground (use a spice or coffee grinder)
150g/ml milk
150g caster sugar
1 tbsp honey
2 tbsp dried currants
zest of a lemon
35g unsalted butter
1 egg

Combine the poppy seeds with the milk and caster sugar in a medium saucepan over a low heat, stirring to dissolve the sugar. Once the mix has come together in a gloopy paste, add the honey, currants and lemon zest. Bring to a slow boil, stirring occasionally. When it starts to bubble, remove from the heat and stir in the butter until it melts. Set aside for 15–30 minutes, then mix in the egg until the filling is shiny and well-combined.

Place the chilled dough on a lightly floured surface and roll into a rectangle of about 40cm x 30cm. Spread the filling over the dough, reaching right to the corners, then roll up tightly from one of the longer sides, so that you end up with a 40cm-long log.

Lift the log onto a tray and place in the fridge for 15–20 minutes to chill and firm up. While you are waiting, lightly grease a 23cm round cake tin and line with baking parchment.

Use a pastry cutter or sharp knife to cut the log into seven slices, each about 5cm wide. Place one in the centre of the tin with the filling spiral facing upwards, then place the others (also spiral-upwards) in a circle around it, leaving a little space between each. Leave to prove in a warm place until the dough is fluffy, soft and doubled in size (this should take about 1–1½ hours).

Preheat the oven to 220°C/200°C fan/gas mark 7. If you are using the egg wash, brush over the surface of the dough spirals. Bake in the oven for 10 minutes, then turn the tin around for an even bake and leave for another 10 minutes.

Remove from the oven and immediately pour the sugar syrup all over the hot cake. Leave to rest in the tin. It will be ready to eat in 10 minutes, but beware: it will be hot. To serve, simply cut a wedge or pull a rose out.

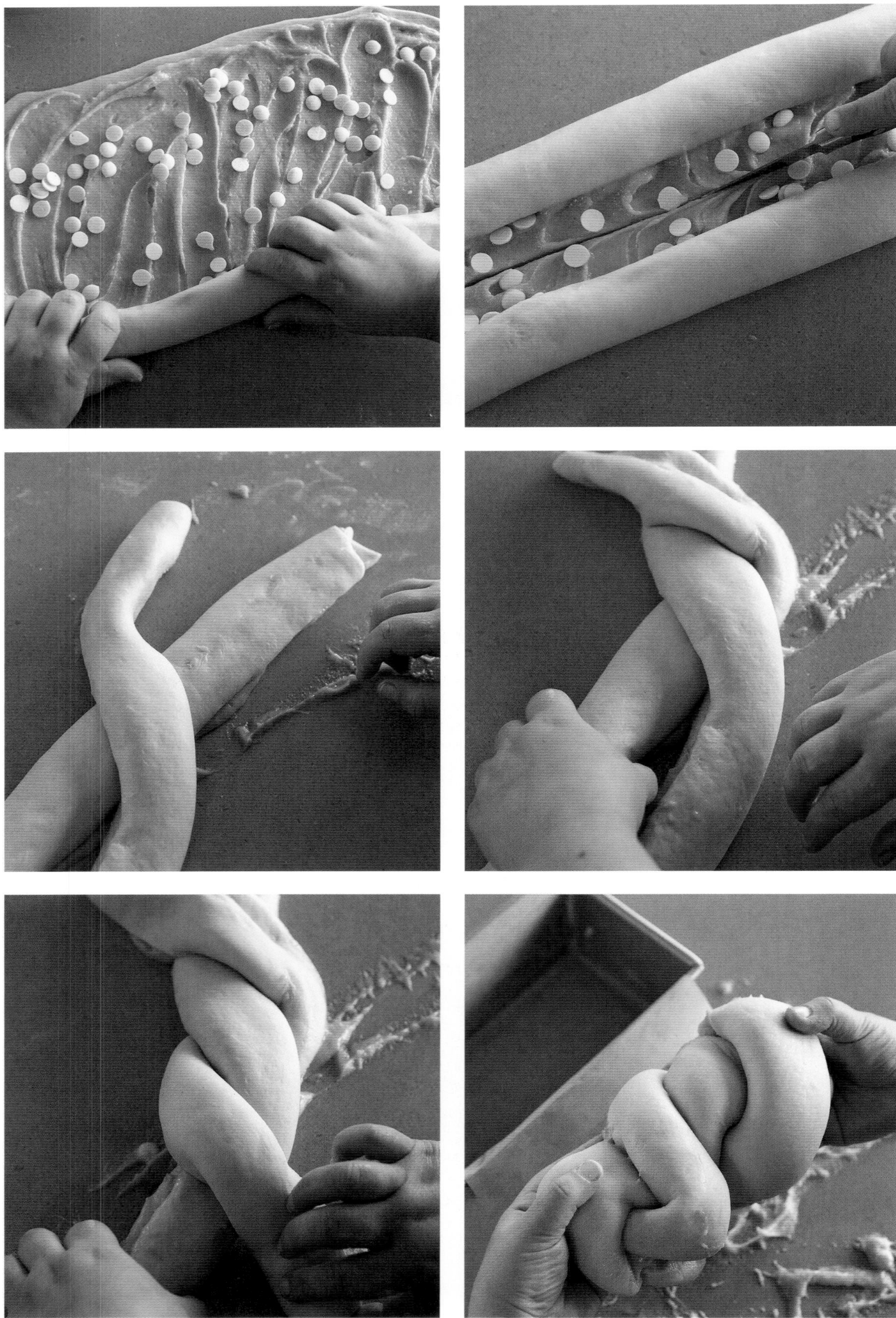

Tahini & white chocolate plait

Fills a 1kg (2lb) loaf tin

1 batch yeast dough
a little egg wash (1 egg beaten with a pinch of table salt), if you like
200g/ml base sugar syrup (page 59)

For the filling
200g tahini paste
200g/ml double cream
100g caster sugar
100g white chocolate, cut in small pieces

Mix the tahini with the cream and sugar in a bowl until combined. Butter the loaf tin and line the base and long sides with a sheet of baking parchment, making sure that there is an overhang so that you will be able to lift the baked plait out easily.

Place the chilled dough on a lightly floured surface and roll into a rectangle of about 40cm x 60cm (the longer edge closest to you). Spread the filling over the dough, then sprinkle with the pieces of white chocolate. Roll up the dough from the long edge closest to you until you reach the centre of the rectangle, then stop. Now roll down from the long edge furthest away from you, continuing until you meet the first log in the middle. The two logs should be of the same thickness. Use a sharp knife to cut through the dough connecting the logs and separate them. Then simply twist the two logs over each other to create a plait. Lift into the lined baking tin and leave to prove in a warm place until the plait looks taut, feels soft and has doubled in size (about 1½ hours).

Preheat the oven to 220°C/200°C fan/gas mark 7. If you are using the egg wash, brush over the surface of the plait. Bake in the oven for 10 minutes, then turn the tin around for an even bake and leave for another 10 minutes. Reduce the heat to 180°C/160°C fan/gas mark 4 and bake for a further 20 minutes.

Remove from the oven and immediately pour the sugar syrup all over the hot plait. You can make a couple of holes with a skewer or toothpick to speed this up, or just be patient and allow the syrup to seep slowly in. Once all the syrup has been absorbed and the cake has rested in the tin for at least 30 minutes, it is ready to eat.

Chocolate, hazelnut & cinnamon krantz loaf

Fills a 1kg (2lb) loaf tin

1 batch yeast dough
a little egg wash (1 egg beaten with a pinch of table salt), if you like
200g/ml base sugar syrup (page 59)

For the filling
100g unsalted butter
190g caster sugar
80g 70% dark chocolate
40g dark cocoa powder
1 tsp ground cinnamon
60g roasted hazelnuts, roughly chopped

Melt the butter in a small saucepan over a medium-low heat. Remove from the heat, tip the sugar in and stir to dissolve. Add the chocolate, cocoa and cinnamon and mix to combine. Set aside to cool a little at room temperature (don't place it in the fridge, as it will set solid).

Place the chilled dough on a lightly floured surface and roll into a rectangle of about 50cm x 30cm. Spread the filling over the dough, reaching right to the corners, then sprinkle with the hazelnuts. Roll up tightly from one of the longer sides, so that you end up with a 50cm-long log. If the dough has softened too much for you to handle it, place on a tray and chill in the fridge for 10 minutes to firm up. While you are waiting, butter the loaf tin and line the base and long sides with baking parchment, making sure that there is an overhang so that you will be able to lift the baked loaf out easily.

Use a pastry cutter or sharp knife to cut the log in half along its length to expose the layers. Place the halves with the cut sides facing upwards. Lift one halved log over the other so that they form a cross at their midpoints, with the filling layers still pointing upwards. Continue to twist the strands over each other until the dough looks like a lovely twisted plait. Place in the lined baking tin and leave to prove in a warm place until the dough is fluffy, soft and doubled in size. This will take about 1½ hours in a warm kitchen, or up to 2 hours if it is chilly.

Preheat the oven to 220°C/200°C fan/gas mark 7. If you are using the egg wash, brush all over the surface. Bake in the oven for 10 minutes, then turn the tin around for an even bake and leave for another 10 minutes. Reduce the heat to 190°C/170°C fan/gas mark 5 and bake for a further 10 minutes.

Remove from the oven and immediately pour the sugar syrup all over the hot cake. You must let this cool in the tin or it will fall apart. I know this is hard, but practise some restraint. It will be worth the wait.

5 a day

The '5 a day' campaign was created to improve the nation's health by encouraging us to eat more fruit and vegetables. We are not campaigners, nor are we claiming that the following five cakes will improve your health. We eat fruit and vegetables because we like them, and we make these cakes because they are delicious. But if you are inclined to believe that these five are better for you than other cakes, we will not ruin it for you.

Putting fruit or vegetables in the batter adds plenty of flavour and moisture to your cake, but should be done with care – too much moisture will ruin it, and while a tiny earthy note is nice, nobody wants their cake to taste too veggie or (God forbid) healthy. The five here have proved a big hit with our customers, perhaps all convincing themselves that a slice of cake can count as one of their '5 a day'.

Icing is a bone of contention in our kitchen: Sarit is against, I am wholly in favour. I think most cakes need at least a finger-thick layer of frothy icing on top. We've kept the following cakes dairy-free, but if you're an icing fiend like me, here are two that work well with these cakes. Both can be made either in a mixer or by hand (we use a mixer).

Cream cheese icing

Makes enough to top 1 cake

125g unsalted butter, at room temperature
150g icing sugar
300g full fat cream cheese, at room temperature

Place the butter and icing sugar in a mixer bowl with a paddle attachment and cream together on a medium speed until very light and fluffy. Keep mixing as you feed in the cream cheese a little at a time until fully incorporated. Do make sure the cream cheese is at room temperature (you can heat it for about 10 seconds in the microwave if it is fresh from the fridge), as this gives a nice fluffy texture to the icing.

Mascarpone icing

Makes enough to top 1 cake

200g mascarpone cheese
150g full fat cream cheese
150g icing sugar
50g/ml double cream
seeds from 1 vanilla pod

Place all the ingredients in a mixer bowl with a paddle attachment. Cream together on a slow speed until the icing thickens. Don't use a whisk or you risk splitting it.

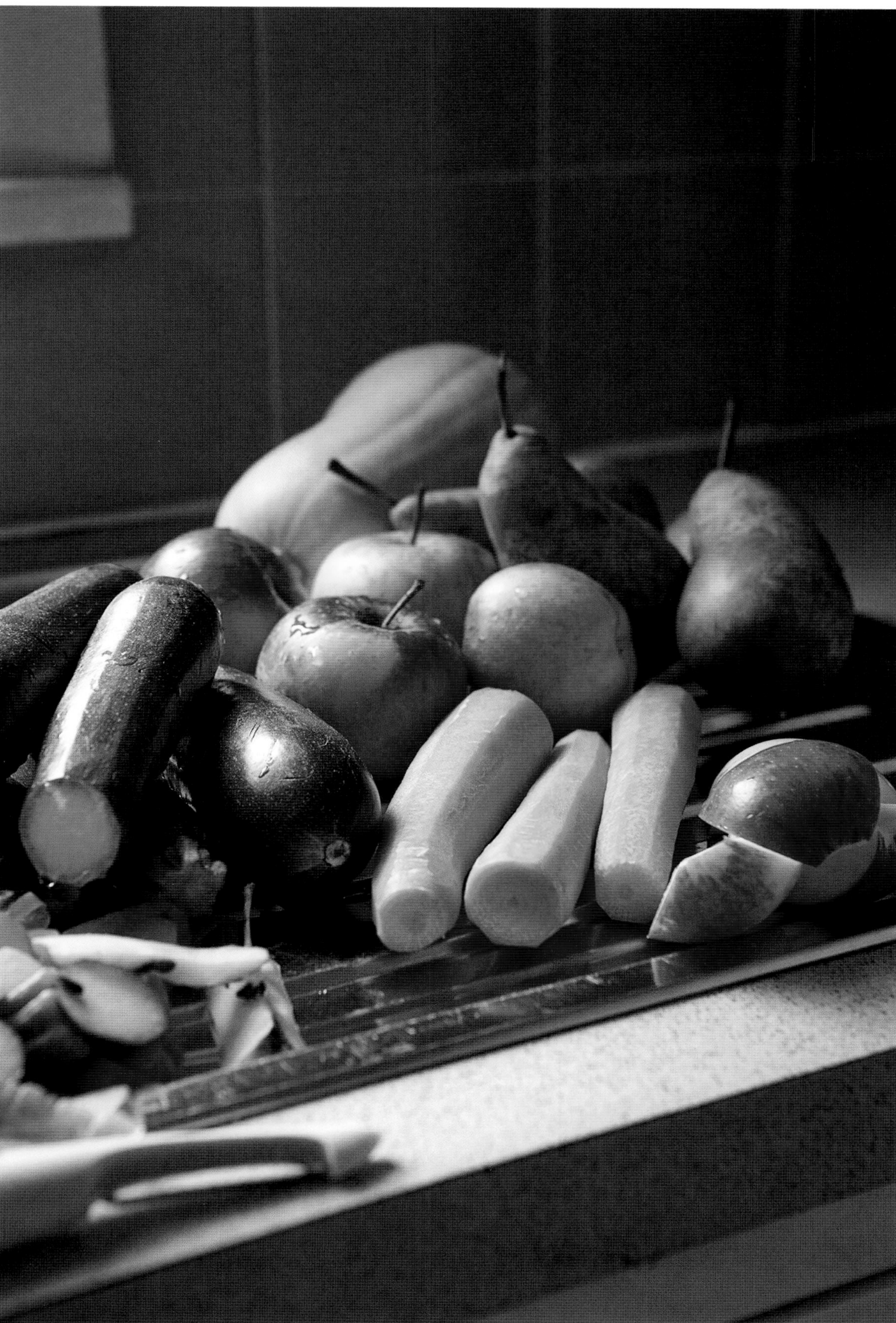

Apple cake with lemon & chocolate flecks

This is the cake I would choose above all others. It is my mother's go-to cake, the one that was always on the kitchen counter. Although my wife made a few changes to the recipe, the essence and goodness are unchanged.

Makes a 1kg (2lb) loaf cake

2 tbsp whisky
zest and juice of 1 lemon
2 apples (200g once diced, skin-on) – I use Pink Lady apples
40g bitter chocolate (70% cacao works best here)
2 eggs
160g caster sugar
120g/130ml vegetable oil
150g plain flour
1½ tsp baking powder
1 tsp ground nutmeg
1 tsp ground fennel seeds (I always grind my own)
a pinch of table salt

Preheat the oven to 180°C/160°C fan/ gas mark 4. Butter a 1kg (2lb) loaf tin and line the base and long sides with a sheet of baking parchment, making sure that there is enough of an overhang to ease removal of the cake later.

Mix the whisky in a bowl with the lemon juice and zest. Cut the apples in small cubes (the size of playing dice) and toss them in the whisky mixture. I like to leave the peel on, especially when using red-skinned apples, as it looks so pretty in the final result. Set aside until later.

Chop the chocolate into slivers like little flecks and set in the fridge to stay cold. In a large bowl, or using a mixer with a whisk attachment, whisk the eggs with the sugar until they start to puff up and go pale. Slowly pour in the oil until it has all been incorporated. Get rid of the whisk and use a spatula or wooden spoon to fold in the flour, baking powder, nutmeg, fennel and salt to a smooth consistency. Then fold in the diced apple and whisky mixture, and finally fold in the chilled chocolate flecks.

Transfer the batter to the lined tin and bake for 35 minutes. Turn the tin around for an even bake, then leave for another 15–20 minutes. It should be bouncy to the touch and the house should be filled with the aroma of baking apples. Allow to cool in the tin for at least 15 minutes before devouring.

To me this cake needs no topping at all. But if you are making it at teatime and you want to spoil yourself, use one of the icings on page 138 or whip up a small tub of double cream with a tablespoon of whisky and a tablespoon of icing sugar for a double treat.

Spiced carrot & walnut cake

Makes a 1kg (2lb) loaf

80g walnuts
100g plain flour
75g wholemeal flour
1 tsp ground cinnamon
1 tsp ground ginger
a pinch of table salt
1 tsp bicarbonate of soda
3 carrots, peeled and grated (175g)
1 large apple, peeled and grated (50g)
250g caster sugar
175g/185ml vegetable oil (such as sunflower or rapeseed)
2 eggs

Preheat the oven to 190°C/170°C fan/ gas mark 5. Butter a 1kg (2lb) loaf tin and line the base and long sides with a sheet of baking parchment, leaving a little overhang at the sides. Once the oven is hot, roast the walnuts for 10 minutes. Leave to cool a little before chopping roughly.

Mix the flours, spices, salt and bicarbonate of soda together in a bowl. In a separate bowl mix the grated carrot, grated apple and chopped nuts. Place the sugar and oil in a large bowl (or you could use a mixer with a whisk attachment if you are super-lazy) and whisk together until combined. Whisk in the eggs one at a time and keep whisking until you have a lovely emulsified texture, a little like mayonnaise. Get rid of the whisk. Use a spatula or large spoon to stir in the carrots, apple and nuts. Fold in the remaining ingredients and combine to an even consistency.

Transfer the batter to the lined loaf tin and bake for 35 minutes. Turn the tin around for an even bake and leave for a further 20–25 minutes. The end result should be lovely and springy to the touch.

Allow to cool in the tin before removing. This will keep in an airtight container for up to 5 days.

Butternut squash, currant & pecan loaf

This recipe was born when a squash that was meant to be coarsely grated for fritters ended up on the fine grater. What a happy mistake that was, as this cake has turned out to be hugely popular with our customers.

Makes a 1kg (2lb) loaf

80g pecans
175g plain flour
1 tsp bicarbonate of soda
a pinch of table salt
2 tsp sweet spice mix (page 48)
80g dried currants
200g butternut squash, peeled and grated
250g dark brown soft sugar
175g/185ml rapeseed oil
2 eggs

Preheat the oven to 190°C/170°C fan/ gas mark 5. Butter a 1kg (2lb) loaf tin and line the base and long sides with a sheet of baking parchment, leaving a little overhang at the sides. Once the oven is hot, roast the pecans for 8 minutes. Leave to cool a little before chopping roughly.

Mix the chopped pecans, flour, bicarbonate of soda, salt, spice mix, currants and grated squash together in a bowl so that you don't forget anything later on. Place the sugar and oil in a large bowl (or you could use a mixer with a whisk attachment if you are super-lazy) and whisk together until combined. Whisk in the eggs one at a time and keep whisking until you have a lovely emulsified texture, a little like mayonnaise. Get rid of the whisk, add the remaining ingredients and use a large spoon or spatula to fold and combine to an even consistency.

Transfer the batter to the lined loaf tin and bake for 35 minutes. Turn the tin around for an even bake and leave for a further 25–30 minutes. The end result should be lovely and springy to the touch.

Allow to cool in the tin before removing. This will keep in an airtight container in the fridge or a cold pantry for up to 5 days.

Courgette, golden raisin & pistachio cake

At the end of our street is the head office of Caprice Holdings Ltd, the group that operates some of the best and glitziest restaurants in London. Alvin and Kate work there, and treat us as their canteen. We know Alvin's weird coffee order, and that Kate will have hot chocolate in winter and sparkling lemonade in the warmer months. They are both great lovers of cake, and whenever there is a birthday in the office we get an order for one with some silly writing on it – 'Cheers, all the best' or 'Shiiiiiiiit' – often private jokes that only they understand. This cake is their absolute favourite (they have a horrible nickname for it – 'the green goddess' or 'green velvet'), so this recipe is for them, in the hope that they will never bake it themselves, but instead keep on coming to us for it.

Makes a 1kg (2lb) loaf

60g pistachios
175g self-raising flour
a pinch of table salt
1 tsp ground ginger
½ tsp ground star anise
200g light brown soft sugar
50g caster sugar
175g/185ml olive oil
2 eggs
60g golden raisins
3 courgettes, unpeeled but trimmed, grated (200g)
zest of 1 lemon

Preheat the oven to 190°C/170°C fan/ gas mark 5. Butter a 1kg (2lb) loaf tin and line the base and long sides with a sheet of baking parchment, allowing a little overhang at the sides. Once the oven is hot, roast the pistachios for 8 minutes. Keep them whole and leave to cool a little.

Mix the flour, salt, ginger and star anise together and add the pistachios. Place the sugars and oil in a large mixing bowl (or you could use a machine with a whisk attachment if you are super-lazy) and whisk together until combined. Whisk the eggs in one at a time and keep whisking until you have a lovely emulsified texture, a little like mayonnaise. Now add the rest of the ingredients, get rid of the whisk and use a large spoon or spatula to fold and combine to an even mixture.

Transfer the cake batter to your lined loaf tin and bake for 35 minutes. Turn the tin around so that it bakes evenly and leave for a further 15–20 minutes. The end result should have a lovely springy feel. Allow to cool in the tin before removing. This will keep in an airtight container for up to 3 days and for up to a week if you store it in the fridge.

Pear, ginger & olive oil cake

Makes a 1kg (2lb) loaf

2–3 pears, peeled and diced (350g)
1 tbsp lemon juice
zest of 1 lemon
200g caster sugar
150g/160ml olive oil
2 eggs
50g crystallised ginger, finely chopped
350g plain flour
1 tsp ground ginger
1 tsp bicarbonate of soda
1 tsp baking powder
½ tsp table salt

To garnish
1 pear, skin-on and cut in wedges
1 tbsp demerara sugar

Preheat the oven to 180°C/160°C fan/ gas mark 4. Butter a 1kg (2lb) loaf tin and line the base and long sides with a sheet of baking parchment, leaving a little overhang at the sides.

Mix the diced pears in a bowl with the lemon juice and zest and set aside. Place the sugar and oil in a large bowl (or you could use a mixer with a whisk attachment if you are super-lazy) and whisk together until combined. Whisk in the eggs one at a time and keep whisking until you have a lovely thick texture. Get rid of the whisk, add the pear–lemon mixture and use a spatula or wooden spoon to combine. Add the remaining ingredients and fold until combined, but try not to overwork the mixture – it is OK to have a couple of lumps.

Transfer the batter to the lined loaf tin. Top with the pear wedges and sprinkle with the demerara sugar. Bake in the centre of the oven for 40 minutes. Turn the tin around for an even bake and leave for another 25 minutes, then check to see if it is done. As this is a very fruit-heavy cake, it can be hard to be sure it is cooked through. The best way is to slide in a knife tip at the midpoint of the loaf; if there is wet batter on it when you pull it out, leave the cake to bake for another 10 minutes. But make sure you are looking at uncooked batter and not simply moisture from the fruit.

Leave to cool in the tin. This cake is best stored in the fridge and will keep for 5–6 days. Allow it to come up to room temperature before eating.

High
noon

Lunch

Sometimes the lunchtime crowd blows in like a whirlwind at 12 noon sharp; sometimes before that; and sometimes it trickles in slowly in dribs and drabs from midday onwards. However it may start, by 1pm the shop is jumping, full of people engrossed in the serious business of eating. Some rush in for a quick bite, then rush out again to get on with their day; others sit deep in conversation, discussing opinions and decisions. Some people simply walk past and decide to give us a go; others have booked well in advance, and are determined to try everything on the menu in a leisurely fashion. Friends, colleagues, new business, family business; the drama of London life plays out for us, and all we need to do is serve the food.

The kitchen fires on all cylinders during lunch; in two and a half hours the chefs can send out up to 70 meals. In order for things to go smoothly, every bit of prep needs to taste right, look right and be in the right place. The porters gallop up the stairs carrying hot food. The girls shout down for extra bread, or dessert, or to check progress on main courses. The bar sends out iced tea, wine, coffee and beer, and water bottles are in constant need of refilling.

Things start to wind down towards the tail end of service. If everything has gone well, we see a dining room full of happy people finishing their meals, debating whether or not they should have dessert (of course they should!). Then off they go to continue with the rest of their day, happy and replete.

Whether you work on the floor or in the kitchen, there is nothing to compare with the satisfaction you feel at around 2.30pm or 3pm, knowing that in a small but significant way you have helped to fuel the London machine.

Our pastry section produces quite a variety of baked goods, and though many are sweet or breakfast items, all our breads and a few savouries are made there too. It would be remiss of us not to include a few traditional Middle Eastern recipes in this chapter, along with some of our go-to savoury bakes to whet the appetite, but we are keeping it short. If you want more of our savoury dishes, you will simply have to refer to our previous book, or come to the restaurant and let us cook for you (easier, and far less washing up).

Su böreği (aka a bake named Sue or Turkish lasagne)

Istanbul is one of our favourite places in the world. We go there whenever we can, and though we've been quite a few times, we feel as if we've barely scratched the surface of this magnificent metropolis, with the amazing food it has to offer. Every time we go, we seem to add to our list of favourite restaurants – Balıkçı Sabahattin for fish, Hamdi for kebabs... One of our first discoveries was a great bakery right on the waterfront near Eminönü, where we first tried this glorious bake, with its layers of delicate pastry and creamy cheese. We always think of it as 'Turkish lasagne'. Sarit has worked hard to recreate the recipe, and makes this whenever we want a taste of Istanbul in London. Her version is as good as theirs, but the bakery by the water is still one of the first places we visit whenever we go back.

Fills a 18–20cm (7–8 inch) spring-form tin or frying pan

For the pastry

250g strong white bread flour
a pinch of table salt
2 eggs
2–3 tbsp water
1 tbsp vegetable oil

For the filling

320g/ml double cream
3 eggs
½ tsp ground nutmeg
½ tsp table salt
½ tsp freshly ground black pepper
250g ricotta cheese
120g feta cheese, crumbled

You can put all the ingredients for the pastry in a mixer with a paddle attachment or work this by hand in a bowl. Combine until lovely and smooth. Shape into a ball, wrap in cling film and chill in the fridge for at least one hour. In the meantime, mix the cream with the eggs, ground nutmeg, salt and pepper in a bowl. Combine the ricotta with the crumbled feta in a separate bowl.

Preheat the oven to 200°C/180°C fan/gas mark 6. Line the baking tin or ovenproof frying pan with a single large sheet of baking parchment (at least 25cm x 25cm), which you push into the tin or pan in one piece (it needs to be in one piece to stop any liquid leaking out). You can stick it down with a little butter, or make sure it stays in place the French way: fold the sheet in half diagonally so that you have a triangle, then fold in half again to make another triangle, and repeat twice more. Open it up again and place in the pan. The folded paper should slide in easily and sit neatly in place. ›››

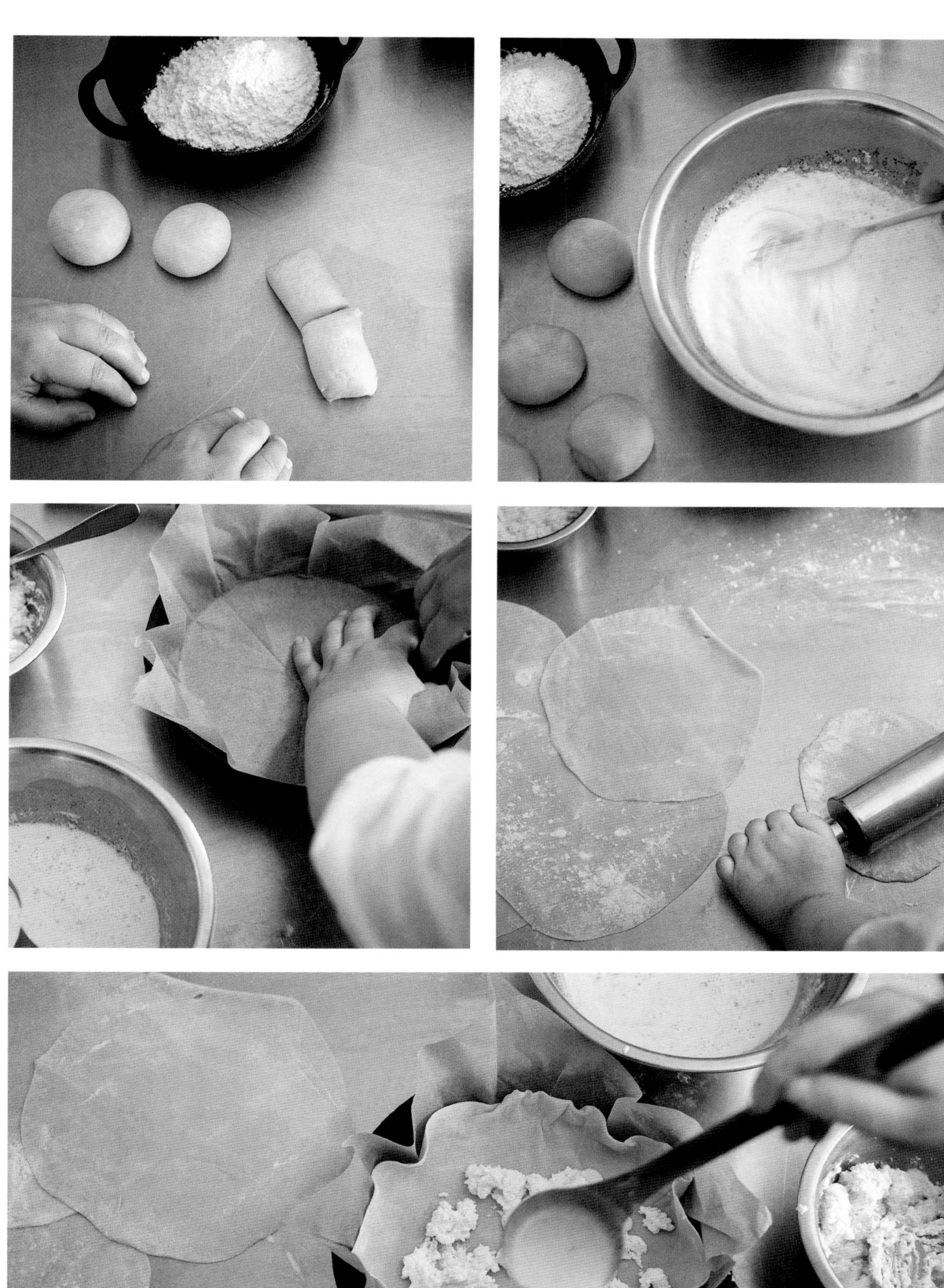

Divide the rested pastry into six equal pieces and form each one into a ball. Dust your work surface with some flour and start rolling out a piece of pastry as thinly as you can. You should end up with a large disc at least 20cm in diameter. This isn't easy to achieve, but is well worth the effort. If you are struggling to reach 20cm, roll the sheets as thinly as you can, then set aside for 5 minutes before rolling again (this allows the pastry to rest a little and makes it easier to make the last stretch).

Place a single sheet of pastry in the base of the tin, letting any excess drape up the sides. Pour 3 tablespoons of the cream mixture on top and sprinkle with about a sixth of the ricotta-feta mix. Top with another sheet of pastry and follow with more cream and cheese. Repeat until you have layered all the pastry and cheese, then pour the remaining cream mixture over the top.

Bake in the centre of the oven for 15 minutes, then reduce the heat to 180°C/160°C fan/gas mark 4 and bake for a further 20 minutes or until dark golden all over.

Remove from the oven and leave to rest for 10 minutes before serving. This is great eaten hot with a side salad, but would also be tasty cold at a picnic.

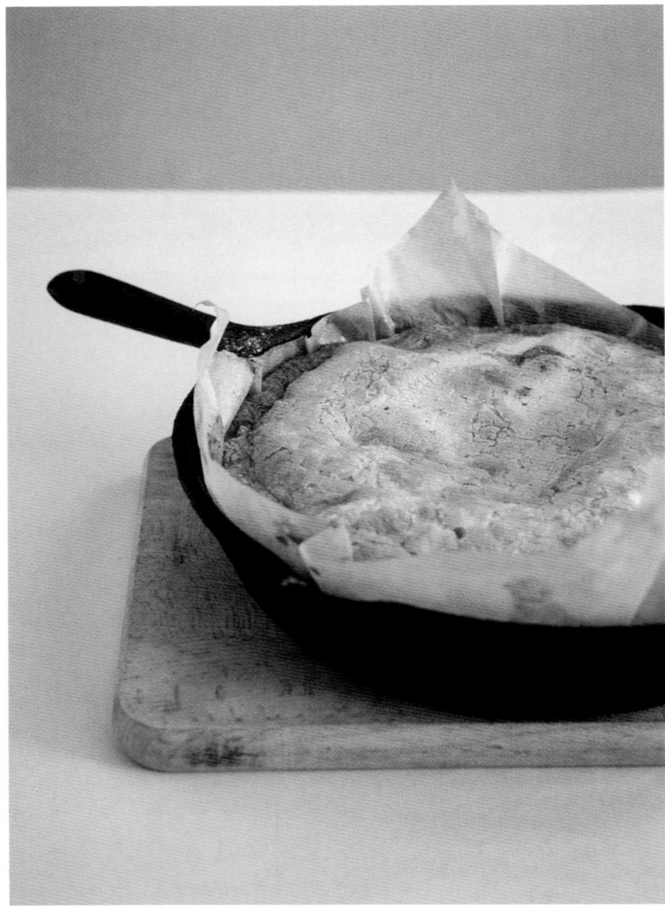

Phylas puff pastry

Mornings never were my strong suit, much to my wife's dismay. My first head chef allowed me to keep my job only on condition that every time I was late for a shift, I brought a box of burekas from Nissim as breakfast for the entire kitchen. Nissim's bakery was at the end of our street, at the entrance to Tel Aviv's Carmel Market, and his burekas were unrivalled in Tel Aviv, in both quality and price. In fact I don't think I have ever tasted better. In time I knew everyone's favourite order: aubergine for Moosh; potato for Ben; extra pickle for Tatjana. Some months my entire meagre commis chef's salary would go on rent and burekas. I never quite managed to get a handle on timekeeping, but I did manage to cling to the job for five years. Even though I got really friendly with Nissim, he never agreed to teach me the secret of his perfect burekas.

This is a basic puff pastry used all over the Middle East for filled pies, pastries and burekas. It involves a fair amount of work but freezes well, so it's worth making a full batch and keeping some in the freezer for another day. You can simply buy pre-rolled puff pastry if you prefer. It will take a fraction of the time, but be sure not to skimp – buy the best all-butter puff out there.

Makes about 1kg

500g strong white bread flour
1 tsp table salt
1 tsp lemon juice
1 tsp white wine vinegar
2 tbsp vegetable oil
200–220g/ml water
250g unsalted butter
2 tbsp plain flour, for flattening the butter

You can make this dough by hand or use a mixer with a paddle attachment. Place the bread flour and salt in the mixer bowl. Combine the lemon juice, vinegar, oil and 200g/ml of the water in a jug. Tip it into the flour all at once and mix at a medium speed until the pastry dough comes together. If you think it is looking very dry, add a touch more water, but it should be quite firm, so don't overdo it. Work the dough for about 2 minutes until it is smooth. Remove from the bowl, wrap in cling film and place in the fridge for at least 1 hour and up to 24 hours.

Remove the butter from the fridge about 15–20 minutes before you want to roll the pastry. Sprinkle the workbench with half the plain flour, place the butter on top and sprinkle it with the remaining flour. Pound the butter with a rolling pin to flatten it into a square about 10cm x 10cm.

Roll the chilled dough on a lightly floured surface to form a rough square about 20cm x 20cm. Place the butter in the centre of the dough at a 90 degree turn, so that you have a diamond of butter on a pastry square. Fold the pastry corners into the centre, stretching them a little to make sure they meet. The pastry should completely cover the butter and should now look like a sealed envelope. Turn the pastry over and roll the dough into a long rectangle of about 50cm x 20cm. Now for the 'three-fold': place the pastry with one of the long sides closest to you; fold the left-hand third into the centre; then fold the right-hand third over the top. You should end up with the pastry in a block about 20cm x 16cm and three layers thick. Lightly wrap in cling film and place in the fridge for 1–6 hours.

Place the chilled dough on the work surface with one of the 20cm sides closest to you. Roll away from you to create a fresh rectangle of about 50cm x 20cm. We then use a 'book fold': place the pastry with one of the long sides closest to you; fold the left-hand quarter into the centre; ›››

fold the right-hand quarter in to meet it; then fold the left-hand doubled-up piece of pastry over the right-hand one (as if you were closing a book). You should now have a pastry block about 20cm x 12cm and four layers thick. Wrap the pastry and refrigerate again for 1 hour.

Roll out once again to 50cm x 20cm, then fold in a 'three-fold'. Wrap and chill the pastry for at least an hour (and up to 2 days).

The pastry is now ready to use. You can freeze it (still in cling film) for up to a month – just thaw before rolling and filling. If you are using it after it has been in the fridge for a while, you may need to let it warm a little at room temperature before rolling, but I find it is best to work with it while still cold so the butter stays in the layers.

Smoky aubergine 'S' phylas

2 aubergines (about 600g before burning)

Makes 6 'S's

For the roux sauce

30g unsalted butter
30g strong white bread flour
½ tsp nutmeg
½ tsp table salt
½ tsp freshly ground black pepper
220g/ml milk
100g kashkaval or pecorino cheese, finely grated
1 small bunch of parsley, chopped

½ batch phylas puff pastry (page 155) or 500g ready-made puff pastry
egg wash (1 egg beaten with a pinch of table salt)

I like to burn the aubergines directly on the gas hob. Remove the rack and cover the surface of the hob with aluminium foil. Return the rack and turn the gas flame to high. If you have an extractor fan, turn it on, or open a window. Place the aubergines directly over the flame and allow to burn fully, first on one side, then the other. Use a pair of tongs to turn the aubergines, so that they burn all over. Repeat until the flesh caves in and the aubergine feels completely soft. This takes about 12 minutes in total.

Remove the burned aubergines to a colander until cool enough to handle. Place one on a chopping board and use a knife to remove the stem and slit all the way down to expose the flesh. Scoop out the pulp with a spoon, scraping as close to the skin as possible to capture all that smoky flavour. Place in the colander to drain away as much of the liquid as possible and repeat the process with the other aubergine. You should end up with about 300–350g aubergine flesh, depending on how wet they are.

Melt the butter in a small pan, then add the flour, nutmeg, salt and pepper. Stir well to combine and cook for 30 seconds. Pour in the milk in a steady stream, whisking all the time to combine and create a really smooth, very thick sauce. Once the first bubbles appear, stir really well. Allow to cook for another minute, stirring all the time, before pouring into a large bowl. Add the aubergine flesh, grated cheese and chopped parsley and stir well to combine. Place cling film directly on the surface of the roux (to avoid it developing a skin) and place in the fridge until completely cold and quite stiff.

Preheat the oven to 210°C/190°C fan/gas mark 6–7. Line a large tray with baking parchment. Roll out the pastry on a lightly floured surface to form a large rectangle about 50cm x 30cm. Cut in thirds lengthways to create three long strips, each about 50cm x 10cm.

I like to use a large piping bag to fill the pastries but you can use a spoon, if you prefer. Pipe or spoon a third of the filling along one of the long edges of a strip, to cover the entire length. Fold the pastry over the filling and roll up until you have a filled pastry 'snake' about 50cm long. Turn so that the seam is underneath. Cut the 'snake' in half and pinch the cut edges together really well to seal. Coil each 25cm 'snake' into a tight 'S' shape and place on the lined tray. Repeat the process with the remaining two strips to give you six 'S's in total. You can freeze these unbaked for up to a month. Simply thaw before baking.

Brush the pastries generously with egg wash and bake for 20 minutes until really golden and crisp, then reduce the heat to 190°C/170°C fan/gas mark 5 and bake for a further 15–20 minutes. Remove to a wire rack. These are best eaten hot, or at least warm, with a dish of goats' yogurt or ayran (a slightly salted Turkish yogurt drink), but they also travel well for a picnic or packed lunch.

Meat & spinach coiled phylas

Makes 4 large coiled pastries

A generous lunch for 4 very hungry people

1 tbsp olive oil
2 onions, peeled and diced (about 300g)
1½ tsp table salt
750g lamb mince
4 tbsp pine nuts
1 tbsp ground cumin
½ tsp turmeric
1 tsp ground cinnamon
1 tsp ground fennel seeds (I always grind my own)
½ tsp chilli flakes
1 small bag of baby spinach (about 200g), washed

½ batch phylas puff pastry (page 155), or 500g ready-made puff pastry
egg wash (1 egg beaten with a pinch of table salt)

Heat the olive oil in a large deep frying pan over a medium heat. Add the onions and half a teaspoon of the salt and sauté until soft (about 8–10 minutes). Increase the heat to high and add the lamb mince. Move it around to break it up so that it browns all over (about 5 minutes), then add the pine nuts, spices and remaining salt. Mix until well combined and continue cooking for about 5 minutes. Fold the spinach into the hot meat (you may need to do this in batches, wilting a little at a time). Remove to a bowl or other container and allow to cool entirely before using to fill the pastries. You can make this in advance and store in the fridge overnight.

Line a large tray with baking parchment. Roll out the pastry on a lightly floured surface to form a large rectangle of about 60cm x 25cm. Cut in quarters across its width to create four smaller rectangles, each about 25cm x 15cm.

Spoon a quarter of the meat filling along one of the long edges of a rectangle, then fold the pastry over the filling and roll up tightly until you have a filled pastry 'snake' about 25cm long. Turn so the seam is underneath, then coil into a tight spiral and place on the lined tray. Tuck the loose end under the coil to keep the shape. Repeat the process with the remaining three rectangles to give you four coils in total. You can freeze these unbaked for up to a month. Simply thaw before baking.

Preheat the oven to 210°C/190°C fan/gas mark 6–7. Brush the pastries generously with egg wash and bake for 25 minutes until really golden and crisp, then reduce the oven temperature to 190°C/170°C fan/gas mark 5 and bake for a further 15–20 minutes. Remove to a wire rack. I think these are great eaten hot, and are best served with a lovely green salad on the side.

Balkan cheese bread

We lived in a flat across the hall from a Bulgarian widow called Smella and her Siamese cat Ninja. The cat amazed us with his skills (he could open doors and turn on lights), while Smella amazed us with her wonderful cooking. She gave us a proud introduction to her country's cuisine: rice fragrant with cinnamon and bay; mutton stewed slowly with green peppers; and an endless parade of cheesy pastries, which we could never get enough of. We haven't been to Bulgaria yet, but we know we will have a delicious time there.

It is hard to explain exactly what this is. A very doughy pie? A very rich bread? Whatever you call it, it is incredibly nice to eat, especially if you have it with some good yogurt and chopped vegetables on the side.

Makes a 23cm (9 inch) round cheesy loaf

For the dough

20g fresh yeast or 1½ tsp dried yeast
150g/ml lukewarm water
2 tsp caster sugar
300g plain flour
½ tsp table salt
1 egg yolk
2 tbsp vegetable oil, plus 1 tbsp for the top

For the filling

25g unsalted butter
1 leek, sliced and washed (about 200–250g)
a pinch of table salt
a pinch of freshly ground black pepper
1 tsp nigella seeds
½ tsp chilli flakes
100g feta cheese, crumbled
70g kashkaval or pecorino cheese, roughly grated

For the topping

egg wash (1 egg beaten with a pinch of table salt)
30g kashkaval or pecorino cheese, finely grated
a pinch of sweet paprika

Put the yeast in a jug or small bowl with the water and sugar and stir to dissolve. Place the rest of the dough ingredients in a large bowl or a mixer with a hook attachment. Add the yeasty liquid to the other ingredients and combine to form a smooth, supple dough. This will take 2–3 minutes in a mixer or about 8 minutes by hand. Bring together to a ball and smooth the top with the remaining tablespoon of oil. Set aside in a covered bowl and allow to prove until doubled in size. This should take 1–2 hours in a warm kitchen (maybe longer if it is a very cold day). In the meantime lightly butter the sides of a 23cm round baking tin and line the base with baking parchment.

Melt the butter in a large frying pan and add the leek. Sauté for 2–3 minutes, then season with the salt and pepper and continue cooking for another 10–15 minutes until the leek is soft. Remove from the heat and stir in the nigella seeds and chilli flakes. Once the leek has cooled down a little, mix in the cheeses.

Carefully transfer the dough to the lined baking tin. Spoon the leek mixture on top and use your fingertips to push the filling into the dough. Some of the mixture can be left exposed, but don't be scared to really get it in there. Cover lightly with some cling film or a damp cloth and allow to prove again. This stage should only take about 30–40 minutes, as the leek mixture will still be warm, which should help the dough to rise. After 20 minutes preheat the oven to 220°C/200°C fan/gas mark 7.

Once the dough has risen, it should cover most of the filling. Egg-wash the loaf and sprinkle with the grated cheese and paprika. Bake in the centre of the oven for 15 minutes, then turn the tin (to bake evenly) and reduce the heat to 200°C/180°C fan/gas mark 6. Bake for another 15 minutes.

Allow to cool in the tin for 10–15 minutes before lifting the loaf out and eating all that cheesy goodness. You can make this bread in advance and simply reheat it in the oven, or slice and toast it, before serving.

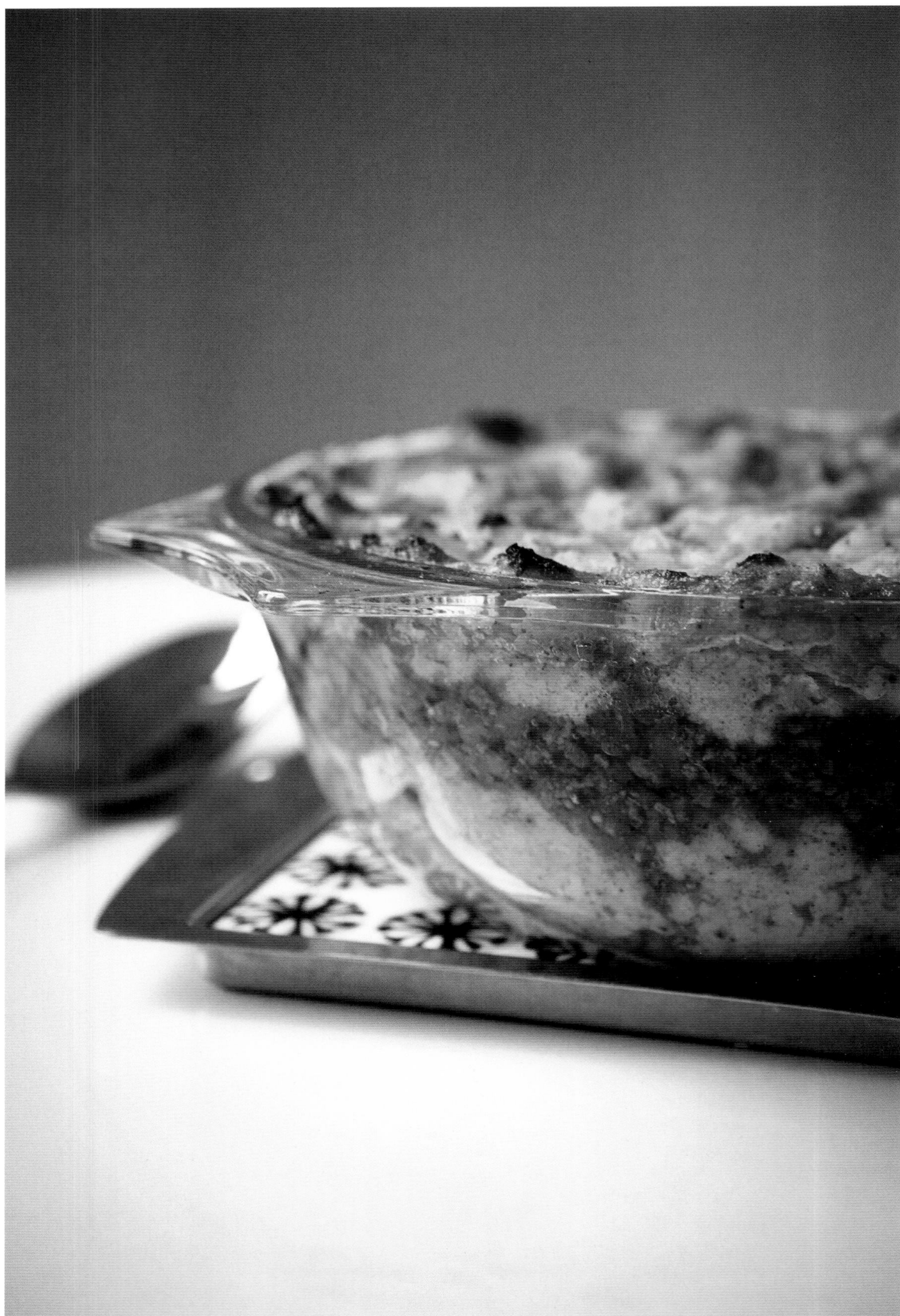

Large pastel

Traditionally pastelicos are small canapé-sized stuffed pastries. You flatten potato dough in the palm of your hand, place a bit of filling inside and fold over to create a little disc that you flour and deep-fry. Delicious and so much fun, but they belong to a different era. We try to keep traditions alive. If this means we need to adapt a bit – increase the size and bake rather than fry – so be it. The result is just as tasty, and the old recipe gets a new lease of life. If you ever find yourself with time to kill before a big party (yeah, right), you can make these the old-fashioned way, but if you're looking for a truly great lunch for fairly little effort, look no further.

Serves 4

Use a 22cm (8½ inch) casserole dish or similar

For the potato dough

- *1.5kg medium-large potatoes (Maris Piper and Desiree work really well)*
- *¼ tsp ground white pepper*
- *½ tsp turmeric*
- *1 tsp table salt*
- *2 tsp ras el hanut spice mix*
- *2 eggs*
- *3 tbsp plain flour*
- *1 tbsp olive oil*

For the filling

- *1 large onion, peeled and diced*
- *2 tbsp oil*
- *800g beef mince*
- *1 tsp table salt, plus more to taste*
- *½ tsp freshly ground black pepper*
- *1 tsp ground pimento (allspice)*
- *½ tsp ground cinnamon*
- *1 tsp ground fennel seeds (I always grind my own)*
- *1 tsp sweet paprika*
- *250g/ml water*
- *2 bay leaves*

olive oil, for brushing

Preheat the oven to 220°C/200°C fan/ gas mark 7. Bake the potatoes on a tray for about 1 hour or until soft. Check by inserting the tip of a knife; it should go through without any resistance. Allow to cool.

While the potatoes are baking, fry the onion in the oil over a high heat until soft and starting to colour (about 8–10 minutes), then add the mince. Break it up so it can colour all over. Stir in the salt, pepper and spices and fry for 2 minutes – keep stirring so they are well distributed. Add the water and bay leaves and reduce to a simmer. Cook for about 20–30 minutes until most of the water has gone. Taste and see if you wish to add a little more salt.

As soon as the potatoes are cool enough to handle, cut in half and scoop out the soft flesh (you should have about 700g). You can discard the skins (or fry them, toss in some salt and paprika and eat with some plain yogurt). Place the potato in a large bowl and use a potato ricer or grater to break it down. Add the other dough ingredients and mix well to combine. Don't be tempted to use a food processor, as it will make the mixture very gluey and not so pleasant to eat.

Place half the potato dough in the bottom of the casserole and flatten into a smooth layer. Tip the mince mixture on top and spread evenly, pressing down to flatten. Top with the remaining potato dough and flatten down again. You can prepare to this stage up to a day in advance and keep the unbaked pastel in the fridge until you are ready to cook.

Preheat the oven to 200°C/180°C fan/ gas mark 6 and brush the top layer of dough with some olive oil. Bake for 20–30 minutes (or 50–60 minutes if it has just come out of the fridge) until a light brown crust forms. Remove from the oven and serve hot.

Greek moussaka

There are loads of stages involved in making a good moussaka, which can often seem too much effort for something that is available to buy from the supermarket freezer, but a good moussaka is a feast of a dish, a real centrepiece you can serve with pride. The care you take in preparing each step will show from top to bottom: a smooth golden crown of creamy, cheesy topping; a layer of aubergine neatly arranged and roasted to a soft submission; the meat in the middle delicately spiced and scented; and the potatoes underneath it all, cooked in all those lovely juices (probably the nicest part of all).

Fills a large casserole

Dinner for 4, with some left for tomorrow's lunch

3 aubergines
60g/ml olive oil to brush

For the mince
2 tbsp olive oil
2 medium-sized onions, peeled and diced
3 cloves of garlic, crushed
600g minced beef (or lamb, if you prefer)
2 tbsp dried oregano
1 tsp sweet paprika
a pinch of dried chilli flakes or cayenne pepper
2 tsp table salt
½ tsp freshly ground black pepper
1 tin peeled tomatoes (400g)
1 small bunch of thyme, tied with string
2 tbsp tomato purée

For the base
2 large potatoes (about 500g)
olive oil to drizzle
2 plum tomatoes

For the béchamel sauce
50g unsalted butter
50g plain flour
½ tsp table salt
a pinch of freshly ground black pepper
500g/ml milk

To sprinkle
50g kashkaval or pecorino cheese, grated

Preheat the oven to 240°C/220°C fan/ gas mark 9 and line two large trays with baking parchment. Cut the aubergines into long, finger-thick slices (about 1.5cm wide), brush generously on both sides with the olive oil and lay on the lined trays. Season with salt and black pepper, then roast in the oven for 20–25 minutes until nice and golden.

In the meantime, place the olive oil in a large pan on a high heat and fry the onions and garlic for about 8–10 minutes until softened. Add the meat and, keeping the heat high, smash the mince around until it crumbles and breaks up. Stir in the oregano, spices, salt and pepper, and cook for 30 seconds, then mix in the tinned tomatoes, thyme and tomato purée. Reduce the heat to low and allow to cook slowly for 30 minutes. You may need to add about 120g/ml of water if the mince gets a little dry, but not too much as you want a dry-ish mixture. Once the meat sauce is cooked, remove and discard the thyme bundle.

While you are waiting for the mince to cook, peel the potatoes and slice as thinly as you can (use a mandolin if you have one). Lay them in a single layer to cover the bottom of the casserole dish. Drizzle with a touch of olive oil, and season with salt and pepper. Place half the aubergines in a layer on top of the potatoes, and follow with a meat layer, using half the mince. Slice the fresh tomatoes and lay them on top. Place the remaining aubergines in a layer on the tomatoes, and finish with a second meat layer, using the rest of the mince.

Melt the butter in a small pan, then add the flour, salt and pepper and cook for 30 seconds. Use a small whisk to incorporate the milk, whisking all the time as you pour it in a steady stream. Keep whisking until you have a lovely thick béchamel sauce. Heat until the first bubbles appear, then pour on top of the meat in the casserole. Spread the béchamel out to create a smooth layer and sprinkle with the grated cheese. You can bake this now or set it in the fridge for up to 24 hours.

You need the oven at 200°C/180°C fan/gas mark 6, so either lower the temperature (if it is still on after roasting the aubergines) or preheat (if you made the moussaka in advance). Bake for 30 minutes if you just finished preparing the dish, or 60 minutes if it has been in the fridge (to make sure that it will be heated right through). Either way, it should have a great golden crust once cooked.

Any leftovers can be refrigerated and then reheated until piping hot, either in the microwave or in the oven on a tray covered with aluminium foil.

Pigeon pastilla

In Morocco this is traditionally made with warka pastry. In the West we tend to substitute filo, which is more readily available. While warka pastry is quite easy to make at home, it does require you to use a brush to paint batter on a griddle that is set on a pan of boiling water. This is just as painful and boring as it sounds, but if you feel so inclined, there are plenty of recipes online (check out the video of a grey-haired lady cooking warka and explaining how to do it while inhaling helium from a balloon – the joys of the internet). In my opinion, these kinds of pastry are never ever worth making at home. All that my hard work at it ever got me was a messy kitchen, aching arms and pastry that wasn't as thin as it should be. Some things should be left to the pros.

Enough for lunch for 6 or a very hungry 4 (pigeon is very rich)

1 packet (or 6 sheets) of filo pastry
100g unsalted butter, melted

For the pigeon
- *4 pigeons*
- *1 orange, cut in half*
- *2 bay leaves*
- *2 cloves*
- *4 whole pimento peppers*
- *1 cinnamon stick*
- *enough water to cover*
- *3 tbsp vegetable oil*

For the filling
- *cooked pigeon meat (about 500g)*
- *120g hazelnuts (skins removed), roughly chopped*
- *200g dried figs, diced*
- *40g unsalted butter*
- *40g plain flour*
- *400g/ml strained poaching liquid (reserved)*

Place the pigeons, halved orange, bay leaves and spices in a large pan. Cover with water, season with salt and pepper, and bring to a boil over a high heat. Skim off any foam, then add the vegetable oil, reduce the heat to low and cover. Simmer slowly for about an hour, then remove the pigeons from the liquid and set on a plate to cool. Strain the poaching liquid into a measuring jug. You need to reserve about 400g/ml for the filling, but you can discard the rest.

Once the birds are cool enough to handle, carefully pick the pigeon off the bones, making sure you don't leave any small bones in with the meat. Place the meat in a large bowl with the chopped hazelnuts and figs.

Heat the butter and flour together in a small pan until the butter has melted. Stir well while it browns a little, then add the reserved poaching liquid and continue to cook, stirring all the time, until the first bubbles appear. Remove from the heat, pour over the pigeon mixture and stir to combine.

Preheat the oven to 200°C/180°C fan/gas mark 6. Line a 18–20cm (7–8 inch) frying pan or round baking tin with baking parchment. Open the packet of filo and lay the sheets on the work surface. Butter one sheet. Lay another sheet across it at 90 degrees. Butter a third sheet, fold it in quarters, and place in the centre of the two sheets you've already buttered, to provide a stronger base. Butter the remaining three sheets and layer them on top, changing the angle slightly every time to fill in the gaps between the sheets and create a large filo disc. Lift carefully and slide into the lined pan or tin, leaving the excess pastry hanging over the sides. Place the pigeon mixture in the centre, then fold the edges over it in a crinkly mess to create a pastry parcel. Bake in the centre of the oven for about 25–30 minutes until a lovely golden colour. Serve hot.

Fricassée bread

I love the great British sandwich: a world of civilisation between two slices of bread, and the ultimate snack for clean-fingered folk. Tunisians take a different view: the sandwich is not a light snack you have on the go; it is a feast of a meal, with all manner of possible fillings, spreads and salads, served at the table with a stack of fried(!) buns, so that each person can create their own. If you are lucky or smart enough to have Tunisian friends, and are invited to fricassée night, your views of what a sandwich can be will change forever, and for the better. The fried buns are not greasy – just lovely bread in a crisp shell, but if frying them seems too indulgent (or too much work), any soft bread rolls will do. Or give the bread a miss altogether and have a make-your-own salad lunch.

Makes 6 large fried bread rolls

320g plain flour
½ tsp table salt
15g fresh yeast or 1 tsp dried yeast
½ tsp caster sugar
180g/ml water
1 tbsp vegetable oil

vegetable oil for coating, oiling and frying

Place the flour and salt in a mixing bowl. Put the yeast in a jug or small bowl with the sugar and water and stir to dissolve. You can use an electric mixer with a dough hook to make the dough, but it is just as easy to work this amount by hand. Pour the yeast mixture into the salted flour, combine and knead to a smooth consistency. Add the oil and continue kneading until you have a supple and shiny dough – this should take about 6–8 minutes. Divide the dough into six pieces, each about 85–90g. Shape the pieces into rough logs of about 15cm long. Brush with lots of oil and set on an oiled tray to prove and double in size (about an hour at room temperature, or faster if the weather is hot). Make sure to leave space between them so they don't stick to each other.

Heat about 5cm of oil in a large, deep frying pan (or if you own a deep fat fryer, use that). The oil should be about the depth of the top two segments of your finger if you stick it in – but do test the depth before you heat the oil, otherwise you will be very sore and the thought of a sandwich will no longer inspire you.

You can test that the oil is up to temperature either with a thermometer (it should be about 170°C) or by flicking in a little flour (it should fizz). You want to keep a nice, steady, medium heat so that the dough cooks through while developing a crispy exterior. Gently and very carefully place two or three dough logs in the oil, one at a time. Don't crowd the pan – it's fine to fry these in two or three batches. And don't worry about leaving a few fingerprints in the dough; it is all part of the charm – your personal touch. Fry until the logs are golden on the underside (about 2–3 minutes), then flip and fry the other side for 2–3 minutes. Use a pair of tongs to remove carefully from the oil and transfer to a plate covered with some kitchen paper to absorb any excess oil. Repeat the process with the remaining dough logs.

As soon as the rolls are at a temperature that you can handle, fill and eat them. (See the following page for two of our favorite fillings.)

Fricassée roll fillings

Filling the fricassée sandwich is an art all of its own. Like the sabich (aubergine, egg, parsley, tahini and lemon) and the falafel pitta (falafel, salad, tahini and pickles), this satisfying sandwich is a popular street snack, intended to sustain you during the long day ahead. There are two fillings here: first the traditional tuna, and a slightly lighter one using an excellent little trick for preparing egg salad. Do try the egg filling; it may sound simple and a bit ordinary, but that is deceptive, as it is pure genius. I owe the method to the mum of my best friend at high school, Liat.

Tuna filling

6 fricassée rolls (page 168)

Makes enough to fill 6 sandwiches

2 tins of tuna in oil, drained
6 tsp harissa paste
3 tbsp preserved lemons, chopped and seeds removed
2 tbsp capers

To top
6 hard-boiled eggs (see recipe below if you need guidance), peeled and quartered
a handful of pitted green olives
1 bunch of fresh parsley, leaves picked
2 large tomatoes, thinly sliced
sea salt

Mix the tuna, harissa, preserved lemons and capers in a bowl. Cut the rolls in half and divide the tuna mixture between them. Top each heap of tuna with an egg, some olives, parsley leaves, and a couple of pieces of tomato. Sprinkle with a little sea salt and devour.

Egg salad filling

The rich eggs, crunchy bread and fresh cucumber work together like a dream in this.

6 fricassée rolls (page 168)

Makes enough to fill 6 sandwiches

12 eggs
1 small bunch of dill, fronds chopped
3 tbsp grapeseed oil (or another mild-flavoured vegetable oil)
a generous pinch of table salt
a pinch of freshly ground black pepper
3 small Lebanese cucumbers (or 1 large cucumber), peeled in thin ribbons

Place the eggs in a saucepan large enough to contain them comfortably, add 2 teaspoons of table salt and cover with cold water. Bring to the boil, then cook for 5 minutes. Remove from the heat and allow to sit in the hot water for 4 minutes, then rinse with cold water and peel.

Grate the eggs on a coarse grater (this is easier than it sounds – just pretend they are carrots) and place in a bowl. Add the dill, oil, salt and pepper and mix well. Slice the rolls in half and fill each with some egg salad, topped with cucumber ribbons. Sprinkle on a touch of sea salt and eat.

Leek & goats' cheese pie

They say real men don't eat quiche but this does not apply to Itamar. He is not one to let gender bias keep him away from the good stuff. Quiche is a French dish and has nothing to do with Middle Eastern food, aside from the fact that this recipe combines versions from our two favourite cafés in Tel Aviv.

Makes a large rectangular pie (20cm x 30cm – 8 inch x 12 inch – or thereabouts)

A loose-bottomed tin is best for this

For the pastry

200g plain flour
100g cold butter, diced
30g full fat cream cheese
20g kashkaval or pecorino cheese, grated
1 egg
1 tbsp olive oil
1 tbsp vinegar
a pinch of table salt

For the filling

2 small leeks (about 400g raw should result in about 250g cooked)
2 cloves of garlic, peeled and halved
20g unsalted butter
1 tbsp olive oil
a pinch of table salt
a pinch of pepper
2 sprigs of thyme

For the topping

2 eggs
200g/ml double cream
½ tsp table salt
a generous pinch of freshly ground black pepper
150g goats' cheese

I make the pastry in a food processor with either the metal blade or the plastic blade attachment (you can also make it by hand, but try not to overwork it as you want a lovely short texture). Place the ingredients in the processor and pulse until they come together in a rough ball. Flatten the pastry slightly and wrap it in cling film. Chill for at least 30 minutes (up to 48 hours).

Slice the leeks thinly and wash well to get rid of any grit. I usually submerge them in cold water for 10 minutes, then shake them about and lift them out, rather than drain, so the dirt stays in the bowl. Sauté the leeks in a frying pan over a medium-low heat with the garlic, butter, oil, salt, pepper and thyme for about 10–15 minutes until soft, stirring occasionally. Allow to cool, then remove the thyme.

Preheat the oven to 200°C/180°C fan/gas mark 6. Lightly flour the workbench and roll the pastry to a large rectangle of about 35cm x 25cm. Line the tin with the pastry, allowing a little overhang to avoid shrinkage (this will also help you fill the pie as fully as possible without the mixture spilling out). Set in the fridge for 15–30 minutes.

Cover the chilled pastry with baking parchment and fill with baking beans, rice or any beans/pulses that you have lurking at the back of the cupboard and will never use. Bake for 15 minutes, then remove. Carefully lift off the baking beans and parchment.

Mix the eggs with the double cream, salt and black pepper. Place the leeks in a layer covering the bottom of the pie base. Slice or crumble the goats' cheese and distribute it over the leeks so that every slice will get some, then top with the egg mixture.

Reduce the oven to 180°C/160°C fan/gas mark 4 and place the pie tin in the centre. Bake for about 25–30 minutes until the pastry at the edges is lovely and golden and the filling is set when you shake the tray slightly, turning it around halfway through to make sure it gets a nice even colour. Allow to cool in the tin for at least 20–30 minutes.

Trim any excess pastry from the rim of the tin and carefully push the base up to release. Serve warm or cold, as you prefer. It really needs nothing else, but if you are feeling virtuous, serve with a fresh green salad.

Big kubbeh

I'm not sure what the exact definition of kubbeh is. So many Middle Eastern dishes bear that name, from those deep-fried torpedoes you get in Lebanese restaurants to the various soft, filled dumplings served in soup. And of course this pie-like creation. All very different, with only the minced meat and bulgar wheat in common. This version is quite easy to prepare and tastes gorgeous – the bulgar wheat gives the crust a great texture, while the onion and fruit keep the filling incredibly moist. Use a mince with at least 20% fat to give this dish plenty of flavour.

Fills a 22–24cm (8½–9½ inch) round casserole dish

Will easily feed 6

For the casing

200g bulgar wheat
300g/ml boiling water
1 tsp table salt
250g minced lamb
1 tsp ground cinnamon
pinch of cayenne pepper
pinch of white pepper

For the filling

2 onions, peeled and diced
4 cloves of garlic, peeled and crushed
1 tsp table salt
2 tbsp vegetable oil
25g pine nuts
25g pistachios, roughly chopped
1 cinnamon stick
500g minced lamb
1 tsp ground nutmeg
1 tsp ground coriander seeds
1 tsp ground pimento (allspice)
1 tsp sweet paprika
½ tsp cayenne pepper
a pinch of white pepper
100g pitted prunes, roughly chopped
500g/ml water

Place the bulgar wheat in a bowl. Pour in the boiling water, stir in the salt, cover with cling film and set aside for 10 minutes.

Break up the bulgar wheat a little with a fork. Add the lamb mince, cinnamon, cayenne and white pepper and combine well. Do this while the bulgar is still warm to get the best results. Work the ingredients together just as you would a flour-based dough, then divide in two. Flatten each half between two sheets of baking parchment cut to fit the dish you will be baking it in. You can use a rolling pin to do this and treat it just as you would any other dough. Set aside until the filling is ready.

Sauté the onions, garlic and half a teaspoon of salt in the oil in a frying pan over a medium heat for about 5 minutes. Stir in the pine nuts, pistachios and cinnamon stick, and continue cooking for another 8–10 minutes. Increase the heat to full and add the minced lamb. Break it up as it cooks so that it can caramelise all over. Sprinkle with the spices and remaining half-teaspoon of salt, mix well and cook for 5 minutes. Add the prunes and water, reduce the heat to medium-low and cook for about 40 minutes until most of the water has gone and the meat is soft.

Preheat the oven to 200°C/180°C fan/gas mark 6. Place the first disc of bulgar wheat mixture in the base of the casserole dish, then peel off the top layer of baking parchment (the bottom layer of parchment stays under the bulgar wheat base to line the dish). Spread the lamb mixture over the bulgar wheat base. Peel the top layer of parchment off the second disc of bulgar wheat mixture. Very carefully flip it onto the meat to seal it into the casserole. Once the disc is in place, peel off the remaining layer of baking parchment. Press down to secure the bulgar wheat lid – don't worry if it breaks a little.

Bake in the centre of the oven for 15 minutes, then turn the casserole around for an even bake and leave for another 15 minutes until the top layer is all golden. This is best served with loads of tahini and a chopped salad.

Even if you don't want to serve it straight away, I would recommend that you bake this as soon as it has been assembled as otherwise you risk the bulgar wheat absorbing all the moisture from the filling and drying everything out. If you are making it in advance, simply leave to cool after baking, then cover and refrigerate until needed. To serve, reheat in the casserole (covered this time, so that it doesn't dry out) for 15–20 minutes at 200°C/180°C fan/gas mark 6, or in a microwave if you prefer.

Before sunset

oney & Co.
From the Middle East

Teatime

If you come for a late lunch at Honey & Co, you can almost hear all of us catching our breath after the lunchtime madness. Downstairs the kitchen will be sending up the last lunch orders while cleaning and filling the pass for the dinner shift team who are about to arrive. Julia will be in the walk-in fridge with her clipboard, going through every single container, trying to assess how much food we need to prepare for that evening, as well as what and how much we need to order for the next day; or on the phone, when she sees what time it is, rushing to get the fish order in before 4pm. The porters will be doing a thorough clean of the kitchen, stairs, bathroom and dining room (when they are done, it's as if lunch had never happened). Upstairs post-lunch espressos will be downed in one, and bills requested and paid. Dee will be by the door saying goodbye to an old customer who has become a friend, or to a new customer who may yet become one. The sunlight will be creeping into our north-facing window, the rays in the eyes of the last diners at the window bar, prompting them to ask for the bill, or move to a table.

Once the bar has been cleared and cleaned, the cake parade starts. We move them from the small counter in the back of the restaurant (their exile home during lunch and dinner) to the bar by the front window, centre stage. They make their way through the little dining room like catwalk models, turning heads. Diners who have just finished their lunch will have cakes flashed under their noses on the way – this one is lemon drizzle, this one coffee & walnut. Even the strongest of wills bends, and diets die a swift, sweet death. You may be able to resist one cake passed before you, but not a whole procession.

Giorgia will peek upstairs to see how many of her cakes lasted through lunch. While the kitchen was sending up meals, she was baking in her section, the shelves next to her oven slowly filling up, getting ready for teatime – the official time for cakes. They are all by the window now, beautifully arranged, ready to do their job.

General baking guidelines

I have said this before, but it is worth saying again – always *read the entire recipe* before starting. I can't stress this enough. Make sure you have a clear idea of what is required, and where possible I strongly advise collecting all your recipe ingredients before you start, if only because it reduces the chance of leaving out something vital.

Baking is quite different from cooking generally and I therefore advise sticking to the recipes as written, at least for the first time you prepare them. Once you get the gist it'll be easier for you to put your own creative stamp on things – that's how the best recipes are created.

When baking cakes I always heat my oven to the required temperature and make sure it is hot before I put the cake in. I bake in the centre of the oven unless the recipe specifies otherwise. I also try not to overcrowd the oven in order to ensure an even bake.

I've been training pastry chefs for years and one of the biggest challenges is teaching them how to judge when a cake is baked. It isn't as easy as it sounds since so many factors go into the equation: the temperature of your base ingredients; the heat of your oven; the tin you are using. Always use your own judgement as well as the time suggested. Incidentally, I never use the skewer method, since some cakes should be moist when they come out of the oven, and some cakes contain fruit, which makes it impossible to tell. I decided a long time ago that this method simply doesn't work for me.

Here are my guidelines for telling when a cake is baked:

- It should have a lovely smell of baked goods – the first indication that a cake is baked is the fragrance of caramelising sugar and flour running through the house.

- The colour should be nice and golden and ideally even all over. If the centre is a much lighter colour the cake may not be baked all the way through. If you are worried about the sides over-colouring, create a little aluminium foil jacket that will cover and protect the sides while leaving the centre exposed.

- The texture should be the same all over. Use the tip of your finger to poke the cake gently in the centre and at the outer edges of the cake's surface. In most cases (I will always mention when there is an exception) the cake should feel rather firm, so if your finger sinks in a little the cake isn't baked. The reason you press on the rim as well as the centre is to get a feel for what a baked cake feels like.

- Always turn the cake tin around halfway through the baking time. Every oven I have encountered in my life bakes unevenly, so turning the tin will help you to achieve the most even result possible.

- The last and strangest of all my guidelines is to listen to your cake. You may think I'm mad but give it a go. Take the cake out, lower your ear towards the surface and listen: if you hear crackling, bubbling and hissing, put it back in the oven – it isn't baked. If you don't hear anything, it is most likely ready.

I tend to use a butter spray to grease my tins and moulds as it is hassle-free and easy to apply evenly, but you can, of course, use soft or melted butter and brush it on instead.

For some recipes I suggest lining your tins with baking parchment or dusting with flour. This will help you to get a better

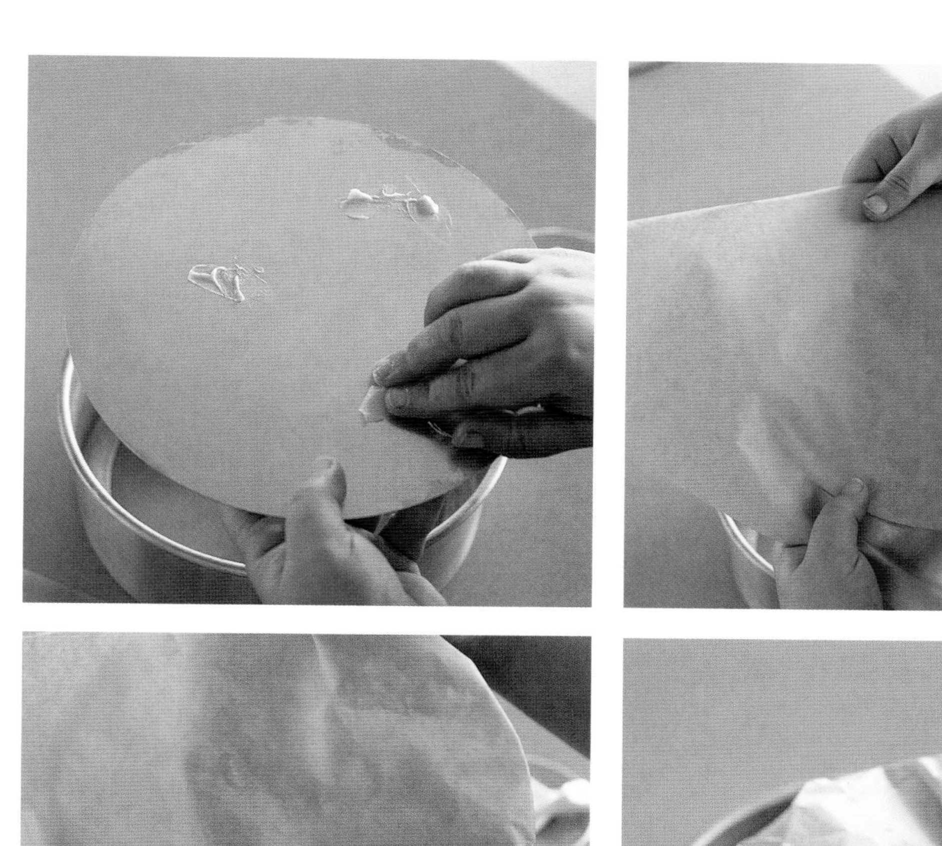
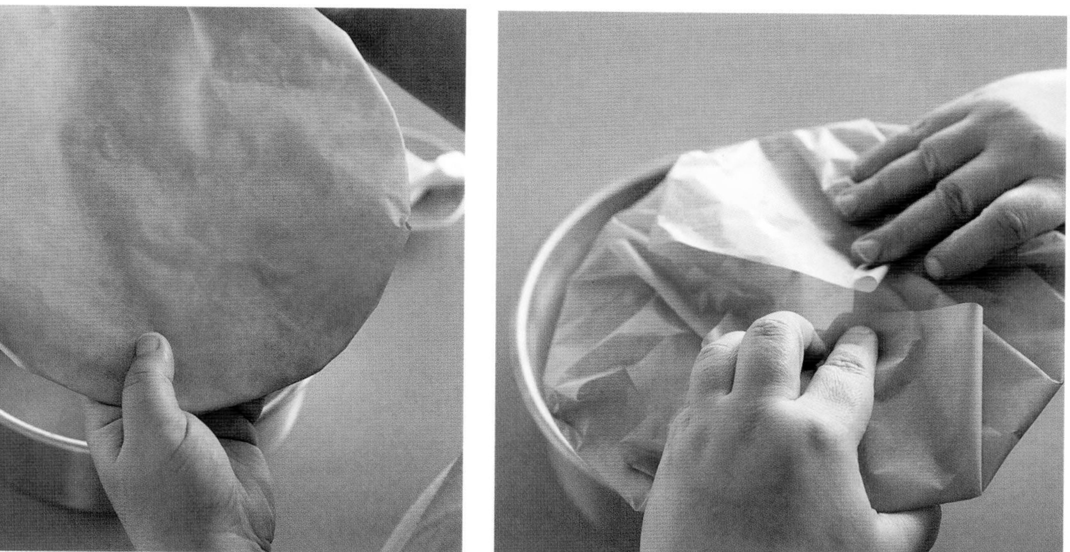
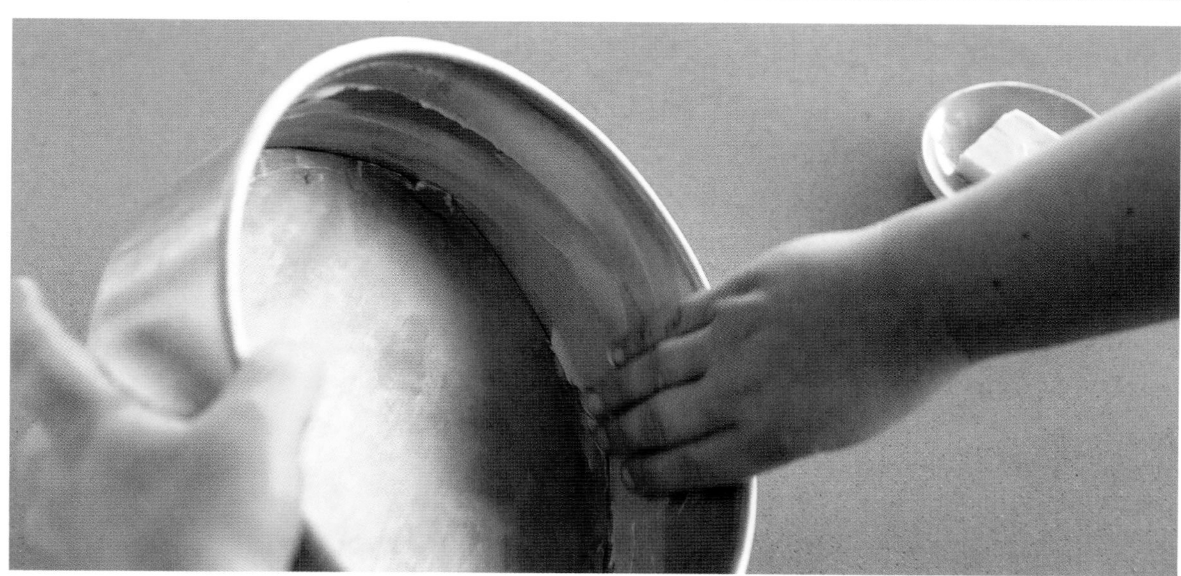

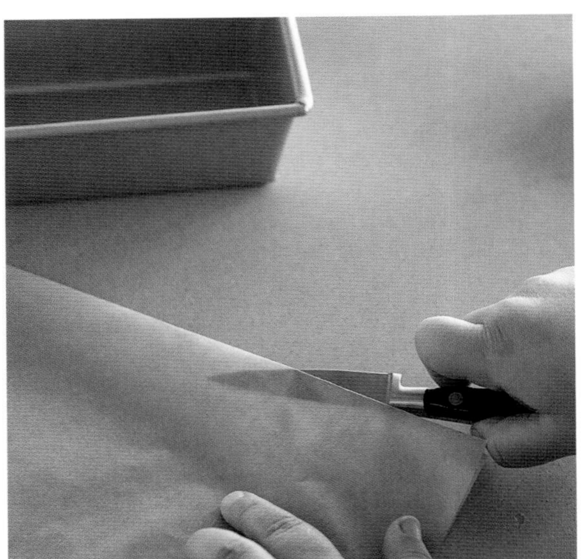

result with cake mixes that are harder to remove from their tins. There can be many reasons for this, including the amount of butter and sugar in the batter and the end crumb consistency. You will just have to trust me on this.

These pictures show you my usual lining methods. Leaving the excess baking parchment hanging over the sides of the loaf tin will help you to lift the baked cake or loaf out.

In general I only really like to use silicone moulds for specific cakes (like financiers), as I find that most cakes benefit from the even distribution of heat that a classic metal tin provides. I will always note in the recipe if I think it is a cake that bakes well in silicone; I recommend that otherwise you stick to metal tins (unless you have a silicone mould you love and trust and you want to take your chances with it).

I have specified the size and shape of the moulds I use in each recipe and have tried not to use a huge variety. If you really like the sound of a cake but don't have the correct tin, try it in a different one or bake one large cake instead of small individual ones (but then please take into account that baking times will vary).

Small cakes

These are the little jewels of the pastry world. They are meant to impress, plus they allow each person to have their own perfect cake without sharing it – the best kind of cake. Weighing the amount that goes into the individual tins or moulds will ensure that you achieve the best-looking, most evenly baked cakes possible. The selection at Honey & Co is constantly changing, but here are a few of our favourites.

Spiced chocolate & prune cakes

The first flat we shared in Tel Aviv was a short walk from the buzzing Carmel Market. One of our biggest pleasures was stocking up the kitchen with edible treats for the weekend. On Friday mornings we would nip down to the market for fresh fruit and vegetables. We got to know all the stallholders and learnt who brought the best produce: peaches from the desert; mushrooms from the cool north; preserved bitter olives sold by the Druze lady; cured fish and feta from the Turkish deli. Our next stop might be the fishmonger or butcher, and on the walk home we would stop for flowers. We would always end up at Erez Komarovsky's (a wonderful baker and chef). A visit to his bakery was the highlight of our weekend run; full of breads and bakes that were all so tempting that choosing just one was sheer agony. This combination of chocolate and prunes is shamelessly stolen from him. It makes so much sense and is so delicious that I'm surprised not to see it everywhere.

Makes 6 small bundt cakes

Gluten-free

For the prunes

200g stoned prunes
150g/ml boiling water
1 Earl Grey tea bag
1 tbsp brandy

For the cake batter

4 eggs
100g caster sugar
250g unsalted butter
250g dark chocolate
25g cornflour
25g cocoa powder
½ tsp ground cinnamon
½ tsp ground ginger
½ tsp ground cardamom
a pinch of freshly ground black pepper

The prunes need to soak for at least an hour (or overnight, if you are feeling organised). Put the prunes in a bowl. Make a strong cup of tea with the boiling water and tea bag, and pour it (bag and all) over the prunes. Allow to sit for 15 minutes before adding the brandy, then infuse for a minimum of 45 minutes at room temperature (or place in the fridge for tomorrow).

Remove the tea bag and use a stick blender or food processor to blitz the prunes with the soaking liquid until you have a rough, chunky purée with some bits of prune still visible. Preheat the oven to 190°C/170°C fan/gas mark 5 and lightly grease the bundt tins (use butter spray or brush with melted butter).

Use an electric whisk to beat the eggs and sugar at very high speed until they go thick and very fluffy, so that you have a strong sabayon (more notes on this on page 18). Melt the butter and chocolate together to form a smooth mixture (instructions on page 17). Place the dry ingredients in a separate bowl and mix together.

Fold the chocolate paste and then the prune purée into the sabayon. Add the dry ingredients and fold carefully to retain as much air as possible. Divide the batter between the baking tins (about 150g in each).

Bake in the centre of the oven for 10 minutes, then turn the tins around and leave for a further 6 minutes. Allow to cool in the tins for at least 30 minutes. The cakes may not seem set when you remove them from the oven, but don't worry – baking with chocolate sometimes has this effect. They will set once cold, so stick to the baking times here.

Once the cakes have cooled, flip them out of the tins. Serve with whipped cream or just as they are. These will keep in the fridge for a week or so, but bring them up to room temperature before eating to taste them at their best.

Bleeding hearts (vanilla, rose & strawberry cakes)

The name may be cheesy, but that is the only criticism you could make of these cakes, which are as pretty on the outside as they are within. Cut open to reveal the red heart of the matter. The batter needs to rest for at least an hour – you can keep it in the fridge for up to a week and bake variations on these cakes using different jams, fruits and nuts. This strawberry one is my favourite. The only other version that comes close in our kitchen is one with Nutella piped inside and hazelnuts sprinkled on top.

Makes 6 muffin-sized cakes

These work beautifully in silicone moulds

For the cake batter

- *140g unsalted butter*
- *200g icing sugar*
- *110g ground almonds*
- *50g plain flour*
- *seeds from ½ vanilla pod*
- *120g egg whites*

For the filling

- *6 tsp strawberry & rose jam (page 33), or ordinary strawberry jam with a couple of drops of rose water added*

For the icing

- *170g icing sugar*
- *1–2 strawberries (or ½ tsp strawberry jam)*
- *½ tsp rose water*
- *a few vanilla seeds (¼ pod) or 1 tsp vanilla extract*
- *1 tbsp glucose or honey*

Melt the butter in a small pan on a high heat and cook until it starts to foam, turns golden and catches a little at the bottom, then remove from the stove.

A food processor will give the best results for these cakes (if you don't have one you can make the batter by hand, but you will need to be quite vigorous). Place the dry ingredients and vanilla seeds in the food processor and mix together. With the food processor running, pour in the egg whites in a constant steady stream and mix to combine thoroughly. Follow with the hot burnt butter, pouring it slowly into the processor as it works, making sure to scrape in the sticky brown bits at the bottom of the saucepan too – they add great flavour. Set the batter in the fridge to cool for at least an hour (and up to a week).

When you are ready to bake, preheat the oven to 190°C/170°C fan/gas mark 5. Lightly grease the silicone moulds with butter spray (if using metal moulds, lightly butter and flour them). Divide the batter between the moulds. It should reach about 2cm below the top. Insert a teaspoonful of jam into the heart of each one: simply use the teaspoon to push some batter aside, then slide the jam off. As you pull the spoon out, the batter should rise up and cover the jam.

Place the moulds on a baking tray and bake for about 25–30 minutes until the smell is irresistible and the cakes are set to the touch (in this case you can only test the edges, as the centre will sink because of the jam underneath). Lay a large piece of baking parchment on top of the tins, set a baking tray on top of that, and very carefully flip them over and allow to sit for 20 minutes.

Mix the icing ingredients together in a bowl, squashing the strawberries a little to extract their juice and colour. The icing should be the texture of thick honey, so if it seems a little thick, add a couple of drops of water.

Remove the cakes from the moulds and leave to cool entirely on a wire rack before spooning or piping the icing on generously. Let the natural flow of the icing gently trickle down the sides and set. If you want, you can top each one with some fresh rose petals or a strawberry. Once set, these keep at room temperature for 2–3 days, staying lovely and moist.

Peach, vanilla & fennel seed mini loaves

This cake was created while we were working on our first book. We would have long afternoon meetings with Elizabeth, our publisher, in her office across the road from our restaurant. Tea was always involved and, inevitably, cakes. One autumn afternoon she produced a humble-looking loaf cake, delicately flavoured with caraway seeds, which we both went mad for. I had never heard of or tasted seed cake before, and this one was particularly good (it's a Delia recipe, and it's perfect). Seeds and spices are right up our alley, so we adopted the idea with gusto and experimented a lot, with varying degrees of success. Not to replace the traditional recipe, just to offer another option. This one proved to be a great triumph.

Makes 8 little loaf cakes (or a large 1kg (2lb) loaf)

1 tsp fennel seeds
125g unsalted butter, at room temperature
seeds of ½ vanilla pod
zest of 1 lemon
zest of 1 orange
225g caster sugar, plus 1 tbsp for sprinkling
a pinch of table salt
3 eggs
120g mascarpone
160g plain flour
½ tsp baking powder
2 peaches

Preheat the oven to 190°C/170°C fan/ gas mark 5. Butter eight small loaf tins and line each with a sheet of baking parchment to cover the base and long sides, allowing a little overhang at the sides. Don't worry about lining the ends too, just make sure they're greased. Lightly toast the fennel seeds in a dry frying pan over a medium heat for about 5 minutes, then allow to cool before crushing.

I use an electric mixer to make the batter, but if you don't have one, you can make it by hand. Beat the butter, vanilla seeds, zests, fennel seeds, sugar and salt together until just combined in a ball. Don't overbeat or cream. Add the eggs one at a time, mixing each egg in well, so that the batter is completely smooth before the next goes in. Add the mascarpone, flour and baking powder in one go and mix at full speed for a few seconds to make sure everything is well combined.

Slice two 'cheeks' off each peach (one from either side of the stone), cutting as close to the stone as possible. Chop the remaining fruit into small dice and mix into the cake batter. Cut the peach 'cheeks' into thin long slices. Divide the batter between the lined tins. Top each cake with four or five peach slices spread out like a small fan and sprinkle with the additional sugar.

Bake for 20–25 minutes or until risen and a lovely golden colour. It is a little tricky to tell when a cake containing fresh fruit is fully baked, but the surface should feel nice and bouncy.

These are great to eat warm. They keep well at room temperature for 24 hours but after that they start to deteriorate, so be sure to gobble them up quickly.

Spice cakes with marzipan cream filling & raspberries

This is like a Middle Eastern rum baba made with fragrant spices. The amount of spice in this recipe is just a starting point. Stick to it the first time you bake this; the second time you may want to add some more, or take some out. Even if you aren't going to make this cake, do give the marzipan cream a try – it is a nifty little trick that works well with lots of cakes and desserts (or on its own). If you fancy it, serve these with fresh raspberries or cherries; the combination works really well.

Makes 6 small bundt cakes (or a classic 1kg (2lb) bundt)

You can use silicone moulds here to great effect

For the cake batter
- *110g unsalted butter*
- *200g icing sugar*
- *80g ground almonds*
- *150g plain flour*
- *¾ tsp baking powder*
- *1½ tsp sweet spice mix (page 48) or ½ tsp each of ground ginger, cinnamon and cardamom*
- *200g egg whites (from about 6–7 eggs)*

For the brandy syrup
- *220g/ml water*
- *2 tbsp honey*
- *250g caster sugar*
- *2 tbsp brandy*

For the marzipan cream
- *30g marzipan (page 265 or ready-made)*
- *30g/ml milk*
- *150g/ml double cream*

fresh raspberries or cherries to serve (if you like)

Set the butter to burn in a small pan on a high heat – it should start to go golden and catch a little at the bottom. This browning process adds a very rich, nutty flavour that is so much more than simply melting butter, so don't be tempted to use the microwave here.

Combine the icing sugar, ground almonds, flour, baking powder and sweet spices in a mixer bowl with a paddle (you can also stir them together by hand with a large spoon, but be quite vigorous as you want them well mixed).

Set the mixer on a slow speed and add the egg whites to the dry ingredients in a constant steady stream. Once the egg whites have been fully incorporated, keep mixing and gradually add the hot butter in a constant slow stream, allowing it to be absorbed into and combine with the mixture. Make sure you get all the residue of sticky brown bits that will have formed at the bottom of the pan – they contain loads of flavour. Transfer the lovely smooth batter to the fridge to rest for at least an hour (it can be kept in the fridge for up to a week before baking).

When you are ready to bake, preheat the oven to 190°C/170°C fan/gas mark 5. Lightly grease the silicone moulds with butter spray (if using metal moulds, lightly butter and flour them). Pipe or spoon the mix into six small bundt tins (about 120g batter in each). Bake in the centre of the oven for 20–25 minutes, or until the cakes feel very springy to the touch. (If you are baking a single large cake, it will take 40–50 minutes.)

While the cakes are baking, bring the water, honey and sugar to the boil in a small pan on a high heat. Skim off any impurities that form on top and continue boiling for 1 minute, then remove from the heat and add the brandy.

As soon as the cakes come out of the oven, flip them and remove from the tins – be careful, as they will be hot. You want to douse them in syrup straight away, so don't be tempted to wait until they cool. Use a large pastry brush to soak them generously or pick each one up carefully and dip it in the syrup, then allow them to rest for at least 15 minutes before filling with the cream (if you are using it).

Mix the marzipan with the milk until you have a thick paste, then add the double cream and whisk to a nice soft consistency. Fill the hole in the centre of each cake with the cream and, if you wish (and I am sure you do), top with some fresh raspberries or cherries.

Citrus & us

We come from a country where citrus fruit is king. In Hebrew citrus trees are called 'glory trees', and if you ever visit a citrus orchard in fruit you'll know why: the sight of the heavy, brightly coloured orbs bobbing in a sea of dark green foliage, shining in the winter sun; the scent of the leaves as you scrunch one in your hand; the flavour of the fruit...

Lemons and oranges are a cornerstone in our cooking and baking. We use the flesh and juice in many different ways, and the fresh zesty peel brings its own special aroma to our food. The skin is always candied in our kitchen and we love cooking entire fruits in jams, cakes and sauces. And a glug of orange blossom water adds a delicious floral note to both sweets and savouries. We could fill an entire book with our recipes for citrus cakes, but we have whittled it down to these.

Blood orange & pistachio cakes

While these are perfectly delicious made with regular oranges, this particular combination really comes into its own in late January with the musky, more grown-up flavour of blood oranges. These look sensational as well, as everything made with blood oranges does.

Makes 10 large muffin-sized cakes

Silicone moulds work well here

For the cake batter
250g unsalted butter
250g caster sugar
zest of 1 blood orange
125g ground almonds
125g ground pistachios
4 eggs
250g self-raising flour
a pinch of table salt

For the topping
120g caster sugar
1 tbsp cornflour
3–4 blood oranges

Preheat the oven to 190°C/170°C fan/ gas mark 5 and lightly spray or butter ten large muffin tins. Mix the sugar and cornflour for the topping together and spoon a teaspoonful into each muffin tin. Shake the tins a little so you have a sugared layer on the base of each one.

Use a sharp knife (I think serrated is best for this job) to cut away the skin from the oranges for the topping, then cut the flesh into slices about as wide as your finger – you should get 3–4 full slices from each orange (eat the end bits). Place a slice of orange flat in the base of each tin.

I use an electric mixer to make the batter, but if you don't have one, you can make it by hand. Cream together the butter, sugar and orange zest until paler and a little aerated. Add the ground almonds and pistachios and mix until it all comes together and starts to stick to the side of the bowl. Add the eggs one at a time, »»

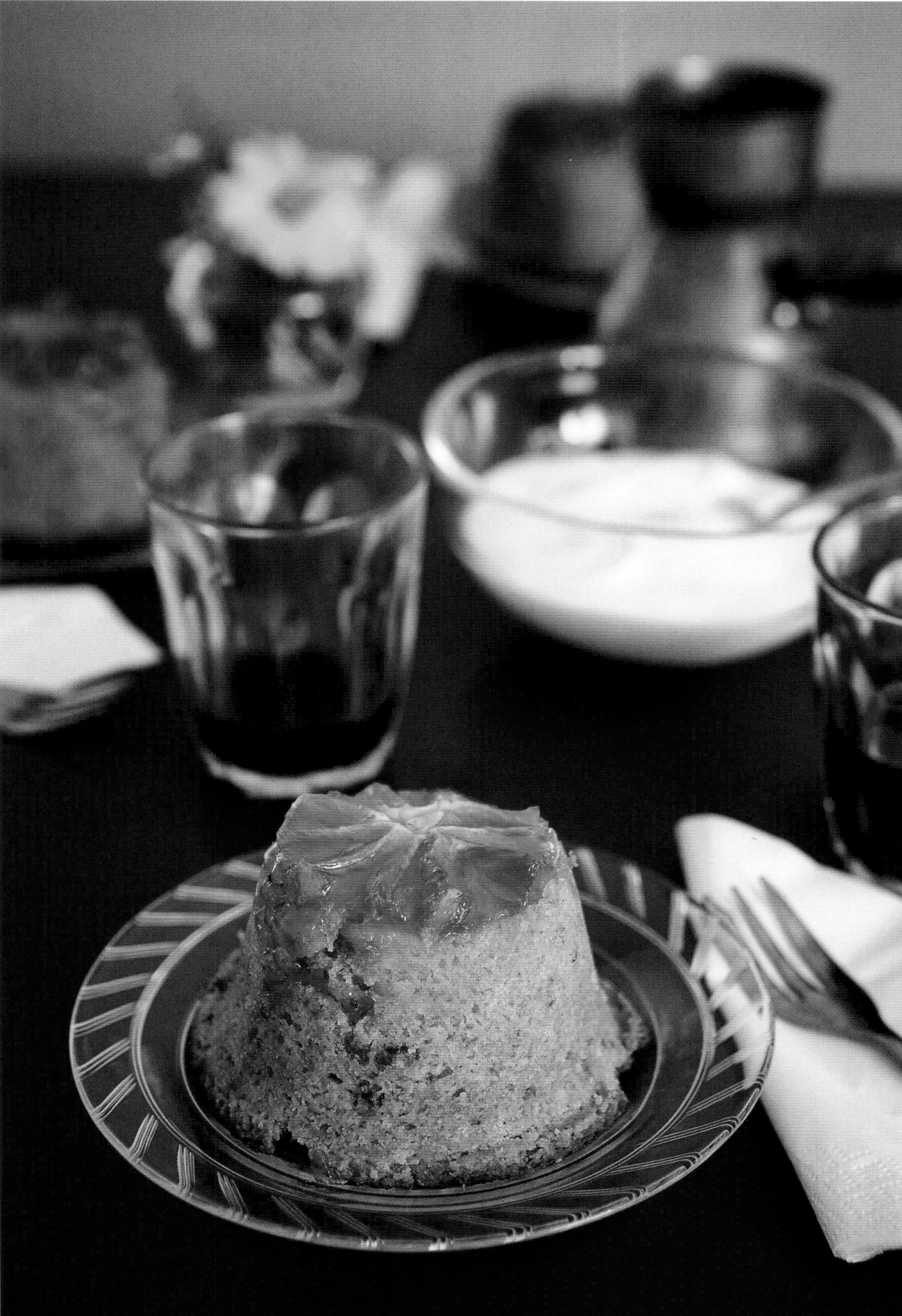

mixing well to combine each one before adding the next. Once you have a smooth paste, scrape it down the sides of the bowl all the way to the bottom, then add the flour and salt in one go. Mix again at a high speed until you have a nice, smooth, well-combined batter.

I usually transfer it to a piping bag at this stage but you can also use two spoons to scoop the batter instead. Divide it between the tins. You can weigh them if you want to be specific; there should be about 80g in each. Place the tins on a baking tray and bake in the centre of the oven for 15 minutes, then turn them around for an even bake and leave for a further 10–15 minutes until the cakes are set. You can check this by pressing lightly with your finger. The cakes should have a slight bounce and your finger shouldn't sink at all.

Remove from the oven and flip the moulds onto a tray lined with baking parchment. Allow to cool slightly upside-down (5–10 minutes will do) before you remove the cakes from the tins. Don't let them get too cold or it will be really hard to keep the orange slices intact (the cornflour thickens with the orange juice and sticks the slice to the tin when cold).

These are best eaten straight away, as they are delicious warm. They also keep well in the fridge for a few days, but for best results let them come up to room temperature before eating.

Orange blossom & marmalade cakes

The quadruple orange dose in these cakes – in the form of fresh orange, orange marmalade, orange blossom water and orange syrup – gives them the most delicious smell. The soft, slightly crumbly texture and bright orange flavour make them not only a good companion for tea or coffee, but also a great dessert to end a meal. I love to fill the centre of the bundts with rich Greek yogurt and an extra teaspoon of marmalade, but you can have them just as they are.

Makes 6 small flower-shaped bundt cakes (or 1 classic 1kg (2lb) bundt)

For the cake batter

200g unsalted butter, at room temperature
250g caster sugar
seeds from ½ vanilla pod or 1 tsp vanilla essence
zest of 1 orange
60g ground almonds
4 eggs
200g plain flour
60g semolina
1 tsp baking powder
a pinch of table salt
60g whole orange marmalade (page 41)
2 tsp orange blossom water

For the syrup

juice of 1–2 oranges (about 60g/ml)
150g caster sugar
100g water
1 tbsp orange blossom

Preheat the oven to 190°C/170°C fan/ gas mark 5. With this cake I advise using old-fashioned metal bundt tins, as the crust that forms is great and you will get a lovely shape for the cakes. Lightly grease the tins with butter spray, or lightly butter and flour them if you prefer.

I use an electric mixer with a paddle attachment to make the batter, but if you don't have one, you can make it by hand. Cream the butter, sugar, vanilla, orange zest and almonds together until they start to fluff up and stick to the sides of the bowl, but don't overwork or allow the mixture to go white. Scrape down the sides of the bowl and mix in the eggs one at a time, making sure each is fully combined before adding the next. Then add the flour, semolina, baking powder, salt, marmalade and orange blossom water and combine to a nice, even consistency. Take care to not over-mix, as this can result in a tougher texture that isn't as nice to eat.

Pipe or spoon the batter into the tins – you end up with about 150g in each (or use a single large bundt tin). For the small cakes, bake for 10 minutes, then turn the tins around and leave for a further 10–12 minutes until just set to the touch. They will firm up later, so don't be tempted to leave them in the oven for longer. (If you are using a large bundt, it will need an additional 15–20 minutes until it is set.)

While the cakes are baking, mix the orange juice, sugar and water together in a small saucepan and bring to the boil over a high heat. Skim any impurities that form on top and continue boiling for 1 minute, then remove from the heat and add the orange blossom water.

As soon as the cakes come out of the oven, brush generously with the syrup and allow to soak in. Repeat until you have used all the syrup. Don't be tempted to leave any – it may look like a lot but it will be absorbed and make the cakes like little syrupy rum ››› babas (without the rum). Flip the tins as soon as you can handle touching them and gently release the cakes onto a wire cooling rack. These keep well for up to 3 days (because of the syrup) and are best kept at room temperature, rather than in the fridge.

If you fancy my serving idea, fill the centre of each cake with Greek yogurt and a touch of marmalade. Alternatively, simply serve the yogurt on the side.

Lemon drizzle cake with elderflower & mascarpone icing

This cake is the result of an experiment that took some strange turns along the way. I had a glut of lemon marmalade and wanted to create a cake recipe to use it up. I thought I had struck gold on my first attempt when I looked in the oven and saw a beautiful golden dome rising, but when it cooled down it sank horribly in the middle – my heart sinking with it. I left it for the staff lunch without even trying it. Our staff members are always appreciative when they get cake with their lunch, but the reactions to this one were like nothing before: they were all raving about it. I tried a slice and could immediately see why: it had a soft texture, dense without being heavy, and a lovely fresh taste. The only problem was its sunken appearance, which we easily fixed with a creamy elderflower icing. This is now one of our best-loved cakes.

Makes a 23cm (9 inch) round cake

For the cake batter
- *225g unsalted butter*
- *400g caster sugar*
- *zest of 2 lemons*
- *4 eggs*
- *120g plain flour*
- *10g baking powder*
- *a pinch of table salt*
- *150g/ml double cream*
- *50g/ml elderflower cordial*
- *100g whole lemon marmalade (page 41)*

For the syrup
- *100g/ml base sugar syrup (page 59)*
- *50g/ml lemon juice*

For the icing
- *200g mascarpone*
- *150g full fat cream cheese*
- *50g icing sugar*
- *50g/ml elderflower cordial*

Preheat the oven to 180°C/160°C fan/ gas mark 4. Line the base and butter the sides of the cake tin.

It is best to use an electric mixer with a paddle attachment to make this. You can make it by hand, but you will need to be very vigorous. Cream the butter with the sugar and lemon zest until fluffy and white. Add the eggs one by one, along with a tablespoon of flour each time. Make sure that each egg is well mixed in before adding the next. Mix in the remaining flour along with the baking powder and salt. Keep mixing as you slowly pour in the cream and elderflower cordial until fully incorporated. Add the lemon marmalade and mix around to soften and ripple through the batter. Transfer to the baking tin and smooth the surface a little.

Bake in the centre of the oven for 40 minutes, then turn the tin around for an even bake and leave for another 20 minutes. Remove from the oven to check whether it is done. This is a very wet, rich batter so the best way is by pressing lightly in the centre of the cake – it should feel firm but not springy. If it feels very wet, return it to the oven for a further 10 minutes. Being a rich cake, it will colour quickly. It should have a really dark golden crust once baked (if you feel it is going too dark, cover the top with aluminium foil).

Mix the sugar syrup with the lemon juice. As soon as the cake comes out of the oven, make a few holes using a skewer or toothpick and pour the lemon syrup all over. Leave to cool in the tin. The cake will sink in the centre, that's for sure, but that space will be filled with the lovely creamy icing.

Place the icing ingredients in a mixer with a paddle attachment and combine at slow-medium speed until the cream thickens and holds its shape. You can mix this by hand if you like, but don't use a whisk or you will split the cream. Spread all over the cake or pipe in a pattern, whichever you prefer.

Keep this cake in the fridge until you are ready to serve. It lasts well for 4 days un-iced, but once iced you should really finish it within 2 days.

Clementine cake (inspired by Claudia Roden)

You are often disappointed when you meet someone whose work you admire. We had the opposite reaction when we met Claudia Roden; we were trembling with excitement when she came to the restaurant and she turned out to be the gentlest, warmest, most charming person you are ever likely to meet. Her flourless orange cake is legendary; we had it on our dessert menu, proud to have her name gracing it. If you haven't tried her cake before, then you really must. And if you already know and love it, as we do, you can try this take on it.

Makes a 23cm (9 inch) round cake

Gluten-free

2 whole ripe clementines
3 eggs
130g caster sugar
150g ground almonds
½ tsp baking powder
½ tsp ground ginger
1 tbsp cornflour
a pinch of table salt

Cut a cross into the top of each clementine where the stem is, so that you reveal the flesh slightly, but keep the fruit intact. Place in a saucepan and cover with plenty of water. Bring to the boil, then drain and discard the water. Repeat the process twice more until you have boiled and drained the fruit three times.

Place the boiled clementines in a colander and allow to cool a little. Split the fruit and remove any seeds and the central white pith. You should end up with about 200–220g.

Preheat the oven to 190°C/170°C fan/gas mark 5 and line the base of the cake tin with baking parchment.

Place the clementines in a food processor with a metal blade, and purée until the texture resembles baby food. Keep the processor running and add the eggs and sugar to incorporate. Mix the remaining ingredients in a large bowl, then pour the clementine mixture on top. Fold together until well combined. Transfer the batter to the tin and smooth the top.

Bake in the centre of the oven for 30 minutes, then turn the tin around for an even bake and leave for another 5–10 minutes. The end result should be springy to the touch. Allow to cool in the tin before turning out and serving. This cake keeps well for a few days and is best kept in the fridge.

Lemon, blueberry & cream cheese squares

We are not proud of it, but we know that Louisa (in charge of our catering and running our office) works in quite harsh conditions. Her realm is a tiny cramped office tucked behind our pastry ovens, which make it impossibly hot in summer and impossible to heat in winter. This is where she answers a seemingly endless stream of emails and phone calls, her work constantly interrupted by random queries and requests from chefs, shift managers and the two of us. She takes it all with good-spirited calm and a great smile, and enjoys one of the few perks of her job – the occasional piece of cake that lands on her desk.

Makes a 23cm (9 inch) square cake

125g full fat cream cheese
200g caster sugar
3 eggs
zest and juice of 2 lemons
150g self-raising flour
a pinch of table salt
60g butter, melted
60g whole lemon marmalade (page 41)

For the topping
200g blueberries
20g caster sugar

Preheat the oven to 190°C/170°C fan/ gas mark 5. Butter and line the square cake tin.

Place the cream cheese and sugar in a mixer with a paddle attachment (or fold together by hand with a spatula) and cream until they are combined and the sugar has dissolved. Mix in the eggs one by one, followed by the lemon zest and juice. Add the flour and salt, and stir to combine. Finally fold in the melted butter and marmalade.

Mix half the blueberries into the batter, then transfer to the tin. Top with the remaining blueberries and sprinkle with the sugar. Bake for 20 minutes, then turn the tin around for an even bake and leave for a further 15–20 minutes until the cake is golden and the blueberries have started to explode.

Allow to cool in the tin before cutting the cake into squares. This keeps well for a couple of days at room temperature and about 4 days if kept in the fridge.

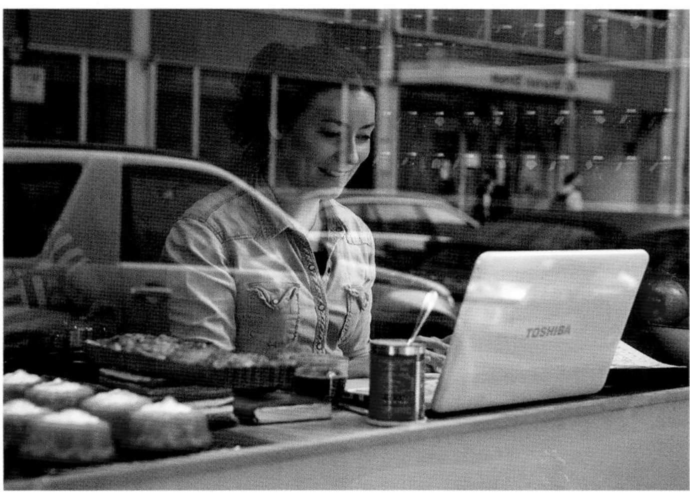

Good cookies

Itamar discourages me from making cookies for the shop for many reasons. They are very labour-intensive, taking up much of our pastry time; plus the rest of the kitchen, seeing a tray coming out of the oven, will flock around to try to damage the little things so they can have them. The main point of disagreement, however, is that he doesn't see them as dessert. I most definitely do. I think there is nothing nicer as a treat, and a bowlful of indulgent cookies passed around the table can be the perfect finish to a rich dinner. They contain just the right amount of sweetness, and if one isn't quite enough, you can always have another, and then just one more... Maybe I can see the problem with them after all.

Chocolate & pistachio cookies

Mel will be very happy to see this recipe here. She is one of our most loyal regulars, and may come for breakfast, lunch and dinner on the same day, and then return the day after that. She lives in Toronto, where she runs a gallery, and visits London a few times a year. When she is in town we see her every day, and before she leaves she usually stops in to buy something to eat on the plane and a pack of these biscuits. We refused her the recipe many times, but only so we can indulge her now in a big way. The appeal of these cookies is tremendous – soft fudgy chocolate encased in mega-crunchy nuts. They are hugely popular among our more local customers as well.

Makes 12 large cookies (or 24 bite-sized ones)

250g chocolate (I use a 60% cacao dark chocolate)
50g unsalted butter
2 eggs
175g light brown soft sugar
60g strong white bread flour
½ tsp baking powder
a pinch of table salt
about 200g pistachios, very roughly chopped, to coat

Melt the chocolate and butter together in a bowl in the microwave or over a double steamer (see page 12 for more information about melting chocolate). In the meantime, whisk the eggs and sugar to a sabayon – that is, until the mixture is very thick and fluffy. Line two baking trays with baking parchment.

Fold the melted chocolate into the eggs. Add the flour, baking powder and salt, then fold together until you have a lovely even mixture. Allow to rest for about 30 minutes in a cool place or pop in the fridge for 10–15 minutes (you want the dough to be manageable but not set). If you forget about it in the fridge and it sets solid, you will have to bring it back up to temperature in a warm place so that you can handle it easily.

Divide the dough into 12 and, using two spoons or a piping bag, shape into balls of about 50g each. I usually use weighing scales, but you can be more relaxed if you prefer and just estimate the size.

Spread the chopped pistachios on a flat tray and drop the balls of chocolate goodness onto them. Flip them to coat all over, then transfer to the baking trays, allowing about 5cm between them as they will spread in the heat of the oven. You can keep the unbaked cookies in the fridge until you are ready to bake or, alternatively, freeze them for up to 2 weeks and simply thaw before baking.

Preheat the oven to 200°C/180°C fan/gas mark 6. Place the trays in the centre of the oven for 8–9 minutes (allow 12 minutes if the cookies have been chilled). Remove and leave to cool on the trays while the chocolate sets fully. Once the cookies are cool you will be able to pick them up quite easily, but the middle will stay nice and soft like a moist chewy brownie, so handle with care. These keep well for up to a week in an airtight container or sealed bag.

Chocolate, pistachio
fudge cookies
BB
Marzipan
Cookies
BB

Date & pine nut maamool cookies

There is a recipe for traditional maamool cookies in our previous book. Filling, closing and decorating individual balls of dough requires the patience of a Buddhist monk, a clear schedule and years of practice to get it just right. In contrast, this recipe uses a short cut inspired by the very British sausage roll. I pipe the date filling through the entire dough and slice off individual cookies when I want to bake them, rather like an American freezer cookie-log. This allows me to have a fresh cookie whenever I wish. And if the presentation of these is less elaborate than the original, the flavour is still excellent.

Makes about 40–45 cookies

For the cookie dough

125g icing sugar
1 egg
zest of ½ lemon
a pinch of table salt
250g unsalted butter at room temperature, diced
380g plain flour
½ tsp table salt

For the filling

400g pitted dates
400g/ml boiling water
100g pine nuts, roasted
2 tsp ground cinnamon
1 tsp ground cardamom
1 tsp ground ginger
1 tbsp honey

egg wash (1 egg beaten with a pinch of table salt) or a little milk
sesame seeds to sprinkle

Cream the cookie dough ingredients together in a mixer with a paddle attachment (or by hand, if you prefer) until they form a nice smooth dough. Shape into a ball and wrap in cling film. Chill in the fridge for at least 1 hour.

Soak the dates in the boiling water for 30 minutes, then drain and chop finely (you can purée them in a food processor if you prefer a smoother filling). Mix with the pine nuts, spices and honey, then transfer to a piping bag with a very wide nozzle.

Dust your work surface with some flour and roll out the dough to a large rectangle about 40cm x 30cm. You can roll the dough between two sheets of greaseproof paper if you are worried it will stick. If it gets too warm and soft, return the dough to the fridge for 10 minutes to chill. Make sure the dough is at a good, workable temperature before you start assembling the cookies.

Pipe a long strip of the date filling (about as thick as your thumb) along one of the 40cm sides of the rectangle, about 1–2cm in from the edge. Fold the edge of the dough over the filling and roll to wrap it up. Stop rolling once the filling is encased – it should resemble a very long, thin sausage roll. Cut the rolled log free of the rest of the cookie dough and set to one side. Repeat the piping, rolling and cutting until you have used up all the cookie dough. Carefully transfer the filled logs to a tray lined with baking parchment and chill in the fridge for at least 1 hour (up to 48 hours). Alternatively, put some or all of them in the freezer to bake another day.

Preheat the oven to 200°C/180°C fan/gas mark 6. Brush the logs with egg wash or a little milk and sprinkle with sesame seeds. Cut at an angle to create short logs, each about 2.5cm long, and place on a baking tray.

Bake for about 15–20 minutes until lovely and golden. Allow to cool a little on the tray before gobbling, as the filling will be very hot. These keep for a few days in an airtight container and some say they actually improve with time, but personally I like them warm, fresh from the oven.

Tahini sandwich cookies filled with white chocolate & rose

A traditional childhood treat for us was a slice of bread spread with tahini and either honey or silan (date molasses). The combination of very rich and very sweet is pleasing at any age – rather like the American combo of peanut butter and jelly (jam). The tahini gives these cookies a delicate nuttiness and a short texture unlike any other. Sandwiching them may feel a bit indulgent and special occasion-y, so if you want to give it a miss, that's fine – these cookies can proudly stand alone.

Makes 10–12 sandwich cookies

For the dough
- *150g unsalted butter, diced*
- *150g caster sugar*
- *270g strong white bread flour*
- *½ tsp mahleb (or ground cardamom)*
- *150g tahini paste*

For the filling
- *100g/ml double cream*
- *250g white chocolate, chopped in small chunks*
- *2–3 tsp rose water*

dried rose petals for decoration (if you like)

Preheat the oven to 190°C/170°C fan/ gas mark 5 and line a baking sheet with baking parchment. Place all the dough ingredients in a mixer with a paddle attachment (or you can make it by hand, but it will be a sticky affair). Start slowly until the dough comes together, then increase the speed to high and work for a few seconds until it is really shiny and supple.

Divide the dough into pieces roughly the size of a walnut in its shell (about 30g each). There should be between 20 and 24 pieces, although this really depends on whether you are the type of person who eats cookie dough (this one is especially delicious). Roll each piece between your palms to form a ball, then place on the baking sheet and press down to flatten slightly. Leave about 3–4cm between each one as they will spread a little during baking.

Bake in the centre of the oven for 10 minutes, then turn the tray around and bake for a further 6–8 minutes until light golden. They will still be a little soft when you remove them from the oven, so let them cool on the tray. Don't worry, they will harden once cold, so don't be tempted to allow them to colour too much.

Boil the cream in a small pan, then pour over the chocolate in a bowl. Leave for 30 seconds before stirring from the centre until all the chocolate has melted. If it refuses to melt entirely, you can pop the bowl in the microwave for a couple of seconds or put it over a double boiler to melt fully, but don't overheat it – it's really easy to burn white chocolate. Stir in 2 teaspoons of the rose water, then taste to see that you are happy with the amount. If you like, you can add a little extra but be cautious: the mixture should taste slightly floral; not like soap.

Leave in a cool place or in the fridge until nicely thickened but not completely set – you want it to be the texture of fondant icing or peanut butter. In the meantime, arrange the cookies in pairs and flip them so that their flat bases are facing upwards. If you have an uneven number, quickly eat one before someone notices.

Divide the filling between half the upside-down cookies, using a piping bag or teaspoon to place it in the centre of the flat base. Use the other cookie in each pair to close the sandwich, pushing down slightly until the filling reaches the edges. If you are using the rose petals to decorate, simply dip the side of each cookie in the petals. Leave in a cool place until fully set before serving.

Once assembled, the sandwich cookies will only last for a day or so before they go soft, but you can always prepare the cookies in advance and store them unfilled for up to a week. Make the filling when you are ready to assemble the sandwiches (or eat the cookies just as they are).

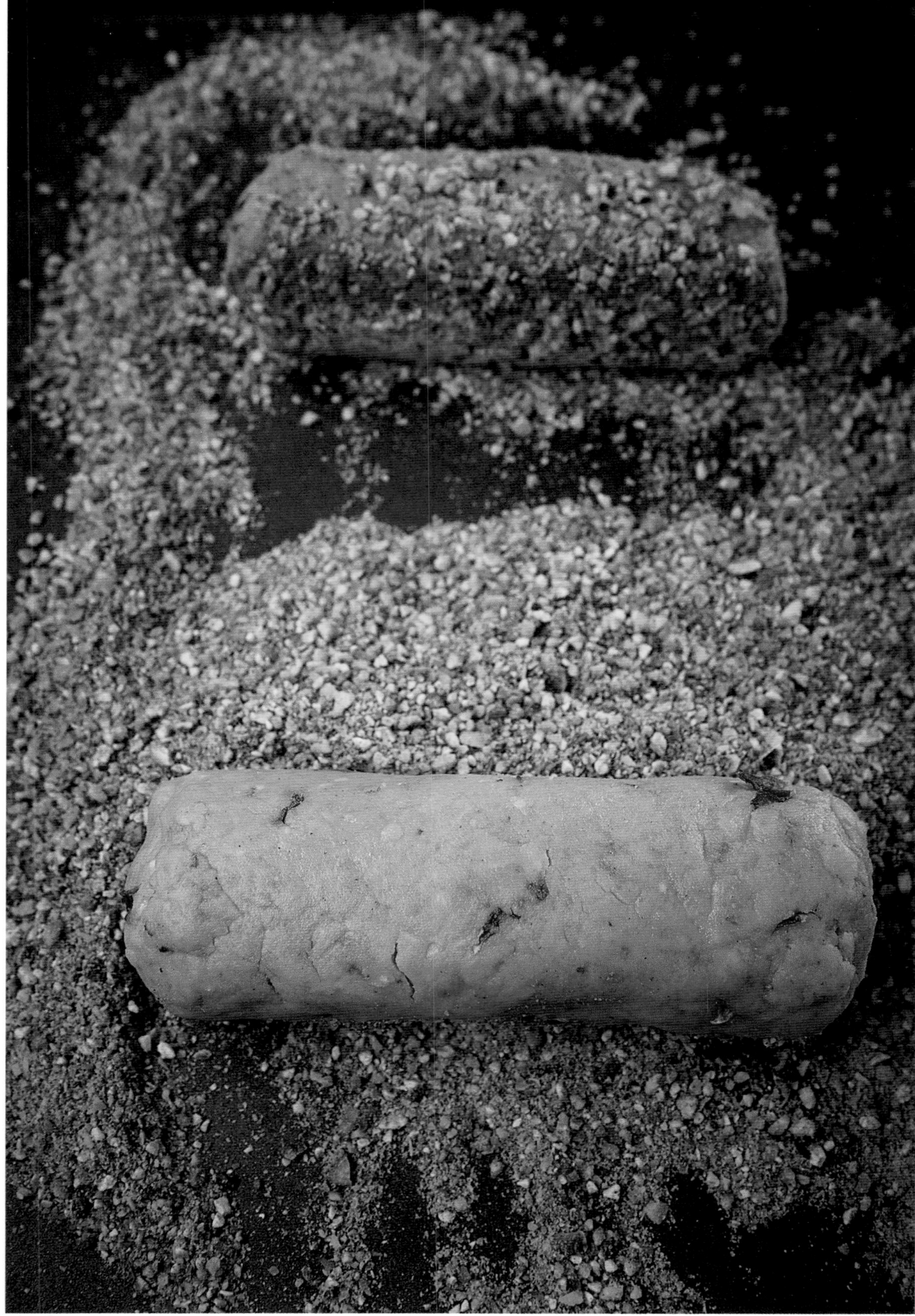

Gram flour shortbread

This is one of the best shortbread recipes I have encountered. I stumbled across the idea of using gram (chickpea) flour for shortbread while browsing through a book or magazine. I was dogged by the idea for the longest time, but was not encouraged to pursue it, as every time I mentioned it to my husband he voiced his utter disgust with the idea of chickpea sweets (surely you can see his point). I eventually tried it – magic! The chickpea flour gives these a very special crumb and a delicate back note that works so well with heady rose and cardamom. The fact that they are gluten- and dairy-free is incidental; they will please everyone (my husband included).

Makes about 16–18 cookies

Gluten-free

125g icing sugar
150g/160ml grapeseed oil, plus 1–2 tbsp if needed
250g gram (chickpea) flour
½ tsp ground cardamom
a pinch of table salt
1 tbsp dried rose petals
1 egg yolk
1 tsp rose water
80g pistachios, roughly chopped, for rolling

Put all the ingredients apart from the pistachios in a mixer with a paddle attachment (or mix by hand in a large bowl) and work them slowly until they come to a rough crumb consistency. Increase the speed to medium and work for a few seconds. The dough should come together into a ball, but I sometimes find that it stays in crumbs (gram flour can be drier than wheat flour); if this is the case, add another tablespoon or two of oil until the dough forms a ball.

Transfer the dough to the work surface and form into a log about 25–26cm long. As this is a gluten-free dough, you will need to be very firm with it to show it who's boss.

Lay a large sheet of cling film flat on the work surface and sprinkle with the chopped pistachios. Lift the dough log onto the nuts and roll and turn it to coat all over. Fold the cling film over and around the dough to cover, then roll up really tightly – this will help stick the pistachios securely in place. Twist the ends of the cling film to seal. Place in the fridge to chill for at least an hour (up to 3 days).

Preheat the oven to 190°C/170°C fan/gas mark 5 and line a baking sheet with baking parchment. Remove the dough from its cling film wrapper and cut in slices of about 0.5cm. Lay them flat on the baking tray.

Bake for 10 minutes, then turn the tray around and bake for a further 8–10 minutes until the cookies are a lovely golden colour and smell like roasted nuts. Allow to cool on the tray before packing away in an airtight container.

Cranberry, orange & almond caramel cookies

This looks great coming out of the oven: golden pastry with a layer of filling bubbling crazily on top, rather like pizza. When the topping cools you can see all the pretty shapes and colours of your fruit and nuts set in a crunchy caramel. Lovely.

Makes about 30 cookies

For the pastry

200g unsalted butter at room temperature, cubed
100g icing sugar
1 egg
zest of 1 lemon
300g strong white bread flour
½ tsp table salt

For the topping

30g unsalted butter
30g glucose syrup
150g caster sugar
100g/ml double cream
50g slivered almonds, lightly roasted
50g candied orange peel (page 44, or shop-bought)
50g dried cranberries

Combine all the ingredients for the pastry together to a lovely smooth dough, either by hand or using a mixer with a paddle attachment. Cover with cling film and chill in the fridge for at least 1 hour and up to 48 hours.

Roll the chilled pastry between two sheets of baking parchment to create a rectangle of about 40cm x 30cm. Peel off the top layer of parchment and cut the pastry lengthways to create two rectangles, each of around 40cm x 15cm. Fold the edges of the rectangles to create sides about 1cm high, as the unbaked caramel topping will be very runny. If you want these to look fancy, you can crimp them.

Transfer to a baking tray lined with baking parchment and make holes all over the base with the tines of a fork (this is called docking and stops the base from rising while it bakes). Set the tray in the fridge to chill for at least 30 minutes.

Preheat the oven to 200°C/180°C fan/gas mark 6. Bake the bases for 10–15 minutes until lightly golden. Remove from the oven and lower the temperature to 190°C/170°C fan/gas mark 5.

Combine the butter, glucose syrup, sugar and cream in a saucepan, bring to a rapid boil over a high heat and cook for 2 minutes. Stir in the almonds, candied peel and cranberries. Remove from the heat and divide the topping between the two pastry rectangles, then use a spatula to distribute evenly and smooth as much as possible.

Bake for 10–15 minutes or until the topping has caramelised to a lovely golden colour. Allow to cool on the tray for 10–15 minutes before removing to a chopping board to cut into fingers. Don't wait too long as the caramel will set once cold, making these really hard to slice. Once cut, leave to cool entirely before eating or storing. These will keep in an airtight container for up to a week.

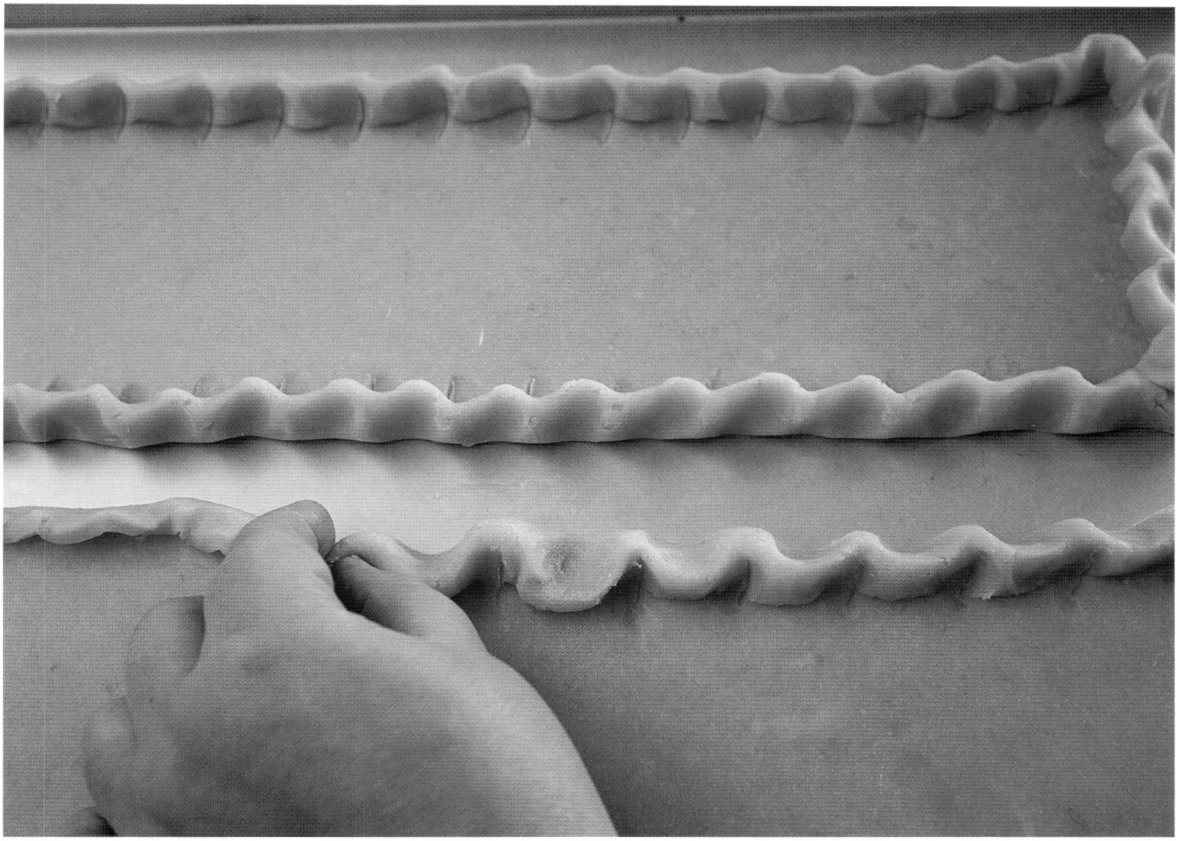

Chocolate sandwich cookies filled with tahini cream

Even if you are a hopeless baker like I (Itamar) am, you need to have one or two killer desserts in your repertoire. This one is mine. I found the chocolate cookie recipe in a magazine and followed it religiously. I was very impressed with the results, Sarit less so. She went on to change the recipe completely and add the tahini cream. No matter. These are good enough (and rich enough) to serve as dessert on their own and are dead easy to make. Do not be tempted to over-bake them; their greatness lies in their gooey centre.

Makes 7 sandwiches (or 14 individual cookies)

Gluten-free

For the dough

40g unsalted butter
250g 70% dark chocolate
2 eggs
150g light brown soft sugar
20g cocoa powder
50g 70% dark chocolate, chopped

For the filling

40g tahini paste
50g full fat cream cheese
50g/ml double cream
25g icing sugar

Preheat the oven to 200°C/180°C fan/ gas mark 6 and line two trays with baking parchment. Melt the butter and chocolate together in the microwave or over a double steamer (see notes on page 12).

Whisk the eggs and sugar to a really fluffy, white, peaky sabayon. Fold the melted chocolate mixture into the sabayon. Add the cocoa powder and chocolate chunks and fold to combine.

Use a piping bag or two spoons to make about 14 heaps of cookie dough (each about 30–35g) on the baking trays. Allow plenty of space (at least 5cm) between each one as they spread quite a bit during baking.

Bake for 9 minutes until they have formed a crust but are still really soft. Remove from the oven and allow to cool completely on the tray before filling.

Combine all the filling ingredients in a mixer with a paddle attachment, working the mixture at a really slow speed until smooth, creamy and able to hold its shape. Alternatively, you could whisk the ingredients together by hand, but be very careful not to over-whisk.

Pair the cookies and flip them base-upwards. Place a spoonful of filling in the centre of half the upturned cookies, then use the other cookie in each pair to close the sandwich, pressing lightly until the filling reaches the edges. You can eat these straight away or keep them in the fridge for a few days, if you can resist for that long.

Coconut & chocolate cake

Our first year in London was coconut-flavoured. We lived in a small but perfectly formed studio flat in Clapham. We had a tiny kitchen, a tiny dining table that could seat four very snugly, a massive bay window and a strange obsession with coconut cake. I think it was Sarit's thrifty nature that brought it about; we had bought a bag of coconut to bake a cake, so then we had to make another to use up the rest because it's a shame to throw away good food – but we had to buy a second bag as there wasn't quite enough left in the first one to make a whole cake... and so on, until we moved to a bigger place with enough room in the kitchen to store the ingredients for more than one cake. We tried many variations, but this was the one we stayed with. It is just moist enough to be a great cake but not so damp that it resembles a Bounty bar. The coconut strips make for a really funky-looking topping, so don't be lazy – make some (page 46) and use them here.

Makes a 23cm (9 inch) round cake

For the cake batter

250g unsalted butter
250g caster sugar
4 eggs
125g self-raising flour
125g desiccated coconut
zest of 1 lime

For the chocolate mousse topping

2 eggs
70g light brown soft sugar
50g unsalted butter
120g 70% dark chocolate

Preheat the oven to 190°C/170°C fan/ gas mark 5. Butter and line a 23cm (9 inch) cake tin.

Cream the butter and sugar together until light and fluffy. Gradually mix in the eggs one at a time until well combined. Add the rest of the ingredients and combine well. Transfer to the cake tin and smooth the top.

Bake in the centre of the oven for 15 minutes, then turn the tin around and bake for a further 15–20 minutes until the cake is set and spongy to the touch. Allow to cool slightly in the tin, then turn out and leave to cool entirely on a wire rack.

Whisk the eggs and sugar for the topping in a mixer with a whisk attachment until really fluffy. Melt the butter and chocolate together (on a double burner or in the microwave – see notes on page 12), then fold into the egg sabayon. Allow to set in the fridge for an hour or so, then spread over the top of the cake. Top with crystallised coconut strips (page 46), if you fancy making them.

Coffee, cardamom & walnut cake

Coffee and walnut is a classic British combo, and one of our favourite cakes – the kind you have in the café at the Tate gallery or a National Trust property. Coffee with cardamom is a Middle Eastern staple. It made sense to me that the three flavours would work well together, and they do. Even though the spice adds a tiny exotic note, this cake could take pride of place in any cafeteria across the land.

Makes a 23cm (9 inch) square cake (or a round one, if you prefer)

This works well in a silicone mould

For the cake batter

- *330g icing sugar*
- *120g ground almonds*
- *130g self-raising flour*
- *a pinch of table salt*
- *80g roasted walnuts, plus 50g extra to garnish (if you like)*
- *1 tsp ground coffee (Turkish coffee powder is best)*
- *½ tsp ground cardamom*
- *3 whole eggs*
- *150g egg whites (from about 4 eggs)*
- *140g burnt butter (method on page 18)*

For the syrup

- *2 tbsp honey*
- *60g/ml water*
- *50g caster sugar*
- *a double espresso or 60g/ml strong coffee*

For the coffee cream icing

- *120g unsalted butter, at room temperature*
- *140g icing sugar*
- *400g full fat cream cheese, at room temperature*
- *30g date molasses or maple syrup*
- *1 tsp ground coffee (Turkish coffee powder is best)*

Heat the oven to 190°C/170°C fan/ gas mark 5. Butter a 23cm (9 inch) cake tin and line with baking parchment.

Stir the dry ingredients together in a large bowl, then add the eggs and egg whites and mix really well until smooth. Pour in the warm melted butter and stir carefully until fully combined. Transfer to the prepared tin and allow to sit for 10 minutes to rest the batter a little, then bake for about 30–35 minutes until the cake is set.

While the cake is baking, bring the syrup ingredients to the boil in a pan, then remove from the heat. Once the cake comes out of the oven, brush it generously with half the syrup, reserving the remainder for later. Chill the cake (still in its tin) in the fridge for at least an hour (and up to 24 hours).

Put the butter and icing sugar in a mixer with a paddle attachment and cream together on a high speed until really light and fluffy. Mix in the cream cheese a little at a time, allowing each addition to combine and aerate before adding the next. Finally mix in the date molasses or maple syrup together with the ground coffee. Scrape the sides and bottom of the bowl to check the icing is well combined with no lumps.

Remove the cake from the tin, place on a serving platter and use a large serrated knife to cut it in half to create two layers. This can seem a little scary, but it is just a question of confidence. Use the knife to score around the sides of the cake at the midline to give you a guideline to follow. Holding the knife firmly in one hand, place the other hand flat on the top of the cake (to keep it steady) and use little sawing motions to cut through it, all the way to the other side.

Very gently slide the top layer onto your work surface or a flat tray. Brush the cut surface of the bottom layer with the remaining syrup, then cover with half the icing, spreading it all over, right up to the edges. Very carefully lift up the top layer of cake and slide it to sit on the iced bottom layer. Spread the rest of the icing over the top in little waves and garnish with walnuts (if using).

You will need to keep this cake in the fridge. It will be tasty for 2–3 days, but make sure to bring it back up to room temperature before eating for the best result.

Poppy seed cake with lemon icing

This cake – much like the other well-known derivative of the poppy plant – is totally addictive. With its humble black and white appearance, it has been on our cake counter from the start and has a loyal following among our customers, who keep coming back for their fix. Grinding the seeds is important to the flavour and texture of this cake. The only problem with it is the risk of social death – poppy seeds in between your teeth. If you want to keep this cake dairy-free you can substitute orange juice or almond milk for the milk in the batter; it'll still be delicious.

Makes a large flower-shaped bundt or a 23cm (9 inch) round cake

This works well in a silicone mould

For the cake batter

- *190g/ml vegetable oil (e.g. sunflower or linseed)*
- *300g caster sugar*
- *4 eggs*
- *180g plain flour*
- *1 tsp baking powder*
- *200g/ml milk*
- *150g poppy seeds, ground*
- *juice and zest of 1 lemon*
- *juice and zest of 1 orange*

100g/ml base sugar syrup (page 59)

For the lemon icing

- *250g icing sugar, plus more if needed*
- *1 tsp glucose syrup (this gives the icing a great shine, but omit it if you can't get hold of it)*
- *juice of 1 lemon (you may not need it all)*
- *poppy seeds for sprinkling*

Preheat the oven to 190°C/170°C fan/ gas mark 5. Lightly spray a silicone mould with butter spray, or lightly butter and flour a metal tin.

Whisk the oil with the sugar in a large bowl until combined. Add the eggs one at a time, whisking well after each one to create an emulsion (similar to making mayonnaise). Once you have a smooth, silky-looking mixture, add all the remaining batter ingredients at once and whisk until well combined. The batter will seem very runny, but don't worry, it will set solid once baked. Pour into the prepared mould or tin.

Bake in the centre of the oven for 25 minutes, then turn the cake and bake for a further 15–20 minutes until firm and springy to the touch (check this carefully: push down on the middle with your finger and make sure there is no liquid centre lurking within). Brush the sugar syrup all over the cake while it is still hot, then allow to cool in the tin for 20 minutes before turning out onto a wire rack and cooling entirely.

Combine the icing sugar and glucose (if using) in a small bowl. Mix in the lemon juice, a couple of drops at a time, until you have quite a thick icing. Check the consistency – it should be quite heavy and take some time to fall off a spoon. If it drips or runs off quickly, add a little more icing sugar to thicken it to the right consistency. Spoon or pipe it all over the top of the cake and allow it to drip naturally down the sides. Sprinkle with a few poppy seeds, then leave the icing to set before cutting.

This is a really moist cake and keeps well for 3–4 days at room temperature, and more than a week in the fridge.

Blueberry, hazelnut & ricotta cake

Recipes are nomads: they travel from one person to the next and, like Chinese whispers, they change a bit each time they pass. We don't know where this recipe started its journey, but it came to us from Laura Jane, a wonderful Australian baker with whom we worked for a spell. She used to bake it with chocolate flakes – delicious – which we changed to blueberries. This is in fact a cheesecake in disguise. The ricotta keeps it extremely moist and juicy while the ground hazelnuts bring texture and flavour, and work terrifically well with the fruit. After you have made it once or twice, why not experiment with the fruit-nut combo – walnut and date perhaps, or strawberry and almonds?

Makes a 23cm (9 inch) round cake

115g unsalted butter
125g caster sugar
3 eggs
25g plain flour
½ tsp table salt
zest of 1 lemon
1 tsp ground ginger
150g ground hazelnuts
250g ricotta cheese
1 punnet of blueberries (150g)
100g hazelnuts, roughly chopped
2 tbsp demerara sugar

Preheat the oven to 180°C/160°C fan/ gas mark 4. Butter the bottom of a 23cm (9 inch) cake tin, line with baking parchment and butter the sides.

Cream the butter and sugar together until light and fluffy – you can use an electric mixer with a paddle attachment or do it by hand with a large spatula. Add the eggs one at a time, making sure each is well combined before adding the next. Scrape down the sides of the bowl. Add the flour, salt, lemon zest, ground ginger and ground hazelnuts and mix until fully incorporated. Fold the ricotta and half the blueberries into the batter and scoop into the prepared tin. Top with the remaining blueberries and the roughly chopped hazelnuts, and sprinkle with the demerara sugar.

Bake for about 55–65 minutes or until the cake has set, the blueberries have exploded a little and oozed blue syrup, and the hazelnuts are golden. Allow to cool in the tin. Once cooled, place in the fridge to help it set so that you can transfer it to a serving platter.

The cake keeps well in the fridge for 3–4 days, but it's best to bring it up to room temperature before eating so that you can enjoy all the flavours to the full.

Baking cheesecake

Israel is a strange mixture of ancient, biblical traditions and modern-day living. For some reason the ancient festival of Pentecost, which has deep religious meaning in Judaism, is now celebrated in Israel with cheesecake. For one day in spring the entire country – religious and secular people alike – bakes and eats cheesecake. The newspapers are filled with cheesecake recipes and there are cheesecake-baking competitions. Some families unite under one recipe; others divide between different baking traditions (east v. west, new v. old). I am unclear how this custom came about or what the exact connection is between the holy day and the divine bake. Perhaps it is just an easy way to create something rich and festive.

I have great love for cheesecake (and quite a few recipes). It is as much of a joy to eat as it is to make, and almost fail-safe. There are just a few things you need to look out for:

• All your ingredients should be at room temperature, including the cheese, cream and eggs. Simply put everything on the work surface about 30 minutes before you start making the cake.

• Use a base that works well with the flavour of the filling. I like to bake an appropriate biscuit for each one, but then I work in a restaurant kitchen. At home this may be a bit of a tall order, so use shop-bought biscuits instead: I think plain digestive or Rich Tea biscuits work best. The neatest way to crush them is to place them in a plastic bag and use a rolling pin or mallet to smash them to bits inside it. In general terms 250–300g of biscuit crumbs will make a good base. Don't be tempted to make it any thicker as it will drink in moisture from the filling and expand, and a heavy doorstop base can be the downfall of a good cheesecake.

• Use a mixer with a paddle attachment to make the filling, or combine with a large spatula or spoon. Don't use a whisk as this aerates the mixture too much, causing it to rise quickly in the oven and then sink, and it will lose that lovely creamy texture.

• Bake the cheesecake until it is just wobbly in the centre – it should jiggle like soft jelly. If you've made custard tart or crème brûlée before, then you already know how it should look. The filling will continue to set as it cools, so there's no need to bake until firm. If it is colouring too quickly, reduce the heat of the oven and cover for the remainder of the cooking time (most cheesecakes should stay rather pale). Try to avoid baking until the filling cracks, as it makes the texture crumbly. That said, some people are crazy for that in a cheesecake. If you are one, knock yourself out.

• Cheesecakes, like revenge, are best served cold, and I prefer to bake them at least a day in advance. They will keep for a day at room temperature, but it's better to store them in the fridge, where they can last for up to a week in perfect shape.

• Always use a hot knife (chef's or palette knife) to loosen around the edges of the tin to release the cake. Use a hot knife to slice, if you want a clean 'restaurant cut'.

• Cheesecakes are richer than other cakes and a 23cm (9 inch) one should provide 12 slices unless you are extremely greedy. All the recipes here require this size cake tin and I strongly advise using one with a removable base. Butter and line the base with baking parchment, then when the cake is cold, you should simply be able to lift it off the paper and onto your serving plate.

• All these cheesecake recipes can be easily adapted to be gluten-free: just use a gluten-free biscuit for the base and replace any flour in the filling with rice flour or cornflour.

Cheesecake with white & dark chocolate

I was twelve when I made this for the first time and didn't know there was such a thing as white chocolate, so I just used the milk chocolate we had at home. There were no lovely layers, but it was delicious all the same. I know now of white chocolate, and though I am not generally a huge fan I think it works really well here, adding a smoothness to the cake and a gentle flavour. Itamar says this cheesecake is too sweet for him, but I notice that he always finishes his portion.

Makes a 23cm (9 inch) round cake

For the base
200g biscuit (or sweet pastry) crumbs
1 tbsp sugar (I tend to use light or dark brown soft sugar, but caster works as well)
1 tbsp cocoa powder
30g unsalted butter, melted

For the filling
500g full fat cream cheese
120g caster sugar
120g/ml double cream
4 eggs
200g white chocolate, melted

For the topping
300g/ml soured cream
100g dark chocolate, melted

Preheat the oven to 180°C/160°C fan/ gas mark 4. Line a loose-based 23cm (9 inch) cake tin with baking parchment.

Mix the biscuit crumbs, sugar and cocoa powder together in a bowl, pour over the melted butter and stir to combine. Tip the mixture into the cake tin and spread around to cover the entire base lightly. Flatten a little but don't compress it too much; if you do, you will create a very dense base that is hard to cut through.

Bake for 10 minutes, then remove from the oven to cool. This allows the base to dry a little so it can absorb some of the moisture from the cheesecake.

Use a mixer with a paddle attachment (or a large spoon, if making by hand) to make the filling. Don't use a whisk, as it will simply aerate the mixture, which will then collapse after baking. Place the cream cheese, sugar and cream in the mixer bowl. Mix at a medium speed until well combined, then add the eggs one at a time. Finally, pour in the melted chocolate (see page 12 for more information about melting chocolate) and mix to combine. Pour the filling onto the baked base and return the tin to the oven to bake for about 25–30 minutes. Remove from the oven and allow to rest and cool for 10 minutes.

While it cools, make the topping. Mix the soured cream with the warm melted dark chocolate until you have a smooth paste. Pour over the top of the baked cheesecake, making sure not to pour it all in one spot as it may sink in. Then use the back of a spoon or a small spatula to spread it evenly to cover the filling. Return to the oven for a final 10 minutes.

Remove and cool in the fridge overnight or for at least 6 hours before cutting and eating.

ZUCCA
STAGIONATA
ALTA QUALITÀ GARANTITA e CERTIFICATA
PRODOTTO DA LOTTA INTEGRATA

Butternut squash & spice cheesecake

Our friend Bridget introduced us to the joys of American home cooking. She is the kind of cook who makes exactly the type of food you want to eat: chicken cacciatore; Southern-fried chicken drizzled with maple syrup; buttermilk mash and gravy; proper, potent chillies – the good stuff. She introduced us to this unbelievably tasty cheesecake, which is possibly the best cake in this book. We used to bake a large batch in big trays and cut it into portions (the offcuts were the most coveted food in the kitchen), but for you at home, this size should suffice.

Makes a 23cm (9 inch) cake

For the base

100g whole hazelnuts
25g unsalted butter
25g light brown soft sugar
½ tsp sea salt
1 tsp ground cinnamon
200g biscuit (or sweet pastry) crumbs

For the filling

1 butternut squash, to yield 360g when cooked (or a tin of pumpkin purée)
375g full fat cream cheese
265g caster sugar
1 tsp ground cinnamon
1 tsp ground ginger
½ tsp ground cardamom
3 eggs
2 tbsp plain flour
150g/ml soured cream

For the topping

300g/ml soured cream
50g caster sugar
seeds from ½ vanilla pod

Preheat the oven to 240°C/220°C fan/ gas mark 9. Line a loose-based 23cm (9 inch) cake tin with baking parchment.

Halve the butternut squash (you can leave the skin on) and remove the seeds. Wrap loosely in aluminium foil and roast in the oven, cut-side facing upwards, for 40–50 minutes until the flesh is soft. Once cool enough to handle, scoop out the pulp, place in a bowl and mash with a fork or potato ricer. You can do this a day in advance if you like and store the mashed squash in the fridge until needed.

Reduce the oven temperature to 180°C/160°C fan/gas mark 4. Roast the hazelnuts on a tray for 8 minutes before removing. Rub with a clean towel to get rid of some of the papery brown skins, then crush to a rough crumb (you can use a food processor or chop with a knife). Melt the butter. Put the chopped hazelnuts and other remaining ingredients for the base in a bowl, pour in the melted butter and stir to combine. Tip the mixture into the tin and spread around to cover the base. Flatten a little but don't compress too much. Bake for 10 minutes, then allow to cool.

Place the cream cheese, sugar and spices in a mixer with a paddle attachment (or use a large spoon, if making by hand). Work at a medium speed until well combined, then add the eggs one at a time. Finally add the butternut purée, flour and soured cream and mix well. Pour over the base and bake for about 25–30 minutes. Remove from the oven and allow to rest and cool for 10 minutes.

Mix the soured cream for the topping with the sugar and vanilla seeds until you have a smooth paste. Pour over the top of the baked cheesecake, making sure not to pour it all in one spot as it may sink in. Then use the back of a spoon or a small spatula to spread evenly over the top. Return to the oven for a final 10 minutes.

Cool in the fridge for at least 6 hours (or overnight) before cutting and eating.

Yogurt cheesecake with quince topping

This cake, like many other things in this book, is tailored to my husband's taste. He is always badgering me for cheesecake with quince. It is tangy and light, juicy with fruit and not too sweet – I have to admit that he is on to something here. You can change the topping according to season and availability: gently roasted peaches work a treat, as does stewed rhubarb.

Makes a 23cm (9 inch) cake

For the base
40g unsalted butter
250g biscuit (or sweet pastry) crumbs

For the cheesecake
300g full fat cream cheese
300g Greek yogurt
200g caster sugar
zest of 1 orange
zest of 1 lemon
4 eggs
50g plain flour

For the quince wedges
2–3 quince (about 500g)
300g caster sugar
juice of 1 lemon
1 cinnamon stick
500g/ml water

Preheat the oven to 180°C/160°C fan/ gas mark 4. Line a loose-based 23cm (9 inch) cake tin with baking parchment.

Melt the butter and combine with the biscuit crumbs. Tip the mixture into the tin and spread around to cover the base. Flatten a little but don't press it too much; if you do, you will create a dense base that is hard to cut and eat. Bake for 10 minutes, then allow to cool.

Cut each quince into 8–10 wedges and remove the cores. I like to leave the skin on for flavour (and it helps the wedges hold their shape) but you can peel them if you prefer. Place in a deep roasting dish, sprinkle with the sugar and lemon juice, add the cinnamon stick and cover with the water. Place in the oven to cook for around 40–45 minutes.

Use a mixer with a paddle attachment on medium speed (or a large spoon, but definitely not a whisk) and beat the cream cheese with the yogurt, sugar and zests. Mix in the eggs one at a time, then fold in the flour. Pour over the base and place in the oven with the quince.

Bake the cheesecake for 30–35 minutes until it rises and goes a light golden brown colour. Remove from the oven and allow to cool for at least 3–4 hours. The quince wedges may take a little longer to roast, so leave them there until they are soft, then remove and allow to cool in the cooking liquid.

Remove the wedges from the liquid and arrange them on top of the cheesecake. Tip the roasting liquid into a pan and reduce over a high heat until it thickens. Use some to brush over the quince wedges so they are shiny and lovely.

Nutella cheesecake

On the shelf of our pastry section there is always a jar of Nutella. Our pastry chef Giorgia (like most Italians, I suspect) is obsessed with the stuff from childhood, and will usually have some on a scrap of pitta or milk bun for her breakfast. Over time it has made its way into our pastry, permeating our sweet offerings, much to Giorgia's delight. If, like her, you are a Nutella fan, this cake is for you. If, like me, you are a peanut butter lover, try it here instead of the Nutella, and use peanuts instead of hazelnuts in the base and praline garnish.

Makes a 23cm (9 inch) cake

Gluten-free

For the base

- *100g ground hazelnuts*
- *1 tbsp cocoa powder*
- *1 tbsp cornflour*
- *25g dark brown soft sugar*
- *½ tsp sea salt*
- *25g butter, melted*

For the filling

- *375g full fat cream cheese*
- *200g caster sugar*
- *60g/ml double cream*
- *3 eggs*
- *115g Nutella*
- *1 tbsp cornflour*
- *1 tbsp ground coffee beans*

For the topping

- *200g/ml soured cream*
- *100g melted milk chocolate*

For the praline garnish (not strictly necessary, but great)

- *50g caster sugar*
- *1 tsp butter*
- *40g roasted hazelnuts*

Preheat the oven to 180°C/160°C fan/ gas mark 4. Line a loose-based 23cm (9 inch) cake tin with baking parchment.

Mix all the ingredients for the base together in a bowl. Tip into the tin and spread around to cover the base. Flatten a little but don't compress too much (if you do, you will create a very dense base that is hard to cut through). Bake for 10 minutes, then remove from the oven to cool.

Make the filling in a mixer with a paddle attachment, or in a bowl with a large spoon. Don't use a whisk, as it will aerate the mixture, which will then collapse after baking. Combine the cream cheese, sugar and cream on a medium speed, then mix in the eggs one at a time. Add the Nutella, cornflour and coffee and mix well until combined. Pour over the base and bake for about 25–30 minutes. Remove from the oven and allow to rest and cool for 10 minutes.

Mix the soured cream with the warm melted chocolate (see notes on melting on page 12) until you have a smooth paste. Pour over the top of the baked cheesecake, making sure not to pour it all in one spot as it may sink in. Then use the back of a spoon or a small spatula to spread evenly over the top. Return to the oven for a final 10 minutes. Cool in the fridge for at least 6 hours (or overnight) before cutting and eating.

If you are making the praline, line a baking tray with baking parchment. Set a pan over a high heat and allow it to warm up for a minute, then sprinkle in the sugar and stir until it melts and becomes a dark caramel. Mix in the butter, then add the roasted nuts and stir well to coat. Quickly tip onto the lined tray and allow to cool entirely before chopping to a chunky crumb. Sprinkle over the rim of the cake just before serving to add some crunch and additional sweetness.

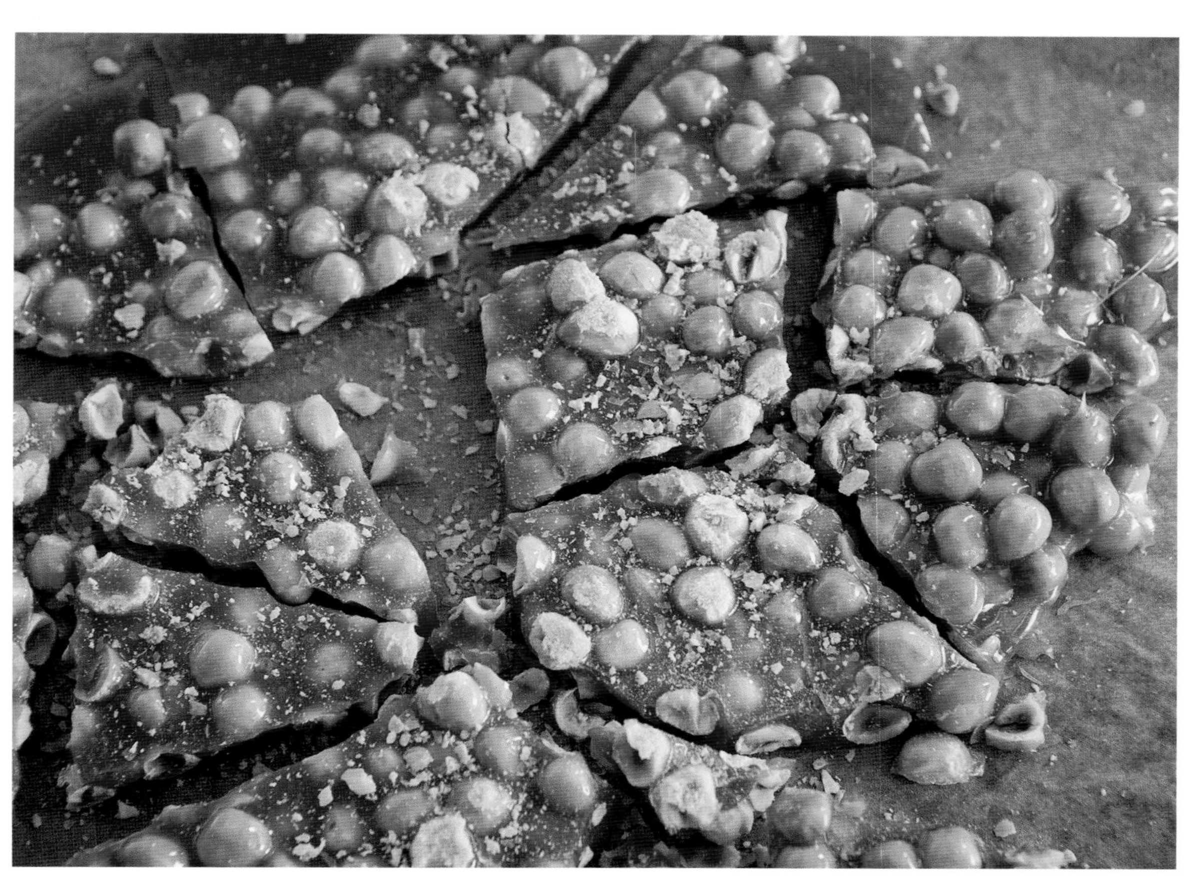

Rose-scented cheesecake on a coconut base with berry compote

This one owes its existence to Sarah Randell – a great cook and writer of great cookbooks – who asked us to do a summer baking piece for the food magazine she edits. We wanted something that would look glitzy and glam for the press. We came up with this, and it is as glossy as one of our cakes can be. The combination of coconut, roses and berries makes for the most spectacular mouthful. While some people are attracted to rose-scented desserts, they can occasionally be a bit soapy. That is definitely not the case here; the rose is just a gorgeous, exotic back note in this creamy white cheesecake, exactly as it should be.

Makes a 23cm (9 inch) cake

For the coconut base

50g butter
100g desiccated coconut
75g caster sugar
½ tsp sea salt
1 egg

For the rose-scented cheesecake

500g full fat cream cheese
100g/ml soured cream
200g caster sugar
zest of 1 lemon
4 eggs
1 tbsp rose water
50g plain flour

For the compote topping

300g raspberries, plus 100g extra to fold in at the end
180g caster sugar
1 lemon, halved
1 tbsp rose water
100g strawberries, cut in quarters, to fold in at the end

Preheat the oven to 190°C/170°C fan/ gas mark 5 and line a loose-based 23cm (9 inch) cake tin with baking parchment.

Melt the butter and mix with the coconut, sugar, salt and egg until well combined. Transfer to the cake tin, smooth out and bake in the oven for 10 minutes until the coconut goes a light golden colour. Remove from the oven to cool.

Make the filling in a mixer with a paddle attachment, or in a bowl with a large spoon (but not a whisk). Combine the cream cheese with the soured cream, sugar and lemon zest on medium speed. Add the eggs one at a time, then gradually mix in the rose water. Finally fold in the flour. Pour over the coconut base and bake for 30–35 minutes until the cake rises and goes a light golden brown. Remove from the oven and cool in the fridge for at least 4 hours before topping.

Mix 300g of the raspberries in a pan with the sugar and lemon halves. Set on a very high heat, bring to a rapid boil and cook for about 3–4 minutes until the compote thickens. Remove from the heat. Take out the lemon halves and squeeze them into the compote so that you don't lose any juice, then discard. Stir in the rose water, transfer to a bowl and chill in the fridge for at least an hour until set.

When you are ready to serve, gently fold the additional 100g of raspberries and the quartered strawberries into the chilled compote and use to top the cheesecake (or serve on the side).

After
dark

Honey & Co.

Traditional desserts

Our evening starts when Sanaa arrives. Our little French firecracker is a nocturnal creature; she comes to life as the day fades out. Every day at 4pm, she ties her golden pushbike to the pole outside the shop, wearing some outrageous outfit that she unearthed in a second-hand shop, something that only she could pull off. A quick look at the booking sheet and the wine fridge, and the evening can start. The restaurant is set up around the last tea-timers. Tables are joined and separated to suit different-size parties; the lights are dimmed; whatever cakes are left from the afternoon are returned to the counter at the back (these cakes move a lot); and as the room fills with the soft glow from little tea lights, Sanaa comes into her own, her eyes and smile twinkling in the candlelight.

Dinner explodes on us like a firework display. Between 6pm and 6.30pm all our tables and the five bar seats fill up, and in the summer the tables outside too. The first dinner service is the fast one; pre-theatre, post-work, these people are in a rush. It's a tempest in the kitchen, all hands on deck. Tray after laden tray of mezze heads upstairs. This is where we really go to town. Our dinner mezze selection is a taste of almost everything we make in the kitchen: three types of bread, two or three dips (one is always hummus), falafel with a dipping sauce, olives, seasonal pickles and salads. Each of our tables will be laden with a dozen small plates, little bites to start the meal, with a warning not to fill up on bread.

After that first rush, things become more relaxed. As some customers head out and others trickle in, we can all relax into the evening. Hopefully, the restaurant will fill up again at least once during the night. There will be time to laugh and chat a bit. Something funny will happen, or something strange; ideally nothing bad, although inevitably sometimes it does: computers break, drinks spill, customers get upset – that's just restaurant life. If all goes well, then by 9pm our room feels like a lovely dinner party, with chatter filling each table, sometimes overflowing to the neighbouring one, and plates of food and bottles of wine passing around. Our little Sanaa oversees it all, smiling at each guest and looking like the proudest host in town.

As the night moves on, dessert options are discussed – cake from the counter or dessert from the kitchen? Cheesecake again or something new? One dessert and two forks, or do we get one each? Then finally it is time for bills and goodbyes. As the last customers leave, we snuff out the candles on another day and the cleaners turn up the lights to make sure they don't miss a thing, getting Honey & Co ready for tomorrow, when it starts all over again.

Desserts

You can have cake for pudding – there's nothing wrong with that – but sometimes you want something different, a bit more elegant perhaps, or just a bit lighter. Dessert is not about massive portions or mounds of cream, but rather about complementing your dinner, and spoiling yourself and others. Each of the following can be made in advance, then assembled just before you want to serve (a really 'chef-y' thing to do, which should be done more at home). This way you can nip into the kitchen and get everything ready in a jiffy, before coming back with a fabulous dessert to bask in the glory.

Some of these desserts take a little time and effort to prepare but don't worry if they aren't perfect; they will taste delicious even if they look a bit crooked. And if things really do go south, just remember Nigella's advice: apologise once, then let it pass (advice equally good for baking disasters and life in general).

Knafe

This is the dessert I crave when I go home to Israel for a visit. Not just any knafe but the one in Acre market, though if I don't have the time to head to Acre, the knafe in downtown Haifa will do the trick. It is one of those specialist products that you seek out, find your favourite pastry shop and stick to it for years. I have tried others – in fact I try them whenever I can. There is something about the combination of really sweet syrup, salty cheese and pastry with a crispy and yielding texture that just makes so much sense to me. Itamar has always claimed this isn't his favourite but it truly is mine. And whenever I make it, thinking that I can finally have a dessert all to myself, I notice that he manages to eat his fair share, making me doubt the truth of his claim.

Fills an 18–20cm (7–8in) frying pan

Enough for 4–6, depending on your ability to consume sweet things

For the syrup

- *5 whole cardamom pods*
- *3 wide strips of orange zest (use a peeler)*
- *250g caster sugar*
- *140g/ml water*
- *1 tbsp orange blossom water*

For the filling

- *125g (1 small log) rindless goats' cheese*
- *150g feta cheese*
- *100g mascarpone or full fat cream cheese*
- *½ tsp freshly ground cardamom pods*
- *zest of ½ orange (use the remaining zest from the orange for the syrup)*

For the base

- *200g kadaif pastry*
- *100g unsalted butter, melted*

To garnish (if you like)

- *20g chopped pistachios*
- *1 tbsp dried rose petals*

Start by making the syrup so that the flavours have time to infuse. Press the cardamom pods to open slightly and expose the seeds in the centre, then pop into a small saucepan, pods and all. Add the other syrup ingredients and mix well to start the sugar dissolving, so that it doesn't catch when you heat it.

Set the pan on a high heat and bring the syrup ingredients to the boil. Skim off ›››

any foam that forms on the top, then remove from the heat. Leave to cool in the pan with the orange zest and cardamom pods still in it until you are ready to assemble the knafe (you can prepare the syrup a few hours in advance if you wish). This syrup is very thick and will need to be strained before using.

To make the filling, crumble the goats' cheese and feta into a bowl and add the mascarpone, cardamom and orange zest. Mix to combine, but allow the cheeses to stay in rough clumps. Don't worry that no sugar is added at this point, as the filling will get plenty of sweetness from the syrup.

Preheat the oven to 200°C/180°C fan/gas mark 6. Place the kadaif pastry in a large bowl and pull apart a little to separate the strands. Pour over the melted butter and mix it in, using your hands to rub it all over so that the pastry is well coated (a little like putting conditioner in your hair). Place half the pastry in an 18–20cm (7–8in) frying pan and flatten down to cover the base of the pan. Evenly distribute the cheese filling all over and then top with the rest of the pastry as a second layer.

I always start by giving the knafe some colour on the stove top: set the frying pan on a low to medium heat and swivel the pastry around in it every 20 seconds to start it crisping. After 2 minutes, press down on the top layer with the lid of the frying pan or a plate that fits into the pan, and (holding firmly onto the lid or plate) carefully turn upside-down. The knafe will now be sitting on the plate or lid, crispy side uppermost. Set the frying pan down and very carefully slide the knafe back into the pan so that you can crisp the other side for 2 minutes before transferring the pan to the oven for 10 minutes to complete the baking. Alternatively, if this sounds too much like hard work, just set the whole thing straight in the oven for 20 minutes without browning in the pan first – you won't get all the tiny crispy strands of pastry top and bottom, but this is definitely the easier option.

Once the knafe is baked, remove from the oven and carefully pour all the syrup over it, using a sieve to catch the orange and cardamom pods (you can discard them now that they have done their job). Allow 5 minutes for the syrup to absorb, then sprinkle the pastry with chopped pistachios and rose petals (if using). Serve straight away – you can carefully cut it into wedges or use a large spoon to scoop out portions. This really isn't a dessert to eat cold; you want to have it while the cheese is still oozing and the pastry is warm.

If you are making this for a dinner party, follow all the stages up to the point where it is ready to put in the oven, then keep in the fridge until needed (up to 24 hours). Simply add an extra 5 minutes to your baking time when you come to heat it up.

Raspberry & rose kadaif nests

Junior works for the company that supplies us with Greek produce – he brings us olive oil, our beautiful Kalamata olives, delicious honeys and the kadaif pastry we love so much. I first met him some years back in my old job. A dour man, he would drop by every Wednesday, leave his stuff and go without as much as a hello or goodbye. We decided to rebrand him; we changed his name to Sunny and made a point of chatting to him every time he came. When we finally got to know him, we discovered a lovely guy with a lovely smile, and everyone's Wednesdays became better.

This is a beautiful little treat. It may seem rather complex at first glance, but really it is all about planning: you make the different parts in advance and simply assemble when you want to eat. If you decide to make the pistachio praline, and I recommend that you do, you'll find that this makes about double the amount you need here. However, it will keep for up to 2 weeks in a sealed container and is extremely tasty, so don't worry about it – just keep the rest to nibble on another time.

Makes
8 small nests

For the kadaif nests
150g kadaif pastry
60g caster sugar
120g unsalted butter, melted

For the rose cream
200g/ml double cream
100g white chocolate
1 tsp rose water

For the macerated raspberries
120g/ml base sugar syrup (page 59)
1 tbsp vodka (or 2, if you feel so inclined)
1 tsp rose water
2 punnets of fresh raspberries (about 200g)

For the pistachio praline (if you like)
75g caster sugar
10g unsalted butter
60g whole roasted pistachios

Preheat the oven to 190°C/170°C fan/ gas mark 5. Place the kadaif pastry in a bowl and add the sugar and melted butter. Mix around and make sure the pastry is coated well. Divide into eight (about 30–40g each), then shape in shallow muffin moulds to resemble birds' nests – you know what I mean: the pastry should be higher at the sides, coming to just above the rim of the muffin mould, and flat at the bottom to create a nest shape. ›››

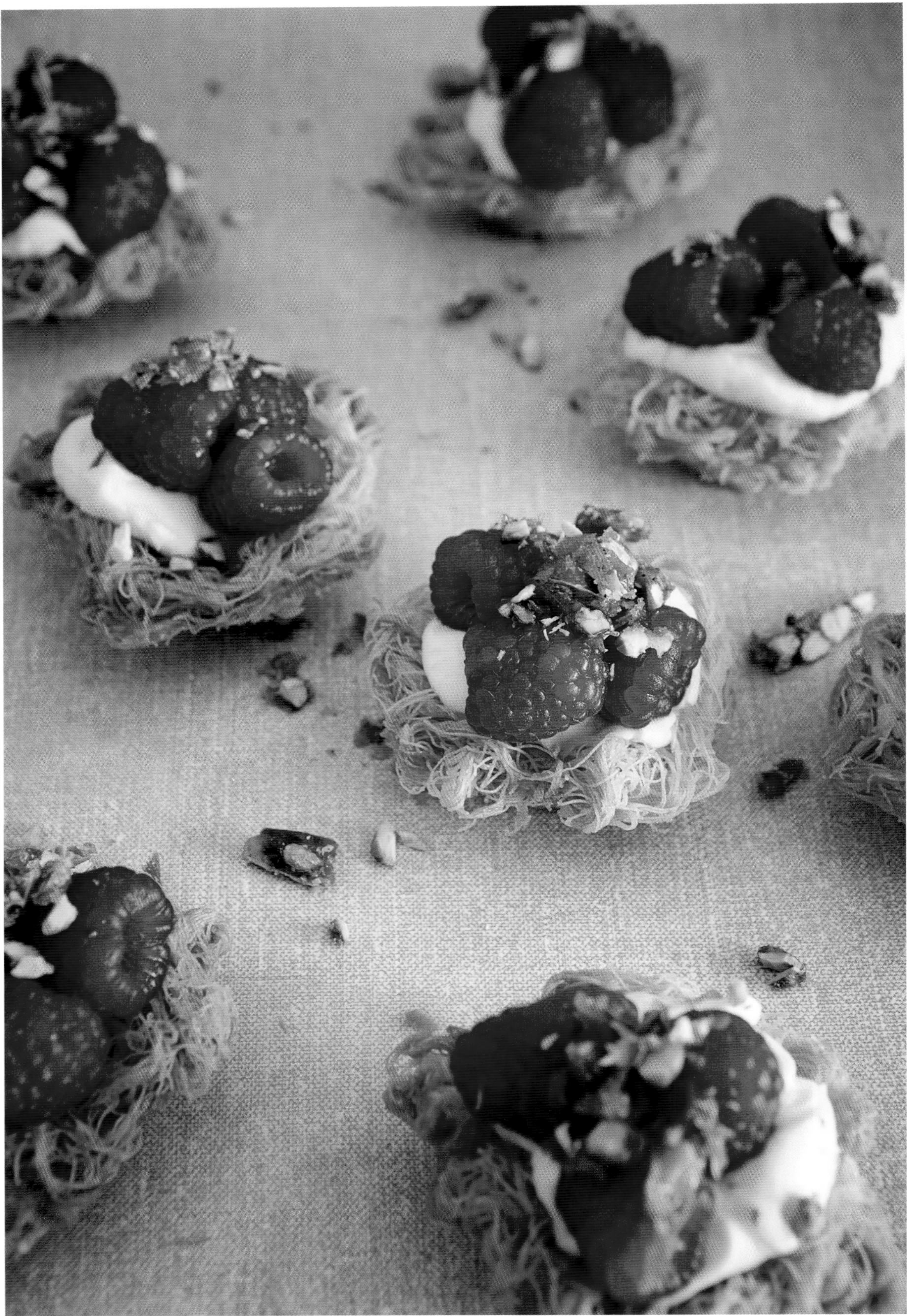

Bake the nests in the centre of the oven for about 20 minutes until golden brown, then remove from the moulds and cool on a wire rack. You can make the nests up to 2 days in advance. Keep them in an airtight container, but make sure not to put them in the fridge, as they will soften and you want them nice and crispy.

Boil the cream for the filling in a small pan, then pour it over the white chocolate in a bowl and leave for 30 seconds. Stir to combine before mixing in the rose water. Cover and place in the fridge to cool for at least 2 hours (and up to 2 days). When you are ready to use, whisk to create a lovely thick, fluffy cream, but be careful not to over-whisk as it can split and become too buttery.

To macerate the fruit, mix the sugar syrup with the vodka and rose water and pour over the raspberries in a bowl. Leave to soak for a minimum of 2 hours. You can keep them in the fridge for a day or two to let the flavour really intensify.

If you are making the praline, line a baking tray with a sheet of greaseproof paper and put a small frying pan on a high heat. Sprinkle in the sugar and stir around with a wooden spoon until it is all melted and the colour starts to deepen to a rich caramel, then remove from the heat and add the butter. Mix until it is thoroughly combined, then stir in the pistachio nuts. Quickly transfer to the lined tray and leave to cool and set entirely before chopping up. You can make this up to 2 weeks in advance and keep it in a dry airtight container.

To assemble, place the little nests on a serving platter and spoon some of the rose cream into the centre of each one. Top with soaked raspberries, sprinkle with pistachio praline (if using) and serve immediately.

Dilute any remaining macerating syrup with some sparkling water and serve alongside for an excellent accompaniment.

Strawberry semolina spliffs (aka znoud el sett or lady's arms)

Global markets and imports mean that what grows when is no longer as clear-cut as it used to be. At Honey & Co we try to use what is in season locally. In the United Kingdom strawberries mean summertime, but the delicate fruit cannot survive Israel's fierce summer sun, so the season there is in the dead of winter. Every January my mum would splash out and buy some of the first strawberries to make my birthday cake. A month later they would cost a fraction of the price, available to buy everywhere, including the side of the road, but those first few berries were precious. I wanted to recreate one of my childhood favourites, a bowl of semolina pudding with a generous teaspoon of strawberry jam in the middle, but felt that it needed a lighter touch if we were to serve it in summer. So here is a very grown-up version of semolina and strawberries. Serve the spliffs hot with cold berry salad on the side for the best results.

Makes 6 very generous portions (or 8 slightly less generous but perfectly sufficient portions)

For the casing

1 small packet (or 6–8 sheets) of filo pastry, about 200g
100g unsalted butter, melted

For the filling

250g/ml milk
75g/ml double cream
60g caster sugar
seeds from ½ vanilla pod or 1 tsp vanilla extract
50g semolina
10g cornflour

For the strawberry compote

250g strawberries
100g caster sugar

For the strawberry salad

1 small punnet of strawberries
3–4 sprigs of mint
½ tsp ground sumac
½ tsp caster sugar
1 tbsp olive oil

Line a small tray (about 18cm x 11cm) with baking parchment. If you only have a larger tray don't worry; just use part of it. There are two ways to line the tray depending on whether you are feeling scientific or laid-back. If you are feeling scientific: cut an 18cm x 22cm rectangle of baking parchment and fold in half so that it is 18cm x 11cm; open it out again and put one half in the base of the tray with the other half hanging over the side (the scientific bit comes later). If you are feeling more relaxed about things: simply line the tray with a large piece of baking parchment.

Place the milk, cream, sugar and vanilla in a small saucepan over a medium heat and stir to start dissolving the sugar. Combine the semolina and cornflour in a small bowl, then gradually add to the vanilla milk, whisking all the time. Cook for 2–3 minutes, whisking continuously, until the mixture thickens and large bubbles start to form. Quickly pour the thickened pudding onto the prepared tray. If you are taking the scientific approach, pour the semolina into the tray, then fold the overhanging parchment over to cover it. If you are taking the more relaxed approach, pour it onto the lined tray, spread into a rectangle about the thickness of a slice of bread and cover the surface directly with baking parchment or cling film (to stop it forming a crust). Leave to cool in the fridge for at least 40 minutes to set entirely.

Cut the semolina into six fat fingers (or eight more dainty ladylike fingers, depending on how many you are feeding), each about 11cm long. Store the semolina ›››

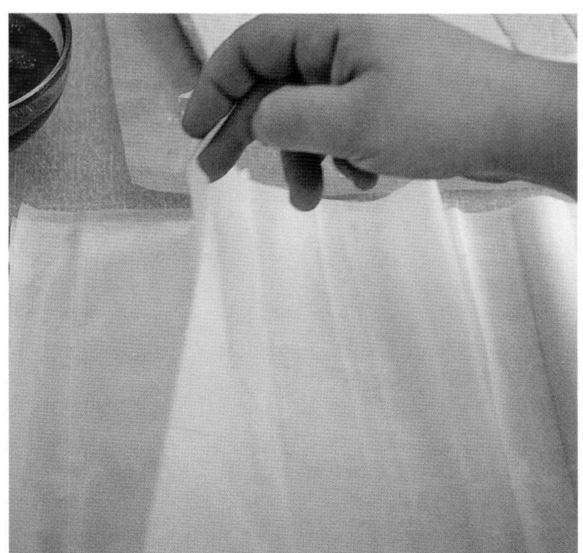

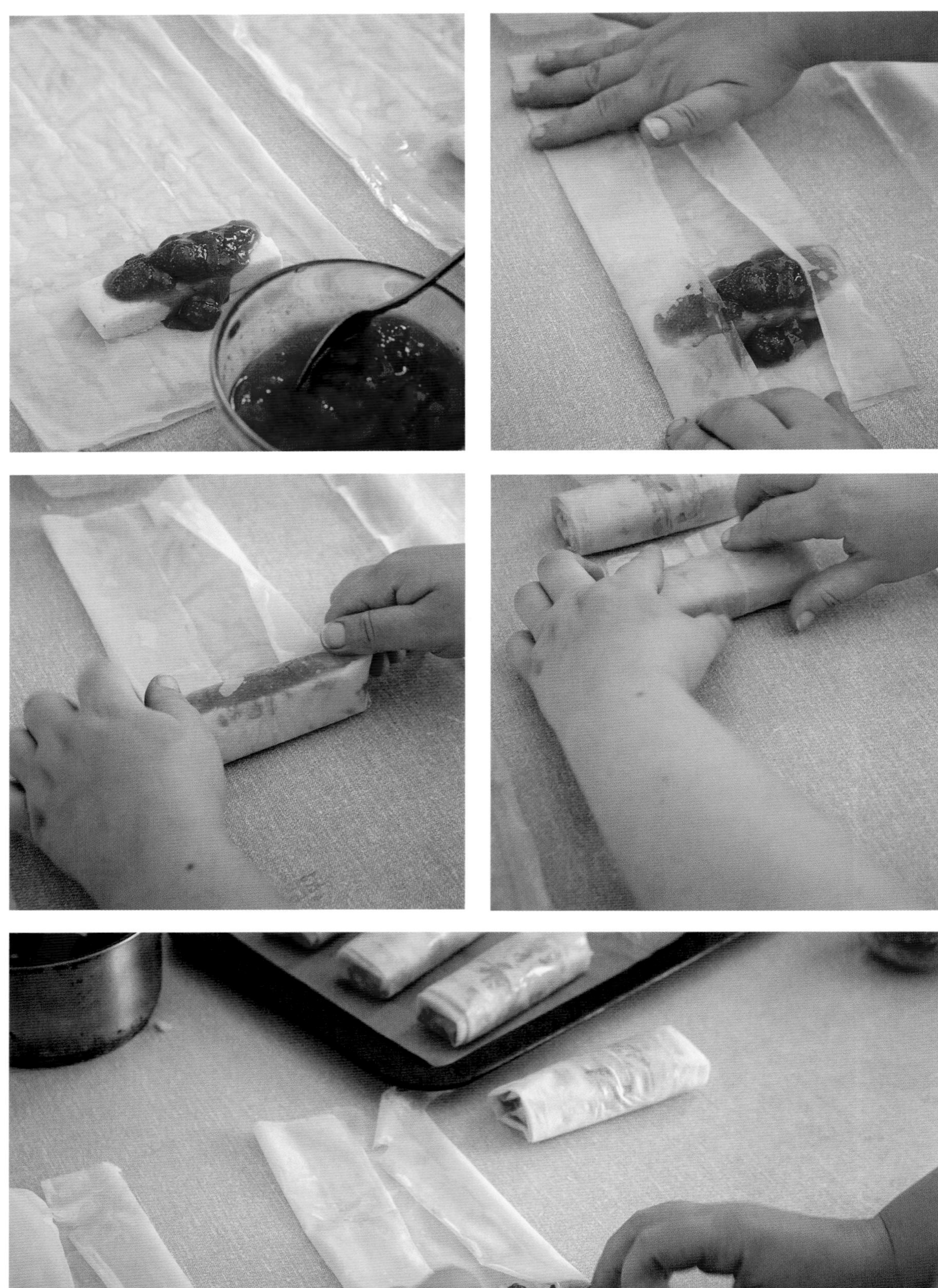

fingers in the fridge until needed (they can be kept overnight if you want).

To make the compote, remove the green stems from the strawberries and cut into large dice. Place in a large frying pan (you want a good-sized surface exposed to heat), sprinkle the sugar all over and set on a very high heat. Liquid will ooze out of the strawberries. Bring to the boil, stir well and continue to boil for 4–6 minutes or until the strawberry liquid starts to thicken. Pour into a small bowl and cool in the fridge until required (this will keep in the fridge for a couple of days, if you wish to prepare it in advance).

Lay the filo pastry sheets out on the workbench. Brush each one with butter and fold in half. Place a finger of semolina pudding on each sheet about 5cm from one of the shorter edges and top each one with a spoonful of strawberry compote. Fold the long sides in to cover the ends of the semolina finger, then roll up like an eggroll to create logs. Brush the tops with some more butter and place on a baking tray. The spliffs will keep like this for up to 2 days in the fridge, or you can bake them straight away if you prefer.

Preheat the oven to 200°C/180°C fan/ gas mark 6. While it is warming up, make the strawberry salad. Remove the green stems from the strawberries, quarter them and place in a bowl. Pick the mint leaves and rip them up, dropping the shreds into the bowl. Add the sumac, sugar and olive oil and mix well.

Bake the spliffs for 10 minutes or until golden brown. Serve hot, one per person, with the fresh strawberry salad.

Hazelnut milk pudding

Milk pudding, or malabi as we know it best, is the most common dessert in the Middle East. In Turkey they use rice flour to thicken it; elsewhere they use other starches, including cornflour. I was talking to Itamar in the office one day about introducing a Honey & Co version and was saying we wanted something a little richer and more complex. I saw Giorgia's ears prick up at the mention of a hazelnut version, and when I mentioned warm chocolate sauce, she literally jumped over to us, nodding her head in excitement (she is Italian and Nutella is her favourite food). The milk pudding is lovely just as it is without the addition of chocolate, but for those of you feeling the need for indulgence, make the quick chocolate sauce too. At the restaurant we serve it in a little jug on the side, allowing the guest to decide whether or not it will join the party in the glass.

Makes 6 glasses of pudding

For the pudding
- *100g whole hazelnuts (skin on)*
- *200g/ml single cream*
- *500g/ml whole milk, plus about 100g/ml to top up*
- *30g caster sugar*
- *50g honey*
- *70g cornflour*

For added texture and crunch (optional)
- *40g currants, soaked in 100g/ml boiling water*
- *50g blanched roasted hazelnuts (roasting notes on page 20), roughly chopped*

For the chocolate sauce (if you feel like it)
- *100g dark chocolate*
- *80g/ml double cream*
- *30g/ml whole milk*
- *1 tsp hazelnut oil, if you like*

To make the milk puddings, you need a hazelnut infusion. Preheat the oven to 200°C/180°C fan/gas mark 6. Roast the nuts for about 15–18 minutes until very dark but not burnt. Smash them up a little, then add to the cream and milk in a saucepan and set on a medium heat. Mix in the sugar and honey and bring to the boil, then remove from the stove and set aside. Allow to infuse for at least 1 hour and up to 24 hours. The first hour should be at room temperature, but after that transfer to the fridge.

Strain through a fine sieve into a bowl or measuring jug, making sure to drain the nuts completely to capture all the liquid. You can now discard the hazelnuts; it may seem harsh, but they have served their purpose and won't have any flavour left in them. In contrast, the milk they have left behind will be lovely and nutty. Measure how much liquid you have (some will have been lost while infusing) and top up with fresh milk to make 700g/ml.

Put six nice glasses (or dessert bowls) on a tray, ready to be filled as soon as the pudding is cooked (it sets really quickly).

Mix about 100g/ml of the hazelnut infusion with the cornflour in a small bowl. The cornflour will go hard and seize up at first, but be persistent and stir until it forms a smooth paste, adding a little more of the cold hazelnut milk if needed. Put the remaining infusion in a small pan and bring to the boil. When the first bubbles appear, whisk in the cornflour paste in a slow, steady stream and keep whisking until fully combined. The mixture will thicken and become gloopy. Continue whisking until bubbles start to appear again (they will look like massive molten lava eruptions), then quickly remove from the heat and pour about 100g into each of the waiting glasses (or bowls). Set the glasses in the fridge as soon as they have been filled, in order to cool the puddings quickly and achieve the best texture. They will take a minimum of 2 hours to set completely and can be kept in the fridge for up to 48 hours.

If you are making the chocolate sauce, now's the time. Break the chocolate into pieces and place in a bowl. Put the cream and milk in a small pan, bring to the boil over a high heat, then pour over the chocolate and whisk until it has melted entirely. If you are adding the hazelnut oil, mix it in now.

I like to serve the puddings with warm chocolate sauce alongside to pour over them at the table before sprinkling with chopped hazelnuts and drained currants. The hazelnuts add crunch, the currants add moisture and sharpness, and the chocolate sauce is pure indulgence.

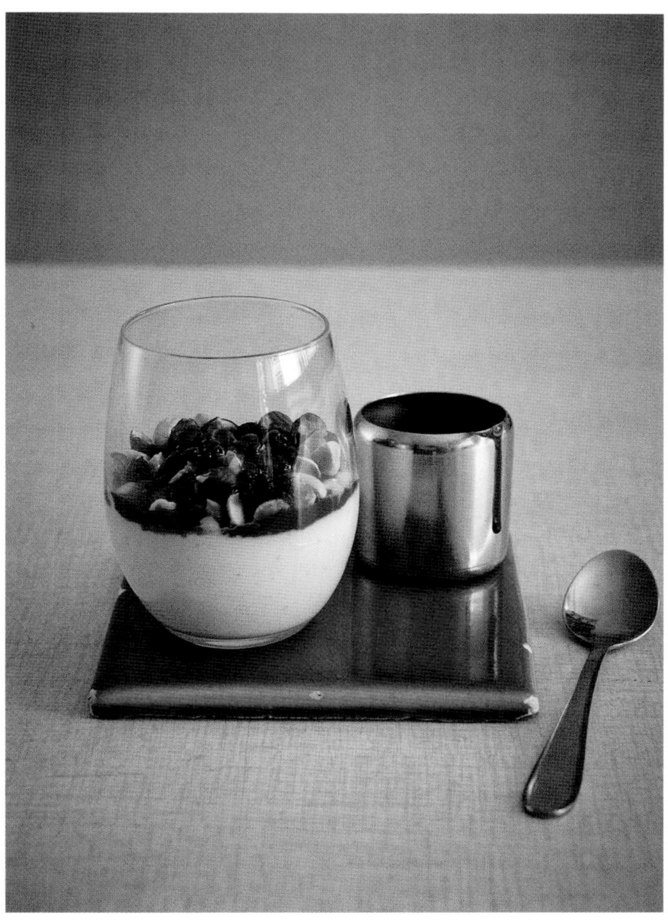

Quince trifle

My wife is an extremely competent pastry chef and baker, but I do believe she prefers trifle to any other dessert. Even the simplest shop-bought mass-produced trifle in a plastic cup can give her the greatest joy. Me? I like a trifle as much as the next guy, but it's the quince here that really rocks my boat. Working and living together, there are plenty of things we don't agree on, and there's always plenty to argue about. However, this dessert is a good place for us to put our differences aside.

Makes 6 individual trifles or 1 large trifle

For the quince
- *2 quince, cored and diced but the skin left on (500g)*
- *250g caster sugar*
- *½ cinnamon stick*
- *2 cardamom pods, crushed*
- *500g/ml water*
- *juice of 1 lemon*

For the jelly
- *150g/ml water*
- *250g/ml quince cooking liquid*
- *4 gelatine leaves (see notes on page 20)*

For the ginger custard
- *200g/ml milk*
- *3 cardamom pods, crushed*
- *50g caster sugar*
- *2 egg yolks*
- *25g plain flour*
- *½ tsp ground ginger*

Toppings (if you like)
- *diced sponge cake (the vegan loaf cake on page 128 works really well here) or crushed ginger nuts to sprinkle*
- *double cream for pouring*

Put the quince dice in a saucepan with the sugar, spices, water and lemon juice and bring to the boil on a high heat. Skim off any foam that forms on the top, then reduce the heat to medium and cook at a constant simmer for 5 minutes. Ladle out 250g/ml of the cooking syrup and set aside to use for the jelly. Reduce the heat to very low and continue cooking the quince in the remaining liquid for about 20 minutes until the fruit has turned dark orange and the poaching syrup around it has become really thick and sticky. Spoon the quince pieces into the trifle bowl(s) to cool. (You should end up with about 80g in each bowl if making individual trifles.) You can use the remaining syrup to make a lovely quince Bellini with sparkling wine, or use it as a cordial.

To make the quince jelly, add the water to the 250g/ml of poaching liquid set aside earlier (to make up to 400g/ml). Pour into a small pan and warm over a medium heat for a minute or two, taking care not to boil, then remove from the heat. While the quince liquid is warming, soak the gelatine leaves in plenty of cold water until softened, then lift out, squeeze to remove any excess water and add to the now warm liquid in the pan. Stir until all the gelatine has dissolved, then pour over the quince cubes to cover. (If you are making individual portions and want to be scientific about it, pour about 60g/ml of jelly into each bowl.) Place in the fridge for at least 4 hours to cool and set (see gelatine notes on page 20). You can leave the trifle preparation at this stage for up to 2 days.

Put 150g/ml of the milk with the crushed cardamom pods and sugar in a pan and bring to the boil slowly over a medium heat. Combine the remaining milk with the yolks, flour and ground ginger in a small bowl. When the first bubbles start to appear on the surface of the milk, slowly pour in the yolk mixture, stirring continually. Keep stirring and cook until the custard thickens and bubbles start to appear again. Remove from the heat and pass through a sieve into a bowl. Cover the surface with cling film (touching the custard so that it can't form a skin) and chill in the fridge for at least 30 minutes.

To serve, top the jelly / jellies with the thick custard and, if you are going to town, sprinkle with the diced sponge or crumbled ginger nuts. Then let people pour cream all over for themselves before eating.

Chocolate, coffee & cardamom cake

This recipe is our version of one we found in a booklet by *Australian Women's Weekly*. Their cakes are exactly the kind you want to eat, and their recipes are always reliable. Adding coffee and cardamom to the chocolate cake gives this a distinctively Middle Eastern twist. It is somewhere between a cake and a pudding, and works as an excellent solution when you need something gluten-free. You will have to plan ahead, though, as this cake really needs to rest for at least 24 hours before serving.

Makes a 23cm (9 inch) round cake

Enough for 10–12 as dessert

Gluten-free

6 eggs
100g dark brown soft sugar
400g dark chocolate
250g/ml double cream
1 tsp ground cardamom
1 tbsp Turkish coffee powder (or freshly-ground coffee beans, as finely ground as you can)
2 tbsp cocoa powder to dust (if you wish)
whipped cream to serve (if you like)

Heat the oven to 190°C/170°C fan/ gas mark 5. Butter a 23cm (9 inch) round cake tin and line with baking parchment, set in an ovenproof tray with a rim and fill the tray with two fingers (about 3cm) of hot water.

Use the whisk attachment in a mixer to whisk the eggs and sugar together until you have a strong sabayon; they should look really fluffy and hold a ribbon shape on the surface. Reduce the mixer speed to low. Melt the chocolate until smooth and warm (see notes on melting chocolate on page 12). Whisk into the eggs in a steady stream and keep whisking to combine. Fold in the double cream, ground cardamom and coffee powder until fully incorporated and beautifully smooth. Pour into the cake tin.

Place the tray containing the tin and the water in the centre of the oven. Bake for 15–20 minutes until the cake begins to rise and develop a crust. Turn the oven off and leave the cake inside for 10 minutes, then carefully remove. Take the tin out of the water bath and chill in the fridge overnight.

The next day, carefully remove the cake from the tin and dust the top with cocoa powder if using. I like to serve this with a large dollop of whipped cream and a small cup of Turkish coffee. The cake will keep well in the fridge for up to a week, and is best cut with a knife dipped in boiling water to get a clean, smooth cut.

Pistachio nougat parfait

I'm not sure why this is called pistachio nougat parfait, as it doesn't have any nougat in it, but this is what we called it at the Orrery, the restaurant where I picked up this dessert. This was one of the first recipes that made it into my famous purple folder, and more than a decade later it still tastes great, so no alteration is required to the method or the name. The only liberties I have taken are to replace the glacé maraschino cherries in the original with sour cherries, and to make fresh pistachio paste instead of using the commercial stuff we had back in the day. This parfait is lovely served with fresh cherries, and keeps in the freezer for up to a month, so any that is left over can be enjoyed another day.

Fills a 1kg (2lb) loaf tin

Enough for up to 10 slices

100g pistachios
25g/ml cherry brandy or brandy
100g sour cherries
400g/ml double cream
4 eggs
100g caster sugar
100g honey
50g glucose syrup (or honey, if you can't get any glucose syrup)
2–3 tbsp water

For the pistachio paste
200g pistachios
30g caster sugar

Roast 100g of pistachios for 10 minutes at 190°C/170°C fan/gas mark 5. Pour the brandy over the sour cherries in a bowl and leave to soak. Line a 1kg (2lb) loaf tin with cling film or greaseproof paper (I use two strips set at right angles, one lengthways and one widthways), allowing enough excess that the lining overhangs on all sides. Or make life easier and use a silicone mould if you have one, as it requires no lining at all.

Lightly whip the cream until it forms ribbons – it needs to be very soft-whipped, so be careful not to overwork it. Chill in the fridge until needed.

Put the eggs in a mixer with a whisk attachment and start whisking at a slow-medium speed. Combine the sugar, honey and glucose syrup in a small saucepan, then mix in enough of the water to create a wet paste. Moisten your finger or a brush with some water and run it around the sides of the pan to clean away any sugar crystals, then set on a high heat to bring to a rapid boil. Don't be tempted to stir it. If you have a sugar thermometer, use it now; you need to bring the mixture up to 'hard-ball' stage (121°C). If you don't have one, you can judge this by eye; boil for about 2–3 minutes until the bubbles become bigger and the mixture starts to thicken but doesn't colour.

Whisk the hot sugar syrup into the eggs in a slow, steady stream, then increase the speed to high and whisk for about 10 minutes until very fluffy and partially cooled. You can check whether it is cool enough by placing your hands on the mixing bowl; it should feel slightly warmer than your palms. This mixture will form a nice strong base for your parfait.

While the base is whisking, grind 200g of pistachios in a food processor with 30g of sugar for 1–2 minutes until the nuts start to produce oil and become a little wet. Stir in some of the parfait base to loosen, then fold into the rest of the fluffy egg mixture to combine. Next fold in the soft-whipped cream, then add the roasted pistachios and soaked cherries (plus soaking liquid) and stir to distribute evenly throughout. Pour the mixture into the lined loaf tin and fold the overhang over the top to cover; if using a silicone mould, cover with a piece of cling film or greaseproof paper. Set in the freezer for at least 12 hours. This keeps well for up to a month.

To serve, peel the cling film or greaseproof paper off the top and flip the parfait onto a chopping board. Lift the loaf tin off and carefully peel away the lining (you don't have to worry about this if you are using a silicone mould). Dip a large, sharp knife in boiling water (to give you a clean, smooth finish) and use to cut one slice per person (I allow about one tenth each). Accompany with some fresh cherries in season or, if you want to take this to the next level, pour over some dark chocolate sauce (from the hazelnut milk pudding recipe on page 248)... mmmm.

Rice pudding with wine-poached grapes

There is no guidebook to running a restaurant. The only certainty is that whatever can go wrong (however improbable) in time will go wrong. If the telephone rings when we aren't in the shop, we now know to expect the unexpected. One winter evening one of our chefs called to say, 'We have a situation here.' Two girls had come to the restaurant as walk-ins, really keen to eat with us. As all our tables were full, they were about to leave but asked to use the toilet first. When they saw the spare table we keep on the little patio next to the bathroom, they decided to stay and have their dinner there. Asia, who was managing the shift, tried to dissuade them, but in the end could not refuse their pleas (she has the kindest heart). And so they sat and had a three-course meal in what is essentially the bathroom. I can only imagine what all the diners who went to use the bathroom that night must have thought. We were mortified, of course, but there was nothing we could do. Now we explain to every server starting work with us that we do not serve food in the bathroom, just in case it's not obvious.

Enough for 4 people depending on greediness

Any leftovers make a great breakfast

For the grapes
- *250g red seedless grapes, well washed*
- *2 star anise*
- *100g/ml light white wine (we use Chardonnay)*
- *2 tbsp light brown soft sugar*

For the rice pudding
- *25g unsalted butter*
- *125g risotto rice*
- *85g/ml light white wine (the same type as for the grapes)*
- *4 cardamom pods, split*
- *½ vanilla pod, split*
- *500g/ml whole milk*
- *1 small tin of condensed milk (about 200g)*

Put the grapes in a small saucepan, add the star anise, cover with the wine and bring to the boil. As soon as it boils, stir in the sugar, then boil for a further 5 minutes. Allow to cool in the pan.

Melt the butter in a thick-based pan over a medium heat. Add the rice, stir to coat and cook for 1 minute before adding the wine. Stir well, then add the cardamom pods and half vanilla pod. Allow the wine to cook and evaporate, then pour in half the milk. Bring to the boil and mix well. Pour in the remaining milk, bring back to the boil and simmer for about 15–20 minutes, stirring every now and then, until most of the liquid has been absorbed. Remove from the heat, add the condensed milk and stir till combined.

You can serve this straight away with a spoonful of cold poached grapes on top of the hot rice pudding, but I prefer to eat them both cold.

Poached peaches with rose jelly & crystallised rose petals

We make this dessert in summer when peaches and roses are in high season. Since finding a constant supply of good unsprayed roses can be tricky, all our staff are under clear instructions to loot whatever gardens they have access to, so everyone comes to their shift bearing gifts of roses for Giorgia.

Makes 4 portions of the lightest, prettiest dessert

For the poached peaches

200g caster sugar
200g/ml water
some strips of peel and the juice of 1 lemon
some strips of peel and the juice of 1 orange
1 cinnamon stick
1 tsp rose water
4 flat white peaches
50g/ml vodka

For the jelly

160g/ml peach cooking liquid
3 gelatine leaves (or the appropriate quantity for about 330g/ml liquid, according to the manufacturer's instructions)
160g/ml cold water
1–2 tsp rose water

For the crystallised rose petals (if you like)

1 egg white
caster sugar
fresh garden roses

To elevate this dessert to something heavenly

a good splash of sparkling wine for each plate

To poach the peaches, place all the ingredients apart from the peaches and vodka in a saucepan and bring to the boil. Score the skin at the base of each peach with a little cross to just pierce the skin but not cut through the flesh. Once the liquid is boiling, place the peaches in it and cook for 1 minute. Take the pan off the heat and use a slotted spoon to remove the peaches to a bowl. Once they are cool enough to touch, peel off the skin; it should come away easily.

Return the peeled peaches to the cooking liquid in the pan and bring to the boil again. Once it has come to the boil, turn the heat off (if the peaches you are using are very hard, you may want to cook them for 2–3 minutes before turning off the heat). Add the vodka, then leave the peaches and their poaching liquid in the pan to cool.

While the peaches are cooling, strain 160g/ml of the poaching liquid into a small bowl (leave the peaches in the remainder). Soak the gelatine in cold water (follow the manufacturer's instructions), then remove, squeeze out the excess water and add the gelatine to the hot poaching liquid to melt. Once it has melted, stir in the cold water and rose water. Pour into four individual moulds and place in the fridge to chill until the jelly sets. This will take at least 2 hours and anything up to 5 hours, depending on the gelatine used.

If you are crystallising the rose petals, start by mixing the egg white with a pinch of sugar in a small bowl. Tip some caster sugar into a shallow saucer or dish. Dip a petal in the egg white mixture, then in the sugar, coating both sides. Lay the petals on a wire rack or a tray lined with baking parchment and leave to crisp and dry – this will take at least 6 hours, and up to 8 if the room is very cold. You can then keep them in an airtight container for up to 2 weeks, but make sure not to refrigerate as they will soften.

When you come to serve, the best way to get the jelly out of the moulds is to find a bowl that the jelly mould can fit into easily and to fill it with boiling water. Dip the mould in the hot water for 2 seconds and remove, then use your finger to pull the jelly a little to the side. This will allow air to come between the jelly and the mould; if you then flip the mould onto a serving plate, the jelly will slide out. Repeat with the other jellies. Place a peach at the side of each jelly and pour over a little of the cooking liquor. Then just splash with some sparkling wine and garnish with the rose petals, if using.

Baked apricots with marzipan filling & almond crumble

It feels silly giving a recipe for baked apricots. They are so delicious eaten ripe in season that they really need no addition, and their season is so short they seem to vanish in a blink. However, their unique, floral flavour works beautifully with our marzipan (page 265), and for us this dish is one of the highlights of their brief appearance.

For 6 guests (2 apricots per person)

For the roasted apricots

120g marzipan (page 265 or ready-made)
12 fresh ripe apricots
60g very soft butter
100g demerara sugar

For the almond crumble

100g almonds, roughly chopped
20g sesame seeds
a pinch of fennel seeds
a pinch of ground mahleb or cardamom
a pinch of sea salt
50g honey
1 tsp oil

For the brandy cream

100g/ml double cream
100g/ml soured cream
2 tbsp brandy

Preheat the oven to 200°C/180°C fan/ gas mark 6. Divide the marzipan into 12 pieces (10g each), roll into balls and flatten slightly. Open the apricots by pulling the cheeks apart. Remove the stones, replace each with a ball of marzipan and press the apricot halves together again to enclose.

Brush the fruit all over with the soft butter, then roll in the sugar to cover. Place in an ovenproof pan and roast for 8–10 minutes until the apricots are soft.

Mix the crumble ingredients together and spread on a baking tray lined with baking parchment. When the apricots come out of the oven, put the crumble in and bake for 8 minutes. Set aside to cool.

Mix the brandy cream ingredients together in a bowl until well combined. I don't add sugar as I feel the dish is sweet enough, but if you have a very sweet tooth, stir in a little icing sugar.

Serve two apricots per person with a splash of brandy cream and some crumble sprinkled on top.

Fig carpaccio with frozen goats' cheese cream, honey & thyme

Our cookery book collection is now well into the hundreds. Every room in our flat is littered with them, all except the kitchen. Strange as it may seem, we very rarely cook from them. We consider a cookbook worth its purchase price and a place on our shelves if it inspires just one good idea. The inspiration for this fig dessert (and many others) came to us from a massive, very serious tome about French patisserie called *Au Cœur des Saveurs*. It was one of the first cookbooks we got, and one of the few that actually gets used in the kitchen (with the dirty pages to prove it).

Makes 6–8 portions (2 figs per person)

12–16 figs
zest of 1 lemon
3–4 sprigs of thyme, leaves picked
3 tbsp good-quality honey (thyme honey would work beautifully here)
a little olive oil to drizzle

For the frozen cream
50g soft rindless goats' cheese
100g/ml double cream
70g honey
½ tsp ground cardamom

Whip the goats' cheese with the cream, honey and cardamom until just softly set. Use a teaspoon or piping bag to spoon or pipe in little mounds (about the size of a penny) on a tray lined with a sheet of greaseproof paper. Place in the freezer for at least 2 hours.

Cut 12 –16 sheets of greaseproof paper (depending on how many portions you are making) to the size of the plates you'll be serving this on.

Peel the figs: nip off the stalk and pull or cut the skin away. Cut each into four slices.

Place eight slices (two figs) on a piece of greaseproof paper, spacing them out a little. Cover with another sheet of paper and use a rolling pin or a flat wooden spoon to pound, flatten and spread the figs until you have a thin layer sandwiched between the sheets. Repeat with the other fig slices. Chill in the fridge until you are ready to serve. If you want to prepare this a day or two in advance, you can freeze the sheets of figs, then just thaw for 10 minutes before serving.

When you are ready to serve, peel off the top layer of paper. Flip one carpaccio (fig-side-down) onto each serving plate and carefully peel away the remaining greaseproof paper. Grate the lemon zest directly onto the carpaccios so each gets a dusting, then sprinkle with the thyme leaves and drizzle with the honey and a little olive oil. At the last minute remove the cream dollops from the freezer and divide between the plates. Serve immediately.

Marzipan

This marzipan is ridiculously easy to make and far more delicious than any you could buy. As with almost everything else, freshness is key. You will need some electrical assistance to grind the almonds. A small electric coffee grinder works best, as it gives you a very fine-textured marzipan. The problem is that it can only work a small amount at a time, so you have to make this in several batches and knead them together on the workbench. For an easier life and marzipan with a little more texture, follow the method here and blitz it in a food processor with a blade attachment.

Makes 10 small balls (30g each)

200g whole almonds (skin-on)
boiling water to cover
200g icing sugar
zest of ½ orange
1 tsp orange blossom water, plus more if needed
cornflour to dust, if needed
10 whole almonds to garnish, if you wish

Place the almonds in a bowl and pour over enough boiling water to cover. Leave to soak for about 10 minutes or until the water has cooled enough that you can handle the almonds. Peel the soaked nuts – the skin should just pop off if you pinch them – and lay on a clean cloth to dry for a few minutes.

Use a food processor to blitz the almonds to a crumb. Add the icing sugar and orange zest and work the mixture until it starts turning into a paste. Keep working it as you add the orange blossom water.

The marzipan should come together in a ball. Remove from the food processor and knead on the workbench until nice and smooth. If it seems rather wet, dust your palms with a little cornflour; if it seems a little dry, use a touch more orange blossom water to bring it together.

Divide into 10 pieces (30g each) and roll into balls. If garnishing, stick an almond in the top of each one. It's as simple as that.

Kadaif baklava with almonds & sour cherries

This is our take on a very traditional type of pastry. It is difficult to do justice to classic baklava. People have been making it for generations and if you want the genuine article, you need to buy it from one of those baklava masters who make tray upon tray of glistening sugary nuggets that stick to your teeth and give you a sugar rush like nothing else. Once you've eaten one of these, accompanied by some really good unsweetened black coffee, it will suddenly become clear why there are so many different recipes. This is my homage to baklava, bringing a little tartness, in the form of sour cherries, to balance the intense sweetness.

Makes 22–25 pieces

For the pastry
- *1 x 200g packet of kadaif pastry*
- *140g butter, melted*

For the filling
- *150g whole almonds (I like them skin-on but use blanched if you prefer)*
- *2 tbsp icing sugar*
- *1 tsp sweet spice mix (page 48)*
- *a pinch of sea salt*
- *2 tbsp almond oil (or any other nut oil will do)*
- *100g dried sour cherries*

For the sugar syrup
- *250g caster sugar*
- *125g/ml water*
- *1 tsp orange blossom water*

Put the almonds in a food processor with the icing sugar, spice and salt and blitz for 1 minute. Add the almond oil and sour cherries and pulse until the mixture comes together in a thick paste.

Spread a large sheet of cling film (at least 45cm x 35cm) on the work surface. Carefully open the packet of kadaif pastry and lift and unfold the strands a few at a time, keeping them intact (rather than mixing them up to loosen) so that the pastry stays in one piece. Lay it flat on the cling film and keep lifting and unfolding strands until you have one thin continuous sheet of about 40cm x 30cm. Pour the melted butter all over and pat to spread around a little. Use scissors to cut the pastry sheet in half lengthways so you end up with two rectangles of about 20cm x 30cm.

Remove the almond paste from the food processor and divide in two. Roll each half to a long 'snake' of about 30cm; don't worry if it cracks a little. Place a 'snake' along one of the long sides of a pastry rectangle, slightly in from the edge. Pick up the cling film closest to that side and lift the pastry over the nut paste, then use to roll up the pastry to enclose the filling. Wrap the filled pastry log in the cling film. Hold the ends of the cling film and roll the log on the table a couple of times to tighten and condense it as much as possible, then twist the ends firmly to secure. Repeat with the remaining paste and pastry. Set the cling-wrapped pastry logs in the fridge to chill and harden for at least 30 minutes and up to 48 hours.

Preheat the oven to 200°C/180°C fan/gas mark 6. Remove the pastry logs from the fridge and take off the cling film. Wrap both logs together in a sheet of baking parchment, then wrap that in aluminium foil. Bake on a tray in the centre of the oven for 20 minutes. In the meantime heat the sugar and water for the syrup together in a small pan, stirring as it comes up to the boil. Once boiling, remove from the heat and mix in the orange blossom water.

Remove the pastry logs from the oven and carefully open (but don't remove) the wrapping, leaving the logs sitting inside. Return to the oven for 15–20 minutes until lightly golden and then remove from the oven again. Carefully pour half the syrup over the logs inside their baking parchment and foil basket and leave to cool for about 20 minutes.

Once the logs are cool enough to handle, remove from their wrapping, place on a chopping board and slice into 3cm pieces. Place the pieces neatly next to each other in a small tray with a rim, sitting them upright so that the filling is facing upwards. Pour the remaining syrup all over, then allow to sit and absorb for at least 20 minutes before eating. These keep well for up to 3 days as long as you keep them covered.

Almond crescent cookies (aka kourabiedes or Greek ash cookies)

There is no ash in these, just a heavy coating of icing sugar that makes them look ash-covered, and (if done properly) leaves your face and fingers coated in a dusty layer. Although the ingredients are quite simple, the taste of these cookies is so much more than the sum of the parts. If you cannot find mahleb, use a few drops of rose water for a different, but still wildly delicious, result.

Makes about 36 bite-sized cookies or 18 larger ones (how I like my cookies)

For the cookie dough

110g cold butter, diced
60g icing sugar
1 tsp ground mahleb
a pinch of sea salt
85g plain flour
1 tbsp cornflour
110g ground almonds

To coat

about 200g icing sugar

Put the cookie dough ingredients in a mixer with a paddle attachment (or rub the butter into the dry ingredients, if making by hand). Mix on a low speed to a breadcrumb consistency, then increase the speed to bring the dough together, continuing until large clumps form (this may take a little time). Remove from the bowl to your workbench and bring the dough together into a ball.

Divide into 36 pieces of roughly 10g or 18 pieces of roughly 20g, depending on what size cookies you want. (I think around 20g makes a satisfying cookie, but Itamar always says that good things come in small packages so he prefers 10g ones.) Roll each piece into a ball between your palms, then roll a little more at the ends to create a zeppelin shape (the ends should be thinner than the middle). Bend slightly to resemble a crescent moon and lay on a flat baking tray lined with baking parchment (you may need two trays, depending on the number of cookies). Allow 2–3cm between each one, as they will spread a little while baking.

Preheat the oven to 190°C/170°C fan/gas mark 5. Bake one tray of cookies in the centre of the oven for 8 minutes, then turn the tray for an even bake and leave for another 5 minutes for the small cookies, or 8–9 minutes for the large ones. They should still be pale but going golden around the edges.

Remove the tray from the oven and set a timer for 5 minutes. Place the icing sugar in a wide, shallow bowl. When the timer rings, carefully lift a couple of cookies at a time into the icing sugar and toss to coat all over. Return the coated cookies to the tray to cool entirely.

Now repeat the process with the second trayful of cookies (if they didn't all fit on the first).

Once the cookies are cold, they can be stored in an airtight container for 3–4 days, but are best eaten fresh and buttery on the day of baking.

Halva

Pippa has worked with us for almost two years now; she started in the savoury side of the kitchen and is now doing a great job in the pastry section. Her Aussie palate is completely hooked on Middle Eastern flavours, so on her holidays she travels to explore the flavours of Istanbul, the markets of Marrakesh and the sights of Jerusalem, then comes back to London with bags of sweets for everyone, full of inspiration, and wanting to learn more.

Sesame halva is a confection that is hard to describe but very easy to fall in love with; if you get hooked on it during a trip east then this recipe is for you. If you haven't tried it yet, give it a go – you are in for a treat.

Makes 36 squares

50g pistachios, roasted (see page 20) and roughly chopped
1 tbsp dried rose petals
200g tahini paste
300g caster sugar
100g/ml water

Line a small (roughly 15cm x 15cm) plastic container or shallow square baking tin with baking parchment and sprinkle with the chopped pistachios and the rose petals. Fill a large bowl (or part-fill the sink) with cold water, ready to chill the sugar syrup pan when it comes off the heat.

Place the tahini paste in a small saucepan and set on a low heat. Stir constantly while the tahini thins and becomes shinier. Once it feels quite warm when tested against your lip, remove from the heat. Leave in the pan to keep warm.

Put the sugar in a separate pan, pour in the water around the sides and mix lightly to create a damp paste. Moisten your finger or a brush with some water and run it around the sides of the pan to clean away any sugar crystals (see notes on caramel on page 15). Place on a high heat and bring to the boil, then cook for 5 minutes or, if you have a sugar thermometer, until the mixture reaches 'soft-ball' stage (118°C). Take the pan off the heat and plunge it into the bowl of water (or half-filled sink) to cool it rapidly from outside. Don't let the water overflow into the sugar syrup.

Transfer the warm tahini to a wide bowl and stir with a spatula. Slowly pour in the sugar syrup, stirring all the time. The halva will start to thicken immediately and will continue to do so as it cools. Keep stirring and when it gets really thick, get rid of the spatula, put on some disposable gloves (if you have any) and use your hands to mix and knead the halva as you would dough.

Once it is as thick as marzipan, transfer to the lined container or tin containing the pistachios and roses. Press down to flatten, then cover and place in the fridge to cool for at least 2 hours before cutting into 36 small squares (about 2.5cm x 2.5cm).

Hazelnut truffles

When Dee joined us, we knew immediately we had a keeper; she is beautiful, quiet and calm, but full of energy and charisma and with a great passion for food. At first we thought she might be one of those foodies who never actually eats. She always gives the staff meal a miss at lunch, and instead piles her plate with leaves and carrot peelings she finds somewhere, plus a mound of salt. Later we realised where her passion lies. Once she has finished her meagre lunch, she goes sniffing around the pastry trolley, looking for sweet stuff; a spoonful of chocolate mousse, a broken chestnut cake. This is when her eyes light up, and never more so than when she eats these little treats.

Makes 20 truffles

150g whole blanched hazelnuts
3 tsp honey
2 tsp hazelnut oil (or vegetable oil), plus a little more for oiling
a pinch of sea salt

To coat (if you want to spoil someone special)
100g–150g dark chocolate, broken or chopped in small pieces

Preheat the oven to 180°C/160°C fan/ gas mark 4. Roast the hazelnuts for 14 minutes, then allow to cool on the tray. Once cool, place them in a food processor with a metal blade attachment (or use a spice grinder to do this in a couple of batches). Set on the highest speed and blitz for 1 minute. Add the remaining ingredients and blitz for another 2 minutes until the mixture comes together in a thick, praline-like paste.

Lightly oil your palms. Scoop out about 10g of paste, roll into a small ball and set on a small tray or a plate. Repeat with the rest of the praline paste; you should get 20 truffles out of this mixture. Chill in the fridge until needed. You can of course just eat them like this, but for a special occasion, coat them in chocolate.

There are two ways, which are equally tasty. The first uses 100g of chocolate; the second uses 150g for a slightly thicker coating.

Place 70% of the chocolate in a small bowl (70g or 105g depending on which coating method you are using). Pour some boiling water into a small pan and place the chocolate bowl over it (the pan should not be on the heat). Leave for 30–40 seconds, then stir the chocolate and continue stirring until it has all melted. Add the remaining chocolate, remove the bowl from the pan of hot water and continue to stir to melt the rest of the chocolate. Once it is all combined, it is time to dip.

This first method is the one I prefer, as it is more economical and creates a lovely pattern on each truffle. Put some melted chocolate in your hand and rub your palms together, then roll a ball of hazelnut praline between your palms to coat. Return to the plate or tray and repeat with the other truffles. Once they have all been coated, return them to the fridge until you are ready to eat. If you have a pair of disposable gloves, you can wear them to coat the truffles, but if not, hot water and soap will remove the chocolate from your palms.

If you are more fastidious about these things, use this method instead. Stab a toothpick securely into a truffle and use it to dip and swirl the praline ball around in the melted chocolate to coat. Return to the plate or tray and pull out the toothpick before the chocolate sets. Once you have coated all the truffles, return them to the fridge to set completely. Store in the fridge for up to a week.

Pocky sticks

We fell in love with Pocky sticks during a trip to Japan, where we had these little sweet-salty treats on a daily basis. It seemed a good idea to us to scale them up a bit, and it was in fact a great idea – this way one is enough.

Makes about 30–35 large sticks

250g strong white bread flour
½ tsp table salt
½ tsp caster sugar
2 tsp fennel seeds, roughly ground
60g cold butter, diced
60g/ml water, plus a tiny bit more if needed
300g dark chocolate
1 tsp vegetable oil
sea salt for sprinkling

Place the flour, salt, sugar and ground fennel seeds in a mixing bowl, add the cold, diced butter and rub to a crumb consistency (you can do this by hand or in a mixer with a paddle attachment). Start mixing in the water little by little until you have a tight dough that comes together in a ball. If necessary, add another couple of drops of water, but not too much as this dough should be quite firm. Wrap in cling film and place in the fridge to rest for at least 1 hour and up to 48 hours.

Very lightly dust your work surface with flour and roll the dough into a 25cm x 35cm rectangle. Place on a tray and return to the fridge to chill and set for a minimum of 10 minutes. Preheat the oven to 190°C/170°C fan/gas mark 5 and line a baking sheet with baking parchment.

Cut the chilled dough into 25cm-long thin sticks, each about 1cm wide, and lift carefully onto the lined baking sheet. Allow just a little space between each one so they don't stick to each other when baking. You should end up with about 30–35 sticks. Bake for 10 minutes, then turn the tray around and leave for another 5–6 minutes until the sticks are golden. Allow to cool on the tray.

While they are cooling, melt 250g of the chocolate over boiling water or in the microwave (see notes on page 12). When it is fully melted, add the remaining 50g of chocolate and stir until it melts in too, then stir in the teaspoon of oil.

Transfer the melted chocolate to a tall, dry glass. Dip the sticks in one at a time, coating them about halfway up their length, then pull out, shake off any excess chocolate and lay back on the tray to set. Once you have dipped a few, sprinkle with some sea salt so that it sticks to the setting chocolate. Keep dipping and sprinkling until you have coated them all. Set the tray in the fridge for 10–15 minutes, just to harden the chocolate fully, and then store at room temperature in an airtight container. These keep well for a few days.

Sugar-crusted candied peel

This is not a recipe as much as a serving suggestion for our home-made candied orange peel (page 44).

Remove as much candied peel as you require from the syrup and place on a clean cloth to drain away some of the liquid. Put some caster sugar in a small bowl. Dip the orange peel pieces in the sugar to coat both sides, then set on a wire rack to dry overnight.

You can eat these as they are or dip them in dark chocolate (see notes on melting chocolate on page 12).

Honey & Co.
Food From the Middle East
HSBC
VISA

Thanks

Working on this book has been a particularly pleasurable experience, steeped in sugar, cream and friends; a true labour of love. But with love there often comes sadness, and this year has seen many of us – at Honey & Co, at Saltyard Books and amongst our friends – dealing with illness or the loss of a loved one. We hope to offer this book as a small comfort, because cakes and baking are nothing if not about love.

Every day we are in awe of the joy, dedication and care brought to work by the motley crew that makes up Honey & Co. They inspire us, push us forward and keep us from falling. Most of them are mentioned already in this book, but they all deserve to be mentioned again. Our chefs, with their leader Julia (Yulcah), Hernan David (HD), Hussein (Juice), Mirko (the meerkat) and Marco (di pasta). Our floor staff, Rachael (Ray), Dorit (Dee), Sanaa, Camille, Meave, Anja and Sabrina, all equally welcoming and kind to customers and colleagues. Louisa (Lou-lou) in the office, so capable, calm and forever smiling. Last but by no means least, in the pastry section Bridget and Pippa (the other Georgia), and a very special thanks to our wonderful Giorgia Di Marzo, who is so much more than our pastry chef, and who has done so much to help this book come to life with her endless enthusiasm and love of sweets.

When it comes to the making of this book (and its predecessor), the stars have aligned for us in the most generous way; we could not have asked for a better team. The magnificent Luigi who set it all up, Patricia (the red mullet) whose happy light shines on everything she does, and Alice who would cross London to see artwork we had discussed, and then bring back the most wonderful visions. Thanks go to the meticulous Bryony, for making sure that if (when) we embarrass ourselves, we do it in proper English; to Lesley for pointing out the difference between 'but' and 'however' and many invaluable insights; to Annie for checking and double checking; to Rosie, for not being scared to pick up the tannoy, amongst many other things; to Kate (Katrina) Miles, for treating everything to do with this book, from the big things to the small, with such tremendous care; and to all at Hodder, for their support and custom.

To the great Elizabeth Hallett: working with you has been a privilege. You are a true master of your craft and the world of book-making will be less without you.

We want to thank our recipe testers: Bren, who is a real pro; Charissa, a gifted pastry chef; and Jaap Parqui, a zealous home cook. Your comments have made us, and this book, better. Major thanks to our chief recipe taster and great friend Shachar (Couscousul); stay hungry!

To our dear friends: Erez and Yonit, Inbal and Ben, Illill, Nirit, Savarna, Stephanie, Liat, Oshrat and Gal and to the members of the Bonne Bouche Parliament – Yotam, Cornelia and Dianne. Our breakfasts mean so much to us.

We would like to thank our families: mothers, fathers, brothers, sister, nephews and nieces. You could have done better, but we couldn't.

To Amit and Nikki et al at Pilates Junction, for keeping Sarit sane(ish).

A half-hearted thank you to Andy: you are great, but you drive us crazy.

The biggest thank you is to our customers – those who come to us and those who let us, via our books, into their homes. We are forever grateful. You have the best of us, and we hope so much that you enjoy it.

GREEK PRODUCT
NO PRESERVATIVES

Index

First published in Great Britain in 2015 by Saltyard Books
An imprint of Hodder & Stoughton
An Hachette UK company

1

A CIP catalogue record for this title is available from the British Library.

ISBN 978 1 444 73500 0
eBook ISBN 978 1 444 73502 4

'I got hunger' on page v is taken from the song 'Got the Hunger?' from the album *Pot of Gold*. Written by Alice Russell & Alex Cowan. Appears courtesy of 5MM Publishing.

Book design by Aka Alice
Typeset in Miller, Capita and Bohemian Typewriter

Copy editors Bryony Nowell and Lesley Levene
Proof reader Annie Lee
Indexer Caroline Wilding

Printed and bound in Germany by Mohn Media

Hodder & Stoughton policy is to use papers that are natural, renewable and recyclable products and made from wood grown in sustainable forests. The logging and manufacturing processes are expected to conform to the environmental regulations of the country of origin.

Saltyard Books
Carmelite House
50 Victoria Embankment
London EC4Y 0DZ

www.saltyardbooks.co.uk